TRANSFORMING MISSION

The American Society of Missiology Series, in collaboration with Orbis Books, seeks to publish scholarly works of high merit and wide interest on numerous aspects of missiology—the study of mission. Able presentations on new and creative approaches to the practice and understanding of mission will receive close attention.

**Previously published in
The American Society of Missiology Series**

American Society of Missiology Series, No. 16

TRANSFORMING MISSION

Paradigm Shifts in Theology of Mission

David J. Bosch

ORBIS BOOKS

Maryknoll, New York 10545

Twenty-first Printing, October 2005

The Catholic Foreign Mission Society of America (Maryknoll) recruits and trains people for overseas missionary service. Through Orbis Books, Maryknoll aims to foster the international dialogue that is essential to mission. The books published, however, reflect the opinions of their authors and are not meant to represent the official position of the society.

Library of Congress Cataloging-in-Publication Data

Bosch, David Jacobus.
    Transforming mission : paradigm shifts in theology of mission /
David J. Bosch.
        p. cm. — (American Society of Missiology series ; no. 16)
    Includes bibliographical references and index.
    ISBN 0-88344-744-4 — ISBN 0-88344-719-3 (pbk.)
    1. Missions — Theory. 2. Missions — Theory — History of doctrines.
3. Christianity and other religions. I. Title. II. Title:
Paradigm shifts in theology of mission. III. Series.
BV2063.B649   1991
266'.001 — dc20   90-21619
                                                                   CIP

For Annemie

Contents

Part 1
New Testament Models of Mission

vii

Part 2
Historical Paradigms of Mission

Part 3
Toward a Relevant Missiology

In Memoriam
David J. Bosch, 1929-1992

On April 15, 1992, just one year after *Transforming Mission* was published, David J. Bosch died in an automobile accident in South Africa. At the age of 62, a preeminent Protestant missiologist, his contribution and influence in mission studies globally was immense.

After missionary service in Transkei from 1957 to 1971, David was professor of missiology at the University of South Africa from 1971. He served as dean of the faculty of theology in 1974-1977 and again in 1981-1987. He was general secretary of the Southern African Missiological Society from its founding in 1968 and editor of its journal *Missionalia* from its inception in 1973. He served as national chairman of the South African Christian Leadership Assembly in 1979 and as chairman of the National Initiative for Reconciliation from 1989, as part of his tireless ministry to bring about reconciliation among racial, denominational, and theological groups in South Africa and across the world.

A prolific author and eloquent lecturer, fluent in Xhosa, Afrikaans, Dutch, German, and English, Bosch lectured widely in Europe, Britain, and North America. His doctorate from Basel was in New Testament, and he brought profound biblical insights to his work in missiology. He was a "bridge person," respected as much in the World Council of Churches as in the World Evangelical Fellowship and the Lausanne Committee for World Evangelization.

When *Transforming Mission* first appeared, it was received with critical acclaim, recognized as a monumental, magisterial work and a superb teaching tool. It was selected as one of the "Fifteen Outstanding Books of 1991 for Mission Studies" by the *International Bulletin of Missionary Research*. But it is more than that. *Transforming Mission* is in a class by itself. It has become a standard reference in studies of the Christian world mission, perhaps the most widely used textbook in mission courses. David Bosch's *magnum opus* has become his enduring legacy to all who seek to understand, to serve, and to spread the cause of Christ in the world.

One of my lasting memories of David Bosch is from his visit with me a few years before *Transforming Mission* was published. He had received an invitation to join the faculty of one of the leading seminaries in the United States as professor of world mission. As we walked along the ocean beach in Ventnor, New Jersey, he discussed the pros and cons of leaving South Africa and coming to this attractive post, where he could devote himself more fully to teaching and writing, removed from the stress and struggle going on in South African society, events in which he was deeply involved. I encouraged him to accept the invitation. But at the end of our long conversation, he said, "No, I don't think I can leave my colleagues and the struggle in South Africa. It is a critical moment and that is where God has placed me."

It was this kind of "bold humility" that characterized David Bosch, and it is what he calls for in *Transforming Mission*.

GERALD H. ANDERSON

Preface to the Series

The purpose of the ASM Series—now in existence since 1980—is to publish, without regard for disciplinary, national, or denominational boundaries, scholarly works of high quality and wide interest on missiological themes from the entire spectrum of scholarly pursuits, e.g., biblical studies, theology, history, history of religions, cultural anthropology, linguistics, art, education, political science, economics, and development, to name only the major components. Always the focus will be on Christian mission.

By "mission" in this context is meant a passage over the boundary between faith in Jesus Christ and its absence. In this understanding of mission, the basic functions of Christian proclamation, dialogue, witness, service, worship, and nurture are of special concern. How does the transition from one cultural context to another influence the shape and interaction between these dynamic functions? Cultural and religious plurality are recognized as fundamental characteristics of the six-continent missionary context in East and West, North and South.

Missiologists know that they need the other disciplines. And those in other disciplines need missiology, perhaps more than they sometimes realize. Neither the insider's nor the outsider's view is complete in itself. The world Christian mission has through two millennia amassed a rich and well-documented body of experience to share with other disciplines. The complementary relation between missiology and other learned disciplines is a key of this Series, and interaction will be its hallmark.

The promotion of scholarly dialogue among missiologists may, at times, involve the publication of views and positions that other missiologists cannot accept, and with which members of the Editorial Committee do not agree. Manuscripts published in this series reflect the opinions of their authors and are not meant to represent the position of the American Society of Missiology or of the Editorial Committee for the ASM Series. The committee's selection of texts is guided by such criteria as intrinsic worth, readability, relative brevity, freedom from excessive scholarly apparatus, and accessibility to a broad range of interested persons and not merely to experts or specialists.

On behalf of the membership of the American Society of Missiology we express our deep thanks to the staff of Orbis Books, whose steadfast support over a decade for this joint publishing venture has enabled it to mature and bear scholarly fruit.

James A. Scherer, Chair
Mary Motte, FMM
Charles R. Taber
ASM Series Editorial Committee

Foreword

The title of this book — first suggested to me by Eve Drogin of Orbis Books — is ambiguous. "Transforming" can be an adjective describing "mission". In this case, mission is understood as an enterprise that transforms reality. "Transforming" can, however, also be a present participle, the activity of transforming, of which "mission" is the object. Here, mission is not the enterprise that transforms reality, but something that is itself being transformed.

I must admit that I had some misgivings about the suggested title. Then, one day, I discussed it with Prof Francis Wilson of Cape Town University who, together with Dr Mamphela Ramphele, coordinated the Second Carnegie Inquiry into Poverty and Development in Southern Africa. Wilson pointed out to me that the title of their book on the project, *Uprooting Poverty*, reflects the same ambiguity. It depicts poverty as something that uproots while, at the same time, articulating the challenge that poverty is something that has to be uprooted. Since this discussion I have had peace of mind about an ambiguous title for my own book!

The ambiguity in the title in fact reflects the subject matter of the book very accurately. With the aid of the idea of paradigm shifts I am attempting to demonstrate the extent to which the understanding and practice of mission have changed during almost twenty centuries of Christian missionary history. In some instances the transformations were so profound and far-reaching that the historian has difficulty in recognizing any similarities between the different missionary models. My thesis is, furthermore, that this process of transformation has not yet come to an end (and will, in fact, never come to an end), and that we find ourselves, at the moment, in the midst of one of the most important shifts in the understanding and practice of the Christian mission.

The study is, however, not only descriptive. It does not set out merely to portray the development and modifications of an idea, but also suggests that mission remains an indispensable dimension of the Christian faith and that, at its most profound level, its purpose is to transform reality around it. Mission, in this perspective, is that dimension of our faith that refuses to accept reality as it is and aims at changing it. "Transforming" is, therefore, an adjective that depicts an essential feature of what Christian mission is all about.

A few observations about the genesis of this book may be in order here. In 1980 I published *Witness to the World: The Christian Mission in Theological Perspective*. At the formal level, the present book deals, to some extent, with the same subject matter as my book of a decade ago. That book has been out of print for a number of years, and I originally set out to write a revision of it. It soon became clear, however, that I had "outgrown" my previous book and that, in any case, a book for the early eighties would not address the challenges of the early nineties. Too much had happened in the eighties, in respect of theology, politics, sociology, economics, etc. Of course, there are essential continuities between my previous book and the present one, just as there are continuities between the world of the early eighties and that of the early nineties. Some of these continuities, together with the important discontinuities, are — I hope — reflected in the present study.

The writing of this book has preoccupied me since at least 1985. In 1987 the University of South Africa, together with the (South African) Human Sciences Research Council, made a research grant available which enabled me to spend six months of virtually uninterrupted research at Princeton Theological Seminary in New Jersey. I would like to express my gratitude to my university and the HSRC for the grant, but also to Princeton Theological Seminary and its president, Dr Tom Gillespie, for providing me and my family with accommodation as well as superb resource facilities.

For the successful completion of my writing project I am deeply indebted to more people than I could possibly mention by name. Some of them, however, have to be singled out. I am thinking of my colleagues in the Department of Missiology at the University of South Africa — Willem Saayman, J.N.J. ("Klippies") Kritzinger, and Inus Daneel, together with our two splendid secretaries, Hazel van Rensburg and Marietjie Willemse — who have not only continually stimulated my own theological thinking but have also created space and time for me to pursue my research. Other friends and colleagues who have also read sections of my manuscript and interacted with me on its contents include Henri Lederle, Cilliers Breytenbach, Bertie du Plessis, Kevin Livingston, Daniël Nel, Johann Mouton, Adrio König, Willem Nicol, Gerald Pillay, J. J. ("Dons") Kritzinger and several others. Some of them also participated in the January 1990 meeting of the Southern African Missiological Society which was devoted to my theological oeuvre (cf J.N.J. Kritzinger and W. A. Saayman [eds], *Mission in Creative Tension*: *A Dialogue with David Bosch*. Pretoria: S. A. Missiological Society, 1990]). It is indeed a joy to work with such colleagues!

A word of appreciation should also go to Orbis Books for its readiness to publish this book. Eve Drogin, Senior Editor at Orbis, guided me through the early stages of writing and of negotiations with the publishers. My sincerest thanks to her. During the final and crucial stages of preparing and editing the manuscript, William Burrows, Orbis's Managing Editor, took personal charge. His detailed and incisive commentary on my first draft revealed to me his superb qualities as skillful editor, articulate theologian, and sensitive interlocutor. Subsequent communications between us confirmed my first impressions. Nobody could have wished for a better editor.

The book appears in the *American Society of Missiology Series*. I deem this a great honor and wish to express my gratitude to the members of the editorial committee (the names of Gerald H. Anderson [New Haven] and James A. Scherer [Chicago] should be singled out in this respect) and, in fact, to the entire American Society of Missiology. I have had the privilege of attending several of its annual meetings and will always cherish those memories.

Last but not least: This book is dedicated to my wife of thirty-something years, Annemarie Elisabeth. For several years she has had to put up with the writing of this book and to forfeit holidays as well as adequate support from me in family and other matters. She remained encouraging and understanding, however, and was, throughout, the "help meet" on whom I could bounce off my ideas and from whom I could always expect intelligent and sympathetic feedback. I owe her more than I can express in words.

Abbreviations

AG	*Ad Gentes* (Decree on the Church's Missionary Activity [Vatican II])
CMS	Church Missionary Society (Anglican)
CWME	Commission for World Mission and Evangelism of the World Council of Churches
CT	*Catechesi Tradendae* (Apostolic Exhortation of Pope John Paul II, 1979)
EATWOT	Ecumenical Association of Third World Theologians
EN	*Evangelii Nuntiandi* (Apostolic Exhortation of Pope Paul VI, 1975)
FO	Faith and Order (Commission of the World Council of Churches)
GS	*Gaudium et Spes* (Pastoral Constitution on the Church in the Modern World [Vatican II])
IMC	International Missionary Council
LC	The Lausanne Covenant (produced by the International Congress on World Evangelization, Lausanne, 1974)
LCWE	Lausanne Committee for World Evangelization
LG	*Lumen Gentium* (Dogmatic Constitution on the Church [Vatican II])
LMS	London Missionary Society
ME	Mission and Evangelism—An Ecumenical Affirmation (World Council of Churches' Document on Mission and Evangelism, published in 1982)
NA	*Nostra Aetate* (Declaration on the Relation of the Church to Non-Christian Religions [Vatican II])
NEB	New English Bible
NIV	New International Version (of the Bible)
RSV	Revised Standard Version (of the Bible)
SPCK	Society for the Propagation of Christian Knowledge
SPG	Society for the Propagation of the Gospel
SVM	Student Volunteer Movement
WCC	World Council of Churches
WEF	World Evangelical Fellowship
WSCF	World Students Christian Federation

Introduction

Mission: The Contemporary Crisis

BETWEEN DANGER AND OPPORTUNITY

Since the 1950s there has been a remarkable escalation in the use of the word "mission" among Christians. This went hand in hand with a significant broadening of the concept, at least in certain circles. Until the 1950s "mission", even if not used in a univocal sense, had a fairly circumscribed set of meanings. It referred to (a) the sending of missionaries to a designated territory, (b) the activities undertaken by such missionaries, (c) the geographical area where the missionaries were active, (d) the agency which despatched the missionaries, (e) the non-Christian world or "mission field", or (f) the center from which the missionaries operated on the "mission field" (cf Ohm 1962:52f). In a slightly different context it could also refer to (g) a local congregation without a resident minister and still dependent on the support of an older, established church, or (h) a series of special services intended to deepen or spread the Christian faith, usually in a nominally Christian environment. If we attempt a more specifically theological synopsis of "mission" as the concept has traditionally been used, we note that it has been paraphrased as (a) propagation of the faith, (b) expansion of the reign of God, (c) conversion of the heathen, and (d) the founding of new churches (cf Müller 1987:31-34).

Still, all these connotations attached to the word "mission", familiar as they may be, are of fairly recent origin. Until the sixteenth century the term was used exclusively with reference to the doctrine of the Trinity, that is, of the sending of the Son by the Father and of the Holy Spirit by the Father and the Son. The Jesuits were the first to use it in terms of the spread of the Christian faith among people (including Protestants) who were not members of the Catholic Church (cf Ohm 1962:37-39). In this new sense it was intimately associated with the colonial expansion of the Western world into what has more recently become known as the Third World (or, sometimes, the Two-Thirds World). The term "mission" presupposes a sender, a person or persons sent by the sender, those to whom one is sent, and an assignment. The entire terminology thus presumes that the one who sends has the *authority* to do so. Often it was argued that the real sender was God who had indisputable authority to decree that people be sent to execute his will. In practice, however, the authority was understood to be vested in the church or in a mission society, or even in a

Christian potentate. In Roman Catholic missions, in particular, juridical authority remained, for a long time, the constitutive element for the legitimacy of the
missionary enterprise (cf Rütti 1972:228). It was part of this entire approach
to view mission in terms of expansion, occupation of fields, the conquest of
other religions, and the like.

In Chapters 10 to 13 of this study I will argue that this traditional interpretation of mission was gradually modified in the course of the twentieth century.
Much of what follows will be an investigation of the factors that have led to
this modification. Some introductory remarks may, however, serve to set the
scene for our investigation, not least because—more than ever before in its
history—the Christian mission is in the firing line today.

What is new about our era, it seems to me, is that the Christian mission—
at least as it has traditionally been interpreted and performed—is under attack
not only from without but also from within its own ranks. One of the earliest
examples of this kind of missionary self-criticism is Schütz (1930). Another and
even more trenchant censure of mission, particulary as it was conducted in
China, was conducted by Paton (1953). Similar publications followed. In one
year alone, 1964, four such books appeared, all written by missiologists or mission executives: R. K. Orchard, *Missions in a Time of Testing*; James A. Scherer,
Missionary, Go Home!; Ralph Dodge, *The Unpopular Missionary*; and John Car-
den, *The Ugly Missionary*. More recently, James Heissig (1981), writing in a
missiological journal, has even characterized Christian mission as "the selfish
war".

These circumstances alone necessitate and justify reflection on mission as a
permanent item on the agenda of theology. If theology is a "reflective account
of the faith" (T. Rendtorff), it is part of the task of theology critically to consider
mission as one of the expressions (however warped an expression it may be in
practice) of the Christian faith.

The criticism of mission should not, in itself, surprise us. It is, rather, *normal*
for Christians to live in a situation of crisis. It should never have been different.
In a volume written in preparation for the 1938 Tambaram conference of the
International Missionary Council (IMC), Kraemer (1947:24) formulated this as
follows, "Strictly speaking, one ought to say that the Church is always in a state
of crisis and that its greatest shortcoming is that it is only occasionally aware
of it". This ought to be the case, Kraemer argued, because of "the abiding
tension between (the church's) essential nature and its empirical condition"
(:24f). Why is it, then, that we are so seldom aware of this element of crisis
and tension in the church? Because, Kraemer added, the church "has always
needed apparent failure and suffering in order to become fully alive to its real
nature and mission" (:26). And for many centuries the church has suffered very
little and has been led to believe that it is a success.

Like its Lord, the church—if it is faithful to its being—will, however, always
be controversial, a "sign that will be spoken against" (Lk 2:34). That there were
so many centuries of crisis-free existence for the church was therefore an abnor-
mality. Now, at long last, we are "back to normal" . . . and we know it! And if
the atmosphere of crisislessness still lingers on in many parts of the West, this

is simply the result of a dangerous delusion. Let us also know that to encounter crisis is to encounter the possibility of truly being the *church*. The Japanese character for "crisis" is a combination of the characters for "danger" and "opportunity" (or "promise"); crisis is therefore not the end of opportunity but in reality only its beginning (Koyama 1980:4), the point where danger and opportunity meet, where the future is in the balance and where events can go either way.

THE WIDER CRISIS

The crisis we are referring to is, naturally, not only a crisis in regard to mission. It affects the entire church, indeed the entire world (cf Glazik 1979:152). As far as the Christian church, theology, and mission are concerned, the crisis manifests itself, *inter alia*, in the following factors:

1. The advance of science and technology and, with them, the worldwide process of secularization seem to have made faith in God redundant; why turn to religion if we ourselves have ways and means of dealing with the exigencies of modern life?

2. Linked to the former point is the reality that the West — traditionally not only the home of Catholic and Protestant Christianity, but also the base of the entire modern missionary enterprise — is slowly but steadily being dechristianized. David Barrett (1982:7) has calculated that, in Europe and North America, an average of 53,000 persons are permanently leaving the Christian church from one Sunday to the next. He confirms a trend first identified almost half a century ago, when Godin and Daniel (1943) shocked the Catholic world with the publication of *France: pays de mission?*, in which they argued that France had again become a mission field, a country of neo-pagans, of people in the grip of atheism, secularism, unbelief, and superstition.

3. Partly because of the above, the world can no longer be divided into "Christian" and "non-Christian" territories separated by oceans. Because of the dechristianization of the West and the multiple migrations of people of many faiths we now live in a religiously pluralist world, in which Christians, Muslims, Buddhists, and adherents of many traditional religions rub shoulders daily. This proximity to others has forced Christians to reexamine their traditional stereotypical views about those faiths. Moreover, the devotees of other faiths often prove to be more actively and aggressively missionary than the members of Christian churches are.

4. Because of its complicity in the subjugation and exploitation of peoples of color, the West — and also Western Christians — tends to suffer from an acute sense of guilt. This circumstance often leads to an inability or unwillingness among Western Christians to "give an account of the hope they have" (cf 1 Pet 3:15) to people of other persuasions.

5. More than ever before we are today aware of the fact that the world is divided — apparently irreversibly — between the rich and the poor and that, by and large, the rich are those who consider themselves (or are considered by the poor) to be Christians. In addition, and according to most indicators, the

rich are still getting richer and the poor poorer. This circumstance creates, on the one hand, anger and frustration among the poor and, on the other, a reluctance among affluent Christians to share their faith.

6. For centuries, Western theology and Western ecclesial ways and practices were normative and undisputed, also in the "mission fields". Today the situation is fundamentally different. The younger churches refuse to be dictated to and are putting a high premium on their "autonomy". In addition, Western theology is today suspect in many parts of the world. It is often regarded as irrelevant, speculative, and the product of ivory tower institutions. In many parts of the world it is being replaced by Third-World theologies: liberation theology, black theology, contextual theology, *minjung* theology, African theology, Asian theology, and the like. This circumstance has also contributed to profound uncertainties in Western churches, even about the validity of the Christian mission as such.

Naturally, these and other factors also have a positive side, and much of the last part of my study will be an attempt to identify this. It is, in fact, the thesis of this book that the events we have been experiencing at least since World War II and the consequent crisis in Christian mission are not to be understood as merely incidental and reversible. Rather, what has unfolded in theological and missionary circles during the last decades is the result of a fundamental paradigm shift, not only in mission or theology, but in the experience and thinking of the whole world. Many of us are only aware of the crisis we are facing now. It will, however, be argued that what is happening in our time is not the first paradigm shift the world (or the church) has experienced. There have been profound crises and major paradigm shifts before. Each of them constituted the end of one world and the birth of another, in which much of what people used to think and do had to be redefined. Those earlier shifts will also be traced in some detail, insofar as they had a significant bearing on missionary thought and practice. It will, furthermore, be proposed that such a paradigm shift does not—to paraphrase Koyama—confront us only with a danger but also with opportunities. In earlier ages the church has responded imaginatively to paradigm changes; we are challenged to do the same for our time and context.

FOUNDATION, AIM, AND NATURE OF MISSION

The contemporary crisis, as far as mission is concerned, manifests itself in three areas: the *foundation*, the *motives and aim*, and the *nature* of mission (cf Gensichen 1971:27-29).

As regards the foundation for mission, one has to concede that, for a long time, the missionary enterprise had to make do with a minimal basis. This emerges, *inter alia*, from the publications of both Gustav Warneck (1834-1910) and Josef Schmidlin (1876-1944), respectively the founders of Protestant and Catholic missiology. Warneck, for instance, distinguished between a "supernatural" and a "natural" foundation for mission (cf Schärer 1944:5-10). As regards the first, he identified two elements: mission is founded on Scripture (particularly the "Great Commission" of Matthew 28:18-20) and on the monotheistic nature of the Christian faith. Equally important are the "natural" grounds for mission: (a) the absoluteness and superiority of the Christian religion when compared with others; (b) the acceptability and adaptability of Christianity to all peoples and conditions; (c) the superior achievements of the Christian mission on the "mission fields"; and (d) the fact that Christianity has, in past and present, shown itself to be stronger than all other religions.

The reflections on missionary motives and the aim of mission were often equally ambiguous. Verkuyl (1978a:168-75; cf Dürr 1951:2-10) identified the following "impure motives": (a) the imperialist motive (turning "natives" into docile subjects of colonial authorities); (b) the cultural motive (mission as the transfer of the missionary's "superior" culture); (c) the romantic motive (the desire to go to far-away and exotic countries and peoples); and (d) the motive of ecclesiastical colonialism (the urge to export one's own confession and church order to other territories).

Theologically more adequate but in their manifestation often also ambiguous are four other missionary motives (cf Freytag 1961:207-17; Verkuyl 1978a:164-68): (a) the motive of conversion, which emphasizes the value of personal decision and commitment—but tends to narrow the reign of God spiritualistically and individualistically to the sum total of saved souls; (b) the eschatological motive, which fixes people's eyes on the reign of God as a future reality but, in its eagerness to hasten the irruption of that final reign, has no interest in the exigencies of this life; (c) the motive of *plantatio ecclesiae* (church planting), which stresses the need for the gathering of a community of the committed but is inclined to identify the church with the kingdom of God; and (d) the philanthropic motive, through which the church is challenged to seek justice in the world but which easily equates God's reign with an improved society.

An inadequate foundation for mission and ambiguous missionary motives and aims are bound to lead to an unsatisfactory missionary practice. The young churches "planted" on the "mission fields" were replicas of the churches on the mission agency's "home front", "blessed" with all the paraphernalia of those churches, "everything from harmoniums to archdeacons" (Newbigin 1969:107). Like the churches in Europe and North America, they were communities under the jurisdiction of full-time pastors. And they had to adhere to confessions prepared centuries before in Europe, in circumstances and in response to challenges fundamentally different from those that faced the young churches of India or Africa. At the same time they were regarded as remaining under the tutelage of Western mission agencies, at least until the latter should decide to grant them a "certificate of maturity", that is, until the younger churches had proved that they were fully self-supporting, self-governing, and self-propagating.

It was this ecclesiastical export trade that caused Schütz to cry out in protest, "The house of the church is on fire! In our missionary outreach we resemble a lunatic who carries the harvest into his burning barn" (1930:195—my translation). Schütz located the problem not "outside", on the mission field, but in the heart of the Western church itself. So he calls the church back from the mission field where it did not proclaim the gospel but individualism and the values of the West, back to become what it was not but should be: church of Jesus Christ in the midst of the peoples of the earth. *"Intra muros!"* he shouted, "the outcome is determined by what happens inside the church, not outside, on the mission field".

Because of the inadequate foundation and ambiguous motivation of the missionary enterprise few advocates and supporters of mission were able to appreciate the challenges presented by Schütz or, twenty-three years later, after the "missionary débâcle" in China, by David Paton (1953). Most felt content with the performance of Western agencies. In fact, their "accomplishments" were, ironically, often used to undergird the shaky foundations of mission; looking with approval upon the practice of mission, the champions identified their missionary projects with what they saw in the pages of the New Testament, which in turn became the theological justification for the continuation of the enterprise.

By means of such circular reasoning, the success of the Christian mission became the foundation for mission. Other religions were regarded as moribund; they would all soon disappear. To mention a couple of examples of this reasoning: In the year 1900 the General Secretary of the Norwegian Missionary Society, Lars Dahle, having compared statistics of the numbers of Christians in Asia and Africa in 1800 and 1900 respectively, was able to devise a mathematical formula which revealed the growth rate of Christianity, decade by decade, during the nineteenth century. It was only logical that Dahle would apply the formula also to successive decades of the twentieth century. On the basis of this he could calmly predict that, by the year 1990, the entire human race would be won for the Christian faith (cf Sundkler 1968:121). A few years later Johannes Warneck, son of Gustav Warneck, wrote a book entitled *Die Lebenskräfte des Evangeliums* (2d impression 1908), in which he demonstrated the power of the Christian mission vis-à-vis other faiths. The American translator of the book was even more sanguine than Warneck himself had been: he published it under the title *The Living Christ and Dying Heathenism* (1909).

Indeed, Christianity's successes proved its superiority! Today, however, we know that those optimistic predictions were unfounded. There are no longer any signs of what J. Warneck called "dying heathenism". Virtually all world religions display a vigor nobody would have credited them with some decades ago. The confident predictions of Dahle and others concerning the triumphal march and imminent total victory of Christianity have come to nothing. The Christian faith is still a minority religion, at best holding its own in relation to the overall world population. And if Christianity is no longer successful, is it still unique and true?

FROM CONFIDENCE TO MALAISE

It is circumstances like these that have led to the confidence about imminent victory being replaced by a profound malaise in some missionary circles. Toward the end of his life Max Warren, for many years General Secretary of the Church Missionary Society in Great Britain, referred to what he termed "a terrible failure of nerve about the missionary enterprise". In some circles this has led to an almost complete paralysis and total withdrawal from any activity traditionally associated with mission, in whatever form. Others are plunging themselves into projects which might just as well – and more efficiently – be undertaken by secular agencies.

Again, in some Christian circles there is no sign of such a failure or nerve. Quite the contrary. It is "business as usual" as regards the continuation of one-way missionary traffic from the West to the Third World and the proclamation of a gospel which appears to have little interest in the conditions in which people find themselves, since the preachers' only concern seems to be the saving of souls from eternal damnation. Here the right of Christians to proclaim their religion is beyond dispute since the Bible clearly commands world mission. To even suggest that there is a fundamental crisis in mission would be tantamount to making concessions to "liberal" theology and to doubting the abiding validity of the faith once handed down to us.

Whilst the zeal for mission and the self-sacrificing dedication evidenced in these circles must be applauded, one cannot help wondering whether they are really rendering a valid and long-term solution. Our spiritual forebears may perhaps be pardoned for not having been aware of the fact that they were facing a crisis. Present generations, however, can hardly be excused for *their* lack of awareness.

A "PLURIVERSE" OF MISSIOLOGY

If there is no possibility of ignoring the present crisis in mission, nor any point in trying to circumvent it, the only valid way open to us is to deal with the crisis in utmost sincerity yet *without allowing ourselves to succumb to it*. Once again: crisis is the point where danger and opportunity meet. Some see only the opportunity and rush on, oblivious of the pitfalls on all sides. Others are only aware of the danger and become so paralyzed by it that they back off. We can, however, only do justice to our high calling if we acknowledge the presence of both danger and opportunity and execute our mission within the field of tension engendered by both.

I suggest, then, that the solution to the problem presented by the present failure of nerve does not lie in a simple return to an earlier missionary consciousness and practice. Clinging to yesterday's images provides solace, but little else. And artificial respiration will yield little beyond the semblance of returning life. Neither does the solution lie in embracing the values of the contemporary world and attempting to respond to whatever a particular individual or group chooses to call mission. Rather, we require a new vision to break out of the present stalemate toward a different kind of missionary involvement – which need not mean jettisoning everything generations of Christians have done before us or haughty condemnations of all their blunders.

The bravest among missionary thinkers have already for some time begun to sense that a new paradigm for mission was emerging. More than thirty years ago Hendrik Kraemer ([1959] 1970:70) said that we had to recognize a crisis in mission, even an "impasse". And yet, he said, "we do not stand at the end of mission"; rather, "we stand at the definite end of a specific period or era of mission, and the clearer we see this and accept this with all our heart, the better". We are called to a new "pioneer task which will be more demanding and less romantic than the heroic deeds of the past missionary era".

The world of the 1990s is undoubtedly different from that of Edinburgh 1910 (when advocates of mission believed that the entire world would soon be Christian), or from that of the 1960s (when many predicted confidently that it was only a matter of time before all humankind would be free from want and injustice). Both manifestations of optimism have been destroyed, fundamentally and permanently, by subsequent events. The harsh realities of today compel us to re-conceive and reformulate the church's mission, to do this boldly and imaginatively, yet also in continuity with the best of what mission has been in the past decades and centuries.

The thesis of this book is that it is neither possible nor proper to attempt a revised definition of mission without taking a thorough look at the vicissitudes of missions and the missionary idea during the past twenty centuries of Christian church history. A major part of this study will therefore be devoted to tracing the contours of successive missionary paradigms, from the first century to the twentieth. It should soon become clear that at no time in the past two millennia was there only one single "theology of mission". This was true even for the church in its pristine state (as the next four chapters will hopefully illustrate). However, different theologies of mission do not necessarily exclude each other; they form a multicolored mosaic of complementary and mutually enriching as well as mutually challenging frames of reference. Instead of trying to formulate one uniform view of mission we should rather attempt to chart the contours of "a pluriverse of missiology in a universe of mission" (Soares-Prabhu 1986:87).

I am not suggesting that each historical missionary model can be reconciled with every other such model. Frequently different understandings of mission are at odds with one another. Because of this, it will be necessary to look critically at the evolution of the missionary idea, to take a stand for one and against another interpretation. It means, of course, that the scholar, too, operates with certain presuppositions (which, naturally, must remain revisable!), and it would only be fair to state these in advance. This is what I would like to do on the next few pages. I shall not, at this stage, attempt to substantiate my convictions about mission in any detail—these will only emerge in the course of the study. Still, I believe that one cannot really embark on a project of this nature without sharing with the reader some of the assumptions operating when surveying and evaluating the vicissitudes of mission and missionary thinking in the course of twenty centuries. I am aware of the fact that, in following this route, I have—to some extent—anticipated views which will emerge in clearer profile only in the final part of this study. There I shall, however, develop them within the framework of what I shall call the emerging ecumenical paradigm of mission.

MISSION: AN INTERIM DEFINITION

1. The Christian faith, I submit, is intrinsically missionary. It is not the only persuasion that is missionary. Rather, it shares this characteristic with several

other religions, notably Islam and Buddhism, and also with a variety of ideologies, such as Marxism (cf Jongeneel 1986:6f). A distinctive element of missionary religions, in contrast to missionary ideologies, is that they all "hold to some great 'unveiling' of ultimate truth believed to be of universal import" (Stackhouse 1988:189). The Christian faith, for example, sees "all generations of the earth" as objects of God's salvific will and plan of salvation or, in New Testament terms, it regards the "reign of God" which has come in Jesus Christ as intended for "all humanity" (cf Oecumenische inleiding 1988:19). This dimension of the Christian faith is not an optional extra: Christianity is missionary by its very nature, or it denies its very *raison d'être*.

2. Missiology, as a branch of the discipline of Christian theology, is not a disinterested or neutral enterprise; rather, it seeks to look at the world from the perspective of commitment to the Christian faith (see also Oecumenische inleiding 1988:19f). Such an approach does not suggest an absence of critical examination; as a matter of fact, precisely for the sake of the Christian mission, it will be necessary to subject every definition and every manifestation of the Christian mission to rigorous analysis and appraisal.

3. We may, therefore, never arrogate it to ourselves to delineate mission too sharply and too self-confidently. Ultimately, mission remains undefinable; it should never be incarcerated in the narrow confines of our own predilections. The most we can hope for is to formulate some *approximations* of what mission is all about.

4. Christian mission gives expression to the dynamic relationship between God and the world, particularly as this was portrayed, first, in the story of the covenant people of Israel and then, supremely, in the birth, life, death, resurrection, and exaltation of Jesus of Nazareth. A theological foundation for mission, says Kramm, "is only possible if we continually refer back to the ground of our faith: God's self-communication in Jesus Christ" (1979:213 — my translation).

5. The Bible is not to be treated as a storehouse of truths on which we can draw at random. There are no immutable and objectively correct "laws of mission" to which exegesis of Scripture gives us access and which provide us with blueprints we can apply in every situation. Our missionary practice is not performed in unbroken continuity with the biblical witness; it is an altogether ambivalent enterprise executed in the context of tension between divine providence and human confusion (cf Gensichen 1971:16). The church's involvement in mission remains an act of faith without earthly guarantees.

6. The entire Christian existence is to be characterized as missionary existence (Hoekendijk 1967a:338) or, in the words of the Second Vatican Council, "the church on earth is by its very nature missionary" (AG 2). In light of this it is tautological to refer to a "universal gospel" (Hoekendijk 1967a:309). The church begins to be missionary not through its universal proclamation of the gospel, but through the universality of the gospel it proclaims (Frazier 1987:13).

7. Theologically speaking, "*foreign* missions" is not a separate entity. The missionary nature of the church does not just depend on the situation in which it finds itself at a given moment but is grounded in the gospel itself. The jus-

tification and foundation for foreign missions, as for home missions, "lies in the universality of salvation and the indivisibility of the reign of Christ" (Linz 1964:209 – my translation). The difference between home and foreign missions is not one of principle but of scope. We therefore have to repudiate the mystical doctrine of salt water (Bridston 1965:32); that is, the idea that travelling to foreign lands is the *sine qua non* for *any* kind of missionary endeavor and the final test and criterion of what is truly missionary (:33). Godin and Daniel's publication (1943) was the first serious study to have destroyed the "geographical myth" (Bridston) of mission: it proved that Europe, too, was a "mission field". The book did not go far enough, however. To the concept of mission as the first preaching of the gospel to pagans it simply added the idea of mission as the reintroduction of the gospel to neo-pagans. It still defined mission in terms of its addressees, not in terms of its nature, and suggested that mission is accomplished once the gospel has been (re)introduced to a group of people.

8. We have to distinguish between *mission* (singular) and *missions* (plural). The first refers primarily to the *missio Dei* (God's mission), that is, God's self-revelation as the One who loves the world, God's involvement in and with the world, the nature and activity of God, which embraces both the church and the world, and in which the church is privileged to participate. *Missio Dei* enunciates the good news that God is a God-for-people. *Missions* (the *missiones ecclesiae*: the missionary ventures of the church), refer to particular forms, related to specific times, places, or needs, of participation in the *missio Dei* (Davies 1966:33; cf Hoekendijk 1967a:346; Rütti 1972:232).

9. The missionary task is as coherent, broad and deep as the need and exigencies of human life (Gort 1980a:55). Various international missionary conferences since the 1950s have formulated this as "the whole church bringing the whole gospel to the whole world". People live in a series of integrated relationships; it is therefore indicative of a false anthropology and sociology to divorce the spiritual or the personal sphere from the material and the social.

10. It follows from the above that mission is God's "yes" to the world (cf Günther 1967:20f). When we speak about God, the world as the theater of God's activity is already implied (cf Hoekendijk 1967a:344). God's love and attention are directed primarily at the world, and mission is "participation in God's existence in the world" (Schütz 1930:245 – my translation). In our time, God's yes to the world reveals itself, to a large extent, in the church's missionary engagement in respect of the realities of injustice, oppression, poverty, discrimination, and violence. We increasingly find ourselves in a truly apocalyptic situation where the rich get richer and the poor poorer, and where violence and oppression from both the right and the left are escalating. The church-in-mission cannot possibly close its eyes to these realities, since "the pattern of the church in the chaos of our time is political through and through" (Schütz 1930:246 – my translation).

11. Mission includes *evangelism* as one of its essential dimensions. Evangelism is the proclamation of salvation in Christ to those who do not believe in him, calling them to repentance and conversion, announcing forgiveness of sin, and inviting them to become living members of Christ's earthly community and

to begin a life of service to others in the power of the Holy Spirit.

12. Mission is also God's "no" to the world (cf Günther 1967:21f). I have suggested, above, that mission is God's "yes" to the world. This was submitted in the conviction that there is continuity between the reign of God, the mission of the church, and justice, peace, and wholeness in society, and that salvation also has to do with what happens to people *in* this world. Still, what God has provided for us in Jesus Christ and what the church proclaims and embodies in its mission and evangelism is not simply an affirmation of the best people can expect in this world by way of health, liberty, peace, and freedom from want. God's reign is more than human progress on the horizontal plane. So if, on the one hand, we assert God's "yes" to the world as expression of the Christian's solidarity with society, we also have to affirm mission and evangelism as God's "no", as an expression of our opposition to and engagement with the world. If Christianity blends with social and political movements to the point of becoming completely identified with them, "the church will again become what is called a religion of society . . . But can the church of the crucified man from Nazareth ever become a political religion, without forgetting him and losing its identity?" (Moltmann 1975:3).

God's "no" to the world does not, however, signify any dualism, just as God's "yes" does not imply any unbroken continuity between this world and God's reign (cf Knapp 1977:166-168). Therefore, neither a secularized church (that is, a church which concerns itself only with this-worldly activities and interests) nor a separatist church (that is, a church which involves itself only in soul-saving and preparation of converts for the hereafter) can faithfully articulate the *missio Dei*.

13. The church-in-mission—as will be argued in detail later—may be described in terms of sacrament and sign. It is a *sign* in the sense of pointer, symbol, example or model; it is a *sacrament* in the sense of mediation, representation, or anticipation (cf Gassmann 1986:14). It is not identical with God's reign yet not unrelated to it either; it is "a foretaste of its coming, the sacrament of its anticipations in history" (Memorandum 1982:461). Living in the creative tension of, at the same time, being called out of the world and sent into the world, it is challenged to be God's experimental garden on earth, a fragment of the reign of God, having "the first fruits of the Spirit" (Rom 8:23) as a pledge of what is to come (2 Cor 1:22).

PART 1

NEW TESTAMENT MODELS
OF MISSION

Chapter 1

Reflections on the New Testament as a Missionary Document

THE MOTHER OF THEOLOGY

Introductions to missiology tend to begin with a section called something like "Biblical Foundations for Mission". Once these "foundations" have been established—so the argument seems to go—the author can proceed by developing his or her exegetical findings into a systematic "theory" or "theology" of mission.

In this volume I wish to proceed in a different manner. By means of a brief overview of the missionary character of the ministry of Jesus and the early church, followed by an in-depth discussion of the ways in which three prominent New Testament authors interpreted mission, I will argue that, in this respect, the New Testament witnesses to a fundamental shift when compared with the Old Testament. In surveying paradigm shifts in missionary thinking I wish to suggest that the first and cardinal paradigm change took place with the advent of Jesus of Nazareth and what followed after that. It is the contours of this first and foundational shift that I shall attempt to trace in the next four chapters, before turning to a second shift, less fundamental but also important—that of the "patristic" Greek church.

The missionary character of the New Testament has not always been appreciated. For a very long time it was customary, says Fiorenza (1976:1), to consider the New Testament writings primarily as "documents of an inner-Christian doctrinal struggle" and early Christian history as "confessional" history, "as a struggle between different Christian parties and theologians". In what follows I would like to submit that this approach to the New Testament is, at least to some extent, misguided. Instead I suggest, with Martin Hengel, that the history and the theology of early Christianity are, first of all, "mission history" and "mission theology" (Hengel 1983b:53). Hengel applies this description in the first place to the apostle Paul, but he certainly implies that the same is true of other New Testament writers as well. Other New Testament scholars, such as Heinrich Kasting and Ben Meyer, affirm this. Kasting states: "Mission was, in the early stages, more than a mere function; it was a fundamental expression of the life of the church. The beginnings of a missionary theology are therefore also the beginnings of Christian theology as such" (1969:127—my translation). Ben Meyer interprets: "Christianity had never been more itself, more consistent with Jesus and more evidently en route to its own future, than in the launching of the world mission" (1986:206, cf 18). In its mission, early Christianity took an astonishing "leap of life" from one world to another (Dix 1955:55), since it understood itself as the vanguard of a saved humankind (Meyer 1986:92).

Contemporary New Testament scholars are thus affirming what the systematic theologian Martin Kähler said eight decades ago: Mission is "the mother of theology" (Kähler [1908] 1971:190; my translation).[1] Theology, said Kähler, began as "an accompanying manifestation of the Christian mission" and not as "a luxury of the world-dominating church" (:189). The New Testament writers were not scholars who had the leisure to research the evidence before they put pen to paper. Rather, they wrote in the context of an "emergency situation", of a church which, because of its missionary encounter with the world, was *forced* to theologize (Kähler [1908] 1971:189; cf also Russell 1988). The gospels, in particular, are to be viewed not as writings produced by an historical impulse but as expressions of an ardent faith, written with the purpose of commending Jesus Christ to the Mediterranean world (Fiorenza 1976:20).

It is important to note that the New Testament authors also differed from one another, not least in their understanding of mission—as the ensuing three chapters will illustrate. We should, however, not be surprised if the New Testament does not reflect a uniform view of mission but, rather, a variety of "theologies of mission" (Spindler 1967:10; Kasting 1969:132; Rütti 1972:113f; Kramm 1979:215). As a matter of fact, no single overarching term for mission can as such be uncovered in the New Testament (Frankemölle 1982:94f). Pesch (1982:14-16) lists no less than ninety-five Greek expressions which relate to essential but frequently different aspects of the New Testament perspective on mission. So perhaps the New Testament authors were less interested in definitions of mission than in the missionary existence of their readers; to give expression to the latter they used a rich variety of metaphors, such as "the salt of the earth", "the light of the world", "a city on a hill", and the like. We may therefore, at best, succeed in creating a "semantic field" of New Testament perspectives on mission (Frankemölle 1982:96f). Hopefully the contours of this will become clearer as we proceed.

I shall return to the reasons for the differences between New Testament authors in respect of their understanding of mission. For the moment, however, let me briefly turn to the Old Testament.

MISSION IN THE OLD TESTAMENT

It might be asked whether one should not begin with the Old Testament in the search for an understanding of mission. This is a legitimate question. There is, for the Christian church and Christian theology, no New Testament divorced from the Old. However, on the issue of mission we run into difficulties here, particularly if we adhere to the traditional understanding of mission as the sending of preachers to distant places (a definition which, in the course of this study, will be challenged in several ways). There is, in the Old Testament, no indication of the believers of the old covenant being sent by God to cross geographical, religious, and social frontiers in order to win others to faith in Yahweh (cf Bosch 1959:19; Hahn 1965:20; Gensichen 1971:57,62; Rütti 1972:98; Huppenbauer 1977:38). Rzepkowski may therefore be correct when he says: "The decisive difference between the Old and the New Testament is mission. The New Testament is essentially a book about mission" (1974:80). Even the book Jonah has nothing to do with mission in the normal sense of the word. The prophet is sent to Nineveh not to proclaim salvation to non-believers but to announce doom. Neither is he himself interested in mission; he is only interested in destruction. Contrary to what earlier scholars have suggested, not even Second Isaiah is to be regarded as a book about mission (Hahn 1965:19).

Even so, the Old Testament is fundamental to the understanding of mission in the New. There is, first, the decisive difference between the faith of Israel and the religions of the surrounding nations. Those religions are hierophanic in nature; they express themselves as manifestations of the divine at specified holy places, where the human world can communicate with the divine. This occurs in cults or rituals, in which the threatening powers of chaos and destruction can be neutralized. At the same time the religions are caught up in the cycle of the seasons, where winter and summer follow each other in an eternal battle for supremacy. The emphasis, throughout, is on the reenactment of what has once been, on repetition and remembrance.

Not so with the faith of Israel. The essence of this faith is the firm conviction that God has saved the fathers and mothers from Egypt, led them through the desert and settled them in the land Canaan. They have only become a people because of God's intervention. What is more, God has made a covenant with them at Mount Sinai, and this covenant determines their entire subsequent history. In the religions of Israel's neighbors God is present in the eternal cycle of nature and at certain cultic places. In Israel, however, *history* is the arena of God's activity. The focus is on what God has done, is doing and is yet to do according to his declared intention (cf Stanley 1980:57-59). God is, in the words of the title of the well-known book by G. E. Wright (1952), the "God who *acts*". It may therefore be more accurate to refer to the Bible as the Acts of God rather than call it the Word of God (Wright 1952:13). For the people of Israel (unless they allow themselves, as in fact often happens, to be seduced by the hierophanic religions) faith can never be a religion of the status quo. Dynamic change is to be expected since God is a dynamic being, engaged in the active direction of history (:22). The Old Testament surely knows of the immediate awareness of God's presence in worship and prayer, but its "main emphasis . . . is certainly on his revelation of himself in historical acts" (:23).

As the God of history God is, secondly, also the God of promise. This becomes evident once we reflect on the Old Testament understanding of *revelation*. We often interpret this as merely a making public or an unveiling of something that has always been there but was kept hidden. Revelation is, however, an event in which God commits in the present to be involved with his people in the future. He reveals himself as the God of Abraham, Isaac, and Jacob, in other words as the God who has been active in past history and who precisely for this reason will also be the God of the future. Nature festivals such as those of the first fruits and of the harvest are therefore, in line with this logic, gradually transformed into festivals of historical events such as the exodus from Egypt and the sealing of the covenant at Sinai; that is, the festivals of nature become celebrations of events in the history of salvation. And these celebrations are more than just occasions to remember; they are, at the same time, celebrations in anticipation of God's future involvement with his people, of God being *ahead* of his people (Rütti 1972:83-86, with reference to Th.C. Vriezen, Gerhard von Rad, and other Old Testament scholars).

God as revealed in history is, thirdly, the One who has elected Israel. The purpose of the election is service, and when this is withheld, election loses its meaning. Primarily Israel is to serve the marginal in its midst: the orphan, the widow, the poor, and the stranger. Whenever the people of Israel renew their covenant with Yahweh, they recognize that they are renewing their obligations to the victims of society.

From an early stage, furthermore, there has been the conviction that God's compassion embraces the nations also. There is an ambivalent attitude toward the other nations in the Old Testament. On the one hand they are Israel's political enemies or at least rivals; on the other hand God himself brings them into Israel's circle of vision. The story of Abraham is an illustration of this. It follows hard on the Babel episode, which dramatizes the foundering of the nations' own schemes. And then God begins all over again—with Abraham. What Babel has been unable to achieve is promised and guaranteed in Abraham, namely the blessing of all nations. In the Abraham stories of the Yahwist there is not one which does not, in one way or another, illustrate Abraham's (and therefore Israel's) relationship with the nations (Huppenbauer 1977:39f). The entire history of Israel unveils the continuation of God's involvement with the nations. The God of Israel is the Creator and Lord of the whole world. For this reason Israel can comprehend its own history only in continuity with the history of the nations, not as a separate history.

At this point the Old Testament's dialectical tension between judgment and mercy comes into play—judgment and mercy of which both Israel and the nations are the recipients. Second Isaiah (Is 40-55) and Jonah illustrate two sides of the same coin. Jonah symbolizes the people of Israel, who have perverted their election into pride and privilege. The booklet does not aim at reaching and converting Gentiles; it aims, rather, at the repentance and conversion of Israel and contrasts God's magnanimity with the parochialism of his own people. Second Isaiah, on the other hand, particularly in the metaphor of the suffering servant, paints the picture of an Israel which has already been the recipient of God's judgment and wrath, and which now, precisely in its weakness and lowliness, becomes a witness to God's victory. Just at the moment of Israel's deepest humiliation and despondency we see the nations approach Israel and confess: "The Lord . . . is faithful, the Holy One of Israel . . . has chosen *you*" (Is 49:7).

Thus, as Yahweh's compassion reaches out to Israel and beyond, it gradually becomes clear that, in the final analysis, God is as concerned with the nations as with Israel. On the basis of its faith Israel can draw two fundamental conclusions: Since the true God has made himself known to Israel, he is to be encountered only in Israel; and since the God of Israel is the only true God, he also is the God of the whole world. The first conclusion emphasizes isolation and exclusion from the rest of humankind; the second suggests a basic openness and the possibility of reaching out to the nations (cf Labuschagne 1975:9).

Israel would, however, not actually go out to the nations. Neither would Israel expressly call the nations to faith in Yahweh. If they do come, it is because God is bringing them in. So, if there is a "missionary" in the Old Testament, it is God himself who will, as his eschatological deed *par excellence*, bring the nations to Jerusalem to worship him there together with his covenant people. The prophecies alluding to the future worship of Yahweh by all nations are, however, few; in addition, they are not always free from ambiguity. Still we may, with Jeremias (1958:57-60), piece together some evidence in this regard. The most positive composite picture — positive, that is, from the point of view of the nations — might have looked something like the following:

The nations are waiting for Yahweh and trusting in him (Is 51:5). His glory will be revealed to them all (Is 40:5). All the ends of the earth are called upon to look to God and be saved (Is 45:22). He makes his servant known as a light to the Gentiles (Is 42:6; 49:6). A highway is constructed, from Egypt and Assyria to Jerusalem (Is 19:23); the nations encourage each other to go up to the mountain of the Lord (Is 2:5), and they carry precious gifts with them (Is 18:7). The purpose of all of this is to worship at the temple in Jerusalem, the sanctuary of the whole world, together with the covenant people (Ps 96:9). Egypt will be blessed as God's people, Assyria as the work of his hands, and Israel as his heritage (Is 19:25). The visible expression of this global reconciliation will be the celebration of the messianic banquet upon the mountain of God; the nations will behold God with unveiled faces, and death will be swallowed up forever (Is 25:6-8).

There is, however, also a dark backdrop to this positive picture. As the nations journey to Jerusalem, Israel *remains* the center of the center and the recipient of "the wealth of the nations" (Is 60:11). Even in Second Isaiah, which represents the high-water mark of Old Testament universalism, there are traces of this Israel-centeredness. The Sabeans, for instance, will come to the people of Israel in chains and bow down before them (45:14). Elsewhere, too, when judgment is announced on some nations (e.g. Is 47), it is not always clear whether they are seen as people who have refused God's merciful overtures or, rather, primarily as enemies of Israel.

It is therefore not strange that, in the course of time, it is the negative attitude toward the nations that prevails. As the political and social conditions of the people of the old covenant deteriorate, there increasingly develops the expectation that, one day, the Messiah will come to conquer the Gentile nations and restore Israel. This expectation is usually linked with fantastic ideas of world domination by Israel, to whom all the nations will be subject. It reaches its peak in the apocalyptic beliefs and attitudes of the Essene communities along the shores of the Dead Sea. The horizons of apocalyptic belief are cosmic: God will destroy the entire present world and usher in a new world according to a detailed and predetermined plan. The present world, with all its inhabitants, is radically evil. The faithful have to separate themselves from it, keep themselves pure as the holy remnant, and wait for God's intervention. In such a climate even the idea of a missionary attitude to the Gentiles would be preposterous (Kasting 1969:129). At best God would, without any involvement on the part of Israel, by means of a divine act, save those Gentiles he had elected in advance.

To a large extent Jewish apocalyptic spells the end of the earlier dynamic understanding of history. Past salvific events are no longer celebrated as guarantees and anticipations of God's future involvement with his people; they have become sacred traditions which have to be preserved unchanged. The Law becomes an absolute entity which Israel has to serve and obey. Greek metaphysical categories gradually begin to replace historical thinking. Faith becomes a matter of timeless metahistorical and carefully systematized teaching (Rütti 1972:95).

BIBLE AND MISSION

This is the context and climate into which Jesus of Nazareth was born. And he clearly and unequivocally understood his mission in terms of the authentic Old Testament tradition.

Until fairly recently it has been customary in Christian and particularly missionary circles to view Jesus in purely idealistic terms. In the course of time, so the argument goes, all this-worldly, national, social, and historical aspects of the Old Testament faith were overcome and the way prepared for a truly universal religion for all humankind. This universal tendency, which was always, even if only latently, present in the Old Testament, then reached perfection in Jesus' teaching. The center of his teaching—so this understanding of Jesus is classically summarized by the Catholic missiologist, Thomas Ohm, in his *magnum opus*—was his message about God's reign as being of "a purely religious, supra-national, other-worldly, predominantly spiritual and inward nature" (1962:247; my translation). It was something infinitely "higher" than the Old Testament and was no longer tied to the people of Israel.

Today we know that this view can no longer be maintained. Even so, it may still come as a surprise to many to be told that, during his life on earth, Jesus ministered, lived, and thought almost exclusively within the framework of first-century Jewish religious faith and life. He is introduced to us, particularly in the Gospel of Matthew, as the One who has come to fulfill what had been promised to the fathers and mothers of the faith. It could not have been immediately clear to his early followers that the door of faith would soon be opened to the Gentiles too.

Of course, we no longer have any direct access to the story of Jesus. The only access we have to that story is through the New Testament authors, particularly those who wrote our four gospels. The subdiscipline of form criticism, which dominated (Western) New Testament scholarship from the 1920s to the 1950s has, however, taught us to be very skeptical about the historical reliability of our gospels and to accept as authentic only those sayings of Jesus which could in no way have been "invented" by subsequent tradition. For the "Jesus of history" all this had a devastating effect. Rudolf Bultmann chose to say virtually nothing about him. His story was covered under so many layers of *Gemeindetheologie* (the theology of the early Christian communities) that it would be a Sisyphean task to piece it together again.

Meanwhile, however, we have left the heyday of form criticism behind us. Redaction criticism has helped us to concentrate not so much on uncovering authentic sayings of Jesus as to concentrate, rather, on the evangelists' witness to him. We have discovered that there is no "Jesus of history" divorced from the "Christ of faith", since the evangelists — in witnessing about him — could not but look through the eyes of faith at Jesus of Nazareth. Indeed, the sayings *of* Jesus in the gospels are already and at the same time sayings *about* Jesus (Schottroff and Stegemann 1986:2, cf 4). Precisely from this perspective the "historical Jesus" has again become crucial as we begin to rediscover him, and the context in which he lived and labored, through the eyes of faith of the four evangelists. Today scholars show a greater confidence in the earthly Jesus than was customary some decades ago (Burchard 1980:13; Hengel 1983a:29). Consequently, the "practice of Jesus" (Echegaray 1984) has become the focus of much contemporary theologizing. Jesus, as Echegaray puts it (1984:xv-xvi), inspired the early Christian communities to prolong the logic of their own life and ministry in a creative way amid historical circumstances that were in many respects new and different. They handled the traditions about him with creative but responsible freedom, retaining those traditions while at the same time adapting them.

That the first Christians proceeded in this way should not trouble us. If we take the incarnation seriously, the Word has to become flesh in every new context. For this very reason the contemporary theologian's task is not really different from what the New Testament authors set out so boldly to do. What they did for their time, we have to do for ours. We too must listen to the past and speak to the present and the future (LaVerdiere and Thompson 1976:596). At the same time, our task today is far more difficult than that of the New Testament authors. Matthew, Luke, Paul, and the others lived in cultures radically different from ours and faced problems of which we have no idea (just as we face problems of which they knew nothing). Moreover, they used notions their contemporaries immediately understood but we do not.

There have, of course, always been those who attempted to cut the Gordian knot by setting up a direct relationship between the Jesus of the New Testament and their own situation, applying the ancient words uncritically and on a one-to-one basis to their own circumstances. Others have, with the aid of all the critical tools at their disposal, set out to reconstruct "objective" histories of Jesus. Surprisingly, however, there was often little difference between the Jesus of conservative authors and the Jesus of critical scholarship. Only too frequently

Jesus was re-created in the image of the contemporary theologian and made subservient to the latter's interests and predilections (cf Schweitzer 1952:4). Small wonder then that the many books written on Jesus during the past two centuries or so picture an absolute bewildering variety of Jesuses, some of whom are literally poles apart from others. Jesus may turn out to be a benign middle-class American, the "founder of modern business," the executive who proved that dedication to one's task and a spirit of servanthood guarantee success (cf Barton 1925). Or he may be a Jesus of the right-wing establishment who like some latter-day Führer leads his nation to a position of domination over others (see examples in Hengel 1971:34f). Again, he may be a revolutionary Jesus, who broadcasts Marxist slogans, has a carefully worked-out strategy, in three stages, for overthrowing the politico-economic system, and who assiduously cultivates a following in preparation for that great moment (Pixley 1981:71-82). In each case the "Jesus of history" turns out to be the Jesus of the historian concerned.

Christians are, however, not at liberty to talk about Jesus in any way they choose. They are challenged to speak about him from within the context of the community of believers, "the whole people of God", past and present (Schottroff and Stegemann 1986:vi). The variety of Christian utterances can therefore not be unlimited. It is, in fact, limited—not only by the community of believers but, even more fundamentally, by the community's "charter of foundation", the event of Jesus Christ. It is the events at the origin of the Christian community—the "agenda" set by Jesus living, dying, and rising from the dead—that basically and primarily established the distinctiveness of that community, and to those events we too have to orientate ourselves. God comes to us primarily in the history of Jesus and his deeds (Echegaray 1984:9). There remains a difference between the first decisive dimensions of a historical event and its subsequent evolution; in light of this we may indeed, as Schleiermacher suggested (cf Gerrish 1984:196), regard the New Testament as norm for what is authentically Christian. A crucial task for the church today is to test continually whether its understanding of Christ corresponds with that of the first witnesses (Küng 1987:238; cf also the perceptive discussion of Smit 1988).

This implies, naturally, that we cannot, with integrity, reflect on what mission might mean today unless we turn to the Jesus of the New Testament, since our mission is "moored to Jesus' person and ministry" (Hahn 1984:269). As Kramm puts it,

> A theological foundation for mission is only possible with reference to the point of departure of our faith: God's self-communication in Christ as the basis which logically precedes and is fundamental to every other reflection (1979:213—my translation).

To affirm this is not to say that all we have to do is to establish what mission meant for Jesus and the early church and then define our missionary practice in the same terms, as though the whole problem can be solved by way of a direct application of Scripture. To do this would be to succumb to "the temptation of concordism, which equates the social groups and forces within first-century Palestine with those of our own time" (G. Gutiérrez, in Echegaray 1984:xi). In some circumstances, as a matter of fact, such an approach would be even more unwarranted than in others; the historical gap of two millennia between our time and the time of Jesus may turn out to be of less importance than the social gap that separates today's middle-class elite from the first Christians or, for that matter, from many marginalized people today (Schottroff and Stegemann 1986:vii). One only has to read the several volumes of Ernesto Cardenal's *The Gospel in Solentiname* to discover that the socio-political circumstances of the Nicaraguan peasants who made up Cardenal's basic Christian community were closer to the context of the early church than the situation of many Christians in the West is to that of the early church. The same may be true of some indigenous African independent churches or the house-churches of mainland China.

Yet even where the socio-cultural gap between today's communities and those of the first Christians is narrow, it is there, and it should be respected. A historico-critical study may help us to comprehend what mission was for Paul and Mark and John but it will not immediately tell us what *we* must think about mission in our own concrete situation (Soares-Prabhu 1986:86). The text of the New Testament generates various valid interpretations in different readers, as Paul Ricoeur has often argued. Thus the meaning of a text cannot be reduced to a single, univocal sense, to what it "originally" meant.

The approach called for requires an interaction between the self-definition of early Christian authors and actors and the self-definition of today's believers who wish to be inspired and guided by those early witnesses. How did the early Christians as well as subsequent generations understand themselves? How do we, today's Christians, understand ourselves? And what effect do these "self-understandings" have on their and our interpretation of mission? These are the questions I wish to pursue.

In recent decades scholars such as G. Theissen, A. J. Malherbe, E. A. Judge, L. Schottroff, W. A. Meeks, and B. F. Meyer have helped us tremendously in gaining a better understanding of the social world of early Christianity. By subjecting the contexts in which those Christians lived to careful sociological analysis these scholars have added significantly to our understanding of the early church and its mission. It seems to me, however, that—without in any sense disparaging the important work that has been done in this field—we are now in need of going beyond sociological analysis to an approach which may be termed critical hermeneutics (cf Nel 1988). The bias of most social analysis (as Meyer 1986:31 has shown) is toward a view from the outside. The bias of critical hermeneutics, on the other hand, is toward a view from the inside—in other words, toward inquiring into the *self*-definitions of those with whom we wish to enter into dialogue. Indeed, self-definition becomes a key concept in this approach. In his study on the early Christians' "world mission and self-discovery" Ben Meyer has (in my view, convincingly) shown that it was because of a new self-definition that at least some first-century disciples felt urged to get involved in missionary outreach to the surrounding world. Meyer then sets about tracing the contours of this new self-definition by attempting answers to questions such as the following (Meyer 1986:17),

> How is it that, alone of the parties, movements, and sects of first-century Judaism, Christianity discovered within itself the impetus to found gentile religious communities and to include them under the name "the Israel of God" (Gal 6:16)? How can we explain the dynamics of the decision in favor of this impetus? ... How can we account for the origins of the conception of Christ not only as the fulfillment of the promises to Israel but as ... the first man of a new mankind?

The critical hermeneutic approach goes beyond the (historically-interesting) quest of making explicit early Christian self-definitions, however. It desires to encourage dialogue between those self-definitions and all subsequent ones, including those of ourselves and our contemporaries. It accepts that self-definitions may be inadequate or even wrong. So its aim is that those self-definitions be extended, criticized, or challenged (cf Nel 1988:163). It assumes that there is no such thing as an objective reality "out there," which now needs to be understood and interpreted. Rather, reality is *intersubjective* (:153f); it is always *interpreted* reality and this interpretation is profoundly affected by our self-definitions (:209). It follows from this that reality changes if one's self-definition changes. This is precisely what happened with early Christians and, in a variety of comparable ways, with later generations of Christians. The changes in self-definition were not always adequate; as a matter of fact, they were often warped, as I hope to show in the course of my exploration. Still, they have to be taken seriously and should be challenged by the self-definitions of other Christians, particularly those who first experienced a "paradigm shift" in their understanding of reality. In light of this the challenge to the study of mission may be described (in the words of van Engelen 1975:310) as relating the always-relevant Jesus event of twenty centuries ago to the future of God's promised reign by means of meaningful initiatives for the here and now.

Naturally, if we explore what I have here referred to as the self-definition of early Christians, we will be forced also to ask about the self-definition of *Jesus* (cf Goppelt 1981:159-205). This is a quest we have to pursue even if, as has been said above, we only know Jesus via the witness of the early church, that is, via the self-definitions of those believers. The point is that there are no simplistic or obvious moves from the New Testament to our contemporary missionary practice. The Bible does not function in such a direct way. There may be, rather, a range of alternative moves which remain in deep tension with each other but may nevertheless all be valid (Brueggemann 1982:397, 408). As the *Inter-Anglican Theological and Doctrinal Commission* (1986:48) says,

> The Holy Spirit who guides into all truth, may be present not so much exclusively on one side of a theological dispute as in the very encounter of diverse visions held by persons ... who share a faithfulness and commitment to Christ and to each other.

JESUS AND ISRAEL

In his classic book on conversion, A. D. Nock has demonstrated that the era from Alexander the Great to Augustine was a time of unprecedented economic, social and religious ferment and change. Greek religions and Greek philosophy spread eastward, into Central Asia. At the same time many Eastern religions, particularly those of Egypt, Syria, and Asia Minor penetrated into the Greco-Roman world and won thousands of converts there (Nock 1933; cf Grant 1986:29-42).

The Jewish faith was one of those which had permeated the entire region. There was little evidence of any active going out to Gentiles in order to win them over to the faith. Still, Gentiles were often attracted to the Jewish faith. The very term used for such converts to Judaism, "proselytes",[2] illustrated this; individual Gentiles, more or less on their own initiative, approached Jews, submitted to the Torah, and asked to be circumcised. Outside of this circle of people who had made the transition to Judaism, there was another category, the "God-fearers" who, though attracted to Judaism, did not take the final step of asking for circumcision.[3] On the whole, however, the attention of pious Jews was not focused on Gentiles. Frequently their concern was not even with all members of their own race. For several centuries prior to the birth of Jesus the conviction was gaining ground that not all Israel but only a faithful remnant would be saved. Several religious groups within Judaism regarded themselves as this remnant and all others, even fellow Jews, as being beyond the pale. This was particularly true of the Essene communities along the Dead Sea.[4] In most of these circles there was little concern for recruiting others even of their own kind, let alone Gentiles.

Still, all these endeavors have to be seen within the horizon of the struggle for the true Israel, for the sake of the restitution of the people of the covenant. In this context we also have to see the ministry of John the Baptist. He appeared on the scene as a prophetic preacher sent by God to call Israel to repentance and conversion. In the Baptist's view it could no longer be assumed that all Israel was elected. The Jews of his time were a "brood of vipers" (Mt 3:7; Lk 3:7) and equated with pagans. Only a remnant would be saved if they repented and produced fruit in keeping with repentance (Mt 3:8; Lk 3:8). To underscore the fact that all Israel were Gentiles in the eyes of God, outside the covenant, the repentant had to submit to the rite of baptism in the same way Gentile converts to Judaism did.

This, then, was the religious climate into which Jesus was born: it was a time of sectarianism and fanaticism, of religious traffic between East and West, of merchants and soldiers carrying home new ideas, of experimenting with new faiths. Socio-politically the period was no less volatile. Palestine was under Roman occupation. One of the results of this was a system of large estates spreading gradually but irresistibly throughout the country, at the expense of communal property. The already poor peasants were soon transformed into a labor pool for the estate owners and managers; these are the "day laborers" we frequently meet in the gospel parables.

Rome consolidated its hold on the Jews by organizing a census (in AD 6), followed by the actual collection of taxes. For the Jews this was more than an irritation, it was an assault on their ancestral rights and their holy land, which was now degraded to a mere province of the vast Roman Empire. It was understandable that, at such a time, the memories of the past would be revived: the liberation from Egypt, the glorious reign of David, the Maccabean revolt, etc. Small wonder then that, precisely during the various stages of the census, there often were disturbances. We read in Acts 5:37 that Judas the Galilean led a band of people in revolt "in the days of the census". The fact that Jesus' birth was linked to the taking of the census (Lk 2:1-2) perhaps also contributed to the view that he might be the expected Messiah, that precisely in Israel's darkest hour God would send a deliverer.

Jesus' life and ministry have to be seen within this concrete historical context. If not, we will not begin to understand him. He stands in the tradition of the prophets. Like them and like John the Baptist his concern is the repentance and salvation of Israel.

> As . . . Jew he understands himself as being sent to his own people. His call for repentance concerns this people. . . . His life's work is limited to them. That he is sent only to Israel, is already evident in Matthew 1:21 and Luke 1:54. According to the reports of all the gospels he finds himself virtually always on the soil of the Holy Land. He appears to enter Gentile and Samaritan territories only with some reluctance. He restlessly moves around in the land of the Jews, back and forth. . . . Precisely as Son of Man he has to fulfill the calling of the son of David: to liberate his people . . . He devotes himself to Israel with unconditional devotion while declining every other solicitation (Bosch 1959:77; translated from the German).

Still, the question about the earthly Jesus' attitude to Gentiles is important but secondary, as we hope to illustrate below (cf also Bosch 1959:93-115; Jeremias 1958; Hahn 1965:26-41). There undoubtedly is a difference between Jesus and the Jewish religious groups of his time, between his self-definition and theirs. All of them (including, apparently, John the Baptist) concern themselves with the salvation of only a *remnant* of Israel. Jesus' mission is to *all* Israel. This is expressed, first, in his constantly being on the move, throughout the entire Jewish land, as a wandering preacher and healer, without permanent ties to family, profession, or residence. The fact that he selects twelve disciples to be with him and that he sends them out into the Jewish land points in the same direction: their number refers back to the ancient composition of the people of Israel and their mission to the future messianic reign, when "all Israel" will be saved (cf Goppelt 1981:207-213; Meyer 1986:62).

Jesus' attitude to the Pharisees appears to constitute a special case. The earliest tradition does not present them as Jesus' implacable enemies. They were not yet the leaders of Judaism; they would establish their undisputed hegemony only after the destruction of Jerusalem (in AD 70). Like Jesus, they attempted to deal theologically with Israel's distress, even if in a very different manner. There can, therefore, be no doubt that Jesus sought to win them over (Schottroff and Stegemann 1986:35 and 125, note 94).

More important than Jesus' plea to the Pharisees, however, is his "consistent challenge to attitudes, practices and structures that tended arbitrarily to restrict or exclude potential members of the Israelite community" (Senior and Stuhl-mueller 1983:154). This applies particularly to those who are marginal to the Jewish establishment. The Jesus story mentions them by many names: the poor, the blind, the lepers, the hungry, those who weep, the sinners, the tax-collectors, those possessed by demons, the persecuted, the captives, those who are weary and heavy laden, the rabble who know nothing of the law, the little ones, the least, the last, the lost sheep of the house of Israel, even the prostitutes (Nolan 1976:21-29). As happens in our own time, the affliction of many of those on the periphery of society is occasioned by repression, discrimination, violence, and exploitation. They are, in the full sense of the word, victims of the society of the day. Even the "sinners" are not without ado to be understood in modern terms. We should not beatify them either. They are probably at one and the same time victims of circumstances, practitioners of despised trades, *and* shady characters (Schottroff and Stegemann 1986:14f). The point is simply that Jesus turns to all people who have been pushed aside: to the sick who are segregated on cultic and ritual grounds, to the prostitutes and sinners who are ostracized on moral grounds, and to the tax-collectors who are excluded on religious and political grounds (Hahn 1965:30). Tax-collectors and prostitutes may even be praised by Jesus as models to emulate, since they heed his call while others do not (Mt 21:31; cf Schottroff and Stegemann 1986:33).

Jesus' socializing with tax-collectors must have been particularly offensive to the religious establishment. Tax-collectors were regarded as traitors to the Jewish cause, as collaborators with the Romans and exploiters of their own people (Ford 1984:70-78; Schottroff and Stegemann 1986:7-13; Wedderburn 1988:168), but Jesus does not pass them by. He invites himself to the home of Zacchaeus, a wealthy chief tax-collector (Lk 17:1-5). And he invites Levi (or Matthew) to leave his booth and follow him (Mt 9:9 par.). The call is an act of grace, a restoration of fellowship, the beginning of a new life—even for tax-collectors (Schweizer 1971:40).

Preeminently, however, the tradition (particularly as retained in Luke's gospel) tells of Jesus as "the hope of the poor" (Schottroff and Stegemann 1986). "The poor" is a comprehensive term, which often includes some of the other categories already mentioned. What makes them "the poor" is the fact that circumstances (or, perhaps more precisely, the wealthy and powerful) have treated them unkindly. They are the ones who cannot but be anxious about tomorrow (cf Mt 6:34) and worry about what to eat and to wear (Mt 6:25). The standard wage for a laborer was a silver denarius a day, which was barely enough to keep a small family at a subsistence level. If such a laborer did not find work for several days, his family was destitute. In such circumstances the fourth petition in the Lord's Prayer ("Give us today our bread for this day") takes on a poignancy many of us no longer experience. It is a prayer for survival.

In the ministry of Jesus, God is inaugurating his eschatological reign and he is doing it among the poor, the lowly, and the despised. "No greater religious claim could have been made in the context of Jewish religion" (Schottroff and Stegemann 1986:36). The wretched life of the poor is contrary to God's purposes, and Jesus has come to put an end to their misery.

AN ALL-INCLUSIVE MISSION

What amazes one again and again is the *inclusiveness* of Jesus' mission. It embraces both the poor and the rich, both the oppressed and the oppressor, both the sinners and the devout. His mission is one of dissolving alienation and breaking down walls of hostility, of crossing boundaries between individuals and groups. As God forgives us gratuitously, we are to forgive those who wrong us — up to seventy times seven times, which in fact means limitlessly, more often than we are able to count (Senior and Stuhlmueller 1983:148f).

The inclusiveness of Jesus' mission is highlighted particularly in the *Logia* or Sayings-Source (also known as Q).[5] The wandering prophets[6] who make use of the Logia, undoubtedly have *all* of Israel in mind as they move around in the Jewish land and proclaim the words of Jesus to all they meet (Schottroff and Stegemann 48f). This is the only aspect from the rich and varied theology of Q I wish to accentuate here.

There can be no doubt that a primary concern of the *Logia* is the preaching of love even to enemies in order that, if at all possible, such enemies may be won over. Mark 2:16 (which does not come from Q) already illustrates a basic problem the Pharisees have with Jesus (even those who do not *a priori* feel negatively toward him) — the fact that he does not lay down any conditions. We can still detect the amazement in their voices when they say to the disciples: "Why does he eat with tax-collectors and sinners?" The Q prophets are in basic continuity with this element in the early tradition about Jesus. They are perhaps persecuted for their beliefs. Yet in spite of this (or because of this?) they turn their full attention to their persecutors and to all others who have rejected the message of Jesus. The self-understanding of this group of messengers of Jesus is, as far as we know, "without sociological or religio-sociological parallel" (Schottroff and Stegemann 1986:61, cf 58).

The injunction to love one's enemies has rightly been described as the most characteristic saying of Jesus (references in Senior and Stuhlmueller 1983:159). Even Lapide (1986:91), an Orthodox Jew, says that this was "an innovation introduced by Jesus". And the Q prophets faithfully retain and observe it. It would appear that these preachers are reviled, interrogated, ostracized, and threatened like sheep among wolves, yet they continue to offer their message of peace and love to the very people who treat them so unjustly. Even the persistent rejection of their message does not cause them to give up.

Some of the sentiments conveyed by the *Logia* are indeed deeply moving and at the same time eminently missionary. "This generation" — those who oppose the preachers and spurn their message — "is like children to whom other children call out: " 'We piped to you, and you did not dance; we wailed, and you did not mourn' " (Mt 11:16f). Again and again invitations go out to them, but they refuse to respond. Another Q-saying is directed to Jerusalem as symbol of all Israel, which kills the prophets and stones those sent to her. Yet still the flow of prophets to Israel continues unabated: "How often would I have gathered your children together as a hen gathers her brood under her wings, and you would not!" (Mt 23:37 par). Like Noah of old the *Logia* prophets face people who are unaware of the impending judgment and indifferent to their urgent warnings, yet they continue to issue these warnings (cf Mt 24:37-39). People only have to ask, the preachers say, and God will respond; they only have to knock and the door will be opened. God is the Father of all Israel; and which father will give his son a stone instead of bread, or a snake if he asks for a fish? "If you then, who are evil, know how to give good gifts to your children, how much more will your Father who is in heaven give good gifts to those who ask him!" (Mt 7:11 par). Once again the addressees (those who are "evil"—v 11) are the enemies of the message of Jesus, but God has not turned his back upon them. He still makes his sun rise even on them (Mt 5:44 par). In keeping with God's magnanimity the followers of Jesus do not define their identity in terms of opposition to outsiders. They remind themselves of Jesus' words: "If you love those who love you, what reward have you? Do not even the tax collectors do the same? And if you salute only your brethren, what more are you doing than others? Do not even the Gentiles do the same?" (Mt 5:46f).

The Q prophets certainly also announce judgment. The towns that reject their message, they say, face a fate more terrible than the fate that befell Sodom and Gomorrah (Mt 10:11-15 par). Yet the preachers of the Sayings-Source are not latter-day Jonahs who look forward with glee to the disaster they prophesy. Rather, their announcements of doom are intended as a kind of shock treatment, as a last urgent call to repentance and conversion, as an expression of their deep concern for those who oppose and revile them. "They practice love of enemies and proclaim judgment; in fact, they practice love by means of their proclamation of judgment" (Schottroff and Stegemann 1986:58). Their call for conversion is implicit in each of the judgment sayings. They continue to pursue those who refuse to listen, and they are prepared to persevere with this ministry until the last headstrong and wayward Israelite has been found and returned to the fold. Does not, as a matter of fact, a good shepherd do the same? Does he not leave the ninety-nine and go after the one sheep that has gone astray? (Mt 18:12 par). And would God expect less of the followers of Jesus?

This is the way in which the Q prophets emulate their Master. Evidently their compassion for all Israel, like their Master's, is total. And like him, their proclamation knows nothing of coercion. It always remains an invitation. Is it possible to imagine a more ardent and compelling missionary spirit?

AND THE GENTILES?

The preachers of the *Logia* still operate within a limited horizon. Jesus' own mission, they believe, was restricted to Israel. So is theirs. Of course, like Jesus, their concern is with *all* Israel, not just with a remnant. But the Gentile world really falls outside of their purview, although they are aware that a mission among Gentiles has already begun and it is most unlikely that they oppose this ministry. Moreover, the very nature of their commitment to Israel, even to the point of loving their worst enemies and inviting them to follow Jesus, gives witness to the fact that, in the long run, their message cannot be confined to Israel. They know that John the Baptist already proclaimed that God was able to raise up children for Abraham out of stones and that he was therefore not bound to Israel (Mt 3:9 par). They also repeat sayings of Jesus according to which Gentiles may become an indictment to Jews: the people of Nineveh will condemn "this generation", for they repented at the preaching of Jonah whilst the Jews of their own time do not, in spite of the presence of "something greater than Jonah" (Mt 12:41 par).

The Gentiles thus do appear in Q, but mainly within the framework of judgment sayings or as a warning to Israel that it may jeopardize its position of privilege. The prophets know that some non-Jews have already, during Jesus' own ministry, put Jews to shame. One of the best-known examples is that of a centurion from Capernaum who amazed Jesus and caused him to exclaim: "Truly, I say to you, not even in Israel have I found such faith" (Mt 8:10 par). In like manner a Canaanite woman's conduct prompts him to say: "O woman, great is your faith!" (Mt 15:28). Small wonder, then, that Gentiles can some- times be portrayed as substitute guests at the eschatological banquet. People will come from east and west and north and south and take their places at the feast, while "those who were born to the kingdom" will be thrown out (Mt 8:11-13, NEB; cf Lk 13:28-30). They are, in the metaphoric language of the parable of the great banquet, the guests who have refused the invitation on the basis of incredibly flimsy excuses and now have to look on while the Gentiles take their places, not because of any merit such Gentiles may have, but simply because they have responded positively. Such Gentiles are perhaps prefigured in the tax collectors and prostitutes who "go into the kingdom of God" ahead of the religious establishment (Mt 21:31) and in the parable of the prodigal son, which Jesus tells precisely because the Pharisees are upset when he wel- comes tax-collectors and sinners and eats with them (Lk 15:1f).

What is it that gave rise to the many sayings, parables, and stories that seem, at the very least, to nourish the idea that, one day, God's covenant will reach far beyond the people of Israel? In my view there can be no doubt: the primary inspiration for all these stories could only have been the provocative, boundary-breaking nature of Jesus' own ministry.

For a long time New Testament scholars tended to deny the fundamental missionary dimension of Jesus' earthly ministry (often on the basis of the argu- ment that we know too little about the historical Jesus to make any such claim) and to attribute the entire phenomenon of the Gentile mission after Easter to a variety of socio-religious circumstances or impute it almost exclusively to individual Christian leaders such as Paul. Although such views are occasionally still being mooted it would, I believe, be correct to say that scholars are today far more ready to credit Jesus himself with laying the foundations for the Gen- tile mission. In the words of Martin Hengel (1983b:61-63; cf Senior and Stuhmueller 1983:141f; Hahn 1984:269, 272):

It is necessary to stress the obvious fact that without the activity of the earthly Jesus it becomes absurd to speak of "Jesus' concern"; and the church founded by Easter which, for whatever reason, no longer dares to ask after the earthly Jesus, is separated from its starting point. One can speak meaningfully of Easter only if one knows that here the *man Jesus of Nazareth is raised*, someone who in his human life, with its activity and suffering, is not just any interchangeable blank sheet. We therefore have to look for the earthly Jesus if we want to elucidate "the beginnings of the earliest Christian mission" . . . the content of the preaching of Jesus had just as much "missionary" character as that of his disciples after Easter . . . Here we are confronted with the real starting point of the primitive Christian mission: it lies in the conduct of Jesus himself. If anyone is to be called "the primal missionary", he must be . . . The ultimate basis for the earliest Christian mission lies in the messianic sending of Jesus.

SALIENT FEATURES OF JESUS' PERSON AND MINISTRY

The above quotation from Hengel shows that Jesus' "self-definition" was such that he consistently challenged the attitudes, practices, and structures which tended arbitrarily to exclude certain categories of people from the Jewish community. I shall now endeavor to uncover, in some detail, the salient features of his ministry in order better to appreciate the missionary thrust of his person and work. I do this in the conviction that it will also help us to discern the meaning of mission for our own time. Four of these features will be highlighted: Jesus' proclamation concerning the reign of God, his attitude to the Jewish law, the calling and commissioning of his disciples, and the significance of the Easter event.

Jesus and the Reign of God
The expression "reign of God" (*malkuth Yahweh* in Hebrew) does not appear in the Old Testament (Bright 1953:18). It is first encountered in late Judaism, though the idea itself is older. It developed through several stages. At one point it was believed that the royal rule of God would manifest itself in the Davidic dynasty (cf 2 Sam 7:12-16). At another stage it was thought that God would reconcile and rule the world from the temple through the priesthood (cf Ezek 40-43). Both these expectations came to nothing (Bright 1953:24-70). So the conviction grew, particularly during periods of foreign domination, that God's kingdom was an entirely future entity and would manifest itself in a complete turning of the tables, with Israel at the top and the oppressors becoming the oppressed (cf Bright 1953:156-186; Boff 1983:56f). It was this last view that was dominant during Jesus' earthly ministry. It is still captured, for instance, in the words of the disciples after Easter: "Lord, will you at this time restore the kingdom to Israel?" (Acts 1:6).

The reign of God (*basileia tou Theou*) is undoubtedly central to Jesus' entire ministry.[7] It is, likewise, central to his understanding of his own mission. One may even say that, for Jesus, God's reign is the "starting point and context for mission" (Senior and Stuhlmueller 1983:144) and that it puts "the traditional values of ancient Judaism in question at decisive points" (Hengel 1983b:61).

It is not easy to define Jesus' view of the *basileia*. He speaks of it mainly in parables. And parables are a form of discourse which deliberately veils the mystery of God's reign (in the sense of Mark 4:11), at the same time that it discloses it (cf Lochman 1986:61).

Two features in Jesus' preaching of God's reign are of particular importance if we wish to appreciate the missionary nature of Jesus' self-understanding and ministry. Both are fundamentally different from those of his contemporaries.

First, God's reign is not understood as exclusively future but as both future and already present. We today can hardly grasp the truly revolutionary dimension in Jesus' announcement that the reign of God has drawn near and is, in fact "upon" his listeners, "in their very midst" (Lk 17:21, NEB). According to both Mark and Matthew he inaugurates his public ministry with an announcement about the nearness of God's reign (Mk 1:15; Mt 4:17). Something totally new is happening: the irruption of a new era, of a new order of life. The hope of deliverance is not a distant song about a far-away future. The future has invaded the present.

There remains, however, an unresolved tension between the present and the future dimensions of God's reign. It has arrived, and yet is still to come. Because of the latter, the disciples are taught in the Lord's Prayer to pray for its coming.

Such apparently conflicting sayings are an embarrassment to us. Small wonder that, throughout the history of the church, Christians have attempted to resolve the tension. Under the influence of Origen and Augustine the expectation of God's reign in the future was made to refer either to the spiritual journey of the individual believer or to the church as the kingdom of God on earth. Future eschatology was gradually pushed out of the mainstream of church life and thus relegated to the ranks of heretical aberration (cf Beker 1984:61). For nineteenth-century liberal theology God's kingdom was more or less the equivalent of the ideal moral order couched in categories of Western civilization and culture. At the turn of the century Johannes Weiss and Albert Schweitzer went to the opposite extreme: they eliminated all references to God's reign as present and regarded Jesus, in typical apocalyptic fashion, as proclaiming only a future coming of the kingdom. According to Schweitzer Jesus in the end provoked his own execution which would then, so Jesus believed, precipitate the coming of the kingdom, which, sadly, did not happen.[8] Today, however, most scholars agree that the tension between the "already" and the "not yet" of God's reign in Jesus' ministry belongs to the essence of his person and consciousness and should not be resolved; it is precisely in this creative tension that the reality of God's reign has significance for our contemporary mission (Burchard 1980).[9]

The missionary nature of Jesus ministry is also revealed in a second fundamental characteristic of his kingdom ministry: it launches an all-out attack on evil in all its manifestations. God's reign arrives wherever Jesus overcomes the power of evil. Then, as it does now, evil took many forms: pain, sickness, death,

remain a reality. They continue to declare themselves as the real absolutes. So we remain both impatient and modest. We know that our mission will not usher in God's reign. Neither did Jesus. He inaugurated it but did not bring it to its consummation. Like him, we are called to erect signs of God's ultimate reign — not more, but certainly not less either (Käsemann 1980:67). As we pray "your kingdom come!" we also commit ourselves to initiate, here and now, approximations and anticipations of God's reign. Once again: God's reign *will* come, since it has *already* come. It is both bestowal and challenge, gift and promise, present and future, celebration and anticipation (cf Boff 1983:16). We have the firm assurance that its coming cannot be thwarted. "Even rejection, the cross and sin are not insuperable obstacles to God. Even the enemies of the kingdom are at the service of the kingdom" (Boff 1983:60).

Jesus and the Law (the Torah)

We can only appreciate Jesus' attitude toward the Torah if we view it as an integral element of his consciousness of being the one who inaugurates the reign of God. It is in this sense that the theme "Jesus and the Law" acquires significance for our understanding of both Jesus' mission and our own.

Moltmann (1967:193) aptly summarizes:

> The central place of the Torah in late Jewish apocalyptic is . . . taken by the person and the cross of Christ. The place of life in the law is taken by fellowship with Christ in the following of the crucified one. The place of the self-preservation of the righteous from the world is taken by the mission of the believer in the world.

Even so, according to the gospels, particularly Matthew, Jesus seems to view the Torah in a way that is not essentially different from that of his contemporaries, including the Pharisees (Bornkamm 1965a:28). At closer look, however, there are some fundamental dissimilarities. For one thing, Jesus attacks the hypocrisy of allowing a discrepancy between accepting the Law as authoritative and yet not acting according to it. For another, he radicalizes the Law in an unparalleled manner (cf Mt 5:17-48). Third, in supreme self-confidence he takes it upon himself simply to abrogate the law, or at least certain elements in it.[11]

Why does he do that? This, of course, is the question his contemporaries also ask, either in utter amazement or in bitter anger. The answer lies in several mutually related elements, all of which involve Jesus' understanding of his mission.

First, the reign of God and not the Torah is for Jesus the decisive principle of action. This does not imply the annulment of the Law or antinominianism as though there could be a basic discrepancy between God's reign and the God's Law. What happens, rather, is that the Law is pushed back in relation to God's reign (Merklein 1978:95, 105f). And this reign of God manifests itself as love to all. The Old Testament knows of God's unfathomable and tender love to Israel — dramatized, *inter alia*, in the enacted parable of the prophet Hosea's marriage to a prostitute. Now, however, God's love begins to reach out beyond the boundaries of Israel. This, says William Manson, was an absolutely new thing in the religious history of humankind (1953:392).

Second, and intimately related to the point just mentioned: in Jesus' ministry people matter more than rules and rituals. The individual commandments are interpreted *ad hominem*. This is why sometimes the Law's rigor is increased whereas, at other times, some commandments are simply abrogated. With magnificent freedom Jesus disregards all regulations when, for instance, love for people in need require him to heal even on the Sabbath (cf Schweizer 1971:34). In this way he demonstrates that it is impossible to love God without loving one's neighbor. Love for people in need is not secondary to love for God. It is part of it. Years later the first letter of John would formulate this in a way that could not be misunderstood: "If any one says, 'I love God', and hates his brother, he is a liar" (4:20). Love of God, in Jesus' ministry, is interpreted by love of neighbor. This also involves new criteria for inter-human relations. The disciples of Jesus should reflect, in their relations with others, a different standard of high and low, of great and small. They should do this by serving others rather than ruling over them. In this they would emulate their Lord who washed their feet. Jesus gives himself in love to others; so should they, constrained by his love. Does this not reveal a profoundly missionary stance?

Jesus and His Disciples

In Mark's and Matthew's gospels Jesus' public ministry begins with the proclamation: "The time is fulfilled, and the kingdom of God is at hand; repent and believe in the gospel!" (Mk 1:14f; Mt 4:17). Immediately following this announcement, both evangelists relate the calling of the first four disciples (Mk 1:16-20; Mt 4:18-22).

This sequence of events cannot have been accidental. Mark, in particular, clearly has an explicitly missionary purpose in mind in his account of the calling of the disciples. The calling takes place on the shores of Lake Galilee. This territory is, in Mark's gospel, the true scene of Jesus' preaching and the lake is for him a bridge toward the Gentiles. Mark thus puts a missionary stamp on his gospel from the very first chapter. The disciples are called to be missionaries. In a study on Mark 1:16-20, Pesch puts it as follows: "Their mission would take the fishers of humans across the lake to the Gentiles, to the people for whom Jesus was to die (9:31;10:45)" (Pesch 1969:27; my translation). "The calling of the disciples is a call to follow Jesus and a being set aside for missionary activities. Calling, discipleship and mission belong together" (:15) — not only for the first disciples who walk with Jesus but also for those who would respond to this call after Easter (:29). In light of this it is appropriate that we reflect on the missionary significance of Jesus having gathered around him a band of disciples.

The rabbis of Jesus' time also had disciples (Aramaic: *talmidim*; Greek: *mathetai*). On the surface there appears to be very little difference between the disciples of the rabbis and those of Jesus. In both cases a disciple is always attached to a particular teacher. In substance, however, the two types are fundamentally different. When we take a closer look at some of these differences we shall notice that all of them, in one way or another, have to do with the way the evangelists understand Jesus' and his disciples' mission (cf Rengstorf 1967:441-455; Goppelt 1981:208f).

1. In the Judaism of Jesus' time it was the *talmid*'s prerogative to choose his own teacher and attach himself to that teacher. None of Jesus' disciples, however, attaches himself of his own volition to Jesus. Some try to do so but are discouraged in no uncertain terms (Mt 8:19f; Lk 9:57f, 61f). Those who do follow him are able to do so simply because they are called by him, because they respond to the command, "Follow me!" The choice is Jesus', not the disciples'.

Moreover, the call does not seem to expect anything but an immediate and positive response. And the response is recorded as if it is the most natural thing in the world, without any suggestion of the possibility of reservations and difficulties on the part of those who are called (Schweizer 1971:40). There is no hint at any compromise; the one called, leaves "everything", whether his tax-collector's booth, as in the case of Levi (Mt 9:9), or their fishing boats, as in the case of the first four disciples. For both Matthew and Mark, then, the response of the first four disciples to Jesus' calling—following, as it does, hard on the one-sentence summary of his first preaching—suggests that they are the first who "repent and believe". Getting up and following Jesus is the same as repenting and believing. In the synoptic gospels repentance (*metanoia*) is not a psychological process but means embracing the reality and the presence of the reign of God (Rütti 1972:340). The call to discipleship is a call into God's reign and is, as such, an act of grace (Schweizer 1971:40: cf Lohfink 1988:11).

2. In the case of late Judaism, it was the Law, the Torah, that stood in the center. It was for his knowledge of the Torah and only for this, that would-be disciples approached a particular rabbi. "The personal authority which a teacher of the Torah enjoys he owes, for all the recognition of his own personal gifts, to the Torah which he sacrificially studies" (Rengstorf 1967:447f). The authority was the Torah's, not the teacher's. Jesus, however, waives any legitimation of his authority on the Torah, or on anything else, for that matter. He expects *his* disciples to renounce everything not for the sake of the Law but for his sake alone: "He who loves father or mother more than me is not worthy of me; . . . and he who does not take his cross and follow me is not worthy of me . . . and he who loses his life for my sake will find it" (Mt 10:38f). No Jewish rabbi could say this. Here Jesus takes the place of the Torah.

3. In Judaism discipleship was merely a means to an end. Being a *talmid*, a student of the law, was no more than a transitional stage. The student's goal was to become a rabbi himself. The rabbi was, in this process, certainly indispensable, but he himself looked forward to the crowning of his own efforts— the day his disciples would become teachers like himself. With this in mind, he guided and helped them eventually to master the Torah.

For the disciple of Jesus, however, the stage of discipleship is not the first step toward a promising career. It is in itself the fulfillment of his destiny. The disciple of Jesus never graduates into a rabbi. He may, of course, become an apostle, but an apostle is not a disciple with a degree in theology. Apostleship is not, in itself, an elevated status. An apostle is, essentially, a witness to the resurrection.

4. The disciples of the rabbis were only their *students*, nothing more. Jesus' disciples are also his *servants* (*douloi*) something quite alien to late Judaism (Rengstorf 1967:448). They do not just bow to his greater knowledge; they obey him. He is not only their teacher, but also their Lord. He says to them: "A student is not above his teacher, nor a servant above his master" (Mt 10:24).

At the same time, however, the Master is also a servant. So John tells us of Jesus performing the most menial task — that of washing the feet of his disciples. The culmination of his service is, of course, his death on the cross. A key saying of Jesus in Mark's gospel is found in chapter 10:45: "For the Son of Man also came not to be served but to serve, and to give his life as a ransom for many". Thus servanthood, as a matter of course, involves suffering, also for the followers of Jesus. In fact, "the tradition is unanimous that . . . Jesus left His disciples in no doubt that they were committing themselves to suffering if they followed Him" (Rengstorf 1967:449). In Mark 10:45 "the Son of Man calls (his disciples) to walk the road on which he precedes them" (Breytenbach 1984:278; my translation).

5. What, however, do they become disciples *for*? First, as Mark puts it, they are called to be disciples simply "to be with him" (3:14). Schweizer (1971:41) elucidates:

> It means that the disciples walk with him, eat and drink with him, listen to what he says and see what he does, are invited with him into houses and hovels, or are turned away with him. They are not called to great achievements, religious or otherwise. They are invited as companions to share in what takes place around Jesus. They are therefore called not to attach much importance to themselves and what they accomplish or fail to accomplish, but to attach great importance to what takes place through Jesus and with him. They are called to delegate their cares and worries and anxieties.

Mark says more, however. Jesus also appoints them "to be sent out to preach and have authority to cast out demons" (3:14f). Following Jesus or being with him, and sharing in his mission thus belong together (Schneider 1982:84). The call to discipleship is not for its own sake; it enlists the disciples in the service of God's reign. The peculiar expression "fishers" of human beings is in this respect of particular importance. The phrase is a key one in Mark's gospel and undoubtedly points to the disciples' future involvement in mission (Pesch 1969).

Again the difference between the disciples of Jesus and the *talmidim* of the Jewish teachers is striking. To follow Jesus does not mean passing on his teachings or becoming the faithful custodians of his insights, but to be his "witnesses".

Jesus sent out his disciples to preach and heal during his own lifetime — about this there can be little doubt, even if the stories about these missions, as related in all three synoptic gospels, reveal evidence of the church's missionary experience *after* Easter (Hahn 1965:40; Hengel 1983b:178, note 75; Pesch 1982:27). What is clear from these commissions is that Jesus endows his disciples with full authority to do his work. As a matter of fact, in most cases the synoptic gospels use the same words for the activities of both Jesus and the disciples, for instance, in respect of preaching, teaching, evangelizing, exorcising, and healing. The disciples have simply to proclaim and do what Jesus proclaims and does (Frankemölle 1974:105f). They are, in Paul's language, Christ's ambassadors through whom God is making his appeal (2 Cor 5:20).

6. Another, and final, difference between the *talmidim* of the Jewish teachers and the disciples of Jesus is that the latter are the vanguard of the messianic people of the end-time. The gospel of Mark, in particular, puts discipleship within the force field between the passion of the earthly Jesus and the parousia of the coming Son of Man; to be a disciple means to follow the suffering Jesus *and* look forward to his return in glory (cf Breytenbach 1984:passim). It is the expectation of the parousia which provides the motivation for discipleship and compels it to express itself in mission (:338). The expectation of the future is an integral element in Mark's understanding of discipleship-in-mission (:280-330).

Precisely as vanguard of the messianic people of the end-time, en route toward the parousia, the disciples should not regard themselves as an exclusive group of super-followers of Jesus. Therefore the term *mathetes* is not restricted to them. They are simply the first fruits of the kingdom, which is clearly not to be "under the management of hereditary administrators" (Lochman 1986:69). They are essentially members of the Jesus community just like everybody else. Paul Minear (1977:146) comments,

> In the early Church the stories of the disciples were normally understood as archetypes of the dilemmas and opportunities that later Christians experienced. Each Gospel pericope became a paradigm with a message for the Church, because each Christian had inherited a relationship to Jesus similar to that of James and John and the others.

Naturally this applies to their mission also. The "ordinary" members of the first Christian communities cannot appropriate the term "disciple" to themselves unless they are also willing to be enlisted in Jesus' fellowship of service to the world. The entry point for all alike is receiving forgiveness and accepting the reality of God's reign; this determines the whole life of the disciple and of the community to which he or she belongs.

Mission from the Perspective of Easter

For the disciples of Jesus the Easter experience was pivotal. They interpreted the cross as the end of the old world and the resurrection of Jesus as the irruption of the new. The resurrection was ultimately viewed as the vindication of Jesus (Senior and Stuhlmueller 1983:158; Meyer 1986:48) as putting a seal of approval on the practice of Jesus (Echegaray 1984:xvi).

It is only because of Easter that our gospels were written. Without Easter they make no sense. Even more particularly, they were written from the perspective of Easter; the glow of that experience permeates all the gospels (not only the fourth). The stories about pre-Easter events express the message of an ardent faith more than the chronicles of past events. Yet, even if the memory of the deeds and words of the earthly Jesus is colored by the Easter experience, it is not blurred by it (Echegaray 1984:17). It is, in fact, precisely the Easter faith that enables the early Christian community to see the practice of Jesus in a specific light—as the criterion for understanding their own situation and calling (cf Kramm 1979:216; Breytenbach 1984:336). "It is only on the basis of Easter that the Jesus affair had a future. Easter had a creative significance for the church" (Kasting 1969:126—my translation).

It is equally clear that it was the Easter experience that determined the early Christian community's self-definition and identity. Nothing else suffices to account for its coming into being (Meyer 1986:36). Not that its self-understanding was the product solely of the Easter experience. Rather, having been initiated by the historic mission of Jesus, the apostles' self-understanding was consummated and sealed by the Easter experience (:43, 49). It was also Easter that kept the community alive. It is therefore only natural that all our gospels would link Easter with mission and that this event would play a key role in the origins of the mission of the early church (cf Kasting 1969:81,127, Rütti: 1972:124). It is the exalted Christ who draws all people to him (cf Jn 12:32; cf also the hymn which Paul quotes in 1 Tim 3:16 and which likewise links Easter with mission).

In terms of the New Testament the exaltation of Jesus is the sign of the victory Jesus has already won over the evil one. Mission means the proclamation and manifestation of Jesus' all-embracing reign, which is not yet recognized and acknowledged by all but is nevertheless already a reality. So the church's mission will not inaugurate God's reign, but neither will the possible failure of that mission thwart it. The reign of God is not a program but a reality, ushered in by the Easter event. The first Christians respond to this reality, which has overpowered them in the Easter experience, by mission. They feel themselves challenged to declare the praises of God who has called them out of darkness into his wonderful light (cf 1 Pet 2:9).

Intimately related to the resurrection, almost part of the Easter event itself, is the gift of the Spirit, which is equally integrally linked to mission. Roland Allen (1962) was one of the first theologians to have stressed the missionary dimension of pneumatology. Subsequently Harry Boer (1961) undertook a thorough study in which he demonstrated the indissoluble link between Pentecost and mission. Berkhof (1964:30; cf 30-41) regards mission as the first activity of the Spirit. Newbigin (1982:148; 1987:17) calls mission "an overflow from Pentecost". Thus, if it was the experience of the resurrection that gave the early Christians certainty, it was Pentecost that gave them boldness; only through the power of the Spirit did they become witnesses (Acts 1:8). The Spirit is the risen Christ who is active in the world. On the day of Pentecost Christ, through the Spirit, throws open the doors and thrusts the disciples out into the world.

Where this occurs, so the New Testament authors bear witness, the forces of the future world stream in. Easter is "the dawn of the end-time" (Kasting 1969:129; cf Rütti 1972:240), and a high-strung expectation of the end characterizes the early Christian community. The time is short. The eschatological people of God has to be gathered immediately. The commissionings reported in the synoptic gospels, particularly in Matthew 10 and Luke 10, reflect much of this—the disciples have to travel light, keep moving, and waste no time on the road.

Even so, scholars tend to overemphasize the early Christian community's *Naherwartung* (its expectation of the imminent end of the world) or, rather, to misinterpret it. It differs fundamentally from the expectations of the end prevalent among apocalyptic groups of the time for whom *all* salvation was still future.[12] For the Jesus community, on the contrary, the resurrection of Christ and the coming of the Spirit are tangible proof of the "already-ness" of God's reign. The future dimension of God's reign and of salvation is nurtured by the present reality of that reign. The "not yet" feeds on the "already". Two orders of life, two ages, have come to co-exist. The new age has begun, but the old has yet to end (Manson 1953:390f; cf also Rütti 1972:104,240). It is therefore incorrect to claim that the so-called delay of the parousia plunged the early church into an extreme crisis; this was not the case (Kasting 1969:142; Pesch 1982:32). This is not to deny that the delay of the parousia did not put the early Christian community under considerable strain. What I do deny is that it had a paralyzing effect on the early church. The very opposite was true, at least in the first decades.

The early church understood its missionary engagement with the world in terms of this end-time, which had already come and is at the same time still pending. As a matter of fact, its missionary involvement was itself a constitutive element of its eschatological self-understanding. The expectation of the imminent end was a component of and presupposition for mission; at the same time it expressed itself in mission (Pesch 1982:32). It is not true that, in the early church, mission gradually *replaced* the expectation of the end. Rather, mission was, in itself, an eschatological event.

THE EARLY CHRISTIAN MISSION

Having briefly surveyed what I have termed four salient features of Jesus' person and ministry, which may help us better to understand the missionary thrust of his person and work, I now turn to the beginnings of the Christian mission.

In the years immediately following the first Easter, the early church's missionary engagement remained confined to *Israel*, as Jesus own ministry had been. Jerusalem remained the center of the new community, the members of which continued to visit the temple regularly. The restoration of God's covenant people took priority; in this final hour it had to be gathered and renewed (Kasting 1969:130). To abandon Israel now would be to be unfaithful to the intention of Jesus. The disciples had "the sacred duty to proclaim to apostate Israel its last chance of repentance before the coming of the Son of man" (Hengel 1983b:58).

During the early stages there was clearly no intention to form a separate religion. The Judaism of the time exhibited a degree of pluralism which permitted Jewish Christianity to exist as one group among many without severing its links with the main body. The members of the Jesus community continued to worship in the temple and the synagogues. The situation only changed after the Jewish War and the destruction of Jerusalem in AD 70 (Brown 1980:209,212; Schweizer 1971:123).

But what about a mission to Gentiles? The first Christian community was not opposed to the conversion of Gentiles. Contemporary Judaism was not averse to winning proselytes, and it would have been extremely odd if Jewish *Christians* had not at least matched other Jews in this respect. Many of the first Gentile converts to Jesus were, in fact, proselytes or "God-fearers". One of the attractions of the Christian church was that, whereas proselytes were never fully integrated into Judaism (cf Malherbe 1983:67), they were embraced without reserve by Christians (Hahn 1984:269). Yet the Jewish Christian community did not, in these early stages, go out of its way to win Gentiles. The first conversions of Gentiles came about as a spin-off of a mission directed primarily at Jews (Kasting 1969:109).

In the general spirit of the time it would, moreover, have been the most natural thing in the world to require Gentile converts to be circumcised. It is, however, possible that there were occasional exceptions to this rule from a fairly early stage. We simply know too little about the origins of the Gentile mission to make any categorical statements about its nature and scope; it is therefore advisable to be circumspect and reserved in our claims (cf Pesch 1982:45). Certainly many Gentiles regarded circumcision as an insurmountable stumbling block to becoming Christians. We know that this was a problem for converts to Judaism and it is only logical that the same would be true of prospective converts to the Jesus movement. Gradually, however, it became the practice in some circles to accept Gentiles into the Christian fold without first circumcising them.

This did not come about without controversy, as is evident from a reading of the Book of Acts. In order to appreciate something of this controversy and its significance for the early Christian mission, it is necessary to take cognizance of the differences in self-understanding between the *hebraioi* ("Hebrews", or Aramaic-speaking Jewish Christians) and the *hellenistai* ("Hellenists", or Greek-speaking Jewish Christians) (cf Hengel 1983a:passim; Meyer 1986:53-83).

The "Hebrews", initially under the leadership of Peter and embracing all the "apostles", understood themselves as embodying and anticipating the restoration of Israel. Calling the nation to enter into its rightful heritage, they insisted that there was no entry into this heritage except through confessing the risen Messiah and being baptized (Meyer 1986:169). At the same time, Torah piety belonged to their horizon, and they assimilated the experience of salvation in Christ in a way that left allegiance to the Torah intact (:175). This made it possible for them to remain in Jerusalem when persecution broke out (Acts 8:1). They believed that their mission was limited to the house of Israel and that the salvation of the Gentiles would take place by means of the eschatological pilgrimage of the nations to Jerusalem, as depicted in the Old Testament (:67, 82). Their self-definition made it impossible for them to embark on a mission to the world outside Israel (:67).

The Hellenists differed from the Hebrews at decisive points. In their case, a paradigm shift was much more clearly in evidence. By translating Jesus' message into the Greek language, this community became the "needle's eye" through which the earliest Christian *kerygma* found a way into the Greco-Roman world (Hengel 1983a:26f). The Hellenists believed that the Easter experience had by-passed Torah and temple. It would be "the Spirit" rather than the Law that would guide the believers' life. It was this attitude which brought them into conflict with the Jewish authorities and precipitated the murder of Stephen and the subsequent persecution of the Hellenists (cf Hengel 1986:71-80).

The Hellenists' critical attitude toward the Law and the temple reflected the attitude and ministry of the historical Jesus (Hengel 1983a:24, 29; 1986:72f, 84). The same was true of their openness to Samaritans and Gentiles. Thus, when they were expelled from Jerusalem, they as a matter of course began to preach among the despised Samaritans as well as among the Gentiles in Phoenicia and Syria as far as Antioch. It was equally a matter of course that they proclaimed a gospel which no longer required circumcision and the observance of the ritual law (Hengel 1986:100; Meyer 1986:82f; Wedderburn 1988:163).

It was in Antioch that the decisive breakthrough occurred (Hengel 1986:99-110). Antioch was the third largest city in the ancient world, after Rome and Alexandria, and capital of the combined Roman province of Syria and Cylicia during this period. It became the first great city in which Christianity gained a footing, when the "largely anonymous, extraordinary assured, open, active, pneumatic, city-oriented, Greek-speaking Jewish Christian heirs of Stephen" (Meyer 1986:97), exiled from Jerusalem, arrived there and founded a church made up of both Jews and Gentiles.

The Antioch church was, by any standards, a remarkable body of people. In Jerusalem the Jesus movement had still been regarded as a Jewish sect, by Jews and Romans alike. In Antioch it soon became clear that the community was neither Jewish nor "traditionally" Gentile, but constituted a third entity. Luke mentions that it was here that the disciples were first called "Christians" (Acts 11:26).

The Antioch community was indeed amazingly innovative. Soon Barnabas was sent there by the Jerusalem church (Acts 11:22), not least to keep an eye on developments which already at that stage were causing some alarm in the parent community. Yet instead of censuring the Antiochians for what he saw, Barnabas was himself caught up in the events there and "encouraged" the believers (11:23). Luke describes him as "a good man, full of the Holy Spirit and of faith", and adds that, after his arrival, even more people were "added to the Lord" (11:24). Barnabas then remembered Paul, whom he had first introduced to the church leadership in Jerusalem (Acts 9:27), and now went to Tarsus to persuade Paul to join him in Antioch. In addition to the rapid growth of the Christian community, startling things were happening there. There was, to begin with, no church apartheid in Antioch. Jews and Gentiles ate together —

something unparalleled in the ancient world, particularly since those Gentiles were not circumcised. It was evident that, whereas the Hebrews found their identity in the past of Israel and of Jesus, the Hellenists understood themselves as the link with the future, not as heralds only of a renewed Israel but as vanguard of a new humanity.

Even so, the Hellenists did not immediately launch a worldwide mission from Antioch (cf Hengel 1986:80). When it did come to that, it was Paul who became the catalytic factor. *He* was the one who provided the theological basis for the Torah-free self-definition of Gentile Christianity; it was his message that made the Christian *kerygma* intelligible and viable in the Mediterranean world and that prepared the way for a far-flung missionary program (cf Hengel 1983a:29; Meyer 1986:169). Through the ministry of Paul and Barnabas the Antioch church became a community with a concern for people they had never met — people living on Cyprus, the mainland of Asia Minor, and elsewhere. They decided to send missionaries there . . . and went ahead and commissioned their two most gifted and experienced leaders to go (Acts 13:1f). This far-reaching decision and action was, however, not peripheral to the early Christian community, a kind of expendable extra. Rather, in retrospect it becomes clear "that Christianity had never been more itself, more consistent with Jesus and more evidently en route to its own future, than in the launching of the world mission" (Meyer 1986:206).

Meanwhile, in Jerusalem, the situation was apparently different. There was little joy when Cornelius was converted, only horror over the fact that Peter had entered the house of uncircumcised men and eaten with them (Acts 11:2f). Later, James sent some men from Jerusalem to inspect the situation in Antioch and report on it (Gal 2:12). They immediately demanded that the Gentile converts be circumcised (Acts 15:1) and refused to have table fellowship with them until they were. Peter and some other Jewish Christians who had shared fully with the Antioch believers until then, were so unnerved and intimidated by the uncompromising attitude of the Jerusalem delegation that they, too, separated themselves from the Gentile Christians (Gal 2:12f).

Still, the differences between the *hebraioi* and the *hellenistai* should not be exaggerated. Early Christianity was a living organism, developing all the time; it cannot be frozen into two mutually exclusive positions (cf Meyer 1986:195f). Both groups confessed Jesus as the risen Messiah and practiced baptism as condition for incorporation into the new community; both agreed that they shared an identity that was new and distinctive and normative (cf Meyer 1986:169). One has to add that the inclusion of the Gentiles in God's saving act was integral to the faith convictions of both *hebraioi* and *hellenistai*. Whereas the former expected their inclusion to be brought about by the eschatological pilgrimage of the nations to Jerusalem, promised in the Old Testament, the latter believed that the Gentiles would be brought in through an historical missionary outreach of the church (Meyer 1986:67, 82, 206). The two communities certainly had different self-understandings: the *hebraioi* considered themselves as the beginning of the restoration of Israel; the *hellenistai* regarded themselves as launching-pad for a new humanity. It is, however, unwarranted to deduce two gospels from two self-understandings (Meyer 1986:99).

Yet even *within* each community there were differences. This was particularly true of the *hebraioi*. It is difficult to piece together a coherent picture of the situation, but it may be correct to surmise that this group consisted of a center (represented by James, the brother of Jesus), a "left wing" (represented by Peter and John), and a "right wing" made up of those who were not prepared to concede the possibility of Gentiles being incorporated into the community without circumcision (cf Meyer 1986:107). Peter's willingness (if only after some hesitation!) to go to Cornelius and baptize uncircumcised Gentiles, as well as the Jerusalem elders' fierce reaction to this (Acts 11:2f), surely indicate that he really stood closer to Paul than is often recognized (cf Dietzfelbinger 1985:139). He was not a typical representative of a Jewish Christianity practicing strict observance of the Law, but occupied a mediating position, although he tended to vacillate under pressure (cf Hengel 1986:92-98). All of this may have led to him being replaced by the more conservative James as leader of the Jerusalem church (around AD 43/44). In subsequent years the "right wing" became ever more influential: in Acts 21:20 Luke refers to a situation in the mid-fifties, when "all" believers had become "zealous for the law" (cf Hengel 1983a:25; 1986:95-97). The "Judaizers," who opposed Paul's work in the fifties and sixties, have to be located somewhere on the fringe of this "right wing".

It is hard to know whether the Judaistic viewpoint had been there from the very beginning. Perhaps it only developed in the late forties of the first century (Kasting 1969:116). On the other hand, it could have been present latently since a very early stage. Still, there was little cause for anxiety then. The Judaizers only really became alarmed when the unprecedented growth of the Gentile Christian community came to their attention. They had previously been irritated by the views and activities of the Hellenists, but not really threatened since there were so few Gentile converts. By the late forties, however, they had reason to fear that the very character and composition of the Jewish Christian community was in jeopardy. Recruitment from the Jewish community had probably already passed its peak, but the Christian church had remained essentially Jewish since circumcision still provided a hurdle to Gentiles who might not be prepared to embrace the Jewish lifeview and worldview. With this hurdle gone, and Gentiles pouring into the church, the Judaizers balked. Their primary targets were Paul, Barnabas, and the Antioch community, where they detected antinominian tendencies and where Jewish and Gentile Christians were living in full fellowship. A major crisis was on hand and it was decided to attempt to resolve it at what became known as the "Apostolic Council". It is not easy to establish in detail how the crisis actually unfolded and was dealt with. We can, however, piece together some of its major elements from Luke's report in Acts 15 and Paul's reflections in Galatians 2, in spite of some discrepancies between the two accounts. In spite of the fact that many scholars are rather skeptical about the historical trustworthiness of Luke's account that an agreement was reached at the Council (cf Brown 1980:208-210; Sanders 1983:187; Martyn 1985:307-324), others believe that substantial progress toward the resolution of a particularly thorny issue was indeed reached (cf Holmberg 1978:20-32).

According to this latter view, the fact that the meeting had to take place in Jerusalem and that the apostles had a crucial role to play in the debate, was not something accepted grudgingly by Paul and the rest of the Antiochian delegation, nor a mere conciliatory gesture on their part; rather, the unique position of Jerusalem and the apostles was part and parcel of their self-understanding (cf Holmberg 1978:26-28). This "concession" was not exploited by the "pillars" in Jerusalem; like Paul, they recoiled from division and were prepared to take every possible step to retain unity. There was a general desire to listen to each other. The Jerusalem leaders did not wish to do anything that would jeopardize Gentile Christian communities, some of which had been in existence for more than a decade at this time (Hengel 1986:116). They were able to differentiate between Torah piety and the heart of the Christian experience. All these factors together prepared the way for the decision taken at the council, which Meyer (1986:101) identifies as "by all odds the cardinal policy decision of the first-century church".

It goes without saying that there were, both before and after the council, Christian *hebraioi* who were stubbornly critical of the very idea of a Torah-free mission (Meyer 1986:99). At the council they were still in a minority. In subsequent years they were to gain more and more influence in the Jerusalem church; Luke's account of the conflict-ridden situation that obtained during Paul's last visit to Jerusalem (Acts 21:17-26) seems to underline this (Hengel 1986:116f).

Differences about the issues debated during the council persisted until the Jewish War. Even before the destruction of the temple and the fall of Jerusalem, however, most Jewish Christians had left Judea. By the time the war broke out, the Sadducee movement was losing popularity and support. When the temple was destroyed, the Sadducees lost the last foothold they had had. The turmoil of the war spelled the end for them, but also for the Zealots and the Essenes as separate organized groups. Only the Pharisees survived the crisis, partly because their strength lay in the synagogues, scattered throughout the Jewish land and farther afield. In the years immediately after the war they managed to gain control over virtually all of Judaism. As they rose to ascendancy they began to introduce restrictions on Jewish Christians who were still members of local synagogue communities. It became increasingly difficult to remain both a practicing Jew and a Christian. Eventually, around AD 85, it was made impossible. The *Eighteen Benedictions*, promulgated by the Pharisees at their new center at Jamnia, included a clause which anathematized both Christians ("Nazarenes") and heretics (*minim*) and excluded them from the synagogues.[13]

This did not spell the end of the Jesus movement. It had by that time survived its first major challenge: whether it was to remain essentially within the confines of Judaism or live up to the logic of Jesus' own ministry and transcend all barriers. It chose the latter. The community's sense of mission made it impossible for its members to do otherwise; once their horizon had been widened infinitely there really was no possibility of turning back. The church had irrevocably taken its "leap for life", and it did so only just in time (Dix 1953:55).

THE MISSIONARY PRACTICE OF JESUS AND THE EARLY CHURCH

Let me now attempt to draw together some major ingredients of the missionary ministry of Jesus and the early church.

1. First and foremost, the early Christian mission involved the person of Jesus himself. It remains impossible, however, to fit Jesus into a clearly circumscribable framework. Schweizer rightly calls him "the man who fits no formula" (1971:13). What he said and did, says Schweizer (1971:25f),

> shocked all his contemporaries. They would have understood and tolerated an ascetic who wrote off this world for the sake of the future kingdom of God. They would have understood and tolerated an apocalypticist who lived only for hope, completely uninterested in worldly affairs ... They would have understood and tolerated a Pharisee who urgently summoned people to accept the kingdom of God here and now in obedience to the law, for the sake of participating in the future kingdom of God. They would have understood and tolerated a realist or skeptic who took his stand in this life with both feet on the ground, declaring himself an agnostic with respect to any future expectations. But they could not understand a man who claimed that the kingdom of God came upon men in what he himself said and did, but nevertheless with incomprehensible caution refused to perform decisive miracles; healed individuals, but refused to put an end to the misery of leprosy or blindness; spoke of destroying the old temple and building a new one, but did not even boycott the Jerusalem cult like the Qumran sect to inaugurate a new, purified cult in the cloister of the desert; who above all spoke of the impotence of those who can only kill the body, but refused to drive the Romans from the country.

In all our discussions about Jesus' mission we should keep this perspective in mind.

2. The early Christian mission was political, indeed revolutionary. Ernst Bloch, the Marxist philosopher, once said that it was difficult to wage a revolution without the Bible. To this Moltmann (1975:6) adds, referring to Acts 17:6f, "It is even more difficult not to bring about a revolution with the Bible".

In his definitive three-volume study of political metaphysics from Solon (sixth century BC) to Augustine (fifth century AD), the German jurist, Arnold Ehrhardt, has demonstrated the subversive nature of the early Christian faith and documents (1959:5-44). An authority on Roman and Greek jurisprudence and politics in antiquity, Ehrhardt was able to identify many early Christian sayings and attitudes that were outright seditious at the time but which we no longer experience as such. This applies not only to the Jesus movement in Palestine around AD 30, but also to Paul, Luke and other New Testament writers. The Christian movement of the first centuries was a radically revolutionary movement "and ought to be that today also" but, adds Ehrhardt, we should then keep in mind that revolutions are not to be evaluated in terms of the terror they spread, nor of the destruction they cause, but rather in terms of the alternatives they are able to offer (:19). In its missionary outreach into the Greco-Roman world the early church offered such alternatives. It rejected all gods and in doing this demolished the metaphysical foundations of prevailing political theories. In a great variety of forms, all of which made sense in the religio-political context of the time, Christians confessed Jesus as Lord of all lords — the most revolutionary political demonstration imaginable in the Roman Empire of the first centuries of the Christian era. The idea of "religion as a private affair", of divorcing the "spiritual" from the "physical", was an unthinkable attitude in light of the all-embracing nature of God's reign ushered in by Jesus.

3. The revolutionary nature of the early Christian mission manifested itself, *inter alia*, in the new relationships that came into being in the community. Jew and Roman, Greek and barbarian, free and slave, rich and poor, woman and man, accepted one another as brothers and sisters. It was a movement without analogy, indeed a "sociological impossibility" (Hoekendijk 1967a:245). Small wonder that the early Christian community caused so much astonishment in the Roman Empire and beyond. The reaction was not always positive. In fact, the Christian community and its faith was so different from anything known in the ancient world that it often made no sense to others. Suetonius described Christianity as a "new and malevolent superstition"; Tacitus called it "vain and insane", blamed Christians for their "hatred of the human race," and referred to them as "reprobate characters" because they despised the temples as morgues, scorned the gods, and mocked sacred things (references in Harnack 1962:267-270; for an excellent survey of pagan views of Christians during the first Christian centuries, cf Wilken 1980:passim). What Christians were and did simply fell outside of the frame of reference of many philosophers of the period. At the same time, it should be remembered that, during the first century, Christians were criticized for social rather than political reasons. Only as Christianity began to assume a separate identity as a potentially powerful movement was political action directed against it (cf Malherbe 1983:21f).

Still, many of their contemporaries began to see something more positive in the Christians. Tertullian mentioned that they were referred to as a "third race", after the Romans and Greeks (the first race) and the Jews (the second). About the year 200 the designation third race for Christians was perfectly common on the lips of pagans in Carthage. It soon became a term of honor on the lips of the Christians themselves (Harnack 1962:271-278), and was perhaps the most revolutionary notion of all used at that time (Ehrhardt 1959:88f). Christians — so we read in the second century *Letter to Diognetus* — are not distinguished from the rest of humankind as regards their speech, their customs, and where they live. There remains a critical distance between them and reality around them, however. They are kept in the world as in a prison-house, and yet they are the ones who hold the world together.

The way in which they held the world together was, preeminently, through their practice of love and service to all. Harnack devotes an entire chapter of his book on the mission and expansion of the early church to what he calls "the gospel of love and charity" (1962:147-98). Through meticulous research he pieced together a remarkable picture of the early Christians' involvement with the poor, orphans, widows, the sick, mine-workers, prisoners, slaves, and travellers. "The new language on the lips of Christians", he summarizes, "was the language of love. But it was more than a language, it was a thing of power and action" (:149). This was a "social gospel" in the very best sense of the word and was practiced not as a stratagem to lure outsiders to the church but simply as a natural expression of faith in Christ.

4. In their mission the early Christians did not usher in utopia, nor did they attempt to do so. Their invocation, *"Marana tha!* ("Our Lord, come!") expressed an intense hope that had not yet been fulfilled. Injustice had not yet vanished, oppression had not yet been eliminated, poverty, hunger, even persecution were still very much the order of the day.

The same was of course true of Jesus' own earthly ministry. He did not heal and liberate everyone who came to him: In the words of Ernst Käsemann (1980:67):

> The earthly paradise in no way began with him, and what he actually did brought him in the end to the cross. Through him, the reign of God was carried into the demonic kingdom but not finally and universally completed there. He established signs showing that this kingdom had drawn near and that the struggle with the powers and authorities of this age had begun.

In his earthly ministry, death, and resurrection, and in the outpouring of the Spirit on the day of Pentecost, the forces of the future world began to stream in. But the counter-forces also rushed in—the destructive forces of alienation and of human rebellion—in an attempt to thwart the irruption of God's new world. God's reign did not come in all its fullness.

Jesus' ministry of erecting signs of God's incipient reign was emulated by the early church. Christians were not called to do more than erect signs; neither were they called to do less.

5. When the infant Jesus was presented to God in the Jerusalem temple, so Luke tells us, the aged Simeon blessed him and said to Mary, "This child is set ... for a sign that is spoken against" (Lk 2:34). So even the signs that he did erect and the sign that he himself was were ambiguous and disputed. It was not possible to convince everybody of the authenticity of Jesus. He ministered in weakness, under a shadow, as it were. This is, however, how authentic mission always presents itself—in weakness. As Paul says, in defiance of all logic: "It is when I am weak that I am strong" (2 Cor 12:10).

It was, we are told, by the marks of his passion that the disciples were able to identify the risen Lord (Jn 20:20). It happened again, says John, when Thomas was with the others, a week later. Similarly, Cleopas and his friend recognized Jesus when he broke the bread and they saw his hands (Lk 24:31f). The risen Lord still carries in his body the scars of his passion. The Greek word for "witness" is *martys*. From this our word "martyr" is derived, for in the early church the *martys* often had to seal his *martyria* (witness) with his blood. "Martyrdom and mission", says Hans von Campenhausen (1974:71), "belong together. Martyrdom is especially at home on the mission field".

WHERE THE EARLY CHURCH FAILED

I am, of course, not suggesting that everything was well in the early church. It certainly was not! We only have to read Paul's first letter to the Corinthians and the letters to the seven churches of Asia Minor (Rev 2-3) to realize that the early Christian communities were as far from being ideal as our own churches are. Neither was this phenomenon the result of a late development, say only toward the end of the first century AD. No, the flaws were there from the beginning. There is, for instance, evidence of rivalries at an early stage among the disciples of Jesus. To mention only one example: James and John asked for special seats of honor in Jesus' kingdom (Mk 10:35-41), to the indignation of the others. There are, moreover (and particularly in Mark), many examples of the disciples' lack of understanding and faith (cf Breytenbach 1984:191-206). And the book of Acts, in spite of presenting, on the whole, an idealized picture of the early church, does not hide from us some of the tensions, failures, and sins of early Christians, including the leadership.

I shall not say more about these general shortcomings in early Christianity. Yet I do wish to attend, very briefly, to some more specific weaknesses of the first Christians in the area of mission—weaknesses which threatened, in different degrees, to undo the integral nature of the first paradigm shift.

1. I have suggested that Jesus had no intention of founding a new religion. Those who followed him were given no name to distinguish them from other groups, no creed of their own, no rite which revealed their distinctive group character, no geographical center from which they would operate (Schweizer 1971:42; Goppelt 1981:208). The twelve were to be the vanguard of all Israel and, beyond Israel, by implication, of the whole ecumene. The community around Jesus was to function as a kind of *pars pro toto*, a community for the sake of all others, a model for others to emulate and be challenged by. Never, however, was this community to sever itself from the others.

This high level of calling was, however, not maintained for long. Already at a very early stage Christians tended to be more aware of what distinguished them from others than of their calling and responsibility toward those others. Their survival as a separate religious group, rather than their commitment to the reign of God, began to preoccupy them. In the words of Alfred Loisy (1976:166), "Jesus foretold the kingdom and it was the Church that came". In the course of time the Jesus community simply became a new religion, Christianity, a new principle of division among humankind. And so it has remained to this day.

2. Intimately linked to this first failure of the early church is a second: it ceased to be a movement and turned into an institution. There are essential differences between an institution and a movement, says H. R. Niebuhr (following Bergson): the one is conservative, the other progressive; the one is more

or less passive, yielding to influences from outside, the other is active, influencing rather than being influenced; the one looks to the past, the other to the future (Niebuhr 1959:11f). In addition, we might add, the one is anxious, the other is prepared to take risks; the one guards boundaries, the other crosses them.

We perceive something of this difference between an institution and a movement if we compare the Christian community in Jerusalem with that of Antioch in the forties of the first century AD. The Antioch church's pioneering spirit precipitated an inspection by Jerusalem. It was clear that the Jerusalem party's concern was not mission, but consolidation; not grace, but law; not crossing frontiers, but fixing them; not life, but doctrine; not movement, but institution.

The tension between these two self-understandings led, as we have seen, to the convening of the "Apostolic Council" in AD 47 or 48. According to Luke's report in Acts 15 and also according to Paul in Galatians 2, the Gentile point of view prevailed at that juncture. The situation remained volatile, however, and the tendency in early Christianity to become an institution appeared, in the long run, to be irresistible — not only in Jewish Christian communities but certainly also in Gentile ones. At an early stage there were indications of two separate types of ministry developing: the settled ministry of bishops (or elders) and deacons, and the mobile ministry of apostles, prophets, and evangelists. The first tended to push early Christianity toward becoming an institution, the second retained the dynamic of a movement. In the early years in Antioch there was still a creative tension between these two types of ministry. Paul and Barnabas were at the same time leaders in the local church and itinerant missionaries, and apparently they resumed their congregational duties as a matter of course whenever they returned to Antioch. Elsewhere, however (and certainly at a later stage also in Antioch), the churches became ever more institutionalized and less concerned with the world outside their walls. Soon they had to design rules for guaranteeing the decorum of their worship meetings (cf 1 Cor 11:2-33; 1 Tim 2:1-15), for establishing criteria for the ideal clergyman and his wife (1 Tim 2:1-13), and for addressing cases of inhospitality to church emissaries and of hunger for power (3 Jn; cf Malherbe 1983:92-112). As time went by, intra-ecclesial issues and the struggle for survival as a separate religious group consumed more and more of the energy of Christians.

3. The third respect in which the early church failed was one we have already touched upon: it proved unable, in the long run, to make Jews feel at home. Beginning as a religious movement that worked exclusively among Jews, it changed, in the forties of the first century, to a movement for Jews and Gentiles alike, but wound up proclaiming its message to Gentiles only.

There were two catalytic events in this regard, one religio-cultural (the issue of circumcision of Gentile converts), the other socio-political (the destruction of Jerusalem and the temple in AD 70). After the war Pharisaic Judaism became far too xenophobic to tolerate anything but a hard-line, exclusive Jewish approach. Jewish Christians were forced to choose between the church and the synagogue, and it appears that many chose the latter. In addition, the mood of the time made it virtually impossible to recruit further converts from Judaism.

In the fifties of the first century Paul still felt himself passionately and unconditionally committed to the conversion of the Jews. Even some decades later,
long after the Jewish war, both Matthew and Luke still tried to make clear "the
necessity of mission to the Jews and the lasting precedence of Israel" (Hahn
1965:166). In the long run, however, the tension snapped. The church
responded with anti-Jewishness to Judaism's anti-Christian stance.

WERE THERE ANY ALTERNATIVES?

Looking back today to the early church's mission, we cannot but lament the
three failures we have briefly highlighted. However, we have to ask ourselves
whether they were really avoidable, given the total context in which early Christianity found itself. Most probably they were not.

First, we have to ask whether it is fair to expect a movement to survive only
as movement. Either the movement disintegrates or it becomes an institution —
this is simply a sociological law. Every religious group that started out as a
movement and managed to survive, did so because it was gradually institutionalized: the Waldensians, the Moravians, the Quakers, the Pentecostals, and
many more. The same was bound to happen to the early Christian movement.
It could not, in the long run, survive merely in the shape of a charismatic leader
with his band of lower-class artisans from the periphery of society. Actually, it
probably took that form only during the first months of Jesus public ministry.
Whereas earlier New Testament scholars (such as Adolf Deissmann) and some
contemporary Marxist ones hold that, during the first century or so, the overwhelming majority of Christians came from the lower strata of society and that
Christianity, therefore, was essentially a proletarian movement, recent studies
are pointing in another direction. Scholars now agree that the church in Corinth
was, by and large, a lower-class church, but they believe that this was not true
of the majority of other churches (cf Malherbe 1983:passim; Meeks 1983:51-
73).

Also prominent members of the Jewish establishment showed a keen interest
in the Jesus movement from an early stage. Two names come to mind: Joseph
of Arimathea, and Nicodemus. We may criticize both of them for their hesitancy
in this matter and blame their slowness to rally openly to Jesus' cause on their
exaggerated sense of bourgeois respectability, but would it be fair to do that?
After all, both Joseph and Nicodemus did make a move before Easter, without
knowing that Jesus would rise from the dead. This was perhaps as strong a
stand as men in their position could be expected to take, what with all the
middle-class responsibilities they had (cf Singleton 1977:31). We might say that
they were halfhearted, that they should have left wife, children, and the Sanhedrin (of which they were members) and follow Jesus around as he visited the
hamlets of Galilee, but would it be fair to expect that? The point is that very
few people can be both at the periphery and at the center at the same time.
And even if they do manage that, they usually do so only for a very short while.

Be this as it may, the Josephs and Nicodemuses helped to smooth the transition from a charismatic movement to a religious institution. In this way they

also helped to guarantee the survival of the movement. Without that, and speaking humanly and sociologically, the Jesus movement would perhaps have been absorbed into Judaism or have disappeared, "leaving but a vague souvenir of a bizarre, millennial movement" (Singleton 1977:28).

We cannot have it both ways, then: purely and exclusively a religious movement, yet at the same time something that will survive the centuries and continue to exercise a dynamic influence. Our main point of censure should therefore not be that the movement became an institution but that, when this happened, it also lost much of its verve. Its white-hot convictions, poured into the hearts of the first adherents, cooled down and became crystallized codes, solidified institutions, and petrified dogmas. The prophet became a priest of the establishment, charisma became office, and love became routine. The horizon was no longer the world but the boundaries of the local parish. The impetuous missionary torrent of earlier years was tamed into a still-flowing rivulet and eventually into a stationary pond. It is this development that we have to deplore. Institution and movement may never be mutually exclusive categories; neither may church and mission.

This brings us to the second failure of the early church in the area of mission: the break with the Jewish people. Once again we have to ask whether that development was avoidable. How could the early church do anything but follow through on the logic of Jesus' ministry and still, in the long run, embrace the Jewish law as a way of salvation? By the same token, how could Judaism have remained both true to itself and open to a mission to Gentiles free from the requirements of the law? Given these circumstances, was there, in the long run, any alternative to a parting of the ways? Given, in addition, the events of the Jewish War (AD 66-70) and the fact that Judaism was almost wiped out by it, is it fair to blame post-war Pharisaic Judaism for having developed into a xenophobic religious club and having conceived the *Eighteen Benedictions*?

The sociological (and therefore human) answer to all these questions can only be a resounding no. The die was, in fact, already cast in the earthly ministry of Jesus of Nazareth. Forty years later, at the end of the Jewish War, the fate of both Judaism and Christianity was finally sealed; they would henceforth go their separate ways.

Even so, this is not a story Christians can tell with joy, particularly in light of subsequent Christian-Jewish relations. And we have to admit that the seeds of anti-Jewishness were already sown at a very early stage. The apostle Paul who, on the one hand, could wish that he himself were cursed and cut off from Christ for the sake of Israel (Rom 9:3f), could also, on the other hand, accuse the Jews of having killed Jesus, of displeasing God, and being hostile to all people, thus heaping up their sins to the limit and invoking the eternal wrath of God upon themselves (1 Thes 2:15f). This attitude became the model for later views on Judaism. Twice in the book of Revelation the Jewish religious assembly is referred to as "a synagogue of Satan" (2:9; 3:9). The Epistle of Barnabas (*circa* AD 113) and Justin's *Dialogue with Trypho the Jew* (*circa* AD 150) for all practical purposes excluded Jews from the church's field of vision, calling them the worst, most godless and God-forsaken nation on earth, the devil's own people, seduced by a wicked angel from the very first and having no claim whatsoever to the Old Testament (references in Harnack 1962:66f). In the writings of Tertullian and Cyprian we encounter the view that, at most, some individual Jews could be converted. This too was finally to disappear with the anti-Jewish edicts of Emperor Theodosius in 378. Harnack (1962:69) comments:

> Such an injustice as that done by the Gentile church to Judaism is almost unprecedented in the annals of history. The Gentile church stripped it of everything; she took away its sacred book; herself but a transformation of Judaism, she cut off all connection with the parent religion. The daughter first robbed her mother, and then repudiated her!

•

I began this chapter with the claim that the New Testament has to be understood as a missionary document. The profile of the missionary nature of this document and of the early church has, I hope, become somewhat clearer as we gradually uncovered the evidence. There is a degree of ambivalence about the nature and scope of mission, we found, and this seems to have been the case virtually from the beginning. Some firm and enduring elements of mission appear, however, to have emerged in the course of our investigation. The mission of the church is rooted in God's revelation in the man from Nazareth who lived and labored in Palestine, was crucified on Golgotha, and, so the church believes, was raised from the dead. For the New Testament mission is determined by the knowledge that the eschatological hour has dawned, bringing salvation within reach of all and leading to its final completion (Hahn 1965:167f). Mission is "the Church's service, made possible by the coming of Christ and the dawning of the eschatological event of salvation . . . The Church goes in confidence and hope to meet the future of its Lord, with the duty of testifying before the whole world to God's love and redemptive deed" (Hahn 1965:173; cf Hahn 1980:37). The New Testament witnesses assume the possibility of a community of people who, in the face of the tribulations they encounter, keep their eyes steadfastly on the reign of God by praying for its coming, by being its disciples, by proclaiming its presence, by working for peace and justice in the midst of hatred and oppression, and by looking and working toward God's liberating future (cf Lochman 1986:67).

A careful study of the New Testament and the early church may help us to come to greater clarity about what mission meant then and might mean today. So we shall now, as it were, retrace our steps, listen to the testimony of three New Testament writers, Matthew, Luke, and Paul, who each represents a subparadigm of the early Christian missionary paradigm, discover how they interpreted mission for their communities, and emulate the imaginative way in which they did this as a model for our missionary involvement today.

I should, perhaps, very briefly explain why I have chosen to concentrate on the three New Testament witnesses just mentioned. I could, of course, have surveyed the entire New Testament and also other early Christian writings. For two reasons I have decided to limit my reflections to Matthew's gospel, Luke-Acts, and the letters of Paul. First, a thorough and creditable treatment of all the material we have from the first century AD would have called for more than just one volume and made it impossible to include an in-depth discussion of today's missiological issues. Second, and perhaps more important, I believe that the three New Testament authors chosen for my survey are, on the whole, representative of first-century missionary thinking and practice. A few words on this may elucidate what I mean.

Matthew wrote as a Jew to a predominantly Jewish Christian community. The entire purpose of his writing was to nudge his community toward a missionary involvement with its environment. The Protestant missionary enterprise of the past two centuries or so has therefore rightly appealed to Matthew's "Great Commission" when it had to give an account of its outreach to people across the globe. Unfortunately, however, as I hope to illustrate, the appeal to the "Great Commission" usually took no account of the fact that this pericope cannot be properly understood in isolation from the gospel of Matthew as a whole.

Luke was selected because he did not only write a gospel, as Mark, Matthew and John did, but actually a two-part volume: the Gospel of Luke *and* the Book of Acts. Since John's gospel is, in our Bibles, inserted between Luke and Acts, we easily overlook the fact that Luke-Acts was written as a unit and should be read as such. In the way he structured his two volumes, Luke wished to demonstrate the essential unity between the mission of Jesus and that of the early church. This fact alone makes the inclusion of Luke-Acts indispensable in a survey of this kind.

The decision to include *Paul*'s letters should speak for itself. No discussion of the early church's missionary thinking and practice is even conceivable without a study of the writings and activities of the "apostle to the Gentiles".

Chapter 2

Matthew: Mission as Disciple-Making

A "GREAT COMMISSION"?

The gospel of Matthew reflects an important and distinct sub-paradigm of the early church's interpretation and experience of mission. However, in missionary circles much of the discussion about Matthew has, unfortunately, been obfuscated by the high prominence given (especially, but not exclusively, in Protestant circles) to the significance and interpretation of the so-called "Great Commission" at the end of the gospel (28:16-20) (for a survey, cf Bosch 1983:218-220).

Interestingly enough, New Testament scholarship for a long time appeared to have been very little interested in this passage. Even in commentaries on Matthew little attention was paid to it. In his monumental work, *The Mission and Expansion of Christianity in the First Three Centuries*, Harnack even toyed with the idea that these words might be a later addition to the gospel, since he could not understand why Matthew would have added them (Harnack [1908] 1962:40f, note 2). Even so, in the fourth edition of his book in German, he added that this "manifesto" (as he now calls it) was a "masterpiece". He summarized his comments on the passage by saying, "It is impossible to say anything greater and more than this in only forty words" (Harnack 1924:45f, note 2 — my translation).

It was, however, not until the 1940s that biblical scholarship, pioneered by Michel (1941 and 1950/51) and Lohmeyer (1951) began to pay serious attention to Matthew 28:18-20. Since then there has been a sustained and, in fact, expanding interest among New Testament scholars in the closing lines of Matthew's gospel. Scores of theologians have tried to lay bare the origins and significance of this majestic passage. In 1973 Joachim Lange devoted a monograph of 573 pages to a tradition- and redaction-critical study of the pericope (Lange 1973). A year later Benjamin Hubbard published another major monograph on it (Hubbard 1974). And still, so it appears, there remains more to discover about the "Great Commission". John P. Meier comments, "There are certain great pericopes in the bible which constantly engender discussion and research, while apparently never admitting to definite solutions. Mt 28:16-20 seems to be such a pericope" (Meier 1977:407). On one thing scholars agree, however, says Meier: "The pivotal nature of these verses".

This is a significant shift away from the earlier position. Michel (1950/51:21), for instance, says that the entire gospel was written only from the perspective of the presuppositions embodied in this pericope (Michel 1950/51:21). In a more recent essay, Friedrich (1983:177, note 114) lists some phrases scholars have used to give expression to the importance of these verses for understanding Matthew's gospel: "the theological program of Matthew" (J. Blank); "a summary of the entire gospel of Matthew" (G. Bornkamm); "the most important concern of the Gospel" (H. Kosmala), "the 'climax' of the gospel" (U. Luck); "a sort of culmination of everything said up to this point" (P. Nepper-Christensen); "a 'manifesto'" (G. Otto); and "a 'table of contents' of the gospel" (G. Schille). Friedrich himself says that "Matthew has, as if in a burning-glass, focused everything that was dear to him in these words and put them as the crowning culmination at the end of his gospel" (Friedrich 1983:177 — my translation). Today scholars agree that the entire gospel points to these final verses: all the threads woven into the fabric of Matthew, from chapter 1 onward, draw together here.

All this means that the way the "Great Commission" has traditionally been utilized in providing a biblical basis for mission has to be challenged or at least modified. It is inadmissible to lift these words out of Matthew's gospel, as it were, allow them a life of their own, and understand them without any reference to the context in which they first appeared. Where this happens, the "Great Commission" is easily degraded to a mere slogan, or used as a pretext for what we have in advance decided, perhaps unconsciously, it should mean (cf Schreiter 1982:431). We then, however, run the risk of doing violence to the text and its intention. One thing contemporary scholars are agreed upon, is that Matthew 28:18-20 has to be interpreted *against the background of Matthew's gospel as a whole* and unless we keep this in mind we shall fail to understand it. No exegesis of the "Great Commission" divorced from its moorings in this gospel can be valid. It should therefore come as no surprise if we discover that, as far as use of language is concerned, the "Great Commission" is perhaps the most Matthean in the entire gospel: virtually every word or expression used in these verses is peculiar to the author of the first gospel.

In what follows I shall argue that we shall only understand what this pericope means if we first ask about the self-definition of the author of this gospel and his community. From that we might be able to make some inferences about Matthew's overall missionary paradigm.

MATTHEW AND HIS COMMUNITY

Our first gospel is essentially a missionary text. It was primarily because of his missionary vision that Matthew set out to write his gospel, not to compose a "life of Jesus" but to provide guidance to a community in crisis on how it should understand its calling and mission.

I accept, together with the majority of contemporary scholars, that the author of the first gospel was a member of a Jewish Christian community which had left Judea before the Jewish war and settled in a predominantly Gentile environment, probably Syria. In Judea the community had most likely shared some of the insularity of other Jewish Christians and had participated, at least to some extent, in the general cultural and cultic life of Judaism inasmuch as that was possible before the war. The Christians had not yet understood themselves as being members of a separate religion over against Judaism but primarily as a renewal movement within it. They had, of course, known about the vigorous missionary expansion among Gentiles but this happened outside of their experience and range of vision.

However, by the late seventies or early eighties of the first century AD, the situation was fundamentally different. At Jamnia (as has been mentioned in the previous chapter) the Pharisees, with Johannan ben Zakkai their leader, were assuming exclusive control. The synagogue worship was regulated and partly structured on that of the now defunct temple. The rabbinate was introduced as authoritative interpreter of the law. Even more important, a bitter polemic had developed between Jamnia Pharisaism and Jewish Christianity and was inexorably moving, around AD 85, toward the formulation of the Twelfth Benediction: "Let the Nazarenes and the heretics be destroyed in a moment . . . Let their names be expurgated from the Book of Life and not be entered with those of the just".

Apparently this moment of final and absolute break with the synagogue had not yet arrived when Matthew wrote his gospel (cf Bornkamm 1965a:19; LaVerdiere and Thompson 1976:585; Brown 1980:216; Frankemölle 1982:122f). The community still defends its right to be viewed as the true Israel (cf the title of Trilling 1964), but it faces a crisis of unprecedented magnitude as regards its self-understanding. What should its identity be in the coming years? Can it continue as a movement within Judaism? What attitude should it adopt toward the Law? Can it give up on viewing Jesus as more than just a prophet? And can it give up on a mission to fellow Jews? It is for this community that Matthew writes, a community cut off from its roots, its attachment to Judaism exposed to the harshest test possible, divided in itself as to what its priorities should be, groping for direction in the face of previously unknown problems. And his primary concern is not simply to help his people cope with the new pressures they confront, but to assist them in developing a missionary ethos that will match the challenges of a new epoch. He does this in an exemplary fashion by prolonging the logic of Jesus' ministry into the historical circumstances he is facing.

Not everybody in Matthew's community agrees on the direction that should be taken at the present juncture. Some emphasize faithfulness to the Law, even to the smallest letter; others claim to have the Spirit through whom they perform miracles (cf Friedrich 1983:177). With his remarkable pastoral style and with the aid of a dialectic approach, Matthew shows, on the basis of the Jesus tradition, that both are right . . . but at the same time wrong. This accounts, *inter alia*, for the many apparent contradictions in his gospel. He does not gloss over the differences but points beyond both. In this manner he prepares the way for reconciliation, forgiveness, and mutual love within the community; and he seems to suggest that the confusion, tension and conflict that divide them one from another can only be overcome if they join hands and hearts in a mission to the Gentiles among whom they live (LaVerdiere and Thompson 1976:574).

Matthew desires his community no longer to regard itself as a sectarian group but boldly and consciously as the church of Christ (he is the only evangelist who uses the word *ekklesia*, "church") and precisely therefore as the "true Israel" (although Matthew himself does not use this expression; cf Trilling 1964:95f; Bornkamm 1965a:36). To substantiate this claim he includes a plethora of explicit quotations from the Old Testament and even more indirect allusions, more than any of the other evangelists. The purpose of the so-called formula quotations is to prove that Jesus is the Messiah and as such the fulfillment of Old Testament promises. Matthew therefore uses the Old Testament as witness *against* the Jewish theologians of his day and their use of Scripture (Frankemölle 1974:288). He does this by casting "the aura of fulfillment over his entire portrait of Jesus" and by applying "the label of fulfillment to practically every dimension of Jesus' life" (Senior and Stuhlmueller 1983:241). The genealogy with which he opens his gospel plants Jesus deep within the heritage of Judaism. His infancy narrative, which Matthew does not share with any of the other gospels, is replete with Old Testament references. Each event here — the visit of the magi, the flight to Egypt, the massacre of the innocents, the return to Nazareth — is presented as the fulfillment of an Old Testament text. Throughout the gospel titles forged in the Hebrew Scriptures are applied to Jesus: Immanuel, Christ, Son of David, Son of Man, etc (cf LaVerdiere and Thompson 1976:596; Senior and Stuhlmueller 1983:241). At the same time Jesus is subtly cast in the role of a new Moses (Hubbard 1974:91-94), not only in the infancy narrative (Jesus' escape from Herod's execution order and his return from exile), but also in the forty days and forty nights he spent in the desert, in the Sermon of the Mount where he reveals the new "law" (Luke situates this event in a *plain*) and in the transfiguration (where Matthew adds: "And his face shone like the sun" — 17:2). At the same time there can be no doubt in the minds of Matthew's readers that "more than Moses is here".

Throughout, then, Matthew's use of the Old Testament is not just polemical — to counter rabbinic claims to the Old Testament — but deeply pastoral and missionary — *pastoral*, in that he wishes to convey self-confidence to a community facing a crisis of identity; *missionary*, in that he wishes to embolden the community members toward seeing opportunities for witness and service around them.

CONTRADICTIONS IN MATTHEW

It is against this general background that we have to see the apparent contradictions in Matthew's gospel. On the one hand, scholars argue, this is clearly the most Jewish of all our gospels. E. von Dobschütz (1928:343) once even

called Matthew "a converted Jewish rabbi". Stendahl (1968) and others claim
that he has arranged his gospel in such a way that it would resemble the first
five books of the Old Testament. Still others contend that he has often "reju-
daized" the tradition handed down to him (Brown 1977:25-28). By contrast,
others argue that Matthew's gospel consistently and systematically engages in
polemics against the Jews and their leadership, a stance that clearly demonstrates his "Gentile bias," which would be natural only if he were "a Gentile
author" (Clark 1980:4; cf Strecker 1962:15-35).

Matthew's gospel is indeed, in many respects, baffling. I have argued that
the "Great Commission" at the end of the gospel is to be understood as the
key to Matthew's understanding of the mission and ministry of Jesus. Matthew
has, stronger than any other evangelist, emphasized Jesus' activities among
Gentiles (cf Hahn 1965:103-111). Still, in the central section of his gospel he
includes some particularistic sayings which must have been extremely offensive
to Gentile readers. Chapter 10 relates the sending out of the twelve apostles
(v 2) to whom Jesus says, "Go nowhere among the Gentiles, and enter no town
of the Samaritans, but go rather to the lost sheep of the house of Israel" (v 5f).
What Jesus says to the Canaanite woman according to Matthew 15 must have
been even more disagreeable to Gentiles. Matthew has taken this episode over
from Mark, but he introduces important changes. Jesus repeats what he has
said to the Twelve, "I was sent only to the lost sheep of the house of Israel"
(v 24; this saying has no parallel in any of the other gospels). When the woman
insists that Jesus help, he adds, "It is not fair to take the children's bread and
throw it to the dogs" (v 26). It is clear that in Matthew's two major sources
(Mark and the *Logia*) there is no trace of absolute exclusivism and particularism. Why then has this issue become a problem in Matthew's gospel (cf Frankemölle 1974:109)?

Many attempts have been made to solve the contradictions in Matthew (cf
Hahn 1965:26-28; Frankemölle 1982:100-102). It is probably best to assume that
Matthew deliberately included both sets of conflicting sayings in the service of
the overall purpose of his gospel. It is indeed possible that the different sayings
also reflect opposing views and traditions in Matthew's community and were,
we may deduce, responsible for some sharp differences. Matthew, however,
chooses to include both. This certainly speaks for his pastoral concern; he does
not simply play off one group against another. But it also reflects his theological
position: a mission to Israel and one to Gentiles need not exclude but ought
rather to embrace each other.

So Matthew does not just advocate a chronological sequence of the two
missions (as Mark appears to do: cf the "first" in Mk 7:26) but upholds a
theological correlation of one to the other. Hahn uses the metaphor of two
concentric circles (the larger one signifying the Gentile mission, the other the
mission to Israel) which necessarily belong together but, of course, in such a
way that the Gentile mission becomes the all-embracing and over-arching one
(Hahn 1965:127; cf Frankemölle 1982:113). Matthew achieves this by means of
the skillful way in which he organizes his material, for instance by having Gentiles play a role from the beginning to the end (the four non-Israelite women

in Jesus' genealogy [ch 1]; the visit of the magi [2:1-12]; the centurion of Capernaum, who prompts Jesus to say that many Gentiles will one day take their places with the patriarchs in the kingdom of heaven [8:5-13]; the Canaanite woman [15:21-28]; the statement in the eschatological discourse that the gospel will be preached to all the nations [24:14; cf 26:13]; and the reaction of the Roman centurion and those with him at the crucifixion of Jesus, who exclaim, "Truly he was the Son of God" [27:54; Mark mentions the reaction of the centurion only, not that of his division of soldiers also]).

Perhaps even more important are the not-so-obvious allusions to Gentiles and a future mission to them: God's "people" (*laos*) who will be saved from their sin (1:21; this points to the "nation" [*ethnos*] who will take Israel's place as inheritors of God's reign, cf 21:43); the identification of Galilee as "Galilee of the Gentiles" (4:15; at the end of the gospel it is again in Galilee, semi-Gentile territory to Matthew, that the disciples are commissioned); the summary of Jesus' activities in 4:23-25, which adds that news about him "spread throughout all Syria" (in 9:35-38 Matthew has an almost identical summary, where he adds Jesus' word about a plentiful harvest, an obvious allusion to a wider mission; again, Matthew's readers [in Syria] could not have overheard the assertion that the earthly Jesus had been known in Syria); the reference to the disciples as the salt of the *earth* and the light of the *world* (5:13f); the quotation from Isaiah in 12:18-21 with its twofold mentioning of Gentiles; the saying that the field on which the "sons of the Kingdom" are sown is "the world" (13:38); the cleansing of the forecourt of the temple (also known as the forecourt of the Gentiles) as indication that salvation is at hand for Gentiles also (cf Hahn 1984:273); Jesus' spontaneous willingness to enter Gentile homes (cf 8:7; in Luke's gospel Jesus does not seem prepared to do this: cf Frankemölle 1974:113), etc.

In these and other ways Matthew nourishes universalism and skillfully conditions his reader toward a mission to the Gentiles. He does it with a remarkable degree of consistency without ever allowing his reader to wander off (Frankemölle 1982:112; Senior and Stuhlmueller 1983:152). Even particularistic sayings such as Matthew 15:24, and 26 do not permit his Jewish reader a sigh of relief, since Jesus immediately praises the Canaanite woman's remarkable faith (15:28). As a matter of fact, one thing about Gentiles that Matthew frequently stresses is their faith in Jesus, their spontaneous and positive response to him, which is so different from that of (the majority of) Jews. In addition to the Canaanite woman we may refer to the Capernaum centurion (Jesus says of him, "Truly, I say to you, not even in Israel have I found such faith" — 8:10) as well as to the centurion with his contingent of soldiers who were watching the crucifixion (27:54; no word is said about the reaction of the Jewish crowds). The magi even confess their faith in Jesus before having seen or heard him. The faith response of Gentiles, compared to the lack of such a response among Jews, is a recurring theme in Matthew (cf Hahn 1965:35; Frankemölle 1974: 114,118).

Even so, Matthew never tells of Jesus actually taking the initiative and going out to Gentiles. *They* approach *him*, not he them—the magi, the centurion of

Capernaum, the Canaanite woman. Matthew here clearly follows the tradition about Jesus handed down to him and also reflected in the other gospels, including John (cf, for instance, Jn 12:32). There is no evidence of a conscious Gentile missionary outreach, "even though such evidence would have been highly useful for the ... evangelists who were writing to an increasingly Gentile church" (Senior and Stuhlmueller 1983:142).

MATTHEW AND ISRAEL

Throughout, Matthew's judgment on Jews is severe. This may, in part, reflect the confrontations his community had with Jamnia Pharisaism at the time of writing but was certainly also a recurring theme in the tradition he uses. His judgment of the Jews is, in virtually every instance, more negative than that of Mark and Luke (e.g. in 11:16-19; 11:20-24; 12:41-45; 22:1-14; 23:29-39; cf Frankemölle 1974:115). The parable of the two sons (21:28-32) is told by Matthew only. In his rendering of Jesus' own exposition of the parable (v 31f), the "chief priests and the elders of the people" (v 23) are the son who said he would go and work in his fathers vineyard but did not, whereas the "tax-collectors and the harlots" (v 31) — those of whom one would least expect it — are the son who first said that he would not go but eventually went. (Since the pairing of tax-collectors and prostitutes obviously no longer has any immediate and concrete significance for Matthew's readers, they understand this as an implicit reference to a positive response to Jesus from Gentiles [cf Schottroff and Stegemann 1986:33]).

The parable of the tenants that follows immediately (21:33-44) exposes the central (but still hidden) thrust of the parable of the two sons. Once again Jesus' listeners are the Jewish religious establishment; as a matter of fact, at the end of the parable "they perceived that he was speaking about them" (v 45). The tenants have failed in their duty; they did not produce any fruit. So the landowner brings "those wretches to a miserable death" and will rent his vineyard "to other tenants, who will give him the fruits in their seasons" (v 41). Matthew shares this parable with Luke (20:9-10) and Mark (12:1-12), but he goes further than both and puts an interpretation of the parable in Jesus' mouth: "Therefore I tell you, the kingdom of God will be taken away from you and given to a nation producing the fruits of it" (v 43). Thus Matthew here takes up the theme of the substitution of Israel by a new covenant people, a theme which, in fact, is present under the surface throughout his gospel. It is, indeed, a central theme of Matthew and this parable occupies a pivotal place in his theology (cf Trilling 1964:55-65). In the old covenant God's kingdom was entrusted to a nation; now once again his reign is entrusted to a "nation". For Matthew the fact that the kingdom has been taken away from Israel is the real punishment, not so much the physical judgment on the Jews, for instance, the destruction of Jerusalem (Trilling 1964:65).

The supreme transgression of the tenants in the parable is, however, not just that they refused to send the landowner his share of the crop, but that they maltreated and killed his servants and, ultimately, his son, in a scandalous attempt to arrogate the vineyard to themselves. This detail Matthew takes over from Mark; the only difference he introduces is to say that the son was killed outside the vineyard (21:39), thus modelling the parable even more explicitly on what happened to Jesus. In his gospel Matthew emphasizes the involvement of the Jewish leaders in the betrayal, arrest, and condemnation of Jesus, reaching a climax in his rendering of the trial before Pilate (27:11-26). The fact that leaders and people chose Barabbas is stressed much more forcefully than in Mark's account. Also, only Matthew reports the pleas of Pilate's wife on behalf of "that righteous man" (27:19). Pilate is distracted for a moment and the chief priests use this opportunity to persuade the crowds to ask for Barabbas's release (cf Senior and Stuhlmueller 1983:245). The concern of Pilate's wife for Jesus and Pilate's washing of his hands in public (27:24; again only Matthew reports the latter) once more serve to underline the difference in attitude between Jews and Gentiles, particularly when all the people (not just the chief priests) boldly declare, "His blood be on us and on our children!" (27:25; once again only Matthew relates this).

Certainly Matthew's portrayal of the Jews and their leadership contains an anti-Semitic potential which we, particularly after the Holocaust, should not brush aside too lightly. However, Matthew himself is no anti-Semite; after all, he was, in all probability, himself a Jew. Donald Senior (1983:246) interprets his purpose correctly, I believe:

> Matthew is trying to fit a series of baffling, even tragic events into his conviction that God acts in and through history. These tragic events, from Matthew's viewpoint, included the death of Jesus, the failure of the Christian mission to Israel, and the intransigence of Christians in his own church who were opposed to accepting Gentiles.

Senior adds, however, that "these considerations do not completely remove the dark potential of Matthew's formulations in 27:24-25" (ibid), even if his overall concern is a positive one; namely, that Israel's rejection of its Messiah has become a paradoxical impulse to a new life-giving stage in God's plan of history. "From the death of Jesus comes the birth of a resurrection community; from the failure of the mission to Israel comes the opening to the Gentiles" (:244).

MATTHEW AND "THE NATIONS"

It may shed some light on the issue under discussion if we, at this point, look at the phrase *panta ta ethne* in the "Great Commission". Following through on the supposition that, for Matthew, the Jews have — by their conduct — forfeited the "right" to be preached to, some scholars (particularly those who believe that the author of our first gospel was a Gentile) suggest that these words refer to all nations *excluding* the Jews: those who had not been called before may now become Jesus' disciples; those who had been called previously are now rejected (Clark 1980:2; cf Walker 1967:111-113).

I believe, with many New Testament scholars, that this is a misinterpretation of Matthew (cf Michel 1950/51:26; Strecker 1962:117f; Trilling 1964:26-28; Hahn 1965:125; Zumstein 1972:26; Frankemölle 1974:119-123; 1982:112-114; Matthew 1980:168, note 14; Friedrich 1983:179f). The Jews are included among "all the nations"—no longer, however, as a specially privileged people. "Israel" as a theological entity belongs to the past (Frankemölle 1974:123). "Israel" is no longer the "church". In what happened to Jesus, the ancient notion of "Israel" has been ruptured and God's eschatological community ushered on to the stage of history. All restrictions have been lifted.

It is true that *ethne* in Matthew's gospel mostly refer to Gentiles only. But, in almost all these cases we have to do with either Old Testament quotations or material of non-Matthean origin. To this we must add that, where Matthew adds *panta*, "all", to *ta ethne*, an important nuance is added. Matthew uses *panta ta ethne* four times, and all of these are in the final part of his gospel (24:9,14; 25:32; and 28:19), where the Gentile mission comes into focus ever more clearly. The various parallels to Matthew's fourfold use of *panta ta ethne* also evoke universalist imagery: *hole he oikoumene* (the whole inhabited world), *holos (hapas) ho kosmos* (the whole [human] world) and *pasa he ktisis* (the entire [human] creation). It is clear, then, that Matthew was simply trying to say that Jesus was no longer sent only to Israel but had, in fact, become the Savior of all humankind. If Matthew had intended his readers (many of whom were Jews, still part of the wider Jewish community) to understand him as saying that Jews could no longer be recipients of the gospel, he would have had to say it much more unambiguously. An unbiased reader of chapters 24 to 28 of his gospel can only understand them as suggesting that Matthew's concern was with all of humankind, including the Jews.

Therefore, despite his strong views on the hardheartedness of Jews, Matthew never doubts the continued validity of a mission to his compatriots. This remains the inalienable task of himself and his community; they continue to regard themselves as inwardly and outwardly tied to Israel (Hahn 1965:125). Yet he is equally committed to the Gentile mission. Between the two missions there exists a unity full of tension, a kind of contrasting interdependence (Frankemölle 1982:113, 120) to which Matthew remains obligated, since it is the only way in which he can hold on to both his "text" (God's promises to his covenant people in the Old Testament) and his "context" (God's obvious endorsement of the Gentile mission).

In his view the Gentile mission is, however, only a possibility after the death and resurrection of the Messiah of the Jews. Prior to those events it can be referred to only in the future tense (8:11; 24:14; 26:13). The parable of the tenants graphically illustrates that the vineyard can only go to others *after* the son has been killed. The two demon-possessed men from the region of the Gadarenes (Gentile territory!) therefore rightly complain that Jesus has come to torture them "before the (appointed) time", in other words, before his death and resurrection (Mt 8:29; only Matthew has this phrase; cf Frankemölle 1974:115).

The risen Jesus, however, boldly and unreservedly, sends his followers to disciple "all nations" (*panta ta ethne*: Mt 28:19). The reign of God has been entrusted to God's new people (cf 21:43).

KEY NOTIONS IN MATTHEW'S GOSPEL

From what has been said so far, one should not deduce that Matthew's entire gospel exhausts itself in an attempt to solve the enigma of the relationship between Jews and Gentiles. To narrow his understanding of mission down to this aspect alone would be totally unwarranted (Frankemölle 1982:100). Yet it certainly forms a backdrop to virtually everything else Matthew tells us and has to be kept in mind constantly.

Matthew, I have said, fights a battle on two fronts: Pharisaic Judaism and the inroads it was making into his community, and the antinominianism of an enthusiastic Hellenistic Jewish Christianity. This has led to much confusion in the interpretation of Matthew's gospel. An example of this was the publication, more or less simultaneously, of two books that came to almost exactly opposite conclusions: Strecker (1962) who understood Matthew as a gospel written from a Gentile Christian bias, and Hummel (1963) who interpreted Matthew as being in close proximity to Pharisaic Judaism (cf also Bornkamm 1965b:229,306).

All this makes it hard really to get to the bottom of Matthew's "theology of mission". I believe that we shall only understand it (and even then only approximately) if we see Matthew as attempting to move beyond both positions he is opposing. In this respect there are a number of key concepts in his gospel which are all intimately interrelated and also supremely significant for interpreting his missionary consciousness. The most important of these concepts are: the reign (*basileia*) of God (or of heaven), God's will (*thelema*), justice (*dikaiosyne*), commandments (*entolai*), the challenge to be perfect (*teleios*), to surpass or excel (*perisseuo*), to observe or keep (*tereo*), to bear fruit (*karpous poiein*), and to teach (*didasko*). At first glance, most of these concepts appear to support a kind of rabbinic salvation by works. They have a different function, however. Sometimes one concept is a synonym for another, sometimes not. Throughout, they appear to be intimately linked to and dependent upon each other. All taken together, they are like plaited strands woven into the very fabric of the entire gospel.

Some of these ideas (such as that of the reign of God) I have already touched upon in the previous chapter. I shall therefore, in this chapter, only (and briefly) attend to such key concepts insofar as they are central to *Matthew* and his perception of mission.

"TEACHING THEM TO OBSERVE ALL . . ."

The final part of the "Great Commission" makes mention of "teaching them to observe all that I have commanded you" (Mt 28:20). On the face of it, this "teaching them", together with the preceding "baptizing them", appears to be the real content of disciple-making, and therefore of mission, in Matthew's understanding. It moreover appears to be something rather different from mission in parallel passages in the other gospels and in Acts. In Luke 24:47 the message proclaimed to the nations is one of repentance and forgiveness of sins in the name of Jesus. In Acts 1:8 the disciples are told that they will be witnesses to the Easter events, empowered by the Holy Spirit. In John 20:21-23 the disciples are likewise promised the Holy Spirit and sent into the world by the risen Christ with the authority to forgive sins. Matthew, it seems, has nothing of all this. The Matthean Jesus sounds extremely didactic and legalistic and is an embarrassment, particularly to Protestants, who would prefer to hear about proclamation rather than teaching, about forgiveness of sins and the power of the Holy Spirit rather than the keeping of commandments.

Let us, however, look more closely at what Jesus says according to Matthew, and at how these words, in a truly extraordinary way, summarize some of the basic concerns Jesus has expressed throughout the gospel. Beginning with the words in the latter part of the "Great Commission" we shall, as it were, move from smaller to larger concentric circles as we attempt to trace Matthew's missionary concern.

Three terms in the "Great Commission" summarize the essence of mission for Matthew: make disciples, baptize, teach. I shall return to the first two below and turn, for the moment, to the third. Whereas Mark uses "proclaim" (*kerysso*) and "teach" (*didasko*) as synonyms, Matthew consistently distinguishes between the two activities (cf Trilling 1964:36; Hahn 1965:121; 1980:42). In Matthew, "preach" or "proclaim" always refers to a message addressed to outsiders; it is frequently used together with "the gospel of the kingdom". The expression "proclaim the gospel (of the kingdom)" is sometimes also used with specific reference to a future (Gentile) mission (24:14; 26:13; cf 10:7). Jesus never "preaches" to his disciples; them he "teaches". Similarly, in the synagogues and in the temple (that is, among "believers") Jesus never "preaches" but always "teaches". Why then does he drop this overtly missionary terminology in his "Great Commission?" Why no word about "preach" (nine times in Matthew), "proclaim the gospel" (four times), "evangelize" (once)? This is the kind of terminology Jesus used in the commissioning narrative in Matthew 10. So why not here, in a commissioning which involves a universal outreach?

The extremely sober vocabulary of the "Great Commission" certainly is, at least in part, to be attributed to the evangelist's differences with the enthusiasts in his community. Surely, however, polemics is not his only consideration. Behind his choice of terms there are important theological (read: missiological) considerations. To appreciate these, it is important to recognize that, for Matthew, teaching is by no means a merely intellectual enterprise (as it often is for us and was for the ancient Greeks). Jesus' teaching is an appeal to his listeners' will, not primarily to their intellect; it is a call for a concrete decision to follow him and to submit to God's will (cf Frankemölle 1982:127f). Moreover, teaching does not merely involve inculcating the precepts of the Law and obeying them, as contemporary Judaism interpreted it (cf also Jesus' very "Jewish" advice to the rich young man in Matthew 19:17). No, what the apostles should "teach" the new disciples according to Matthew 28:20, is to submit to the will of God as revealed in Jesus' ministry and teaching. There is no gospel that may distance itself in an enthusiasm of the Spirit from the earthly Jesus. His instructions remain valid and authoritative, also for the future. Continuity must be maintained between the earthly Jesus and the exalted Christ. Those made disciples and baptized by Christ's messengers are to follow Jesus just as the eleven did (Friedrich 1983:181). He himself is now the content of his own earlier teaching, the embodiment of God's reign, the gospel (Lohmeyer 1956:418). Discipleship is determined by the relation to Christ himself, not by conformity to an impersonal ordinance. The context of this is not the classroom (where "teaching" usually takes place for us), nor even the church, but the world.

We have to say more, however, by way of fleshing out this teaching, these "commandments" of Jesus. The Matthean term that comes to mind first when we attempt this, is "the will of the Father" (cf Giessen 1982:224-235). More than the other evangelists Matthew highlights the centrality of God's will for Jesus and the disciples. Parallels in other gospels are rare. Virtually all occurrences of the expression are restricted to Matthew and they are all remarkable. Matthew's version of the Lord's Prayer, taken over from the *Logia*, resembles Luke's version in almost every detail, yet only Matthew has the petition "Thy will be done" (6:10). In addition, whereas all the other petitions of the Lord's Prayer have parallels in Judaism, this one has none (Frankemölle 1974:276 and note 15). In Matthew 7:21 the reference to the Father's will appears in an eschatological context, against the dark backdrop of the last judgment: "Not every one who says to me, 'Lord, Lord,' shall enter the kingdom of heaven, but he who does the will of my Father." In similar vein "it is not the will of my Father who is in heaven" that any of the little ones should be lost (Mt 18:14). And as mentioned before, only Matthew has the parable of the two sons (21:28-31) who differ in one respect only: the one did the will of his father; the other did not.

For Israel the will of God is contained in the Torah or, for the Qumran community, in their manual (Frankemölle 1974:277-280, 282, 287). Not so for Jesus and his disciples. The expression is particularly crucial for our understanding of the Sermon on the Mount, in the very center of which Matthew places the Lord's Prayer. It is the heart of the Sermon just as the Decalogue is the heart and center of the Torah. What precedes the Prayer is recapitulated in the first three petitions; what follows it is extrapolated from the last three (cf also Frankemölle 1974:274f). The Sermon on the Mount is, however, not a new code, a new Torah. The critical corrective for any law that tends to hypostatize itself is the twofold commandment of love. This becomes the principle of interpretation in the face of the nascent legalism in Matthew's own community (:278f). The criterion for every act and attitude is love of God and neighbor (cf Mt 22:37-40).

As a matter of fact, love of neighbor may be regarded as the litmus test for love of God. The same is true of *deeds*. They are the test for the authenticity of *words*. To "believe", to "follow Jesus", to "understand", all contain an element of active commitment that flows into deeds. The actual commandments themselves are hereby relativized since they are contingent upon the context and circumstances of the neighbor. This dimension of proper response is a major theme in Matthew (Senior and Stuhlmueller 1983:247). He addresses himself to both opposing groups in his community; enthusiasts and legalists are equally prone to majoring in words rather than deeds.

It is particularly in the Sermon on the Mount, the first of Matthew's five great compositions of Jesus' teaching, that this concern surfaces, notably in the final section (cf 7:21): "Not every one who *says* to me, 'Lord, Lord', shall enter the kingdom of heaven, but he who *does* the will of my Father," and 7:24, "Everyone then who hears these words of mine and *does* them . . ."). Matthew himself summarizes Jesus' entire ministry with the words "the *deeds* of the Christ" (*ta erga tou Christou* — 11:2). This summary appears in the important central section of his gospel, after the first two discourses and prior to the last three. In prison John the Baptist hears about "the deeds of the Christ" and sends his disciples to Jesus. This episode introduces a series of narratives about rejection and acceptance in preparation for the third and central discourse (ch 13: the parables of the reign of God) and is crucial to the overall structure of the gospel. The expression "the deeds of the Christ" may be regarded as the caption of the entire first half of the gospel (Wilkens 1985:37) and clearly has a missionary connotation; indeed, it is a key missionary concept and one that puts its stamp on Matthew's basic understanding of mission (Frankemölle 1982:98; 126-128). Orthopraxis is hereby made into a critical yardstick for orthodoxy and becomes the norm for God's covenant people (cf, again, 7:21; 12:50; and 21:31) (Frankemölle 1974:279f).

The true disciples of Jesus are challenged to "bear fruit". The Baptist already preached, "Bear fruit that befits repentance" (3:8). Matthew has found this reference in the *Logia* but then uses it, in one form or another, elsewhere in his gospel as well. I have already referred to 7:16-20. Matthew takes up the same metaphor in 12:33 and also uses it more extensively than the other synoptic gospels do in the parable of the tenants (21:33-46); in fact, it becomes the dominant theme in Matthew's rendering of this parable (Frankemölle 1974:279f).

It is in this context that we have to appreciate Matthew's understanding of sin or failure, or, more specifically Matthean, *hypocrisy*. The context reveals that it means the absence of good deeds, of fruit, even if one might have the right words. A near synonym for hypocrisy is *anomia* ("iniquity"; Matthew, the only evangelist who employs this word, uses it four times). This shows that, for Matthew, hypocrisy is more than pretending or sanctimoniousness. Hypocrisy is evil-doing. It is a failure of conduct with reference both to people and to God. Not doing good means doing evil; not bearing fruit means bearing wrong fruit. The hypocrites have failed to obey God's will; they live outside God's covenantal relationship; they are no longer heirs to God's reign. Over against the evildoers and hypocrites stand the *dikaioi*, the righteous, the fruit-bearers (Mt 13:41-43; 23:27f) (cf Frankemölle 1974:284-286; Giessen 1982:202-224; Senior and Stuhlmueller 1983:248).

THE SERMON ON THE MOUNT

In the previous section several references were made to the so-called Sermon on the Mount (Mt 5-7). A few additional comments about this remarkable body of literature may help us to grasp the missionary dimension of Matthew's gospel, not least because, through the ages, this passage has fascinated both Christians and people of other faiths. In the eyes of many people it embodies something like the final will of Jesus.

Matthew's gospel contains five major sermons or discourses (forming, according to some scholars, Matthew's "pentateuch"). They are the sermons on (1) discipleship (ch 5-7); (2) the apostolic mission (ch 10); (3) how the reign of God comes (ch 13); (4) church discipline (ch 18); and (5) false teachers and the end (ch 23-25). The phrase "teaching them to observe all that I have commanded you" (Mt 28:19) refers back primarily to the first of these discourses, the Sermon on the Mount. Indeed, this sermon expresses, like no other New Testament passage, the essence of the ethics of Jesus. Through the ages, however, Christians have usually found ways around the clear meaning of the Sermon on the Mount. Strecker (1983:169) mentions three misinterpretations, whereas Lapide (1986:4-6) lists no fewer than eight. I enumerate only some of these:

a. Already the early church, and later on particularly Thomas Aquinas, believed that not all Christians need to obey the injunctions of Matthew 5-7; they are intended only for a special category of Christians, more particularly the clergy.

b. The Lutheran Orthodoxy of the seventeenth century argued that it was impossible to obey the demands of Jesus in these chapters, but that this was, strictly speaking, not their purpose. The very unrealizability of these superhuman demands should, rather, expose our own inadequacy and sinfulness and cause us to put all our trust only in Christ rather than in our own ability to do God's will.

c. During the nineteenth century, with its emphasis on individualism, it was believed that what counted was not the concrete obedience of these demands but rather the correct disposition of heart. Individual attitudes were more important than actual deeds.

d. Yet another explanation was to write off the injunctions of the Sermon on the Mount as manifestations of an "interim ethic". Such extraordinary accomplishments as are expected here, it was argued, only make sense in the context of an expectation of the parousia as imminent. Only during a very short interim period can anyone live up to such high expectations.

Today, however, most scholars agree that these and similar interpretations are inadequate, that there is no getting around the fact that, in Matthew's view, Jesus actually expected all his followers to live according to these norms always and under all circumstances (cf Strecker 1983:169; Lapide 1986:6f). If we recognize this we also, however, have to concede that, down through the centuries, precious few followers of Jesus have actually lived up to these expectations. There is a discrepancy between what Jesus taught and what actually happened to his teaching. This is particularly true of his injunction to love our enemies which, more than any other command, reflects the true nature of Jesus' boundary-breaking ministry (Lapide 1986:96-104). It forms the culmination of Jesus' ethic of the reign of God. Yet at this point "the eschatological prophet of

Nazareth represents a stumbling block for both his Jewish contemporaries and the church of all times"; as a matter of fact, the history of the church may very well be written "as a history of those who have shut themselves off from this command" (Strecker 1983:167 – my translation).

The failure of Christians to live according to the standards of the Sermon on the Mount does not, however, absolve them from the challenge to do so. Particularly in our contemporary world of violence and counter-violence, of oppression from the right and the left, of the rich getting richer and the poor poorer, it is imperative for the church-in-mission to include the "superior justice" of the Sermon on the Mount (cf Mt 5:20) in its missionary agenda. Its mission cannot concern itself exclusively with the personal, inward, spiritual, and "vertical" aspects of people's lives. Such an approach suggests a dichotomy totally foreign to the Jesus tradition as interpreted by Matthew.

I have argued in the previous chapter that Jesus had no intention of establishing a political kingdom in Israel. This does not mean, however, that his ministry was apolitical. It certainly was not. The Sermon on the Mount, in particular, is eminently political since it challenges almost every traditional societal structure. His politics was, however, one of peace-making, of reconciliation, of justice, of refusing vengeance (I shall return to this aspect in more detail in the next chapter) and, above all, of love of enemy. To quote Lapide again: "(Jesus) was a threefold rebel of love, much more radical than revolutionaries of our day" (1986:103). This was the case particularly since there was no tension between what he *said* and what he *did*.

Frankemölle therefore rightly regards the expression *ta erga tou Christou* (the works or deeds of Christ) in Matthew 11:2 as a "nodal point in Matthew's gospel" where the various strands of the missionary practice of Jesus flow together. The expression *ta erga tou Christou* forms a kind of *Oberbegriff* (generic term) which illuminates the various aspects of Jesus' mission (Frankemölle 1982:98, 128). His supreme "work" of selfless love was, of course, his dying on the cross. Without this, the instruction on the Mount remains an eloquent but hollow sermon. "It gets its true binding force only through the exemplary life, sufferings, and death of the Nazarene who sealed its validity with his own blood" (Lapide 1986:141).

GOD'S REIGN AND JUSTICE-RIGHTEOUSNESS

We can no longer circumvent two other Matthean expressions which have all along been hovering in the background, as it were, and have been pressing themselves upon us as eminently missionary notions. I am referring to the terms *basileia* ([God's] reign) and *dikaiosyne* (justice or righteousness).

The *basileia* concept has been explored in the previous chapter and will be referred to here only insofar as it relates to *dikaiosyne* and insofar as it has a particularly Matthean flavor. Compared to eighteen times in Mark, Matthew uses the term *basileia* fifty-one times, mostly with the addition "of heaven". It is the dominant theme in the proclamation of the Matthean Jesus, in his parables (cf particularly the parable discourse of chapter 13), his healings and his exorcisms (cf 12:28). Twice, in summaries about the ministry of Jesus, Matthew uses the expression "preaching the gospel of the kingdom" (4:23; 9:35). "Good news" or "gospel" here refers to the entire event of Jesus' coming. The *basileia* which then follows (in the genitive construction "gospel *of* the *basileia*") appears to refer to Jesus himself. "From Matthew's perspective, to encounter the kingdom is to encounter Jesus Christ" (Senior and Stuhlmueller 1983:237f). In Jesus, the reign of God has drawn near to humankind. The unique phrase, "the gospel of the *basileia*", "underlines the inherent universal and missionary character of the kingdom ministry of Jesus. This universal horizon of the kingdom metaphor is implicit in Mark but comes much closer to the surface in the mission theology of Matthew" (:238).

Linked with God's reign in a mysterious way is the concept *dikaiosyne*, which is perhaps the most characteristically Matthean notion of all. A careful analysis shows that it is unlikely that Matthew has found this term in his sources; it is introduced by himself at each point, usually in such a way that it contrasts clearly with what he had encountered in his sources (cf Strecker 1962:149-158).

The translation of *dikaiosyne* poses problems, however, at least in English. It can refer to *justification* (God's merciful act of declaring us just, thus changing our status and pronouncing us acceptable to him), or to *righteousness* (a preeminently religious or spiritual concept: an attribute of God or a spiritual quality that we receive from God), or to *justice* (people's right conduct in relation to their fellow human beings, seeking for them that to which they have a right). Most English New Testament translations reveal a bias toward the second meaning. Often the word "justice" does not appear at all in an English New Testament—with important consequences. One discovers this if one translates *dikaiosyne* in the sayings of Jesus alternatively with "righteousness" and "justice". The fourth beatitude (Mt 5:6) may then refer either to those who hunger and thirst after (spiritual) righteousness and holiness, *or* to those who long to see that justice be done to the oppressed. By the same token, the "persecuted" of Matthew 5:10 may be suffering because of their religious devoutness (righteousness), *or* because they champion the cause of the marginalized (justice). Again, according to Matthew 5:20, either the disciples' religiosity or, alternatively, their practice of justice has to surpass that of the Pharisees. Likewise, if we translate Matthew 6:33, "But seek first his kingdom and his righteousness, and all these things shall be yours as well" (RSV), it may mean that the spiritual is more important than the material and that, if only we have our priorities right (putting God's reign and his righteousness above this-worldly concerns) God will bless us materially as well. If, on the other hand, we translate, "set your mind on God's kingdom and his justice before everything else, and all the rest will come to you as well" (NEB), it may mean that Jesus asks us not to be concerned with our own desires and interests but with the practice of justice in respect of those who are the victims of circumstances and society, that this is what God's reign is all about. To find the correct translation is, therefore, crucial. A wrong translation may in fact prove the aptness of the Italian saying, *traduttore traditore* — "The translator is a traitor!"

Perhaps, however, we should not allow ourselves to choose between "righteousness" and "justice" when seeking for the meaning of *dikaiosyne*. Our problem may, rather, lie in the fact that the English language is unable to embrace the wide scope of the concept *dikaiosyne* in *one* word. Maybe, then, we should translate it with "justice-righteousness", in an attempt to hold on to both dimensions. Michael Crosby, for instance, translates *dikaiosyne* alternatively as "justice", "holiness", "piety", and "godliness" (1981:118-124). He believes that *dikaiosyne* contains both a "constitutive" and a "normative" dimension: "With 'the Spirit of the Lord God' anointing us (Is 61:1), we are clothed with a robe of justice; we are wrapped in a mantle of justice (Is 61:10). The robe and the mantle enable us to experience God in the depths of our being as *our* justice". This is the *constitutive* dimension: God justifying us, making us righteous and holy in his sight. Once constituted in God's justice, "God uses us to 'make justice and praise spring up before all the nations' (Is 61:11)". This is the *normative* dimension: God raising up people who become ministers to others of the same justice they have experienced from God (Crosby 1981:118f; quotations on p 118). *God's* justice, then, is his saving activity on behalf of his people. *Human* justice is the effort *we* make to respond to God's goodness by carrying out his will (:139).

If Matthew's Jesus calls his disciples to the practice of *dikaiosyne* it is primarily this second dimension he has in mind, but in such a way that the first dimension remains constitutive (cf Giessen 1982:259-263). To emphasize only the ethical aspect would hardly be in keeping with Matthew's fierce polemic against legalism (cf Frankemölle 1984:281, 287). *Dikaiosyne* is *faith* in *action*, the *practice* of *devotion* or, as Matthew 6:1 suggests, an act of right conduct "before your Father" (:283); it is *doing* the *will of God*. Like the Decalogue and its summary (Mt 22:37-40), *dikaiosyne* relates to both God and neighbor (:281f). It manifests itself in active faith in God's involvement in history. It is, first of all, gift, and only then obligation. In this respect it resembles the original intention of the Decalogue: Israel understood and celebrated the announcement of the ten commandments as a salvific event of the first order, since "Yahweh proved his covenantal faithfulness to Israel" in this experience (G. von Rad, quoted by Frankemölle 1974:292 – my translation).[1]

Matthew's pleas for a justice that "surpasses" that of the Pharisees and for being "perfect" have to be seen in the same light (cf Giessen 1982:122-146). It makes no sense to see these injunctions in the context of moral superiority or higher accomplishments. If that were the way Matthew uses it, how could anyone dare use an expression such as "you must be perfect, as your heavenly Father is perfect" (5:48)? "Perfect" is never an attribute of God in the Septuagint, yet Matthew puts this expression—which is without parallel also in the Qumran texts and the Judaism of his time (cf Frankemölle 1974:282, 288)— into the mouth of Jesus. He does not, however, have any quantitatively higher fulfillment of the Law in mind, but a qualitative transforming or transcending of it. "Perfection is, for Matthew, a strictly theocentric concept which leaves any traditional understanding of the Law far behind" (Frankemölle 1974:293 – my translation; cf 283,292). The *dikaiosyne* of God's reign is particularly expressed in a series of statements where Jesus contrasts his commands with what his listeners have heard was said to the people of old (Mt 5:21-46). None of these injunctions can merely be seen as a tightening of the Law; they refer to obedience of another kind, of another order, since they are spawned by the irruption of God's reign in the life of Jesus. Merely performing superlative acts of sacrifice is not enough and will not do it. The rich young man was not just asked to give all his possessions to the poor, but also to follow Jesus. The latter summons is the really decisive one; the "being perfect" manifests itself in discipleship (cf Barth 1965:90, 93).

"MAKE DISCIPLES . . ."

My survey of the intimate interrelatedness of notions such as commandment, teaching, the will of the Father, the reign of heaven, justice-righteousness, and being perfect may have helped the reader to understand the commission "teaching them to observe everything I have commanded you" (Mt 28:20). I have illustrated how these words draw together in one phrase a major portion of the theological wealth and depth of Matthew's gospel and may open missionary perspectives to us. We have, however, not yet exhausted Matthew's missionary message and significance. So we turn to another key expression of the "Great Commission". I refer to the entire semantic field of the terms "disciple" (*mathetes*) and "make disciples" (*matheteuein*).

The theme of discipleship is central to Matthew's gospel and to Matthew's understanding of the church and mission. " 'The disciples' is *the* specifically ecclesiological concept of the evangelist" (Bornkamm 1965b:300 — my translation; cf Bornkamm 1965a:37-40). Let us, however, first turn to the verb, *matheteuein*, "to make disciples". The verb occurs only four times in the New Testament, three of these in Matthew (13:52, 27:57; 28:19) and one in Acts (14:21).

The most striking use of the verb *matheteuein* is encountered in the "Great Commission" (28:19). It is also the only instance in which it is used in the imperative sense: *matheteusate*, "make disciples!" It is, moreover, the principal verb in the "Great Commission" and the heart of the commissioning. The two participles "baptizing" and "teaching" are clearly subordinate to "make disciples" and describe the form the disciple-making is to take (Trilling 1964:28-32; Hahn 1980:35; Matthey 1980:168). The overall "aim of mission is the winning of all people to the status of being true Christians" (Trilling 1964:50 — my translation). With this in view and in opposition to both the enthusiast and the antinominian elements in his community, Matthew employs the sober injunction, "Make disciples", *matheteusate*!

In contrast to the rareness of the verb "to make disciples", the noun "disciple" (*mathetes*) is common, at least in the four gospels and Acts, for it is not found anywhere else in the New Testament. Paul, for instance, never uses it.

"Disciple" is far more central in Matthew than in the other synoptic gospels. The term occurs seventy-three times in Matthew, compared to forty-six times in Mark and only thirty-seven times in Luke. It is, in fact the only name for Christ's followers in the gospels. The verb that most commonly goes with "disciple" is the verb *akolouthein*, "to follow (after)". This verb is also more common in Matthew than in his sources; at several points he has introduced it into the narrative (cf Strecker 1962:193; Kasting 1969:35f; Frankemölle 1974:153; Friedrich 1983:165). (The English word "discipleship" is therefore a correct rendering of the German *Nachfolge*, "following after" [cf the translation of the title of Dietrich Bonhoeffer's *Nachfolge* as *The Cost of Discipleship*].)

More important than the difference between Matthew, Mark, and Luke as regards the frequency of the term *mathetes* is the difference in nuances of meaning. For Matthew, the expression "disciples" does not refer to the Twelve only (as it does in Mark and Luke). It is used in a less exact way, although the Twelve are always presupposed when the word is used. Put positively, for Matthew the first disciples are prototypes for the church. The term thus expands to include the "disciples" of Matthew's own time. His gospel is known, and for a very good reason, as the gospel of the church.

The link between Jesus' own time and the time of Matthew's community is, in fact, given in the command "Make disciples!" (28:19). In other words, the followers of the earthly Jesus have to make others into what they themselves are: disciples. In the final analysis, therefore, there is, for Matthew, no break, no discontinuity between the history of Jesus and the era of the church. The community of believers of Matthew's time does not constitute a new period in the economy of salvation. The past relation between the Master and his first disciples is being transformed into something *more* than history—it aims at nourishing and challenging the present hour. Faith takes effect in what Kierkegaard has called *contemporaneity*, that is to say, in the unceasing yet irreversible recurrence of the foundational and exemplary history of the Master and the disciples. It is precisely this indispensable dialectic between the history of Jesus and the life of the church of his own time that justifies, for Matthew, the writing of his gospel (cf Zumstein 1972:31-33; Minear 1977:145-148).

The notion of the first disciples as prototypes for the later church manifests itself in many forms. The members of Matthew's community, too, are the ones who expect God's reign (5:20). They too are the salt of the earth and the light of the world (5:13f). They too are the blessed ones, for many reasons, all of which are summarized in the "on my account" of Matthew 5:11. God is their Father, and they are the children of God (5:9; 5:42) and of God's reign (13:38); as such children they are free (17:25f). They are, moreover, *adelphoi* (brothers) among one another (5:22, 23, 24, 47; 18:15, 21, 35; 23:8), even servants of one another (Frankemölle 1974:159-190, with detailed references and argument). The "disciples" of Matthew's time are thus not just linked to the first disciples but also to one another. Every disciple follows the Master, but never alone; every disciple is a member of the fellowship of disciples, the body, or no disciple at all.

MODELLED ON JESUS, AND YET...

The "disciples" of Matthew's own time, then, are modelled on Jesus' first disciples, just as those first disciples are modelled on Jesus himself. I have, in the previous chapter, argued that the relation between Jesus and his disciples was fundamentally different from that between the Jewish rabbis and their students. We have to go further, however. According to Matthew it is not just a case of the disciples having to teach what Jesus has taught (28:20), nor of them being Jesus' fellow-workers and not merely his messengers (Hahn 1965:41). There is an even more profound correspondence and solidarity here. This becomes particularly evident in the central part of the gospel, chapter 9:35-11:1, which can be subdivided into eleven short sections. At the center of these eleven paragraphs we have Chapter 10:24f: "A disciple is not above his teacher nor a servant above his master; it is enough for the disciple to be like his teacher, and the servant like his master". Around this centerpiece Matthew has arranged a whole series of sayings which all illuminate one fact only: what applies to Jesus applies to his disciples also. Their sharing becomes apparent particularly in two seemingly contradictory respects: Jesus and his disciples share in *suffering* and in *missionary authority* (cf Brown 1978:76-79 and Frankemölle 1974:85-108, both with detailed references; cf also Frankemölle 1982: 125-129).

Even if the disciples are modelled so carefully and consistently on Jesus, there is no indication of a blurring of the essential difference between him and them. Two small but nevertheless important details in Matthew illustrate this. The first is Matthew's use of the verb *proskynein*, "to worship" or literally "to fall prostrate". It occurs, *inter alia*, in the "Great Commission" pericope: when the disciples saw Jesus, "they worshiped him" (28:17). *Proskynein* is a favorite word of Matthew. He uses it no less than thirteen times (compared to twice each in Mark and Luke). He frequently introduces *proskynein* where he follows Mark, for instance in Matthew 8:2; 9:18; 15:25 and 20:20 (Hubbard 1974:75). The verb refers to a gesture that should be reserved for expressing submission to and adoration of God alone, as Jesus' answer to Satan in the temptation episode explicitly states (Mt 4:10, with a reference to Deut 6:16). After Jesus has walked on the water only Matthew has the disciples fall at his feet and exclaim, "Truly, you are the Son of God" (Mt 14:33) (cf also Lange 1973:472-474; Matthey 1980:164). Jesus is clearly for Matthew much more than somebody to be emulated. He is, in the ultimate sense of the word, the Lord.

This brings us to the other significant detail which illustrates the difference between Jesus and the disciples: Matthew's use of the expression *Kyrios*, "Lord". In Matthew this appellation is reserved for use by the disciples and by those who suffer and come to Jesus for help; Jesus' opponents, on the other hand, always address him as "Teacher" or "Rabbi". This differentiation is carried through consistently. Where Matthew's sources have "teacher" or "rabbi" in the mouth of the disciples, he has changed this to "Lord". The result is that Jesus' opponents never address him as "Lord" and the disciples never in any way other than "Lord". There is one exception, however—Judas Iscariot twice calls him "Rabbi", both times in the context of his betrayal of Jesus (Mt 26:25,48) (cf Strecker 1962:33, 123f; Bornkamm 1965a:38; 1965b:301f; 33, 123f; Lange 1973:218-229). *Kyrios* was, of course, at the time not only a royal or divine title but also simply used as an appellation of showing respect. Even so, it can hardly be doubted that Matthew understood it primarily as a divine title (Bornkamm 1965a:39).

It has often been pointed out that Matthew tends to idealize the disciples, particularly in comparison to Mark (for details, cf Strecker 1962:193; Frankemölle 1974:150-155). Let us not, however, rashly accuse Matthew of misconstruing history, but rather remember that, as I have repeatedly argued, he is, in his unique way, prolonging the logic of Jesus' ministry into his own time and circumstances. His concern is both pastoral and missionary—pastoral, in that he holds up the first disciples as models for his own community, as ideals to emulate; missionary, in that he urges his community to "make disciples" who should resemble those first ones. It is, however, important also to note that Matthew does not remove all negative traits (Strecker 1962:193f; Frankemölle 1974:152-155). The disciples are sometimes referred to as being "of little faith" or "afraid" or "full of doubt". The last of these, *distazein*, appears only in Matthew. Particularly striking is its appearance in the context of the "Great Commission": "When they saw him, they worshiped him; *but some doubted*" (28:17).

Clearly these references to the weakness of the disciples have an important meaning for Matthew's readers. Being a disciple of Jesus does not signify that one has, as it were, arrived. Matthew's gospel records several parables about the need for remaining vigilant to the last moment (cf LaVerdiere and Thompson 1976:580f). Even the brother or the servant in God's household may turn out to be a "hypocrite" (7:5; 24:51). The separation between the saved and the lost is reserved for the day of judgment, as the parables of the wheat and the tares and of the fish net (both only in Matthew; cf 13:24-30 and 13:47-50) make clear (Bornkamm 1965a:16f, 40). The call to constant vigilance is certainly intended as warning against any possible self-exaltation, but also as motivation to an eager engagement in mission (cf LaVerdiere and Thompson 1976:581; Frankemölle 1982:127).

The weaknesses of the disciples in Matthew's gospel do not, however, have a dark side only. In Matthew 28:17 the disciples' doubt is strangely juxtaposed to their worship: "They (all!) worshiped him; but some doubted". The same two verbs are closely connected in Matthew 14:31,33 (cf Zumstein 1972:20, 24; Hubbard 1974:77; Matthey 1980:165). As Matthew looks at the members of his own community—living at a frontier, experiencing difficulty in defining their own identity on the borderline between increasingly hostile Jews and as yet alien Gentiles—he reminds them of a rather bewildered band of simple folk on the slopes of a mountain in Galilee, just across the border from Syria where they are now living, and he wishes his community to know that mission never takes place in self-confidence but in the knowledge of our own weakness, at a point of crisis where danger and opportunity come together. Matthew's Christians, like the first disciples, stand in the dialectical tension between worship and doubt, between faith and fear.

Almost as if he refuses to come to their aid and help them combat their doubt, Matthew portrays the risen Jesus' final appearance to his disciples in starkly sober language. He simply says that the eleven disciples went to the mountain in Galilee where Jesus had told them to go. Then Jesus came to them and commissioned them (28:16-18). He is simply Jesus, the same name given to him in the gospel narrative; he is the same one who walked the dusty roads of Palestine with them. He is now risen from the dead, yes, but his glory is hidden, wrapped in a mystery. No ascension into heaven or outpouring of the Holy Spirit is reported or even anticipated (cf Trilling 1964:43; Bornkamm 1965b:290; Schneider 1982:86). There is a remarkable restraint in the way Matthew describes the entire scene; the concentration is almost exclusively on Jesus' words (cf Bosch 1959:188; Matthey 1980:166). Whereas Matthew is usually given to quoting the Old Testament in order to authenticate what Jesus is and does, no such formula quotation appears here; the readers have to accept the validity of the words of the risen Jesus on the basis of their own authority (cf Hahn 1980:32). Nothing spectacular! Nothing for the enthusiasts!

In his characteristically dialectical style, however, Matthew contrasts the sobriety of this scene with two other elements: Jesus' statement about his all-embracing authority (v 18) and his very last words, with which Matthew concludes his gospel, "And lo, I am with you always, to the close of the age" (v 20). We turn, first, to this latter saying.

The expressions "with you" and "the close of the age" are typically Matthean. Once again, as he so often does in this final pericope, Matthew reaches back to themes he has developed in the earlier part of his gospel. In the case of "I am with you" he takes up the words from Isaiah 7:14, which he has used in chapter 1:23, "And his name shall be called Immanuel (which means, God with us)". At the beginning of the gospel Jesus' presence was promised primarily to Israel; here at the end it pertains to all disciples wherever they may be (cf also 8:23-27 and 18:20). His presence is, moreover, permanent—until the end of the age. It is for this reason that no ascension, no outpouring of the Spirit, and no parousia need to be mentioned. "The interest in that appears to be absorbed by the experience of the always immediate, comforting and empowering presence of the Lord ... The consciousness of the present experience of the Lord is so intense that it can embrace the entire future. What is a reality now remains valid for ever. Here speaks the faith of the church, not apocalyptic speculation" (Trilling 1964:43f—my translation). In this way the conclusion of the gospel signals a new beginning (Legrand 1987:12).

Jesus' abiding presence is, however, intimately linked to his followers' engagement in mission. It is as they make disciples, baptize them, and teach them, that Jesus remains with those followers (Matthey 1980:172; Schneider 1982:85f). In the Old Testament the Lord's presence with his people is particularly emphasized where a dangerous mission is to be undertaken (cf Josh 1:5; Is 43:1f, 4f). The same assistance Yahweh has assured his people of old, Jesus now promises his disciples as they go out on their hazardous mission and encounter rebuffs and persecution (cf Zumstein 1972:28; Senior and Stuhlmueller 1983:242). The clause "I am with you always" is, however, not logically subordinated to the "go ... and make disciples." It is, rather, the other way round—because Jesus continues to be present with his disciples, they go out in mission (Legrand 1987:12).

The second feature with the aid of which Matthew counterbalances his sober depiction of the final appearance of Jesus is expressed in the words with which Jesus prefaces the actual "Great Commission": "All authority in heaven and on earth has been given to me" (28:18). Now, after his resurrection, Jesus is given *all* authority, not only on earth (cf 9:6) but also in heaven. What is new is the universal extension of his authority (cf Strecker 1962:211f; Zumstein 1972:24; Lange 1973:96-169; Meier 1977:413; Matthey 1980:166f). Again Matthew takes up a theme from the earlier part of his gospel: in 4:8f the devil offered Jesus "all the kingdoms of the world and the glory of them" if Jesus would only bow down and worship him. But Jesus refused. Now, in the final scene of the gospel, the disciples worship *him* and he announces that God has given him much more than the devil has promised. "The Crucified has become the Lord of the cosmos" (Friedrich 1983:179 — my translation; cf also Lohmeyer 1951: passim).

This announcement appears to be contradicted immediately, however, by Jesus' next words: "Go therefore and make disciples . . ." (28:19f). Is Jesus then still not really and fully the universal Lord? Do his followers have to *make* him that, through their discipling, baptizing, and teaching of the nations? Does his sovereignty still have to be ratified by the nations acknowledging him as King? And is his reign in jeopardy if they do not?

Or, conversely, if his lordship is already established beyond any dispute, why is it still necessary to go into all the world and persuade the nations to submit to him? Are they not already his subjects? If Jesus has "all authority in heaven and on earth", what is the point in trying to manifest that authority still further?

An insignificant and often overlooked word (and another one of Matthew's favorite expressions; cf Lange 1973:306f; Friedrich 1983:174) provides the answer: the word "(go) *therefore*" (Greek: *oun*).[2] It links the announcement of a reality (Jesus' universal authority) with a solemn challenge: "Make disciples". If Jesus is indeed Lord of all, this reality just *has* to be proclaimed. Nobody who knows of this can remain silent about it. He or she can do only one thing — help others also to acknowledge Jesus' lordship. And this is what mission is all about — "the proclaiming of the lordship of Christ" (Michel 1941:262). Jesus' enthronement inaugurates and makes possible a worldwide mission inconceivable up to now. The universal and unlimited dominion of the risen Jesus evokes an equally universal and limitless response from his ambassadors (cf Friedrich 1983:180). Mission is a logical consequence of Jesus' induction as sovereign Lord of the universe. In the light of this, the "Great Commission" enunciates an empowerment rather than a command (Hahn 1980:38). It is a creative statement in the manner of Genesis 1:3, "Let there be . . ."

The phrase "baptizing them in the name of the Father and of the Son and of the Holy Spirit" (28:19) has to be seen in the same light. The fact that Matthew puts the baptismal command before the command to teach, whereas the missionary practice of many centuries has been adhering to the exactly opposite sequence, has led some missionaries and missiologists to advocate a return to the original *modus operandi*: first baptize converts, then teach them. It is, however, seriously to be doubted whether Matthew can be used in this way. The Matthean Jesus makes a theological statement, as it were. In the words of Gerhard Friedrich (1983:182 – my translation; cf 183):

> The sequel "baptizing" and "teaching" is not a doctrinal oversight but consciously chosen by Matthew. Through baptism people are called into becoming disciples of Jesus. Baptism is no human act or decision, but a gift of grace. Through baptism the one who is baptized is made to partake of the entire fullness of the divine promise and the reality of the forgiveness of sins.

This may also explain the absence of any explicit reference to forgiveness of sins which, as I have previously mentioned, is emphasized in corresponding passages in both Luke (24:47) and John (20:21-23). Forgiveness of sins is a central idea in Matthew's gospel (*contra* Strecker 1962:148f). As early as 1:21 Matthew quotes an angel saying to Mary, "You shall call his name Jesus, for he will save his people from their sins". Immediately following the Lord's Prayer – which contains the petition, "Forgive us our debts as we also have forgiven our debtors" (Mt 6:12) – Matthew has Jesus say, "For if you forgive people their trespasses, your heavenly Father also will forgive you" (6:14f). Furthermore, at the institution of the Lord's Supper the Matthean Jesus says, "For this is my blood of the covenant, which is poured out for many for the forgiveness of sins" (26:28). The reference to forgiveness does not occur in the other synoptic gospels' accounts of the Last Supper (cf also Trilling 1964:32).

In view of all this it would have been redundant expressly to mention the forgiveness of sins in the "Great Commission". For Matthew, this was self-evidently included in the baptismal formula: "One becomes a disciple through baptism in that one's sins are pardoned" (Friedrich 1983:183 – my translation). As Paul also says (precisely in the context of a baptismal text!), "Consider yourselves dead to sin and alive to God in Christ Jesus" (Rom 6:11); in other words, accept as real what God has already done, and act accordingly! What God has done in Christ – the forgiveness of sins – is the point of departure of the new life of the disciple (*contra* Strecker 1962:149) and is being sealed in the act of baptism.

MATTHEW'S PARADIGM: MISSIONARY DISCIPLESHIP

I wish to conclude this chapter by highlighting some of the elements which are unique to the Matthean paradigm of mission, as they have begun to emerge in our exposition above. What was it that the author of the first gospel contributed to the understanding of mission?[3]

Much has undoubtedly changed since Jesus' earthly ministry and also since the Christian church, from the late forties of the first century onward, has increasingly become a Gentile rather than a Jewish body. If my dating of Matthew's gospel (the eighties of the first century) is correct, then the devastation of the Jewish War already lies almost twenty years back and Pharisaic Judaism is increasingly adopting a fiercely negative stance toward the Christian community. Matthew's own community is, however, still predominantly (or exclusively?) Jewish; its members no longer live in their ancestral homeland but lead a ghetto-like existence in Syria. They are a community in transition (cf LaVerdiere and Thompson 1976), rejected by their compatriots yet without, as yet, having embraced a new identity. They are also a divided community, made up of enthusiasts and legalists, with the main body probably somewhere in between.

1. In attempting to articulate an identity for this community, Matthew draws on the tradition about Jesus of Nazareth. He clarifies the community's identity as an identity-in-mission by writing a gospel permeated, from beginning to end, by the notion of a mission to Jews and Gentiles (cf Michel 1950/51:21) and by designing it in such a way that it would culminate in the "Great Commission". Virtually every word of this commission reaches back to the story of Jesus as told in earlier passages of the gospel: the fact that the meeting took place on a mountain in Galilee; the disciples' wavering between worship and doubt; the references to Jesus' authority, to making disciples, and teaching, and expressions such as "go", "therefore", "observe", "command", "I with you", and "the close of the age" (cf Lange 1973; Hubbard 1974:73-99; Meier 1977:408-410). It also appears that Matthew has fashioned the "Great Commission" in such a way that it would constitute a counterpart to the temptation narrative (4:8f). Both episodes take place on a mountain, in both cases the issue of power is central, both times the verb "to fall prostrate" or "to worship" (*proskynein*) is employed. Thus, says Matthey (1980:163), "we have placed at the beginning and at the end of Jesus' ministry two texts which describe alternative understandings of his mission as Son of God, alternative methods to incarnate the kingdom of heaven" (cf Friedrich 1983:178, note 115).

2. Matthew seems to espouse a "low" christology in that he portrays Jesus in terms reminiscent of Moses, without, however, in the least casting any doubt on his conviction that Jesus is the *Lord* who has to be *worshiped*. His low christology enables him to depict the disciples in such a way that they are, on the one hand, very similar and close to Jesus, almost as students following a rabbi; on the other hand, he stresses, more than the other synoptic gospels, the disciples' attitude of reverence and dependence.

The first emphasis enables him to represent the risen Jesus not as the One who has ascended into heaven and sits at the right hand of God, and who will one day return (cf Acts 1:11), but as the One who remains with his disciples always, until the end of the age. Jesus is Immanuel, God with us (1:23). Matthew does not find it necessary to say that Jesus will return; how could he, if he always remains with his disciples?! It was precisely because of such bold fusion of the awareness of the present lordship of Christ with his empowering his followers to make disciples of all nations that the delay of the parousia did not cause a catastrophe in the early church (cf Bornkamm 1965b:295). The community's involvement in mission was in itself an integral part of the parousia expectation, a kind of "proleptic parousia" (Osborne 1976:82). Matthew has his eyes on the contemporary situation, not on the "end of the age" (cf Trilling 1964:45). The experience of the presence of Christ is so overpowering that it embraces the future. Today's reality remains permanently valid (:43f), since the incarnation continues in the disciples' self-giving service to the world. "The resurrected Jesus is present among the missionaries" (Matthey 1980:166). They go to the ends of the earth in the confidence that "those who receive you, receive me", just as "those who receive me, receive the One who sent me" (10:40). All of this highlights the close proximity between Jesus and the disciples. Throughout the final pericope he remains "Jesus", the One whom they had known in the flesh, on whom their entire ministry is modelled, and who stays with them always.

The second emphasis enables Matthew to highlight the fact that Jesus is not just a leader in the manner that Moses was, but the disciples' *Lord* (for this is how they invariably address him) and the One who has been given all authority in heaven and on earth. For Matthew, missionary discipleship unfolds itself in the creative tension between these two emphases and has far-reaching consequences for his understanding of mission.

3. In developing his missionary paradigm, Matthew is both traditional and innovative, a disposition which enables him to communicate with both "wings" of his community: those who emphasize continued faithfulness to the Law, and those who claim that they rely only on the guidance of the Spirit (cf Friedrich 1983:177).

One way of responding creatively to this dual challenge is the manner in which Matthew underscores *orthopraxis* — an approach which probably brought him in tension with both main groups in his community. He selects, from the Jesus tradition, stories and sayings about deeds (especially the "deeds of the Christ", 11:2), about bearing fruit, about doing God's will, about keeping his commandments, about being perfect, about practicing justice. All these clearly point toward a very specific understanding of mission. Neither a legalistic insistence on right doctrine nor an enthusiastic claim that one is led by the Spirit serves any purpose if it is not corroborated by the bearing of fruit "that befits repentance" (3:8). After all, a good tree is known only by its fruits (7:19f).

For Matthew, then, being a disciple means living out the teachings of Jesus, which the evangelist has recorded in great detail in his gospel. It is unthinkable to divorce the Christian life of love and justice from being a disciple. Discipleship involves a commitment to God's reign, to justice and love, and to obedience to the entire will of God. Mission is not narrowed down to an activity of making individuals new creatures, of providing them with "blessed assurance" so that, come what may, they will be "eternally saved". Mission involves, from the beginning and as matter of course, making new believers sensitive to the needs of others, opening their eyes and hearts to recognize injustice, suffering, oppression, and the plight of those who have fallen by the wayside. It is unjustifiable to regard the "Great Commission" as being concerned primarily with "evangelism" and the "Great Commandment" (Mt 22:37-40) as referring to "social involvement". As Jacques Matthey (1980:171) puts it,

According to Matthew's "Great Commission", it is not possible to make disciples without telling them to practice God's call of justice for the poor.

The love commandment, which is *the* basis for the church's involvement in politics, is an integral part of the mission commandment.

To become a disciple means a decisive and irrevocable turning to both God and neighbor. What follows from there is a journey which, in fact, never ends in this life, a journey of continually discovering new dimensions of loving God and neighbor, as "the reign of God and his justice" (Mt 6:33 — my translation) are increasingly revealed in the life of the disciple.

4. Matthew's tendency to opt for creative tension, of combining the pastoral and the prophetic, is also evidenced by the way in which he portrays the call to a mission to both Jews and Gentiles. I have referred to the many and serious contradictions in his gospel, in particular the manifest irreconcilability between sayings such as 10:5f and 15:24 on the one hand and 28:18-20 on the other. Matthew keeps both sets of sayings, probably because he wishes to hold on to the tension. Nothing is sorted out neatly. It is, as yet, uncertain which way things will go. The attitude of the synagogue is a harsh and painful reality. But does this mean that God has abandoned his people? Matthew cannot bring himself to saying that. So, while on the one hand affirming and promoting the Gentile mission, also among the members of the his own community, he on the other hand portrays Jesus as having been sent to Israel only. He does not devise a "theology" to accommodate these contradictory positions (the way Paul did — cf ch 4); he simply affirms and holds on to both.

5. Bornkamm (1965a) and others have pointed out that no other gospel is as manifestly stamped by the idea of the church as Matthew's and as clearly shaped for ecclesial use. Matthew is also the only evangelist who puts the word *ekklesia*, church, into the mouth of the earthly Jesus (on two occasions: Mt 16:18 and 18:17).

We should, however, guard against reading into Matthew's gospel our contemporary use of the word "church", particularly in the sense of "denomination". Where he identifies mission as "making disciples", Matthew does not have in mind the adding of new members to an existing "congregation" or "denomination". To be a disciple is not just the same as being a member of a local "church" and "making disciples" does not simply mean the numerical expansion of the church. We should therefore not overemphasize the *gemeindemässige* (ecclesial) tone of the verb *matheteuein*, "to make disciples" (Trilling 1964:32). There is, for Matthew, a certain tension between church and discipleship; at the same time they may never be divorced from each other (Kohler 1974:463). Ideally, every church member should be a true disciple, but this is obviously not the case in the Christian communities Matthew knows; he therefore reminds them of the parable of the tares among the wheat (13:24-30) and of the fact that worthless fishes are sometimes caught in the net of the kingdom (13:47-50). Some converts are shallow and abandon the faith when persecutions come; others succumb to the temptations or pressures of this world (13:20-22).

Matthew's interest, then, is in costly discipleship. If this attitude scares some would-be converts away from the church, so be it. In Matthew's understanding the church is only to be found where disciples live in community with one ish Christian community in the wake of the momentous events around AD 70. Luke, on the other hand, was perhaps the only Gentile author of a New Testament book and wrote for Christians who were predominantly of Gentile origin. Moreover, he appears to have had in view many communities rather than one single community, as did Matthew (cf LaVerdiere and Thompson 1976: 582f).

Even so, there are enough similarities between Luke's and Matthew's gospels to warrant a worthwhile comparison. For one thing, both gospels were written in approximately the same period, probably in the eighties of the first century, that is, during the reign of the Roman emperor Domitian. Second, Luke and Matthew, to quite a large extent, made use of the same sources, namely the Gospel of Mark and the Sayings-Source (or Q). Third, both Matthew and Luke wrote for communities in transition (cf the title of LaVerdiere and Thompson 1976). Matthew's concern was with a predominantly (perhaps even exclusively) *Jewish* Christian community which, in the wake of the Jewish War and in the face of the increasingly hostile attitude toward the church displayed by Pharisaism, was facing both an identity crisis and an uncertain future. Luke also had a crisis situation in mind when he set out to write his two-volume work—which brings us to the question about the factors that occasioned his writings.

More than half a century had passed since those momentous events concerning Jesus of Nazareth. Very much had happened during these years. The Zealot movement within Judaism had precipitated the Jewish War which, in turn, had led to the destruction of Jerusalem and almost totally changed the face of Judaism. The Christian church, which began as a renewal movement within Judaism had, during the preceding four decades or so, undergone an almost complete transformation. It was no longer winning any significant numbers of Jews to faith in Jesus Christ. It had, in fact, for all intents and purposes become a Gentile church. The vigorous missionary program of Paul, in particular, was responsible for the predominantly Gentile character of the church of the eighties. Yet the heyday of missionary expansion and of Paul's energetic outreach in all directions already lay a quarter of a century back and a degree of stagnation had set in. The church was now a church of the second generation and revealed all the characteristics of a movement that no longer shared the fervor and dedication of recent converts. The return of Christ, which was so fervently expected by the first generation of believers, did not take place. The faith of the church was tested in at least two ways: from within, there was a flagging of enthusiasm; from without there were hostility and opposition from both Jews and pagans. In addition, Gentile Christians were facing a crisis of identity. They were asking, "Who are we really? How do we relate to the Jewish past, particularly in view of the manifest animosity of contemporary Judaism? Is Christianity a new religion or a continuation of the faith of the Old Testament? And above all, how do we relate to the earthly Jesus, who is gradually and irrevocably receding into the past?"

Luke decided to come to the aid of these Christians. Anyone who acted as though nothing had happened since Jesus' ministry in Galilee and Judea would be untrue to that very Jesus. A naive equation of the discipleship practiced by the Christian communities of Luke's time with that of the first disciples was no longer possible. Luke, more than most of his contemporaries, saw the problem posed by the passage of time and of the transformation of the Christian community from being exclusively Jewish to being predominantly Gentile. The history of half a century could not simply be passed over but needed to be reinterpreted (cf Schweizer 1971:137-146). Luke provided this reinterpretation in a unique manner. He argued that the Christians of his time were not really in a less advantageous position than Jesus' first disciples were, that the risen Lord was still with them, particularly through his Spirit who was continually guiding them into new adventures. Jesus was still present in his community, in his "name" and in his "power", through which the past became efficacious. This happened where Jesus was obeyed and truly accepted as Lord, and also where the community followed the lead of his Spirit into new situations of mission.

As Luke retells the story of Jesus and of the early church there are certain themes to which he returns again and again: the ministry of the Holy Spirit, the centrality of repentance and forgiveness, of prayer, of love and acceptance of enemies, of justice and fairness in inter-human relationships. There are also particular categories of people who are prominent in his writings. Heading the list (at least as far as the gospel is concerned) are the poor. Also to be mentioned is his emphasis on Jesus' association with women — a stunning crossing of a social and religious barrier in the patriarchal society of his day (cf Senior and Stuhlmueller 1983:261) — tax-collectors, and Samaritans. The entire ministry of Jesus and his relationships with all these and other marginalized people witness, in Luke's writings, to Jesus' practice of boundary-breaking compassion, which the church is called to emulate.

In order to appreciate Luke's unique contribution to the understanding of mission it is necessary to say a few words about Hans Conzelmann's seminal studies on Luke, particularly his book *Die Mitte der Zeit* (ET: *The Theology of St Luke*), first published in 1953. Conzelmann argued that Luke had consistently toned down the expectation of an imminent eschatological consummation that characterized the early Christian community. The Holy Spirit was, in Luke's writings, "no longer the eschatological gift, but the substitute in the meantime for the possession of ultimate salvation" (Conzelmann 1964:95). In this way the coming of the Holy Spirit solved, for Luke, the problem caused by the delay of the parousia. This means, for Conzelmann, that Luke had introduced the idea of *Heilsgeschichte*, "salvation history", which he regarded as comprising three distinct epochs: (1) the epoch of Israel, up to and including John the Baptist; (2) the epoch of Jesus' ministry, which Luke regarded as past and as constituting the middle period of salvation (hence the German title of his book); and (3) the epoch of the church, which was inaugurated on the day of Pentecost.

There is undoubtedly a degree of validity to Conzelmann's reconstruction of Luke's overall plan. I have already mentioned that Luke was, more than the other evangelists, painfully aware of the fact that he and the church of his time lived in an era which differed in crucial respects from the period of Jesus' earthly ministry. Yet most scholars today agree that Conzelmann has overstated

his case, that it is hardly possible to maintain that Luke had systematically recast his sources in order to squeeze them into a preconceived overall theological framework.

It is, moreover, incorrect to maintain that Luke regarded the church's mission in the power of the Spirit as a *substitute* for eschatological expectation. Luke preserves the tension between eschatology and history and does not place the *eschaton* as terminus at the end of a salvation-historical era (cf Rütti 1972:171f, and Nissen 1984:92, note 12, where further bibliographical references can be found).

More important, it is incorrect to subdivide the three periods of salvation history as absolutely as Conzelmann does (cf Schweizer 1971:142). LaVerdiere and Thompson have reminded us that the Holy Spirit is prominent not only in Acts but also in Luke's gospel. To a very real extent then, Luke unites the time of Jesus and the time of the church in one era of the Spirit. The two times are certainly not identical but neither can they be divorced from each other. For Luke's ecclesiology, both the distinction and the close relationship between the time of Jesus and the time of the church are significant: Jesus and the church belong to one and the same era. The historical life of Jesus was not purely and simply relegated to the past. The church lives in continuity with the life and work of Jesus.

Still, even if we cannot subscribe to Conzelmann's entire interpretation of Luke's writings, we have to agree that Luke was first and foremost a theologian who wanted to communicate a specific understanding of Jesus and his coming. He was not a mere chronicler or historian (in spite of what he himself said in the introduction to his gospel, 1:1-4). He was not interested in retelling the stories of Jesus and the church "as they actually happened". In the words of Eduard Schweizer, "He was too good a witness to let this happen" (Schweizer 1971:144). In chapter 1, I attempted a brief reconstruction of the main flow of the origins of the Christian mission. This was not what Luke tried to do in Acts. His interest was in the way the Gentile mission was to be motivated theologically, not in an historical report of the origins and course of the mission (cf Jervell 1972:42). Naturally this does not mean that his rendering is without value as a historical source; it still remains the best and most reliable source we have of the beginnings of Christianity (cf Hengel 1983a:2; 1986:35-39, 59-68; Meyer 1986:97). The thrust of his concern was not historical detail, however, but the restructuring of the tradition in such a way that it conveyed a message and a challenge to his contemporaries. What Haenchen (1971:110) says about the differences between Luke's three accounts of Paul's conversion may perhaps be said about the entire corpus of his writings,

That a writer should thus make free with tradition must at first strike us as irresponsible, as an unwarranted license. But evidently Luke has a conception of the narrator's calling different from ours. For him, a narration should not describe an event with the precision of a police-report, but must make the listener and reader aware of the inner significance of what happened, and impress upon him unforgettably the truth of the

power of God made manifest in it. The writer's obedience is indeed fulfilled in the very freedom of his rendering.

JEW, SAMARITAN, AND GENTILE IN LUKE-ACTS

The Difference between the Gospel and Acts

Wilson (1973:239) suggests that the description of Luke's approach to the Gentiles as theological is misleading; the most striking characteristic of Luke-Acts, he believes, is precisely the lack of any consistent theology of the Gentiles. This statement as it stands is saying too much. Luke most certainly has an overall theological understanding of a mission to Jews and Gentiles, even if the way in which he develops this might not always satisfy modern Western demands for logical consistency.

The principal manner in which Luke attempts to articulate his theology of mission is by writing not only one book, but two. Most scholars agree that the writing of the Book of Acts was not an afterthought but that, from the outset, Luke intended to write two volumes (cf Stanek 1985:17). This emerges clearly when we look at the overall structure of the two writings. Luke regards Jesus' mission as universal in intent but incomplete in execution (LaVerdiere and Thompson 1976:595). A mission to Gentiles is mentioned explicitly only once in the gospel: in Luke 24:47, that is, in the final pericope. The Gentile mission would be the task of the church, not of the historical Jesus (cf Hahn 1965:129; Wilson 1973:52f). The gospel takes us to the very threshold of the Gentile mission; the Book of Acts would tell that story in detail (compare Luke 24:47 with Acts 1:8). This is certainly not just a Lukan theological construct but a historical fact. It is striking, throughout Luke's gospel, how reserved Jesus is in relation to Gentiles. Only once explicit mention is made of a visit to non-Jewish country, to the land of the Gerasenes (8:26-39); for the rest Jesus apparently remains on Jewish soil (cf Bosch 1959:108).

Luke also uses other strategies to reveal the inner unity of his understanding of mission. One of these is geography. In the gospel, Jesus' ministry unfolds in three stages: Galilee (4:14-9:50), his journey from Galilee to Jerusalem (9:51-19:40), and finally the events in Jerusalem (19:41 to the end of the gospel; it is striking that Luke does not mention any appearances of the risen Christ in Galilee—everything is concentrated in Jerusalem). In Acts, the church's missionary ministry likewise evolves in three phases, indicated in 1:8, "You shall be my witnesses in Jerusalem and in all Judea and Samaria and to the end of the earth". The opening chapters of Acts relate the birth and growth of the church in Jerusalem; the second part portrays the expansion of the church into Samaria and the coastal plains until it reaches Antioch; the third section relates the missionary outreach in several directions, concluding with Paul's arrival in Rome, at which point the book comes to a rather abrupt end.

Thus the overall outline of the two books is geographical, from Galilee to Jerusalem and again from Jerusalem to Rome, but this doubtless has more than geographical significance. Geography simply becomes a vehicle for conveying theological (or missiological) meaning. Luke employs it so as to disclose the

relationship between the mission of Jesus and the mission of the church. Jeru-salem, in particular, is for Luke much more than a geographical center (cf Dupont 1979:12f; Dillon 1979:241, 246; Senior and Stuhlmueller 1983:255).

The Gentile Mission in Luke 4:16-30

An *implicit* reference to the future Gentile mission does, however, surface in the so-called Nazareth episode (Lk 4:16-30). At least three fundamental concerns of Luke are expressed here: (1) the centrality of the poor in Jesus' ministry; (2) the setting aside of vengeance; and (3) the Gentile mission. For the moment I turn to this last aspect only; I shall return to the other two.

Luke takes up an event Mark relates much later in his gospel (6:1-6; Mt 13:53-58) and presents it as the story about the beginning of Jesus' public ministry, at the same time modifying the story almost beyond recognition. It is clear both from the context in which Luke places this event and from its con-tents that Luke himself regards the incident as exceptionally significant. It stands as a "preface" to Jesus' entire public ministry (Anderson 1964:260), even as a condensed version of the gospel story as a whole (Dillon 1979:249). It is a "programmatic discourse" which fulfills the same function in Luke's gospel as the Sermon on the Mount does in Matthew's (Dupont 1979:20f). This is under-lined by Jesus confidently and emphatically appropriating an Old Testament prophecy to his person and ministry. The Spirit of the Lord is upon *him* and has anointed him. The final messianic future is now operative. Isaiah's prophecy is being fulfilled.

Luke tells the reader very little of what Jesus said at this occasion. He concentrates, rather, on the reaction of the synagogue congregation of Jesus' hometown. It is clear from this reaction that Jesus must have said something that antagonized them. I shall return to this point in more detail. For the moment it suffices to note that the people of Nazareth refused to believe Jesus' claim and rejected him. Jesus then challenged the congregation's "ethics of election" (Nissen 1984:75). What he communicated to them, *inter alia*, was that God was not only the God of Israel but also, and equally, the God of the Gentiles. He reminded them of the fact that the prophet Elijah had bestowed God's favor upon a Gentile woman in Sidon and that Elisha had healed only one leper, Naaman, a Syrian. God was, therefore, not irrevocably bound to Israel. Dupont rightly points out that this incident reveals a striking parallel with several stories in Acts where, time and time again, the gospel of Jesus is offered to Jews who refuse it, with the result that the apostles then go to the Gentiles (Dupont 1979:21f). There can, therefore, be little doubt that, in Luke's mind, the Nazareth episode has a clearly Gentile mission orientation and serves to highlight this fundamental thrust of Jesus' entire ministry at his very first appearance in public (cf LaVerdiere and Thompson 1976:589, 593; Senior and Stuhlmueller 1983:268).

Encounters with Samaritans

Luke's accounts of encounters between Jesus and Samaritans fulfill a similar function. Once again a comparison with Mark and Matthew reveals a striking

difference. Mark gives no reference to Samaritans or Samaria, whereas Matthew records only Jesus' prohibition to enter any Samaritan town (10:5). Luke, on the other hand, has several such references, of which at least some are highly significant for his purpose in Luke-Acts; namely, to show that the Samaritan mission was the beginning of the Gentile mission and was part of the divine plan (cf Ford 1984:79-95).

These encounters are all reported in Luke's central section, that is, in the part of the gospel which recounts Jesus' journey from Galilee to Jerusalem (9:51-19:40). Actually, this part of the gospel *opens* with an episode in which Jesus encounters Samaritans (9:51-56). Jesus sends out messengers to prepare lodgings for himself and his disciples in a Samaritan town, but the inhabitants refuse them accommodation. James and John are furious and, like latter-day Elijahs, immediately wish to call down fire from heaven and burn up the Samaritans, but Jesus rebukes the two disciples and goes to another town.

In order to understand this episode, and particularly Jesus' reaction, one must keep in mind that, for nationalistic Jews, Samaritans were worse than Gentiles (cf Hengel 1983b:56). This attitude was due, to a large degree, to the Samaritan defilement of the Jewish temple and the killing of a company of Jewish pilgrims by Samaritans (for details, cf Ford 1984:83-86). The Jewish reader of Luke's gospel would therefore fully understand the attitude of James and John, not however the reaction of Jesus. It is clear from the context that Jesus' conduct reflects an explicit and active denial of the law of retaliation (cf Ford 1984:91), and is, precisely as such, also a pointer toward a mission beyond Israel.

Luke's next reference to Samaritans is even more important for our theme. I refer to the parable of the good Samaritan (10:25-37). The fact that this parable follows hard on the sending out and the return of the seventy(-two) disciples further emphasizes a future mission to all nations. The parable marks a significant, highly provocative, and novel step in the mission of Jesus (Ford 1984:93). Jesus' audience, including his disciples, must have found this parable unpalatable, indeed obnoxious. The Samaritan in the narrative, says Mazamisa, represents profanity; even more, he stands for non-humanity. In terms of Jewish religion the Samaritans were enemies not only of Jews, but also of God. In the context of the narrative the Samaritan thus has a negative religious value. He is furthest removed from the fulfilling of the law (it was a question about this which provoked Jesus to narrate the parable), at the bottom of the religious and moral hierarchy, whereas the priest and the Levite are at the top (Mazamisa 1987:86). Jews were forbidden to receive works of love from non-Jews and were not allowed to purchase or use oil and wine obtained from Samaritans (cf Ford 1984:92f). Yet it is not the "human" in Jewish society who takes pity on the man who has fallen among robbers, but the "non-human". He offers the victim a "beatific comradeship" (cf the title of Mazamisa's book on this parable).

Luke relates one more incident about Samaritans in his central section: the healing of ten lepers (17:11-19). This happens in the borderland of Samaria and Galilee (17:11). The horror of leprosy has served to erase the differences between Jews and Samaritans here, for the story suggests that of the ten lepers

nine are Jews and one is a Samaritan. All are sent to show themselves to the priests, but only one returns to thank Jesus—the Samaritan. Jesus' words to him, "Go on your way; your faith has cured (or "saved", *sesoken*) you," are another clear pointer to the fact that salvation has also come to this despised people.

In his next volume Luke then brings his "Samaritan theology" to a close. The resurrected Lord announces that, after Jerusalem and Judea, Samaria will be the recipient of the gospel (Acts 1:8). The Samaritan mission suggests a fundamental break with traditional Jewish attitudes.

Luke's "Great Commission"

I said above that a mission to Gentiles and Samaritans remains only implicit in Luke's first volume. All the references—in the infancy narratives (2:31f; 3:6 [cf Schneider 1982:89]), in Jesus' sermon in his home town, in his encounters with Samaritans—remain ambiguous and open to more than one interpretation. In the final pericope of the gospel, however, the curtain is lifted. The risen Jesus meets his disciples in Jerusalem (not in Galilee, as in Matthew), and opens their minds to understand the scriptures.

> Thus it is written, that the Christ should suffer and on the third day rise from the dead, and that repentance and forgiveness of sins should be preached in his name to all nations, beginning from Jerusalem. You are witnesses of these things. And behold, I send the promise of my Father upon you; but stay in the city, until you are clothed with power from on high (Lk 24:46-49).

I have argued, in the previous chapter, that Matthew's entire gospel can only be read and understood from the perspective of the final pericope. The same is true of Luke's gospel. From its first verse this gospel moves toward the climax at the end (cf also Dillon 1979:242; Mann 1981:67). Jesus' words quoted above reflect, in a nutshell, Luke's entire understanding of the Christian mission: it is the fulfillment of scriptural promises; it only becomes possible after the death and resurrection of the Messiah of Israel; its central thrust is the message of repentance and forgiveness; it is intended for "all nations"; it is to begin "from Jerusalem"; it is to be executed by "witnesses"; and it will be accomplished in the power of the Holy Spirit. These elements constitute the "fibers of Luke's mission theology" running through both the gospel and Acts, binding this two-volume work together (Senior and Stuhlmueller 1983:259). Luke presents all this, not in the form of a mandate or commission, as Matthew does, but rather in the form of a fact and a promise; as such the words of Jesus at the end of the gospel corresponds to what he says in the beginning of Acts (1:8) (cf Schneider 1982:88).

The Jewishness of Luke

It has for a long time been customary among scholars to interpret Luke's two-volume work almost exclusively in terms of the Gentile mission only. The suggestion is that the Jews, at most, form a dark backdrop to Gentiles and the Gentile mission: Luke describes the rejection of the Christian proclamation on the part of the Jewish people, and he dwells extensively on this subject only because, in his thinking, the Jews' rejection of Jesus forms a decisive presupposition for the Gentile mission, which is the real area of Luke's interest. Haenchen, one of the most accomplished scholars on Luke-Acts, says that, from the first page of Acts to the last, Luke is wrestling "with the problem of the *mission to the Gentiles without the law*. His entire presentation is influenced by this" (1971:100; italics in the original).

This interpretation, even if it contains an element of truth, seems to me to be oversimplified and one-sided, as the subsequent exposition will hopefully show. A careful reading of his gospel reveals that Luke has an exceptionally positive attitude to the Jewish people, their religion and culture. Let me mention only a few aspects of this and further refer to the illuminating article of Irik on this subject, where detailed references are to be found (1982: passim).

To begin with, Luke does not, to the same degree as the other evangelists, emphasize the difference between the teaching of Jesus and that of the scribes. Jesus does criticize the Pharisees, but not as severely as in Matthew; they are never called "hypocrites" or "blind guides". Luke relates three instances of Jesus having been invited to meals in the houses of Pharisees. He omits controversial passages (such as Mk 7:1-20), which might have been experienced as unpleasant by Jews. He does not apply the parable of the tenants to the chief priests and the Pharisees, as Matthew does. In his passion narrative the crowd does not cry out, "His blood be on us and on our children!" (Mt 27:25); instead, Luke mentions that "a great multitude of the people" mourned and lamented over Jesus (23:27). Only Luke has the Crucified pray, "Father, forgive them; for they know not what they do" (23:34), and it is highly unlikely that he intends to suggest that Jesus is praying only for his Roman executioners. Actually, Luke frequently emphasizes that the Jewish authorities did what they did *out of ignorance* (cf Acts 3:17; 13:27).

The Greek Luke writes is also of significance for the subject under discussion. It is, on the whole, the Hebraized Greek of the Septuagint and of the synagogues of the Jewish diaspora (cf also Tiede 1980:8, 15). This fact, too, seems to indicate that Luke wrote his two-volume work for the benefit of Jews as much as Gentiles.

At the same time, his two books serve to reassure Gentile Christians about their origins; Luke makes it abundantly clear that the Gentile mission is in no way an illegitimate offshoot of renegade Christians but deeply rooted in God's ancient covenant (cf Wilson 1973:241), even though he distinguishes carefully between Jews and Gentiles. The difference between the two is not historical or national, but theological (cf Wilckens 1963:97).

It is particularly in his infancy narrative that Luke highlights the theological significance of Israel. I have referred to the allusions to a (future) Gentile mission in these stories. Such allusions remain vague, however. Not so the references to *Israel*'s salvation! Luke, the non-Jew, here presents Jesus as first and foremost the Savior of the old covenant people. In the Magnificat (Lk

1:54f) Mary sings, "(God) has helped his servant Israel, in remembrance of his mercy, as he spoke to our fathers, to Abraham and to his posterity for ever".

In Zechariah's hymn (1:68f) the same sentiments are expressed, "Blessed be the Lord God of Israel, for he has visited and redeemed his people, and has raised up a horn of salvation for us in the house of his servant David". And Simeon is "looking for the consolation of Israel" (2:25); he praises God for the "salvation" he is privileged to see with his own eyes (2:30) and for the light that will be "glory to thy people Israel" (2:32). Again, the prophetess Anna talks about the child Jesus to all who are looking "for the redemption of Jerusalem" (2:38).

From the entire context it is clear that these utterances can in no way be interpreted symbolically or "spiritually"[2] — Luke has the empirical Israel in mind (cf Irik 1982:286; Tannehill 1985:71f; Schottroff and Stegemann 1986:28f). And it is not only in the infancy narrative that we find these references (although they are particularly abundant there). At the end of the gospel the two travellers to Emmaus, referring to the death of Jesus, say, "And we had hoped that he was the one to redeem (or liberate) Israel" (24:21). Similarly, at the beginning of Acts the disciples ask the risen Jesus, "Lord, will you at this time restore the kingdom to Israel?" (1:6). The disciples are talking about the same hope as the travellers to Emmaus. It surfaces again in later chapters of Acts. In 3:19 Peter, addressing a Jewish crowd at the temple, refers to the "times of refreshing" (*apokatastasis*) God may still grant Israel. Even in the final pericope of the book we hear Paul say to the Jews in Rome that it is "because of the hope of Israel" that he is in chains (28:20).

Jerusalem

The importance Luke attaches to Israel is borne out by the central role he ascribes to Jerusalem in his narrative. The city is, for Luke, a highly concentrated theological symbol — an understanding he shares with the Judaism of his time, for which Jerusalem was the sacred center of the world, the place where the Messiah would make his appearance, and where not only the Jewish diaspora but all the nations would gather to praise God.

The entire central section of Luke's gospel (9:51-19:40), as remarked earlier, can be put under the rubric of "Jesus en route to Jerusalem" (cf Bosch 1959:103-111; Conzelmann 1964:60-65). It is also in this section that Luke includes the pericopes on Samaria and the Samaritans, none of which are found in Mark and Matthew. Luke describes the beginning of Jesus' journey in an unusually solemn, indeed awesome manner: "And it came to pass, when the days were fulfilled for him to be received up, he resolutely set his face to go to Jerusalem" (9:51, NIV). There immediately follows the story about his rejection by a Samaritan town (9:52-56), which forms a pendant to the first episode of Jesus' Galilean ministry where he was rejected by his own people. The first pericope of the middle section of the gospel thus emphasizes two elements: Jesus' approaching passion, and the fact that both Jew and non-Jew have rejected him; and both these are linked intimately with Jerusalem. The journey itself is, however, sketched in a most extraordinary manner. Luke 9:51 solemnly announces the journey's beginning; Luke 19:41 dramatically heralds its end: "And when he drew near and saw the city he wept over it". The narrative covers ten chapters, more than one-third of the entire gospel, but it contains the absolute minimum of geographical details. The reader is, however, continually reminded of the fact that Jesus is on his way to Jerusalem (in 9:51; 9:53; 13:22; 13:33; 17:11; 18:31; 19:11; 19:28; and 19:41), that is, to his passion. In 13:33 Luke has Jesus say, "I must go on my way today and tomorrow and the following day, for it cannot be that a prophet should perish away from Jerusalem". Conzelmann summarizes correctly: "Jesus' awareness that he must suffer is expressed in terms of the journey ... he does not travel in a different area from before, but he travels in a different manner" (1964:65; cf Dillon 1979:245f).

All that follows — passion, death, resurrection, appearances, and ascension — take place in Jerusalem. In the final passage Jesus announces that repentance and forgiveness of sins will be proclaimed to all nations, "beginning from Jerusalem" (24:47). The holy city is thus not only the destination of Jesus' wanderings and the place of his death, but also the location from which the message will go out in concentric circles to Judea, Samaria, and the ends of the earth (Acts 1:8). The Christian mission "beginning from Jerusalem" is a substantive, keynote "beginning", not just a matter of geographical fact (Dillon 1979:251). First and foremost, however, it is the center for a mission to Israel: "Anyone who wanted to address all Israel had to do so in Jerusalem" (Hengel 1983b:59). The equipment "with power from on high" (Lk 24:49) also takes place in Jerusalem, on the day of Pentecost, and immediately the missionary outreach begins — among Jews. Luke tells us, at various intervals in Acts, about large numbers of Jews who were converted; it is evident, however, that the most spectacular conversions take place in Jerusalem. It is here, in the center of Israel, that the gospel celebrates its greatest triumphs (Jervell 1972:45f).

To the Jews First, and to the Gentiles

Equally significant in Luke's account is the incontrovertible Jewishness of Jesus, of those around him, and of the Jewish converts of Acts. Jesus' parents are Jews faithful to the Torah and traditional Jewish practices (Lk 2:27, 31). The temple in Jerusalem is Jesus' proper place (2:49f) and he participates in synagogue worship (4:16-21). In Acts, Luke emphasizes that the early Jerusalem Christians live as pious Jews: they frequent the temple, live in strictest observance of the law and in accordance with the customs of the fathers (cf 2:46; 3:1; 5:12; 16:3; 21:20). Many of the Gentiles who become Christians have been proselytes or "God-fearers", that is, people who were previously related to Israel; it is the Gentiles of the synagogue who accept the gospel (cf Jervell 1972:44f, 49f). A comparison between Luke 7:1-10 and Matthew 8:5-13 is also illuminating in this respect. In Luke the centurion is clearly a "God-fearer" — he sends Jewish elders to speak to Jesus on his behalf, and they tell Jesus that he deserves a favor from him, "for he loves our nation, and he built us our synagogue" (Lk 7:5) (cf Bosch 1959:95).

In light of all this we can comprehend why, throughout the Book of Acts, it is emphasized that the gospel first has to be proclaimed to Jews, and only then to Gentiles. This is not merely a reference to an actual historical sequence. Neither is it just a matter of communications strategy, on the basis of the argument that the Jews, particularly those in the synagogues of the diaspora, would be more likely converts than the pagans. No, it was due to theological reasons, to the priority of the Jews in the light of salvation history (cf Zingg 1973:205; Irik 1982:287). This explains why, according to Acts, even Paul, the "apostle to the Gentiles", spends as much, if not more, of his time preaching to Jews as to Gentiles (Wilson 1973:249). It also clarifies why—even after he has solemnly declared that, since the Jews have rejected the gospel, he is now turning to the Gentiles—Paul continues, with almost monotonous repetition, to go to the synagogue first in every city where he arrives (cf Acts 14:1; 17:1, 10, 17; 18:4, 19, 26; 19:8) (for the likely historical kernel in this, cf Bornkamm 1966:200; Hultgren 1985:138-143).

The emphasis on salvation for the Jews and their theological priority is, however, never divorced from the Gentiles and a mission to them. The risen Lord has entrusted the *Gentile* mission to the apostles (Lk 24:47; Acts 1:8); they execute this mission by turning, first, to the *Jews*! The Gentile mission is not secondary to the Jewish mission. Neither is the one merely a consequence of the other. Rather, the Gentile mission is coordinated to the Jewish mission.

It is therefore incorrect, or at the very least insufficient, to say (as is still being suggested by some scholars, *inter alia* Anderson 1964:269, 272; Hahn 1965:134; Sanders 1981:667) that the Gentile mission only became possible after the Jews had rejected the gospel. In its more extreme form this view suggests that Luke's whole purpose was to prove beyond any doubt that the Jews had, through their own decision, forfeited any hope of salvation. According to this view the Jews are, for Luke, "mere theological pawns"—people who are obstinate and perverted, and only serve to justify the Gentile mission and the formation of a Gentile church (Sanders 1981:668).[3]

The Division of Israel

Undoubtedly the Jews' resistance to the gospel forms an important and recurring theme in Acts. What many Jews would do with the proclamation of the apostles is, in fact, foreshadowed in the Nazareth episode in the gospel (4:16-30) and in the parable of the pounds where Luke's version tells us that the fellow-citizens of the newly appointed king refused to accept him as their sovereign (19:14). In Acts, then, Luke repeatedly emphasizes that many Jews rejected Jesus. Frequently, after such an episode, the Christian preacher would say that, in view of the fact that the Jews had rejected the message, he was now going to the Gentiles. Strangely, however, the apostles continue to preach to Jews even after such an incident—which only makes sense if we accept that Luke wishes to say that the apostles are warning their Jewish listeners not to miss the opportunity for salvation offered to them (cf Paul's words to the Jews in Pisidian Antioch: Acts 13:40; see further Jervell 1972:61).

More important, the many incidences of rejection by Jews have to be seen in relation to their counterpart: the stories about Jews accepting the gospel.

Jervell has shown that wherever Acts tell us about Jewish rejection of the message it also reports that there were those who responded positively (Jervell 1972). Luke has already, in his gospel, indicated a more positive response of Jews to Jesus than did the other gospels (cf Irik 1982:283f). Acts reveals a similar tendency. Mass conversions of Jews are again and again reported, particularly of Jews in Jerusalem (which, as indicated above, occupies a very special position in Luke's theology) but also of those in the diaspora. There is, moreover, a clear progression in these reports: in Acts 2:41, three thousand Jews are converted; in 4:4 there are five thousand; in 5:14 "multitudes both of men and women" are added; in 6:7 the number of disciples in Jerusalem has "multiplied greatly"; in 21:20 Paul is informed about "many thousands" (*myriades*, "tens of thousands") of believing Jews (cf Jervell 1972:44-46).

In light of these oft-repeated reports it can, thus, hardly be maintained that it was the Jewish rejection of Jesus which precipitated the Gentile mission. On the other hand, Jervell goes too far when he says, "It is more correct to say that only when Israel has accepted the gospel can the way to Gentiles be opened" (:55). Rather, what Luke wants to communicate is that it is the combination of acceptance and rejection by Jews, or more precisely, it is the division within Judaism, between the repentant and the unrepentant, which opens the way for the Gentile mission. The difference in their response, and not just the story of their obduracy, is told again and again, up to the very last passage of Acts. Israel has not rejected the gospel, but has become divided over the issue (Jervell 1972:49; cf Meyer 1986:95f).

I have proposed that Luke, from the very beginning of his gospel, is interested in the "restoration" of Israel. It may now be said, with some justification, that the restoration has taken place in the conversion of (a significant part of) Israel. This constitutes the purified, restored, and true Israel, from which those who have rejected the gospel are purged. Through their negative response the latter have excluded themselves from Israel. Luke does not describe the Christian church as a kind of "third race", in addition to Jews and Gentiles. Rather, for him the Christian community consists of the converted Jews, after the obdurate ones have consciously excluded themselves and to which the Gentile converts are added. The Christian church did not begin as a new entity on the day of Pentecost. On that day many Jews became what they truly were — Israel. Subsequently Gentiles were incorporated into Israel. Gentile Christians are part of Israel, not a "new" Israel. There is no break in the history of salvation. Not to be converted means to be purged from Israel; conversion means a share in the covenant with Abraham. The promises to the fathers have been fulfilled. The church is born from out of the womb of Israel of old, not as an outsider laying claims to Israel's historic prerogatives (cf Schweizer 1971:150; Jervell 1972:49, 53f, 58; Dillon 1979:252 and 268, note 85; Tiede 1980:9f, 132).

A Tragic Story

Does this mean that the reaction of unrepentant Jews constitutes no problem for Luke, that the struggle for all Israel now belongs to history, that he has eliminated the possibility of a further mission to Jews for the church of his time because the judgment by and on the Jews has been irrevocably passed and the unbelieving portion of Israel is rejected for all times? May the church now wash its hands of Israel? This is the verdict Jervell (1972:54f, 64, 68) reaches. Robert Tannehill and others have, however—I believe quite rightly—denied that this is the case (cf Tannehill 1985:passim). The infancy narrative of Luke's gospel, in particular, stands in an unresolved tension with the book of Acts, particularly the latter's conclusion; the expectations raised in the gospel are largely *not* fulfilled in the subsequent narrative. Tannehill (:73f) considers various possible explanations and then comes to the conclusion that Luke is deliberately and consciously guiding his readers to experience the story of Israel and its Messiah as a tragic story. What the reader was given to expect did not happen. There has been an unanticipated turn in the plot, a reversal of fortunes (:78). With the aid of the repetition of key words or word roots (such as the word *soterion*, "salvation") Luke points to the tragic disparity between the great promise of Israel's beginnings and the failure of its later history (:81).

Already in the gospel the element of tragedy is underscored through the recurrent awakening of hope and the repeated failure of fulfillment. There is, for instance, the sadness of the travellers to Emmaus, who say, "But we had hoped that he was the one to redeem Israel" (24:21; cf Tannehill 1985:76). Even more striking are the four texts in Luke which speak of Jerusalem's rejection of Jesus and its coming destruction: 13:33-35; 19:41-44; 21:20-24; and 23:27-31. All of these passages, except the first, are unique to Luke. None of these stories reveals any trace of vindictiveness or gloating on the part of Luke, as though he experiences glee over the judgment on the Jews and their city (as Sanders 1981 suggests). Rather, the tone is pathetic, the emotions aroused in the reader are those of anguish, pity and sorrow (Tannehill 1985:75, 79, 81; cf Tiede 1980:15). The reader senses that, in spite of all indications to the contrary, Luke has not absolutely and finally given up on the Jews. One might perhaps even say that his entire two-volume work is conceived on the basis of the conviction that the final decision has not yet fallen and the definite answer not yet given (Stanek 1985:25). Jesus weeps for Jerusalem; so does Luke. Jesus' yearning for Israel's salvation remains unfulfilled; so does Luke's. But "times of relief" and "restoration" may yet come, in spite of all indications to the contrary. The complete disappearance of this hope would leave Luke with an unsolvable theological problem, since he has, in many different ways, depicted salvation for Israel as a major aspect of God's purpose. So he does not give up this hope. Jerusalem—he has Jesus say—will be trampled by foreigners "until the times of the Gentiles are fulfilled" (Lk 21:24; this saying probably does not refer to a future Gentile mission); Jerusalem will not "see" its king until the time comes when it will say, "Blessed is he who comes in the name of the Lord" (Lk 13:35) (cf Tannehill 1985:85). Sure, the hope beyond tragedy is expressed only in vague terms, but it is there. Even in the final scene in Acts 28:23-28 Paul is still preaching to the Jews (:82f).

In light of the above, I believe that Jervell, Tannehill, and others are correct in assigning a central place in Luke's theology of mission to the salvation-historical relationship between Jews and Gentiles. We would, however, be going too far if we were to insist that Luke's entire mission theology can be interpreted as an effort to solve this mystery. Rather, the turn to the Gentiles follows upon the rejection by Israel and the acceptance of the gospel by a significant portion of Israel, *but is not wholly explained by it* (cf Senior and Stuhlmueller 1983:272). Evidently, Luke is no systematic theologian in the modern sense of the word. He has several intermingling missionary motifs. The first is certainly the relationship between the mission to Jews and the mission to Gentiles. Other major themes include Luke's message to the poor and the rich; his understanding of repentance, forgiveness, and salvation; and his emphasis on Jesus' ministry of superseding vengeance. To these we now turn.

GOSPEL FOR THE POOR—AND THE RICH

The Poor in Luke's Gospel

It is common knowledge that Luke has a particular interest in the poor and other marginalized groups. Already in the Magnificat (Lk 1:53) we read: "(God) has filled the hungry with good things, and the rich he has sent away empty".

This sentiment is sustained throughout the gospel. We need to think only of the beatitude of the poor and the parallel woe-saying on the rich (6:20, 24), the parable of the rich fool (12:16-21), the story of the rich man and Lazarus (16:19-31), and the exemplary conduct of Zacchaeus, the chief tax-collector of Jericho (19:1-10). All of these are unique to Luke. In addition, he has frequently edited the tradition handed down to him in such a way that a bias toward the dispossessed becomes evident. He is, for instance, the only evangelist who has John the Baptist spell out in practical terms what it means to "bear fruits that befit repentance" (3:8), and he does this in terms of economic relations (3:10-14). The term *ptochos* ("poor") occurs ten times in Luke, compared to five times each in Mark and Matthew.[4] Not only the word *ptochos*, but also other terms referring to want and need abound in Luke. The same is true of terms referring to wealth, such as *plousios* ("rich") and *hyparchonta* ("possessions") (cf Bergquist 1986:4f). "If we did not have Luke", comments Schottroff and Stegemann (1986:67), "we would probably have lost an important, if not the most important, part of the earliest Christian tradition and its intense preoccupation with the figure and message of Jesus as the hope of the poor". Mazamisa (1987:99) summarizes,

> [Luke's] concern is with the social issues he writes about: with the demons and evil forces in first century society which deprived women, men and children of dignity and selfhood, of sight and voice and bread, and sought to control their lives for private gain; with the people's own selfishness and servility; and with the promises and possibilities of the poor and the outcasts.

Much has been written in recent years in an attempt to identify the poor to whom Luke refers. In particular, the difference between Matthew's and Luke's first beatitude (Mt 5:3, "Blessed are the poor in spirit"; Lk 6:20, "Blessed are you who are poor") has long fascinated scholars and ordinary Bible readers. This is not the place to reopen the debate or to attempt a novel contribution. Suffice it to say that not even the Matthean version of the first beatitude may be understood only in a spiritual sense. In Luke such a spiritualization is still more unwarranted. This does not, however, mean that such nuances are excluded. They are not. The poor are also the devout, the humble (cf *tapeinos* in the Magnificat: Lk 1:47, 52), those who live in utter dependence upon God (cf Pobee 1987:18-20). *Ptochos* ("poor") is moreover often a collective term for all the disadvantaged (cf Albertz 1983:199; Nissen 1984:94; Pobee 1987:20). This emerges from the way in which Luke, when he gives a list of people who suffer, either puts the poor at the head of the list (cf 4:18; 6:20; 14:13; 14:21) or at the end, as a climax (as in 7:22). All who experience misery are, in some very real sense, the poor. This is particularly true of the those who are sick. Lazarus, the exemplary poor person in Luke, is both poor and sick. Primarily then, poverty is a social category in Luke, although it certainly has other undertones as well. It is, however, unwarranted to allow what is secondary to become primary (cf Nolan 1976:23; Fung 1980:91).

And the Rich?

What Luke says about the rich can only be understood against the background of this portrait of the poor. *Plousios* ("rich") is, like *ptochos*, a comprehensive term. The rich are primarily those who are greedy, who exploit the poor, who are so bent on making money that they do not even allow themselves the time to accept an invitation to a banquet (Lk 14:18f), who do not notice the Lazarus at their gate (16:20), who conduct a hedonistic lifestyle but are nonetheless (or, rather, because of this) choked by cares about those very riches (8:14). They are, at the same time, slaves *and* worshipers of Mammon (cf D'Sa 1988:172-175).

From this primary meaning of *plousios* several secondary meanings follow. Luke calls the Pharisees *philargyroi*, "lovers of money" (16:14); this does not simply refer to one trait among others, "but involves the whole moral identity of the person", "the entire orientation of their lives" (Schottroff and Stegemann 1986:96). They are, like the Pharisee in the parable, those who trust in themselves that they are righteous and despise others (18:9). The rich are thus also the arrogant and the powerful who abuse power. They are, supremely, the impious who are bent only on the things of this world and therefore are "not rich toward God" (12:21) or "paupers in the sight of God" (NEB). In essence this means that, through their avarice, haughtiness, exploitation of the poor, and godlessness, they have willfully and consciously placed themselves outside of the range of God's grace. They are only interested in what they can get out of the present moment. The woe-sayings (Lk 6:24f), which contrast the beatitudes, thus become transparent:

> But woe to you that are rich, for you have received your
> consolation.
> Woe to you that are full now, for you shall go hungry.

> Woe to you that laugh now, for you shall mourn and
> weep.

The motif is the same one we encounter in the Magnificat (1:51-53) and also in the story of the rich man and Lazarus (16:25) (cf Schottroff and Stegemann 1986:99) — the motif of reversal, of contrasting present bliss with future agony (and present agony with future bliss). The rich have — not only because they are rich, but also because of the way they behave — used up their portion of happiness (Schottroff and Stegemann 1986:32) and relinquished any hope of blessings in the future.

Jesus in Nazareth

The first words the Lukan Jesus speaks in public (Lk 4:18f) contain a programmatic statement concerning his mission to reverse the destiny of the poor:

> The Spirit of the Lord is upon me,
> because he has anointed me
> to preach good news to the poor.
> He has sent me to proclaim release to the captives
> and recovery of sight to the blind;
> to set at liberty those who are oppressed,
> to proclaim the acceptable year of the Lord.

These words from the Book of Isaiah become, in Luke's gospel, a sort of manifesto of Jesus: "Today this scripture has been fulfilled in your hearing" (4:21). The prisoners, the blind, and the oppressed (or the bruised) are all subsumed under "the poor"; they are all manifestations of poverty, all in need of "good news". The major part of the quotation comes from Isaiah 61:1f, a prophecy first directed to the disappointed Jews shortly after the Babylonian exile. There it is aimed at encouraging them by assuring them that God had not forgotten them but would come to their aid by ushering in "the year of the Lord's favor", namely the Jubilee (cf Albertz 1983:187-189).

Remarkably, however, Luke does not only quote from Isaiah 61:1f. He inserts a phrase from Isaiah 58:6 between Isaiah 61:1 and 61:2, "to let the oppressed go free". Scholars have made many attempts to explain this strange state of affairs, but none of these explanations really satisfies. We have to accept, I believe, that Luke intentionally inserted these words from another chapter of the book of Isaiah in order to communicate something to his readers which was apparently not sufficiently clearly expressed in Isaiah 61 (cf Dillon 1979:253; Albertz 1983:183f, 191). The phrase "to let the oppressed go free" has a distinctly *social* profile in Isaiah 58. It stands in the context of prophetic criticism of social discrepancies in Judah, of the exploitation of the poor by the rich. Even on a day of fasting the latter pursue their own interests, make their employees work the harder (v 3), and wrangle with those who owe them money (v 4; cf Albertz 1983:193). It is in this context that the prophet then exclaims, in v 6f:

> Is not this the fast that I choose:
> to loose the bonds of wickedness,
> to undo the thongs of the yoke,
> *to let the oppressed go free,*
> and to break every yoke?
> Is it not to share your bread with the hungry,
> and bring the homeless poor into your house;
> when you see the naked, to cover him . . .?

The context of Isaiah 58 is also reflected in Nehemiah 5, where we are told of poor Jews who, in order to pay the taxes levied by the Persian king, had to mortgage their vineyards and homes and even sell their children into slavery to rich fellow-Jews who grasped the opportunity to capitalize on the predicament of the poor. In light of this, the "oppressed" or "bruised" or "broken victims" of Isaiah 58:6 are to be understood as those who were economically ruined, those who had become bonded slaves and had no hope of ever again escaping from the throttling grip of poverty. Only a Jubilee, a "year of the Lord's favor", could provide them with a way out of their misery.

The social-ethical thrust of this phrase was undoubtedly familiar to Jesus' listeners, even if they no longer knew the detailed circumstances of the "oppressed" of Isaiah 58:6. The *tethrausmenoi* of Luke 4:18 should therefore equally be regarded as those who have become destitute because of their ever-growing debts (cf Albertz 1983:196f). For them, as well as for the other oppressed groups listed here, the "year of the Lord's favor" is being announced.

What all this meant in the actual historical ministry of Jesus or in the earliest Jesus tradition is not easy to establish. We do not have direct access to that tradition, only to the evangelists' interpretation of it. Still, it is doubtful that Jesus intended to launch a people's movement for political liberation or that his sermon in Nazareth could be regarded as manifesto for a popular uprising. That Jesus announced and exerted himself for fundamental changes in the society of his day cannot, however, be denied. The present form of Luke 4:16-30 still gives clear evidence of that, and the way Luke has incorporated this story into his gospel illustrates this. It is now our task to attempt to interpret the Nazareth episode within the context of Luke's writings and theology.

Evangelist of the Rich?

I begin with Luke's sayings about the rich and what they should do in the face of abject poverty. From the gospel it is evident that Jesus had many dealings with wealthy people; similarly, in Acts we read about wealthy and distinguished people who joined the Christian community. What is Luke hoping to communicate about them? What is he saying to the wealthy of his own time? He intends, apparently, to articulate something very explicit. This he does, *inter alia*, with the aid of a variety of parables, stories, and injunctions. Their situation, before God and in the face of the poor, need not remain what it is. So Luke "wants the rich and respected to be reconciled to the message and way of life of Jesus and the disciples; he wants to motivate them to a conversion that is in keeping with the social message of Jesus" (Schottroff and Stegemann 1986:91; cf D'Sa 1988:175-177).

One such possible response is exemplified by Zacchaeus, the chief tax-collector of Jericho (Lk 19:1-10) (cf Schottroff and Stegemann 1986:106-109; Pobee 1987:46-53), whose conversion takes as concrete a form as his preceding transgression. He will repay those he has exploited and give half of his possessions to the poor. Even if he is not called to follow Jesus physically, he becomes a disciple by putting Jesus' words into practice. He is, in fact, the only rich person in the gospel about whom it is explicitly told that he chose another lifestyle (Nissen 1984:82).

Luke contrasts the story about Zacchaeus with that of the rich young ruler (18:18-30). In both cases, wealthy persons are challenged by Jesus, but they respond differently. The ruler, who otherwise leads an exemplary life according to the letter of the law (and who is also in this respect contrasted with the tax-collector and his disreputable lifestyle) is, however, not prepared to take up Jesus' challenge. He becomes very sad and leaves, "for he was very rich". For Luke, this story is one of an unsuccessful call to discipleship (cf Schottroff and Stegemann 1986:75). It has a parallel in Acts, in the story of Ananias and Sapphira (5:1-11), just as the conduct of Barnabas in Acts (4:36f) is analogous to that of Zacchaeus. The problems facing the wealthy in the post-Easter community are thus obviously not different from those facing the rich who encountered Jesus. Zacchaeus and Barnabas become paradigms of what Luke expects of wealthy Christians.

The attitude the wealthy should adopt toward the destitute is explicated in more detail in other Lukan sayings. Particularly illuminating is the Lukan redaction of some material from Q, included in Jesus' Sermon on the Plain (6:30-35a), and which differs at decisive points from the Matthean redaction:

> Give to everyone who begs from you; and of him who takes away your goods do not ask them again. And as you wish that men should do to you, do so to them. If you love those who love you, what credit is that to you? For even sinners love those who love them ... And if you lend to those from who you hope to receive, what credit is that to you? Even sinners lend to sinners, to receive as much again. But love your enemies, and do good, and lend, expecting nothing in return.

The whole passage is shot through with references to what the conduct of the rich ought to be toward the poor (cf Albertz 1983:202f; Schottroff and Stegemann 1986:112-116). What is particularly remarkable is that the Matthean love of enemies is now interpreted as love toward those who do not repay their debts! Perhaps the "treat spitefully" or "abuse" (*epereazo*) of 6:28 (the parallel in Matthew has "persecute") also refers to the abuse of those who borrow money without repaying it. Luke understands these words as an exhortation to rich Christians. The social ethic of the time suggested that the rich invite only the rich, in order to be invited back (cf 14:12). Precisely this the Lukan Jesus rejects. It is the kind of conduct one would expect of sinners who only do good to those who do good to them and only lend money if repayment is guaranteed (6:32-34). Jesus' disciples, however, should lend without expecting anything in return (6:35a). They are challenged to be merciful, as their heavenly Father is (6:36). This will bring them reward (6:35b): if they acquit (*apolyo*) their debtors, they will themselves be acquitted, that is, forgiven (6:37).[5] All of this is put in the context of the Lukan Jesus' understanding of who my neighbor is. From the parable of the good Samaritan we know that the neighbor is the one in need who makes a demand on me and whom I dare not leave by the roadside. In economic terms, it means that the rich members of Luke's community are challenged to give up a significant portion of their wealth, and also to perform specific unpleasant actions, such as the issuing of risky loans and the cancelling of debts. All this is, of course, also Jubilee language—the idea of the Jubilee indeed permeates Luke's gospel.

Luke's "ethic of economics" also finds expression in the idea of almsgiving. Apart from Matthew 6:1-4 the term *eleemosyne* (almsgiving) occurs in the New Testament only in the Lukan writings (Lk 11:41; 12:33; Acts 3:2, 3, 10; 9:36; 10:2, 4, 31; 24:17). In addition, whereas almsgiving was, at the time, usually understood as charity directed to fellow-believers, whether Jews or Christians, Luke understands it as also directed to outsiders (cf Schottroff and Stegemann 1986:109). Today, of course, charity is a bad word in many circles and often seen as the very antithesis of justice. In the Old Testament and Judaism it was different (:116), as it still is in Islam. Almsgiving is not something that subverts justice and structural change; rather, it is an expression of justice and stands in its service. In the Old Testament the two concepts are often synonyms. Almsgiving (*eleemosyne*) is, furthermore, an expression of having mercy (*eleos*).

In light of all this, we may conclude that Luke cannot really be called the evangelist of the poor; "He can more correctly be called the 'evangelist of the rich'" (Schottroff and Stegemann 1986:117). Albertz, who particularly emphasizes Luke's interest in Isaiah 58, comes to a similar conclusion (1983:203—my translation):

> Both Is 58:5ff and the Gospel of Luke address the wealthy. Both wish to inspire them to perform extraordinary far-reaching accomplishments, to renounce a large portion of their possessions and waive the recovery of debts, and to give alms generally, in this way alleviating the plight of the poor members of the community. Is 58:5-9a spoke to the upper stratum of the community immediately after the Exile, in the midst of a severe social crisis; Luke addresses his two-volume work to the upper stratum of the Hellenistic community.

All Are in Need of Repentance

Luke should, however, not be interpreted as if he knows of only one sin, that of wealth, and only one kind of conversion, that of giving up one's possessions. Both the poor and the rich need salvation. At the same time, each person has his or her specific sinfulness and enslavement. The patterns of enslavement differ, which means that the specific sinfulness of the rich is different from that of the poor. Therefore, in Luke's gospel, the rich are tested on the ground of their wealth, whereas others are tested on loyalty toward their family, their people, their culture, and their work (Lk 9:59-61) (Nissen 1984:175). This means that the poor are sinners like everyone else, because ultimately sinfulness is rooted in the human heart. Just as the materially rich can be spiritually poor, the materially poor can be spiritually poor (:176; cf Pobee 1987:19, 53). Luke undoubtedly wishes to communicate to his readers what is today often referred to as God's preferential option for the poor, but this option cannot be interpreted in any exclusive sense (Pobee 1987:54). It does not exclude God's concern for the rich, but, in fact, stresses it for, in both his gospel and Acts, Luke wishes his readers to know that there is hope for the rich, insofar as they act and serve in solidarity with the poor and oppressed. In their being converted to God, rich and poor are converted toward each other. The main emphasis, ultimately, is on sharing, on community. At various points in Acts, Luke highlights this "communism of love" (cf Acts 2:44f; 4:32, 36f).

Nevertheless, a problem remains. Whereas no serious student of Luke can doubt that the motif of the gospel as good news for the poor is absolutely crucial for the understanding of his gospel, it is equally obvious that this motif appears to have run dry in the Book of Acts (cf Bergquist 1986). In none of the dozen or so speeches of Peter, Stephen, and Paul reported in Acts is there any reference to the poor; as a matter of fact, the word *ptochos*, "poor", does not even occur in Acts. Indeed, the whole thrust of Luke's second volume appears to be elsewhere. This is even more remarkable if we keep in mind that the two volumes were, from the beginning, planned and written as a unit.

Why then would Luke have gone to such lengths in editing his sources (particularly Mark and Q), to include a great variety of explicit and implicit references to the poor and to the responsibility of the rich toward them, only to drop this entire emphasis when he starts writing his second volume? James Bergquist examines several suggested solutions and then concludes that the reason is to be found in the fact that, in Luke's view, the motif of good news for the poor is indeed a central but at the same time an incomplete part of a wider controlling theological purpose in Luke-Acts. This controlling theological motif, he suggests, lies in the announcement of God's final salvation in Jesus. Bergquist finds confirmation for this thesis in the fact that, in Acts, the term "Gentiles" replaces the characteristic gospel terms for the poor and the outsider: the outsiders in Acts become the Gentiles; Luke mentions Gentiles forty-three times in Acts and builds his narrative of mission with them in view (Bergquist 1986:12; cf also Wedderburn 1988:164).

Bergquist's suggestion may have merit. We shall, however, be in a position to judge this only after we have taken a closer look at what salvation meant for Luke. To this we now turn.

SALVATION IN LUKE-ACTS

There can be no doubt that "salvation", as well as its attendant ideas of repentance and forgiveness of sins, are central to Luke's two-volume work. The words *soteria* and *soterion* ("salvation") appear six times each in Luke and Acts, against no occurrences in Mark and Matthew, and only one in John. Four times salvation is mentioned in Luke's infancy narrative. In two of these instances Luke uses the less common form *soterion* which, apart from Acts 28:28 (that is, at the very end of his two-volume work) occurs only in Ephesians 6:17. In a sense then, Luke frames his entire body of writing with the idea of the salvation that has dawned in Christ. Among the synoptics, only Luke calls Jesus *Soter* ("Savior"), once in the gospel (2:11), and twice in Acts (5:31; 13:23).

In similar way, Luke gives prominence to *metanoeo* ("repent") and *metanoia* ("repentance"; sometimes he uses *epistrephein* ["turn about"] as alternative). Mark 2:17, for instance, reads, "I came not to call the righteous, but sinners"; Luke 5:32 adds "to repentance". "Repent" or "repentance" is, in Luke's writings, often linked closely to "sinners" (*hamartoloi*) and "forgiveness" (*aphesis*). It is a message that reverberates in the missionary sermons in Acts (cf 2:38; 3:19; 5:31; 8:22; 10:43; 13:38; 17:30; 20:21; 26:18, 20). This message does not, however, begin only in Acts. At the end of the gospel the risen Jesus tells his disciples, *inter alia*, that "repentance and forgiveness of sins" will be proclaimed in his name to all nations (24:47). Only Luke records the words of the repentant criminal on the cross and Jesus' response to him which, even if the word "forgiveness" is not used here, can only imply forgiveness and salvation ("today you will be with me in Paradise"—Lk 23:43). Only Luke has Jesus' word "Father, forgive them . . ." (23:34). And the parable of the prodigal son (again only Luke relates it) is a dramatic story about repentance and forgiveness. Thus repentance, conversion, and forgiveness become a dominant theme in the ministry not only of Jesus, but also of the apostles and evangelists after him and of John the Baptist before him.

It is not immediately evident, particularly in Acts, what the sins are people have to repent of. Often the apostles just call upon their listeners to repent of their sins, without specifying what they are. The sins of Jews and Gentiles are, however, different. The Jews have to repent of their share in the death of Jesus, following which they will (again) be incorporated in salvation history (cf, in particular, Acts 2:36-40 and 3:19). The sins of Gentiles, who are only now being incorporated in salvation history, consist primarily in their worship of idols (Acts 17:29) (cf Wilckens 1963:96-100; 180-182; Grant 1986:19-28, 49f). In the gospel the situation appears to be somewhat different. Luke uses the word *hamartolos*, "sinner", much more frequently than do the other two synoptic gospels; in addition, even where the word or its cognates do not appear, the idea itself is present. On the basis of the Q-saying about Jesus as "friend of tax-collectors and sinners" (Lk 7:34), Schottroff and Stegemann suggest that, in the earliest Jesus movement, no call of repentance was directed to "the poor, tax-collectors, and sinners, since their 'sin' consisted in their wretched condition rather than their criminality" (1986:33). This view cannot be proved from the sources, however; the two authors in fact admit that "this aspect of the earliest preaching can only be the subject of hypotheses" (:33). Still, an element of validity in Schottroff and Stegemann's conjecture may lie in the fact that, in Luke's gospel, "sin" and "sinners" usually refer to *moral* conduct, particularly in respect of other people — a circumstance which may betray something about the earliest preaching of Jesus. This already becomes evident in Luke's rendering of the ministry of John the Baptist (3:10-14). In like manner, the rich man in the parable (16:19-31) is a sinner because he shows no compassion for Lazarus. The priest and Levite are, by implication, depicted as sinners in that they ignore the plight of the person who has fallen among robbers (10:30-37). The prodigal son has sinned against heaven and against his father by his conduct, but even more by the way he treated his father (15:11-32). The tax-collector of the parable pleads for mercy because of his evil practices of extortion (18:9-14); this was clearly also the sin of Zacchaeus (19:8). And one's sinfulness is greater if one denies being a sinner. This is the case with the Pharisees who appear oblivious of their sins; they are not really righteous but *self*-righteous, particularly in respect of others (cf the elder son in Luke 15:29f and the Pharisee in 18:11f).

If we compare these examples with the missionary sermons in Acts, there is indeed a difference in the understanding of sin. This becomes obvious particularly if we compare the reaction to the preaching of John the Baptist with the reaction to Peter's sermon in Acts 2. In both cases the response of the listeners is expressed in the soul-searching question, "What then shall we do?" (Lk 3:10; 12; 14; Acts 2:37). In Acts, Peter's reply remains vague, with only a hint at the fact that his listeners were accomplices in the death of Jesus (2:38-40). In the gospel, the Baptist's reply is very concrete — it concerns sharing a coat with him who has none, giving food to the hungry, and not robbing people who are at one's mercy (Lk 3:11-14).

Comparing the gospel with Acts on the content of the repentance and conversion required we notice, thus, a certain vagueness in the latter book. The suggestion is that conversion means that Jews accept Jesus as their Messiah and that Gentiles turn from their idols to faith in him. In the gospel conversion is more specific. Zacchaeus undertakes to give half of his possessions to the poor and to repay fourfold all those from whom he has extorted money. The conversion of the prodigal son consists in his coming to his senses and returning to his father. Reasons for the *absence* of conversion are equally important. The elder son experiences no conversion, since he refuses to accept his brother; in addition, in his self-centeredness he calculates and compares, just as the Pharisee does in the parable about forgiveness (18:11f). The rich young ruler refuses Jesus specific injunction, "for he was very rich" (18:23); therefore his conversion miscarries.

Those who repent and whose sins are forgiven, experience *soteria*, "salvation". In the infancy narrative of Luke "salvation" obviously has political undertones: God has raised up a "horn of salvation" for Israel (1:69); he has saved Israel from its enemies (1:71); and will give his people "the knowledge of salvation" (1:77). Perhaps Ford (1984:77) is correct in arguing that Luke has deliberately structured his infancy narrative in terms of political conquest and liberation, so as to contrast Jesus' ministry with that (see below). It is evident that the salvation that has come to Zacchaeus's house is not really political. In his case, as with the prodigal son, salvation means acceptance, fellowship, new life. Often this is expressed in the imagery of a banquet: Jesus has table-fellowship with Zacchaeus, the prodigal son is treated with a feast, and those from the streets and alleys of the town, from the roads and country lanes are invited to the rich man's banquet (14:16-23). Whatever salvation is, then, in every specific context, it includes the total transformation of human life, forgiveness of sin, healing from infirmities, and release from any kind of bondage (Luke uses *aphesis* for both "forgiveness" and "release" or "liberation": compare 24:47 with 4:18).

This comprehensive understanding of salvation is evident in both the gospel and Acts. The mission of the Christian community in Acts is a mission of salvation, as was the work of Jesus (cf Senior and Stuhlmueller 1983:273). Salvation involves the reversal of all the evil consequences of sin, against both God and neighbor. It does not have only a "vertical" dimension. It is therefore incomplete to say, with Mann (1981:69), that the parable of the prodigal son gives no direction for one's earthly conduct but only for one's relationship to God. Zacchaeus is not only inwardly liberated from all the ties of his possessions, but actually does reparation (cf Albertz 1983:202). Liberation *from* is also liberation *to*, else it is not an expression of salvation. And liberation *to* always involves love to God *and* neighbor. "Anyone who reduces the following of Jesus to an enterprise of the heart, the head, and private interpersonal relations restricts the following of Jesus and trivializes Jesus himself" (Schottroff and Stegemann 1986:5f).

There is in the final analysis, therefore, no irreconcilable discrepancy between the gospel of Luke and Acts (although the tension between the emphasis of the two volumes should not be denied). In both, salvation is ultimately tied to the person of Jesus. In her Magnificat, Mary praises God's great deeds because of the child she carries in her womb. The disciples, those of both the gospel and Acts, turn their backs on their previous life and lifestyle because of their extraordinary encounter with Jesus, for the reign of God is already present in him (cf Lk 17:21). In the story of Zacchaeus, it is the presence of Jesus, not the supererogatory performance of the chief tax-collector, which ushers in salvation. Jesus is, really, the person who invites the cripples and the outcasts to a banquet. He is the Samaritan, who takes pity on his Jewish archenemy. He is the father, in whose home and heart there is room for both lost sons. Only in his name and in his power are true repentance, forgiveness of sins, and salvation to be found (cf Acts 4:12).

Seen from this perspective, Luke-Acts becomes a paean of praise to the incomparable grace of God, lavished upon sinners. The thrust of this can only be grasped, and then only partially, if we see it against the background of the understanding of God at the time: omnipotent, terrifying, and inscrutable. He is not to be understood as a pleasant and innocuous God, who is always prepared to forgive even more than people are prone to sin (in the sense of Voltaire's contemptuous remark, "*Pardonner, c'est son métier*," "to forgive is, after all, his profession"; cf Schweizer 1971:146). It is precisely as the omnipotent and inscrutable that he forgives—for the sake of Jesus. The initiative, throughout, remains *God's* (cf Wilckens 1963:183). And it manifests itself in ways that make no sense to the human mind. The prodigal son becomes the recipient of unfathomable and undeserved kindness; sinners are not only sought and accepted but receive honor, responsibility, and authority (Ford 1984:77). God answers the prayer of the tax-collector, not—as Jesus' listeners have anticipated—that of the Pharisee. Salvation comes to a chief tax-collector, of all people, but only after Jesus has taken the initiative and invited himself to the house of Zacchaeus. A Samaritan—the most unlikely candidate imaginable— performs an extraordinary deed of compassion. A contemptible criminal receives pardon and the promise of paradise in the hour of death, without any possibility of making restitution for his wicked deeds. The crucifiers of the innocent man from Nazareth hear him pray for forgiveness for what they are doing to him. And in Acts despised Samaritans and idol-worshiping Gentiles receive pardon and are incorporated into Israel, with whom they form the one people of God. What Jeremias said with reference to Jesus' word that the tax-collector, rather than the Pharisee, went home "justified" (Lk 18:14), can be said about all the examples referred to above: "Such a conclusion must have utterly overwhelmed (Jesus') hearers. It was beyond the capacity of any of them to imagine. What fault had the Pharisee committed, and what had the publican done by way of reparation?" (quoted in Ford 1984:75). The Jesus Luke introduces to his readers is somebody who brings the outsider, the stranger, and the enemy home and gives him and her, to the chagrin of the "righteous", a place of honor at the banquet in the reign of God.

With this observation I have already introduced the theme of the next section.

NO MORE VENGEANCE!

The Inexplicable Volte-Face

I turn, once again, to the story of Jesus' rejection by his home congregation of Nazareth (Lk 4:16-30). It has often puzzled scholars and other Bible readers that there is a shift in the story that seems unaccounted for. In the first part, up to v 22, the encounter unfolds quite amicably. Jesus is obviously welcome in the synagogue, is handed the scroll of the prophet Isaiah, reads from it, and returns the scroll. Luke then continues, "And the eyes of all in the synagogue were fixed on him" (v 20), apparently in expectation of what he was going to say. Of his sermon itself nothing is reported, except the opening lines, "Today this scripture has been fulfilled in your hearing" (v 21). The next verse then recounts the reaction of the synagogue congregation: "And all spoke well of him and wondered at the gracious words which proceeded out of his mouth. 'Is not this Joseph's son?' they asked" (RSV); or, "There was a general stir of admiration; they were surprised that words of such grace should fall from his lips. 'Is not this Joseph's son?' they asked" (NEB). The next verse, however, suggests a decisive shift in the nature of the encounter. Jesus says, "Doubtless you will quote me this proverb, 'Physician, heal yourself!' " (v 23a). He then reminds his listeners of God's mercy on the Gentile widow of Sidon and on Naaman, the Syrian. But by now all in the congregation are infuriated; they leap up, drive him out of the town to the brow of the hill on which it was built and try to hurl him over the edge, but he escapes miraculously.

What baffles the reader is why the Nazareth congregation changes from great admiration of what Jesus is saying to murderous intent in such a short time. Senior and Stuhlmueller (1983:260) refer to the somewhat puzzling exchange of verses 22-29, whereas A.R.C. Leany (quoted by Anderson 1964:266) says that "it is not too much to say that Luke has given us an impossible story". It may therefore be justifiable to look at this story from the perspective of an examination of Luke's "theology of mission".

Isaiah 61 in the First Century AD

Perhaps the solution to the apparent discrepancy between Luke 4:16-22 and 4:23-30 may be found by asking how the portion from Scripture Jesus was reading was understood by the Jews of his time. In order to do so I turn again, briefly, to Luke's infancy narrative. It has already been pointed out that this section — particularly Mary's Magnificat (Lk 1:46-55), Zechariah's song (1:68-79), and the words of Simeon (2:29-32) — contains a plethora of references to liberation for Israel. Ford even devotes a whole chapter to what she calls "revolutionary Messianism and the first Christmas" (1984:13-36). An examination of the infancy narratives, she says (:36), shows that the war angel, Gabriel, appeared to Zechariah and Mary. John the Baptist was to work in the spirit and power of the zealous prophet Elijah. Jesus (Joshua), John, and Simeon are names found among Jewish freedom fighters. The annunciation to Mary and the Magnificat have political and military overtones. The same is true of the story about the shepherds, to whom a heavenly army appears. When Jesus is presented in the temple, two persons appear, Simeon and Anna, who may have been anticipating a political leader.

Thus Luke, so Ford argues, deliberately structures his first few chapters in such a way that the contemporary Jewish messianic expectations are highlighted. This, she believes, is a faithful picture of Jewish life at the time: Palestine was "a seething cauldron" in the first century (Ford 1984:1-12). Galilee, in particular, was rife with revolutionaries and apocalyptic thinkers (:53), and Nazareth was hardly an exception. So what would Jesus' audience have expected when they heard him reading from Isaiah 61? The words were originally addressed to the Jews who had returned from Babylonian exile, and who were "grieving for Zion" (v 3), despondent because of their lost freedom and the destruction of their land. Precisely these former exiles were then, in Isaiah 61, promised a total reversal of their present wretched conditions. Israel would recover, the prophet said, since the Lord will turn their dismal present into a new and permanent Jubilee. Not only that, they would also get even with their powerful oppressors. So the prophet not only predicts "the year of the Lord's favor" (the Jubilee), but also *the day of the vengeance of our God*" (v 2) — vengeance, namely, on Israel's enemies (cf Albertz 1983: 188f). The words anticipated a future state of Israel in which foreigners would serve the Hebrews (verses 5-7) and not the other way round, as was the case at the time of the prophecy. What sentiments would this prophecy evoke in Jesus' audience? Ford

(1984:55) suggests that the text would be heard in a similar way in the first century AD; the audience would, however, be expecting release from Roman, not Babylonian, domination.

Ford also draws attention to a fragment from the Qumran writings, dating back roughly to the first century, called *11 Q Melchizedek*, in which a dramatic change in the concept of the Jubilee has been effected. The Qumran community changed the social notion of the Jubilee to an eschatological and apocalyptic one. However, along with the emphasis on the good news of the Jubilee, and as prominent as that, is the day of vengeance (:57). Among God's agents on that day would be the prophet anointed by the Lord and also Melchizedek, through whom God would usher in a day of vengeance (and slaughter) for the ungodly, particularly Israel's enemies. Thus, when Jesus read Isaiah 61 in the synagogue, the congregation probably expected him to announce vengeance on their foes, especially the Romans—a vengeance which would be a preliminary step toward the time of liberation (:59f). This may explain the initial positive response to Jesus—"and the eyes of all in the synagogue were fixed on him" (v 20). They were fervently expecting a sermon with a revolutionary thrust and perhaps Jesus' opening words, "Today this scripture has been fulfilled in your hearing" (v 21), further fanned these expectations.

Vengeance Superseded!

The eyes fixed on Jesus might, however, also have been filled with *suspicion*! According to Luke, Jesus only reads up to the first part of Isaiah 61:2, "to proclaim the acceptable year of the Lord". He stops short of the words, "and the day of vengeance of our God," which, according to Hebrew parallelism, belong intrinsically to the first part. He also omits the rest of the prophecy, which paints the imminent reversal in glowing colors; by doing this he removes all the elements that refer to Israel and Zion (cf Albertz 1983:190f) as well as all elements that are hostile to Gentiles. "What is he up to?" the congregation wonders. "Why does he leave out the vengeance part? Is he perhaps suggesting that there is no longer any room for retribution?" Apparently he is! Whereas, in *11 Q Melchizedek* and much of contemporary Judaism, salvation was destined only for (a small group of) Jews, Jesus not only omits any reference to judgment on Israel's enemies but also reminds his listeners of God's compassion on those enemies (4:25-27), a fact that fills all in the synagogue with wrath (v 28) (cf Ford 1984:61).

These circumstances have prompted B. Violet and particularly Joachim Jeremias to suggest that the key to the entire enigma of interpreting the Nazareth episode should be looked for in the dramatic way in which the reading from Isaiah 61 is terminated just before the reference to the day of vengeance and the portrayal of the hoped-for reversal—for which the entire congregation must have been waiting. Jesus does the unimaginable by omitting this (cf Jeremias 1958:41-46). Jeremias therefore takes a fresh look at verse 22—which, as indicated above, is usually interpreted in terms of a very positive response to Jesus' sermon—and retranslates it as follows, "They protested with one voice and were furious, because he only spoke about (God's year of) mercy (and omitted the words about the messianic vengeance)".

We cannot repeat Jeremias's detailed argument in support of a translation which so drastically deviates from most other interpretations of Luke 4:22. Suffice it to say that it is probably the only translation that helps us make sense of what Luke writes about the events in the Nazareth synagogue. Several scholars have also, in recent years, and particularly in the light of the Qumran evidence, come out in support of Jeremias (cf, for instance, Albertz and Ford). Ford regards the event in Nazareth and the strategic place it occupies in Luke as a deliberate contrast to the expectations evoked in his infancy narrative. In the first scenes of the gospel Luke dramatically portrays the families of John the Baptist and of Jesus as Jews who expect a prophet and a king who will conduct a holy war on Israel's enemies. In his fourth chapter, then, Luke introduces the awaited leader. He is wholly different from what has been expected. He is the Anointed of God who will announce a year of favor for both Jews *and* their opponents. The Nazareth congregation receives his message with such astonishment and hostility that they try to assassinate him (Ford 1984:136). In this prominent story of Jesus' extraordinary behavior, then, Luke is able to foreshadow the major elements of his theology. This "will be found to be inimical to that of many of (Jesus') contemporaries, especially the revolutionaries, and will lead to repeated rejection and finally a martyr's death" (:54). The Nazareth pericope thus sets the stage for Jesus' entire ministry.

Once one has been made aware of this important thrust of Jesus' sermon in Nazareth, one may discover the same motif throughout Luke. Let me highlight some instances. Jeremias (1958:45f) points out that it is not only in the Nazareth incident that Jesus omits any reference to vengeance. The same happens in Luke 7:22f (par Mt 11:5f). In his reply to John the Baptist Jesus again, as he did in 4:18f, "splices" different passages from Isaiah (in this case Is 35:5f, 29:18f and 61:1). All three of these passages contain, in one form or another, references to divine vengeance (35:4; 29:20; 61:2), but again Jesus omits any references to it. This can hardly be unintentional, moreso because of the added remark, "And blessed is he who takes no offense at me" (Lk 7:23). In other words: Blessed is everyone who does not take offense at the fact that the era of salvation differs from what he or she has expected, that God's compassion on the poor, the outcast and the stranger — even on Israel's enemies — has superseded divine vengeance!

Jesus' attitude toward Samaritans has already been referred to. When, at the beginning of his "journey to Jerusalem", John and James wished to pray down fire from heaven to destroy the Samaritan town which refused them hospitality, Jesus rebuked them. As a matter of fact, all Luke's stories and parables about Samaritans give evidence to Jesus refusal to embrace the vengeful sentiments of his compatriots.

A more controversial incident is the one reported in Luke 13:1-5. Jesus is told about a group of Galileans whose blood the Roman legionaries have "mingled with their sacrifices" (cf Jeremias 1958:41). His audience probably expects him to condemn Pilate, but he does not do so; instead, he uses the occasion to call them to repentance instead of vengefulness. In our understanding today this may suggest that Jesus adopted an apolitical stance and, in doing so, actually condoned what the Romans did. There may indeed be something of that in the way Luke interprets the incident (see below); at the same time it is evidence of his understanding of Jesus as someone who refuses to return evil for evil (cf Ford 1984:98-101). In fact, Jesus' entire conduct throughout his arrest, trial, and execution, as Luke presents them, underscores his unwavering commitment to nonviolence (for details, cf Ford 1984:108-135). Jesus' prayer of forgiveness for his executioners, to which attention has already been drawn, likewise brings out his complete absence of vengefulness. His prayer, together with the word of pardon to the criminal on the cross (both reported only by Luke), show that, even while dying a slave's and criminal's death, Jesus turned in love and forgiveness to outcasts and enemies, thus living out an ethic that was completely contrary to the militant ideology of both oppressor and oppressed (cf Ford 1984:134, 135). The Jubilee year was supposed to begin on the great Day of Atonement. Perhaps, in Luke's understanding, that day commences when Jesus on the cross, as the new high priest on a new day of atonement, intercedes for all sinners—Jews and Gentiles (:133).

The events at the end of his life thus dramatically underscore the thrust of Jesus' words in the Nazareth synagogue. It is against this background—which breathed a relentless, vengeful, and holy wrath against pagans—and the expectation of a second coming of Melchizedek, who would wreak divine vengeance on the Gentiles, that the Lukan pericope as a whole must be understood (Ford 1984:62). The first words of Jesus' public ministry are ones of forgiveness and healing, not wrath and destruction. The Nazareth pericope is, in fact, the basis of Luke's entire gospel and a prelude to Acts, especially in regard to the Gentile mission (:63).

Luke writes his two-volume work in the wake of the devastation of the Jewish War, in which the political hopes of the Zealots were crushed; many of his readers lived in a war-torn country, occupied by foreign troops who often took advantage of the population; violence and banditry have been their meat and drink for many a year (cf Ford 1984:1-12). They have, in a real sense, reaped the whirlwind. And now Luke presents them with a challenge: Jesus and his powerful message of nonviolent resistance and, above all, of loving one's enemy in word and deed. The peace that comes with Jesus is not won through weapons, but through love, forgiveness, and acceptance of one's enemies into the covenant community (:136). "Everyone who believes in him" is welcome—this is the astonishing discovery that Peter makes in his encounter with Cornelius (Acts 10:43). The Lukan Jesus turns his back on the in-group exegesis of his contemporaries by challenging their "ethic of election" (cf Nissen 1984:75f). From the Nazareth episode onward, Luke has his eye on the Christian church, where there is room for rich and poor, Jew and Gentile, even oppressor and oppressed (cf Schottroff and Stegemann 1986:37; Sundermeier 1986:72)—which does not, of course, suggest that conditions should remain what they are.

This may also help to explain the fact that Romans are accorded a singularly sympathetic treatment throughout Luke-Acts (LaVerdiere and Thompson 1976:586). There is, perhaps, a certain ambivalence here: on the one hand, Luke realizes that any further revolutionary opposition to Rome is futile; on the other, there is his deep commitment to Jesus' own preaching and example of forgiveness and peace-making. So he does not wish to antagonize the authorities. They should cause the church no difficulties. By implication, Luke claims for the church the protection of the law and the status of a *religio licita*, an "approved religion" (cf Stanek 1985:10, 16f; Bovon 1985:73f, 127).[6] However, all this is, for Luke, hardly a matter of expediency; he adopts this attitude because he is convinced that the gospel of Jesus is one that puts a supreme premium on peace-making, love of enemies, and forgiveness. There is no room for vengefulness and wrath in the community of Jesus.

THE LUKAN MISSIONARY PARADIGM

Let us now attempt to identify some of the major ingredients of the Lukan missionary paradigm, as these have emerged in our discussion thus far.

1. I turn, first, to Luke's *pneumatology*. More than the other evangelists Luke dealt theologically with the fact that history went on and that Christ did not immediately return. His community knew that Jesus was no longer with them; they realized that the following of Jesus, in completely different circumstances, could not consist in a simple, slavish imitation of the Jesus or a reproduction of the past but had to be reinterpreted (cf Schweizer 1971:150; Schottroff and Stegemann 1986:98). At the same time, they had to be shown that there was no reason for despair. The story of the two disciples who had gone to Emmaus (Lk 24:13-35) was retold by Luke for precisely this reason — since Jesus can now be experienced in an entirely new manner, believers are not left in distressful sadness (LaVerdiere and Thompson 1976:291f).

It was preeminently through the *Spirit* that the risen Christ was present in the community. In Mark and Matthew the Spirit is not particularly prominent and is rarely linked with mission. Not so in Luke. Among the evangelists he may be singled out as the "theologian of the Holy Spirit" (G. Montague, quoted in Senior and Stuhlmueller 1983:277). Luke realized that Jesus' mission and ministry had to reinterpreted for the church of his own time, and he believed that this reinterpretation would be mediated by the Spirit. He did not introduce this notion only at Pentecost. The ministry of the earthly Jesus is already portrayed in terms of the initiative and guidance of the Spirit.

The idea of being led by the Spirit into mission is then, however, applied in a far more comprehensive manner to the ministry of the *disciples*. They will turn into Jesus' witnesses as soon as they are clothed with power from on high (Lk 24:49; Acts 1:8). The same Spirit in whose power Jesus went to Galilee also thrusts the disciples into mission. The Spirit becomes the catalyst, the guiding and driving force of mission. At every point the church's mission is both inspired and confirmed by manifestations of the Spirit (cf Wilson 1973:241; Zingg 1973:207f; Senior and Stuhlmueller 1983:275). The decisive event, of course, is Pentecost (cf Boer 1961:passim). The Spirit has descended upon Jesus at his baptism (Lk 3:21f), and now the Spirit descends for a second "baptism" (cf Acts 1:5); in this way the Spirit's particular ministry is both distinguished from the ministry of Jesus (Pentecost follows a full ten days after the ascension) and intimately coordinated with it. The gift of the Spirit is the gift of becoming involved in mission, for mission is the direct consequence of the outpouring of the Spirit. Luke's pneumatology excludes the possibility of a missionary *command*; it implies, rather, a *promise* that the disciples will get involved in mission. It was these circumstances that prompted Roland Allen to write:

> St Luke fixes our attention, not upon an external voice, but upon an internal Spirit. This manner of command is peculiar to the Gospel. Others direct from without, Christ directs within; others order, Christ inspires . . . This is the manner of the command in St Luke's writings. He speaks not of men who, being what they were, strove to obey the last orders of a beloved Master, but of men who, receiving a Spirit, were driven by that Spirit to act in accordance with the nature of that Spirit (1962:5).

Moreover, the Spirit not only *initiates* mission, he also *guides* the missionaries about where they should go and how they should proceed. The missionaries are not to execute their own plans but have to wait on the Spirit to direct them (cf Zingg 1973:208f). Philip's encounter with the Ethiopian eunuch, for instance, is through the agency of the Spirit (Acts 8:29). Of special importance for the understanding of Luke's second volume is the conversion of Cornelius. The acceptance of this Gentile (without circumcision!) into the Christian fold is confirmed when a second Pentecost is enacted: the Spirit is poured out even on a Gentile and his family (Acts 10:44-48). In his report to the Jerusalem community, Peter explains that it was the Spirit who told him not to hesitate but to go to Cornelius (Acts 11:12). Again, the ratification by the Jerusalem Council of the decision to baptize Gentiles without prior circumcision is also described as having taken place under the impulse of the Spirit (Acts 15:8, 28) (cf Zingg 1973:207; Senior and Stuhlmueller 1983:275). Similarly, it is the Spirit who charges the worshiping and fasting church of Antioch to set Saul and Barnabas apart for a special task (13:2), as it is the Spirit who sends them on their way (13:4). The Spirit prevents Paul from going deeper into Asia (16:6): through the vision of a man from Macedonia the Spirit directs him to Europe (16:9). In all these narratives the emphasis is on the Holy Spirit as catalyst, guide, and inspirer toward mission.

In the Lukan writings the Spirit of mission is also the Spirit of *power* (Greek: *dynamis*). This is true of the mission of both Jesus (Lk 4:14; Acts 10:38) and the apostles (Lk 24:49; Acts 1:8). The Spirit is thus, further, not only the initiator and guide of mission, but also the one who empowers to mission. This manifests itself particularly in the boldness of the witnesses once they have been endowed with the Spirit. In Acts, Luke often uses the words *parresia* and *parresiazomai* ("boldness"; "to speak boldly") (cf 4:13, 29, 31; 9:27; 13:46; 14:3; 18:26; 19:8). The suggestion is always that this has been made possible by the power of the Spirit. It is the Spirit who emboldens previously timid disciples. Through the Spirit, God is in control of the mission (Gaventa 1982:415).

The intimate linking of pneumatology and mission is Luke's distinctive contribution to the early church's missionary paradigm. In Paul's letters — probably written some thirty years before Luke-Acts — the Spirit is only marginally related to mission (cf Kremer 1982:154). By the second century AD the emphasis had shifted almost exclusively to the Spirit as the agent of sanctification or as the guarantor of apostolicity. The Protestant Reformation of the sixteenth century tended to put the major emphasis on the work of the Spirit as bearing witness to and interpreting the Word of God. Only in the twentieth century has there been a gradual rediscovery of the intrinsic missionary character of the Holy Spirit. This came about, *inter alia*, because of a renewed study of the writings of Luke. Undoubtedly, Luke did not intend to suggest that the initiative, direction, and power of the Spirit in mission applied only to the period about which he was writing. It had, in his view, permanent validity. For Luke, the concept of the Spirit sealed the kinship between God's universal will to save, the liberating ministry of Jesus, and the worldwide mission of the church (Senior 1983:269).

2. Another specifically Lukan contribution to the understanding of mission in the first century was his *correlation of the Jewish and Gentile missions*. At the time of Luke's writing Jewish Christianity was probably largely a spent force; very few, if any, conversions of Jews were still taking place. In most Christian communities Gentiles predominated. However, the Gentile church could neither deny nor denounce its Jewish origins. It was Luke, the Gentile, who saw the need for rooting the Gentile church in Israel. He did this in a bold way: Jesus was first and foremost the Messiah of Israel and precisely for this reason also the Savior of the Gentiles!

The Christian church may never forget that it developed organically and gradually from the womb of Israel and that it may therefore not, as an outsider, lay claim to Israel's historic prerogatives (Dillon 1979:252; cf 268). This is, unfortunately, what happened only too frequently as Christians boldly (even rashly) designated themselves as the "new Israel".

With the ascendancy of Gentile Christianity and the virtual disappearance of Jewish believers in Jesus, generations of Gentile Christians have ignored their dependence on the faith of Israel and often boasted of their new faith over against the Jews (Tiede 1980:128). Frequently, this happened on the basis of Luke-Acts; indeed, from the second century to the twentieth most expositors have read the Book of Acts at the expense of the Jews, frequently with disdain for the obvious evidence of the struggle within the Jewish context from which it originates (:128). Gentile Christianity did not, however, *replace* the Jews as the people of God; rather, in the wake of Pentecost thousands of Jews, after embracing the staggering realization that their sacred customs are to give way before the "impartiality" of God (cf Acts 10:15, 34, 47; 11:9, 17, 18), became what they truly were — "Israel". Peter's amazement at what was taking place can still be detected in his words in the house of Cornelius, "Truly I perceive that God shows no partiality!" (10:34). Into this renewed (not new) Israel, Gentile converts were incorporated. There is, for Luke, no break in the history of salvation. The church may therefore never in a spirit of triumphalism arrogate the gospel to itself and in the process turn its back on the people of the old covenant.

3. *"You are witnesses to these things"* (Lk 24:48). The noun "witness(es)" (*martys/martyres*) occurs thirteen times in Acts but only once in Luke's gospel (in the pivotal final pericope). This then, says Dillon (1979:242), is why the group has been kept together since Calvary and what the whole Lukan Easter story is about. It is dedicated to telling us not just how perplexed observers became Easter believers, but how uncomprehending eyewitnesses were made witnesses of the risen Christ, sharers of his messianic destiny, and spokespersons of the word of forgiveness in his name to all the nations.

Undoubtedly the witness terminology is crucial for the understanding of Luke's paradigm for mission. In Acts, "witness" becomes *the* appropriate term for "mission" (Gaventa 1982:416). To some extent the terms "apostle" and "witness" are synonyms. It is the apostles who are told that they will be Jesus' witnesses (cf Acts 1:2, 8). To Cornelius Peter says that Jesus was seen by "us who were chosen by God as witnesses, who ate and drank with him after he rose from the dead" (10:41). Again, in Pisidian Antioch Paul says, "For many days (Jesus) appeared to those who came up with him from Galilee to Jerusalem, who are now his witnesses to the people" (13:31). This understanding of "witness" is similar to what we find in the fourth gospel, where Jesus says to the disciples, "You . . . are witnesses because you have been with me from the beginning" (Jn 15:27).

At the same time, the term "witness" is expanded and applied to others, such as Paul (Acts 22:15; 26:16) and Stephen (22:20). Thus there is already in the Lukan writings an extension of the concept of witness to people other than the apostles. In addition, in Acts 22:20, we already sense an allusion to the "witness" (*martys*) being regarded as a "martyr".

In Acts the content of the witness (the *martyria*) refers, on the whole, to the church's proclamation of the gospel (cf Kremer 1982:147). Primarily, "gospel" alludes to the resurrection of Jesus and its significance. In Acts 1:22 Luke quotes Peter as saying that the task of the new apostle to be elected would be to "become with us *a witness to his resurrection*" (cf also Acts 10:41). Elsewhere, again, Luke seems to suggest that the *martyria* pertains not only to Jesus' resurrection, but to his entire life and ministry (cf Lk 24:48 and Acts 13:31). Jesus himself proclaimed the "(good news of) the kingdom of God" (Lk 4:43; 8:1; 9:11; 16:16). This is essentially what the witnesses in Acts also do (cf 8:12; 19:8; 20:25; 28:23, 31): the good news of the reign of God is Jesus Christ, incarnated, crucified and risen, and what he has accomplished.

The term "witness" is a very fitting one for what Luke wishes to communicate. It is evident, from Acts, that this task is entrusted to very fallible human beings who can do nothing in their own power, but are continuously dependent upon empowerment by the Spirit. But also, in a sense, they are not really called to accomplish anything, only to point to what God has done and is doing, to give testimony to what they have seen and heard and touched (cf 1 Jn 1:1). Paul and the other second generation witnesses have not seen and heard and touched Jesus, but obviously, in Luke's mind, this does not make their witness inferior. It is rendered in the same power, carries the same conviction, and issues in the same call to those who hear it.

4. *"Repentance, forgiveness of sins, and salvation"*. Luke's gospel and Acts are built on the expectation of response. The *martyria* of the missionaries aims at repentance and forgiveness (cf Lk 24:48; Acts 2:38), which leads to salvation (cf Acts 2:40, "save yourselves from this crooked generation!"). Luke formulates this more fully in Acts 26:17f, where Paul refers to what Jesus said to him on the Damascus road, "The Gentiles . . . to whom I send you to open their eyes, that they may turn from darkness to light and from the power of Satan to God, that they may receive forgiveness of sins and a place among those who are sanctified by faith in me" (cf also Kremer 1982:149). In the gospel the hosting of Jesus was equivalent to the hosting of salvation (Lk 19:9) (cf LaVerdiere and Thompson 1976:592). It is not essentially different in Acts, since salvation is in his name only. Salvation is liberation from all bondage as well as new life in Christ. The missionaries witness as people who know that life and death depend on their testimony. Therefore, in spite of all appreciation they may have for the religious life of Gentiles (cf Acts 17:22f), they continue to insist on repentance and conversion. Their urgency certainly has to do with the way they view those "outside Christ": to turn one's back on one's past is tantamount to turning from "darkness to light" (Acts 22:18; cf also the title of Gaventa 1986). Much is at stake and the witnesses cannot possibly be indifferent about the destiny of others. They therefore do not offer the invitation to join their community in a spirit of "take it or leave it" (cf Zingg 1973:209; Kremer 1982:162).

Even so, personal conversion is not a goal in itself. To interpret the work of the church as the "winning of souls" is to make conversion into a final product, which flatly contradicts Luke's understanding of the purpose of mission (Gaventa 1986:150-152). Conversion does not pertain merely to an individual's act of conviction and commitment; it moves the individual believer into the community of believers and involves a real—even a radical—change in the life of the believer, which carries with it moral responsibilities that distinguish Christians from "outsiders" while at the same time stressing their obligation to those "outsiders" (cf Malherbe 1987:49).

5. With Scheffler (1988:57-108), one could say that, for Luke, salvation actually had *six* dimensions: economic, social, political, physical, psychological, and spiritual. Luke seemed to pay special attention to the first of these. We may thus detect a major element in Luke's missionary paradigm in what he writes about *the new relationship between rich and poor*. There are, at this point, parallels between Matthew and Luke; the difference is that, whereas Matthew emphasized justice in general, Luke seemed to have a peculiar interest in *economic* justice.

Jesus' sermon in Nazareth (4:16-30) constitutes the Lukan parallel to Mark's (1:15) and Matthew's (4:17) accounts of the beginning of Jesus' public ministry. In Mark, Jesus says, "The time is fulfilled, and the kingdom of God is at hand; repent and believe in the gospel". Jesus' reading from the Isaiah scroll says essentially the same. If Jesus, anointed by the Spirit of God, proclaims good news to the poor, freedom for prisoners, and sight for the blind, and if he announces the year of the Lord's favor, he is saying that the reign of God is at hand and calling all to repentance and faith. In the context of the early church, salvation and faith in Christ could not possibly exclude succor to those who had fallen by the wayside. The "deeper healing" the disciples experienced through their encounter with Jesus could not remain barren or idle — it strove at "bearing fruit". John the Baptist already challenged those who were only interested in "spiritual" healing (3:10-14). Similarly, in Nazareth Jesus did not soar off into the heavenly heights but drew his listeners' attention to the altogether real conditions of the poor, the blind, the captives, and the oppressed (cf Lochman 1986:66). He championed "God's preferential option for the poor". He announced the Jubilee, which would inaugurate a reversal of the dismal fate of the dispossessed, the oppressed, and the sick, by calling on the wealthy and healthy to share with those who are victims of exploitation and tragic circumstances.

He did this in the teeth of the ideological defense mechanisms of the privileged, who only too frequently convince themselves that Jesus was more interested in the "correct attitude" toward wealth than in its possession and use. These mechanisms then allow free range to the privileged's unsatiable urge to move upward, socially and economically, and to pursue a hedonistic lifestyle devoid of an ethic that exalts values like self-sacrifice, restraint, and solidarity. But where self-centered sentiments reign supreme, the rich cannot claim to be involved in mission and cannot be in continuity with the Lukan Jesus and church.

It is true that, in Acts, there is much less evidence of compassion with poor and marginalized humanity than is the case in Luke's gospel. However, the context might explain at least some of this. In Acts, compassion and sharing were practiced within the Christian fold where many members were poor, so much so that Paul had to appeal to the Gentile churches to come to the aid of the poor Christians in Judea. Luke does not tire of reminding us of the sacrificial attitude that prevailed in the early days of the church in Jerusalem. They shared everything they had, he tells us (Acts 2:44f; 4:32), with the result that there was no needy person among them (4:34). If rich Christians today would only practice solidarity with poor Christians — let alone the billions of poor people who are not Christians — this in itself would be a powerful missionary testimony and a modern-day fulfillment of Jesus' sermon in Nazareth. The gospel cannot be good news if the witnesses are incapable of discerning the real issues and concerns that matter to the marginalized (cf Mazamisa 1987:99). As was the case in Jesus' own ministry, those in pain are to liberated, the poor cared for, the outcasts and rejected brought home, and all sinners offered forgiveness and salvation.

6. *"Preaching the good news of peace by Jesus Christ"* (Acts 10:36). In her fine study on Luke, Josephine Ford has drawn attention to a much-neglected aspect of the mission of Jesus according to Luke: that of *peace-making*, of nonviolent resistance to evil, of the futility and self-destructive nature of hatred and vengeance. Today, few Christians would doubt that peace-making is an intrinsic aspect of the church's missionary message. In the contemporary world, where terrorism, violence, crime, war, and poverty, often intimately related to and caused by one another, are the most important issues of the day, this aspect of

Luke's gospel is acutely pertinent (Ford 1984:137). Our missionary involvement may be very successful in other respects, but if we fail here, we stand guilty before the Lord of mission. Peace-making, I therefore suggest, is a major ingredient of Luke's missionary paradigm. The message that there is no room for vengeance in the heart of the follower of Jesus permeates both the gospel and Acts. It culminates in the account of Jesus praying for his crucifiers (Lk 23:34), which is echoed in the prayer of the dying Stephen (Acts 7:60).

Naturally, we cannot ignore Luke's own context and experience here. The horror of the Jewish War has taught him that the "peace" won through violent means has little to do with the peace Jesus offers. At the time of writing, the fledgling Christian church was still not sanctioned as an approved religion in the Empire. Luke was concerned about this and did not wish to see the church's position jeopardized.[7] His considerations were undoubtedly pragmatic, but they were also more than that. On the basis of his understanding of Jesus he just could not see how followers of Jesus could bring themselves to propagating the way of violence. Peace-making was, for him, integral to the church's missionary existence in the world.

7. Yet another dimension of Luke's missionary paradigm has to do with his *ecclesiology*. We have seen, in the previous chapter, that Matthew's gospel is preeminently the "gospel of the church". There is no church in Luke's gospel, only "disciples", "followers" of the Nazarene. Not so in Acts. One might say that what distinguishes Acts from the gospel is the church. But the two are not unrelated, in the way Conzelmann (1964) depicts it. Luke regards the life of Jesus and the story of the church as being united in one era of the Spirit (LaVerdiere and Thompson 1976:595). The lordship of Christ is not exercised in a vacuum but in the concrete historical circumstances of a community which lives under the direction of the Spirit (cf Schweizer 1971:145).

Luke presents a picture of the church as he thinks it should be, not so much as it really is (cf Schottroff & Stegemann 1986:117). Yet, even if his portrayal is idealized, there can be no doubt that the early Christian community did constitute a remarkable fellowship. The mutual acceptance of Jew and Gentile must have been particularly noteworthy. The Cornelius story demonstrates that receiving Gentiles into the faith meant entering their homes and accepting hospitality from them; the inclusion of Gentiles and table-fellowship with them were inseparably related (cf Gaventa 1986:120f).

Luke's church may be said to have a bipolar orientation, "inward" and "outward" (cf Flender 1967:166; LaVerdiere and Thompson 1976:590). First, it is a community which devotes itself "to the apostles' teaching, fellowship, the breaking of bread, and the prayers" (Acts 2:42). Teaching refers not so much (as it does in Matthew) to the contents of Jesus' preaching as to the resurrection event; fellowship refers to the new community in which barriers have been overcome; the breaking of bread refers to the eucharistic life of the community and is experienced as continuing the meals with Jesus reported in the gospel; and the prayer life of Jesus, a prominent feature in Luke's gospel, is extended into the church. All this is accomplished in the power of the Spirit: "The Church is the place where the exalted one manifests his presence and where the Holy Spirit creates anew" (Flender 1967:166).

Secondly, the community also has an outward orientation. It refuses to understand itself as a sectarian group. It is actively engaged in a mission to those still outside the pale of the gospel. And the inner life of the church is connected to its outer life (cf LaVerdiere and Thompson 1976:593).

Luke paints the picture of the Christian church at a relatively early stage of its development—one of the factors, incidentally, that indicate a composition of Acts not later than the eighties of the first century. There is, as yet, no reference to local churches institutionally united into one structure. The picture is rather that of various, larger or smaller, local associations of believers (cf Flender 1967:166; Bovon 1985:128-138). The term *ekklesia*, "church", refers to individual congregations rather than to a universal church. Only in Acts 9:31 does the term have the later, broader extension ("the church throughout Judea, Galilee, and Samaria"). The pastors of such local churches do not stand in any kind of "apostolic succession", but have been made overseers of their flocks by the Holy Spirit (cf Acts 20:28). There is, as yet, few signs of a settled ministry of bishops or elders and deacons over against the mobile ministry of apostles, prophets, and evangelists. New converts are still not primarily "church members" but "disciples" of Jesus or "believers" (Bovon 1985:137).

This "unstructured" picture of the church has, however, another side to it too. The church is intimately linked to the apostles, in a dual sense of the word. It is founded on the "teachings of the apostles" and like them sent into the world as witnesses. The "apostles" are a fixed body of persons; Matthias is elected to restore the original body of twelve (Acts 1:21f). Only these twelve are apostles, and Luke views them as important for the church. So, when the apostles in Jerusalem heard that Samaria had accepted the word of God, they sent Peter and John there. The suggestion seems to be that the work there, started "unofficially", had to be validated by the apostles—and through their praying and laying on of hands the Samaritans received the Holy Spirit (8:14-17). The first church outside Judea should not arise entirely without apostolic contact and should not become an isolated sect with no bonds of union with the apostolic church in Jerusalem (Ford 1984:95, drawing on F. D. Bruner; cf also Hahn 1965:132f).

The Cornelius episode goes further, however. Peter does not merely provide an endorsement of what others have done; he himself acts as missionary. Apostolic authority in the establishing of churches among the non-Jews is evidently important to Luke. Even Paul's mission to Gentiles (his conversion is recorded in Acts 9) cannot get underway until the apostles have implicitly ratified such a mission. The Cornelius episode and its sequel (Acts 10-12) are therefore interpolated between Paul's conversion and the beginning of his mission to Gentiles; once the apostles, through their most senior member, Peter, have endorsed a mission to Gentiles, the way is clear for the large-scale launch of Paul's lifework. After this Peter features only once more in Luke's account— at the meeting of the "Jerusalem Council", where he defends the Pauline mission (Acts 15:7-11).[8]

In Luke's view mission is, therefore, an "ecclesial" enterprise (cf Kremer 1982:161). The apostles are the nucleus of witnesses who will provide continuity between the history of Jesus and that of the church; their distinctive role is that of providing an authoritative link between Jesus and the church (Senior and Stuhlmueller 1983:266). Luke reveals no churchism, however. The apostles make mistakes and are frequently shortsighted. Often mission takes place in spite of them rather than because of them (cf Gaventa 1982:416). God often overrules them, first in the missionary outreach of the Hellenists, and then, supremely, in the paradigmatic missionary Paul, the "non-apostle", whom Luke, with bold grasp, claims for his own epoch as the great prototype of the church's missionary activity (cf Hahn 1965:134).

8. I mention one last ingredient of Luke's missionary paradigm: the fact that mission, of necessity, encounters *adversity and suffering*. In a variety of ways Luke portrays Jesus' journey from Galilee to Jerusalem (Lk 9:51-19:40) as a journey to his passion and death (cf Scheffler 1988:109-160). Sayings like 9:51; 13:33; 17:25; 18:31-34; and 24:7 underscore this and find support in the words of the two disciples on their way to Emmaus, "Was it not necessary that the Christ should suffer these things?" (24:27).

What is true of the Master is also true of his disciples. Luke shares with Mark many sayings about the future suffering of the disciples (Scheffler 1988:163f), but he adds "daily" to Jesus' words about the need for carrying a cross (9:23). In Acts, the journey of the church-in-mission parallels that of Jesus to Jerusalem. In 13:31 Paul says that the risen Jesus "appeared to those who came up with him from Galilee to Jerusalem". They are his "witnesses", which means that they must do more than report on the Lord's journey to Jerusalem. They must join him on the way and face the mortal threat he faced (Frazier 1987:40). They have to be prepared to embrace the "Jerusalem destiny" as their own (cf Dillon 1979:255), as Stephen did, who was both "witness" and "martyr" (cf Acts 22:20).

Early in Acts, Luke reports the arrest of Peter and John and their questioning by the rulers. Luke characterizes their defense as "bold". As a matter of fact, in Acts boldness *(parresia)* almost always manifests itself in the context of adversity (cf Gaventa 1982:417-420). When the believers gather together after Peter and John have been threatened by the Sanhedrin, they do not pray that their adversaries be struck down (as John and James did with reference to the Samaritans who had refused them hospitality—cf Lk 9:54); instead, they pray for boldness (Acts 4:27-30; cf Gaventa 1982:418). The juxtaposition of adversity and boldness is not accidental but integral to the entire Book of Acts (:419).

It is, however, particularly Paul's ministry that is characterized by adversity. Luke portrays him as a kind of parallel to Jesus. The parallel is, however, incomplete. Luke does not relate Paul's death as a martyr. This has often puzzled scholars, but perhaps Luke has deliberately omitted it in order to show that, for him, Paul was not a second Jesus. Even so, the parallel remains striking. After Paul's conversion the risen Lord says to Ananias, "I will show him how much he must suffer for the sake of my name" (Acts 9:16). And wherever Paul proclaims the gospel, opposition arises: in Pisidian Antioch, in Iconium, in Corinth, and finally in Rome. It is however particularly his fateful journey to Jerusalem which is, like his Master's journey to that city, charged with symbolism. There are even two announcements of the suffering that is awaiting him in Jerusalem (20:22-25; 21:10f) — announcements which remind the reader of similar sayings in the gospel concerning Jesus' passion and death (cf Kremer 1982:159, 163; Senior and Stuhlmueller 1983:276). The disciple is to share the destiny of his Master, as Stephen and James indeed did. Paul and some of the other apostles also shared this destiny; even so, in Acts this is not recorded, only that they continually live in the shadow of death (cf Stanek 1985:17). But they know that they "must enter the kingdom of God through many tribulations" (Acts 14:22).

William Frazier suggests that, on this point, Luke's writings have a significance far beyond the first-century church (1987:46). He refers, in this regard, to the Roman Catholic ritual that usually crowns the sending ceremony of missionary communities, where the new missionaries are equipped with cross or crucifix. Frazier continues:

Somewhere beneath the layers of meaning that have attached themselves to this practice from the days of Francis Xavier to our own is the simple truth enunciated by Justin and Tertullian: the way faithful Christians die is the most contagious aspect of what being a Christian means. The missionary cross or crucifix is no mere ornament depicting Christianity in general. Rather, it is a vigorous commentary on what gives the gospel its universal appeal. Those who receive it possess not only a symbol of their mission but a handbook on how to carry it out (1987:46).

Chapter 4

Mission in Paul: Invitation To Join the Eschatological Community

FIRST MISSIONARY: FIRST THEOLOGIAN

The apostle Paul has always had a special fascination for missionaries. Small wonder that, through the years, several monographs on Paul's significance for the Christian mission have been written by missionaries and missiologists. Roland Allen's *Missionary Methods: St Paul's or Ours?* (1956 [first published 1912]) occupies pride of place in this regard and has had a profound influence particularly in English-speaking missionary circles. A year after Allen, Johannes Warneck published his *Paulus im Lichte der heutigen Heidenmission*, a book which has had a comparable impact among German-speaking missionaries. The main interest of Allen, Warneck, and other missiologists after them (such as Gilliland 1983) was in Paul's missionary methods and what contemporary missionaries may learn from these. This is, of course, a legitimate pursuit, though not my primary focus in this chapter.

My reflections will differ also in another respect from those referred to above. Whereas they (and, for that matter, most earlier Pauline studies by biblical scholars) tended simply to "fuse" the Paul of the letters with the Paul of Acts, I shall concentrate virtually exclusively on the Pauline letters. Not that Acts is devoid of value in this respect; it contains much material that is unquestionably based on reliable tradition (cf Senior and Stuhlmueller 1983:162; Hengel 1986:35-39) and is, after all, our "first commentary on Paul" (Haas 1971:119). For all this, however, Acts remains a secondary source on Paul, and it is methodologically unsound to mix primary with secondary sources.

There is another limitation as regards sources. I shall restrict myself to the seven letters widely regarded as indisputably from Paul's hand: Romans, 1 and 2 Corinthians, Galatians, Philippians, 1 Thessalonians, and Philemon, without however prejudging the issue of the possible Pauline authorship of the other six letters attributed to Paul. These letters will in any case supply us with more food for thought than we can possibly digest in one chapter! It is generally agreed that 1 Thessalonians is Paul's first letter and either Romans or Philippians his last. All seven letters were written during Paul's years of active missionary service after he had left Antioch, a relatively short period of only seven or eight years (cf Hahn 1965:97; Hengel 1983b:52; Ollrog 1979:243-250), stretching from AD 49 to approximately AD 56. This means that Paul wrote his letters some fifteen to twenty years before Mark authored his gospel, and thirty or more years before Matthew and Luke wrote theirs.[1]

The missionary dimension of Paul's theology has not always been recognized. For many years he was primarily regarded as the creator of a dogmatic system. With the rise of the history-of-religions school he was viewed preeminently as a mystic. Later still the emphasis shifted to the "ecclesiastical" Paul (cf Dahl 1977a:70; Beker 1980:304). Only very gradually did biblical scholars discover (what missionaries have always known!) that Paul was first and foremost to be understood, also in his letters, as apostolic missionary. In 1899 a young New Testament scholar in Basel, Paul Wernle, published a tract entitled *Paulus der Heidenmissionar*, which was perhaps the first serious scholarly attempt to look at Paul from the perspective of his missionary calling and ministry. All Paul's letters, said Wernle, supply only one answer to the question who he was and wanted to be — an apostle of Jesus Christ, a missionary. "He knew. . . that God had sent him into the world to proclaim the gospel, not to contemplate and speculate" (1899:5 — my translation).

It was, however, not until the 1960s that the full import of this new perception of Paul was recognized and properly appraised. It is today widely acknowledged that Paul was the first Christian theologian precisely because he was the first Christian missionary (Hengel 1983b:53; cf Dahl 1977a:70; Russell 1988), that his "theology of mission is practically synonymous with the totality of (his) awesome reflections on Christian life" (Senior and Stuhlmueller 1983:161) and "practically coextensive with his entire Christian vision" (:165) so that "there is something wrong in the very distinction between Paul's mission and his theology" (Dahl 1977a:70; cf Hahn 1965:97). The "Sitz im Leben" of Pauline theology is the mission of this apostle (Hengel 1983b:50).

Paul's theology and his mission do not simply relate to each other as "theory" to "practice" in the sense that his mission "flows" *from* his theology, but rather in the sense that his theology is a missionary theology (Hultgren 1985:145) and that mission is integrally related to his identity and thought as such (:125). Paul's understanding of mission is not an abstract construct dangling from a universal principle, "but an analysis of reality triggered by an initial experience that gave Paul a new world-view" (Senior and Stuhlmueller 1983:171). This is particularly true of the epistle to the Romans (cf Legrand 1988:161-165; Russell 1988), the only letter Paul wrote to a church not founded by himself.

If this is true, one cannot really study our theme by looking for and analyzing "mission texts" in Paul's letters. One would have to examine his entire theological *corpus*. This is, of course, an awesome undertaking, not least since Paul is a most complex thinker. Small wonder that already an early Christian author had to complain about Paul's letters that "there are some things in them hard to understand" (2 Pet 3:16)! It is not any easier today, particularly in view of the many disparate interpretations of Paul that the serious student encounters.

PAUL'S CONVERSION AND CALL

Perhaps then we should begin where Paul himself began—with the event of his conversion and call. What is it that changed a Pharisee of the Pharisees (cf Gal 1:4; Phil 3:4-5) into Christ's apostle to the Gentiles, a persecutor of the early Christian movement into its chief protagonist, a person who perceived Jesus as an impostor and a threat to Judaism into one who embraced him as the center of his life, indeed of the universe? Paul himself gives only one answer: it was his encounter with the risen Christ. In his letters Paul never elaborates on this event (as does the Lukan Paul of Acts, who recounts his conversion in great detail at three occasions: Acts 9:1-19; 22:4-16; and 26:9-19; cf Gaventa 1986:52-95). In his letters Paul also refers to this event three times: Galatians 1:11-17; Philippians 3:2-11; and perhaps Romans 7:13-25 (cf Dietzfelbinger 1985:44-75; Gaventa 1986:22-36), but he does so in a manner that differs considerably from the reports in Acts. The references are strikingly sober and only serve to illustrate the non-human origin of his gospel (Beker 1980: 6f).

Several scholars have argued that we should not use the word "conversion" with reference to Paul's Damascus road experience. Their reasons are essentially twofold. First, conversion suggests a changing of religions, and Paul clearly did not change his; what we call Christianity was in Paul's time a sect within Judaism (cf Stendahl 1976:7; Beker 1980:144; Gaventa 1986:18). Second, it is unwarranted to portray Paul, as still happens, as tormented and guilt-ridden because of his sins, as experiencing an inner conflict which eventually led to his conversion. In a now classic essay, first published in Swedish in 1960, Stendahl has persuasively argued that such a "psychological" interpretation of what happened to Paul on the road to Damascus reflects a typical modern understanding of the event (Stendahl 1976:78-96; cf 7-23). The phenomenon of the "introspective conscience", of penetrating self-examination coupled with a yearning to acquire certainty of salvation, is a typically Western one, says Stendahl. It would be totally anachronistic to assume that Paul shared this trait. Truth to tell, it was not until Augustine that such religious introspection really began to manifest itself. He was the first Christian to write something so oriented to the self as a spiritual autobiography, his *Confessions*. This practice was developed and reinforced during the Middle Ages and eventually canonized, as far as Protestantism is concerned, in the "conversion" of Martin Luther who was, not by accident, an Augustinian monk (Stendahl 1976:16f; 82f). For the last several centuries it has been customary to read Paul through the eyes of Luther, as it were, and to universalize the typical Western conversion experience by not only reading it back into the New Testament, but also declaring it mandatory for all new converts to the Christian faith. Such an experience is not what interests Paul, however. Neither is it what he expects of the people to whom he proclaims the gospel (cf also Krass 1978:70-72; Beker 1980:6-8; Senior and Stuhlmueller 1983:169-171).

This circumstance has led Stendahl and others to suggest that it is preferable not to use "conversion language" for what happened to Paul (and, by implication, for what Paul expected to happen in his mission work). Instead of referring to Paul's "conversion" we should, rather, talk about his "call". "Paul does not speak biographically of his 'Damascus experience', but theologically of his being called to be an apostle to the Gentiles" (Wilckens 1959:274 — my translation; cf Hengel 1983b:53; Beker 1980:6-10; Hultgren 1985:125; and particularly Stendahl 1976:7-23 and Dietzfelbinger 1985:44-82, 88f). Whenever Paul refers to the appearance of Christ to himself, he claims that he was thereby called and commissioned as an apostle, and he does this with unmistakable allusions to the prophetic calls of Isaiah and Jeremiah. Like them, his vocation originated in a decisive act of God and was communicated to him through a revelation and a vision (cf Gal 1:15f). What is often referred to as his conversion experience is absorbed by the greater reality of his apostolic calling.

The emphasis on Paul's calling is certainly a most important correction to the traditional understanding of Paul's conversion. Even so, Stendahl and others go too far by regarding what happened to Paul exclusively in terms of a call. In a recent study on conversion in the New Testament, Gaventa has distinguished between *alternation* (a relatively limited form of change which actually develops out of one's own past), *transformation* (a radical change of perspective which does not require a rejection or negation of the past or of previously held values, but nevertheless involves a new perception, a re-cognition of the past — in the language of Thomas Kuhn "a paradigm shift"), and *conversion* (a pendulum-like change in which there is a rupture between past and present, with the past portrayed in strongly negative terms) (Gaventa 1986:4-14). Stendahl seems to understand what happened to Paul in terms of an alternation. Paul is in basic continuity with his past to which is added "only" a calling to the Gentile mission. However, what Paul himself describes in Galatians 1:11-17 does not suggest that what has occurred to him can be subsumed under this category. Paul underwent a radical change in values, self-definition, and commitments. "Where in the orthodoxy of the Torah was there room for a crucified Christ?" asks Meyer (1986:162), and he answers, "Nowhere". Paul experienced a fundamental revision of his perception of Jesus of Nazareth and of the salvific value of the Law; and in spite of the many and important elements of his worldview that remained essentially unaltered (to which I shall return) it is preferable to use the term "conversion" (or, at least, "transformation") for what happened to him, as Gaventa demonstrates in a very thorough analysis of the evidence (1986:17-51; cf Senior and Stuhlmueller 1983:168). It was indeed a primordial experience and one that Paul understood to be paradigmatic of that of every Christian (Gaventa 1986:38).

So even Peter, Paul, and John, who had lived as righteous Jews, had to experience something else in order to be members of the people of God; they had to have faith in Christ (Sanders 1983:172). The Christ-event signifies the reversal of the ages and denotes, for Paul, the proclamation of the new state of affairs that God has initiated in Christ (cf Beker 1980:7f). The Law as way of salvation is superseded by the crucified and risen Messiah. One of the things those who wish to follow Christ have to die to is the law (Rom 7:4), which means that they have to abandon or give up something — and this is conversion language (cf Sanders 1983:177f).

The encounter with Jesus radically altered Paul's understanding of the course of history; that Jesus was the Messiah could only mean for a Jew that the final age had indeed begun (cf Senior and Stuhlmueller 1983:169). Paul understands this to mean that salvation in Christ is now to be offered to the Gentile world. In his experience, and according to his own testimony, his conversion and his call to the Gentile mission coincide (Zeller 1982:173). Hahn puts it well: "His concept of apostleship is characterized by the fact of his being simultaneously converted, entrusted with the gospel, and sent to the Gentiles" (1965:98). The risen Christ transformed the erstwhile persecutor into his special ambassador: God, he says "was pleased to reveal his Son to me, in order that I might preach him among the Gentiles" (Gal 1:16). There is indeed, in light of Paul's own testimony, no reason to doubt his claim that his conversion and commissioning coincided (cf Dietzfelbinger 1985:138, 142-144).[2]

Paul, or rather Saul, was from the school of Hillel, which was more open to Gentiles than other rabbinic schools. It is therefore possible that, before he became a Christian, Paul had been well-acquainted with and perhaps even actively involved in Jewish proselytism. This factor most probably had a formative influence also on Paul the Christian (cf Hengel 1983b:53). More important, Saul's opposition to the Jesus movement had focused specifically on the Greek-speaking diaspora synagogues in Jerusalem and elsewhere, and it was in these circles, originally under the leadership of Stephen, that the first steps toward a Christian outreach to Gentiles were taken (cf Hengel 1983b:53f; Ollrog 1979:155-157). Paul inherited the gospel he was to proclaim from the very people he had persecuted (Beker 1980:341; Zeller 1982:173; for a detailed interpretation and evaluation of Paul's persecution of Jewish Christians, cf Dietzfelbinger 1985:4-42). By the time he embarked on his missionary journeys, Christian missionary activity had already spread across the Empire, at least as far as Rome. Thus, even if Paul himself claims that the call to the Gentile mission coincided with his conversion, it is clear that his Pharisaic past and his contacts with Hellenistic Jews played a role in this. It is also likely that he only gradually embraced the full significance of his call; the most energetic part of his mission to the Gentiles only began some years after his Damascus experience, in the wake of the events described in Galatians 2:11ff and the apostles' council in Jerusalem (cf Hengel 1983b:50; Zeller 1982:173; Senior and Stuhlmueller 1983:169).

It is important to note that the response of Hellenistic Jews to the gospel was varied. Many Greek-speaking Jews were filled with contempt for and abhorrence of the pagan world, and were fiercely loyal to their own tradition; they were therefore extremely hostile to the new "sect". It was from these circles that Paul originated. Other Hellenistic Jews reacted more positively. They were the ones Paul began to emulate after his Damascus road experience; they constituted the real bridge between Jesus and Paul. All three "groups" (Jesus, the Hellenists, and Paul) had in common an unconditional openness to the outsider (cf Hengel 1983a:29; Dietzfelbinger 1985:141; Wedderburn 1988: passim). It is equally important to point out that Paul never abandoned the theological views he inherited from the *hellenistai*; at the same time, he soon went beyond those (cf Dietzfelbinger 1985:141; Meyer 1986: 117, 169f, 206; Hengel 1986:82-85).

If it is true that Paul is not the initiator of the Christian mission to Gentiles, it is equally true that he had no intention of breaking with the Jerusalem leadership. His relationship with Jewish Christianity is often misconstrued, says Beker, who adds:

> (Liberal scholarship) portrayed Paul as the lonely genius who, after the apostolic council in Jerusalem and his quarrel with Peter and Barnabas in Antioch . . . breaks entirely with Jerusalem. He is described as one who turns his back on Judaism and Jewish Christianity and is intent on making Christianity an entirely Gentile religion based on a law-free gospel (1980:331).

On several occasions Paul, in fact, clearly reveals his passionate desire to remain in full fellowship with the Jerusalem church, particularly as represented by the three "pillars" (Gal 2:9); in 1 Corinthians 15:11 he even claims that he is preaching the same gospel they preach (cf Haas 1971:46-51; Dahl 1977a:71f; Senior and Stuhlmueller 1983:164). Paul is not the "second founder" of Christianity, the person who turned the religion of Jesus into the religion about Christ. He did not invent the gospel about Jesus as the Christ—he inherited it (cf Beker 1980:341).

Paul's reasons for maintaining cordial relationships with the Jerusalem leadership are both practical and theological (cf Holmberg 1978:14-57). To begin with, he lays his gospel before "those who were of repute", lest somehow, he says, "I should be running or had run in vain" (Gal 2:2). This practical consideration—the success of his mission work among Gentiles should not be jeopardized by the possibility of opposition to it—is, however, intimately related to theological reflections, particularly to Paul's passionate convictions about the indestructible unity of the church made up of Jews and Gentiles: "The mission of the church cannot succeed without the unity of the church in the truth of the gospel" (Beker 1980:306; cf 331f; Hahn 1984:282f; Meyer 1986:169f). Paul's collection from his Gentile congregations for the poor Christians in Jerusalem is one way of symbolizing that unity (cf Haas 1971:52f; Beker 1980:306; Hultgren 1985:145; Meyer 1986:183f); it is, at the same time, a recognition of the privileged position of the Jerusalem community in salvation history (cf Brown 1980:209).

Paul is, however, not interested in unity for its own sake, or in unity at all costs. He does not hesitate to "oppose Peter to his face" (Gal 2:11) or to pronounce a curse on Judaizers in Galatia (Gal 1:7-9) and on the "different gospel" in Corinth (2 Cor 11:4), even if such action may, in the eyes of some, jeopardize the unity of the church (cf Beker 1980:306). "Paul cannot bear to be repudiated by the Jerusalem authorities, but he is equally unable to accept their right to pass judgment on his preaching" (Brown 1980:206). He therefore passionately defends his right to be called an apostle, completely on a par with any of those who have walked with Jesus. Like them, his apostleship is derived not from tradition but from an encounter with the risen Lord, who commissioned him to be his ambassador and representative (cf Wilckens 1959:275; Dahl 1977a:71f; Hengel 1983b:59f).

Paul's ministry thus unfolds in a creative tension between loyalty to the first apostles and their message on the one hand and an overpowering awareness of the uniqueness of his own calling and commission on the other. In Paul's usage, contrary to that of the other apostles, "the words 'gospel' and 'apostle' are correlates, and both are missionary terms" (Dahl 1977a:71). It should therefore come as no surprise that, of all New Testament writers, Paul gives the most profound and most systematic presentation of a universal Christian missionary vision (cf Senior and Stuhlmueller 1983:161).

I shall now attempt to trace some of the distinctive features of this vision and practice.

PAUL'S MISSIONARY STRATEGY

Mission to the Metropolises

The characteristics of the Pauline understanding of mission just mentioned, and others, manifest themselves first of all in what one (for lack of a better term) may call Paul's "missionary strategy".

During the first decades of the early Christian movement there were, speaking in general, three main types of missionary enterprises: (1) the wandering preachers who moved from place to place in the Jewish land and proclaimed the imminent reign of God (exemplified in the prophets of the Sayings-Source whom we met in chapter 1); (2) Greek-speaking Jewish Christians who embarked on a mission to Gentiles, first from Jerusalem (often forced to leave the city because of persecutions) and then from Antioch; and (3) Judaizing Christian missionaries who, according to 2 Corinthians and Galatians, went to already existing Christian churches in order to "correct" what they regarded as a false interpretation of the gospel.[3] For his own missionary program Paul takes over elements from the first two types mentioned above; at the same time he modifies these elements decisively (cf Ollrog 1979:150-161; Zeller 1982:179f). Perhaps one could say that his own understanding of his mission is best expressed in a passage toward the end of his letter to the Romans (15:15-21; cf Legrand 1988:154-156, 158-161):

But on some points I have written to you very boldly by way of reminder, because of the grace given me by God to be a minister of Christ Jesus to the Gentiles in the priestly service of the gospel of God, so that the offering of the Gentiles may be acceptable, sanctified by the Holy Spirit. In Christ Jesus, then, I have reason to be proud of my work for God. For I will not venture to speak of anything except what Christ has wrought through me to win obedience from the Gentiles, by word and deed, by the power of signs and wonders, by the power of the Holy Spirit, so that from Jerusalem and as far round as Illyricum I have fully preached the gospel of Christ, thus making it my ambition to preach the gospel, not where Christ has already been named, lest I build on another man's foundation, but as it is written, "They shall see who have never been told of him, and they shall understand who have never heard of him".

From Acts one may get the impression that Paul was, almost exclusively, an itinerant preacher. This is not correct, particularly in view of the fact that in some places he stayed for longer periods (about one and a half years in Corinth, two to three years in Ephesus). It may therefore be more appropriate to say, with Ollrog (1979:125-129; 158), that Paul was engaged in *"Zentrumsmission"*, that is, mission in certain strategic centers. He frequently speaks of his mission as directed toward various countries and geographical regions (Gal 1:17, 21; Rom 15:19, 23, 26, 28; 2 Cor 10:16) (cf Hultgren 1985:133). There is undoubtedly a certain method in his selection of these centers (even if Wernle goes too far when he says, "With a veritable eagle's view he studies the missionary map from his vantage point and traces in advance his route on it" [1899:17 — my translation]). He concentrates on the district or provincial capitals, each of which stands for a whole region: Philippi for Macedonia (Phil 4:15), Thessalonica for Macedonia and Achaia (1 Thes 1:7f), Corinth for Achaia (1 Cor 16:15; 2 Cor 1:1), and Ephesus for Asia (Rom 16:5; 1 Cor 16:19; 2 Cor 1:8) (Hultgren 1985:132; cf Kasting 1969:105-108; Haas 1971:83-86; Hengel 1983b:49f; Ollrog 1979:126; Zeller 1982:180-182). These "metropolises" are the main centers as far as communication, culture, commerce, politics, and religion are concerned (cf Haas 1971:85). To say that Paul "did not think in terms of individual 'gentiles' so much as 'nations' " (Hultgren 1985:133; cf Haas 1971:35) is, however, misleading and, actually, an anachronism. Paul thinks regionally, not ethnically; he chooses cities that have a representative character. In each of these he lays the foundations for a Christian community, clearly in the hope that, from these strategic centers, the gospel will be carried into the surrounding countryside and towns. And apparently this indeed happened, for in his very first letter, written to the believers in Thessalonica less than a year after he first arrived there (Malherbe 1987:108), he says, "The word of the Lord (has) sounded forth from you in Macedonia and Achaia" (1 Thes 1:8).

Paul's missionary vision is worldwide, at least as regards the world known to him. Up to the time of the apostolic council (AD 48) the missionary outreach to Gentiles was probably confined to Syria and Cilicia (cf Gal 1:21; the church in Rome, which perhaps dates back to the early forties of the first century AD, began as a Jewish Christian church). Soon after the Council, however, Paul begins to see mission in "ecumenical" terms: the entire inhabited world has to be reached with the gospel.[4] And since Rome is the capital of the empire, it is natural that he would contemplate a visit to this metropolis (cf Rom 1:13); however, when he is informed of the existence of a Christian community there, he postpones his visit to a later period when he would call upon the Roman Christians en route to Spain (Rom 15:24) (cf Zeller 1982:182). Meanwhile he concentrates his efforts in the predominantly Greek-speaking parts of the empire, in a region extending from Jerusalem to Illyricum (Rom 15:19). Soon, however, he would attempt to go to Spain.

Does this mean that Paul rushes breathlessly through the Roman Empire as an announcer of the imminent end of the world, as is sometimes suggested (Conzelmann, quoted by Hengel 1983b:169, note 22; cf Wernle 1899:18)? Most scholars disagree (cf, *inter alia*, Bieder 1965:31f; Kasting 1969:107f; Beker 1980:52; Zeller 1982:185f; Hultgren 1985:133; Kertelge 1987:372f). Indeed, several important circumstances militate against such an interpretation. To begin with, the end remains, for Paul, always incalculable—the day of the Lord will come like a thief in the night (1 Thes 5:2). At another occasion, some years later, he says no more than that "salvation is nearer to us now than when we first believed" (Rom 13:11). Furthermore, Paul is founding local churches, which he seeks to nurture through occasional pastoral visits and lengthy letters, and by sending his fellow-workers to them. He intercedes on behalf of his congregations and counsels them about a great variety of very practical and down-to-earth matters; he waits for them to grow in spiritual maturity and stewardship, and to become beacons of light in their environment. All of this obviously takes time. Nevertheless, it takes place within the framework of a fervent eschatological expectation. Whereas, in some early Christian circles, an ardent expectation of the imminent end tended to dampen the idea of a wide-ranging missionary outreach, exactly the opposite is true in Paul's case: "He is the herald of the gospel, Christ's ambassador to the Gentiles, an example for his churches and their intercessor and counselor, *and all of this is part of his eschatological mission*" (Dahl 1977a:73; emphasis added). There is, then, no abiding conflict between apostolicity and apocalyptic in Paul, only a creative tension. In the words of Beker (1980:52):

> There is passion in Paul—but it is passion of sobriety; and there is impatience in Paul—but it is impatience tempered by the patience of preparing the world for its coming destiny, which the Christ-event has inaugurated... apocalyptic fervor and missionary strategy go hand in hand... (They) do not contradict each other, as if the one paralyzes the strength of the other.

These observations may also help us to understand Paul's strange statement in Romans 15:23, "I no longer have any room for work in these regions" (he refers to the whole region from Jerusalem to Illyricum). He therefore, he says, has to move on to other regions, since he has made it his ambition to preach the gospel not where Christ has already been named, "lest I build on another man's foundation" (Rom 15:20). Hengel (1983b:52) puts this down to Paul's "ambition", which is hardly an adequate explanation. Why then does Paul make these two statements? Probably for two reasons: (a) In view of the shortness of time and the urgency of the task it would be bad stewardship to go to places where others have already evangelized; (b) he is not suggesting that the work of mission is completed in the regions where he has worked, but simply that there are now viable churches, which may reach out into their respective hinterlands; therefore he has to move on to the "regions beyond".

Paul and His Colleagues

Another characteristic of Paul's missionary practice lies in the way in which he makes use of a variety of associates. Ollrog has argued for the view that these men (and women, such as Priscilla) were not just Paul's assistants or subordinates but truly his colleagues (Ollrog 1979:passim). Ollrog distinguishes among three categories of associates: first the most intimate circle, comprising Barnabas, Silvanus, and particularly Timothy (:92f); second, the "independent co-workers", such as Priscilla and Aquila, and Titus (:94f); and third, and perhaps most important, representatives from local churches, such as Epaphroditus, Epaphras, Aristarchus, Gaius, and Jason (:95-106). The churches, Ollrog argues, put these persons at Paul's disposal for limited periods (:119-125). Through them the churches themselves are represented in the Pauline mission and become co-responsible for the work (:121). As a matter of fact, not being represented in this venture constitutes a shortcoming in a local church; such a church has excluded itself from participating in the Pauline missionary enterprise (:122).

In his fellow-workers Paul embraces the churches and these identify with his missionary efforts; this is the primary intention of the cooperative mission (:125). Where members of the community are chosen for this work they put their charisma for a certain period at the disposal of the mission (:131), and through their delegates the churches themselves become partners in the entire enterprise (:132). The role of the co-workers only becomes transparent if seen in relation to the churches (:160). This ministry demonstrates the coming of age of the churches (:160, 235). The foundational relationship between the co-workers and their local churches has to be taken into account at all times (:234). Theologically this signifies that Paul regards his mission as a function of the church (:234f).

Paul's Apostolic Self-Consciousness

Of particular significance in this respect is Paul's apostolic self-consciousness and the way in which he presents himself as model to be emulated, not only by his fellow-workers, but by all Christians. Referring to 1 Thessalonians 1:6 ("And you became imitators of us and of the Lord"), Malherbe writes, "Paul's method of shaping a community was to gather converts around himself and by his own behavior to demonstrate what he taught" (1987:52). He adds that, in doing so, Paul follows a method widely practiced at the time, particularly by moral philosophers. As with serious philosophers, Paul's life cannot be distinguished from what he preaches; his life authenticates his gospel (:54; cf 68). In spite of remarkable similarities between him and the moral philosophers in this respect there are, nevertheless, also some distinctive differences, both as regards the philosophers' understanding of themselves and their tasks and with respect to the way they carry out their responsibilities. In their exhortations the philosophers point to other individuals as examples; Paul however offers *himself* as a model to be emulated. But, and this is important, Paul's confidence in offering himself as archetype does not reside in himself and his own accomplishments; rather, he continually refers to *God*'s initiative and power in his life (:59). By the same token Paul's boldness is not, as is the case with the philosophers, based on a moral freedom gained by reason and exercise of the will; it is, as he clearly states in 1 Thessalonians 2:1-5, given by God. This enables him to emphasize his own self-giving to a degree that the philosophers could not (:59). Since he does not think that his life can be distinguished from his gospel (:68), he is convinced that, through his life and ministry, God is calling people into the divine kingdom and glory (:109).

Paul's amazing self-confidence and self-consciousness has been a stumbling block for many. How can he be proud of or boast about his work (Rom 15:17 and several other references)? Is boasting (cf the word-group *kauchaomai/kauchema/kauchesis* in Paul's letters, particularly 2 Corinthians) a Christian virtue? And dare mortal beings summon others to "imitate" (cf the references to *mimeomai* and *mimetes* in Paul's letters, as well as Haas 1971:73-79) them? This certainly conflicts with proprieties as we understand them today unless we keep in mind that the unconditional obedience on which Paul insists and the authority to which he lays claim are not for himself, but for the gospel, that is, for Christ (cf Ollrog 1979:201). And the demands he makes on himself are far greater than those he makes on others: "I pommel my body and subdue it, lest after preaching to others I myself should be disqualified" (1 Cor 9:27). It is fully in line with this when he says that he would rather boast of his weaknesses, since Christ has taught him, "My grace is sufficient for you, for my power is made perfect in weakness" (2 Cor 12:9). He can even say, "For when I am weak, then I am strong" (2 Cor 12:10), an expression Ernst Fuchs once referred to as "the most famous paradox in the entire New Testament".[5] His decision to support himself through the work of his own hands and not to accept any financial support from the churches he has founded (except, interestingly enough, the church in Philippi; cf Phil 4:15) has to be understood in the same spirit. He worked day and night, he writes to the Thessalonians, that he might not burden any of them while he preached to them the gospel of God (1 Thes 2:9). The thrust of the argument lies in the last part of the phrase just referred to; he forfeits his right (for this is what it is; cf 1 Cor 9:4-12) in this respect, so as to make the gospel he proclaims more credible. He asserts this in yet another way in 1 Corinthians 9:19, "For though I am free from all men, I have made myself a slave to all, *that I might win the more*" (cf Haas 1971:70-72). Necessity is laid upon Paul: "Woe to me if I do not preach the gospel!" (1 Cor 9:16).

PAUL'S MISSIONARY MOTIVATION

We have in the meantime, almost imperceptibly, moved from Paul's missionary *strategy* to his missionary *motivation*. Michael Green (1970:236-255) has suggested that three main missionary motives were operative in the early church, all of which are particularly clearly identifiable in Paul: a sense of gratitude, a sense of responsibility, and a sense of concern. It may not really be possible to subdivide missionary motives in this way since they very frequently overlap in Paul. Even so, Green's analysis may help us to get a better grasp of Paul's understanding of mission, so I shall use it, but in reverse order.

A Sense of Concern

It is important to realize that, in his assessment of paganism, Paul concurs with the views of the Judaism of his time. This judgment is decidedly negative, not least because of what Jews considered to be the low morality of Gentiles; catalogs of their vices appear in 1 Corinthians 5:10; 6:9-11, and elsewhere (cf Green 1970:249f; Bussmann 1971:120f; Zeller 1982:167; Meeks 1983:94f; Malherbe 1987:95).[6] It is, however, above everything else, *idolatry* that Paul deems reprehensible. Idols are fabrications of the perverted human mind (cf Rom 1:23, 25), and yet, in spite of the fact that they are human creations, they take control of people, who are "led astray to dumb idols" (1 Cor 12:2) and are "in bondage to beings that by nature are no gods", slaves of "weak and beggarly elemental spirits" (Gal 4:9f). Their being in bondage to idols is therefore due not to ignorance (as the Stoics would argue) but to willfulness. In fact, "idolatry" is not limited to worship of idols but includes a broader sense of allegiance to anything that is false (cf Bussmann 1971:38-56; Senior and Stuhlmueller 1983:186; Hultgren 1985:139f; Grant 1986:46-49; Malherbe 1987:31f).

Over against this pervasive idolatry of the Greco-Roman world Paul proclaims (in full harmony with his Jewish religious roots) the uncompromising message of one God who lays exclusive claim to people's loyalty.[7] In absolute contrast to the idols Paul describes God as "living and true" (1 Thes 1:9). We know this, not simply because we infer it from God's miraculous creation and governance of the existing world together with his continuing revelation through his prophets; no, we know it above all because God has revealed himself to us through his Son (Gal 4:4f) (cf Bussmann 1971:75-80; Senior and Stuhlmueller 1983:186; Grant 1986:47).

This is the point where Paul's concern comes into play. He sees humanity outside Christ as utterly lost, en route to perdition (cf 1 Cor 1:18; 2 Cor 2:15), and in dire need of salvation (see also Eph 2:12). The idea of imminent judgment on those who "do not obey the truth" (Rom 2:8) is a recurring theme in Paul. Precisely for this reason he allows himself no relaxation. He has to proclaim, to as many as possible, deliverance "from the wrath to come" (1 Thes 1:10). He is Christ's ambassador; God makes his appeal to the lost through Paul and his fellow-workers: "We beseech you on behalf of Christ, be reconciled to God!" (2 Cor 5:20) (cf also Lippert 1968:148; Zeller 1982:167f, 185; Meeks 1983:95; Senior and Stuhlmueller 1983:186; Hahn 1984:275; Boring 1986:277f; Malherbe 1987:32f).

The primary concern of Paul's preaching is not, however, the "wrath to come" (cf Legrand 1988:163). He never dwells in any detail on this. God's wrath is, rather, the dark foil for the positive message he proclaims: salvation through Christ and the imminent triumph of God. His gospel is *good news*, addressed to people who have willfully sinned, who are without excuse, and who deserve God's judgment (Rom 1:20, 23, 25; 2:1f, 5-10), but to whom God in his kindness is providing an opportunity for repentance (Rom 2:4) (cf Malherbe 1987:32).[8] Where his listeners indeed respond positively, they turn, says Paul in his very first letter, "to God from idols, to serve a living and true God" (1 Thes 1:10). "Conversion has brought the converts from the realm of death and unreality to the realm of the life and reality of God" (Grant 1986:46f). This is a metamorphosis far more fundamental than anything the philosophers envisage; for Paul, "the goal is not the achievement of one's natural potential but the formation of Christ in the believer" (Malherbe 1987:33, referring to Gal 4:19 and Rom 8:29). The expression "turning to God from idols" in 1 Thessalonians 1:10 is language inherited from the Jewish diaspora, "but it is immediately reinforced by an eschatological clause with distinctive Christian content: 'And to await from the heavens his Son, whom he raised from the dead, Jesus who rescues us from the wrath to come'" (Meeks 1983:95). Salvation is, for Paul, the experience of undeserved liberation through the encounter with the one God and Father of Jesus Christ (Walter 1979:430). Other expressions he uses in this regard include "adoption as sons", "the redemption of our bodies", "being called to freedom", "delivered from a deadly peril", "knowing God", and (frequently) "justified".

The purpose of Paul's mission, then, is to lead people to salvation in Christ. This anthropological perspective is, however, not the ultimate objective of his ministry. In and through his mission he is preparing the world for God's coming glory and for the day when all the universe will praise him (cf Zeller 1982:186f; Beker 1984:57).

A Sense of Responsibility

Paul's sense of concern for the Gentiles of the Roman Empire evinces itself in a deep awareness that it is his *obligation* to proclaim the gospel to them. It is a charge laid upon him, an *anangke* ("inescapable necessity"): "Woe to me if I do not preach the gospel!" (1 Cor 9:16). In the epistle to the Romans he frequently employs the words *opheilema* and *opheiletes* ("debt"; "debtor") in this regard. Romans 1:14 is particularly pertinent here: "I am under obligation (*opheiletes eimi*) both to Greeks and to barbarians, both to the wise and to the foolish". This is, as Paul Minear (1961:42-44) has shown, a rather puzzling expression. A sense of debt presupposes (a) a gift from one person to another, and (b) knowledge and appreciation of both the gift and the giver. But Paul neither knows his "creditors" nor have they given him anything. So the normal way in which the expression "debt" is used would make no sense here. Paul is, however, indebted to *Christ*, and this is transmuted into a debt to those whom Christ wishes to bring to salvation. Obligation to him who dies produces obligation to those for whom he died. Faith in Christ creates a mutuality of indebtedness; it recognizes that the believer is as deeply indebted to unbelievers as to Christ. Yet in no sense does it depend upon the tangible contributions of the creditors to the debtors, only and wholly upon the gift of God in Christ. Precisely for this reason the idea of "reward" does not enter into the picture; that would presuppose that Paul is of his own choice engaged in mission in order to gain something from it (cf, once again, 1 Cor 9:16).

In his second letter to the Corinthians Paul employs another term in an attempt to give expression to the "debt" he has: "Therefore, knowing the fear of the Lord, we persuade men" (2 Cor 5:11). Green interprets correctly, "This ... is not the craven fear of the underdog, but the loving fear of the friend and trusted servant who dreads disappointing his beloved Master" (1970:245). Here also is to be found the reason why Paul dreads the possibility that "after preaching to others I myself should be disqualified" (1 Cor 9:27).

All these references emphasize an indebtedness to both Christ and the people to whom Paul is sent. The latter element becomes more prominent in the famous passage in 1 Corinthians:

> I have made myself a slave to all, that I might win the more. To the Jews I became as a Jew, in order to win Jews; to those under the law I became as one under the law—though not being myself under the law—that I might win those under the law. To those outside the law I became as one outside the law—not being without law toward God but under the law of Christ—that I might win those outside the law. To the weak I became weak, that I might win the weak. I have become all things to all men, that I might by all means save some. I do it all for the sake of the gospel, that I may share in its blessings (9:19-23).

These verses really say more about Paul's sense of responsibility than about his missionary methods. No doubt they suggest that Paul's manner of preaching the gospel is "one of flexibility, sensitivity, and empathy" (Beker 1984:58), and that, for him, mission means neither the Hellenization of Jews nor the Judaization of Greeks (Steiger 1980:46; Stegemann 1984:301f). However, in the entire context this is peripheral to what Paul is saying. He is not offering guidelines for cross-cultural missionary accommodation (Bieder 1965:32-35). The last phrase quoted shows "how little this passage has to do with a mere art of adjustment or a successful missionary technique. The freedom of his service is not a matter of his discretion; it is a matter of his obedience to the gospel, so much so that his own eternal salvation is at stake" (Bornkamm 1966:197f). Paul is essentially saying two things here: the gospel of Jesus Christ is intended for all, without any distinction; and he, Paul, is under an inescapable obligation to try to "win"[9] as many as possible. Precisely for this reason Paul insists that no unnecessary stumbling blocks be put in the way of prospective converts or of "weak" believers, for instance in 1 Corinthians 8-10 where he argues the case about eating or not eating meat offered to idols (cf Meeks 1983:69f; 97-100, 105). It is not necessary for Christians from different backgrounds to become carbon copies of one another.

It may be instructive to turn, at this point, to what Paul has to say about the believers' attitude and conduct toward "outsiders", as this may throw additional light on his understanding of his own and other Christians' responsibility. First, he impresses upon his readers that they are a community of a special kind. Meeks has highlighted several features which are significant for the self-understanding of Christians in Paul's letters (1983:84-96; cf van Swigchem 1955:40-57). They constitute a community with boundaries, a fact which finds expression in Paul's use of "the language of belonging" (which emphasizes the internal cohesion and solidarity of the group—Paul uses a great variety of special terms for believers) and "the language of separation" (to distinguish them from those who do not belong). They have to behave in an exemplary way, because they are "saints", God's "elect", "called", and "known" by God.

The suggestion therefore is that, simply because of their unique status as

God's children, their conduct should be exceptional. However, and this is the second point, very frequently Paul says that an exemplary demeanor is required for the sake of the Christian witness toward outsiders. It is true, of course, that Paul often portrays non-members of the community in rather negative terms. I have already referred to some of the expressions he uses in this regard. Other terms include "unrighteous", "nonbelievers", and "those ... who obey wickedness". And yet, it is not words like these, or others such as "adversaries" or "sinners", which become technical terms for non-Christians. There are, says van Swigchem, really only two such technical terms in the Pauline letters: *hoi loipoi* ("the others") and *hoi exo* ("outsiders"). Both of these carry a milder connotation than some of the other more emotive expressions Paul sporadically uses (1955:57-59, 72)[10] and are remarkably free from condemnation.

Paul would rather criticize those who profess to be believers: "For what have I to do with judging outsiders? Is it not those inside the church whom you are to judge? God judges those outside" (1 Cor 5:12f). So the weight of his emphasis is put on the conduct of "insiders" in relation to "outsiders" and for the latter's sake. Christians should not jeopardize relationships with outsiders by irresponsible, disorderly lives. They should live in such a way that they "command the respect of outsiders" (1 Thes 4:12). Paul admonishes them "to live quietly" (1 Thes 4:11), but not in the Stoic sense of retiring into contemplation for its own sake or in the Epicurean sense of contemptuously shunning society; rather, Christians should, by living quietly, aim at earning the approval of society at large (Malherbe 1987:96-99, 105; cf Meeks 1983:106). In addition, Christians are to love all people (1 Thes 3:12). Lippert lists the concrete ways in which this love ought to manifest itself: Christians should relinquish all desires to judge others; their behavior should be exemplary over against the civil order; they should be ready to serve others; they are called upon to forgive, pray for, and bless others (1968:153f; cf Malherbe 1987:95-107).

Earning the respect and even admiration of outsiders is, however, not enough. The Christians' lifestyle should not only be exemplary, but also winsome. It should attract outsiders and invite them to join the community. Put differently, the believers should practice a missionary lifestyle. It is true that the Christian community is exclusive and has definite boundaries (Meeks 1983:84-105), but there are "gates in the boundaries" (:105). Meeks correctly points out that a sect which claims to have a monopoly on salvation usually does not welcome free interchange with outsiders. A case in point is the Essene communities at Qumran. The Pauline churches, however, are manifestly different. They are characterized by a missionary drive which sees in the outsider a potential insider (:105-107). Their "exemplary existence" (Lippert 1968:164) is a powerful magnet that draws outsiders toward the church.

On the other hand, the missionary dimension of the conduct of the Pauline Christians remains implicit rather than explicit. They are, to employ a distinction introduced by Hans-Werner Gensichen (1971:168-186), *"missionary"* (*"missionarisch"*) rather than *"missionizing"* (*"missionierend"*). References to specific cases of direct missionary involvement by the churches are rare in Paul's letters (cf Lippert 1968:127f, 175f).[11] But this is not just to be seen as a deficiency.

Rather, Paul's whole argument is that the attractive lifestyle of the small Christian communities gives credibility to the missionary outreach in which he and his fellow-workers are involved. The primary responsibility of "ordinary" Christians is not to go out and preach, but to support the mission project through their appealing conduct and by making "outsiders" feel welcome in their midst.

A Sense of Gratitude

Only now do we reach the deepest level of Paul's missionary motivation. He goes to the ends of the earth because of the overwhelming experience of the love of God he has received through Jesus Christ. "The Son of God ... loved me and gave himself for me", he writes to the Galatians (2:20), and to the Romans he says, "God's love has been poured into our hearts" (5:5). The classical expression of Paul's awareness of God's love as a motivation for mission is to be found in 2 Corinthians 5. In verse 11 he says, "Therefore, knowing the fear of the Lord, we persuade men". As I have argued, "fear" here refers to Paul's desire not to disappoint his beloved Master (cf Green 1970:245). In verse 14 he then articulates the positive side of what he says in verse 11, "For the love of Christ controls us".

For Paul, then, the most elemental reason for proclaiming the gospel to all is not just his concern for the lost, nor is it primarily the sense of an obligation laid upon him, but rather a sense of *privilege*. Through Christ, he says, "I received the privilege of a commission in his name to lead to faith and obedience men in all nations" (Rom 1:5, NEB). Again, in Romans 15:15f, he refers to "the grace given me by God to be a minister of Christ Jesus to the Gentiles".

Privilege, grace, gratitude (*charis* is the New Testament Greek word used for all three of these terms) – these are the notions Paul employs when referring to his missionary task. In his letter to the Romans he establishes an intimate relationship between "grace" or "gratitude" and "duty"; put differently, Paul's acknowledgment of indebtedness is immediately translated into a sense of gratitude. The debt or obligation he feels does not represent a burden which inhibits him; rather, recognition of debt is synonymous with giving thanks. The way Paul gives thanks is to be a missionary to Jew and Gentile (cf Minear 1961:passim). He has exchanged the terrible debt of sin for another debt, the debt of gratitude, which manifests itself in mission (cf Kähler [1899] 1971:457).

Paul sometimes uses cultic language to give expression to his own and his fellow-believers' "debt of gratitude". In Romans 15:16, to which I have already referred several times, he speaks of himself as a *leitourgos* ("minister") to the Gentiles and of his missionary involvement as "priestly service" (*leitourgein*, "to function as a priest") (cf Schlier 1971:passim). In Philippians 2:17 he designates this a *thysia* ("libation") and *leitourgia* ("sacrifice"). The Gentile converts he is taking to Jerusalem, together with the collection for the poor Christians there, he calls a *prosphora* ("sacrificial offering": Rom 15:16). In similar fashion he appeals to his readers to present their bodies to God as a "living and holy sacrifice", which, he says, is their "spiritual worship"; and the collection the Philippians sent to him through Epaphroditus he labels a "fragrant offering" (Phil 4:18).

Behind all these expressions lies the idea of a sacrifice or offering that is given out of love and because of the love Paul and his communities have received from God through Christ. The cultic-sacrificial language of the mystery religions is transformed metaphorically and applied soberly and concretely to the daily lifestyle of believers (cf Beker 1980:320; cf also Schlier 1971 and, particularly, Walter 1979:436-441). Perhaps some of Paul's recent converts were puzzled by his insistence on cult-free worship; to them he gives the assurance that all cultic practices have been antiquated by God himself. Even so, Christians do have a form of *latreia*; their exemplary conduct for the sake of the salvation of others is "a living sacrifice, holy and acceptable to God", their "spiritual worship" (Rom 12:2) rendered in their day-to-day existence; this is their substitute for all cultic practices. Also, Paul does not use the expression *hilaskesthai* ("to propitiate" or "make expiation for sins"; in the New Testament this verb occurs only in Hebrews 2:17). He prefers the words *katallassein* ("reconcile") and *katallage* ("reconciliation"). However, he turns both the Gentile and the Jewish use of these terms upside down.[12] It is not a case of God having to be propitiated by people because of their transgressions against him. Rather, God himself "pleads to be reconciled with us, his enemies. So low does God bow in partnership with human beings" (Walter 1979:441 — my translation). This is the boundless and inexpressible love that Paul and his communities experience. Is it conceivable that they could respond to it with anything but a profound "debt of gratitude"?

MISSION AND THE TRIUMPH OF GOD

The Apocalyptic Paul

In endeavoring to portray the distinctive features of Paul's missionary theology we have to go beyond what I have termed his missionary strategy and motivation. This is a hazardous enterprise, since Paul's world of thought is exceedingly complex. It is therefore impossible to select one single element as *the* fundamental motif of Paul's theology. There are, rather, several important motifs, all of which are interrelated. To mention only some of those which are associated with his understanding of his mission: his interpretation of the Law; of justification by faith; of the interdependence of a mission to Jews and Gentiles; of the absolute priority of the Gentile mission for the present moment; of the universal, indeed cosmic, significance of the gospel; of the incontestable centrality of Christ and the meaning of Christ's death and resurrection; and of the relevance of his mission for paving the way for God's coming triumph.

I shall begin with this last-mentioned motif, with the qualification, however, that the other motifs have to be presupposed throughout.

Significant advances in Pauline studies during the last decade or two have shown many of the traditional assumptions about Paul's theology to be erroneous or at least incomplete. Important Pauline studies published since the middle of the 1970s include Sanders (1977 and 1983), Beker (1980 and 1984) and Räisänen (1983). Scholars now tend to agree that Paul has to be understood not only in opposition to his Jewish past but also in continuation with that past.

This applies to his appreciation for the Law and the abiding validity of God's promises to Israel (to which I shall return), as well as to his eschatological convictions.

In an essay published in 1959, Wilckens suggested that Paul (or Saul) before his conversion was not to be regarded as a typical orthodox rabbinic Pharisee (as countless generations of Christians have portrayed him). Rather, Saul (as Pharisee!) stood in the Jewish *apocalyptic* tradition from Daniel onward, a tradition which decisively influenced the theology of Paul the Christian; we will never understand Paul until this is fully recognized (Wilckens 1959:passim; see, however, Sanders 1977:479). Ernst Käsemann has also, in several publications since 1960, argued in favor of understanding Paul in the context of apocalyptic (cf particularly Käsemann 1969a; 1969b; 1969c; 1969e). In more recent years Beker (1980 and 1984) has left no stone unturned in an effort to rehabilitate the original "apocalyptic Paul". In contrast to E. P. Sanders, who tends to fuse apocalyptic into the mainstream of rabbinic Judaism (Sanders 1977:423f; but cf Sanders 1983:5, 12, note 13), Beker distinguishes between the apocalyptic ambience of Judaism before the Jewish War and the negative reaction to apocalyptic in the wake of the war. Classical Judaism of the post-Jamnia period made apocalyptic responsible for the destruction of Jerusalem and the temple, because of its messianic speculations. Since the Jamnia council of AD 90, the rabbinic-Hebrew canon, because of its distaste for apocalyptic, had excluded both the Apocrypha and the apocalyptic Pseudepigrapha (Beker 1980:345, 359). Paul, however, belongs to pre-war Judaism and should be read and understood against that background. Small wonder, therefore, that many of the stock themes of Jewish apocalyptic are to be detected in Paul. These include the four basic motifs of "vindication", "universalism", "dualism", and "imminence" (Beker 1984:30-54), all of which were linked with the peculiar perception of the Law operative in Jewish apocalyptic (cf Wilckens 1959).

Before I turn to the profound way in which Paul, in spite of all continuity, modifies Jewish apocalyptic, it may be of interest to point out that just as the Judaism of the period after AD 70 turned its back on its apocalyptic heritage, so also has most of "main-line" Christianity, down through the ages, refused to accept an "apocalyptic" Paul. Paul was understood as though he was reacting to (Christianity's interpretation of) classical post-war rabbinic Judaism.

Apocalyptic is often characterized by the supposition that the present is empty and that all salvation lies only in the future. The despair and frustration people experience in the present propel them to long for total redemption in the future, which is usually understood to be both imminent and calculable. Montanism, a late second- and early-third century heresy, is one of the earliest examples of a Christian apocalyptic movement and bears resemblance to many other millenarian sects that flourished in the Middle Ages, at the time of the Reformation, and later. The cultural climate of our own time appears to be particularly conducive to such movements, as the writings of Hal Lindsey (such at *The Late Great Planet Earth* and *The 1980's: Countdown to Armageddon*) testify. As Beker has cogently argued, such movements are, however, totally out of tune with the essence of the Christian faith. He highlights several grave distortions of the gospel which characterize Lindsey's updated version of Montanism. Lindsey's descriptions of the future are deterministic in the extreme; his apocalyptic is devoid of a christological focus; the biblical materials he cites are totally divorced from their proper historical contexts; his hope for the future is self-centered in the extreme; and there is no theology of the cross in his apocalyptic (Beker 1984:26f).

The Christian Church and Apocalyptic

In light of the above, it should not surprise us if the Christian church, down through the centuries, has often reacted negatively if not violently to any manifestation of apocalyptic. It was either silenced or neutralized by the established church,[13] which resulted in future eschatology being largely pushed out of the mainstream of Christianity and into heretical aberrations. Whereas the apocalypticists at least kept alive the conviction of a fundamental reordering of reality in time at some future moment, the main body of the church soon came under the spell of Platonic thinking. This manifested itself in several ways, particularly under the influence of Origen and Augustine. The resurrection of Christ was viewed as a completed event and severed from the hope of a future resurrection of believers. Christian history after the Christ-event was regarded as little more than the working out of God's once-for-all action in Christ. The expectation of a "new heaven and a new earth" was spiritualized away. The emphasis was laid on the spiritual journey of the individual believer and on a post-mortem afterlife rather than on a future resurrection from the dead. The church was increasingly identified with the kingdom of God; it became the dispenser of sacraments and the place where, through the sacraments, souls were won for Christ (Beker 1980:303f, 356; 1984:73f, 85-87, 108f; cf also Lampe 1957:passim).

Modern theologians have produced their own variations of the solutions offered in early Christianity. Nineteenth-century liberal theology, for instance, summarily removed Paul's future eschatological expectation as an ornamental husk (cf Beker 1984:61). Again, in Protestantism (particularly in its Lutheran branch) there has been a tendency to declare Paul's basic motif, virtually to the exclusion of all others, "to be found in his understanding of law and grace, that is, in his message of justification" (Bornkamm 1966:201), often also at the expense of an expectation of the future.[14] Bultmann's program of demythologizing the New Testament and particularly its eschatology, and of substituting an existentialist interpretation, thus restricting it to hope in a God who "is always One who comes" in "permanent futurity", is a variation of the justification-by-faith theme and an attempt at dealing with the reality of the delay of the parousia, but again at the expense of any future orientation in Paul (cf Beker 1980:17, 355). The "realized eschatology" program of C. H. Dodd and others had a similar effect — once again the embarrassing consciousness of the ongoing and apparently never-ending history of this world caused theologians to adjust Paul's teachings to what he "really meant". Dodd saw Paul developing from an apocalypticist in his earliest letters to embracing a more mature "realized eschatology" in Colossians and Ephesians. Paul, Dodd suggested, thus replaced apocalyptic with ecclesiology (cf Beker 1980:303, 361; 1984:49, 86). Oscar Cullmann's proposition of understanding Paul (and the entire New Testament) from a salvation-history perspective, according to which the decisive battle for God's kingdom (the "D-Day") has already been won, even if the ratification of the victory (the "V-Day") may still be far off, appears, at the first glance, to present a real alternative to the solutions of Bultmann, Dodd, and others. Cullmann's emphasis on Christ as the "midpoint" means, however, that in his thinking the Christ-event, as the center of Christian theology, has effectively displaced the event of God's coming glory and, in Cullmann's own words, dethroned eschatology (cf Beker 1980:355f).

Beker therefore pleads for the rehabilitation of the much maligned term "apocalyptic" over against "eschatology", which has simply become a hermeneutical term for "ultimate", and the use of which is "multivalent and often chaotic". By contrast, "apocalyptic" clarifies the future-temporal character of Paul's gospel and denotes an end-time occurrence that is both cosmic-universal and definitive (1980:361; 1984:14). Precisely for this reason, says Beker, the term "apocalyptic" has to be reinstated as a valid theological concept and reclaimed from the groups which have given it such a bad name.[15]

Apocalyptic's New Center of Gravity

As mentioned above, one of the basic errors of much apocalyptic, ancient or modern, lies in the fact that it minimizes the central significance of Christ. It is precisely at this point that Paul's apocalyptic goes an entirely different route. Paul, the Christian, still formulates his spirituality in terms of his inherited (Jewish) apocalyptic, but apocalyptic is given a new "center of gravity", Jesus Christ (Dahl 1977a:71). Precisely where the Law stood in Judaism the Christ-event now stands (Wilckens 1959:280, 285f; Hengel 1983b:53; cf also Moltmann 1967:192). The proclamation of Christ's death-resurrection (and not the life and ministry of the earthly Jesus or Jesus' preaching about God's reign) forms the center of Paul's missionary message, as 1 Corinthians 15 clearly attests (cf Zeller 1982:173; Grant 1986:47; Kertelge 1987:373). In the words of Beker 1984:35 (cf Zeller 1982:171; Senior and Stuhlmueller 1983:171, 174),

> The division in humankind is constituted not by those faithful to the Torah and those who are wicked and "Gentile sinners" (Gal 2:15) but rather by the death of Jesus Christ as the focal point of God's universal wrath and judgment. The death of Christ signifies the apocalyptic judgment on all humankind, whereas the resurrection signifies the free gift of new life in Christ for all.

The Christ-event is, however, not a closure or completed event; it is not "the end of history". Rather, Paul struggles with the problem that although the Messiah has come, his kingdom has not (Beker 1980:345f). The emphasis is not just on the messiahship of Jesus, but also on the salvation-historical turning point. The death and resurrection of Christ mark the incursion of the future new age into the present old age (cf de Boer 1989:187, note 17; Duff 1989:285-

289). This event signifies the inauguration and the anticipation of the coming triumph of God, the overture to it, and its guarantee. It is a decisive sign, which determines the character of all future signs and indeed of the Christian hope itself. Paul can therefore designate Christ as the "first fruits" of the final resurrection of the dead, or the "first-born among many brethren" (1 Cor 15:20, 23; Rom 8:29). The resurrection of Christ necessarily points to the future glory of God and its completion. This means that Paul's theology is not unifocal, but bifocal; coming from God's past act in Christ it moves toward God's future act. Indeed, both events stand or fall together, and both converge on Christian life in the present: "For as often as you eat this bread and drink the cup, you proclaim the Lord's death until he comes" (1 Cor 11:26). The imminence motif is intensified by the death and resurrection of Christ; the believers therefore pray, *"Marana tha"* — "Our Lord, come!" (1 Cor 16:22; cf 2 Cor 6:2).

Compared to the Jewish apocalyptic of the time Paul's expectation of God's imminent intervention in human history is intensified. He expects the interim period to be completed during his own lifetime (cf 1 Thes 4:15, 17; 1 Cor 7:29). The form of this world is already passing away (1 Cor 7:31). It is full time now for believers to wake from sleep, "for salvation is nearer to us now than when we first believed; the night is far gone, the day is at hand" (Rom 13:11f). Christians belong to those "upon whom the end of the ages has come" (1 Cor 10:11). Having the first fruits of the Spirit, they groan inwardly as they wait for the adoption as children, the redemption of their bodies (Rom 8:23) (cf Aus 1979:232, 262; Beker 1980:146f; 1984:40f, 47). In the case of Paul, then, apocalyptic is indeed the "mother of theology" (Käsemann 1969a:102; 1969b:137).

New Life in Christ

It should, however, once again be emphasized that Paul's focus is not only on an event that is still outstanding. The hope he talks about is hope only because of what God has already done. The dualistic structure of Jewish apocalyptic thought has been profoundly modified (cf Beker 1980:143-152; 1984:39-44). Even if salvation is, for Paul, unmistakably future (cf Zeller 1982:173; Senior and Stuhlmueller 1983:177), it casts its powerful rays into the present. Now already Christians are "holy" and challenged to (greater) sanctification (Rom 6:19, 22). Those who used to be in bondage (Gal 4:8) have been set free from sin and from the present evil age and have become "slaves of righteousness" or "of God" (Rom 6:18, 22; Gal 1:4; 5:1). Through the atonement they have been pronounced righteous (*dikaios*); this means that they enjoy the eschatological gift of justification already, even while living in the present age (cf Zeller 1982:188; Hultgren 1985:144). Paul never uses the notion of "being born again" and rarely employs the verb "repent" (cf Koenig 1979:307; Beker 1980:6; Gaventa 1986:3, 46). He says rather that people should acknowledge that, though living in the midst of a world whose form is perishing and doomed to pass away, they have become part of God's new creation (2 Cor 5:17; Gal 6:15). The whole direction and content of their existence has undergone a metamorphosis. They have "turned to God from idols, to serve a living and true God" (1 Thes 1:10), which means that they have passed from death to life,

from darkness to light (cf Gaventa 1986:passim). They have been transformed
and are enjoined to continue to "be transformed" (Rom 12:2 — *metamor-
phousthe*, "submit to transformation"; cf Koenig 1979:307, 313). Paul's preaching has engendered faith in their hearts (cf Rom 10:8-10, 14), which they confess
through the Spirit (1 Cor 12:3). Indeed, the eschatological gift of the Spirit is
powerfully at work in Paul and his converts. The Spirit dwells in the believer,
sealing him or her as a possession of Christ. The Spirit is alive and life-giving,
since it is the Spirit of him who raised Jesus from the dead (Rom 8:9-11) (cf
Minear 1961:45). This evidence of the Spirit's active presence guarantees for
Paul that the messianic age has dawned. In fact, "the Spirit is the agent of the
future glory in the present; it is the first down payment or guarantee of the
end-time (Rom 8:23; 2 Cor 1:22)" (Beker 1984:46f; cf Senior and Stuhlmueller
1983:178).

   To be reconciled to God, to be justified, to be transformed in the here and
now, is not something that happens to isolated individuals, however. Incorporation into the Christ-event moves the individual believer into the community
of believers. The church is the place where they celebrate their new life in the
present and stretch out to what is still to come. The church has an eschatological
horizon and is, as proleptic manifestation of God's reign, the beachhead of the
new creation, the vanguard of God's new world, and the sign of the dawning
new age in the midst of the old (cf Beker 1980:313; 1984:41). At the same time
it is precisely as these small and weak Pauline communities gather in worship
to celebrate the victory already won and to pray for the coming of their Lord
(*"Marana tha!"*), that they become aware of the terrible contradiction between
what they believe on the one hand and what they empirically see and experience
on the other, and also of the tension in which they live, the tension between
the "already" and the "not yet". "Christ the first fruits" has already risen from
the dead (1 Cor 15:23) and the believers have been given the Spirit as "guarantee" of what is to come (2 Cor 1:22; 5:5), but there does not seem to be much
apart from these "first fruits" and "pledge". Like Abraham, they believe in
hope against hope (Rom 4:18) and accept in faith the Spirit's witness that they
are children and heirs of God and therefore fellow heirs with Christ — provided,
says Paul, "we suffer with him in order that we may also be glorified with him"
(Rom 8:17). God will triumph, notwithstanding our weakness and suffering,
but also in the midst of and because of and through our weakness and suffering
(cf Beker 1980:364f). Faith is able to bear the tension between the confession
of God's ultimate triumph and the empirical reality of this world, for it knows
that "in all these things we are more than conquerors through him who loved
us" (Rom 8:37) and that "in everything God works for good with those who
love him, who are called according to his purpose" (8:28). Nowhere has Paul
portrayed this unbearable (and precisely for this reason bearable!) tension more
profoundly than in 2 Corinthians 4:7-10:

   But we have this treasure in earthen vessels, to show that the transcendent
   power belongs to God and not to us. We are afflicted in every way, but
   not crushed; perplexed, but not driven to despair, persecuted, but not

forsaken; struck down, but not destroyed; always carrying in the body the death of Jesus, so that the life of Jesus may also be manifested in our bodies.

Our Christian life in this world thus involves an inescapable tension, oscillating between joy and agony. Whereas, on the one hand, suffering and weakness become all the more intolerable and our agonizing, because of the terrifying "not yet", intensifies, we can, on the other hand, already "rejoice in our sufferings" (Rom 5:2). This means that our life in this world must be cruciform; Paul bears on his body "the marks of Jesus" (Gal 6:17; cf Col 1:24), he carries "in the body the death of Jesus", and while he lives he is "always being given up to death for Jesus' sake" (2 Cor 4:10f) (cf also Beker 1980:145f, 366f; 1984:120).

Lesslie Newbigin suggests that nowhere in the New Testament is the essential character of the church's mission set out more clearly than in the passage quoted above (2 Cor 4:7-10). "It ought to be seen", he says, "as the classic definition of mission" (1987:24). This passage, moreover, clearly characterizes the Pauline mission as an eschatological event: only within the horizon of the expectation of the end can the tension between suffering and glory be sustained. Apocalyptic groups are usually sectarian, introverted, exclusivist, and jealous in guarding their boundaries; moreover, the expectation of an imminent end leaves no room for any large-scale missionary enterprise. The Pauline communities, although they are exclusive, are, however, not introverted and sectarian. There are, we have said, gates in their boundaries (Meeks 1983:78, 105-107). Nor does the expectation of the parousia in any way paralyze the zeal for mission.

There is another difference between Paul and most apocalyptic groups. Where such groups do get involved in mission, such a venture is usually understood as a precondition for the end, as a means of hastening or precipitating the parousia. Paul, however, can only *proclaim* the lordship of Christ, not inaugurate it; it remains the prerogative of God himself to usher in the end (cf Zeller 1982:186; Beker 1984:52f). Paul only knows that the era between Christ's resurrection and the parousia is the time allotted to him as apostle of the Gentiles, even if he has no guarantee that he himself will bring it to completion; according to Philippians 1:21-24, for instance, he even contemplates the possibility of his own death without any apparent anxiety about the completion of the missionary enterprise (cf Zeller 1982:186, note 75).

The Nations' Pilgrimage to Jerusalem

The apocalyptic context in which Paul sees his mission also emerges from his conviction that, for the moment, the mission to Gentiles rather than to Jews has the highest priority. To Paul's most intense disappointment the Jewish mission, for the present, proves to be a futile enterprise (cf Hengel 1983b:52; Steiger 1980:48). This does not, however, lead him to turning his back on his kinsfolk. He is saying, rather, that God still intends to save Israel, but in a round-about way—via the mission to the Gentiles! Two themes are employed in an effort to give expression to this conviction, and both once again underscore the apocalyptic nature of the Pauline mission. First, there is the collection for the poor Christians in Judea, to which Paul has committed himself (cf Gal 2:10) and to which he seems to have devoted a great deal of his energy during the final years of his ministry (cf Rom 15:25f; 1 Cor 16:1; 2 Cor 8:9). It is possible that Paul and the Jerusalem leadership interpret the significance of the collection differently (cf Brown 1980:209; Beker 1980:332; Meeks 1983:110). For Paul, it clearly symbolizes the unity of the church made up of Jews and Gentiles (Meyer 1986:183f), and this is so important to him that he risks everything in going to Jerusalem personally in order to deliver the gift (it should be noted that this act led to Paul's arrest and the end of his public ministry).

More important, and this is the second theme, a whole retinue of representatives from a variety of Gentile churches accompany him to Jerusalem. It is highly unlikely that Paul just wishes to impress the Jerusalem leadership and prove to them that his mission has borne fruit. Some scholars have therefore suggested that Paul is here taking up a traditional eschatological theme, particularly that of the Gentiles carrying the people of Israel home from all the ends of the earth (cf Is 66:19-23). Paul, however, completely reverses the contemporary Jewish interpretation of the Isaiah 66 prophecy and combines it with another Old Testament prophecy, that of the pilgrimage of the nations to Zion; it is not diaspora Jews, but representatives from all the *Gentiles* who will be gathered from the ends of the earth and brought to Jerusalem. This explains, says Roger Aus, why Paul is so anxious about going to *Spain* (Rom 15:24). Aus argues, in great detail, not only that Spain is undoubtedly the Tarshish of the apocalyptic prophecy Isaiah 66:19, but also that it represents the farthest point in the West, literally "the ends of the earth". Only when the most distant of all the nations mentioned in Isaiah 66:19 also sends its representatives to Jerusalem will the "full number of the Gentiles" (Rom 11:25) have arrived and the time for the parousia come (cf Aus 1979:passim). In this respect Aus also refers to the "offering of the Gentiles" of Romans 15:16. This expression is to be understood not as the money that the Gentiles are sending to Jerusalem; rather, the genitive construction should be translated epexegetically as a genitive of apposition — the "offering of the Gentiles" is the Gentiles themselves (Aus 1979:235-237).[16]

Paul thus blends the theme of the collection with that of the eschatological pilgrimage of the nations to Jerusalem (cf also Bieder 1965:39; Stuhlmacher 1971:560f, 565; Zeller 1982:187; Hofius 1986:313; Kertelge 1987:372). He employs the Hebrew idea of representative universalism. The Gentiles who do come to Jerusalem are the first fruits of redeemed humanity. They stand for the entire crop and through them all the others share in the divine blessing (cf Aus 1979:257-260; Hultgren 1985:135f).

The coming in of the "full number of the Gentiles" (Rom 11:25) is then linked intimately to the salvation of Israel. Paul says that "a hardening has come upon part of Israel" (Rom 11:25), but through the conversion of the Gentiles the Jews may become jealous and also accept Jesus as Messiah (Rom 11:14). Paul cannot for a moment contemplate the possibility of Israel being eternally lost; so, in an astoundingly bold fashion, he envisages the salvation of

Israel after and as a result of the conversion of the Gentiles. His mission to the Gentiles turns out to be "a colossal detour to the salvation of Israel" (Käsemann 1969e:241). The fate of Israel hinges on the Gentile mission. By "bringing in" the Gentiles, Paul will provoke Israel to repentance and so precipitate the final act in the drama of salvation; the restitution of Israel will bring the completion of history (cf Zeller 1982:184f; Senior and Stuhlmueller 1983:183-185). The time of the Gentile mission is "only an interval", and the end can only come when Israel has been saved (Stuhlmacher 1971:565).

However, the Gentile mission as a "prelude" to the salvation of all Israel is, as it were, only one side of the apocalyptic missionary coin. The apocalyptic motif includes the cosmic extension of God's majesty and glory, and this implies a radical break with traditional Jewish soteriology. Jewish apocalyptic certainly expected God's universal reign, but that expectation was firmly anchored in Israel's self-awareness as a privileged people. Even where the Jews anticipated a pilgrimage of the Gentile nations to Jerusalem, their thinking remained introverted and salvation subject to faithfulness to the Law. This, says Beker, "marks Israel as a basically nonmissionary religion and accounts to a large extent for the vengeance motif in its portrayal of the end-time" (1984:35). However, God's intervention in Christ has profoundly modified the Jewish apocalyptic pattern; the Law has been replaced with the crucified Messiah (cf Hengel 1983b:53). Through the death on the cross of Jesus the Jew and in his subsequent exaltation through resurrection, all humanity is offered the possibility of moving from death to life, from sin to God. Paul expounds this in detail in Romans 3:21-30: the righteousness of God has been manifested apart from the Law, through faith in Jesus Christ. There is no longer any distinction between Jew and Gentile. All have sinned and all are justified by God's grace through Christ. God is, after all, the God not only of the Jews, but also of the Gentiles. But precisely because salvation is to be obtained only through Christ, it is intended for all humankind. God allows himself to be found even by those who do not seek him (Rom 10:20). There can no longer be any favorite-nation clause or claim to privilege. A mission that requires conversion to Judaism (and all that this entails) on the part of the Gentiles is, in effect, a denial of the gospel itself. The Messiah of Israel is the exalted Lord (*Kyrios*) of the whole cosmos, and this means that there is no alternative to his claim to Lordship being addressed to all humankind. It is particularly in his letter to the Romans where these cosmic dimensions of the Christian mission are developed. "Salvation *for all*" may appropriately be termed the hermeneutical key to the entire letter (cf further Hahn 1965:99f; Rütti 1972:117f; Mussner 1982:11; Zeller 1982: 171f, 177f; Senior and Stuhlmueller 1983:174-177; Beker 1984:34-38; Legrand 1988:161-165).

Paul's Universalism

In this connection it is crucial to note that Paul's missionary message is not a negative one. He is not charged with announcing an arbitrary apocalyptic blast to the world (Beker 1984:14, 58). He does proclaim the wrath of God, but only as the dark foil of an eminently positive message — that God has already come to us in his Son and will come again in glory. Mission means the announcement of Christ's lordship over all reality and an invitation to submit to it; through his preaching Paul wishes to evoke the confession "Jesus is Lord!" (Rom 10:9; 1 Cor 12:3; Phil 2:11) (cf Zeller 1982:172f, 182). The good news is that the reign of God, present in Jesus Christ, has brought us all together under judgment and has in the same act brought us all together under grace. And yet, this does not mean that the gospel is an invitation to mystical introspection or to the salvation of individual souls, climbing out of a lost world into the safety of the church. Rather, it is the proclamation of a new state of affairs that God has initiated in Christ, one that concerns the nations and all of creation and that climaxes in the celebration of God's final glory (Beker 1980: 7f,354f; 1984:16). So the apostle is commissioned to enlarge already in this world the domain of God's coming world (cf Beker 1984:34, 57).

Does this means that Paul is a "universalist" in the sense that he envisions the ultimate salvation of all humankind? Some of his statements seem to affirm that only a part of the human community will be saved; others seem to suggest that all will finally be saved.[17] Eugene Boring recently published a perceptive and thought-provoking article on this subject (1986; cf Sanders 1983:57, note 64). He points out that a minority of scholars argue that Paul is really a universalist; they then subordinate the particularistic texts to the universalistic ones. The majority appear to be going exactly the opposite way: subordinating the universalistic passages to the particularistic ones they conclude that Paul is really a particularist. Still others attempt to solve the problem by arguing that there is a progressive development in Paul, from "particularism" to "universalism" (cf Boring 1986:271f).

Boring concedes that there are conflicting statements in Paul and that it is virtually impossible to harmonize them. However, the problem only remains insoluble if we pose the issue in terms of conflicting *statements* or *propositions*, not if we regard them as divergent *pictures*. We should therefore understand Paul as a coherent, but not a systematic, thinker; he can be heard as making logically inconsistent, but not incoherent, statements (:288f, 292). In the issue under discussion Paul operates with two seemingly opposing images. In the so-called particularistic passages the encompassing picture is that of God-the-judge. In this image there are "winners" (those who are saved) and "losers" (those who are lost, although even here Paul does not elaborate the fate of the damned; Paul has no doctrine of hell [:275, 281]). In the "universalistic" passages, on the other hand, the dominant motif is that of God-the-king. Where God-the-judge separates, God-the-king unites all in his kingly reign. The once-hostile powers have been overcome and now render homage to the conqueror. God has replaced the reign of sin and death with the reign of righteousness and life; "every knee" acknowledges this and bow willingly before him (Phil 2:10f). This is the language of lordship rather than of "salvation" (:280-284, 290f).

It is indefensible to fuse these two images into one; in fact, we could only do that by choosing between "particularism" and "universalism", and either choice would do an injustice to the delicate nuances of Paul's thinking. Paul can, on the one hand, proclaim with absolute certainty that God will be all in all and that every tongue will confess Jesus as Lord. At the same time he can insist on the Christian mission as a duty that cannot be relinquished. People have to "transfer" from the old reality to the new by an act of belief and commitment, since only Christ can save them (cf Sanders 1977:463-472, 508f). Everybody is dependent on hearing the gospel of justification by faith (Rom 10:14f). God's righteousness does not come into effect automatically, but is dependent upon being appropriated by faith, which is only possible where people have had the gospel proclaimed to them. God has already reconciled the world to himself; however, he does not overpower it, but stretches out his hand in the preaching of his ambassadors who aim at evoking a positive response (cf Zeller 1982:167, 170-173). Thus Paul refrains from any unequivocal assertion of universal salvation; the thrust toward such a notion is balanced by an emphasis on responsibility and obedience for those who have heard the gospel. God's *gift* of righteousness is inseparable from God's *claim* on people (Beker 1984:35-37). The salvation offered by God is thus not universal in the sense that it makes human response inconsequential; "Paul fuses 'qualifiers' onto his statements about salvation such as to those 'who believe,' those 'who are in Christ,' those 'called' " (Senior and Stuhlmueller 1983:175). There is no talk of surrendering the missionary mandate.

At the same time, the significance of Paul's missionary ministry is not exaggerated out of all proportions. He can only *announce* Christ's lordship, not *inaugurate* it. And those who respond positively, do not do so purely "voluntarily". In retrospect their response is seen as a gift of God—hence the language of election, calling, and predestination (cf Zeller 1982:172; Boring 1986:290f; Gaventa 1986:44; Breytenbach 1986:19).

Apocalyptic and Ethics

One question remains in this respect: how does Paul's apocalyptic understanding of mission relate to ethics? This is a crucial question, particularly in light of a charge such as Pixley's, that Paul's (and John's) "spiritual message of individual salvation" may justly be characterized as "a religious opium because it enables a suffering people to endure, by offering private dreams to compensate for an intolerable public reality" (1981:100). What Pixley describes is, of course, true of much apocalyptic, also in our own time. The dualism between "this age" and "the age to come" is often absolute, and where this is the case, believers are not called to engage in working for peace, justice, and reconciliation among people. Their exclusive focus on the parousia is an invitation to ethical passivity and quietism. There is no concern for the here, only for the hereafter. Social conservatism and apocalyptic enthusiasm go hand in hand. Waiting for God's imminent kingdom, people are drawn out of society into the haven of the church, which is nothing but a lifeboat going round and round in a hostile sea, picking up survivors of a shipwreck (cf Beker 1980: 149, 305, 326; 1984:26, 111; Young 1988:6). Moreover, apocalyptic enthusiasts usually display a peculiar self-centeredness. They see themselves as a favored elite. The world is the stage for their own striving for sanctification; the dualism between spirit and body devaluates the created order to a testing ground for heaven – or to a vale of tears. Where they do get involved with others, this usually happens in a condescending manner. They practice an "ethic of excess", in which the "have-nots" become the target for the charity of the "haves" (cf Beker 1980:38, 109; 1984:37, 109).

Paul's apocalyptic is different. It is true that Paul judges the church to be engaged in a battle against the world in view of the fact that "the form of this world is passing away" (1 Cor 7:31). However, Paul perceives the church in a way that fundamentally modifies standard apocalyptic thinking. The church already belongs to the redeemed world; it is that segment of the world that is obedient to God (Käsemann 1969b:134). As such, it strains itself in all its activities to prepare the world for its coming destiny. Precisely because of this the church is not preoccupied with self-preservation; it serves the world in the sure hope of the world's transformation at the time of God's final triumph. The small Pauline churches are so many "pockets" of an alternative lifestyle that penetrates the mores of society around them. In the midst of a "crooked and perverse generation" the Christians are to be "without blemish" and shining "as lights in the world" (Phil 2:15) – sober in judgment, cheerful in performing acts of mercy, patient in tribulation, constant in prayer, practicing hospitality, living in harmony with all, without conceit, serving those in distress (Rom 12). Passion for the coming of God's reign goes hand in hand with compassion for a needy world.

In Paul's thinking, then, church and world are joined together in a bond of solidarity. The church, as the already redeemed creation, cannot boast in a "realized eschatology" for itself over against the world. It is placed, as a community of hope, in the context of the world and its power structures. And it is as members of such a community that Christians "groan inwardly" together with the "whole creation," which is "groaning in travail" (Rom 8:22f). Paul thus resists a narrow individualistic piety and a view that restricts salvation to the church. As long as the creation groans, Christians groan as well; as long as any part of God's creation suffers, they cannot as yet participate in the eschatological glory (cf Beker 1984:16, 36-38, 69).

The life and work of the Christian community are intimately bound up with God's cosmic-historical plan for the redemption of the universe. It most certainly matters what Christians do and how authentically they demonstrate the mind of Christ and the values of the reign of God in their daily lives. Since the forces of the future are already at work in the world, Paul's apocalyptic is not an invitation to ethical passivity, but to active participation in God's redemptive will. He is charged with enlarging in this world the domain of God's coming world. Therefore, precisely because of his concern for the "ultimate", he is preoccupied with the "penultimate"; his involvement is in what is at hand rather than in what will be. Authentic apocalyptic hope thus compels ethical seriousness. It is impossible to believe in God's coming triumph without being agitators for God's kingdom here and now, and without an ethic that strains and labors to move God's creation toward the realization of God's promise in Christ. Opposing the false apocalypses of power politics, Christians strive for those intimations of the good that already foreshadow God's ultimate triumph—even as they know that they may never too easily identify God's will and power with their own will and power, and may never overrate their own capabilities (cf Beker 1984:16, 57, 86f, 90, 110f, 119f).

The intimate link between apocalyptic and ethics is nowhere as pronounced as in Paul's *view of the church*. Although (or rather, precisely because) he regards the church as the community of the end-time, he views it as having tremendous significance for the here and now. Believers cannot accept one another as members of a community of faith without this having consequences for their day-to-day life and for the world. This becomes evident in the Antioch incident to which Paul refers in Galatians 2. He feels compelled to oppose Peter "to his face", an attitude prompted by "religious" as well as "socio-political" reasons—"religious", since Peter's action suggests the possibility of salvation apart from Christ, "socio-political" since his conduct implies that it is conceivable that the Christian community could present itself to the world as a divided body. Paul's vehement reaction signifies that since Christ has accepted everybody unconditionally, it is preposterous even to contemplate the possibility of Jews and Gentiles acting differently on the "horizontal" plane, that is, *not* accepting one another unconditionally. There is, indeed, no longer Jew or Greek, slave or free, male or female (Gal 3:28).

We may, however, ask whether Paul is as uncompromising with respect to slaves and free persons and male and female as he is with respect to Jews and Greeks. Here we have to admit, I believe, that the latter relationship clearly preoccupies him almost to the exclusion of the former two. This means, again, that we have to read Paul in his context. Above all, he believes that the advent of Christ meant that the barrier between Jews and other people, buttressed by a false understanding of the Law, has been torn down; he is prepared to stake his entire ministry on this fundamental tenet of the Christian faith. Since this conviction virtually consumes all his energy, it seems that other divisions are shunted into secondary place. Could it be that he regards these differences as social rather than theological?

Be this as it may, recent studies have shown that women had a much higher profile in the Pauline communities than they had in contemporary Judaism (cf Meeks 1983:81, 220 [Notes 107 and 108] and especially Portefaix 1988:131-173). The situation regarding slaves appears to be more complex. Segundo says that Paul, as child of his times, probably glimpses the real, dehumanizing character of the institution of slavery "only in a vague, remote way" (1986:180). At the same time, Paul is not insensitive to the issue; nor is he an idealist, a utopian dreamer. He is faced with circumstances that he cannot change (:165). Yet he does not endorse slavery, nor is he neutral on the issue. "(I)f in Christ there is no longer any difference between slave and free person, if each is to live and act on behalf of others and not put *obstacles* of any sort in their way, then all that *virtually* implies the abolition of slavery as a societal structure" (165; emphasis in the original). Paul therefore "opts to humanize the slave from within" (:164); the status of slaves "need not prevent them from attaining human maturity" (:180).

This is a helpful analysis. Still, I would suggest that it is possible to go beyond Segundo on Paul's attitude to slavery. In an exhaustive study of Paul's letter to Philemon, Petersen (1985) argues—I believe convincingly—that Paul does not leave open the issue of Philemon setting free his runaway slave Onesimus (cf also Roberts 1983). With the aid of a perceptive analysis of the narrative structure of this exquisitely composed short letter and of Paul's "symbolic universe", Petersen reaches the conclusion that Paul does not really allow Philemon the possibility *not* to set Onesimus free. The letter contains a "thinly veiled command" that Philemon should do more than just receive back his former slave (:288). While not denouncing the institution of slavery as such, Paul clearly "attacks . . . the participation in it of a believing master and his believing slave" (:289). It is, after all, "logically and socially impossible to relate to one and the same person as both one's inferior and one's equal" (ibid.; cf Roberts 1983:64, 66). By writing not only to Philemon but also to the church which regularly meets in his house, Paul places Philemon "between the proverbial rock and hard place" (Petersen 1985:288). Up to now Philemon has led a comfortable double life in the domains of both the world and the church. Now the *worldly* responsibility for acting as a master with his slave is placed in conflict with the *churchly* responsibility for acting as a brother with a brother (:289). Paul does not wish to *force* Philemon into setting Onesimus free, however; the decision must be Philemon's, taken in freedom (Roberts 1983:65). Instead of bludgeoning Philemon into doing what he wishes him to do, he chooses to reveal to Philemon a "more excellent way". Philemon is shown that the financial loss he might suffer by setting free his former slave is negligible compared to what he stands to gain: he has lost a mere slave, he will receive back a dear brother. The "sacrifice" turns out to be no sacrifice at all.

And yet Paul goes beyond such a "soft" approach, particularly toward the end of the letter. He reminds Philemon of the latter's profound indebtedness to him (v 19). He adds: "If you consider *me* your partner, then receive Onesimus *as you would receive me*" (v 17), and he is confident that Philemon would do *even more* than he asks of him (v 21). Then, in the final sentence before he concludes with the customary greetings, he asks Philemon to prepare a guest room for him, since he hopes to visit Colossae soon (v 22). Philemon can now no longer have any doubts about Paul's overall intention—he is coming to check and see how Philemon has handled this thorny question. If he accedes to Paul's "appeal", their meeting will be a very pleasant one; if not, he will confront Paul as one who has publicly defaulted (Petersen 1985:293). So Philemon and the church in his house can no longer be in doubt about the utmost seriousness of this matter, a matter so serious that Paul, contrary to his custom, has devoted an entire letter to this one issue. Philemon (and, with him, the other slave owners in the church in Colossae) is indeed between a rock and a hard place. In Petersen's words

> Paul radically polarizes the options open to Philemon and his church. By representing the polar opposites as acting either in worldly or in properly churchly fashion, Paul forces Philemon and his church to think beyond

narrow self-interest and local sentiments to what being in Christ is all about (:301; cf Roberts 1983:64-66).

Of course, Paul is primarily interested in what happens *within the community of faith*. We would demand too much if we wished him to spell out an ethic for society at large. Christians were a totally negligible factor in the Greco-Roman context of the time. Therefore, given the odds against him and the limitations of his situation, it would be preposterous for Paul (or any other first-generation Christian, for that matter) to attempt to develop a program of liberation for the oppressed of the entire Empire. His base is the *church*; his appeal is to those who have been incorporated into Christ through baptism. At the same time he regards the church as constituting "pockets" of an alternative lifestyle that penetrates the mores of society around it. Precisely because of this, Christians cannot celebrate the advent of God's new world only within the church. Rather, the revolution that is taking place within the church carries within it important seeds of revolution for the structures of society. In the midst of a "crooked and perverse generation" the believers are to be "without blemish" and shining "as lights in the world" (Phil 2:15). They may not withdraw into a sequestered cloister; rather, they constitute a community of hope which groans and labors for the redemption of the entire world (cf Beker 1980:318f; 1984:69). They cannot boast in a "realized eschatology" for themselves over against the world. Church and world are joined together in a bond of solidarity.[18]

In summary Paul is convinced that in Christ God has reconciled the world to himself and that the era between the resurrection of Christ and the parousia is the time allotted to him as apostle to usher in the first stage of the in-gathering of the nations under the lordship of Christ (Hultgren 1985:145). Our survey has revealed that Paul can simultaneously hold together two seemingly opposite realities: a fervent longing for the breaking in of the future reign of God; and a preoccupation with missionary outreach, the building up of communities of faith in a hostile world, and the practicing of a new societal ethic.

Most Christian groups find it impossible to live creatively in this abiding tension between the penultimate and the ultimate. Some succumb to dualism, turn their backs on this world, emphasize "endurance" in the present, and simply wait for the end of suffering in God's glorious new age; where this happens, Jesus tends to become a new prophet or lawgiver, "who merely announces what eventually will come to pass and what must be done in the midst of a wholly unredeemed present" (Beker 1980:346). Others find more sophisticated solutions to the problem of the lapse of time since Christ's first coming. There are those who celebrate the ultimate coming of Christ only in the church, particularly in the sacraments, and who tend to identify God's reign with the church (although we must admit that this position is losing popularity today), and there are others who opt for one of several existentialist positions, or for an almost unqualified participation in the world. In none of these latter instances does it matter any more that time seems to go on interminably. The "delay" of the parousia is no longer of any concern. There is a tendency to "over-celebrate" the present; any hope of a fundamental change in the future is silenced and neutralized (cf Beker 1980:9, 345; 1984:61-77, 118).

Beker, who makes a strong case for rehabilitating apocalyptic, does not suggest that today's church has to follow Paul's views slavishly. He points out that Paul himself sometimes makes adjustments in his expectations (1984:49; he refers, in this respect, to 1 Thessalonians 4:13-18; 1 Corinthians 15:15-21; 2 Corinthians 5:1-10; Philippians 2:21-24). Paul does so, however, without surrendering his expectation of God's triumphal intervention at the end. This is what we, too, must hold on to. And we should do it by providing an answer, in the spirit of Paul's apocalyptic, to at least four fundamental objections to much pedestrian apocalyptic: the obsolete character of the apocalyptic worldview, the misleading "literal" language of apocalyptic for Christian spirituality, the argument that apocalyptic has a purely symbolic significance, and the refutation of future apocalyptic by the ongoing process of history (Beker 1984:79-121). A direct transfer of Paul's formulations of the gospel to our situation cannot succeed (:105). Still, Paul's apocalyptic gospel may help us discern "that the triumph of God is in his hands alone and . . . will transform all our present striving and sighing" (:17). It is precisely the vision of the coming reality of God's glory that compels us to work patiently and courageously in the present, unredeemed world in a manner dictated by the way of Christ. Involvement in the structures of this world and attempts to change them and make them conform, if only to a very limited degree, to the "blueprint" of God's reign, make sense precisely because of our hope for a fundamentally new future. Paul can contemplate a universal mission and yet think in terms of apocalyptic imminence; eschatology and missionary involvement do not contradict each other, since the one does not invalidate the other. God's final triumph is already casting its rays into our present world, however opaque these rays appear to be. Therefore Paul, responding to the inviting power of the apocalyptic hour of righteousness and peace, prepares for that moment by going "to the ends of the earth" and inviting people from all nations to become members of the community of the end-time (cf Beker 1984:51f, 58, 117).

THE LAW, ISRAEL, AND THE GENTILES

I have argued above that Paul finds himself in a paradoxical situation. The Jewish mission appears, for the present, to be a futile enterprise. The Gentile mission, on the other hand, is remarkably successful and Paul now proposes that the salvation of the Jews can only be accomplished via a vigorous missionary effort among Gentiles. I have maintained that this interpretation of his mission only makes sense if we keep in mind that Paul sees himself, through his missionary engagement, as responding to the inviting power of God's ultimate triumph. I now have to go one step further, and relate Paul's apocalyptic mission to his understanding of the Jewish Law and of the relation between Jews and Gentiles.

Paul and Judaism

H. J. Schoeps once called Paul's teaching on the Law "the most intricate doctrinal issue in his theology" (reference in Moo 1987:305). The quest for a trustworthy interpretation of Paul's understanding of the Law has not been made any easier by the vicissitudes of almost twenty centuries of Jewish-Christian relations. If we wish to understand Paul it is therefore of the utmost importance that we attempt to gain as much information as possible on the Judaism of Paul's time and its attitude toward the Law. Recent studies have indeed revealed great diversity within Judaism in the early Roman Empire. This was particularly true of the Judaism of the period prior to the Jewish War; after the war the situation changed to a considerable degree, as the Pharisees attempted to reorganize and consolidate Jewish religious life at the same time as they introduced measures to make it impossible for Jewish Christians to preserve links with the synagogue.

It was particularly the publication of E. P. Sanders's *Paul and Palestinian Judaism* (1977) that marked something like a watershed in Pauline studies (cf Moo 1987:287), although several earlier studies have made proposals similar to those of Sanders. It is today widely held that Paul's teaching on the Law cannot be understood solely within the framework of Luther's attempts to oppose a works-oriented Roman Catholicism with the precept of justification by faith alone. Paul is now often seen as having had a far more positive attitude toward Jews and Judaism in general and toward the Law in particular.

One of the reasons for the new appreciation for the Jewishness of Paul is undoubtedly apologetic. There is today a strong interest in Jewish-Christian dialogue, and since Paul has traditionally been regarded by Jews as the great apostate (because of what he says about the Law, particularly in his letter to the Galatians) and as the originator of anti-Judaism (not least because of what he wrote in 1 Thessalonians 2:14-16!), it is understandable that many Christians would do their best to make Paul more amenable to their Jewish dialogue partners.

Apologetic is, however, not the only reason for the changed image of Paul. A rereading of both Paul and the contemporary Jewish literature has also contributed to a new perception of the "apostle of the Gentiles". For one thing, the views expressed in 1 Thessalonians 2:14-16 must be seen within the context of that letter (the very first one Paul has written) and may not be universalized (Räisänen 1983:262f, 264); in addition, it is clear, particularly from Romans, that the later Paul does not accuse his kinsfolk of having killed Jesus and therefore deserving God's wrath "for ever" (cf Stendahl 1976:5; Steiger 1980:45-47; Mussner 1982:10; Sanders 1983:184). Second, it has been recognized ever more clearly that the letter to the Galatians ("Paul's most hot-tempered letter" — Martyn 1985:309) was written with a specific polemical purpose, namely, to counteract the influence of the Judaizers. Galatians should therefore not be interpreted as a systematic-theological treatise, but as a document written for a very specific context (cf Beker 1980:37-58 and Lategan 1988). Third, Paul shares many religious convictions with his Jewish contemporaries, such as their views on idolatry and their attitude to the Hebrew scriptures (in which his own thought is firmly anchored). A new scripture (a "new testament" contradistinguished from the "old") is to Paul as inconceivable as it is to most early Christians. He is not the "founder" of a new religion but the authoritative interpreter of the old (cf Beker 1980:340f, 343). Fourth, as Sanders (1983:192) has pointed out, the fact that Paul submits to the punishment meted out to him by the Jewish authorities (cf 2 Cor 11:24) shows that he still considers himself (as the Jews who punish him consider him) a member of the Jewish people. Punishment implies inclusion.

The Function of the Law

It is observations such as these, together with the increase in our knowledge of first-century Judaism, that have prompted a scholar like E. P. Sanders to say that

> on the point at which many have found the decisive contrast between Paul and Judaism — grace and works — Paul is in agreement with Palestinian Judaism . . . salvation is by grace but judgment is according to works; works are the condition of remaining "in", but they do not earn salvation (1977:543-552).[19]

Sanders may, however, have overstated his case, as several scholars have since argued (cf, *inter alia*, Moo 1987; Gundry 1987; and du Toit 1988). For one thing, first-century Judaism was not as unified in its "pattern of religion" as Sanders contends (even if we recognize that our knowledge of the Judaism of this period is limited, due to the fact that our sources are rather fragmentary; cf Wilckens 1959; Meeks 1983:32; Moo 1987:292, 298).[20] In addition, and partly in view of the paucity of Jewish sources, it may be a sound policy to accept Paul's writings as part of our source material on Judaism. If it is denied that at least some Jews at that time saw the Law as a way to salvation, Paul's polemic against Judaizers and the like is left dangling in midair; we could then only deduce that Paul has deliberately misunderstood or misrepresented his "opponents" (cf Moo 1987:291-293). So, even if scholars such as Sanders, Räisänen, and others have helped to put an end to some of the more extreme legalistic assumptions about Judaism and to the image of Paul as the lonely genius who has recognized that doing the Law is wrong in and of itself, many scholars still contend that "Paul and Palestinian Judaism look materially different at the point of grace and works" (Gundry 1987:96; cf Moo 1987:292, 298; and du Toit 1988).

I submit, then, that it cannot be denied that Paul experiences a fundamental problem with much of the understanding of the Law in the Judaism of his time and that this has important consequences for his interpretation of mission. It is in any case clear that he quite deliberately does not take the road of many other first-generation Jewish (and Gentile; cf the letter to the Galatians) Christians who experience no conflict between faith in Christ and upholding the Law (cf Wilckens 1959:278f; Beker 1980:248).

It is not easy to establish what precisely Paul's problem with the Law is.[21] To begin with (and this has often not been recognized), Paul sometimes is very positive about the Law. In Romans 9:4 he writes about his kinsfolk: "They are Israelites, and to them belong the sonship, the glory, the covenants, the giving of the law, the worship, and the promises". In Romans 11:29 these assets are referred to as the "gifts" (*charismata*) of God. And in Romans 15:8 he can even call Christ "a servant to the circumcised". Israel was meant to be a manifestation among the nations of a people living by promise and grace, as the case of their forefather Abraham shows (Rom 4; Gal 4) (cf Beker 1980:336). It follows from this that the Law does not oppose the gospel but bears witness to it (Rom 3:21). It is, rather, the summation of all God has given to and done for his people, apart from anything they could have achieved (cf also Räisänen 1987:408-410).

On the other hand, there are sayings in which Paul appears to be extremely negative about the Law, and even more particularly about Jewish practices, above all circumcision, which the "Judaizers" demand of the Gentile converts in Galatia.[22] To accept this means, however, to embrace "a different gospel" (Gal 1:6) or a perversion of the gospel of Christ (1:7); it means being "severed" from Christ" and having "fallen away from grace" (5:4).

Why this vehement attack on the Law? There may be several reasons, and Paul does not set these out logically. First, the demand of the "Judaizers" that the Gentile converts practice the "works of the Law" suggests that they are taught to adhere to outward rituals rather than to what the Law is all about (cf Räisänen 1987:406-408). Second (and this is, in a sense, comprised in the first), Paul's opposition to the Law and its observance is contextual; he sees how Gentile Christians' shallow interpretation of the Law perverts the essence of the gospel of salvation in Christ, and nothing should be allowed to compete with Christ.[23] Third, however (and this may in the final analysis be the most important reason for Paul's negative evaluation not just of the "practices" of the Law but of the Law itself), the Law fosters Jewish exclusiveness and must therefore be abrogated. Since this last observation is particularly germane to Paul's understanding of mission, I turn, briefly, to it.

Paul sees what no orthodox Jew really could see, even if he wished: whether Jews intend it or not, the Law has become a badge of distinction, and therefore of non-solidarity, between Jew and Gentile. It separates and therefore isolates groups from one another. It has become the embodiment of Jewish particularism, introversion, and group identity, and the occasion for pride in being a select people. The Jews have become ignorant of the fact that the Law really stands for "righteousness that comes from God" and, since they have construed it as a domain of segregation from the rest of humankind, they have turned it into their "own" righteousness (Rom 10:3). They misunderstand their own scriptures (cf 2 Cor 3:15) and their role as people of God. The Law has provided the Jews with a "charter of national privilege" (N. T. Wright, quoted by Moo 1987:294; cf also Beker 1980:335f, 344; Zeller 1982:177f). It is this inherently divisive quality of the Law that Paul rejects. Most explicitly he repudiates any "judaizing" of Gentile converts. All differences of social status and gender have fallen away; for Paul, however, the most important distinction that has been annulled is the one between Jew and Gentile (cf Gal 3:28). The "dividing wall" of the Law has been broken down (Eph 2:14) and it is inadmissible to rebuild what has been torn down (Gal 2:18) (cf Beker 1980:250; Zeller 1982:178; Senior and Stuhlmueller 1983:179; Meeks 1983:81).

All this can be formulated in yet another way. Sanders has suggested that Paul works out his mission theology not from plight to solution but from solution to plight (1977:442-447). In other words, it is not that Paul has, because of a particular predicament or plight he had experienced, discovered the inadequacy of the Law and was then driven to Christ as the solution to his plight. It happened the other way round. His encounter with Christ has compelled him to rethink everything from the ground up. The "solution" (Christ) revealed to him his "plight" (the Law's insufficiency unto salvation). For Paul, the real situation of Jews and Gentiles becomes manifest only in the light of the gospel, in the light of the "solution" (Hahn 1965:102, note 1). This is another way of saying what has been said above: no orthodox Jew could see the Law the way Paul sees it, unless he looked at it from Paul's perspective. And Paul was granted this perspective when he met the risen Christ.[24] He did not receive it through any human intervention, nor was he taught it; it came to him as a "revelation" (Gal 1:12-17). That event convinced him that it was through Jesus, crucified and risen, that God was offering salvation to all.

Unconditional Acceptance

Nothing in Jewish tradition has prepared Paul for this revolutionary perception. He now knows that it is not through the Law given at Sinai, but through Christ that all humanity is offered the possibility of moving from death to life, from sin to God. He therefore preaches "Christ crucified, a stumbling block to Jews and folly to Gentiles" (1 Cor 1:23); he has decided, as he writes to the Corinthians, "to know nothing among you except Jesus Christ and him crucified" (2 Cor 2:2) (cf Senior and Stuhlmueller 1983:168f, 171, 174, 179, 187). Christ has superseded the Law. Paul's assertion that Christ is the *telos nomou* (Rom 10:4) probably has to be understood in the sense that Christ is both the "end" and the "goal" of the Law; he is both the substitution for the Law, and the Law's original intention, "the surprising answer to Judaism's religious search" (Beker 1980:336, 341; cf Moo 1987:302-305). His substitutionary death on the cross, and that alone, has opened the way to reconciliation with God. God himself accepts people unconditionally. This is the cornerstone of Paul's mission theology.

From this fundamental cognition Paul draws a conclusion which to us may appear trite, but which constitutes, in fact, a stupendous claim: there is no difference between Jew and Gentile. To begin with, they are all "under the power of sin" (Rom 3:9), and all "fall short of the glory of God" (Rom 3:23). Everyone is under some "lordship" or other—of sin, of the Law, of the flesh, of false gods, etc (cf Rom 1:18-3:20)—and are therefore equally guilty and equally lost; indeed, the wrath of God is revealed from heaven against all ungodliness and wickedness (Rom 1:18) (cf Dahl 1977a:78; Walter 1979:438f; Senior and Stuhlmueller 1983:177; Stegemann 1984:302). No human wisdom, as suggested by the Greeks, and no Law, as the Jews believe, can save from the "wrath to come" (1 Thes 1:10; Rom 3:20; 5:12-14). Since all have sinned, death has spread to all (Rom 7:12).

This negative verdict is, however, counterbalanced with a positive one:

"Since all have sinned and fall short of the glory of God, *they are justified by his grace as a gift*, through the redemption which is in Christ Jesus" (Rom 3:23f; cf Gal 2:15-17). The gospel is indeed "the power of God for salvation, to everyone who has faith" (Rom 1:16). As God was "impartial" in his judgment, he is "impartial" or, better, gracious to all alike (cf Rom 2:11). This is so because God is not only the God of the Jews but the God of the Gentiles also, "since God is one" (Rom 3:29f) and his mercy concerns all (cf 11:30-32; 15:9). After all, both Jews and Gentiles are Abraham's descendants. The line of descent runs from Abraham via Christ to the Gentiles: "If you are Christ's, then you are Abraham's offspring, heirs according to the promise" (Gal 3:29; cf 3:7). Jews and Gentiles together form "the Israel of God" (Gal 6:16). There is "no distinction between Jew and Greek" (Rom 10:12); there is "neither Jew nor Greek . . . for all are one in Christ" (Gal 3:28). The entrance requirement "faith in Jesus Christ" applies to Gentiles and Jews alike (Sanders 1983:172). Only those who have "turned to the Lord" (2 Cor 3:16), whether they are Jews or Gentiles, are inheritors of the promises of Abraham (:174f).

The Problem of Unrepentant Israel

The Gentile mission was making rapid strides in Paul's time. Not so, however, the mission among Jews. It was, for Paul, "the most depressing experience of his life that the majority of his kinsfolk had closed themselves to the gospel" (Mussner 1982:11 – my translation). This bitter experience prompts him to write the deeply moving words of Romans 9:1-3,

> I am speaking the truth in Christ, I am not lying – my conscience bears me witness in the Holy Spirit, that I have great sorrow and unceasing anguish in my heart. For I could wish that I myself were accursed and cut off from Christ for the sake of my brethren, my kinsmen by race.

Paul is the "apostle to the Gentiles" *par excellence*; at the same time he is, among all the New Testament writers, the one most passionately concerned with Israel (Beker 1980:328). This means that, unless one takes into account the question of the salvation of the people of the old covenant, any portrayal of Paul's understanding of the Gentile mission remains fragmentary (Hahn 1965:105). It is Paul's fundamental conviction that the destiny of all humankind will be decided by what happens to Israel. The future of the Jews is, for Paul, not a matter of little consequence, nor is it a special problem of his views on eschatology (Stegemann 1984:300). It hurts him deeply that the Jews are not participating in the pilgrimage to the mountain of God in Jerusalem, "on which, to be sure, the cross now stands" (Steiger 1980:48 – my translation), and he can under no circumstances leave it at that.

So Paul falls back on the pledges of God in the Old Testament and on God's trustworthiness. He writes: "Then what advantage has the Jew? Or what is the value of circumcision? Much in every way. To begin with, the Jews are entrusted with the oracles of God. What if some were unfaithful? Does their faithlessness nullify the faithfulness of God? By no means!" (Rom 3:1-4a). And again: "They are Israelites, and to them belong the sonship, the glory, the covenants, the giving of the law, the worship, and the promises" (Rom 9:4).

Israel's salvation-historical priority thus remains valid and can never be ignored. The advantage of the Jews is real, for it is to them that the promises were entrusted. The Christ-event is primarily an answer to these promises. The gospel Paul proclaims is not a new religion but the answer to Israel's longing for the messianic age (cf Beker 1980:343). "Therefore, eschatological fulfillment of God's promise to Israel remains a lively hope; unless Israel will be saved, God's faithfulness to his promises is invalidated" (:335). For, says Paul, "the gifts and the call of God are irrevocable" (Rom 11:29). If they were not, God's promises, also to the Gentiles, would remain forever ambiguous (cf Stegemann 1984:300).

However, how can Paul maintain such a position in the face of the basic theological claim undergirding his mission to the Gentiles; namely, that there is neither Jew nor Greek in Christ (Gal 3:28), that it is the "children of the promise" rather than the "children of the flesh" who are Abraham's descendants (Rom 9:8), that "true circumcision" is not something "external and physical" but "a matter of the heart", that all have equal access to God and are all alike justified by faith alone? How can Paul hold two opposites at the same time? Senior and Stuhlmueller rightly remark, "Paul's struggle with this dilemma is complex and never entirely resolved" (1983:180). And Räisänen (1987:410) comments about Romans 9-11, where this entire issue comes to a head,

> Romans 9-11 testifies in a moving way to Paul's wrestling with an impossible task, his attempting to "square the circle". He tries to hold together two incompatible convictions: 1) God has made with Israel an irrevocable covenant and given Israel his law which invites the people to a certain kind of righteous life, and 2) this righteousness is not true righteousness, as it is not based on faith in Jesus.

This entire dilemma is really a "dilemma about God", arising, as it does, "from Paul's twin sets of convictions, those native to him and those revealed". Paul's problem is not just one of human anguish evoked by the possibility of eternal judgment on his people whom he loves so profoundly; he also worries "about God, his will, his constancy" (Sanders 1983:197). Paul's problem is indeed one of "conflicting convictions", which can be "better asserted than explained: salvation is by faith; God's promise to Israel is irrevocable" (:198). So Paul desperately seeks a formula which would keep God's promises to Israel intact, while insisting on faith in Christ (:199).

Romans 9-11

It is particularly in Romans 9-11 that Paul "asserts", rather than "explains", his convictions—to use Sanders's expression. These three most difficult chapters are placed in the middle of the letter to the Romans, the dominant theme of which is announced in 1:16, "The gospel . . . is the power of God for salvation

to everyone who has faith, to the Jew first and also to the Greek". The chapters
9 to 11 form the "real center of gravity in Romans" (Stendahl 1976:28) and
constitute a "test case" for understanding Paul and his perception of mission
(Stuhlmacher 1971:555). The inner unity of Paul's mission and theology is
nowhere more obvious than in these chapters (Dahl 1977a:86). It is important,
however, to note that they have not been put in their present position at random, after the first eight chapters. The letter to the Romans is not a theological
treatise on the doctrine of justification by faith in which the chapters 9 to 11
form a kind of "foreign body". Neither can they be attributed to the "speculative fantasy" of Paul, or termed "a kind of supplement," which is not "an
integral part of the main argument" (Bultmann and F. W. Beare respectively,
quoted in Beker 1980:63). This section is, rather, an important "history-of-
missions document that points toward the future"; and within this context, the
section under discussion "elucidates, in particular, the purpose and background
of Paul's mission to the Gentiles" (Stuhlmacher 1971:555 — my translation).

Chapter 11:25-27, as Luz rightly points out (1968:268; cf Hofius 1986:310f),
constitutes the essence of what Paul wishes to say, the culmination, as it were,
of the argument of the three chapters:

> Lest you be wise in your conceits, I want you to understand this mystery,
> brethren: a hardening has come upon part of Israel, until the full number
> of the Gentiles come in, and so all Israel will be saved; as it is written,
> "The Deliverer will come from Zion, he will banish ungodliness from
> Jacob"; "and this will be my covenant with them when I take away their
> sins".

I have said that Paul, and particularly his mission, can only be understood
against the background of Old Testament prophecy and contemporary Jewish
apocalyptic. This observation also applies to Romans 9-11 and especially to
chapter 11:25-27. Nowhere in his letters does Paul base his argumentation more
heavily on the Old Testament than in these three chapters (cf Aus 1979:232f;
Beker 1980:333). Luz (1968:286-300; cf also Rütti 1972:164-169) has argued
that the passage quoted above should not be regarded as referring to chronological events and to any particular sequel but that the references to chronology
should rather be interpreted as affirmations about God's grace and faithfulness.
This is, however, a highly improbable interpretation. Paul employs the style of
apocalyptic revelation here and asserts that the Gentile mission is an enterprise
during an interim period only, that it will come to an end when the "full number
of the Gentiles" has come in, after which "all Israel" will be saved and the
"Deliverer" (Christ at the parousia) will bring history to its end (cf Stuhlmacher
1971:561, 564f; Hengel 1983b:50f; Mussner 1982:12; Hofius 1986:311-320). All
of this is described as the unfolding of an apocalyptic drama.

Paul develops his case from Romans 9:1 onward, in two successive argu-
ments. The first runs from Romans 9:6 to 11:10, the second from 11:11 to 11:32
(Hofius 1986:300-311). Chapter 11:25-27 then forms the punch line, as it were.
It delineates God's salvific "strategy" as a "surprising wavelike or undulating

dynamic" (Beker 1980:334) in three "acts": Israel's hardening and opposition to Christ gives rise to the Gentile mission which, finally, leads to Israel's salvation (cf 11:30f).

A "hardening" (*porosis*) has come "upon part of Israel", says Paul. In 11:28 he even calls the Jews "enemies of God". At the same time he does not doubt their zeal and their good intentions, even if it is "not enlightened" (Rom 10:2). Moreover, drawing on several Old Testament passages, he appears to exculpate them, for he says in 11:8, "*God* gave them a spirit of stupor, eyes that *should* not see and ears that *should* not hear, down to this very day" (cf Mussner 1976:248; Hofius 1986:303f). The dominant motif, then, is that God has *allowed* Israel's hardening, *for the sake of the Gentiles*. This introduces the "second act". Through Israel's trespass "salvation has come to the Gentiles" (11:11); indeed, "their (Israel's) failure means riches for the Gentiles" (11:12), "their rejection means the reconciliation of the world" (11:15). "God shuts the eyes of Israel, so that the Gentiles may see the glory which God has prepared also for them" (Stegemann 1984:306). The hardening that has come upon part of Israel creates room for the Gentile mission and facilitates the coming in of their "full number".

This, then, sets the stage for the "third act"—the salvation of "all Israel". When the "full number of the Gentiles" enters (does Paul think of the representatives from all the Gentile churches who accompany him to Jerusalem to hand over the collection?), the period of Israel's "hardening" will be over; it will greet its "Deliverer" (11:26) and "receive mercy" (11:31). In a final sentence (11:32) Paul then sums up everything ("For God has consigned all to disobedience, that he may have mercy upon all"), and breaks out into a doxology (11:33-36).

How does Paul envisage the "salvation" of "all Israel"? Does he foresee the conversion of Israel to its Messiah? In other words, will Israel embrace Christ in faith? Does Paul expect the salvation of *every* Jew? And does he still see any need for a missionary proclamation to Jews? Scholars differ in their answers to these and similar questions.

Some say that, according to Paul, "all" Israel will be saved through an act of God at the moment of the parousia, *sola gratia*, when Israel will embrace Christ in faith (Stendahl 1976:4; Steiger 1980; Mussner 1976, 1982; Sanders 1983:189-198). Sanders, in particular, emphasizes that this does not imply a kind of "two-covenant theology", according to which Jews will be saved through faithfulness to the Law and Gentiles through faith in Christ. Jews, too, are only saved through faith in Christ. The only way to be part of the olive tree is by faith; Jews and Gentiles must be equal, both before and after being grafted into the olive tree. There are no two economies of salvation. However, so Sanders argues, Israel's coming to faith will not be the result of the apostolic mission; God, not human ambassadors, will accomplish Israel's salvation. This is the "mystery" that has been revealed to Paul. The original scheme has gone awry. God will save Israel not before but *after* the Gentiles have entered (cf Rom 11:13-16), yet on the same condition as the Gentiles—faith in Christ.

Like Sanders, others who adhere to the view that we should understand

Romans 9-11 as saying that "all" Israel will be saved through a divine act at the moment of the parousia are explicit in their conviction that "Gentile" Christians have no mission of converting Jews (cf Beker 1980:334; Steiger 1980:49). They point out that our text says nothing about Israel's *conversion*, only about Israel's *salvation* (Mussner 1976:249). Israel will hear the gospel from the mouth of the Christ of the parousia himself, and then embrace him in faith; "all Israel" will come to faith in exactly the same way Paul himself did—through an encounter with the risen Christ, without any human intervention (Hofius 1986:319f). Any Christian attempt to convert the Jews is, since Paul, theologically and since Auschwitz ethically impossible. In the case of Israel we have to distinguish *strictly* between *missio Dei* and *missio hominum* (Steiger 1980:57; cf Mussner 1976:252f). The church cannot move Israel to faith (Bieder 1964:27f). God alone will save Israel; the church's only involvement is "in the form of . . . a prognosis" (Stuhlmacher 1971:566). The only other obligation the church has is to protect the unbelieving Israel, since the Gentile Christians' present salvation (reconciliation with God) as well as their future salvation (the resurrection) depends on the destiny of the Jews (Steiger 1980:56). Strictly speaking, Romans 9-11 does not contain an indictment of Israel but "a speech for the defence" (:50).

There are indeed, in Romans 9-11, sayings that may lead the reader to interpretations such as the ones just referred to. It is also remarkable that Paul does not use the expressly Christian term *ekklesia*, "church", in the letter to the Romans (with the exception of the greetings in chapter 16 [cf Beker 1980:316]). Equally amazing is the fact that Paul writes the whole section of Romans 10:17 to 11:36 "without using the name of Christ. This includes the final doxology (11:33-36), the only such doxology in his writings without any christological element" (Stendahl 1976:4—he obviously does not understand the "Deliverer" in 11:26 as referring to Christ).

Other scholars judge that the conclusions referred to above are unwarranted. They argue that too much weight is given to just one passage—in fact, just a few verses—and that what Paul says in Romans 11:25-32 has to be seen within the context of what he writes elsewhere. It is also worth noting that Paul includes "qualifiers" even within the argument of chapters 9 to 11. In 11:23, for instance, where he alludes to the "unbelieving" Jews, he says that they, too, may be grafted into the olive tree, "*if* they do not persist in their unbelief". What he says about the salvation of "all Israel" should therefore not be perceived to be in conflict with his statements elsewhere that obedience to the Law, even at its very best, is inadequate (cf Rom 10:2), or with his fundamental thesis in Romans 1:16, namely that the gospel "is the power of God for salvation *to every one who has faith*" (cf also Zeller 1982:184; Senior and Stuhlmueller 1983:180). Christian mission among Jews is therefore not categorically excluded by Romans 9-11 (Kirk 1986).

We may be helped toward finding an answer to the vexing problem presented by Romans 9 to 11 if we keep in mind that an important (perhaps the most important?) motif in these chapters is to warn Paul's Gentile Christian readers in Rome against arrogance and boasting in view of Israel's "hardening". Utilizing the metaphor of the olive tree, Paul says that Gentile Christians might be tempted to exclaim, "Branches were broken off so that I might be grafted in!" (11:19). Paul grants that this is indeed what has happened, but he reminds the Gentile Christians that they have been grafted in "only through faith", and he adds: "so do not become proud, but stand in awe. For if God did not spare the natural branches, neither will he spare you" (11:20f). It is not they who support the root, but the root that supports them (11:18). Gentiles, the "wild olive tree", have been grafted into the "cultivated" tree, Israel, "contrary to nature" (11:24). So they are warned not to be wise in their own conceits (11:25). There is no room for any triumphalism. Only one attitude toward Israel is permitted, indeed advocated, and that is that Gentile Christians, through faith, hope and love, give testimony to Israel's God, and by so doing provoke the Jews to "jealousy". So important is this motif to Paul that he reiterates it in three different ways (Rom 10:19; 11:11; and 11:14), making sure that Gentile Christians fully understand their proper posture toward Israel (cf Mussner 1976:254f; Stegemann 1984:306; Hofius 1986:308-310).

Paul's use of the expression "mystery" (*mysterion*), particularly in Romans 11:25, points in the same direction. The mystery refers to the "interdependence" of God's dealings with Gentiles and with Jews (Beker 1980:334), a process that runs from Gentile disobedience via Gentiles receiving mercy, to Jewish disobedience, to mercy shown to Jews, and, finally, to God having mercy "upon all" (Rom 11:30-32). In Paul's view, then, "the fate of Israel, and therefore the final act in God's plan, hinged on the completion of the Gentile mission" (Senior and Stuhlmueller 1983:185), and on the irrevocable coordination of Jew and Gentile.

Romans 9-11 thus confirms, in yet another way, the dialectical interrelationship between Jews and Gentiles in Paul's thinking. To the *Jews* he is saying that the missionary outreach to Gentiles is the consequence of Israel's historical mission to the world in the new messianic era, which the Christ-event has inaugurated (Beker 1980:333). "Israel must learn to extend God's promise of grace that she has received to all the Gentiles without qualification" (:336f). The gospel is indeed directed to the Jew first, but also to the Greek (cf Rom 1:16; 2:10). Christ has become a "servant to the circumcised" (Rom 15:8) in order that Gentiles might "rejoice ... with his people" (15:10) (cf Minear 1961:45). In Abraham, forefather of the Jews, God has begun a history of promise which aims not only at Jews, but at all people.

To *Gentile Christians* Paul is saying that they would be "wise in their own conceits" (11:25) if they regarded their own existence as Christians in isolation from and severed from Israel (cf Bieder 1964:27). Paul never surrenders the continuity of God's story with Israel. The church cannot be the people of God without its linkage with Israel. Paul's apostolate to the Gentiles is related to the salvation of Israel and does not mean a turning away from Israel. The gospel means the extension of the promise beyond Israel, not the displacement of Israel by a church made up of Gentiles (cf Beker 1980:317, 331, 333, 344). Paul therefore never (not even in Gal 6:16) explicitly says that the church is the "new Israel", as becomes customary from the second century onward, for instance in the writings of Barnabas and Justin Martyr (cf Beker 1980:316f,

328, 336; Senior and Stuhlmueller 1983:173-180). Indeed, the church is not a new Israel, "but an enlarged Israel" (Kirk 1986:258). And Gentile Christians should never lose sight of that.

Has Paul succeeded in "squaring the circle" (Räisänen 1987:410); that is, has he been able to reconcile his views on God's irrevocable covenant with Israel with his conviction that God will save only those who respond in faith to the gospel?

The answer to this question will depend, at least in part, on one's perspective. To the very end these two equally firm beliefs remain in tension with each other, and it would probably be in conflict with the spirit of Paul's ministry to press any of the two to its logical limits. Such logic would ultimately conclude either that faith in Christ does not, in the final analysis, matter so much, or that Israel is lost, in light of the fact that so few Jews have come to faith. Paul cannot bring himself to make either of these two assertions.

THE CHURCH: THE INTERIM ESCHATOLOGICAL COMMUNITY

Ekklesia *in Paul*

Earlier in this chapter, when I discussed Paul's sense of responsibility as a dimension of his missionary motivation, I briefly touched upon what Paul has to say about the believers' attitude and conduct toward "outsiders". We need, however, to take a closer look at his understanding of the *church* in the context of his theology of mission.

Sociologists have pointed out that any social organization, in order to persist, must have boundaries, must maintain structural stability as well as flexibility, and must create a unique culture (Marvin E. Olson, reference in Meeks 1983:84). In the case of an essentially religious organization additional factors enter into the picture, such as those relating to what attracts people to a specific religious persuasion, the changes that take place in their understanding of themselves and of the world, and that which supports them in the new faith (Gaventa 1986:3).

If we wish to apply these criteria to the Pauline churches of the fifties of the first century AD, we should keep in mind that these communities were anything but stable when Paul left them, "relatively unorganized, fraught with distress, with only rudimentary instruction in the faith, and in tension with the larger society" (Malherbe 1987:61; cf Lippert 1968:130f). These numerically small communities assumed the name *ekklesia*, commonly used in the Septuagint as translation for the Hebrew *kahal*. In contemporary Greek, *ekklesia* normally referred to the town meeting of free male citizens of a city of Greek constitution. The Hellenistic-Jewish Christian communities (beginning, perhaps, with the community in Antioch; cf Beker 1980:306) were the first to apply this term to themselves. Paul takes it with him on his missionary travels.

Meeks has offered a careful comparison between the Pauline *ekklesia* and four contemporary models: the Roman or Greek household; the voluntary association (clubs, guilds, and the like); the Jewish synagogue; and the philosophical or rhetorical school (1983:75-84). Malherbe has perused the major philosophical schools (particularly the Cynics, Epicureans, and Stoics) and compared these with Paul's understanding of the church (1987:passim). After careful consideration of the evidence, both scholars come to the conclusion that, in spite of many remarkable similarities between the *ekklesia* and the other groups, there can be no doubt that the *ekklesia* was a community *sui generis*. Since its distinctive characteristics have an important bearing on the understanding of the church as a missionary community, I now turn to these.

In Paul's thinking, the "righteousness of God" (cf Rom 3:21-31) is to be interpreted as gift to the *community*, not to the individual (cf Luz 1968:168-171), for the individual believer does not exist in isolation. This emerges particularly clearly in his two letters to the Corinthians, where some believers interpret their freedom in Christ to mean that each is permitted to do as he or she pleases, an understanding of the Christian life that Paul rejects again and again (cf Gaventa 1986:45). There is indeed no place in the church for the isolated self or for the selfish (Beker 1984:37). When any individual experiences "justification by faith", he or she is moved into the community of believers. "Members of the community of the last days do not live solitary lives" (Malherbe 1987:80). Indeed, Christians "are a community of a special kind" (:94). They are called "saints", the "elect", those "called", "loved", and "known" by God (for references, cf Meeks 1983:85). They have to conduct themselves according to what they are in Christ. This manifests itself particularly in their mutual relationships, they are to admonish those who threaten harmony in the community (:94) and display a practical concern for the material needs of fellow-members (:102). This concern has to be extended far beyond the borders of the local community for, although *ekklesia* in Paul usually refers to the local church (cf Ollrog 1979:126; Beker 1980:314-316), the wider fellowship is always presupposed (Meeks 1983:75, 80, 107-109). Hospitality therefore has to be offered to fellow-believers from other regions as well, and Paul urges the Christians in Rome to "contribute to the needs of the saints" and "practice hospitality" (Rom 12:13) (cf Meeks 1983:109f).

The relationship between believers is particularly clearly displayed in Paul's "language of belonging" (Meeks 1983:85-94). His use of kinship terminology is highly important in this regard. Terms such as "father", "child"/"children", and especially "brother"/"brethren" abound in his letters. Such terms are found elsewhere in the New Testament as well, but both the number and intensity of the affective phrases in the Pauline letters are extremely unusual. The local *ekklesia* clearly becomes the primary group for its members. In his first letter, (the relatively short) 1 Thessalonians, Paul calls the Christians "brethren" no less than eighteen times (cf Meeks 1983:86-88; Malherbe 1983:39f; 1987:48-52). What Alfred Wifstrand (quoted by Malherbe 1983:39) wrote about the New Testament in general is particularly applicable to the Pauline communities: "What is peculiar to the New Testament is that God is nearer and one's fellowmen are nearer than they are to the Jews and Greeks, the conception of community has quite another importance, the valuations are more intense, and for that reason the emotionally tinged adjectives too are more frequent".

Baptism and the Transcending of Barriers

The unity that prevails among believers has its basis in the fact that they are all, through baptism, incorporated into Christ. I have indicated that Paul's preaching, indeed his entire theology, centers in the death and resurrection of Christ. This also explains his understanding of baptism. The believers—not as so many individuals but as a corporate body—are baptized into the death of Christ and are likewise raised from the dead; they are crucified with Christ, have died with him, but now live with him and are alive to God (Rom 6:3-11). They have "put on" Christ, crucified and risen, and have been adopted as children of God (Gal 3:26f; cf Col 3:10).

It is this momentous event of the believers being baptized into Christ that motivates Paul to declare so passionately and vehemently that all human barriers are transcended in the church. Baptism is "the seal of membership in the eschatological people of God" (Käsemann 1969b:119). To the Corinthians Paul says, "By one Spirit we were all baptized into one body—Jews or Greeks, slaves or free" (1 Cor 12:13). To the Galatians he writes in similar vein: "For as many of you as were baptized into Christ have put on Christ. There is neither Jew nor Greek, there is neither slave nor free, there is neither male nor female; for you are all one in Christ" (Gal 3:27f; cf also Eph 3:6).

Baptism thus consciously brings about a change in social relationships and in self-understanding (Malherbe 1987:49). Faith in Christ makes fellowship possible. Because believers are one in Christ, they belong to one another (cf Zeller 1982:180). The fellowship in Christ does not unite only Jews and Gentiles, but people from different social backgrounds as well (I once again refer to Petersen 1985). The contemporary Greek and Roman associations tended to be rather homogeneous sociologically (cf Malherbe 1983:86f; Meeks 1983:79), but Paul insists that divisions be transcended. 1 Corinthians 10-11 offers a sustained argument in support of greater social integration between the rich and the poor (and, by implication, between free citizens and slaves) within the community's celebration of the Lord's Supper. The behavior of the rich collides with Paul's understanding of the nature of community. The conduct of the well-to-do is not simply offensive to the others' sensibilities and cannot be put right just by applying proper etiquette; no, correct behavior in these matters is indicative of the presence of genuine faith (1 Cor 11:19) (Malherbe 1983:79-84).

This explains the vehemence of Paul's reaction to Peter when the latter refused to eat with Gentiles converts (Gal 2:11-21). To object to sharing the table of the Lord with fellow-believers is a denial of one's being justified by faith (cf Räisänen 1983:259). Where this happens, people are trusting in some form of justification by works. The reconciliation with God is in jeopardy if Christians are not reconciled to each other but continue to separate at meals. The unity of the church—no, the church itself—is called in question when groups of Christians segregate themselves on the basis of such dubious distinctives as race, ethnicity, sex, or social status. God in Christ has accepted us unconditionally; we have to do likewise with regard to one another. On the basis of Paul's thinking, it is inconceivable that, in a given locality, converts could comprise two congregations—one of Torah observant Jewish Christians, and another of non-observant Gentile Christians (Sanders 1983:188). In the death and resurrection of Jesus Christ a new age has dawned, in which Jew and Gentile are joined together without distinction in the one people of God. "Is Christ divided?" (1 Cor 1:13). That is inconceivable! Segregation in the church destroys its internal life and denies its grounding in the substitutionary death of Christ. Only *Christ*, not Paul or anybody else (cf 1 Cor 1:13), was crucified so as to reconcile people with God (cf Breytenbach 1986:3f,19). *"One has died for all"* (2 Cor 5:14). And Christ's work of reconciliation does not just bring two parties into the same room that they may settle their differences; it leads to a new kind of body in which human relations are being transformed. In a very real sense mission, in Paul's understanding, is saying to people from all backgrounds, "Welcome to the new community, in which all are members of one family and bound together by love" (cf also Beker 1980:319; Zeller 1982:178; Meeks 1983:81, 92; Hahn 1984:282f; Hultgren 1985:141f; Kirk 1986:252).

For the Sake of the World

This is what the Pauline mission sets out to accomplish. The church is called to be a community of those who glorify God by showing forth his nature and works and by making manifest the reconciliation and redemption God has wrought through the death, resurrection, and reign of Christ (cf 1 Cor 5:18-20). It is true, of course, that the Pauline churches are intensely aware of what distinguishes them from those outside and that Paul also continuously reminds them of their uniqueness. At the same time, this awareness of being a distinctive group does not lead to any encystation; precisely their sense of uniqueness encourages them to share with others. There is a creative tension between being exclusive and practicing solidarity with others.

In Paul's understanding, the church is "the world in obedience to God", the "redeemed ... creation" (Käsemann 1969b:134). Its primary mission in the world is to *be* this new creation. Its very existence should be for the sake of the glory of God. Yet precisely this has an effect on the "outsiders". Through their conduct, believers attract outsiders or put them off (cf Lippert 1968:166f). Their lifestyle is either attractive or offensive. Where it is attractive, people are drawn to the church, even if the church does not actively "go out" to evangelize them. Paul writes to the Thessalonians that the word of the Lord has "sounded forth" from them in Macedonia and that their faith "has gone forth everywhere" (1 Thes 1:8). He reminds the Corinthians that they themselves are his "letter of recommendation ... to be known and read by all men" (2 Cor 3:2). Similarly, of the Christians in Rome it is said that their faith "is proclaimed in all the world" (Rom 1:8) and their "obedience known to all" (16:19). These comments probably do not suggest that the Thessalonian, Corinthian, and Roman churches are actively involved in direct missionary outreach, but rather that they are "missionary by their very nature", through their unity, mutual love, exemplary conduct, and radiant joy.

The church is not other-worldly. It is involved with the world, which means that it is missionary. Christians are called to practice a messianic lifestyle within the church but also to exercise a revolutionary impact on the values of the world. They do not withdraw into a cloister, barricaded against the onslaughts of the world (Beker 1980:318f). For Paul, there is no dualism between the human soul and the external world. "He places the human being in the context of the world and its power structures" and emphasizes "a profound solidarity and interdependence" between the church and the world (Beker 1984:36), which marks the church as a "community of hope while it groans and labors for the redemption of the world" (:69). The church is the church *in* the world and *for* the world (:37), which means that it has "an active vocation and mission to the created order and its institutions" (Beker 1980:326f). The church is that community of people who are involved in creating new relationships among themselves and in society at large and, in doing this, bearing witness to the lordship of Christ. He is no private or individual Lord but always, as Lord of the church, also Lord of the world.

The church is therefore very important to Paul. The believers to whom he addresses his letters are not a "ragtag group of manual laborers formed by an itinerant preacher", but a "community created and loved by God", which as such occupies "a special place in his redemptive scheme" (Malherbe 1987:79). Paul therefore not only founds churches but also sustains them amid all their burdens and conflicts by writing letters and from time to time sending envoys to them. He refers, in this respect, to the daily pressure upon him and to his anxiety for all the churches (2 Cor 11:28). The church is *now* the eschatological people of God and a living witness of the ratification of God's promises to his people Israel, precisely in its having a membership wider than the people of the old covenant. The church is holy, Christ's body on earth, and when believers are insensitive to the needs and circumstances of others, they actually "despise the church of God" (1 Cor 11:22).

In spite of its theological importance, however, the church is always and only a preliminary community, en route to its self-surrender unto the kingdom of God. Paul never develops an ecclesiology which can be divorced from christology and eschatology (Beker 1980:303f; 1984:67). The church is a community of hope which groans and labors for the redemption of the world and for its own consummation (cf Beker 1984:69). It is only the *beginning* of the new age. So Paul never constructs a "doctrine of the church"; *ekklesia* remains, rather, a powerful *image* (Beker 1980:306f). The church is a proleptic reality, the sign of the dawning of the new age in the midst of the old, and as such the vanguard of God's new world. It is simultaneously acting as pledge of the sure hope of the world's transformation at the time of God's final triumph and straining itself in all its activities to prepare the world for its coming destiny (cf Beker 1980:313, 317-319, 326; 1984:41; Kertelge 1987:373). The church knows, after all, that "the form of this world is passing away" and that "the appointed time has grown very short". So,

> from now on, let those who have wives live as though they had none, and those who mourn as though they were not mourning, and those who rejoice as though they were not rejoicing, and those who buy as though

they had no goods, and those who deal with the world as though they had no dealings with it (1 Cor 7:29-31).

THE PAULINE MISSIONARY PARADIGM

As in the preceding chapters, I shall now attempt to trace the outlines of Paul's paradigm of mission. His importance for the understanding of the early Christian mission can hardly be exaggerated. In all of the New Testament — yes, in all of the early church — he is unparalleled in the profound way in which he presents a universal Christian missionary vision (cf Senior and Stuhlmueller 1983:161). There can be no doubt that Paul the theologian cannot be understood unless he is seen primarily as Paul the missionary; any attempt at interpreting Paul must aim at regaining "the unity of theology and evangelism, and of justification by faith and world mission" (Dahl 1977a:88).

Paul's thinking, truth to tell, is so complex that, at the end of a reflection like this, one has the distinct feeling of still standing only at the beginning (cf also Haas 1971:119). There are many trailing edges I have not pursued. It has been impossible to give more than a rough sketch of *one* way in which Paul's understanding of mission may be explicated. I am well aware of the fact that, in several respects, the "real Paul" may often have eluded me. This Paul remains for the most part, says Käsemann (1969e:249), "unintelligible to posterity", also to our own time, and I may, at best, have underlined only *some* of the essential features of his theology.

"One aim of missiology", writes Minear, "is a more adequate understanding of the apostolic task of the Church. One aim of exegetical theology is a more adequate understanding of the mind of the biblical writer". Minear continues, "When, therefore, the exegete deals with the apostle Paul, and when missiology accepts Paul's apostolic work as normative for the continuing mission of the Church, then *these two aims coalesce*" (1961:42; emphasis added). This "coalescence" (H. G. Gadamer would say this "fusion of horizons") is a task fraught with danger. We are easily tempted to draw hasty conclusions and apply these to our contemporary situation, forgetting that Paul developed his missionary theology and strategy in a very specific context. The only way out of the dilemma is once again, as has been suggested in previous chapters, to extrapolate from Paul, to allow him to "fertilize" our imagination and, in dependence on the guidance of the Holy Spirit, to prolong, in a creative way, the logic of Paul's theology and mission amid historical circumstances that are in many respects very different from his. We do not really "understand" Paul if we just "pin him down" in the first century AD. Our quest is not just to establish what Paul's letters meant in the first century, but also what they mean today. We have to bridge the gap between the then and the now. The process of interpretation is basically a unified one in which historical and theological (more precisely, in this case, exegetical and missiological) understandings ultimately blend (cf Beker 1984:63f). Naturally, this can only succeed if we treat the authenticity of the original text with the utmost respect and do not sacrifice it on the altar of "relevance". What we are really called to do, in a nutshell, is "to be faithful to the old text in a new situation" (:106). We have to read Paul historically—that means on his own terms (as far as that is possible)—before we attempt any "application", rather than proof-text him to buttress an understanding to which we happen to be favorably disposed.

It has, hopefully, become clear in the preceding pages that there is more to Paul's "theology of mission" than such an arbitrary (even if time-honored!) interpretation suggests. There may be another problem, however; given the uniqueness of Paul, do we have the right to extrapolate from him? Is it not true, as Hengel (1983b:52f) suggests, that Paul's missionary apostolate is so exceptional that it is not possible to emulate him? Reading Paul's letters, one may indeed gain such an impression. Almost single-handedly he takes on the entire Roman Empire. A "fateful necessity" (*anangke*) is laid upon him (1 Cor 9:16). The labels with which he identifies his person and ministry are indeed awesome. He compares his own call with that of Isaiah and Jeremiah (cf Rom 1:1; Gal 1:15). He portrays his ministry as a "priestly act" and offers the Gentile Christians to God as a sacrifice acceptable to God and sanctified by the Holy Spirit (Rom 15:16). Through Paul God is spreading the "fragrance of the knowledge of him everywhere"; Paul identifies himself as "the aroma of Christ to God among those who are being saved and among those who are perishing" (2 Cor 2:14f). He is Christ's ambassador, through whom God is making his appeal (2 Cor 5:20). He has been made the minister of a new covenant (2 Cor 3:6), even God's fellow-worker (1 Cor 3:9) (cf Senior and Stuhlmueller 1983:182f). In addition he is, as he states in a variety of ways in his letter to the Romans, indebted to both Jews and Gentiles, because he is indebted to Christ (cf Minear 1961).

Dare *we* make such bold claims? Probably not. On the other hand, dare we today read Paul's letters devotionally, dare we preach from them, unless we allow ourselves to be infected with the missionary passion of Paul? And does not Paul himself extend his vision and image of mission to his fellow-workers and to the churches he has founded? I have argued above that he does. Just as Paul is indebted to Christ and to Jew and Gentile, Jewish and Gentile Christians are indebted to Christ and to each other. A "triangular" interdependence is operative here (Minear 1961:44). If we are justified by Christ, this change "will be most authentically indicated by the emergence of a radically new indebtedness/thankfulness" (:48; cf Bieder 1965:30f). The Pauline churches manifest their "debt of gratitude" first and foremost in their being different from others, by commanding the respect of outsiders (1 Thes 4:12), by abstaining from every form of evil (1 Thes 5:22), by giving offense to nobody (1 Cor 10:32), by being "blameless and innocent, children of God without blemish in the midst of a crooked and perverse generation" (Phil 2:15), and by filling their thoughts with all that is true, honorable, just, pure, lovely, and gracious (Phil 4:8). The remarkable chapter 12 of the letter to the Romans is particularly instructive in this regard. There can indeed be no doubt that Paul expects his readers to emulate him.

In this spirit I shall now attempt to identify the characteristics of Paul's missionary paradigm.

1. *The Church as New Community*. The churches that have come into existence as a consequence of Paul's mission find themselves in a world divided culturally (Greeks *v* barbarians), religiously (Jews *v* Gentiles), economically (rich *v* poor), and socially (free *v* slave). In the fledgling churches themselves (particularly the one in Corinth) there are factions, evidenced by disunity and bickering. However, Paul never acquiesces in this. He finds it impossible to give up on the unity of the one body, in spite of all differences. This motif is not just a strategic or pragmatic move against sectarian fragmentation. Rather, it is undergirded by a theological principle: once people have been "baptized into Christ" and have "put on Christ", there can no longer be any separation between Jew and Gentile, between slave and free, between male and female, between Greek and barbarian; now all are "one in Christ Jesus" (Gal 3:27f). We are now "understood in terms of our baptism and not in terms of our birth" (Breytenbach 1986:21). Our unity is, indeed, non-negotiable. The church is the vanguard of the new creation and has, of necessity, to reflect the values of God's coming world.

In light of this, any form of segregation in the church, whether racial, ethnic, social, or whatever, is in Paul's understanding a denial of the gospel (cf Duff 1989:287-289). Reconciliation and justification manifest themselves in interdependence and *philadelphia* between believers. Where this is not the case, something is drastically wrong, and it is unthinkable for Paul to leave it at that. The members of the new community find their identity in Jesus Christ rather than in their race, culture, social class, or sex. Once again, how can it be different, if Gentiles and Jews have been made one by Christ, if he has created "out of the two a single new humanity in himself", and has reconciled them "in a single body to God through the cross" (Eph 2:15f, NEB)?

2. *A Mission to Jews?* Paul's understanding of the relationship between the church and Israel is related to the point just discussed but is also, from another perspective, a special case. Are the Jews perhaps the only religious group in the world to whom the church has no mission of conversion? I have mentioned that several scholars have come to this conclusion, particularly on the basis of their exegesis of Romans 9-11. The church, says Steiger, has no other "mission" toward Jews than to "protect the unbelieving Israel" and safeguard the peace of the Jew in the world (1980:56f; cf Beker 1980:338f).

Even if we grant that Romans 9-11 (and particularly 11:25-32) is to be interpreted in the sense that Paul does not anticipate any further missionary activity among Jews, the conclusion of Steiger and others remains problematic. For one thing, one has to ask whether actual events have not overtaken Paul's expectations so passionately expressed here. And if this is so, would it not be anachronistic to appeal to these verses as the final answer to today's questions (cf also Zeller 1982:189)? Second, do we not perhaps run the risk of over-relying on one single passage, thereby ignoring other statements, not only in the New Testament in general, but also in Paul himself (cf Kirk 1986:249)? Third, can it be denied that much of the contemporary sensitivity to Jewish views and aspirations, along with demands for recognizing "the sacred importance of Jewish survival" (J. T. Pawlikowski, quoted by Kirk 1986:250), are to be attributed to the bad conscience of especially Western Christians after the Holocaust?

In the light of these and similar questions, let me risk a few observations on the subject under discussion.

First, Gentile Christians should never lose sight of the fact that Israel is the matrix of the eschatological people of God; they should therefore never surrender the continuity of God's story with Israel. The Christian faith is "an extension, or fresh interpretation, of what it meant to be Jewish in the first century" (Kirk 1986:253). The church is not the new Israel (in the sense that God has switched the covenant from unbelieving Jews to believing Gentiles); it is, rather, an enlarged Israel (:258). A Gentile Christian existence may never be detached from Israel (Bieder 1964:27). Paul explains this with the aid of a metaphor that defies every horticultural practice; the branches of the *wild* olive tree are grafted, "contrary to nature", into the cultivated olive tree (Rom 11:24).

Second, Gentile Christians have never really behaved like guests in the house of Israel. Rather, the church inverted the order by which the two communities came together; the Jews were locked out of the house and the key thrown away (Fr. Daniel, quoted in Kirk 1986:253). Generations of Gentile Christians have ignored their dependence on the faith of Israel and, in brazen self-justification, boasted of their faith over against "the Jews". Actually, they went further. The relation of Christians to Jews throughout Christian history has been a history of perversion, misunderstanding, hatred, and persecution.

Third, a serious dialogue between Gentile Christians and Jews is of the utmost importance. And yet, we do not meet in a vacuum, but in the shadow of a tragic history, more especially of the Holocaust. However, in spite of the pain and tragedy, we should, in our dialogue, look beyond this event to the fact that Christianity and Judaism share a common root and a common Scripture and yet differ profoundly in the understanding of the revelation of their common God. The age-long history of Christian oppression of Jews will be a silent partner in the dialogue; it should encourage empathy but not lead to a watering down of the issues (cf Beker 1980:337f).

Fourth, any theological dialogue with and discussion about Israel should distinguish between Israel's place in the covenant of God and the empirical modern state or nation of Israel. It is a dangerous theological misconception to lay a direct connection between the unique position of Israel as a theological entity and the survival of the Jews in a separate nation-state – quite apart from the fact that events in recent years have shown that Israel behaves no differently from any other nation (cf Kirk 1986:254-257).

Fifth, the issue of a continuing evangelistic mission to Jews remains an unfinished item on the agenda of the church. What Paul says in Romans 9-11 remains sufficiently ambiguous at least to allow the possibility of interpreting it in the sense of the necessity of a continuing mission to Jews. If Christ is indeed "the surprising answer to Judaism's religious search", if a "conflation of the Torah and Christ" is inadmissible (cf Beker 1980:341, 347), if what matters is not Abraham's flesh but his faith (Gal 3:7; Rom 4:11, 14, 16; 9:8), if zealous observance of religion does not bring salvation (Rom 10:2), if only those who "do not persist in their unbelief" will be grafted back into the olive tree (Rom

11:23), does it not mean that Christians have a responsibility toward Jews beyond safeguarding the peace of Jews in the world? Naturally, any Christian witness to Jews has to be borne in a spirit of profound sensitivity and humility, in light, once again, of the history of the Christian treatment of Jews.[25]

Lastly, Paul's reflections on "the church and Israel" show remarkable similarities with those of Matthew and Luke. They all belong to the same general paradigm. There are, however, also significant differences among the three authors. Paul's reflections, in particular, are characterized by an almost unbearable and yet creative tension.

3. *Mission in the Context of God's Imminent Triumph.* I have given a fair amount of attention to Paul's understanding of his mission within the horizon of Christ's parousia. However, more than nineteen centuries have come and gone since Paul proclaimed the impending end of the world without his expectation being fulfilled. Beker (1984:64) quotes James M. Robinson as an example of widespread disillusionment with Paul in ecclesiastical and theological circles:

> An imminent expectation can no longer be fulfilled, since our time is no longer near to that time. But all other modifications of the time pattern are equally unfulfillable. Anyone who would try to claim that God's reign has already come, that is, that our world is the kingdom of God deserves to be laughed or cried down. But he who seeks a position between those extremes—is also refuted by the non-fulfillment of the consummation. For a thinking person today all temporal alternatives are equally invalid.

The problem is indeed a serious one. Down through the ages, and particularly in modern times, scholars have tried their best to reinterpret or explain away this uncomfortable element in Paul's theology (for examples, see Beker 1980:366; 1984:117). Outside "respectable" church and theological circles the solution was (and still is) often found in exactly the opposite direction—by holding on desperately to the *form* of Paul's apocalyptic, but without its substance, as evidenced by the writings of Hal Lindsey and others.

Beker suggests an opposite approach, that of holding on to the substance of Paul's apocalyptic eschatology without absolutizing its form. Attempts to make the chronological dimension of his expectation absolutely decisive have yielded disastrous results and have acutely distorted the core of Paul's gospel. Chronology is only a (necessary) byproduct of the primary foci of Paul's message— which is not the same as saying that the urgency of (chronological) time can be swept aside in the sense of 2 Peter 3:8 ("But do not ignore this one fact, beloved, that with the Lord one day is as a thousand years and a thousand years as one day"). Still, we cannot simply take for granted chronological time's unending and enduring character. Rather, we must continue to attend to the beckoning power of God's coming triumph without losing ourselves either in chronological speculations or in a denial of the coming actualization of God's promise. With Paul, we must expect an ultimate resolution to the contradictions and sufferings of life in the coming triumph of God. Our life as Christians is only real when it is anchored in the sure knowledge of God's victory: "If for this life only we have hoped in Christ, we are of all men most to be pitied" (1 Cor 15:19). We know and confess that God's triumph is in his hands alone and that it transcends our chronological speculations and anticipations. And precisely because we move toward the dawn of God's indubitable victory we refuse to be conformed to this world; rather, we allow our minds to be remade and our whole nature thus transformed (Rom 12:2). Our mission in the world only makes sense if it is undertaken in the sure knowledge that our puny "accomplishments" will one day be consummated by God (cf further Beker 1980:362-367; and particularly 1984:29-54, 79-121). Here and now believers have the first fruits of the Spirit—not as substitute for eschatological hope but as the One who keeps that hope alive and through whom we groan inwardly as we await redemption (Rom 8:23).

4. *Mission and the Transformation of Society.* A discussion of Paul's apocalyptic raises the issue of the relationship between church and world and the question whether apocalyptic eschatology has anything to say about the church's calling in society.

In reflecting on this, we must remind ourselves that, in Paul's time, the fledgling Christian movement was peripheral to society, a totally negligible entity as far as size was concerned, and its survival—humanly speaking—in jeopardy. These factors explain, at least to some extent, the absence of any trenchant critique of unjust societal structures (such as slavery) in Paul, as well as his basically positive attitude toward the Roman Empire (cf Rom 13).

This is, however, not the full story. One also has to view Paul as one who rejects two mutually contradictory theological interpretations, namely, "pure" apocalyptic and enthusiasm. His reaction to *both* these sentiments reveals the far-reaching societal implications of his gospel.

Jewish apocalyptic, as has been shown, tended to construct an absolute antithesis between this age and the next. Such an understanding almost as a matter of course leads to a withdrawal from this world and its vicissitudes. There can be no doubt that such a basically dualistic apocalyptic was embraced by many first-century Christians. Since the turning of the ages has already begun Paul finds this interpretation utterly impossible. We live *now* in that new space created by the powerful invasion of Christ; therefore we can no longer tolerate Old Age distinctions in the social and political order (cf Duff 1989:285f).

The enthusiasts (particularly those operating in Corinth), adopt essentially the opposite position. In their excitement over what they have already received in Christ, the Corinthian enthusiasts jettison the expectation of an imminent parousia and the hope for a future bodily resurrection of the dead. Christ's resurrection is no longer regarded as harbinger of the universal redemption that is still being awaited, nor the advent of the Holy Spirit as pledge of what is still to come; rather, through baptism and the outpouring of the Spirit believers have already been transferred to the "resurrection" (cf Käsemann 1969b: 124-137; Rütti 1972:282-284). "Expectation of an imminent Parousia thus ceases to be meaningful because everything which apocalyptic still hopes for has already been realized" (Käsemann 1969b:131).

It is fascinating that this theological stance is just as little interested in the

Christian's responsibility in the world as the attitude adopted by the extreme apocalypticists. In the case of the latter, the world is irredeemable and should therefore be shunned; only God will, at the end, put everything right. The enthusiasts, on the other hand, disregard the world since it has already been "overcome" and is no longer a factor to be taken into account; why would one do so, if one's hopes have already been realized?

Paul opposes both postures of non-involvement in society, and he does it with the aid of a radically reinterpreted apocalyptic. Precisely because of God's sure victory in the end Paul emphasizes not ethical passivity but active participation in God's redemptive will in the here and now. Faith in God's coming reign "compels an ethic that strains and labors to move God's creation toward that future triumph of God" (Beker 1984:111; cf 16). The Christian life is not limited to interior piety and cultic acts, as though salvation is restricted to the church;[26] rather, believers, as a corporate body, are charged to practice bodily obedience (cf Rom 12:1) and serve Christ in their daily lives, "in the secularity of the world", thus bearing witness—in the "penultimate"—to their faith in Christ's ultimate victory (cf Käsemann 1969b:134-137; 1969e:250). Paul's ethics is not centered in knowing what is good, but in knowing who is Lord, since the lordship of Christ declares all other claims to lordship illegitimate (Duff 1989:283f).

At the same time, Paul is clearly hesitant about stressing too much participation in the world. This undoubtedly is due, in part, to his context and his expectation of the imminent parousia as well as to his conviction that human exertion will not usher in the new world. Any effort at accomplishing that is a manifestation either of a "romantic illusion" or of a "constrictive demand", "because it collapses God's coming triumph in our present personal stance and will power" (Beker 1984:118). Unless our involvement is a response to the "compelling and beckoning power of God's final theophany" (:109) and "is viewed against the horizon of *God's initiative* in bringing about his kingdom, it threatens to become a romantic exaggeration of the ethical capability of the Christian" (:86). Christian ethics may not be based only "protologically" in what Christ has already accomplished, but also "eschatologically" in what God will still do (cf Beker 1980:366). The church can neglect this dual orientation only at its own peril. So Christians can combat the oppressive structures of the powers of sin and death, which in our world cry out for God's world of justice and peace, as well as the false apocalypses of power politics, which assert themselves on both the left and the right, only by accounting for the hope that is in them (1 Pet 3:15) and by being agitators for God's coming reign; they must erect, in the here and now and in the teeth of those structures, signs of God's new world.

5. *Mission in Weakness*. Paul does not permit his readers an illusory escape from the suffering, weakness, and death of the present hour by means of the enthusiasts' proclamation that Christ has already won the ultimate victory. Nor may his readers, with the apocalypticists, interpret the pain and misery they encounter as evidence of God's absence from the present evil age—which, fortunately, will not last much longer (cf Rütti 1972:167). Rather, Paul's "reval-

uation of all values" (for this is indeed what it is) has its roots elsewhere, in the creative tension of the Christian existence between justification already bestowed and redemption ineluctably guaranteed.

I have argued that Paul's theology is bifocal in that it focuses both on God's past act in Christ and God's future act (cf Duff 1989:286, following J. Louis Martyn). Paul's "near vision" helps him to see that a war is raging between God and the powers of death; his "far vision" enables him to see and already rejoice in the outcome of the battle (cf Rom 8:18).

It is particularly in his second letter to the Corinthians that Paul fleshes out the dialectical tension between his far and near visions. He does this in an astounding way, by linking one set of ideas — weakness (*astheneia*), service (*diakonia*), sorrow (*lype*), and affliction (*thlipsis*) — with a completely opposite set — power (*dynamis*), joy (*chara*), and boasting (*kauchesis*).[27] This dialectic runs through the entire letter, but reaches a climax in chapter 12:9f,

> But he said to me, "My grace is sufficient for you, for my power is made perfect in weakness." I will all the more gladly boast of my weaknesses, that the power of Christ may rest upon me. For the sake of Christ, then, I am content with weaknesses, insults, hardships, persecutions, and calamities; for when I am weak, then I am strong.

Similar contrasting connections are made elsewhere. In chapter 4:8f they are: afflicted — not crushed; perplexed — not despairing; persecuted — not forsaken; struck down — not destroyed. Chapter 6:8-10 features another series of opposites: impostors, yet true; unknown, yet well-known; dying, yet alive; punished, yet not killed; sorrowful, yet rejoicing; poor, yet making many rich; having nothing, yet possessing everything.

For Paul, suffering is not just something that has to be endured passively because of the onslaughts and opposition of the powers of this world but also, and perhaps primarily, as an expression of the church's active engagement with the world for the sake of the world's redemption (cf Beker 1984:41). Suffering is therefore a mode of missionary involvement (cf Meyer 1986:111). Paul bears in his body "the marks of Jesus" (Gal 6:17) he has acquired as servant of Christ (cf 2 Cor 11:23-28). He shares in Christ's sufferings (2 Cor 1:5) and completes in his flesh "what is lacking in Christ's afflictions for the sake of his body, that is, the church" (Col 1:24). Yes, he carries in the body the death of Jesus; death is at work in him, but life in those who have come to faith through him (2 Cor 4:9, 12). If he is afflicted, then, it is for the sake of their salvation (2 Cor 1:6). Toward the end of 2 Corinthians he says it in yet another way, "As for me, I will gladly spend what I have for you — yes, and spend myself to the limit" (12:15, NEB).

6. *The Aim of Mission.* In the opening lines of his letter to the Romans Paul briefly formulates the aims of his apostolate: he has been "set apart for the service of the gospel" by Jesus Christ, through whom he has "received the privilege of a commission in his name to lead to faith and obedience men in all nations" (Rom 1:1, 5, NEB) (cf Legrand 1988:156-158). He is sent to pro-

claim that God has effected reconciliation with himself and also among people. This task carries him around the rim of the Mediterranean world, where he refuses to build on the foundations of others because the time is short and the task urgent (Senior and Stuhlmueller 1983:182). Wherever he arrives he founds *ekklesiai*, churches, which are expected to be manifestations of the new creation which is now "restored to the state from which Adam fell" and in which the powers of the world, other than death, no longer reign (Käsemann 1969b:134).

Important as the church is, it is, for Paul, not the ultimate aim of mission. The life and work of the Christian community are intimately bound up with God's cosmic-historical plan for the redemption of the world. In Christ, God has reconciled not only the church but the world to himself (2 Cor 5:19), and this Paul is called to proclaim: "The universality of the gospel is matched by the universality of the apostle's task, that is, to herald God's saving victory over His creation" (Beker 1980:7). Christ has been exalted by God and given a name which is above every name, so that at the name of Jesus every knee should bow, "in heaven and on earth and under the earth" (Phil 2:9-11), because he has been "declared Son of God by a mighty act in that he rose from the dead" (Rom 1:4, NEB). The salvation of humankind thus finally issues into the praise of God in the mouths of all nations, indeed, of all creation (cf Zeller 1982:186f).

The taproot of Paul's cosmic understanding of mission is a personal belief in Jesus Christ, crucified and risen, as Savior of the world. To proclaim him may be "a stumbling block to Jews and folly to Gentiles", but "to those who are called, both Jews and Greeks", he is "the power of God and the wisdom of God" (1 Cor 1:23f), into whose fellowship they have been called (1 Cor 1:9). Paul's mission is conducted, as Sanders has demonstrated, on the basis of "solution", not of "plight". Only in retrospect could he see what life without Christ meant. Only in light of the experience of the unconditional love of God could he recognize the terrible abyss of darkness into which he would have fallen without Christ. What he writes in 1 Thessalonians 1:4 and 10 ("For we know, brethren beloved by God, that he has chosen you"; and "Jesus who delivers us from the wrath to come") is a *confession* of being saved by God's act in Jesus, not a *pronouncement* about others who do not believe (cf Boring 1986:276f). So Paul does not dwell on the state of those outside the Christian fold. That would be a case of beginning with "plight". Rather, he knows, on the basis of the "solution" he has found — better, which has found *him* — that the gospel he has to preach is one of unconditional love and unmerited grace. His missionary gospel is therefore a *positive* one.

PART 2

HISTORICAL PARADIGMS
OF MISSION

Chapter 5

Paradigm Changes in Missiology

SIX EPOCHS

In the first part of this study I have attempted to introduce the reader to the ways in which three important early Christian witnesses understood the event of Jesus Christ and, flowing from this, the church's responsibility toward the world.

We have to go further, however. It is necessary to write about the meaning of mission for our own time, keeping in mind that the present era is fundamentally different from the period in which Matthew, Luke, and Paul wrote their gospels and letters for the first and second generations of Christians. The profound dissimilarities between then and now imply that it will not do to appeal in a direct manner to the words of the biblical authors and apply what they said on a one-to-one basis to our own situation. We should, rather, with creative but responsible freedom, prolong the logic of the ministry of Jesus and the early church in an imaginative and creative way to our own time and context. One of the basic reasons for having to do this, lies in the fact that the Christian faith is a *historical* faith. God communicates his revelation to people through human beings and through events, not by means of abstract propositions. This is another way of saying that the biblical faith, both Old and New Testament, is "incarnational", the reality of God entering into human affairs.

The implications of acknowledging this will, hopefully, become clearer as I proceed. In considering this, I propose first to reflect on what mission meant in successive periods up to the present and then, in the final part of the book, to draw the contours, in broad strokes, of a contemporary paradigm for mission.

In discussing the manner in which the Christian church has, through the ages, interpreted and carried out its mission, I shall follow the historico-theological subdivisions suggested by Hans Küng (1984:25; 1987:157). Küng submits that the entire history of Christianity can be subdivided into six major "paradigms". These are:

1. The apocalyptic paradigm of primitive Christianity.
2. The Hellenistic paradigm of the patristic period.
3. The medieval Roman Catholic paradigm.

4. The Protestant (Reformation) paradigm.
5. The modern Enlightenment paradigm.
6. The emerging ecumenical paradigm.

Each of these six periods, Küng suggests, reveals a peculiar understanding of the Christian faith. To this I would add that each also offers a distinctive understanding of Christian mission.

I shall, in the following chapters, attempt to outline what mission meant in each of these periods, beginning not with primitive Christianity (since the entire first part of this book was, in fact, devoted to an effort at tracing the missionary paradigm operative in some major representatives of this period) but with the Hellenistic period.

In each of these eras Christians, from within their own contexts, wrestled with the question of what the Christian faith and, by implication, the Christian mission meant for them. Needless to say, all of them believed and argued that their understanding of the faith and of the church's mission was faithful to God's intent. This did not, however, mean that they all thought alike and came to the same conclusions. There have, of course, always been Christians (and theologians!) who believed that their understanding of the faith was "objectively" accurate and, in effect, the only authentic rendering of Christianity. Such an attitude, however, rests on a dangerous illusion. Our views are always only *interpretations* of what we consider to be divine revelation, not divine revelation itself (and these interpretations are profoundly shaped by our self-understandings). I have argued in the preceding chapters that not even the biblical books we have surveyed are, as such, records of divine revelation; they are interpretations of that revelation. It is an illusion to believe that we can penetrate to a pure gospel unaffected by any cultural and other human accretions. Even in the earliest Jesus tradition the sayings *of* Jesus were already sayings *about* Jesus (cf Schottroff and Stegemann 1986:2). And if this was true of the Christian faith in its pristine phase, it should be obvious that it would be even more true of subsequent periods. Nobody receives the gospel passively; each one as a matter of course reinterprets it. There is, truly, no knowledge in which the subjective dimension does not enter in some way or other (Hiebert 1985a:7). Moreover, as will hopefully become clear in the course of my argument, this circumstance is not something we should lament; it is an inherent feature of the Christian faith, since it concerns the Word made flesh.

It is therefore appropriate not to talk about "Christian theology" but about "Christian theologies". Any individual Christian's understanding of God's revelation is conditioned by a great variety of factors. These include the person's ecclesiastical tradition, personal context (sex, age, marital status, education), social position (social "class", profession, wealth, environment), personality, and culture (worldview, language, etc). Traditionally we have recognized the existence (even if not the validity) of only the first factor, that is, the differences caused by ecclesiastical traditions. In more recent years we have begun to accept the role of culture in religion and religious experience. The other factors are, however, equally (if not more) important. A black migrant worker in Johannesburg, for instance, may have a perception of the Christian faith very different from that of a white civil servant in the same city, even if both are members of the Dutch Reformed Church. A peasant in the Nicaragua of President Somoza, as Ernesto Cardenal's *The Gospel in Solentiname* has illustrated so graphically, may understand the gospel in a way that disagrees profoundly from that of a New York businessman, even if they both happen to be Catholics. In each case the individual's self-understanding plays a crucial role in his or her interpretation and experience of the faith.

There is yet another important — and related — factor which affects the ways people interpret and experience the Christian faith: the general "frame of reference" with which they happen to have grown up, their overall experience and understanding of reality and their place within the universe, the historical epoch in which they happen to live and which to a very large extent has molded their faith, experiences, and thought processes. The differences between the six subdivisions of the history of Christianity listed by Küng have to do, to a very large extent, with differences in the overall frame of reference between one era and the other, and only to a lesser extent with personal, confessional, and social differences per se. The "world" of the Hellenistic Christianity of the second and subsequent centuries was simply qualitatively different from the "world" of primitive Christianity, which was still very deeply impregnated with the ethos of the Hebrew Old Testament. And there are comparable disparities between the other epochs referred to above.

Küng's subdivision of the history of Christian thought into six major eras is, of course, not very original. What is original is Küng's fashioning these subdivisions according to Thomas Kuhn's theory of "paradigm shifts". Each of these epochs, Küng suggests, reflects a theological "paradigm" profoundly different from any of its predecessors. In each era the Christians of that period understood and experienced their faith in ways only partially commensurable with the understanding and experience of believers of other eras.

Küng's observations regarding theology in general have a profound effect on our understanding of how Christians perceived the church's mission in the various epochs of the history of Christianity. We therefore have to take a closer look at this entire issue. We do not do this for "archaeological" purposes, that is, just to satisfy our curiosity about the way past generations perceived their missionary responsibility. Rather, we do it also, and primarily, with a view to getting a deeper insight into what mission might mean for us today. After all, every attempt at interpreting the past is indirectly an attempt at understanding the present and the future. So, one important way for Christian theology to explore its relevance for the present is to probe its own past, to allow its "self-definitions" to be challenged by the "self-definitions" of the first Christians. It is in this respect that we may benefit by turning to Kuhn's suggestions about paradigm changes.

THE PARADIGM THEORY OF THOMAS KUHN

This is not the place to enter into a detailed analysis and discussion of the views of Thomas Kuhn, physicist and historian of science. I shall therefore summarize his thesis only insofar as it may have some relevance for theology. I am aware of the fact that Kuhn himself limits his theories to the natural sciences (which he calls "mature sciences") and explicitly excludes references to the social sciences ("proto-sciences" in his view). I am also aware of the extensive critique of his position, from both natural and social scientists (for a brief summary of the criticisms of his views, cf Bernstein 1985:88-93). These two factors alone should suffice to make one cautious about the possibility of applying any of his ideas to theology. If I nevertheless invoke Kuhn in this context, I do it because of the catalytic role he has played in recent years in the theory of scientific research, and I use his views only as a kind of working hypothesis. I believe that Kuhn has, in a sense, uncovered and made explicit what many knew implicitly.

In a nutshell, Kuhn's suggestion is that science does not really grow cumulatively (as if more and more knowledge and research bring us ever closer to final solutions of problems), but rather by way of "revolutions". A few individuals begin to perceive reality in ways *qualitatively* different from their predecessors and contemporaries, who are practicing "normal science". The small group of pioneers sense that the existing scientific model is riddled with anomalies and is unable to solve emerging problems. They then begin to search for a new model or theoretical structure, or (Kuhn's favorite term) a new "paradigm", one that is, as it were, waiting in the wings, ready to replace the old (Kuhn 1970:82f). No individual or group can actually "create" a new paradigm; rather, it grows and ripens within the context of an extraordinary network of diverse social and scientific factors. As the existing paradigm increasingly blurs, the new one begins to attract more and more scholars, until eventually the original, problem-ridden paradigm is abandoned (:84).

This seldom happens without a struggle, however, since scientific communities are by nature conservative and do not like their peace to be disturbed; the old paradigm's protagonists continue for a long time to fight a rearguard action. This is, for instance, what happened in physics when the Copernican paradigm was gradually replaced by the Newtonian and again when the latter gave way to the Einsteinian. In the final analysis, Kuhn argues, the old paradigm and the new are incommensurable; the perspectives of their respective champions are so different that one might even say that they are responding to different realities. Even if the world in which they live is the same for all, they respond to it as though they live in different worlds. Proponents of the old paradigm often just cannot understand the arguments of the proponents of the new. Metaphorically speaking, the one is playing chess and the other checkers on the same board (Hiebert 1985a:9).

It is understandable, says Kuhn, that to abandon one paradigm and embrace another is not simply a matter of taking a rational, "scientific" step. Since there is no such thing as totally objective knowledge, the person of the scholar is deeply involved in this shift from one framework to another. Kuhn even uses religious language to describe what happens to the scientist who relinquishes one paradigm for another. It is a case of "scales falling from the eyes", of responding to "flashes of intuition", indeed, of "conversion" (1970:122, 123,

151; cf Capra 1987:520f). This explains why defenders of the old order and champions of the new frequently argue at cross purposes. Protagonists of the old paradigm, in particular, tend to immunize themselves against the arguments of the new. They resist its challenges with deep emotional reactions, since those challenges threaten to destroy their very perception and experience of reality, indeed their entire world (Hiebert 1985b:12). In Einstein's words (cf Küng 1984:59), "It is more difficult to smash prejudices than atoms".

The term "paradigm" is not without its problems. It is a slippery concept. Kuhn himself has been charged with using the term in at least twenty-two senses in his major work! In the postscript to this work he defines a paradigm as "the entire constellation of beliefs, values, techniques, and so on shared by the members of a given community" (1970:175). Küng uses the concept in the sense of "models of interpretation" (1987:163). T. F. Torrance refers to "frames of knowledge" (cf Martin 1987:372), van Huyssteen to "frames of reference" and "research traditions" (1986:66). Hiebert (1985b:12) suggests the alternative concept of "belief systems", even for the natural sciences, since the personal attitude and commitment of the researcher cannot be expunged from his or her research.

The paradigm theory implies a fundamental break with preceding theories of science, particularly logical positivism's emphasis on "verification" as well as Karl Popper's idea of "falsification" as sure ways in which scientific research advances. It is widely accepted today, in all the sciences (natural as well as social) that total objectivity is an illusion, and that knowledge belongs to a community and is influenced by the dynamics operative in such a community. This means that not only "scientific data" are tested, but also the researchers themselves.

Kuhn's theories have a particular relevance in our own time since, in virtually all disciplines, there is a growing awareness that we live in an era of change from one way of understanding reality to another. Capra suggests that world-views ("macro-paradigms") go through a period of fundamental change every three to five hundred years (1987:519). It is abundantly clear that the twentieth century, particularly after the Second World War, shows evidence of such a major shift in perceiving reality. Since the seventeenth century the Enlightenment paradigm has reigned supreme in all disciplines, including theology. Today there is a growing sense of disaffection with the Enlightenment and a quest for a new approach to and understanding of reality. There is, on the one hand, a search under way for a new paradigm; on the other hand, such a new paradigm is already presenting itself.

PARADIGM SHIFTS IN THEOLOGY

The idea of paradigm changes is of relevance for the study of theology generally and, within the context of this book, for the study and understanding of mission in particular. This is not to suggest that we should uncritically apply Kuhn's ideas to the area of theology (cf also Küng 1987:162-165). To begin with, there are in this respect important differences between theology and the natural sciences. In the natural sciences, for instance, the new paradigm usually *replaces* the old, definitely and irreversibly. After the Newtonian revolution it is simply no longer possible to understand the universe in Copernican, let alone Ptolemaean, categories. In theology (and, for that matter, in the arts; cf Küng 1987:260-265) "old" paradigms can live on. Sometimes one may even have a revival of a former, almost forgotten paradigm; this is evidenced, *inter alia*, in the "rediscovery" of Paul's letter to the Romans by Augustine in the fourth century, Martin Luther in the sixteenth, and Karl Barth in the twentieth (cf Küng 1987:193).

Also, in another sense, the "old" paradigm seldom disappears completely. In Küng's diagram of paradigm shifts in theology (1984:25; 1987:157), he indicates that the Hellenistic paradigm of the patristic period still lives on in parts of the Orthodox churches, the medieval Roman Catholic paradigm in contemporary Roman Catholic traditionalism, the Protestant Reformation paradigm in twentieth-century Protestant confessionalism, and the Enlightenment paradigm in liberal theology. Brauer reminds us that in virtually all denominations today we find, side by side, fundamentalist, conservative, moderate, liberal, and radical believers (1984:12). The matter is further complicated by the fact that people are often committed to more than one paradigm at the same time. Martin Luther, whose break with the preceding paradigm was exceptionally radical, in many respects still harbored important elements of the paradigm he had abandoned. The same was true of Karl Barth. Likewise, people who, by and large, still operate within the old paradigm may already embody significant elements of the new. An excellent example of this was Luther's contemporary, Desiderius Erasmus (1466-1536), who remained within the medieval Roman Catholic paradigm yet at the same time heralded a new era (cf, especially, Küng 1987:31-66).

One of the criticisms of the paradigm theory is that it fosters relativism, that there really are no ultimate norms or values. Thomas Kuhn says, for instance, that each group "uses its own paradigm to argue in that paradigm's defense", that one can only accept a paradigm's validity if one has stepped into its "circle", and that it "cannot be made logically or even probabilistically compelling for those who refuse to step into the circle". Therefore, in paradigm choice "there is no standard higher than the assent of the relevant community" (1970:94). All this indeed sounds rather relativistic! In his "Postscript" Kuhn then responds to his critics' accusations that his position amounts to total relativism (1970:205-207). He qualifies his earlier position by stating that he is a "convinced believer in scientific progress" and that later scientific theories indeed tend to be better than earlier ones.

Perhaps, however, the real point here is that one should in all research, whether in theology or the natural or social sciences, never think in mutually exclusive categories of "absolute" and "relative". Our theologies are partial, and they are culturally and socially biased. They may never claim to be absolutes. Yet this does not make them relativistic, as though one suggests that in theology—since we really cannot ever know "absolutely"—anything goes. It is true that we see only in part, but we do see (Hiebert 1985a:9). We are committed to our understanding of revelation, yet we also maintain a critical distance to that understanding. In other words, we are in principle open to other views, an attitude which does not, however, militate against complete commitment to our own understanding of truth. We preface our remarks with "I believe . . .", or "As I see it . . ." (Hiebert 1985a:9). It is misleading to believe that commitment and a self-critical attitude are mutually exclusive.

Far from leading us into a morass of subjectivism and relativism, the approach I am advocating actually fosters a creative tension between my ultimate faith commitment and my own theological perception of faith. Instead of viewing my own interpretation as absolutely correct and all others by definition as wrong, I recognize that different theological interpretations, including my own, reflect different contexts, perspectives, and biases. This is not to say, however, that I regard all theological positions as equally valid or that it does not matter what people believe; rather, I shall do my utmost to share my understanding of the faith with others while granting them the right to do the same. I realize that my theological approach is a "map", and that a map is never the actual "territory" (cf Hiebert 1985b:15; Martin 1987:373). Although I believe that my map is the best, I accept that there are other types of maps and also that, at least in theory, one of those may be better than mine since I can only know in part (cf 1 Cor 13:12).

For the Christian this means that any paradigm shift can only be carried out on the basis of the gospel and because of the gospel, never, however, against the gospel (cf Küng 1987:194). Contrary to the natural sciences, theology relates not only to the present and the future, but also to the past, to tradition, to God's primary witness to humans (:191f). Theology must undoubtedly always be relevant and contextual (:200-203), but this may never be pursued at the expense of God's revelation in and through the history of Israel and, supremely, the event of Jesus Christ (:203-206). Christians take seriously the epistemological priority of their classical text, the Scriptures.

I realize that, in stating the above, I have hardly solved any problems. Scripture comes to us in the shape of human words, which are already "contextual" (in the sense of being written for very specific historical contexts) and are, moreover, open to different interpretations. In making the affirmation above I am, however, suggesting a "point of orientation" all Christians (should) share and on the basis of which dialogue between them becomes possible. No individual or group has a monopoly here. So, the Christian church should function as an "international hermeneutical community" (Hiebert 1985b:16) in which Christians (and theologians) from different contexts challenge one another's cultural, social, and ideological biases. This presupposes, however, that we see fellow-Christians not as rivals or opponents but as partners (Küng 1987:198), even if we may be passionately convinced that their views are in need of major corrections.[1]

PARADIGMS IN MISSIOLOGY

In the following chapters I shall follow, in broad outline, the subdivision of theology into the periods suggested by Küng (1984:25; 1987:157): primitive

Christianity (already discussed); the patristic period; the Middle Ages; the Reformation; the Enlightenment; and the ecumenical era. It might also have been possible to follow another division. James P. Martin (1987) divides the history of the church and of theology into only three eras. Küng's second, third, and fourth epochs are grouped together and referred to as "pre-critical", "vitalistic", or "symbolic". This is followed by the Enlightenment as the second era, which is characterized as "critical", "analytical" and "mechanistic". The third epoch, now emerging, is described as "post-critical", "holistic", and "ecumenical". Martin's classification has merit, particularly for an understanding of the development of biblical interpretation. Küng's subdivisions will, however, in my view be a more appropriate tool in trying to discern the evolution of the missionary idea.

Even Küng's categorization of the history of theology may, however, still be too general to do justice to all kinds of theological nuances. He therefore rightly calls for a distinction between macro-, meso-, and micro-paradigms (Küng 1984:21). The six historical epochs specified above would then refer to *macro-paradigms*. Each new macro-paradigm represents a reconstruction of the entire field of theology (cf van Huyssteen 1986:83). Within one macro-paradigm theologians indeed share, by and large, one overall frame of reference and a commensurable perspective on God, humans, and the world, even if such theologians do differ substantially from each other in many respects (cf Küng 1984:20f, and 1987: 154f, where examples are given).

The transition from one paradigm to another is not abrupt. A new paradigm has its trailblazers, who still operate in the old. Most contemporary theologians have grown up within the parameters of the Enlightenment paradigm but find themselves today thinking and working in terms of two paradigms at once (cf Martin 1987:375). This produces a kind of theological schizophrenia, which we just have to put up with while at the same time groping our way toward greater clarity. Scholars in all disciplines are overtaxed, and yet there is no way in which we can evade the demands made on us.

The point is simply that the Christian church in general and the Christian mission in particular are today confronted with issues they have never even dreamt of and which are crying out for responses that are both relevant to the times and in harmony with the essence of the Christian faith. The contemporary church-in-mission is challenged by at least the following factors (cf also Küng 1987:214-216, 240f):

1. The West, for more than a millennium the home of Christianity and in a very real sense created by it, has lost its dominant position in the world. Peoples in all parts of the world strive for liberation from what is experienced as the stranglehold of the West.

2. Unjust structures of oppression and exploitation are today challenged as never before in human history. The struggles against racism and sexism are only two of several manifestations of this challenge.

3. There is a profound feeling of ambiguity about Western technology and development, indeed, about the very idea of progress itself. Progress, the god of the Enlightenment, proved to be a false god after all.

4. More than ever before we know today that we live on a shrinking globe with only finite resources. We now know that people and their environment are mutually interdependent. Capra (1987:519) calls the emerging worldview *ganzheitlich-ökologisch*, "comprehensively ecological".

5. We are today not only able to kill God's earth but also—again, for the first time in history—capable of wiping out humankind. If the plight of the environment calls for an ecologically appropriate response, the threat of a nuclear holocaust challenges us to reply by working for peace with justice.

6. If the Bangkok meeting of the Commission for World Mission and Evangelism (1973) was correct in stating that "culture shapes the human voice that answers the voice of Christ", then it should be clear that theologies designed and developed in Europe can claim no superiority over theologies emerging in other parts of the world. This, too, is a new situation, since the supremacy of the theology of the West was taken for granted for more than a thousand years.

7. Again, for many centuries the superiority of the Christian religion over all other faiths was simply taken for granted (by Christians, that is). It was, as a matter of course, regarded as the only true and only saving religion. Today most people agree that freedom of religion is a basic human right. This factor, together with many others, forces Christians to reevaluate their attitude toward and their understanding of other faiths.

Other factors might be added to the seven listed above. The point I am making is simply that, quite literally, we live in a world fundamentally different from that of the nineteenth century, let alone earlier times.. The new situation challenges us, across the board, to an appropriate response. No longer dare we, as we have often done, respond only piecemeal and ad hoc to single issues as they confront us. The contemporary world challenges us to practice a "transformational hermeneutics" (Martin 1987:378), a theological response which transforms us first before we involve ourselves in mission to the world.

We could, conceivably, have moved directly from the primitive Christian paradigm sketched in the first part of this book to the challenge of the contemporary scene. For several reasons this would, however, not be an advisable procedure. The magnitude of today's challenge can really only be appreciated if viewed against the backdrop of almost twenty centuries of church history. In addition, we need the perspectives of the past in order to appreciate the scope of the present challenge and to be able really to understand the world today and the Christian response to its predicament. Like the Israelites of old—who needed to remind themselves, in every period of crisis, of their deliverance from Egypt, their wanderings in the desert, and their ancient covenant with God—we too need to be reminded of our roots, not only in order that we might have consolation but even more that we might find direction (cf Niebuhr 1959:1). We reflect on the past not just for the past's own sake; rather, we look upon it as a compass—and who would use a compass only to ascertain from where he or she has come?[2]

Chapter 6

The Missionary Paradigm
of the Eastern Church

"TO THE JEW FIRST BUT ALSO TO THE GREEK"

Within a very short time the new Christian faith—as it entered the Greco-Roman world—underwent a significant transformation. This metamorphosis was, in scope and character, as profound as any other in the subsequent history of the movement. Paul Knitter (1985:19) succinctly summarizes what happened when Christianity changed from a Jewish into a Greco-Roman religion:

> It was a transformation not only in the liturgical, sacramental life of the church and in the structures of its organization and legislation, but also in its *doctrine*—that is, in the *understanding* of the revelation that had given birth to it. The early Christians did not simply express in Greek thought what they already knew; rather, they discovered, through Greek religious and philosophical insights, what had been revealed to them. The doctrines of the trinity and of the divinity of Christ . . . for example, would not be what they are today if the church had not reassessed itself and its doctrines in the light of the new historical, cultural situations during the third through the sixth centuries.

Naturally, the transition was not abrupt. Neither did it lead to any homogeneous new theology. Far from it. Even so, it is possible to discern the contours of a single, coherent paradigm at least for the Greek Patristic period. In spite of the many and important differences among theologians such as Irenaeus, Clement, Origen, Athanasius, and the three Cappadocians, they all shared a similar view of God, humanity, and the world, and they all differed fundamentally from the apocalyptic-eschatological pattern of primitive Christianity (cf Küng 1984:20; 1987:154). Needless to say, such differences were bound to have a significant effect on the understanding of mission during this period.

It should not bother us that, during the epoch under discussion, the Christian faith was perceived and experienced in new and different ways. The Christian

190

faith is intrinsically incarnational; therefore, unless the church chooses to remain a foreign entity, it will always enter into the context in which it happens to find itself. And the context of the second and subsequent centuries of the Christian era was almost in every respect different from that of the first. The shift from the Hebrew to the Greek world was only one (if extremely important) element of the new setting. It had other decisively different ingredients as well. For one thing, what began as a movement had, long before the end of the first century, irrevocably turned into an institution.

As a matter of fact, as outlined in Chapters 1 to 4 of this book, there already was a notable shift from the historical ministry of Jesus' to the context of the first generations of Christians and the earliest New Testament writings. Subsequent generations would perceive themselves as being even more distant from the birth of the movement. Christianity was still in its infancy, still a minority faith in a pluralistic world, still a *religio illicita*, despised if not always persecuted by the Roman authorities. Yet it had, on the whole, lost much of its early fervor and distinctiveness; it was increasingly resembling the world it wished to win for the faith. More specifically, it gradually lost its apocalyptic-eschatological character, gave up the hope of an imminent parousia, and settled, even if rather awkwardly, into this world. The change took place almost imperceptibly. It is, of course, impossible to draw a hard line between what is sometimes called the New Testament period and the ensuing era. Some of the traits which were to dominate in the second and subsequent centuries are already discernible in some New Testament writings (cf, for instance, Käsemann 1969c).

It has often been claimed (for instance by Frend 1974:32; cf Holl 1974:3-11) that the office, if we may call it thus, of the "itinerant preacher" disappeared with the apostles, that there were, for many centuries, no persons we may justifiably call "missionaries", and that the early church had no missionary method or program. While there is a grain of truth in this view, it falls short of doing justice to the facts. As Kretschmar (1974:94-128) has shown, the significance for the early Christian mission up to the third century of charismatic healer-missionaries, miracle workers, and itinerant preachers should not be underestimated. From the fourth century onward, however, the monk would gradually replace the itinerant preacher as missionary in as yet unevangelized areas (cf Adam 1974:86-93; Kretschmar 1974:99f).

Of far greater significance for mission than the ministry of the peripatetic preacher or the monk was the *conduct* of early Christians, the "language of love" on their lips and in their lives (Harnack 1962:147-198, 366-368), their *Propaganda der Tat* ("propaganda of the deed" — Holl 1974:8). In the final analysis it was not the miracles of itinerant evangelists and wandering monks that impressed the populace — miracle workers were a familiar phenomenon in the ancient world — but the exemplary lives of ordinary Christians (Kretschmar 1974:99). If the conduct of believers in New Testament times had a distinctly missionary dimension (cf van Swigchem 1955), it was not different in the post-apostolic period. In the contemporary Greek world it was Greek philosophy rather than Greek religion which nurtured morality (cf Malherbe 1986). The Greek gods were frequently represented as amoral if not immoral in their conduct. Strictly speaking, ethics was not regarded as a part of religion; the gods did not insist on a total break with the past or on a renunciation of all that was wrong (cf Green 1970:144f). By contrast, the high moral standards of the Christian faith, like those of Judaism, were clearly to be attributed to *religious* influences, and many non-Christians noticed this. Christians were expected to belong, body and soul, to Christ, and this was to show in their conduct (:146).

In the general mood of the time such demeanor could not but be noticeable. Hellenism had long passed its prime. The Marxist philosopher Víteslav Gardavsky says that Rome was still powerful politically and militarily; yet at the same time the "odor of decay" was in evidence everywhere (quoted by Rosenkranz 1977:71). To this Rosenkranz adds,

> In this macabre world, submerged in despair, perversity, and superstition, something new existed and grew: Christianity, bastion of love for God and brother, of the Holy Spirit, and of hope for God's coming reign (:71 — my translation).

The testimonies of enemies of the church (such as Celsus and Julian the Apostate) frequently mentioned the extraordinary conduct of Christians, often with reference to the fact that this conduct had been a factor in winning people over to the Christian faith. Michael Green perhaps gives too romantic a picture of early Christians, and yet the elements of their lives which he reviews (their example, fellowship, transformed characters, joy, endurance, and power) certainly were crucial factors in the phenomenal growth of the new "superstition"[1] during the first few centuries of the Christian era (Green 1970:178-193). And its growth was indeed spectacular; it is estimated that by AD 300 roughly half of the urban population in at least some of the provinces of the vast Roman Empire had turned to the Christian faith (cf Harnack 1924:946-958; von Soden 1974:25). Outside the Empire it was, with some notable exceptions, less successful, for reasons to which I shall return.

THE CHURCH AND ITS CONTEXT

After AD 85 Judaism had to distinguish itself clearly not only from paganism but also from the church. Similarly, Christians had to battle on two fronts: against the synagogue and against Hellenistic religions. In its early stages, Christianity was undoubtedly closer to Judaism; in its later stages it would, in many respects, be closer to the Greek milieu, in spite of initial resistance from theologians such as Tatian and Tertullian. The shift already becomes discernible in the terminology used. Concepts originally typical of the cult of the emperor, the military, the Greek mystery religions, the theater, and Platonic philosophy gradually became common in Christian worship and doctrine (cf van der Aalst 1974:54).

The many parallels between pagan religions and Christianity were, in a real sense, a great help to the church in its mission and defense of the faith. The message about God in human form, about salvific sacrifices, the victory of resurrection, and new life, fell on ears that did not find it entirely unfamiliar. It was easy to regard Christianity as the fulfillment of other religions. For the early Christian faith it was not its dissimilarity with the religions of the environment that was the problem, but its similarity (cf von Soden 1974:26). The new religion could easily slip into the mold of the old without causing much more than a ripple on the surface. The Apologists, in particular, often went out of their way in their efforts to emphasize the resemblance between the new and the old. Justin and Clement adopted a friendly attitude toward the best in paganism and regarded Greek philosophy as a "schoolmaster" leading pagans to Christ. The general spirit of the time was conducive to an almost boundless syncretism of oriental and occidental religions—another factor which induced Christianity to conform. That it did not, in the final analysis, conform, was due not only to its consciousness of being fundamentally different from all other faiths, but to at least two other factors as well.

First, already in its early years the Christian faith had some success among the upper classes, although the majority of Christians were simple folk with little education. The church was not a bearer of culture. As a matter of fact, it was held in contempt by the vast majority of the cultured citizens of the Empire. Celsus combined Platonic philosophical monotheism with Greco-Roman polytheism in his effort to discredit Christianity. From the late second century on the picture gradually began to change. Clement of Alexandria, Origen, and others introduced a new tradition, that of the sophisticated Christian scholar who could match any pagan philosopher, particularly since they could make use of the same type of argument as the Greek teachers did. In the course of time Christian theologians also embraced the typical Hellenistic feelings of superiority, particularly toward the *barbaroi* (cf Holl 1974:14). Even before the persecutions stopped and Christianity was declared the sole legitimate religion in the Roman Empire, the church had begun to be a bearer of culture and a civilizing presence in society. The advent of Constantine put a seal on this development. Henceforth Christians and they alone would be upwardly mobile and cultured. They dominated life in the cities. Non-Christians were now looked down upon as the unenlightened ones; they were "pagans" (*pagani*, "those who lived in rural areas") or "heathen" ("those whose homes were on the heath"). A Celsus was now by definition unthinkable; after all, only *Christians* were civilized and educated. Mission became a movement from the superior to the inferior. Non-Christian faiths were inferior to Christianity, not—primarily—on theological grounds but for socio-cultural reasons (cf Holl 1974: 11f; von Soden 1974:29; Kahl 1978:22f).

Second, and related to the above, the pagan Empire was slowly disintegrating. I have mentioned Gardavsky's reference to the "odor of decay" in evidence everywhere. Fatalism was widespread among the populace, who attempted to find security against the vicissitudes and confusions of life by resorting to magic and astrology (cf Rosenkranz 1977:44f). Christianity was ready to fill the vacuum—and the citizens of the Empire responded. It has been argued that no mass movement into the Christian faith has developed in a culture that was stable and rich in content, but always only in societies which have lost their nerve and were disintegrating. This was true not only of the Greco-Roman world in the fourth and subsequent centuries, but also elsewhere. E. A. Thompson has advocated the view that the success of the Christian mission among the Goths was to be ascribed not so much to the excellent mission work of Ulfilas, but rather to the devastating effect the Goths' encounter with the Roman Empire had on their traditional way of life. He also contends that, apart from the Suevi, no German tribe remained faithful to its traditional religion for longer than one generation after it had invaded the Roman Empire; thus a major reason for the Germans' conversion to Christianity, sociologically speaking, was the disruption of social conditions caused by their migrations (references to Thompson in Frend 1974:40).

THE CHURCH AND THE PHILOSOPHERS

If Christian theologians, by and large, tended to scorn pagan religions, they were far more positive toward pagan philosophy. Like many Jews before them they, consciously or unconsciously, appropriated material from the philosophers. Malherbe has recently published a source-book containing excerpts from Greco-Roman moral philosophers; their writings reveal not only a remarkable affinity with those of Christian authors, but have also undoubtedly influenced the latter (Malherbe 1986). In his study on Paul's first letter to the Thessalonians Malherbe has shown that even Paul's thinking was doubtless affected by several philosophical schools (Malherbe 1987). During subsequent centuries their influence on Christian theologians was to become much more noticeable.

The major philosophical schools during the Hellenistic and Roman periods were the Platonic, Stoic, Cynic, and Epicurean. It was the first-mentioned to whom Christians were most deeply indebted. Platonic influence on Christian thinking manifested itself in at least two respects: the relation between eternity and time, which preoccupied many theologians; and the Platonic distinction between the true and the apparent, the reality and the shadow, which played a role particularly in eucharistic theology (cf van der Aalst 1974:54; Beker 1980:360).

The pervasive impact of Greek philosophy on the infant Christian movement can, however, best be observed in the ever-growing tendency to define the faith and systematize doctrine. The God of the Old Testament and primitive Christianity came to be identified with the general idea of God of Greek metaphysics; God is referred to as Supreme Being, substance, principle, unmoved mover. Ontology (God's being) became more important than history (God's deeds) (cf van der Aalst 1974:110f). It became more important to reflect on what God is in himself than to consider the relationship in which people stand to God. Behind all of this lies the notion that the abstract idea is more real than the historical. Therefore, what pagans were really in need of was an adequate doctrine of God.

For the Greeks the key concept was *knowledge* (*gnosis* or *sophia*) (cf Paul's remark in 1 Cor 1:22). In much of Christian theology this notion gradually replaced that of *event*. The theme, "salvation is to be found in knowledge", was presented in a great variety of ways, in which the original idea of knowledge through experience was increasingly replaced by that of rational knowledge (cf van der Aalst 1974:88f). The Holy Spirit became the "spirit of truth" or the "spirit of wisdom", where one's primary interest was in the Spirit's original *being* rather than *activity in history* (:124f). God's revelation was no longer understood as God's self-communication in events, but as the communication of truths about the *being* of God in three *hypostases* and the *one person* of Christ in two *natures*. The various church councils were intent on producing *definitive* statements of faith; their formulations were conclusive and final rather than references to the ineffable. The unity of the church was regulated by scrutinizing people according to whether or not they subscribed to these formulas. Those who did not were excluded by means of anathemas. A comparison between the Sermon on the Mount and the Nicene Creed confirms the point. The former outlines a mode of conduct without any specific appeal to a set of precepts. The entire tenor of the Sermon is ethical; it is devoid of metaphysical speculation. The latter, in contrast, is structured within a metaphysical framework, makes a number of doctrinal statements, and says nothing about the believer's conduct. Van der Aalst very appropriately summarizes the outcome of this entire development, "The message became doctrine, the doctrine dogma, and this dogma was expounded in precepts which were expertly strung together" (:138 — my translation). One effect of this shift was centuries-long debates on concepts like *ousia, physis, hypostasis, meritum, transsubstantiatio*, etc (ibid).

Some years back it was popular to construct absolute contrasts between Hebrew and Greek worldviews. Today it is widely agreed that the difference was over-emphasized. Many notions regarded as typically Hebrew have been shown to exist in Greek thinking as well, and vice versa. It is too easy to blame all aberrations on the Greeks (cf van der Aalst 1974:150-174, where many similarities between "Hebrew" and "Greek" thinking are discussed; cf also Young 1988:302). Still, an important difference in perspective does exist. I have already referred to the characteristic Greek emphasis on *knowledge* or *gnosis*. To this we have to add the difference between an auditive and a visual approach to reality. Even if the difference is far from absolute, one could say that we can observe a visual rather than an auditive perspective among Greeks and, by the same token, a more auditive than visual approach among Semites (cf van der Aalst 1974:92). For Jews, "faith comes from what is heard" (Rom 10:17), and *dabar* (Hebrew for "word") refers particularly to the *spoken* word. *Logos* (Greek for "word"), by contrast, primarily alludes to knowledge-through-seeing (van der Aalst 1974:98). Whereas Semites (including the Semitic Nestorian Christians) displayed an aversion to plastic art, the Greeks excelled in this art form (:93f).

This has a bearing on the Orthodox understanding of mission. A nineteenth-century Greek Orthodox patriarch underscored the value of images for preaching and added that "seeing more readily guides to faith than hearing" (reference in van der Aalst 1974:99). The allusion is specifically to the liturgy, which non-believers are invited to attend and observe (naturally they cannot participate), and which in the Orthodox tradition is regarded as the main form of witness and mission (cf Stamoolis 1986:85-102).

ESCHATOLOGY

There is probably no area in which the Hellenistic church differed so profoundly from primitive Jewish Christianity as that of its eschatology and understanding of history.

The biblical story is the account of remembrance of encounters with God in real human history and expectations of future encounters. The Christ event is not an isolated occurrence of a totally different kind, but is rooted in God's history with Israel (cf Rütti 1972:95). The significance of Jesus can therefore be grasped only on the basis of the Old Testament history of promise. His resurrection (in which the apostolic mission to the world has its origin) can only be understood within the framework of prophetic and apocalyptic expectation (:103). The proclamation of the reign of God does not introduce a new creed or cult but is the announcement of an event in history, an event to which people are challenged to respond by repenting and believing. In the coming of Jesus and in raising him from the dead, God's eschatological act has already been inaugurated. It is, however, as yet incomplete. Jesus' resurrection and exaltation signify just the beginning of the universal fulfillment still to come, of which the Spirit is a pledge. Only another future intervention by God will wipe out the contradictions of the present. Therefore, in Paul's christology Christ is not so much the fulfillment of God's promises as the guarantee and confirmation of those promises (cf Rom 4:16; 15:8). Christ has not "fulfilled" the Old Testament, but "ratified" it (Beker 1980:345). The end is still to come.

All of this was to change profoundly in subsequent centuries. Apocalyptic expectations were thwarted by the delay of the parousia. The freshness and ardor of the primitive Christian sense of living in the last times dissipated and the perception of urgent and immediate crisis faded in the minds of many believers (cf Lampe 1957:19f). Justin Martyr, living in the middle of the second century, still held to the millennial scheme as part of the doctrine he had inherited, but he placed relatively little emphasis on it. Elsewhere, too, apocalyptic ideas began to assume the role of inherited furniture, handed down to believers and not to be discarded, but no longer treasured (:33). The Christian message was in the process of being transformed from the announcement of God's imminent reign to the proclamation of the only true and universal religion of humankind (cf Rütti 1972:128). Faith in God's promises yet to be fulfilled was replaced by faith in the already consummated eternal kingdom of Christ. His resurrection came to be viewed as a completed event, as the "climactic fulfillment of all God's promises" (Beker 1984:85), and no longer as the "first fruits" of the resurrection of all believers.

In this general mood it should come as no surprise that Paul was soon forgotten or even silenced. Beker (1980:342f) points out that Papias, Hegesippus, Justin Martyr, and the other Apologists do not appeal to Paul at all. Where Paul *is* accepted in the Hellenistic church, he is thoroughly domesticated. Where he is quoted, this is always in terms of his moral injunctions, not of his apocalyptic hermeneutic.

It was in line with this development that the historical continuity between the Old Testament and the New was disregarded and the inherent historical-hermeneutical connection between the two testaments ignored; the Old Testament was gradually dehistoricized and became an allegorical prelude to the event of Christ (cf van der Aalst 1974:118; Beker 1980:359f). Allegory, a rare exegetical method in Paul (cf Gal 4:21-26), became the dominant hermeneutical principle in the Hellenistic church.

The eclipse of eschatology manifested itself in several other respects as well. Historical thinking increasingly made way for metaphysical categories. Believers no longer thought in terms of the distinction between "this age" and "the age to come", but rather of a "vertical" relationship between time and eternity (Lampe 1957:21; Beker 1980:360). People's expectations came to be focused on heaven rather than on this world and God's involvement in history; instead of looking forward to the future they looked up to eternity. The "low" christology of early Jewish Christians, who had put a high premium on the historical Jesus, gave way to Hellenistic Christianity's preoccupation with the exalted Christ, who became identified with the timeless Logos (cf van der Aalst 1974:115-118), an approach which led to a radical spiritualization of the Christ event. The interest shifted from eschatology to protology, to Christ's eternal pre-existence, his relation to God the Father, and the nature of his incarnation (Beker 1980:357, 360; 1984:108). It became more important to know *whence* Christ came than *why*. The interest in his incarnation, so common in this period, therefore had little to do with his entering a human form and identifying with the plight of humanity; rather, it was moved to the level of metaphysics, where discussion centered on the *nature* of the incarnation and its "pedagogical" significance (Irenaeus; cf further Greshake 1983:52-63).

The original eschatological expectation was further devitalized by mysticism, or perhaps more accurately, by pneumatology, that is, by the notion that through the indwelling of the Spirit the soul becomes spiritual and eventually progresses into the angelic order (Lampe 1957:19, 34; Beker 1984:107; cf van der Aalst 1974:144). "Let us become spiritual" (*pneumatikoi*), we read in chapter 4 of the Epistle of Barnabas. And Origen interpreted the reign of God in terms of the apprehension of a spiritual reality, or as the seeds of truth implanted in the soul (for references, cf Lampe 1957:19; 34). Preaching came to focus almost exclusively on the topic of God and the individual soul, without having anything to say about the relation of the gospel to nature and the structures of this world; in the process the cosmic expectation of "a new heaven and a new earth" was spiritualized away (Beker 1980:360; 1984:108).

Whereas the Hebrew concept *yasha*, "to save", primarily means "to save people from danger and catastrophe", or "to free captives" (that is, salvation *for* this world), the Greek concept *soteria* in the period under discussion tended to refer to being rescued from one's bodily existence, being relieved of the burden of a material existence (in other words, salvation *from* this world). Salvation came to be understood exclusively in terms of "eternal life". Sometimes (for instance in Basilides and Marcion) it was said that the soul alone would be saved, to the exclusion of the body; according to Justin Martyr, the soul can see God after its release from the body (cf Lampe 1957:18, 33). The Christian religion saves *from* this earth; it does not change or renew the earth. Involvement in the world took the form merely of charity. Increasingly the emphasis was laid on the immortality of the soul, which Lactantius labelled "the greatest good". The host of the Eucharist became a *pharmakon athanasias*, a "medicine of (or unto) immortality". The vindication of creation in the glory of God made way for the idea of individual bliss and of the immortal heavenly status of the individual after death. Through various degrees and stages of the spiritual life the soul progresses to perfect union with God.

Most commonly, the attainment of salvation was defined in terms of "life". Clement of Rome's list of the gifts of God began with "life in incorruption"; Irenaeus wrote that communion with God renders humans incorruptible. The salvation conferred on people was therefore really to be understood in terms of their divinization (for references, see Lampe 1957:30f, 34).[2]

The abandoning of primitive Christian eschatology together with the idea of the soul gradually and through various stages working its way up toward immortality and incorruptibility had another serious consequence. The emphasis, instead of being on God's future intervention in history, was now on rewards for those who did good and who would win heaven as a prize for their endurance (references in Lampe 1957:20). To escape the perpetual threat of hell, many good deeds had to be performed, many prayers poured forth, and the intercession of many saints invoked. Irenaeus, in particular, portrayed the ascent of the soul in terms of a pedagogic process toward perfection. Martyrdom, in particular, was a sure gateway to immortality. In the *Martyrdom of Polycarp* it is even said that the martyrs were *"purchasing* at the cost of one hour a release from eternal punishment". Many other examples can be given of moralism "spreading itself like blight over Christianity's expectation of the hereafter" (Rosenkranz 1977:61 – my translation).

Much of this development is, of course, understandable. The Apologists, in particular, had to combat a rabid fatalism and they did this by insisting very strongly on free will, repentance, reward, and punishment (cf Lampe 1957:32). Moreover, it would be misleading to suggest that the Greek church jettisoned all eschatological views handed down to it. The church was, in the words of Lampe,

> in large measure kept true to the primitive eschatological convictions by being tied through the Sacraments ... to the historical events in which the Kingdom was manifested, is continually entering into the present order, and will in the future replace it (1957:22).

In addition, elements of primitive eschatology lingered on longer in the thinking of some theologians than they did in the case of others, even if eschatology tended to wilt into a rather one-dimensional thing. In particular, "a realistic eschatology based on the notions of chiliasm, bodily resurrection, and the reign of the saints with Christ" was upheld by those Christians who formed the solid body of the church and contributed the majority of its martyrs (Lampe

1957:24). In times of oppression and persecution, when the battle was proving difficult and casualties were heavy, believers needed more than a teaching about the gradual ascent of the soul to heaven and immortality. A vivid awareness of the reality of Antichrist likewise directed people's hopes to a final judgment of evil and the cataclysmic inauguration of the reign of God (:26, 30f).

Mostly the church was prepared to tolerate this simple, realistic eschatology. Sometimes, however, the protest against the church's inability to appreciate the validity of apocalyptic became so powerful that a schism was unavoidable. This happened, for instance, around the middle of the second century, when Montanus proclaimed a new outpouring of the Holy Spirit and the imminent advent of the New Jerusalem. The movement he led revived in a most vigorous fashion the sense of immediate urgency and crisis characteristic of primitive eschatology. Montanism was, however, particularly in some of its weird excrescences, an aberration from primitive eschatology. After the movement was practically excommunicated in AD 230 the church closed its doors even more resolutely against apocalyptic in any form. It never completely succeeded in doing this, however, and many apocalyptic elements survived, particularly in the monastic movement.

GNOSTICISM

The church had to combat heresy on at least two fronts. On the one hand there were people like Montanus and others, whose teachings may perhaps be regarded as an excessive manifestation of Jewish apocalyptic eschatology. It was, moreover, not unlike the kind of apocalyptic that is flourishing in our own time. Here "linear" eschatology is pushed to the extreme; the present hour is totally empty and people feverishly long for God to intervene in history. All emphasis is put on the "not yet". On the other hand there were those who stressed the reign of God as having already arrived — in the church, in eternal life for the individual, in the guarantee of immortality. Here the stress tended to be on the "already".

The church successfully withstood the first of these two threats (temptations?) and actually immunized itself against any form of apocalyptic. As far as the second danger was concerned the church was more ambiguous. At one point, however, the church (again, only by and large) held firm: in its rejection of Gnosticism. I have argued that, under the influence of popular philosophy, Christian theology tended to put an ever greater emphasis on *gnosis*, knowledge. This may suggest that the church in its entirety fell prey to the movement known as Gnosticism — which, of course, derived its name from *gnosis*. On the whole, however, the philosophical schools were *anti*-gnostic, and so was mainline theology. Even so, Gnosticism made deep inroads into the church and on several occasions struck at its very heart.

In spite of its air of sophistication Gnosticism really was not a philosophy, but a quasi-philosophy, one which despaired of human rationality. It reflected much of the fatalism and superstition of the period. It gave people who felt themselves trapped in the world an excuse for withdrawal from the hard decisions about life, at the same time imputing to them a sense of superiority, of belonging to a special class. The knowledge (*gnosis*) it espoused was, however, not the rational knowledge of the philosophical schools, but esoteric knowledge, special revelations, knowledge of the secrets of the universe, exceptional passwords, a philosophy which had lost confidence in rationality (cf Young 1988:300f).

Gnosticism's most distinctive feature was an irreversible ontological dualism, an opposition between a transcendent God and an obtuse "demiurge" who had created the material world. This material creation was altogether evil and the transcendent God's irrevocable adversary. The world was primarily seen as a threat, as a source of contagion. It follows from this that Gnosticism's christology would be docetic: Christ was not a real human but simply appeared to be one. This pervasive ontological dualism manifested itself in endless pairs of opposites: the temporal and the eternal, the physical and the spiritual, the earthly and the heavenly, the here and the hereafter, the "flesh below" and the "spirit above", etc. Salvation could only mean liberation from the bonds of this alien material world, and those thus saved could treat the material realities with indifference, if not disdain.

Some of these gnostic elements penetrated the church so deeply that they are alive and well even today. On the whole, however, and this is to the church's eternal credit, the church won this life and death struggle. It rejected this extreme form of Hellenization of Christianity as it also rejected extreme Semiticization. Had it not done the first, it would have gone the way of Marcion and Valentinus, and ended in a totally other-worldly and irrelevant esoteric movement. Had it not done the second, Christianity would eventually have retrogressed to an insipid Ebionitism (cf van der Aalst 1974:187f).

In its confrontation with Gnosticism the church, even if it often wavered, held on to the canonicity of the Old Testament, the historical humanity of Jesus, and faith in the bodily resurrection. The result was that, for a while, the church had to forfeit its opportunity for rapid growth; it devoted its time and energy to finding clarity on crucial theological issues and to consolidating internally (cf von Soden 1974:26f).

In this life and death struggle against extreme views on the "right" and the "left", philosophy proved to be a fitting, even if ambivalent, ally. Frances Young may be overstating her case when she says that there was "a genuine kinship between Jewish monotheism and the emerging consensus of the philosophers", and that "early Christianity justifiably claimed the inheritance of Jewish monotheism and Greek rationalism" (1988:302, 304), but in essence she is right. Greek philosophy provided the church with the tools (and more than just the tools) to analyze all kinds of aberrations, to pursue awkward critical questions, to distinguish truth from fantasy, to repudiate magic, superstition, fatalism, astrology, and idolatry, to grapple seriously with epistemological questions which produced a fundamentally rational account of how human beings attain appropriate knowledge of God, and to do all this with a combination of intellectual rigor and a deep faith commitment; in short, to be both "critical" and "visionary" (cf the title of Young's essay).

THE CHURCH IN EASTERN THEOLOGY

There can be no doubt that, as early as the late first century, a shift in the understanding of the church had set in. In fact, some of the New Testament texts already reflect a situation where the mobile ministry of apostles, prophets, and evangelists was beginning to give way to the settled ministry of bishops (elders) and deacons.

The creative tension between these two dynamics of the church's ministry gradually collapsed in favor of the second. Whereas the writings of Luke introduced the Holy Spirit particularly as the Spirit of mission, as the One who equipped the apostles (and Jesus) and guided them into missionary situations, the Spirit's work was now seen almost exclusively as that of building up the church in sanctity. The work of the Spirit was above all to purify and illumine every soul within the church. The Holy Spirit was the Spirit of truth, of light, of life, of love, but there was hardly any consciousness of the Spirit moving outward to bring good tidings to a wider world. The church filled the entire horizon. Ecclesiology became so primary that both eschatology and pneumatology were subsumed under it. Beker (1980:303f) puts it succinctly,

> A mystical doctrine of the church catholic displaces the idea of the church as proleptic reality . . . (It) is now regarded as the company of the spiritual elite, who with their endowment of the Spirit already actualize the kingdom of God in their soul . . . In this setting, the preexistent status of the church, its ontological character, and its status as an imperishable body become the focal concerns.

It was almost a forgone conclusion that in this kind of climate the missionary fervor of primitive Christianity would subside. The first letter of Clemens (chapter 59) makes no mention of mission, only that the Creator of the universe "may guard intact unto the end the number . . . of his elect throughout the whole world". In most of the Apostolic Fathers non-Christians appeared only as dark foil to the church. It was not essentially different in many later theologians. According to Irenaeus, for instance, the church was the bulwark of right doctrine against the heretics. Cyprian regarded the world as in the process of collapse; there was, according to him, only one possibility of obtaining salvation — membership of the church. Christians alone lived in the light of the Lord; he added, "What do we care about pagans who are not yet enlightened, or about Jews, who have turned away from the light and remained in darkness?" (for reference, see Rosenkranz 1977:66). The church had organized itself into an institution for salvation. It was still expanding and enlarging. This was, however, hardly mission in the Pauline sense; rather, it was Christian propaganda (:77). To the church paganism and the absence of "civilization" were synonymous, and mission identical to the spread of culture.

Within this general climate the real bearer of the missionary ideal and practice was the *monastic movement*, which began to flourish particularly during the last quarter of the third and the first quarter of the fourth century and which would eventually lead to the total disintegration of rural paganism in the entire Greco-Roman world (cf Frend 1974:43; Adam 1974). When Christianity became the official religion of the Empire and persecutions ended, the monk succeeded the martyr as the expression of unqualified witness and protest against worldliness. Since the fourth century the history of the church on the move, particularly in the East, was essentially also the history of monasticism. In fact, from the very beginning of monasticism, the most daring and most efficient missionaries were the monks. But even the monk needed the official sanction and oversight of the bishop. Without that, no monk or priest's missionary service could be legitimate; also, only the episcopal office guaranteed the flow of sacramental grace (cf Kahl 1978:22). The missionaries were ambassadors of the bishops, whose task was to incorporate converts into the church.

Until AD 313 (the year in which joint emperors Constantine and Licinius, meeting at Milan, revised the Empire's two-century-old policy toward Christianity and declared that it would henceforth be tolerated) Christians had always been at a disadvantage in the vast Roman Empire. Even when they were not persecuted,[3] Christians suffered discrimination in many ways; they were almost always distrusted and suspected of disloyalty to the state, if not actually of being dangerous politically. Many church leaders and theologians went out of their way in attempting to prove that the church was interested only in spiritual matters; their success was, however, only limited.

After the so-called Edict of Milan the situation was to change drastically. Ostensibly the church still professed sole allegiance to an other-worldly "heavenly Jerusalem"; in practice, however, precisely this avowal implied a compromise to the political system of the day, which was given a free hand in respect of everything not strictly religious. Whereas the church, on the whole, carefully observed this "division of labor", the state was less conscientious. It even happened that emperors got personally involved in "mission" projects, in which religious and political aims were intertwined (cf Frend 1974:38). The subtle compromise was hardly detectable, but manifested itself in various indirect ways. The "high" christology of the church implied that Christ was increasingly depicted in terms reminiscent of the emperor cult. The Council of Nicea, convened in AD 325 by Emperor Constantine, tended—albeit unconsciously—to clothe Christ with the aid of the attributes and titles of the emperor. "Christ became a majestic king who granted an audience in the liturgy, in a monumental basilica the architecture and decorations of which gave expression to his glory" (van der Aalst 1974:120—my translation). The humanity of Christ was not denied; however, his humanness was underexposed in Byzantine devotion, liturgy, and theology (:121f). What began in primitive Christianity as a bold confession in the face of the emperor cult that Jesus was Lord ("*Kyrios Iesous!*"), ended in a compromise where the emperor was to rule in "time" and Christ in "eternity".

MISSION IN NON-ROMAN ASIA

So far in this chapter I have confined myself almost exclusively to theological developments in the patristic period, that is, broadly speaking, to the church of the second to the sixth century. I have, moreover, given more attention to the Greek than to the Latin branch of the church. In addition, my focus was on the church inside rather than outside the Roman Empire, namely, that branch of the church which passed as "orthodox" in doctrine, in contradistinction to groups branded as "schismatic" or "heretic" by the main body. This was, incidentally, also the focus of the main church body itself. Even at the time when it was at loggerheads with the empire, the church experienced and viewed the empire as the primary sphere of its activities and expansion; the "world", the "ecumene", was the Roman Empire. The church's "world mission" would be completed once it had reached the empire's borders (cf Holl 1974:3; von Soden 1974:24). In the final analysis, the boundaries of the empire, of "orthodoxy", and of language would coincide (cf van der Aalst 1974:40).

There were, however, also Christian churches outside the borders of the Roman Empire; what is more, these churches were often far more actively involved in mission than the increasingly monolithic "main" church. Western Christians (both Catholic and Protestant) tend to give attention only to the westward movement of the faith, from the primitive Semitic church, via the Greek church to the Latin and other European churches and those which were founded through their missionary efforts. It is high time that Western Christians took notice also of the missionary fervor and expansion of the Nestorians and other groups further to the East. In the first centuries the church indeed spread its arms widely. It did not incarnate itself only in the cultures and thought-forms of the Greeks and the Romans but also expressed itself through the liturgies of other cultures: Coptic, Syriac, Maronite, Armenian, Ethiopian, Indian, and even Chinese.

There was one fundamental difference between the overall situation of the churches of the East and the church of the West. Whereas the latter (including the largest part of the Byzantine church and its "daughter" churches) profited (at least outwardly) from the effect of the "Constantinian reversal" (that is, the recognition of the main church of the West as state church), the churches of the East, at least in their formative years, never experienced anything of the sort. L. E. Browne says about them, "In Asia . . . never once until the thirteenth century was the favour of the state conferred upon the Church" (quoted in Moffett 1987:481). Even then — in the thirteen century, when a Mongol emperor, son of a Nestorian princess, sat on the throne of China — the respite the church was given was all too brief, for soon these outposts of Christianity were wiped out. So the church in these parts never knew anything like a "Constantinian reversal" of the fortunes of Christianity. The church in Asia was always a minority group within its environment (in fact, it has, with the exception of the Philippines, remained a minority in Asia to this day). Not only was it a minority, it was also always suspected of somehow conniving with the empires of the "Christian" West. For example, in the fourth century King Sapor II of the Sassanid Empire in Mesopotamia regarded the Aramaic Christians within the borders of his state as a fifth column of the Roman Empire. "They live in our territory", he said, "but they share the sentiments of Caesar" (quoted in van der Aalst 1974:59).

This circumstance was both a liability and an asset. It was a liability in that the Christian church always held a most tenuous position in these regions. In Persia, for instance, the church could, in the long run, only survive in the ghetto. "It was a state within a state, a minority enclave of protected but subjugated people ... No Christian, not even the patriarch, had power except within his ghetto, and even there his power was dependent upon the shah" (Moffett 1987:481, 482). As a result, the Christian church always remained a foreign body, an increasingly idiosyncratic subculture, more and more isolated from the population at large and less and less able to communicate with them (Hage 1978).

At the same time the absence of state support was an asset in that the church could be itself and had little reason to attempt to please the powers that be. Its mission was also more credible, since nobody could suspect it of wishing to curry favor with the authorities. The church therefore expanded not only westward, as most Western textbooks would have it, but also eastward. By AD 225, less than two centuries after the earthly ministry of Jesus, the Syrian church had carried the Christian faith halfway across Asia to the edges of India and the western ranges of China (Moffett 1987:484). Its ascetics-turned-missionaries, "homeless followers of the homeless Jesus on ... ceaseless pilgrimage through this world" (Robert Murray, quoted in Moffett 1987:483) healed the sick, fed the poor, and preached the gospel.

Above all it was the Nestorians who were to become the major missionary force in non-Roman Asia. When Nestorius was condemned by the Council of Ephesus (AD 431) and banished to Egypt, his followers fled to Persia where a vital monasticism, an eminent theology (by the sixth century the School of Nisibis had become the most famous center of learning in all Asia outside China; cf Moffett 1987:481), and an imposing missionary activity soon testified to the movement's strength. These three dimensions of Nestorianism—monasticism, theology, and mission—were mutually interdependent, and resulted in the Nestorian church becoming "the 'missionary' church *par excellence* in the overall context of medieval Christianity" (Hage 1978:360). Its monasticism was rooted in its Syriac religious ancestry and was, unlike Egyptian monasticism, missionary through and through. These eccentric hermits may appear almost bizarre to us today, and yet they were the ones who time and again combined the call to ascetic self-denial with the call to go and preach and serve. The Eastern Syrian Nestorians, with missionaries like Alopen (A Lo Pen) may with justification be called the Irish monks of the East (or, if one prefers, the Irish missionaries may be called the Nestorian monks of the West).

By the end of the fourteenth century, however, the Nestorian and other churches—which at one time had dotted the landscape of all of Central and even parts of East Asia—were all but wiped out. Isolated pockets of Christianity survived only in India. The religious victors on the vast Central Asian mission field of the Nestorians were Islam and Buddhism; most of those Christian ghettos which did not perish under the onslaught of one of these two vigorous faiths gradually succumbed to syncretism (Hage 1978:391f). Thus, at the end of the day, it was not the missionary program of the Nestorians and others in

Asia that would put its indelible stamp on world and Christian history—this distinction belongs to the Western church and its mission, to which I now return.

THE PATRISTIC AND ORTHODOX MISSIONARY PARADIGM

Ever since the fourth century, when Constantine the Great moved his head-quarters from Rome to Byzantium on the Bosporus (and renamed that city Constantinople) the empire had to deal with the problem of having two rival capitals. The rivalry was not confined to the political scene; also ecclesiastically Rome and Constantinople were slowly but irreversibly drifting apart, a process which would come to a head with the Great Schism of 1054. After that, the two "wings" of the church, one calling itself "Roman" and "Catholic", the other "Byzantine" and "Orthodox", would go their separate ways. It was the Byzantine Church that would, in the course of many centuries, give birth to and mold Eastern Orthodox theology and mission understanding as we know these today. Since the Great Schism, the Orthodox churches were, for all practical purposes, isolated from theological thinking and developments in the West, at least until very recent times. On the one side Orthodoxy was hemmed in by the Western church; on the other side, it was blocked by the threatening power and advances of Islam. The only area that remained for expansion lay to the north. From the sixth century to the twelfth Orthodox missions advanced mainly among the Slavonian peoples and, even more particularly, into the vast expanses of Russia and its hinterland (cf Hannick 1978).

As we shall see in the next chapter, the Roman Catholic (or Western) Church was almost always compromised to the state. The same was true of the Byzantine Church, only much more so. Eusebius of Caesarea, "herald of Byzantinism" and "founder of political theology" (van der Aalst 1974:59f), constructed a system in which state and church were united in harmony. He combined various early traditions about the divine origin and nature of kings into a new synthesis; monotheism and the monarchy, he suggested, went hand in hand and presupposed each other. In a eulogy on Constantine he became the first theologian who "clearly stated the political philosophy of the Christian Empire, that philosophy of state which was consistently maintained throughout the millennium of Byzantine absolutism" (H. Baynes, quoted in van der Aalst 1974:61f). Jewish monotheism conquered polytheism; in like manner the Roman monarchy had routed earlier polyarchy. The Christian emperor, Constantine, was now called to guide the world back to God. In the Byzantine Empire attempts would time and again be made to let the unity of the empire coincide with the unity of the faith. The *Henotikon* of Emperor Zenon (AD 482), the *Ekthesis* of Heraclius (AD 638), and the *Typos* of Constantius II (AD 648) were all measures taken to assure the indissoluble unity of the interests of church and state (cf van der Aalst 1974:59-62).

In this kind of atmosphere it was to be expected that mission would be as much a concern of the emperor as of the church. As "imitator of God" the emperor united in himself both religious and political offices (Hannick 1978:354). The objectives of the state coincided with the objectives of the church and vice versa, and this applied to mission as well (Stamoolis 1986:56-60). The practice of direct royal involvement in the missionary enterprise would persist throughout the Middle Ages and, in fact, into the modern era. The Russian Orthodox mission of the Kiev princes was a political project and went hand in hand with colonialist expansion northward and northeastward into the interior of Russia (Rosenkranz 1977:188). Evangelization became virtually coterminous with "Russification" (Fisher 1982:22).

Does all this imply that we have to pass an altogether negative verdict on the missionary endeavors of the Orthodox churches? This is frequently what happens, particularly in Western Protestant circles (an example is Rosenkranz 1977:188-190, 242f). At other times one encounters the view that there is, at least in modern times, no such thing as mission in Orthodoxy; these churches are, in one word, non-missionary. Both the negative evaluation and the charge of being non-missionary are, however, misplaced. Both are, rather, to be ascribed to the absolutization of a specific—in this case, a Western—definition of what mission is. But it is possible to look at mission from a different vantage-point. In recent years Christians in other traditions have been helped to appreciate Orthodox mission thinking particularly by the writings of theologians such as Anastasios of Androussa (in Greece), Bria (of Rumania), and Stamoolis. The Eastern church's contribution to an understanding of mission is indeed significant.

It is to the Greeks that we owe the *intellectual discipline of theology* and the classical formulations of the faith. In the Bible and earliest Christian literature any form of systematization was virtually absent. The Alexandrian theologian Origen (ca 185 to ca 254, AD) may well be called the first "systematic theologian" and the first person in whom the Eastern theological paradigm clearly manifested itself (cf Kannengieser 1984:154-156). Is this development, as well as the emergence of Christian dogma, only cause for lament? This is what Harnack (1961:17, 21f) suggested when he said, "Dogma in its conception and development is a work of the Greek spirit on the soil of the gospel". I submit that this paradigm shift was unavoidable and had a very positive side to it. The Greeks provided theology worldwide with the array of concepts which were necessary for the unfolding of a more critical, systematic, and intellectually honest approach in matters of faith (cf van der Aalst 1974:42). There is certainly a danger here—that of rationalization and intellectualization. Origen and his colleagues were, however, not interested in intellect for intellect's sake. They held on to the priority of faith over reason, and undertook rigorous intellectual pursuits precisely for the sake of the faith. Tough-reasoned argument was necessary, for Christians had to understand their faith in a pluralistic world. For Origen, then, faith was the reasoning of the religious mind (cf Young 1988: 306f). That Orthodoxy in subsequent centuries became increasingly inflexible, tended to put its dogma, for all intents and purposes, on a par with biblical truth, and began to think of itself as the (sole?) "defender of the faith" (cf Bria 1980:6), was indeed unfortunate but is not, in and of itself, sufficient reason to reject the discipline of academic reflection and careful formulation. For this legacy bequeathed to us by the Eastern church in its vigorous missionary engagement with the world of its time we should remain forever grateful.

In Orthodox thinking mission is thoroughly *church-centered* (cf Nissiotis 1968:186-197; Anastasios 1989:75, 81-83). This too has its roots in early Eastern theology, where an ever stronger accent was put on ecclesiology. The conviction gradually grew that the church was the kingdom of God on earth and that to be in the church was the same as being in the kingdom.

In Orthodoxy, then, the church is the dispenser of salvific light and the mediator of power for renewal which produces life (cf Nissiotis 1968:195-197). The "ecclesial character" of mission means "that the Church is the aim, the fulfilment of the Gospel, rather than an instrument or means of mission". The church is part of the message it proclaims (Bria 1975:245). Mission is not to be regarded as a function of the church; the Orthodox reject "such instrumental-istic interpretations of the Church". Neither is mission the proclaiming of some "ethical truths or principles"; it is "calling people to become members of the Christian community in a visible concrete form". "The Church is the aim of mission, not vice versa". It is "ecclesiology which determines missiology" (Bria 1980:8). For this reason the basic elements of an answer to the question about the Orthodox understanding of mission must be looked for in its "doctrine and experience of the Church" (Schmemann 1961:251). Mission is "part of the nature of the church"; it is not related exclusively to the church's "apostolicity", "but to all the *notae* of the church" (Bria 1986:12f; cf Stamoolis 1986:103-127).

Such views have far-reaching consequences not only for the understanding, but also for the practice of mission. Under no circumstances may any individual, or group of individuals, embark upon a missionary venture without being sent and supported by the church. If "the Church *as such* is mission" (V. Spiller, quoted in Stamoolis 1986:116), then mission refers to a *collective* task. "Christ must be preached within His historical reality, His Body in the Spirit, without which there is neither Christ nor the Gospel. Outside the context of the Church, evangelism remains a humanism or a temporary psychological enthusiasm" (N. A. Nissiotis, quoted in Bria 1975:245).

This leads us to the next crucial element in Orthodox missiology: the place of *the liturgy in mission*. "Liturgy is the key to the Orthodox understanding of the Church, and therefore the importance of liturgy for the Orthodox viewpoint on evangelism cannot be overemphasized" (Bria 1975:248). Precisely because the church is part of the message, no evangelism or mission should take place "without a definite reference to its spiritual and sacramental existence" (:245). The Orthodox thus subscribe to a "eucharistic ecclesiology" (:247). In the words of K. Rose (1960:456f — my translation),

> As church of the Easter light and liturgy it sees its main task in enlight-ening the pagans who are to receive God's light through the liturgy. The major manifestation of the missionary activity of the Orthodox church lies in its celebration of the liturgy. The light of mercy that shines in the liturgy should act as center of attraction to those who still live in the darkness of paganism.

In the Orthodox perspective mission is thus centripetal rather than centrif-ugal, organic rather than organized. It "proclaims" the gospel through doxology and liturgy. The witnessing community is the community in worship; in fact, the worshiping community is in and of itself an act of witness (Bria 1980:9f). This is so, since the eucharistic liturgy has a basic missionary structure and purpose (cf Stamoolis 1986:86-102) and is celebrated as a "missionary event" (Bria 1986:17f).

If mission is a manifestation of the life and worship of the church, then *mission and unity* go together. Unity and mission (or, for that matter, mission and unity), may never be regarded as two successive stages; they belong inextricably together. In the words of Nissiotis:

> "Mission and unity" mean that no missionary can proclaim the one gospel without being profoundly aware of the fact that he is bringing the historical community of the church and without feeling driven to this witness by the Holy Spirit, on the basis of his personal membership in the one apostolic church (quoted in Rosenkranz 1977:468 — my translation).

For the Orthodox the Great Schism of 1054 had far-reaching consequences. Whereas the Catholic Church continued with its missionary outreach without interruption, particularly after the fifteenth century, and Protestant churches and mission agencies each embarked on their own outreach to those who lived beyond the borders of historical Christendom, the Orthodox could not easily do the same. When the unity was broken, "the Orthodox Church saw its mission altered from evangelism to a search for Christian unity" (Stamoolis 1986:110, summarizing the views of Metropolitan James of Melita). Other Orthodox spokespersons would adopt a less rigid view; instead of arguing that since the Schism mission has become impossible, they would rather say that, in our time, unity is the goal of mission (cf Voulgarakis 1965; Nissiotis 1968:199-201; Bria 1987). For the Orthodox, both unity and mission are ecclesial acts, acts of the whole people of God; they form one ecclesiological reality. In fact, *catholicity* is another name for mission in unity in the Orthodox perspective (Bria 1987:266). Since the church is Christ's body, and there is only one body, the unity of the church is the unity of Christ, by the Spirit, with the triune God. Any division of Christians is therefore "a scandal and an impediment to the united witness of the church" (Bria 1986:69). Tragically, from the Orthodox point of view, we only too often convert people not to this one church, the body of Christ, but to our own denomination, at the same time imparting to them the "poison of division" (Nissiotis 1968:198).

In its deepest sense mission, in the Orthodox perspective, is founded on the *love of God*. If we have to identify *one* text from Scripture that epitomizes the Orthodox position on mission, it would be John 3:16, "For God so *loved* the world that he gave his only Son, that whoever believes in him should not perish but have eternal life". God's love manifests itself in *kenosis*, that is, in "inner, voluntary self-denial which makes room to receive and embrace the other to whom one turns" (Voulgarakis 1965:299-301). And if God's love, disclosed in sending Christ, is the "theological starting-point" of mission (Yannoulatos 1965:281-284; cf Voulgarakis 1987:357f), the same love should find expression in his emissaries; it is because they are motivated by love which, like God's love in Christ, manifests itself in *kenosis*, that they go to those outside the Christian fold. God is not regarded primarily, as he often is in Western theology, as the righteous One who judges the sinful and unrighteous; it is his love rather than his justice that is highlighted. Because God loves humankind he wrought his plan of redemption. "God is the seeking God, looking for the lost sheep; the loving Father, awaiting the Prodigal's return" (Stamoolis 1986:10).

If the ground of mission in the perspective of the Eastern church is love, then the *goal of mission is life* (Lampe 1957:30f). Like love, life is a Johannine theme (cf, once again, Jn 3:16). Eastern Orthodox theology is clearly stamped more by the Johannine than by the Pauline tradition. Christ did not come primarily to put away human sin, but to restore in humans the image of God and give them life. The content of proclamation is "a word of life unto life" (Voulgarakis 1987:359f; cf Schmemann 1961:256). It is in this respect that the characteristic Orthodox doctrine of *theosis* acquires missionary significance. People are not called simply to know Christ, to gather around him, or to submit to his will; "they are called to participate in his glory" (Anastasios 1965:285). The "from one degree of glory to another" (2 Cor 3:18) "defines the process by which the faithful are sanctified during the present life, until the *Parousia*" (:286). *Theosis* is union with God rather than deification; it is "a continuing state of adoration, prayer, thanksgiving, worship, and intercession, as well as meditation and contemplation of the triune God and God's infinite love" (Bria 1986:9). The formula "heaven on earth", familiar to every Orthodox, expresses the actualization in this world of the *eschaton*, "the ultimate reality of salvation and redemption" (Schmemann 1961:252; cf Bria 1987:267). *Theosis* refers to the rescinding of the loss of the image of God and the transformation of the old existence into a new creature, into new, eternal life (cf Rosenkranz 1977:243, 470; Lowe 1982:200-204; Greshake 1983:61-63). Where this takes place, mission has attained its end.

Salvation or life as the goal of mission is not restricted to human beings. It has a *"cosmic dimension"* (Bria 1976:182; 1980:7; Anastasios 1989:83f). Not only humanity, but also the whole universe "participates in the restoration and finds its orientation again in glorifying God". The cross "sanctifies the universe" (Anastasios 1965:286). God has not only reconciled individuals but also "the world" to himself (2 Cor 5:19), even the cosmic forces (Col 1:20). The whole of creation is in the process of becoming *ekklesia*, the church, the body of Christ (Bria 1980:7). This *anakephalaiosis* or "recapitulation" of the universe has not taken place yet but is eagerly expected; it is, truly, an eschatological reality (cf Anastasios 1965:286). For the mission of the church this means that there is, now already, a "messianic movement outside the church", which suggests "an urgent need for the church to increase its understanding of those outside her influence" (Bria 1980:7). As Schmemann puts it,

State, society, culture, nature itself, are real *objects* of mission and not a neutral "milieu" in which the only task of the Church is to preserve its own inner freedom, to maintain its "religious life" . . . In the world of incarnation nothing "neutral" remains, nothing can be taken away from the Son of Man (1961:256, 257).

The observations made in the previous paragraph may help to throw light on yet another aspect of Orthodox missiology, namely, its understanding of mission as *involvement in society*. The Orthodox are frequently viewed as a conservative and contemplative body who wish to escape the difficult realities of history. Rose (1960:457) remarks that Orthodox mission has no "program for the world, for civic life". Viewing the Orthodox understanding of mission from the perspective of the activism of Western Christianity it may indeed appear as though mission in this tradition has no relation whatsoever to the realities of suffering and injustice in the world. Also, there certainly were periods in Orthodox history when the church restricted itself, consciously or unconsciously, to "religious" matters in the narrow sense of the word (Anastasios 1989:70).

On the whole, however, this interpretation of Orthodoxy rests on a misunderstanding of its character; small wonder that, in recent years, Orthodox spokespersons have gone out of their way to clarify their position on this matter. It is, however, crucial to recognize that the Orthodox churches' involvement in society can never be divorced from the practice and experience of their worship. There are two complementary movements in the eucharistic rite: the Eucharist begins as the movement of ascension toward the throne of God, and it ends as the movement of return into the world. "The Eucharist is always the End, the sacrament of the *parousia*, and yet, it is always the *beginning*, the *starting point*: now the mission begins" (Schmemann 1961:255). In recent years it has become customary in Orthodox circles to refer to this second movement as "the liturgy after the Liturgy" (cf Bria 1980:66-71). Both forms may be termed liturgy, worship of God, because both are different yet complementary ways of serving and following him. The mission of the church into the world, the second liturgy, rests upon the radiating and transforming power of the Liturgy. The Liturgy makes the liturgy possible. The eucharistic celebration therefore has to nourish the Christian life not only in its private sphere, but also in the public and political realm; it is impossible to separate the two. According to John Chrysostom (who shaped the order of the eucharistic liturgy usually celebrated by the Orthodox) there is, in addition to the Eucharist, also "the sacrament of the brother", namely, the service which believers have to offer outside the place of worship, in public places, on the altar of their neighbor's heart (:71).

THE FIRST PARADIGM SHIFT: AN INTERIM BALANCE

There can be little doubt that the Greek theology of the early centuries AD and its contemporary heir, Eastern Orthodoxy, represent a paradigm very different from that of primitive Christianity. Origen, in particular, was responsible for a renewal of theology which in many respects was on a par with what Paul did in respect of the tradition he had received (Kannengieser 1984:162); in this respect Origen paved the way for a truly innovative interaction between contemporary culture and Christian self-understanding (:163). The Christian tradition was reworked from the bottom up, and the end result was a way of theologizing that made sense to the Greek mind. In the course of time the Greeks would impart this vision to many other peoples as well: Slavs, Russians, and various Asian groups (cf Hannick 1978), but in such a manner that the essential Byzantine imprint would remain to this day.

In a very real sense this paradigm shift was inevitable. The fledgling Christian movement could either remain within the confines of the small Jewish world or branch out into the *ecumene*. And Hellenism was the cultural form of the world into which Christianity was first introduced. Therefore Hellenization was equivalent to universalization (van der Aalst 1974:185). There was no real alternative to it, if only because it offered the church a more spacious frame of reference (:188f). And even if we may argue that the Hellenization of the faith went too far, we should be reminded of the fact that the church resisted not only the extreme Semiticization of Christianity by the Ebionites, Montanists, and others, but also extreme Hellenization. The "heretics" were often repudiated precisely because they were more hellenistic than the "orthodox" (:188). This was eminently true of Gnosticism. In its opposition to this mortal threat the church, as I have pointed out earlier, held on to the most fundamental and inalienable elements of the Christian faith: the canonicity of the Old Testament, the historicity of the humanity of Jesus, the bodily resurrection of Jesus from the dead. The church did this at a price. It could perhaps have advanced more rapidly throughout the Hellenistic world by abandoning these convictions. However, it resisted being consumed wholly by the Greek spirit (cf von Soden 1974:26f; Lampe 1957:18, 21f).

The monastic movement was another saving element in the patristic and later in the Orthodox missionary tradition. Supremely, however, it has been the simple faith of thousands of ordinary believers that, to this day, gives expression to an essentially missionary dimension in Orthodoxy. The *Letter to Diognetus* 5f, written around AD 200, presents us with an illustration of this dimension at an early stage of Hellenistic Christianity:

> Christians are not distinguished from the rest of humankind either in locality or in speech or in customs. For they dwell not somewhere in cities of their own, neither do they use some different language, nor practice an extraordinary kind of life ... While they dwell in cities of Greeks and barbarians ... and follow the native custom in dress and food and the other arrangements of life, yet the constitution of their own citizenship, which they set forth, is marvelous, and confessedly contradicts expectation. They dwell in their own countries, but only as sojourners ... Every foreign country is a fatherland to them, and every fatherland is foreign ... They find themselves in the flesh and yet they live not after the flesh. Their existence is on earth, but their citizenship is in heaven. They obey the established laws, and they surpass the laws in their own lives ... War is waged against them as aliens by the Jews, and persecution is carried on against them by the Greeks, and yet those who hate them cannot tell

the reason for their hostility. In a word, what the soul is in a body, this the Christians are in the world . . . (they) are kept in the world as in a prison-house, and yet they themselves hold the world together.

The portrayal is admittedly a bit romantic, if not utopian, and yet it can hardly be doubted, even from a secular history point of view, that it was the Christians who had "held the world together". Harnack's meticulous account of their "gospel of love and charity" (1962:147-198) offers an unparalleled testimony to the remarkable witness of life of ordinary Christians in the first three centuries. We shall never be able fully to fathom the significance of this dimension for the mission of the church, yet there can be no doubt that it slowly but surely transformed the entire empire — something Christianity was not able to do further to the East, in non-Roman Asia.

Against this background the characteristic elements of Byzantine and Orthodox mission, which I tabulated above, may be appreciated. The vigorous intellectual discipline was necessary, precisely for the sake of the mission of the church, in a society submerged in syncretism and relativism. The church as sign, symbol, and sacrament of the divine in human life helped to lift people's hearts to God in a world resigned to fatalism and the capriciousness of the gods. The eucharistic liturgy was the place where the faithful were given nourishment which helped them cope with the vicissitudes of life and also equipped them for the "liturgy after the Liturgy". The unity of the church-in-mission not only gave credibility to the church in the context of a divided society, but also signified — to a polytheistic world — that God was one and sovereign. The grounding of mission in the love of God rather than in his justice was a revolutionary message in a world where the gods were ultimately apathetic and unconcerned. The identification of new life as the substance of salvation added an unprecedented quality to the existence of Christians and also served to focus their eyes on what God was still going to put into effect.

Protestants, in particular, are challenged by Orthodox missiology (cf Fueter 1976:passim). They are challenged with respect to their overly pragmatic mission structures, their tendency to portray mission almost exclusively in verbalist categories, and the absence of missionary spirituality in their churches, which often drastically impoverishes all their commendable efforts in the area of social justice.

Still, the Orthodox missionary paradigm is not without its difficulties. It went beyond mere inculturation and contextualization of the faith. The church adapted to the existing world order, resulting in church and society penetrating and permeating each other. The role of religion — any religion — in society is that of both stabilizer and emancipator; it is both mythical and messianic. In the Eastern tradition the church tended to express the former of each of these pairs rather than the latter. The emphasis was on conservation and restoration, rather than on embarking on a journey into the unknown. The key words were "tradition", "orthodoxy", and "the Fathers" (cf Küng 1984:20), and the church became the bulwark of right doctrine. Orthodox churches tended to become ingrown, excessively nationalistic, and without a concern for those outside (Anastasios 1989:77f).

In particular, Platonic categories of thought all but destroyed primitive Christian eschatology (Beker 1984:107f). The church established itself in the world as an institute of almost exclusively other-worldly salvation. Faith in the promises of Christ still to be fulfilled tended to make room for faith in Christ's already accomplished eternal reign, which could henceforth be experienced and manifested only in the cultic-sacramental context of the liturgy. The apocalyptic gospel, which had fervently anticipated God's intervention in history, was replaced by a timeless gospel according to which the delay of the parousia made no vital difference. The element of urgency and crisis was wiped out by the idea of gradually drawing nearer to perfection, through various "pedagogical" phases. Taking their cue from the incarnation of Christ, theologians such as Irenaeus, Clement of Alexandria, and Origen described the believer's ascent from the moment of rebirth, through stages, up to the final point where he or she sees God (cf Beinert 1983:199-202; Küng 1984:53). When all is said and done, this world and its history are not real; it is illusory (Rose 1960:457). The consequence is that, even where believers do get involved in the contingencies of historical life, they do so with reservations and often with a bad conscience (cf Anastasios 1989:69f).

Chapter 7

The Medieval Roman Catholic Missionary Paradigm

CHANGED CONTEXT

The above title refers to the medieval theological paradigm. However, although shaped during the Middle Ages, this paradigm did not disappear after the sixteenth century; as a matter of fact, traces of it can still be found in contemporary Catholicism. Even so, its heyday was the medieval period.

By and large, I shall use the term Middle Ages as referring to the period between 600 and 1500. Broadly speaking, one might say that the epoch commenced with the papacy of Gregory the Great and the emergence and early successes of Islam; it ended with the Muslim seizure of Constantinople (1453) and the Portuguese and Spanish voyages of discovery. The end of the Middle Ages also signalled the era in which Europe had indisputably become Christian: a few centuries earlier, it had only been outwardly Christian, just the "shadow of the Christian symbol" having been cast over it (cf Baker 1970:17-28).

For at least three centuries the Christian church had been stamped almost exclusively by the Greek spirit. Gradually, however, a new mode of Christianity, which bore another imprint, began to develop. Here the dominant language was no longer Greek, but Latin. This external difference concealed many others, which were not immediately apparent. A thousand years after the new religion was first introduced, in 1054, those dissimilarities would lead to the great schism between the churches of the East and the West.

In the Byzantine church—as has been argued in the previous chapter—redemption was a process in which human nature, by means of a "pedagogical" progression, was taken up into the divine; in the West, the emphasis was on the ravages of sin and the reparation of fallen humanity through a crisis experience. The theology of the Eastern church was incarnational; its emphasis lay on the "origin" of Christ, on his preexistence. The theology of the Western church was staurological (from *stauros*, Greek for "cross"); it emphasized the substitutionary death of Christ for the sake of sinners (cf Beinert 1983:203-205).

These are only *some* areas in which each of the two segments of the church went its own way. Given such dissimilarities in accent and interpretation it was only to be expected that the Western mission would differ in many respects from its Eastern counterpart and develop a character of its own. Naturally, there were also many similarities; in fact, these outweighed the differences. For one thing, the Latin church, like the Greek and unlike the Hebrew, had a preference for the visual rather than the auditive. It was interested in the correct formulation of doctrine and could match the Byzantine fathers in their expertise at defining and redefining the tenets of the faith; the thirteen "definitions" of the nature of God, agreed upon by the Fourth Lateran and First Vatican Councils (1215 and 1870) give ample proof of this. The focus, throughout, was on conceptualizing and systematizing doctrines handed down to the church, frequently in a completely ahistorical manner.[1]

Strictly speaking, Augustine of Hippo (354-430) preceded the Middle Ages, at least if one takes this period to have begun around 600. Still, this "first truly Western man" (Stendahl 1976:16) may indeed be regarded as the inaugurator of the medieval paradigm (Küng 1987:258) and the one who placed an indelible stamp on the entire subsequent Western theological history, both Catholic and Protestant. This is to be attributed not only to his genius, but also to his personal history and to the political circumstances in which he found himself. The Christian movement scarcely had the opportunity of adjusting itself to the new religio-political dispensation introduced by Constantine (313) and the proscription of all religions except Christianity by Theodosius (380), when Alaric and his Gothic hordes conquered and sacked Rome in 410. To the entire Mediterranean world Rome was the symbol of civilization, order, and stability. To see it defeated by barbarians could not but create a profound sense of despair and uncertainty. The man of the hour was Augustine who, with his monumental *De Civitate Dei*, succeeded in showing a way forward.

In addition to the crisis the empire faced, Augustine had to respond to two other major crises which were precipitated, respectively, by the Donatists in North Africa and an English monk, Pelagius. These three circumstances and Augustine's reaction to them, influenced deeply by his own personal history, were to shape both the theology and the understanding of mission of subsequent centuries.

THE INDIVIDUALIZATION OF SALVATION

I turn, first, to Augustine's refutation of Pelagianism, since this had the most far-reaching impact on medieval mission and also reveals more clearly the basic difference between the Byzantine and Latin branches of the church.

Pelagius, who was active in Rome at the end of the fourth and beginning of the fifth century, took a decidedly optimistic view of human nature and of the human capacity to attain perfection. While God gets the ultimate credit for having made us so that we are capable of doing what we should, "we have the power of accomplishing every good thing by action, speech and thought". Humanity did not need redemption, only inspiration. This meant that Pelagius did not regard Christ as Savior who died for the sins of humankind, but as master and model whom we are called to emulate. To this Augustine responded with the doctrines of original sin and of predestination. The image of God, impaired by human sin and weakness, could not—as Clement, Origen, and other Greek theologians had taught—be restored by means of a drawn-out, upward pedagogical process culminating in *theosis*; rather, the terrible reality of total human depravity demanded a radical conversion experience and an encounter with the irresistible grace of God in Christ.

Augustine became the first Christian theologian to take Paul's teaching on justification by faith seriously. Our sinful condition is so perilous that only God can change it, without any contribution from us. We are, in this, totally powerless, delivered into Satan's hands, until we are ransomed from his dominion. Since our dilemma is a human one, only a human can satisfy God's demands in this respect; but since all human beings are themselves sinners, only somebody who is sinless and both human and divine can meet this condition and satisfy God vicariously on behalf of other human beings. This is in fact what Christ did, through his vicarious death on the cross. It happened once for all, and now holds true objectively; all that remains is for individuals to appropriate this salvation subjectively—something that only the elect can do. This is, however, not a gloomy or pessimistic message, but one of indescribable joy; after all, only against the somber background of human depravity can the light of God's grace shine truly brilliantly. So one can never talk about human guilt and sin without referring simultaneously to forgiveness, renewal by Jesus Christ, and redemption (cf Greshake 1983:19).

Essentially, Augustine wrestled with an anthropological rather than a theological problem: On what basis does a person find salvation? It was through the lens of this question that he read Paul and found in him the answer. Paul's grappling with the particular salvation-historical problem of Israel's refusal to embrace Christ in faith—an issue so prominent in Romans and Galatians (cf chapter 4 above)—was reapplied by Augustine to a more general and timeless human problem, that of the individual wrestling with his or her conscience. One of the classic ways in which Augustine put this was his saying, "Our hearts are restless until they find their rest in Thee". Elsewhere he wrote, "I desire only to know God and my soul, nothing else". The human soul is lost, therefore it is the human soul that has to be saved. Seven centuries after Augustine, Anselm wrote *Cur Deus Homo? (Why Did God Become Human?)*, and his reply to this question was similar to Augustine's: God became human in order to save human souls that are hurtling to destruction. Not the reconciliation of the universe but the redemption of the soul stands in the center. This redemption is understood to be both other-worldly and individualistic, in contrast not only to much of the Old and New Testament, but also of the traditional religions of Europe, which were exclusively this-worldly and communal (cf Kahl 1978:33).

The theology of Augustine could not but spawn a dualistic view of reality, which became second nature in Western Christianity—the tendency to regard salvation as a private matter and to ignore the world (cf Greshake 1983:20,69). The hope of the kingdom of God was transformed into a hope of "heaven", the place or state of life in which those who have done good will be rewarded and which was to be won as a prize for endurance. To this end an ever more refined penitential practice was developed. Believers were given guidance as to proper ways of conducting spiritual self-examination so as to be better able to analyze their consciences and detect moral weaknesses in their spiritual make-up. Positively, this development helped to give rise to a tradition of integrity and moral vitality in Western Christianity.

Paradoxically, the spiritualization and introversion which began with Augustine also paved the way for large-scale externalization. The cultic-institutional smothered the personal-ethical, since it was the official church which not only sanctioned the penitential practice, but also defined exactly which human thoughts and actions were sins; in addition, of course, only the church, through its ministrations, could guarantee restitution. In this process soteriology tended to get divorced from christology and to be subordinated to ecclesiology. Grace rendered itself autonomous as an ecclesial sacrament. With this remark we are, however, already broaching the subject of Augustine's controversy with the Donatists, to which I now turn.

THE ECCLESIASTICIZATION OF SALVATION

The Donatist movement originated in North Africa, where it had an extensive following during the fourth and fifth centuries. The schism from the Catholic Church was precipitated by the consecration of Caecilian as bishop of Carthage in 311/312. It was alleged that Philip, one of his consecrators, had been a "traitor"[2] during the persecutions under Diocletian, which had immediately preceded Constantine's accession to the throne. Those who protested, called Donatists, stood in the tradition of Tertullian, who had taught that the "seven deadly sins" (idolatry, blasphemy, murder, adultery, fornication, false-witness, and fraud) were unforgivable; a church leader guilty of any of these should therefore not be allowed to stay in office, let alone participate in the consecration of a bishop. His participation could, in fact, render such a bishop's office invalid.

The Donatists thus expressed the anger and despair of those who saw an absolute contrast between the gospel of Christ and the worldliness of the church; true believers should have nothing to do with the world and with a church which allowed itself to become contaminated by the world. The true church must keep itself totally unblemished and perfect; if this does not happen, the sins of individual members and office-bearers will spread like an infection through the entire church. The Donatists were theologically orthodox and, at least formally, stood more explicitly than Augustine in the ancient tradition of strict moral discipline; they also insisted on an absolute separation of church and state (cf Schindler 1987:296-298).[3]

Augustine passionately opposed the Donatists. In doing so, he did not attempt to declare the church and its office-bearers free of any of the sins of which the Donatists accused it. One who enters the church, he said in his *Instructing the Unlearned*, "is bound to see drunkards, misers, tricksters, gamblers, adulterers, fornicators, people wearing amulets, assiduous clients of sorcerers, astrologers ... The same crowds that press into the churches on Christian festivals also fill the theatres on pagan holidays". In the final analysis the difference between Christians and others lies in one thing only: the former are members of the church, the latter not.

There is an important positive side to Augustine's view on this issue, over against that of the Donatists: Augustine insisted that the church was not a refuge from the world but existed for the sake of a world that was hurting. All, including "good church people", were sinners, and the self-righteousness of the Donatists might be more vicious than the sins of others. There is, however, also a more negative side to his stance: authority and holiness were regarded as adhering in the institutional church whether or not these moral and theological qualities were in evidence. Since the worldwide church, founded by the apostles, was the only true church, whoever left it was self-evidently wrong; those who severed their links with the Catholic Church also severed their relationship with God. Visible unity and salvation went hand in hand (cf Schindler 1987:297). As recent as 1919 Josef Schmidlin, the father of Catholic missiology, could say that, for Catholics, the issue of the legitimacy of mission is resolved "by the doctrine of the visible church and its hierarchical structure" (quoted in Rosenkranz 1977:235 – my translation). In the final analysis mission was based on the divinity, holiness, and immutability of the church; in the classical Catholic view mission was, after all, the "self-realization of the church" (cf Rütti 1974:229, 230).

This understanding of mission and the church has its roots in Cyprian's famous dictum, *extra ecclesiam nulla salus* ("there is no salvation outside the [Catholic] church"). The phrase was born during a particularly stormy conflict in the first half of the third century, in the same geographical area where Augustine had to refute the claims of the Donatists two centuries later. Soon, however, the contingent character of Cyprian's utterance was forgotten and the phrase applied universally to the Roman Catholic Church. The papal bull *Unam Sanctam* of Pope Boniface VIII (1302), for instance, endorsed Cyprian's phrase quite literally and closed with the assertion, "We declare, state, define, and proclaim that it is altogether necessary to salvation for every human creature to be subject to the Roman pontiff". In similar vein the Council of Florence (1441) stated, "Not only pagans but also Jews, heretics, and schismatics will have no share in eternal life. They will go into the eternal fire which was prepared for the devil and his angels, unless they become aggregated to the Catholic Church before the end of their lives." Even as recent as 1958 Pope Pius XII, in his encyclical *Ad Apostolorum Principis*, could say that the church of Christ is "one flock under one supreme shepherd. This is the doctrine of the Catholic truth from which no one may digress without ruining his or her faith as well as salvation".

This naturally had important consequences for the understanding of mission. Pope Benedict XV – addressing himself, in his encyclical *Maximum Illud* (1919), to the growth of Protestant missions – wrote, "It would, after all, be a disgrace if, in this respect, the heralds of the truth would be defeated by the servants of error". The Catholic world should therefore not tolerate a situation in which Catholic missions struggle financially, "whereas those who spread error have abundant financial resources at their disposal". In *Rerum Ecclesiae* (1926), Pope Pius XI likewise lamented the "generosity of non-Catholics who liberally support those who spread their false teachings". Again, in the encyclical *Evangelii Praecones* (1951), Pius XII encouraged the work done in Catholic schools, particularly their obligation to refute the errors of non-Catholics and Communists.[4]

Another important consequence of the ecclesiasticization of theology and mission in Cyprian, Augustine, and others was the fundamental change in the understanding of baptism. Augustine himself still emphasized the spiritual formation of converts and their careful preparation for baptism (Rosenkranz 1977:118). In the subsequent period, however, the actual performance of the baptismal rite often tended to become more important than the individual's personal appropriation of the faith. The responsibility of the missionary was reduced to bringing the "convert" to the baptismal font as soon as possible (cf Reuter 1980:76). Once baptized, the new Christian became an object of ecclesiastical discipline; by means of the practice of penance and other rules he or she could gradually be conformed to the Christian pattern.

Eventually Thomas of Aquinas would summarize this practice as one for which the sole condition was "a simple, obedient acknowledgment of that which the church has always taught, even if any more precise knowledge of this teaching is lacking" (quoted in Kahl 1978:49—my translation). Since the act of baptism conferred a *character indelibilis* on the person baptized, nobody could ever undo his or her baptism; even where somebody had *resisted baptism*, he or she became a *fidelis* (believer).

Augustine applied this interpretation of baptism to the Donatists. They could not, even if they wished, cancel their baptism. It would therefore be completely in order to "persuade" them to surrender their erroneous beliefs and return to the Catholic Church. The charge *cogite intrare* ("compel [people] to come in" — Lk 14:23) was applied to them and executed with the help of the state. Augustine believed that state action against schismatics was not persecution but a just *disciplina* (cf Erdmann 1977:9, 237; Rosenkranz 1977:139). By means of this disciplinary exercise the Donatists were to be re-catholicized. Augustine had no qualms about applying pressure on them, although he consistently refused to employ the same methods in respect of pagans (cf Erdmann 1977:9; Rosenkranz 1977:86). Eight centuries later his view on this matter would find its classical expression in Thomas Aquinas's *Summa Theologiae* (II-2, q.10, a.8):

> Unbelievers who have never accepted the faith, Jews and pagans, should under no circumstances be coerced into becoming believers; but heretics and apostates should be forced to fulfil what they have promised.

Even Raymond Lull, who rejected every attempt at forcing Muslims and pagans to convert to the Catholic faith, supported the idea of a crusade, within the boundaries of Christendom, against heretics (cf Rosenkranz 1977:136f).

MISSION BETWEEN CHURCH AND STATE

We have to say more about the long-term effects of Augustine's teachings on the unfolding of the missionary idea and practice during the Middle Ages and beyond. Here not only his controversy with Pelagius and the Donatists, but also his monumental twenty-two volume work, *De Civitate Dei* (*City of God*) is of crucial importance. It was written between 413 and 427 in the wake of the sacking of Rome by the Goths (410). By this time the Roman Empire had been officially Christian for almost a century. Christians tended to look upon the empire, and particularly its capital, as being as unconquerable and permanent as the Catholic Church. They were therefore traumatized by the success of the Goths. Jerome wailed, "If Rome can perish, what can be safe?" Adherents of Rome's traditional religions, on the other hand, were quick to allege that the sacking of the city was the result of the empire's acceptance of Christianity as official religion and its outlawing of Rome's ancient religions. Augustine decided to respond to both the despondency of the Christians and the claims of the pagans.

This is not the place to discuss, in any detail, Augustine's rather disorderly argumentation. Only some aspects of the *City of God*, insofar as they have a bearing on mission, will be singled out.[5] In volume 15 of *City of God* he wrote:

> I classify the human race into two branches: the one consists of those who live by human standards, the other of those who live according to God's will ... By these two cities I mean those two societies of human beings, one of which is predestined to reign with God from all eternity, the other doomed to undergo eternal punishment with the Devil.

These two "societies" or "cities" exist simultaneously and side by side. The first, the *civitas Dei* or city of God, endures forever. It will, however, never be realized fully on earth. It manifests itself in this world as *communio sanctorum* (communion of saints), as a pilgrim people, en route to its heavenly and eternal home.

It is important to note that Augustine did not identify the empirical church with the *civitas Dei*, the reign or kingdom of God. In subsequent centuries, however, the idea of the "city of God" fused virtually completely with that of the empirical Roman Catholic Church; the extension of the latter as a matter of course meant the realization of the first. This inevitably led to an over-emphasis on the empirical church as a Roman institution with papal and curial selfhood and authority.

Augustine's view of the earthly city is, however, not entirely negative. Unlike the Donatists he did not construct an absolute separation between the sacred and the profane. He neither regarded the Roman Empire as God's instrument for salvation (as many of his naive contemporaries tended to do), nor did he declare it to be totally demonic. He acknowledged that the citizens of the *civitas terrena* were striving toward the ideal form of human society where perfect justice and peace might reign. At the same time he was convinced that this ideal state would never be attained in the here and now, but only in the coming kingdom of Christ.

More important, he declared the earthly city to be subservient to the city of God. It was the spiritual society that was supreme; the other was subordinate. Where the earthly ruler was himself a Christian, as was the case with the Roman Empire, this ministry of the earthly city to the heavenly was, if not absolutely guaranteed, at least to be expected. The notion of the supremacy and independence of the spiritual power over against the political authorities was herewith firmly established and would, in subsequent centuries, find its organ of expression above all in the papacy. In the superb intellectual edifice of Thomas Aquinas, reason was lower than faith, nature than grace, philosophy than theology, and the state (emperor or king) than the church (the pope) (cf Küng 1987:223f). In his famous bull, *Unam Sanctam* (1302), Boniface VIII declared that both the "temporal sword" and the "spiritual sword" had been entrusted to the church.

Theoretically, then, Augustine's *magnum opus* intended to safeguard, once and for all, the primacy of the spiritual kingdom and to render it unassailable. In practice, however, Augustine compromised the church to the state and to secular power, also in the church's understanding and practice of mission, not least since the intimate link between throne and altar caused the Catholic Church to become a privileged organization, the bulwark of culture and civilization, and extremely influential in public affairs. The relationship between church and state was actually one of give and take. The regime would be blessed by the church, in exchange for which the state guaranteed to protect and support the church. Of special importance in this respect was the letter Charlemagne wrote to Pope Leo III in 796. His task as emperor, wrote Charlemagne, was to defend the holy church of Christ everywhere against the assault of pagans and the ravages of unbelievers. The pope's responsibility, like that of Moses, was to intercede for the emperor and his military campaigns, "so that, through your intercession and God's guidance and grace, the Christian people may always and everywhere be victorious over the enemies of Christ's name" (cf Schneider 1978:227-248). The relationship between emperor and pope, during the early Middle Ages, was never completely relaxed; there was almost always a silent struggle for supremacy. At the same time each knew that he needed the other. What was true at the highest level was true at the local level as well; every bishop or priest was dependent on the goodwill and support of the authorities, every local ruler required the approval of the church. The church's dependence upon the imperial power, also in its mission work, was both a necessity and a burden (cf Löwe 1978:203, 218f).

An accompanying phenomenon was the tendency to lump together the enemies of the church and the state. After 755 Pippin, and subsequently Charlemagne, often referred to their subjects as *fideles Dei et nostri* ("those who are faithful to God and us"). Naturally, if loyalty to the state meant loyalty to the church, the obverse was also true: opposition to the state was the same as opposition to the church. It is therefore not strange that, from 776 onward, the annals of the empire regularly referred to Charlemagne's Saxon enemies as those who were fighting *adversus christianos* ("against the Christians") (cf Schneider 1978:234f).

Looking back, from our vantage-point today, on this entire development, we may wish to condemn it unconditionally. How *could* the Christian church have allowed itself to become so compromised over against the state? We might, however, do well to take note of Lesslie Newbigin's thoughts on the subject:

> Much has been written about the harm done to the cause of the gospel when Constantine accepted baptism, and it is not difficult to expatiate on this theme. But could any other choice have been made? When the ancient classical world . . . ran out of spiritual fuel and turned to the church as the one society that could hold a disintegrating world together, should the church have refused the appeal and washed its hands of responsibility for the political order? . . . It is easy to see with hindsight how quickly the church fell into the temptation of worldly power. It is easy to point . . . to the glaring contradiction between the Jesus of the Gospels and his followers occupying the seats of power and wealth. And yet we have to ask, would God's purpose . . . have been better served if the church had refused all political responsibility? (1986:100f).

What I have said above should therefore not be regarded as judgment on Augustine and his legacy. Given the historical alternatives he and others had before them, they were the only choices that made sense to them. And it is appropriate to ask whether our choices, in similar circumstances, would have been any better, even if they were different. Let us keep this in mind as we move on to a matter that is, from our perspective, even more controversial.

INDIRECT AND DIRECT "MISSIONARY WARS"

Given the circumstances, it was to be expected that, in the course of time, various methods of coercion would be employed to facilitate conversion to the Catholic Church. I have already mentioned that Augustine appeared to have had few scruples about sanctioning pressure in his attempts at "re-catholicizing" Donatists. The procedure according to which those who had never been Christians were to be converted unfolded in a different manner, however. At the outset Augustine distinguished rigidly between the two categories of people: *pagans* were never subject to the discipline of the church and could therefore not be regarded as *apostates*, who had to be returned to the fold by force.

It was not something entirely different when Gregory the Great encouraged the use of blandishments rather than threats to persuade Jewish peasants on church lands to convert to Christianity (cf Markus 1970:30f). The Franconian rulers of the eighth century were likewise prepared to reward converts (cf Löwe 1978:223f; Schneider 1978:234f). "Encouragement" can, however, take different forms, and increasingly it became customary to use miscellaneous forms of coercion to induce people to embrace the Christian faith. Once again Augustine was the one who paved the way for a new approach. He originally regarded coercive measures inadmissible, or at least inappropriate. After 400, however, he gradually came to the conviction that external pressure had a role to play. To provide the individual with the opportunity to flee eternal damnation could not be wrong and certainly justified the use of pressure. We should, however, keep in mind that Augustine confined coercive measures to fines, confiscation of property, exile and the like. The killing or maiming of dissidents was out of the question (cf also Swift 1983:140-149).

In this mood Gregory the Great, two centuries after Augustine, admonished landowners in Sardinia about the fact that their peasant laborers had not yet been baptized; he suggested that the peasants were to be "so burdened with rent that the weight of this punitive exaction should make them hasten to righteousness". Those who would not listen to reason, if they were slaves, were "to be chastised by beating and torture, whereby they might be brought to amendment". Free men were to be jailed. All of this, of course, was for the non-believers' own good (cf Markus 1970:31-33).

Since its inception in the late Middle Ages, international law tended to deny non-Christians the same rights as Christians. They only had "natural rights" as "creatures of God". Once baptized, however, they were granted the same political rights as their fellow Christians (cf Kahl 1978:60-62). Once again the argument was that it was to their own advantage, also materially and politically, to become Christians.

These developments paved the way for what Erdmann calls "indirect missionary war" (1977:10f, 105) and, in the course of time, also for direct missionary wars. During the first three centuries the church did not sanction war. The issue then was not whether or not war might be justified, but whether individual Christians might participate in any war—a question answered in the negative by Tertullian, Origen, and others (cf Swift 1983:38-46; 52-60). The early Christians "knew only profane wars, conducted for the good of the state, and doubted the propriety of participating in them" (Erdmann 1977:5, following Harnack).

After Constantine the arguments began to change—first in the East, where the contradiction between war and Christianity was soon no longer felt. In the Western church the evolution of a new attitude to this issue was slower and more haphazard, partly because the Latin church never became quite so dependent as the Greek upon the emperor; but here, too, a fundamental shift would manifest itself in the course of time.

It was Augustine who began to charter the course of a Western ethic of war, and who exercised the most lasting influence in shaping its complexities. He grappled with the socio-ethical problem of war on a much more basic level. While stating that war was always evil, he argued that there was nevertheless such a thing as "just war" (*bellum justum*); it could, however, be "just" only on one side, and had to be conducted for self-defense. Augustine's teaching became the cornerstone of European theory of war. For a millennium its validity was unquestioned, even if not faithfully adhered to. Aggressive attitudes were condemned. The purpose of a just or defensive war was peace, not conquest (cf Erdmann 1977:6-8).

Bellum justum was not at first a war of religion, but a moral war. However, it harbored the seeds of the idea of a religious or holy war. Augustine's own attitude toward the Donatists and their forceful reconversion already reveals the fundamental ambivalence of his position. In addition to "just war" he spoke of "war sanctioned by God" (*bellum Deo auctore*), in which the two parties could not be judged according to the same yardstick: one side fought for light, the other for darkness; one for Christ, the other for the devil (Erdmann 1977:8-10).

Augustine did not yet envision the possibility of a religious war against non-Christians (cf Kahl 1978:62). It was Gregory the Great who moved Christian doctrine in this dubious direction, where the defense of Christendom and, often, its extension were held to be the foremost duties of the ruler. Now, for the first time, an aggressive war for the sake of the expansion of Christianity was both justified and practiced. Even in his case, however, the principle involved was "only" that of the *indirect* missionary war (Erdmann 1977:10-12, 105). The immediate aim of the war was the subjugation of the pagans, which was regarded as the basis for *subsequent* missionary activity under the protection of the state; peaceful proclamation of the gospel could now take place (Erdmann 1977:10; Rosenkranz 1977:62f).

The dividing line between "indirect" and "direct" missionary war was, however, very thin. It was only a matter of time before the second would evolve from the first. Augustine's contrast of the city of God and the city of the devil lingered on in people's minds; it was not long before it would be used to characterize the combats of Christians against pagans. As for Augustine's sharp distinction of offensive from defensive war, who was going to decide whether any given war was the one or the other? And since Christian rulers were expected to defend Christendom, could they not also actively further it by means of military campaigns? This is the way Charlemagne saw the situation in his time, so he set out forcibly to subdue the Saxons to the Catholic Church.

There was, of course, another side to this as well, and for Charlemagne this was the more important: in the climate of the time it was inconceivable for a Christian monarch to rule over a pagan people. Thus the enforced baptism of the Saxons was a natural consequence of their defeat at the hands of Charlemagne. They had to be baptized, even against their will if they refused, *because* they had been conquered. Subjection to the stronger God followed subjection to the victorious ruler as a matter of course. Once baptized, the Saxons faced execution if they reverted to their traditional faith; it was inconceivable that they could be politically loyal if their religious loyalty was doubted (cf Schneider 1978:234, 242f). The same pattern would repeat itself elsewhere: Olav Tryggvason's violent Christianization of Norway in the late tenth century, the subjugation, in the twelfth century, of the Wends who lived east and north of the Elbe, and so forth (cf Rosenkranz 1977:110, 118).

Even so, these aggressive and frequently brutal "direct missionary wars" remained the exception. The old ambiguity of the church's attitude toward war restrained it from encouraging this as a normal practice (cf Erdmann 1977:4, 12, 97; Kahl 1978:58f, 68). Such a concept, Erdmann rightly notes, suffered from an internal contradiction: the attitude needed in war against an opponent is so basically different from missionary preaching that no army can ever be inspired by a vision of evangelical service (:11f).

In light of this, it is really impossible to regard the crusades of the eleventh to thirteenth centuries as "missionary wars", even if many ordinary Christians saw them in this light. Pope Urban II, however, had no thought of converting the Muslims by military action; rather, Islam was a menace that had to be defeated before it overwhelmed the church (cf Kedar 1984:57-74, 99-116, who has traced the medieval discussions on the relationship between the crusades and the possibility of a mission to Muslims).

In the process, the precept that killing even in a just war occasioned guilt (a tenet that was basic to Augustine's thinking) came increasingly under pressure (Erdmann 1977:238). One church leader after another — Brun of Querfurt, Manegold of Lautenbach, Bernard of Constance, Bonizo of Sutri, and others — who had persistently paved the way for the First Crusade (1096), differentiated less and less between pagans on the one hand and heretics or apostates on the other. Anybody belonging to any of these categories could be killed with impunity and, in Manegold's judgment, the one who killed such a person would incur no guilt but rather deserved praise and honor. The killing of a heathen or apostate, it was now suggested, was exceptionally pleasing to God (references in Erdmann 1977:12, 236, 238).

One person stood out above all those who prepared the theological climate for the crusades: Anselm of Lucca. Far more subtle in his arguments than Brun, Bonizo, or Manegold, it was he who, in the realm of theory, anticipated the crusades. None of his contemporaries supplied the Gregorian practice of war with a more elevated theological justification, particularly since some of his arguments sounded so genuinely "Christian", for instance his rejection of revenge and of any joy over the defeat of the enemy, and his suggestion that acting against the wicked was not really persecution but an expression of love (cf Erdmann 1977:245-248). These and many other teachings irresistibly led up to the announcement of the First Crusade by Urban II and the enthusiastic response of the masses, who reportedly shouted in unison, *"Deus vult!"* ("God wills it!").

By this time — the high Middle Ages — the structure of human society was finally and permanently ordered and nobody was to tamper with it. Within the divinely constituted and sanctioned order of reality, different social classes were to keep their places. God willed serfs to be serfs and lords to be lords. An immutable, God-given "natural law" ruled over the world of people and things. Everybody and everything was taken care of. All sensible persons were Catholic Christians, and the monopoly of the church, also as regards secular affairs, was undisputed. No "pagan" groups remained in Europe, although there were, here and there, isolated pockets of "heretics" or "schismatics".

Jews constituted a special case. Due to the influence of Paul's and Augustine's theology they were sometimes tolerated and even protected by law (cf Linder 1978:407-413). The scrupulous concern for justice and humanity toward

Jews, which characterized the pontificate of Gregory the Great, was also remembered in some quarters (cf Markus 1970:30). Sometimes Jews, because of their erudition, even aroused the admiration of Christians (Linder 1978:409). More often, however, they were held responsible for the crucifixion of Jesus and persecuted. Insurrections were brutally quelled and synagogues razed. Even where they were not explicitly persecuted, they were discriminated against (:400-407). Prominent theologians, such as Chrysostom, held fiery sermons against them. Where they were allowed to stay, they were generally subject to special rules and restrictions (:421-429, 432-437).

In the early Middle Ages efforts at converting Jews were not dissimilar to those practiced in respect of heretics. Those who refused were sometimes threatened with expulsion, or expropriation, or even execution (:420). Gregory the Great pleaded for Jews to be brought to the Christian faith "by mildness and generosity, by admonition and persuasion", by the "sweetness of preaching" and not by "threats and pressure" (quoted in Markus 1970:30; cf Linder 1978:420f). But Gregory's practice and strategy remained the exception. Waves of forced conversions swept through the Roman Empire from the fourth to the eleventh century (Linder 1978:414-420). Voluntary "group conversions" to the Catholic faith also took place, however; a case in point was the conversion of Jews in Crete in 431 (:414). Sometimes individual Jews also embraced Christianity (:420-439), a step inordinately complicated by the fact that such Jewish Christians were often looked down upon by other Christians and ostracized by fellow-Jews (:430f). By the late Middle Ages Jews were facing unusual difficulties, as the church became increasingly impatient and intolerant; large communities of European Jewry were forcibly resettled or pillaged (:441).

COLONIALISM AND MISSION

During most of the Middle Ages Europe was, for all intents and purposes, a self-contained island, cut off from the rest of the world by Islam. To the East, Islam had penetrated into Central Asia, from where it formed an unbroken chain via Western Asia, the Middle East, and North Africa into Spain and as far as the Pyrenees. Even the crusades did not succeed in breaching this barrier. And Islam was, apparently, still in the ascendancy. In 1453 Constantinople, long the spiritual center of the Eastern church, fell to the Muslims. In the meantime, however, an increasing restlessness made itself felt in Europe, a restlessness which culminated in the Age of Discovery. Vasco da Gama opened a sea route to India, thus outflanking the Muslims, and Columbus "discovered" the Americas. These events, at the close of the fifteenth century, inaugurated a completely new period in world history: Europe's colonization of the peoples of Africa, Asia, and the Americas. This did not happen by accident. In fact, it can be argued that the roots of the later conquistadores and the entire phenomenon of the European colonization of the rest of the world lay in the medieval teachings on just war (Kahl 1978:66). On closer inspection one might even say that colonization was the "modern continuation of the Crusades" (Hoekendijk 1967a:317—my translation). In the words of M. W. Baldwin (quoted by Fisher 1982:23), "Although Crusade projects failed, the Crusade mentality persisted".

Of course, colonization of non-Christian peoples by Christian nations pre-dated modern colonialism by many centuries, but those exploits were launched by Europeans to Europeans, and in each case the vanquished peoples soon embraced Christianity and were assimilated into the dominant culture. Now, however, European Christians met people who were not only physically, but also culturally and linguistically very different from them. One of the most appalling consequences of this was the imposition of slavery on non-Western peoples. In the ancient Roman Empire as well as medieval Europe slavery had little to do with race. After the "discovery" of the non-Western world beyond the Muslim territories this changed; henceforth slaves could only be people of color. The fact that they were different made it possible for the victorious Westerners to regard them as inferior. Spain and Portugal introduced slavery and were soon emulated by other emerging colonial powers (Protestant ones as well), who all claimed a share in the lucrative trade in human bodies. In 1537 the pope authorized the opening of a slave market in Lisbon, where up to twelve thousand Africans were sold annually for transportation to the West Indies. By the eighteenth century Britain had the lion's share of the slave market. In the ten years between 1783 and 1793 a total of 880 slave ships left Liverpool, carrying over three hundred thousand slaves to the Americas. It has been estimated that the number of slaves sold to European colonies amounted to between twenty and forty million. And all along the (assumed) superiority of Westerners over all others became more and more firmly entrenched and regarded as axiomatic.

Perhaps rather incongruously, the colonial period also precipitated an unparalleled era of mission. Christendom discovered with a shock that, fifteen centuries after the Christian church was founded, there were still millions of people who knew nothing about salvation and who, since they were not baptized, were all headed for eternal punishment. "Fortunately", the first two colonial powers and their rulers were stalwart champions of the Catholic faith and could be trusted to do their best to bring the message of eternal redemption to all, even to the slaves. So, hard upon the discoveries of the sea routes to India and the Americas, Pope Alexander VI (in the Papal Bull *Inter Caetera Divinae*) divided the world outside of Europe between the kings of Portugal and Spain, granting them full authority over all the territories they had already discovered as well as over those still to be discovered. This bull (like its predecessor, *Romanus Pontifex* of Nicolas V [1454], which had dealt with privileges granted to Portugal only) was based on the medieval assumption that the pope held supreme authority over the entire globe, including the pagan world. Here lies the origin of the right of patronage (*patronato real* in Spanish, *padroado* in Portuguese), according to which the rulers of the two countries had dominion over their colonies, not only politically, but also ecclesiastically. Colonialism and mission, as a matter of course, were interdependent; the right to have colonies carried with it the duty to Christianize the colonized.

This right to "send" ecclesiastical agents to distant colonies was so decisive that the activities and designation of the envoys were to derive their names from this action; their assignment came to be called "mission" (a term first used in this sense by Ignatius of Loyola), and they themselves "missionaries" (cf Seumois 1973:8-16). Thus far in this book I have used the word "mission" as though it had always been the conventional designation for the activity of proclaiming and embodying the gospel among those who had not yet embraced it. My use of the term has been, however, anachronistic. The Latin word *missio* was an expression employed in the doctrine of the Trinity, to denote the sending of the Son by the Father, and of the Holy Spirit by the Father and the Son. For fifteen centuries the church used other terms to refer to what we subsequently came to call "mission": phrases such as "propagation of the faith", "preaching of the gospel", "apostolic proclamation", "promulgation of the gospel", "augmenting the faith", "expanding the church", "planting the church", "propagation of the reign of Christ", and "illuminating the nations" (cf Seumois 1973:18). The new word, "mission", is historically linked indissolubly with the colonial era and with the idea of a magisterial commissioning. The term presupposes an established church in Europe which dispatched delegates to convert overseas peoples and was as such an attendant phenomenon of European expansion. The church was understood as a legal institution which had the right to entrust its "mission" to secular powers and to a corps of "specialists" — priests or religious. "Mission" meant the activities by which the Western ecclesiastical system was extended into the rest of the world. The "missionary" was irrevocably tied to an institution in Europe, from which he or she derived the mandate and power to confer salvation on those who accept certain tenets of the faith.

The ruling by which the kings of Spain and Portugal were made "patrons" of missionary expansion in their colonies was not without its difficulties. The propagation of the faith and colonial policies became so intertwined that it was often hard to distinguish the one from the other. The dioceses founded in the colonies were given bishops approved by the civil authorities. These bishops were not allowed to communicate directly with the pope; in addition, papal decrees had to be endorsed by the king before they could be made public and acted upon in the colonies. The rulers of Spain and Portugal soon regarded themselves not merely as representatives of the pope, but as immediate deputies of God (cf Glazik 1979:144-146).

The church could not tolerate this indefinitely. The pope's response to the colonial missionary policies of Spain and Portugal was the formation, in 1622, of the *Sacra Congregatio de Propaganda Fide* (Sacred Congregation for the Propagation of the Faith). With the establishment of Propaganda Fide, the Roman Catholic Church's entire ministry among non-Catholics was firmly and exclusively assigned to the pope. During the entire preceding period mission was the responsibility of bishops or, more generally, a task taken upon themselves by monastic communities (to which I shall return) — one did not become a missionary on the basis of ecclesiastical authorization but "under the urge of the Holy Spirit", or (as Francis of Assisi formulated it in chapter 12 of his *Rule*) "on the basis of divine inspiration". All this had now changed, first by granting

Spain and Portugal the right of patronage, secondly by the creation of Propaganda Fide. "The *privilege* of evangelizing the newly-discovered lands (became) the exclusive monopoly of the Roman See" (Geffré 1982:479). The diocesan bishops in the "mission countries" were replaced by titular bishops who had to perform ecclesiastical functions on behalf of the pope. They were therefore referred to as *Vicarii Apostolici Domini,* or "vicars apostolic" (van Winsen 1973:9-11).

This meant, of course, that the colonial churches did not have the autonomy of the dioceses in the "Christian world". They were, in a sense, subsidiaries of Rome, "missions", churches of the second class, daughter churches, immature worshiping communities, frequently the objects of Western paternalism. The vicars apostolic possessed only delegated authority, since the pope alone was the real ordinary. He would, on the basis of the *Jus commissionis* (right of commissioning) "entrust" new mission territories to a specific missionary order or congregation. In this way rivalries between missionaries from different nations and orders were precluded (cf Glazik 1979:145-149).

As a matter of fact, this arrangement applied not only to the new colonial territories, but also to the areas in Europe which Rome had recently "lost" to Protestantism. The activities of the Jesuit settlements in the northern German Protestant region was, for instance, sometimes referred to as "mission". Another example: The Roman Catholic dioceses in Scandinavia were supervised by Propaganda Fide until well into the twentieth century. The Propaganda's activities concerned not only "pagans" but all "non-Catholics". As recently as 1913, Theodor Grentrup advocated the view that mission was "that part of ecclesiastical ministry which concerned itself with the planting of the Catholic faith among non-Catholics" (quoted in Rzepkowski 1983:101 — my translation). Another way of putting it is to say that the activities of Propaganda Fide extended to wherever the Roman Catholic Church was not yet or no longer the dominant confession and where its hierarchical structures were not properly established. This is the view that surfaces clearly in a 1908 document on the reorganization of Propaganda Fide. According to the document *Sapienti Consilio,* the main distinction of a missionary situation is the absence of the hierarchy: "Where the sacred hierarchy has not been constituted, a missionary condition persists" (quoted in Rzepkowski 1983: 102 — my translation). This definition was taken over virtually unchanged in the 1917 Book of Canon Law. The entire missionary enterprise was defined in terms of what Rütti calls a "dogmatic-institutional arrangement" (1974:228). Rütti continues:

> Generally speaking, we have here the principle of sacred-hierarchical mediation. Mission is understood as the mediation of faith (or rather credal truths) and grace. The church as sacral-hierarchical institution is the real bearer and agent of this mediation. Mission is therefore performed by means of a system of authorization and delegation. Juridical authority is the constitutive element of the legitimacy and missionary quality of words and deeds. All other forms of Christian missionary activity are reduced or subordinated to this pattern of authoritative commis-

sioning ... The mediatory structures of mission are therefore in essence structures of reproduction and expansion; consequently mission manifests itself as the "self-realization of the church" ... The absence of the church or, alternatively, the various degrees of its presence, determines the primary criteria for the missionary evaluation of a given historical situation (:228f — my translation).

THE MISSION OF MONASTICISM

The picture I have thus far painted of what I have termed the medieval missionary paradigm is, on the whole, not a pleasant one. For more than a thousand years, says Hoekendijk, Europe played the crusader by maneuvering itself ideologically into a very special position and lording it over the rest of the world (1967a:317). And yet, an authentic Christian culture evolved not only in Europe but also far beyond its borders. The Christian might say that, surely, this was due to the fact that God had overruled human selfishness, shortsightedness, bigotry, and arrogance. Still, it is important to realize that, in spite of what meets the critical human eye, the missionary contribution of the Middle Ages was not only something to lament. I refer again to Newbigin's remark quoted earlier in this chapter. The point is that medieval Christians responded to the challenges they faced in the only way that made sense to them. The interiorization and the ecclesiasticization of salvation, as we identified these processes in Augustine, became vehicles of authentic evangelization and avenues along which the gospel entered Europe and made sense to the European mind. In similar manner the missionary wars, direct or indirect, and the entire project of Western colonization of the rest of the world were — in spite of all the horrors that went with them and even if we, today, find them totally incomprehensible and indefensible — expressions of a genuine concern for others, as Christians understood their responsibility in those years.

Less ambivalent, however, was the *monastic movement* and its contribution to the Christianization of Europe. We may perhaps even say that, humanly speaking, it was because of monasticism that so much authentic Christianity evolved in the course of Europe's "dark ages" and beyond. Only monasticism, says Niebuhr (1959:74) saved the medieval church from acquiescence, petrifaction, and the loss of its vision and truly revolutionary character.

For upward of seven hundred years, from the fifth century to the twelfth, the monastery was not only the center of culture and civilization, but also of mission (cf Dawson 1950:47). In the midst of a world ruled by the love of self, the monastic communities were a visible sign and preliminary realization of a world ruled by the love of God. Therefore any study not only of medieval culture in general but also of the evolution of the medieval missionary paradigm must give an important place to the history of Western monasticism. Henceforth Europe — this "north-western prolongation of Asia" (Dawson 1952:25) — would no longer simply be a geographical concept, but an idea, a historical quality, "the West", an entity steeped in Christianity, shaped and constituted by monasticism and the Christian mission (cf Dawson 1952: passim; Kahl 1978:17f, 20).

Monasticism, as I have indicated in the previous chapter, has its origins in the Eastern church, particularly in Egypt, where it flourished long before it really took root in the West. When it did evolve in the West, it differed from Eastern monasticism in several respects. For one thing, Eastern monasticism was, on the whole, an individual affair. The solitary ascetics of the desert often shunned community life, and perhaps this was one of the reasons why so many of them were in the course of time lost to Orthodoxy. Western monasticism, by contrast, was essentially communal and carefully structured. The monastery was, preeminently, a "school of the service of the Lord". This certainly had to do, among other things, with the Roman penchant for order and discipline. A second, and potentially even more important, difference lies in the fact that Eastern monasticism was very dependent on the state, due to the monastic legislation of Justinian. Western monasticism, by contrast, was far more independent of government interference, perhaps because, as Dawson (1950:51) suggests, "the state was too weak and too barbarous to attempt to control the monasteries". The great legislators here were not, as in the East, the emperors, but monks like Benedict and Gregory the Great.

At the first glance, the monastic movement appears to be a most unlikely agent of mission. The communities were certainly not founded as launching pads for mission. They were not even created out of a desire to get involved in society in their immediate environment. Rather, they regarded society as corrupt and moribund, held together only by "the tenacity of custom". Society was suffering from the "slow fever of consumption", but it was still powerful enough to "seduce and deprave"; serious people should therefore do all they could "to escape from its presence and its sway" (Newman 1970:374). So monasticism stood for the absolute renunciation of everything the ancient world had prized. It was "flight from the world, and nothing else" (:375). Monasticism's one object, immediate as well as ultimate, "was to live in purity and die in peace" (:452), and to avoid anything that could "agitate, harass, depress, stimulate, weary, or intoxicate the soul" (:375).

In light of the above it may therefore sound preposterous to suggest that monasticism was both a primary agent of medieval mission and the main instrument in reforming European society. That this was indeed what happened was due, first, to the high esteem in which monks were held by the general populace. After the Constantinian era had commenced and the supreme test of martyrdom was no longer demanded, the ascetics had come in the eyes of the Christian world to hold the position the martyrs had previously occupied. The eighth century Irish *Cambrai Homily* refers to three types of martyrdom—white, green, and red—which symbolized three stages of Christian perfection: white martyrdom refers to asceticism, green to contrition and penance, whilst red martyrdom signified total mortification for Christ's sake (cf McNally 1978:110); the monks in particular were regarded as the expression of uncompromising Christian life and as the ones who "kept the walls" of the Christian city and repelled the attacks of its spiritual enemies (Dawson 1950:48).

If monks had only been ascetic and eccentric in their behavior, however, they would not have won the devotion and admiration of the people in the way they did. Thus, secondly, their exemplary lifestyle made a profound impact, particularly on the peasants. Their conduct was epitomized in the words of the Celtic monk Columban (543-615), "He who says he believes in Christ ought to walk as Christ walked, poor and humble and always preaching the truth" (quoted in Baker 1970:28). The monks were poor, and they worked incredibly hard; they plowed, hedged, drained morasses, cleared away forests, did carpentry, thatched, and built roads and bridges. "They found a swamp, a moor, a thicket, a rock, and they made an Eden in the wilderness" (Newman 1970:398). Even secular historians acknowledge that the agricultural restoration of the largest part of Europe has to be attributed to them (:399). Through their disciplined and tireless labor they turned the tide of barbarism in Western Europe and brought back into cultivation the lands which had been deserted and depopulated in the age of the invasions. More important, through their sanctifying work and poverty they lifted the hearts of the poor and neglected peasants and inspired them while at the same time revolutionizing the order of social values which had dominated the empire's slave-owning society (cf Dawson 1950:56f).

Third, their monasteries were centers not only of hard manual labor, but also of culture and education. After the existing educational institutions had been swept away by the barbarian invasions, the old tradition of learning found a refuge in the monastery. In an age of insecurity, disorder, and barbarism, the monastery embodied the ideal of spiritual order and disciplined moral activity which in time permeated the entire church, indeed, the entire society. Each monastery was a vast complex of buildings, churches, workshops, stores, and almshouses — a hive of activity for the benefit of the entire surrounding community (cf Dawson 1950:50f, 55, 68f). The citizens of the heavenly city were actively seeking the peace and good order of the earthly city.

There was a fourth way, less easily put into words, in which the monastic movement made a lasting impression on the medieval world, particularly the peasants. I am referring to the monks' patience, tenacity, and perseverance. Wave after wave of invasions swept over Europe, as one warlike barbarian people after the other gained the upper hand. Saracens, Huns, Lombards, Tartars, Saxons, Danes — all of these attacked the unsuspecting peasants and destroyed the monasteries. But monasticism possessed extraordinary resilience and recuperative power. Ninety-nine out of a hundred monasteries could be burnt down and the monks killed or driven out, writes Dawson,

> and yet the whole tradition could be reconstituted from the one survivor, and the desolate sites could be repeopled by fresh supplies of monks who would take up again the broken tradition, following the same rule, singing the same liturgy, reading the same books and thinking the same thoughts as their predecessors (1950:72; cf Newman 1970:410f).

The monks knew that things took time, that instant gratification and a quick-fix mentality were an illusion, and that an effort begun in one generation had to be carried on by generations yet to come, for theirs was a "spirituality of the long haul" and not of instant success (Henry 1987:279f). Coupled with this was their refusal to write off the world as a lost cause or to propose neat, no-loose-ends answers to the problems of life, but rather to rebuild promptly, patiently, and cheerfully, "as if it were by some law of nature that the restoration came" (Newman 1970:411).[6]

All these attitudes and activities were, in a profound sense of the word, *missionary*. Putting it differently (and drawing on a distinction suggested by Newbigin 1958:21, 43f, and Gensichen 1971:80-95): Although the monastic communities were not *intentionally* missionary (in other words, created for the purpose of mission), they were permeated by a missionary *dimension*. Even without knowing it and without intending it, their conduct was missionary through and through. Small wonder then that, increasingly, their implicitly missionary dimension began to spill over into explicit missionary efforts.

To illustrate this point I turn, first, to Irish (or Celtic) monasticism (cf McNally 1978:91-115). In some respects it was the Irish monks who contributed most to creating the tradition of monastic learning and educational activity after the decline of the Byzantine Empire (cf Dawson 1950:58). Columban (543-615), in particular, brought to new life the monasticism of the late Merovingian age, and almost all the great monastic founders of the seventh century were his disciples or influenced by him (:63). However, behind the founding of monasteries in far-away places (Irish monasteries stretched from Skellig Michael, off the west coast of Ireland, right across continental Europe as far as Kiev in Russia), lies something else — the Irish love of roaming. In Christian circles, this *Wanderlust* manifested itself in novel ways. First, it became an expression of ascetic homelessness. The monks undertook journeys to distant places as part of their discipline of penance, and for the sake of their own salvation. Irish monasticism tended to reveal a more austere and uncompromising spirit than its English counterpart; for them *peregrinatio*, pilgrimage, became a way of pushing their renunciation to extreme limits. But the pilgrim must help others he meets on their journeys, so that the concept of pilgrimage often merged into that of mission — even if both pilgrimage and mission remained subordinate to the spiritual perfection of the monk (cf Walker 1970:42; Rosenkranz 1977:93f, 102; Prinz 1978:451-460).

Benedictine monasticism shared with its Celtic counterpart a strong eschatological emphasis, a pronounced moral seriousness, and a profound interest in spiritual perfection. The *Rule of St Benedict* was, however, much more down to earth, and in the course of time virtually replaced the more austere rule of the Celtic monk, St Columban. Benedict (480-547) also put a greater emphasis on the Christian life as being in the service of magnifying God's name. Manual labor was as much religious ministry as prayer, and everything came under the heading *U.I.O.G.D.: Ut in omnibus glorificetur Deus* ("That in all things God may be glorified"). "For St Benedict work was never an end in itself. It must be fitted into the sublime over-all purpose of life: to attain to God by means of the 'Lord's service', by means of obedience" (Heufelder 1983:211). "To please God alone" (*soli Deo placere*) was the ardent desire of this remarkable man, who lived in God *velut naturaliter*, "as it were naturally" (:214, 215). The "ascent to God" evolved in twelve successive "degrees of humility" (on these, cf Heufelder 1983:51-150), and the purpose of his *Rule* (as formulated by Benedict himself in chapter 7) was to help the monk arrive

> at that love of God which, being perfect, casts out fear; whereby he shall begin to keep, without labor, and as it were naturally and by custom, all those precepts which he had hitherto observed through fear: no longer through dread of hell, but for the love of Christ, and of a good habit and a delight in virtue.

Precisely because of its profoundly spiritual yet at the same time eminently practical nature, the Benedictine *Rule* has been "one of the most effective linkages of justice, unity and renewal the church has ever known" (Henry 1987:274). The Benedictine monastery indeed became "a school for the Lord's service". For upward of six centuries these monasteries were the model on which all others were designed and even to this day they exercise a profound influence. Seeking a life free from corruption and free from distraction in its daily worship, in which each day, each hour, would have its own completeness, Benedict introduced a tradition which had far-reaching and enduring consequences. Few scholars have captured the genius and lasting contribution of Benedictine monasticism the way the nineteenth century Cardinal Newman had, as the following lengthy quotation illustrates:

> (St Benedict) found the world, physical and social, in ruins, and his mission was to restore it in the way, not of science, but of nature, not as if setting about to do it, not professing to do it by any set time or by any rare specific or by any series of strokes, but so quietly, patiently, gradually, that often, till the work was done, it was not known to be doing. It was a restoration, rather than a visitation, correction, or conversion. The new world he helped to create was a growth rather than a structure. Silent men were observed about the country, or discovered in the forest, digging, clearing, and building; and other silent men, not seen, were sitting in the cold cloister, tiring their eyes, and keeping their attention on the stretch, while they painfully deciphered and copied and re-copied the manuscripts which they had saved. There was no one that "contended, or cried out," or drew attention to what was going on; but by degrees the wooded swamp became a hermitage, a religious house, a farm, an abbey, a village, a seminary, a school of learning, and a city. Roads and bridges connected it with other abbeys and cities, which had similarly grown up; and what the haughty Alaric or the fierce Attila had broken to pieces, these patient meditative men had brought together and made to live again (Newman 1970:410).

Once again, this may appear at first glance to have little to do with mission. And yet it has, in a profound way. The life and ministry of the Benedictine monasteries were, on closer inspection, missionary through and through; a "missionary dimension" permeated everything the monks did. It therefore should come as no surprise that the Benedictines also became involved in explicit missionary enterprises, in an even more significant way than did the Celtic monks. It was Gregory the Great, himself a Benedictine monk, who first conceived the idea of a planned "foreign mission", when he sent the monk Augustine from the heart of Benedictine monasticism in Italy to the kingdom of Kent on the British isles to initiate a missionary venture among the pagan English. Within a century after the arrival of Augustine at Canterbury the church was firmly established in England — not only because of the Benedictine project, but also due to many pilgrimaging Celtic missionaries (cf Schäferdiek 1978:178).

In the course of time, Benedictine and Celtic monks and their missionary traditions met — and clashed — in Northumbria. It was the meeting of these two traditions which was to produce the deepest and most lasting influence on Western culture (cf Dawson 1950:63-66). Out of the coalescence of these two monastic cultures (in which the Benedictine strand proved to be more enduring) there stepped forward a missionary-monk, Boniface of Crediton, who acquired the epithet of "apostle of Germany" and who has been described as "a man who had a deeper influence on the history of Europe than any Englishman who has ever lived" (Dawson 1952:185), indeed, as "the greatest Englishman" (cf the title of Reuter 1980).

Boniface was not sent by anyone when he undertook his first journey to Frisia; it was a purely personal enterprise, a response to an inward call to mission (Talbot 1970:45). And he was not alone. Other Anglo-Saxon monks, such as Willibrod, Pirmin, and Alcuin of York, either preceded or followed Boniface to the continent (cf Löwe 1978:192-226). All of them had the explicit conviction that one should not remain in the monastery for one's own salvation, but save and serve others. For the Celtic monks preaching and mission were unplanned appendages to their penitential roaming far from home; for the Anglo-Saxons, however, *peregrinatio* (pilgrimage) was undertaken for the sake of mission (Rosenkranz 1977:102). Their travels were not instigated by a penitential urge or a desire for personal perfection; they were conceived solely as attempts to spread the gospel and bring pagans within the bosom of the church. It was with this vision before him that Boniface entered his almost limitless field of labor, the vast country east of the Rhine (cf Reuter 1980:71-94).

There was another respect in which Anglo-Saxon monasticism differed fundamentally from that of the Irish. The latter was much less "ecclesiastical". In Ireland, it was the abbot and not the bishop who was the real source of authority; in fact, the bishop was often a subordinate member of the monastic community. Anglo-Saxon monasticism and mission were, by contrast, explicitly and intensely ecclesiastical. Boniface went to Germany with the full blessing and support of his bishop, Daniel of Winchester, and also maintained his links with his home church (cf Löwe 1978:217). In addition, he secured the backing of the pope in Rome and, in his later years, was able not only to expand the Catholic Church through his missionary apostolate, but also, as the officially sanctioned representative of the pope, to reform and reorganize the Frankish church (Reuter 1980:76-86). Boniface's example was followed by other Anglo-

Saxon missionaries, who consciously acted as emissaries of the pope and whose duty was to incorporate new converts into the only church that guaranteed salvation (cf Rosenkranz 1977:102).

Rosenkranz aptly summarizes the differences between Celts and Anglo-Saxons in this regard: "From itinerant preachers the Irish developed into missionaries; the Anglo-Saxons, however, developed from missionaries into church organizers" (:103 — my translation). It is precisely this dimension of their ministry that brought the Anglo-Saxon missionaries, and indeed the entire Benedictine and subsequent monastic tradition, into the field of force of the missionary paradigm that characterized the medieval period and which I briefly described in the earlier part of this chapter. Still, few of them endorsed any attempt at converting people by force. This was true not only of the Benedictine (and, naturally, the Celtic) monks, but also of a Franciscan such as Raymond Lull (1232-1316), who adopted an attitude to Muslims fundamentally different from that of the crusaders of his time. It was true, supremely, of missionaries such as Antonio de Montesinos and Bartholomé de Las Casas in the age of the Spanish *conquista*. Both these priests, and many other unknown ones, became the champions of the Indians of Latin America, who were ruthlessly oppressed and exploited by the conquistadores. Against the practice of a military conquest of non-Christians Las Casas posited the idea of a *conquista espiritual*. In order to protect Indian converts against the brutality of the Spanish conquerors, he gathered them into so-called reductions or reserves, where missionaries were the only Europeans permitted to enter.

THE MEDIEVAL PARADIGM: AN APPRAISAL

I have said, in the previous chapter, that *the* missionary text of the Greek patristic paradigm was John 3:16. Perhaps one could say that the medieval Roman Catholic missionary paradigm drew, implicitly or explicitly, on another text — Luke 14:23, "and compel them to come in". We first encounter this text in Augustine's controversy with the Donatists, where he argued that it meant that the Donatists had to be *forced* to return to the Catholic fold (cf Erdmann 1977:9; Kahl 1978:55f, note 100). In the course of the Middle Ages the text came to be applied also to the forced conversion (or at least baptism) of pagans and Jews. Even where no explicit appeal was made to Luke 14:23, the idea as such was present and operative (cf also Rosenkranz 1977:118).

That this mentality dominated missionary thinking for centuries is confirmed as late as the sixteenth century, when Las Casas was challenged by opponents of his gentle and non-coercive missionary approach to explain how he interpreted Luke 14:23. *Compellere intrare* ("Compel them to come in"), he responded, did not refer to force but to persuasion; the Indians should be moved by the proclamation of the word to embrace the faith, and not, proverbially speaking, at gun-point (cf Rosenkranz 1977:184). In subsequent centuries the explicit appeal to Luke 14:23 fell into disuse, but the sentiment behind it persisted well into the twentieth century and some of its missionary encyclicals. It could not really be otherwise, as long as one argued that there was no salvation outside the formal membership of the Roman Catholic Church and that it was to people's own eternal advantage if they could be made to join this body.

In the period under discussion in this chapter, the church underwent a series of profound changes. It moved from being a small, persecuted minority to being a large and influential organization; it changed from harassed sect to oppressor of sects; every link between Christianity and Judaism was severed; an intimate relationship between throne and altar evolved; membership of the church became a matter of course; the office of the believer was largely forgotten; the dogma was conclusively fixed and finalized; the church had adjusted to the long postponement of Christ's return; the apocalyptic missionary movement of the primitive church gave way to the expansion of Christendom (cf Boerwinkel 1974:54-64).

Augustine embodied the beginning of this paradigm, Thomas Aquinas its climax (cf Küng 1987:258). In his theology the latter assigned everybody and everything in heaven and on earth a place in the universe, in such a way that the whole constituted a perfect synthesis with no loose ends. The key to it all was a double order of knowledge and being, the one natural, the other super-natural: reason and faith, nature and grace, state and church, philosophy and theology, where the first of each pair refers to the natural foundation, the second to the supernatural "second level". This framework of thinking put the seal on the development of the missionary idea in the high Middle Ages which, in spite of the fact that it experienced several crises, remained essentially intact until the twentieth century. Since the sixteenth century it manifested itself supremely within the context of the European colonization of the non-Western world.

Still, our appraisal cannot only be a negative one. Was anything wrong with the idea of attempting to create a Christian civilization, to shape laws consonant with biblical teaching, to place kings and emperors under the explicit obligation of Christian discipleship (Newbigin 1986:129)? Their can be no doubt that the paradigm we are exploring in this chapter certainly had its dark side, and yet it had its positive contributions as well. In addition, one has to realize that it was only *logical* that things would develop the way they did after Constantine's victory; it was, moreover, and given the particular circumstances, *inevitable* that they would. So, as we criticize our spiritual forebears, and do so relentlessly, let us remind ourselves that we would not have done any better than they did.

Toward the end of the previous chapter I intimated that the Greek patristic missionary paradigm has to a significant extent remained unchanged to the present day. The same is not true of the medieval Roman Catholic paradigm. During the last three decades, in particular, Roman Catholic understanding of mission has undergone a most profound change. The catalytic event was the Second Vatican Council (1962-1965). Stransky is right when he says that in recent decades

no other world church or international confessional body has undergone such an intensive examination of consciousness and conscience about mission as did the Roman Catholic Church during the four years of the Second Vatican Council . . . Each Catholic, and the Catholic Church as a whole, was suddenly required to interiorize and carry out the Council's explicitly theological, pastoral and missionary demands. In hindsight, too much came too soon for too many (1982:344).

Naturally, everything did not happen all of a sudden. The medieval Roman Catholic paradigm was, in the course of time, succeeded by two others: those of the Protestant Reformation and the Enlightenment (which will be discussed in the next two chapters). For several centuries, however, the Catholic paradigm was only marginally affected by these two, so that Hans Küng (1984:23) may be right when he says that Vatican II had to digest simultaneously not one but two paradigms.

Protestants have a saying, *Roma semper eadem est* (Rome will forever remain the same). In light of what has happened in Catholicism since "good Pope John" convened the Second Vatican Council, this aphorism, so it appears to me, has lost its validity. The current Roman Catholic missionary paradigm is fundamentally different from the traditional one. I shall return to this in Chapters 11 and 12.

Chapter 8

The Missionary Paradigm of the Protestant Reformation

THE NATURE OF THE NEW MOVEMENT

The Roman Catholic paradigm experienced a crisis in the late Middle Ages; in time the forces of change would usher in a new era (cf Oberman 1983:119-126; 1986:1-17). The person who became the catalyst in introducing a new paradigm, was Martin Luther (1483-1546).[1] Events in his personal history, together with the climate in which he grew up and the places where he studied, slowly yet inexorably prepared him for his fateful break with the Catholic Church and the launch of a new epoch. These events included his attaching himself to the Nominalist school of William Occam, which was promoted at the University of Erfurt (although he also became a severe critic of Nominalism [cf Gerrish 1962:49-113]); the catalytic role of a terrible thunderstorm in the year 1505; his decision to become an Augustinian monk, the role his teachers played in his formation; his own theological and scriptural studies; etc (cf Oberman 1983:126-138; 1986:52-80).

In spite of the fact that Luther had been an Augustinian since 1505, Augustine's writings at the time played virtually no role in the monasteries of the Augustinian Friars. Luther himself stumbled on Augustine's writings only some years after having joined the order. This helped him to break radically with the entire edifice of Scholasticism and its total dependence on the philosophy of Aristotle with the aid of which the Bible and ecclesiastical teachings were interpreted. Luther opposed Aristotle with Augustine, without, however, capitulating to the latter's Neo-Platonism. What attracted him in Augustine was the Church Father's genuinely theological approach to the Scriptures (cf Gerrish 1962:138-152; Oberman 1983:169). He could therefore say, "The entire Aristotle relates to theology as shade relates to light".

The break with Aristotle signified a break with Thomas Aquinas's theological edifice and its two-story structure, in which faith, grace, the church, and theology occupy the upper, and reason, nature, the state, and philosophy the lower story. This magnificent synthesis was replaced with an emphasis on tension,

sometimes even opposition, between faith and reason (or grace and reason—
cf Gerrish 1962), church and world, theology and philosophy, the *Christianum*
and the *humanum*, a tension which has characterized Protestantism, admittedly
in a great variety of forms, ever since Luther (cf Küng 1987:224, 230).

Augustine had rediscovered Paul for the fifth century; Luther rediscovered
him for the sixteenth. And he found the central thrust of Paul's theology in
Romans 1:16, where "the gospel" is described as "the power of God unto
salvation to everyone who believes", and even more particularly in the next
verse which reads (in the King James Version), "For therein (that is, in the
gospel) is the righteousness of God revealed from faith to faith: as it is written,
The just shall live by faith."

If the "missionary text" of the Greek patristic period was John 3:16 and that
of medieval Catholicism Luke 14:23, then one may perhaps claim that Romans
1:16f is the "missionary text" of the Protestant theological paradigm in all its
many forms. The "rediscovery" of this text and its significance came to Luther
only gradually. His theological studies and particularly his time in the Augustinian monastery had instilled in him the conviction that he had to placate an
angry God by means of self-mortification and the unceasing performance of
good works. Only years later did he realize that God's righteousness did not
mean God's righteous punishment and wrath, but his gift of grace and mercy,
which the individual may appropriate in faith (cf Oberman 1983:135-138, 172-
174). We may not reduce Luther's entire theology to this one "discovery". In
the years 1513 to 1519 he made a whole series of theological breakthroughs.
Still, his reinterpretation of Romans 1:16f remained foundational and the cornerstone or focus of his entire life and theology (:175). He could never again
stop marvelling at the fact that God had accepted him, poor and wretched
human being that he was, mercifully and gratuitously. The last words he scrib-
bled on his deathbed were, "We are only beggars; that is true".

It would be erroneous to argue that the Reformation broke with the medieval
Catholic paradigm in every respect. Some elements of Protestantism were in
fact a continuation, even if in a new form, of what typified the Catholic model
also. For one thing Protestantism, like Catholicism (if not more so), insisted on
correct formulation of doctrine. It became important, particularly for subsequent generations, to uphold the Reformation creeds in an absolutely unaltered
and unalterable form, ascribing to them comprehensive validity for all times
and settings, and using them as much to exclude certain groups as to include
those considered to be orthodox in faith, while dismissing the possibility of any
future doctrinal development.

Second, the Reformation, except in its Anabaptist manifestation, did not
really break with the medieval understanding of the relationship between
church and state. Since Constantine the idea of a "Christian" state and of the
interdependence between as well as the cooperation of church and state was
simply taken for granted. Catholic rulers soon lost their hegemony over certain
parts of Europe, which came to be governed, instead, by Lutheran, Reformed,
or Anglican kings and princes. The only difference was that Protestants seemed
to have believed "that since the exercise of absolute power by the papal church

was wrong its exercise by the opponents of the papacy was right" (Niebuhr 1959:29). "Religious" wars were fought to establish which branch of the Christian faith was to be supreme in a given area. A solution was only achieved at the Peace of Augsburg (1555) and the Peace of Westphalia (1648), where the famous rule *cuius regio eius religio* (freely translated, "each region has to follow the religion of its ruler") was promulgated and overt hostilities brought to an end.

In order to appreciate the Protestant Reformation's unique contribution to the understanding of mission it is important to highlight the areas in which it differed from the Catholic paradigm. To these I now turn, identifying five features which may help us to discern the contours of a "Protestant theology of mission", features which are to be found in all manifestations of sixteenth-century Protestantism, whether Lutheran, Calvinist, Zwinglian, or Anabaptist.

1. It is beyond dispute that for the Protestant Reformation the article of *justification by faith* is the starting point of theology. It is the article by which the church stands or falls (*articulus stantis et cadentis ecclesiae*). This article expresses a basic conviction of the Reformation: there is an awesome distance between God and his creation, but that God nevertheless, in his sovereignty and by grace (*sola gratia*), took the initiative to forgive, justify, and save human beings. To emphasize this is not to suggest that these convictions were absent in contemporary Catholicism. Rather, what "had been habitually believed became a matter of urgent conviction; what had been taught as ancient and accepted doctrine was realized as vital experience; what had been one truth among others became *the* truth" (Niebuhr 1959:18). Thus the doctrine of justification became the one on which all other doctrines hinged (cf Beinert 1983:208). The starting point of the Reformers was not what people could and ought to do for their salvation but what God had already done in Christ.

2. Intimately connected with the centrality of justification was the view that people were primarily to be seen *from the perspective of the Fall*, as lost, unable to do anything about their condition. The Reformation broke with Aquinas's view of the soundness and reliability of human reason; it was corrupt through and through and prone to error. The world was evil, and individuals had to be snatched from it like a brand from the fire. People had to be made conscious of their lost condition so as to be brought to repentance and be released from their heavy load of sin. Whereas Catholicism tended to concentrate on the many sins (plural) of individuals, Protestants emphasized sin (singular) and the essential sinfulness of humanity (cf Gründel 1983:120). In Anabaptism this understanding of human nature, which all Reformers shared, was accentuated even more.

3. The Reformation stressed the *subjective dimension of salvation*. For Thomas Aquinas theology was still *scientia argumentativa* ("reasoned science"); for Luther this was an impossible approach. God was no longer to be regarded as God in himself (*Gott an sich*); he was God for me, for us, the God who, for the sake of Christ, had justified us by grace (cf Beinert 1983:207f; Pfürtner 1984:174f). Luther's personal history and his existential question, "Where do I find a merciful God?", played a role in this, as much as the fact that in the late

Middle Ages the individual was beginning to emerge from the collective. The Reformation "theologized" this development; the question about salvation became the personal question of the individual. This emphasis would never again disappear; in a thousand different forms believers would insist on the personal and subjective experience of a new birth by the Holy Spirit, as well as on the responsibility of the individual over against the group (Pfürtner 1984: 181f).

4. The affirmation of the personal role and responsibility of the individual led to the rediscovery of the *priesthood of all believers* (Holl 1928:238; Gensichen 1960:123). The believer stood in a direct relationship with God, a relationship that existed independent of the church. It is true that in Luther's own case, and because of the way in which the idea of the priesthood of all believers was practiced by the Anabaptists, he was forced to fall back on to a more rigid understanding of office: he denied the validity of any office that was not linked to the existence of geographically defined parishes and rejected the idea of anybody appealing to the "Great Commission" for the justification of an extraordinary and non-territorial ecclesiastical office (cf Schick 1943:15-17). Even so, in reintroducing the concept of the priesthood of all believers he initiated something that could not again be undone, something that has remained a feature of Protestantism to this day.

5. The "Protestant idea" found expression in the *centrality of the Scriptures* in the life of the church. This meant, *inter alia*, that the word prevailed over the image, the ear over the eye. The sacraments were drastically reduced, particularly in the Calvinist tradition, and made subordinate to preaching; as a matter of fact, the sacrament was for Calvin yet another word, a *verbum visibile*, a "visible word". In many Protestant churches the liturgical center was rearranged; the altar (or communion table) had to make way for the pulpit, which was granted center stage.

These five key features of Protestantism, to which several others could be added, had important consequences for the understanding and development of mission, positively and negatively.

The first feature — emphasis on justification by faith — could, on the one hand, become an urgent motive for involvement in mission; however, it could also, as sometimes happened, paralyze any missionary effort. It could, after all, be argued that, since the initiative remains God's, and God is the One who sovereignly elects those who will be saved, any human attempt at saving people would be blasphemy.

Looking at humanity solely from the perspective of the Fall could, on the one hand, safeguard the idea of the sovereignty of God and thus secure mission as, in the first and final analysis, God's own work. A preoccupation with human depravity could however also promote such a pessimistic view of humanity that humans could be regarded, in fatalistic terms, as mere pawns on a chessboard. This could lead to acquiescence and non-involvement, since there was nothing humans could do to change reality.

The emphasis on the subjective dimension of salvation could promote the idea of the worth of the individual — a most important gain over against the

Middle Ages in which the individual was often sacrificed for the sake of the whole. At the same time an overemphasis on the individual could estrange him or her from the group and destroy awareness of the fact that a human being is by definition a being-in-community.

To talk about the priesthood of all believers was to reintroduce the idea of every Christian having a calling and a responsibility to serve God, to be actively involved in God's work in the world, and thus to break with the concept of "ordinary" believers being mere "minors" and immature "objects" of the church's ministry. At the same time it carried within itself the seeds of schism, of different believers interpreting God's will differently and then, in the absence of an ecclesiastical magisterium, each going his or her separate way (cf Oberman 1986:285). To some extent, at least, the multiplying of separate churches in Protestantism has to be seen as the running amuck of the principle of the priesthood of all.

The centrality of the Scriptures as guide for life marked an important advance over the view that all matters of faith and life are to be ruled, sometimes rather arbitrarily, by popes and councils. At the same time it opened the way for a "paper pope" replacing the pope in Rome—hardly an advance over the Middle Ages. Sometimes the Bible was hypostatized and almost regarded as though it was working on its own. It is important, in this regard, to keep in mind that the Reformers did not yet teach biblical inerrancy; they were interested, rather, in the *cause* which Scripture promotes (cf Küng 1987:71f). Luther could say, "God and the Bible are two different things, just as the Creator is different from the creature" (cf Oberman 1983:234-239—my translation). Lutheran and Reformed orthodoxy, and not the Reformers themselves, propagated the idea of the "doctrinal unity" of Scripture, according to which we can deduce one doctrinal system from all biblical sayings (cf Küng 1987:92). This led to the dogma of the verbal inspiration of the Bible, which is found in many branches of Protestantism. Indeed, in Hans Küng's words (:72f—translation, emphasis in the original),

> *biblicism has remained a permanent danger for Protestant theology.* The real foundation of faith is then no longer the Christian message, nor the proclaimed Christ himself, but the infallible biblical word. Just as many Catholics believe less in God than in "their" church and "their" pope, many Protestants believe in "their" Bible. The apotheosis of the church corresponds to the apotheosis of the Bible!

THE REFORMERS AND MISSION

It has often been pointed out that the Reformers were indifferent, if not hostile, to mission. Catholic scholars in particular judged harshly in this respect. Already in the sixteenth century Robert Cardinal Bellarmine said, with reference to the Reformers' manifestly poor missionary record, "Heretics are never said to have converted either pagans or Jews to the faith, but only to have perverted Christians" (quoted in Neill 1966a:221).

Gustav Warneck, the father of missiology as a theological discipline, was one of the first Protestant scholars who promoted this view. We miss in the Reformers not only missionary action, he said, "but even the idea of missions, in the sense in which we understand them today". This is so "because fundamental theological views hindered them from giving their activity, and even their thoughts, a missionary direction" (1906:9). Luther, for instance, never entered into a polemic against foreign mission: he simply did not speak of it (:11). What was particularly sad, said Warneck, was that no lament had been raised by the Reformers about their inability to go out into the world, no word of either sorrow or excuse that circumstances hindered their discharge of missionary duty (1906:8f). And Schick believes that a fundamental affirmation of the missionary duty of the church was simply absent in the Reformers (1943:14).

More recently, however, several scholars have argued that a judgment such as Warneck's implies summonsing the Reformers before the tribunal of the modern missionary movement and finding them guilty for not having subscribed to a definition of mission which did not even exist in their own time. The assumption here is that the "great missionary century" (the nineteenth) had a correct understanding of mission; this definition is imposed on the Reformers, who then have to be judged guilty for not having subscribed to it (Holl 1928; Holsten 1953; cf also Gensichen 1960 and 1961, and Scherer 1987). Would it not be more appropriate, asks Holsten (1953:1f), to summons the nineteenth-century missionary enterprise—victim of Humanism, Pietism, and Enlightenment, and child of the modern mind—before the tribunal of the Reformation and then declare *it* guilty of perverting the missionary idea? After all, mission does not only begin when somebody goes overseas; it is not an "operational theory" *(Betriebstheorie)*, nor is it dependent upon the existence of separate "mission agencies" (:2, 6, 8).

To argue that the Reformers had no missionary vision, these scholars contend, is to misunderstand the basic thrust of their theology and ministry. Luther, in particular, is to be regarded as "a creative and original missionary thinker", and we should allow ourselves to read the Bible "through the eyes of Martin Luther the missiologist" (Scherer 1987:65, 66). In fact, he provided the church's missionary enterprise with clear and important guidelines and principles (Holl 1928:237, 239). The starting point of the Reformers' theology was not what people could or should do for the salvation of the world, but what God has already done in Christ. He visits the peoples of the earth with his light; he furthers his word so that it may "run" and "increase" till the last day dawns. The church was created by the *verbum externum* (God's word from outside humanity) and to the church this word has been entrusted. One might even say that it is the gospel itself which "missionizes" and in this process enlists human beings (Holsten 1953:11). In this respect scholars often quote Luther's metaphor of the gospel being like a stone thrown into the water—it produces a series of circular waves which move out from the center until they reach the furthest shore. In similar way the proclaimed word of God moves out to the ends of the earth (cf Warneck 1906:14; Holl 1928:235; Holsten 1953:11; Gensichen 1960:122; Holsten 1961:145). Throughout, then, the emphasis is on mission not being dependent on human efforts. No preacher, no missionary, should ever dare to attribute to his or her own zeal what is, in fact, God's own work (Gensichen 1960:120-122; 1961:5f).

This does not, however, suggest passivity and quietism. For Luther, faith was a living, restless thing which could not remain inoperative. We are not saved by works, he said, yet added, "But if there be no works, there must be something amiss with faith" (quoted in Gensichen 1960:123). Elsewhere he wrote that if a Christian should find himself or herself in a place where there are no other Christians, "he would be under the obligation to preach and teach the gospel to the erring pagans or non-Christians because of the duty of brotherly love, even if no human being had called him to do this" (quoted in Holsten 1961:145 – my translation).

Other Lutheran theologians of the Reformation period were less clear on the missionary nature of theology. Calvin, on the other hand, was more explicit, particularly since his theology was one which took the believer's responsibility in the world more seriously than Luther's (cf Oberman 1986:235-239). On the whole, then, there can be little doubt that at least Luther and Calvin as well as some of their younger colleagues (such as Bucer) propounded an essentially missionary theology. It is also noteworthy that they broke completely with any idea of using force in Christianizing people. The emperor's sword, Luther said, had nothing to do with faith and no army may attack others under the banner of Christ; in fact, if the pope were really the vicar of Christ on earth, he would preach the gospel to the Turks instead of inciting secular rulers to violent attack on them (for references, cf Warneck 1906:11; Holsten 1953:12f). Coercion has its place in matters of secular power; the church, however, which serves the reign of God, may not utilize it (Holl 1928:240f).

Still, in spite of what Holl, Holsten, Gensichen, Scherer, and others have identified as the fundamentally missionary thrust of the Reformers' theology, very little happened by way of a missionary outreach during the first two centuries after the Reformation. There were, undoubtedly, serious practical obstacles in this regard. To begin with, Protestants saw their principal task as that of reforming the church of their time; this consumed all their energy. Second, Protestants had no immediate contact with non-Christian peoples, whereas Spain and Portugal, both Catholic nations, already had extensive colonial empires at the time. The only remaining pagan people in Europe were the Lapps, and they were indeed evangelized by Swedish Lutherans in the sixteenth century. Third, the churches of the Reformation were involved in a battle for sheer survival; only after the Peace of Westphalia (1648) were they able to organize themselves properly. Fourth, in abandoning monasticism the Reformers had denied themselves a very important missionary agency; it would take centuries before anything remotely as competent and effective as the monastic missionary movement would develop in Protestantism. Fifth, Protestants were themselves torn apart by internal strife and dissipated their strength in reckless zeal and in endless dissensions and disputes; little energy was left for turning to those outside the Christian fold.

All these factors also applied to the *Anabaptists*, and yet they were involved in a remarkable program of missionary outreach (cf Schäufele 1966:passim). It may therefore be of some interest to compare the two movements and their views on mission. The Anabaptists accepted and at the same time radicalized Luther's idea of the universal priesthood of all believers. Whereas Luther still adhered to the concept of territorially circumscribed parishes and of the ecclesiastical office restricted to such a geographically delineated area, the Anabaptists jettisoned both the idea of any special and exclusive office and of any Christian limited for his or her ministry to a given area. This enabled them to regard all of Germany as well as the surrounding countries as mission fields, without any consideration for boundaries of parishes and dioceses; preachers were, in fact, selected and systematically sent to many parts of Europe (cf Schäufele 1966:74, 141-182; Littell 1972:119-123). This "wandering" of Anabaptist evangelists infuriated the Reformers. Orderly ordination and calling to the ministry were vigorously championed against the Anabaptists; whoever preached without an appointment was considered a *Schwärmer* or enthusiast (Littell 1972:115). Likewise, whereas the Reformers no longer considered the "Great Commission" as binding (cf Warneck 1906:14, 17f; Littell 1972:114-116), no biblical texts appear more frequently in the Anabaptist confessions of faith and court testimonies than the Matthean and Markan versions of the "Great Commission", along with Psalm 24:1 (:109). They were among the first to make the commission mandatory for all believers.

Perhaps the most important difference between the two movements, if we look at them from the perspective of their views on mission, lay in their conflicting attitudes toward civil authorities. Anabaptists insisted on absolute separation between church and state and on nonparticipation in the activities of government. This naturally meant that church and state could under no circumstances whatsoever cooperate in mission. The Reformers, on the other hand, could not conceive of a missionary outreach into countries in which there was no Protestant (Lutheran, Reformed, etc) government. It is therefore significant that the only two missionary enterprises embarked upon by "mainline" Protestants during the Reformation era were both undertaken in collaboration with civil authorities. The aborted missionary project by French Protestants in Brazil, launched in 1555, was backed by Admiral Gaspar de Coligny and was part of an effort at founding a colony on the South American mainland. Likewise, the mission to the Lapps (begun in 1559) was promoted by King Gustav Vasa of Sweden, "certainly not without ulterior political motives" (Gensichen 1961:7 — my translation; cf Warneck 1906:22-24).

It is sometimes argued that the absence of any practical mission efforts on the part of the Reformers is to be ascribed to their fervent eschatological expectation. Luther, for instance, expected the last day to come some time in the year 1558. In such a climate, so the argument goes, any "proper missionary ideas" would be out of the question (cf Warneck 1906:15f; Schick 1943:17). It is, however, striking that Luther's eschatology did not prevent him from vigorously promoting his work of reformation. Apocalyptic expectations thus do not necessarily paralyze missionary efforts (as later Protestant missions history also demonstrated). Even more significant is the fact that Luther's contemporaries, the Anabaptists, adhered to eschatological views not essentially different from his, yet in their case precisely these views inspired them to missionary involvement (cf Schäufele 1966:79-97). As in the case of Paul's missionary enterprise (see chapter 4 above) mission itself was considered and experienced as an apocalyptic event (Schäufele 1966:93).

We may indeed, I believe, accept the validity of the arguments concerning the fundamentally missionary nature of the theology of the Reformers. At the same time, and particularly in light of a comparison between the Reformers and the Anabaptists on this point, one may ask whether some of the fierce attempts at exonerating the Reformers (and especially Luther) on this point, did not stem from apologetic considerations. Holl (1928) and Holsten (1953 and 1961), in particular, conduct an impassioned defense of Luther's views on mission and tend to make these normative for all subsequent generations, employing arguments which do not always ring true.[2]

One reason why the Anabaptists subscribed to the "mandate" of the "Great Commission" and the Reformers did not may be found in their contradictory readings of the realities of their time. The Reformers, on the whole, did not deny that the Catholic Church still displayed vestiges of the true church; this becomes evident, for instance, in the fact that they accepted the validity of baptism by Catholic priests. Their concern was the *reformation* of the church, not its *replacement*. The Anabaptists, by comparison, pushed aside with consistent logic every other manifestation of Christianity to date; the entire world, including Catholic and Protestant church leaders and rulers, consisted exclusively of pagans (Schäufele 1966:97). All of Christianity was apostate; all had rejected God's truth. In addition, Catholics and Protestants alike had seduced humanity and introduced a false religion. Europe was once again a mission field. As at the time of the apostles, the Christian faith had to be introduced anew into a pagan environment (:55f). Their project was not the reformation of the existing church but the restoration of the original early Christian community of true believers (:57-59, 71-73). In their understanding, there was no difference between mission in "Christian" Europe and mission among non-Christians. The Reformers, however, could not really bring themselves to such a view.

Still, the Reformation era knew of at least one champion of the idea that the "Great Commission" continued to be binding on the church and had to be understood in the sense of going out to those beyond the boundaries of Christendom: the Dutch theologian Adrian Saravia (1531-1613), a younger contemporary of Calvin (cf Warneck 1906:20-22; Schick 1943:24-29). In 1590 Saravia published a tract in which he argued in favor of the abiding validity of the "Great Commission"; he maintained that we could only appropriate the promise of Jesus in Matthew 28:20 if we also obeyed the commission of Matthew 28:19.[3] Saravia's views were, however, fiercely opposed by Theodore Beza, Calvin's successor in Geneva, as well as by the Lutheran Johann Gerhard.

Communication between Saravia and his opponents was compounded by the fact that he had based his views regarding the continued validity of the "Great Commission" on the conviction that only those bishops who indubitably stood in the apostolic succession were heirs to the commission to the apostles. In a sense this issue was even more important to him than that of enkindling a renewed interest in mission (cf Hess 1962:20). His views on apostolic succession later made him move to England and join the Anglican Church.

LUTHERAN ORTHODOXY AND MISSION

By the time Saravia wrote his tract on the missionary calling of the church, the springtime of the Reformation had already passed. In the German-speaking countries, in particular, efforts at the renewal of the church made way for attempts at keeping it doctrinally pure. The Peace of Westphalia (1648) practically marked the end of the Holy Roman Empire and finally ordered religious matters in the various European territories according to the *cuius regio eius religio* principle. Henceforth Catholicism would be the established religion in Catholic countries, Lutheranism in Lutheran territories, and so on. Only the Anabaptists, the "stepchildren of the Reformation", continued to defy the territorial principle; yet, after having been persecuted ruthlessly during the Reformation century, even they began to concentrate on maintenance rather than mission.

An important factor in this respect was the development in the Protestant understanding of the church in the decades immediately following the Reformation (cf Neill 1968:71-77; Piet 1970:21-29). When the Reformation shattered the ancient unity of the Western church, each of the fragments into which it was now divided was obliged to define itself over against all other fragments. The most famous of the sixteenth-century definitions of the church is the one to be found in the (Lutheran) Augsburg Confession of 1530. Its Article VII describes the church according to two distinguishing marks, namely as "the assembly of saints in which the gospel is taught purely and the sacraments are administered rightly". This forced the Church of Rome, in the Council of Trent (1545-1563), to respond with its own description of the true church, which "consists in its unity" and which has one invisible ruler, Christ, but also a visible one, namely "the legitimate successor of Peter, the Prince of the Apostles", who "occupies the See of Rome". Other Protestant definitions followed, each forced to be more precise than the former. The French Confession (1559) and the Belgic Confession (1561) added a third mark of the true church to the two identified by the Augustana, namely, the exercise of discipline.

Whereas the Catholic definitions of the church in this period tended to emphasize the external, the legal, and the institutional, the Protestant descriptions concentrated on the correctness of teaching and sacraments. Each confession understood the church in terms of what it believed its own adherents possessed and the others lacked, so Catholics prided themselves in the unity and visibility of their church, Protestants in their doctrinal impeccability. The Protestant preoccupation with right doctrine soon meant that every group which seceded from the main body had to validate its action by maintaining that it alone, and none of the others, adhered strictly to the "right preaching of the gospel". The Reformational descriptions of the church thus ended up accentuating differences rather than similarities. Christians were taught to look divisively at other Christians. Eventually Lutherans divided from Lutherans, Reformed separated from Reformed, each group justifying its action by appealing to the marks of the true church, especially correct preaching (cf Piet 1970:26, 30, 58).

In all these instances the church was defined in terms of what happens inside its four walls, not in terms of its calling in the world. The verbs used in the Augustana are all in the passive voice: the church is a place where the gospel *is taught* purely and the sacraments *are administered* rightly. It is a place where something is done, not a living organism doing something.

Neill (1968:75) gives a depiction of the situation in England at the time, a description which in many respects applied to the church in every country of Europe as well. Such definitions of the church, he says,

> call up a vision of the typical English village of not more than 400 inhabitants, where all are baptized Christians, compelled to live more or less Christian lives under the brooding eye of parson and squire. In such a context "evangelization" has hardly any meaning, since all are in some sense already Christian, and need no more than to be safeguarded against error in religion and viciousness in life.

The Reformation had come to its conclusion with the establishment of state churches, and of systems of pure doctrine and conventionalized Christian conduct. The church of pure doctrine was, however, a church without mission, and its theology more scholastic than apostolic (cf Niebuhr 1959:166; Braaten 1977:13).

The first theologian of the era of Lutheran orthodoxy who grappled with the issue of mission was Philip Nicolai (1556-1608) (cf Hess 1962:passim). He is indeed exceptionally important for our theme, not least since, as a transitional figure, his theology reveals the differences between earlier and later orthodoxy. His views on mission—which, in a more extreme form, were to become typical of orthodoxy—were developed especially in his *Commentarius de regno Christi*, published in 1597. I turn to these as well as to the later developments in Protestant Orthodox missionary thinking:

1. Like most theologians of Lutheran orthodoxy Nicolai believed that the "Great Commission" had been fulfilled by the apostles and was no longer binding on the church. Unlike later orthodoxy, however, he did not believe that the church's missionary calling was thereby disposed of. His concern was, rather, to safeguard the uniqueness of the apostles' foundational work and distinguish it from what the church did in later years. The apostles' work he called *missio*, the subsequent extension of the church *propagatio*. The latter expression had no negative overtones for Nicolai and simply served to distinguish what was basic from what was secondary (cf Hess 1962:90-96).

Nicolai's proximity to the momentous events of the Reformation era enabled him to have an essentially positive understanding of his own time. Astounding is, for instance, the fact that he evaluated Roman Catholic missionary efforts in other countries very positively—despite his identifying three great enemies of Christianity (read Lutheranism) in his day, namely the Turks, the papacy, and Calvinism. His positive evaluation of Roman Catholic and Eastern Orthodox missionary efforts (as well as the existence of the Ethiopian church of Prester John and the Mar Thoma Christians in India; details on these in Hess 1962:97-159) may, therefore, not be interpreted as proof of his essentially ecumenical perspective on mission (*contra* Hess). Rather, Nicolai believed that these churches were, involuntarily and unintentionally, "Lutheranizing" the people to whom they went. Even the Catholic missionary enterprise was a *"Handlängerin"* (assistant) in this. This was so because of the power of the word of God, which works independently of what people might intend it to do (cf Beyreuther 1961:5f).

Later generations of orthodox theologians would evaluate the mission work of Catholics and others much more negatively than Nicolai did. Of his views on the "Great Commission" and his distinction between the task of the apostles and that of subsequent missionaries they would retain only the element that declared that present generations of Christians had no business to get involved in a mission to the heathen, since the apostles had completed the task.

2. In opposition to Rome the Reformers emphasized that all initiative unto salvation lay with God alone. This conviction lies at the root of Luther's teaching on justification through faith, by grace, and of Calvin's doctrine of predestination. Luther and Calvin did not, however, interpret the emphasis on God's initiative in any rigid way; God's action did not militate against human responsibility, which was upheld very forcefully. Orthodoxy tended to give up the creative tension between the two and to put all the emphasis on God's sovereignty and initiative.

The attitude was that no human being could undertake any mission work; God would, in his sovereignty, see to this. For Nicolai this meant that we should not arbitrarily traverse the world looking for a mission field. God does not chase us here and there. He confines us to the place where we have grown up and calls us to serve the nearest neighbor to whom we do not have to travel more than a thousand yards (cf Beyreuther 1961:6). In Nicolai's case this rather strict predestinationism was, however, tempered by an exceptionally strong emphasis on love as the primary motive for mission—God has loved us and we are called to love others (Hess 1962:81-85). This accent injected a dynamic element in his missionary thinking which later orthodox theologians, particularly J. H. Ursinus, lacked.

3. It was Nicolai's positive and optimistic disposition which enabled him to judge the Roman Catholic overseas missionary enterprise as benevolently as he did. Any traces of optimism were, however, soon expunged from orthodoxy. It was almost as if pastors and theologians feared that the world might improve. At the same time they believed that there was little cause for such fear—the power of sin and selfishness would see to it that any attempt at improvement was already doomed to failure. This "practical heresy" (as Beyreuther 1961:3 calls it) led to profound pessimism and neutralized any thought of an attempt at changing structures and conditions. It had a similar effect on any talk about a missionary enterprise.

Pessimism and passivity had a yet deeper cause: the dark view of history in Lutheran orthodoxy. Nicolai expected the parousia to take place around the year 1670. The urgency of the imminent end of the world still acted as a motivation for mission in his case. In the course of the seventeenth century this would change. The situation in the church became so lamentable, particularly in the eyes of Gottfried Arnold (1666-1714), that the focus was no longer on the conviction that Christ and his reign would be triumphant, but on the fearful question whether Christ, when he returned, would find any faith on earth. This question destroyed all possibility of joyfully witnessing to Christ (cf Beyreuther 1961:38).

4. Lutheran orthodoxy could not free itself of the view that Lutheran mission could only be undertaken where Lutheran authorities ruled. Nicolai envisaged direct missionary involvement solely as the responsibility of Lutheran colonial masters if and when such colonies should come into existence. Based on this premise, a Lutheran mission could be conducted only in Lappland (cf Beyreuther 1961:6f). Nicolai's views in this respect were shared by virtually all Lutheran theologians and universities of the seventeenth century. A case in point is the "Opinion" on the missionary question released in 1652 by the theological faculty of the University of Wittenberg. It denied that the Lutheran church had any missionary calling; this responsibility rested solely with the state. Significantly, the state's duty in this regard was argued from the Old Testament — the state had to convert pagans *jure belli* ("through martial law") if other means proved to be unsuccessful (cf Warneck 1906:27f).

5. The Wittenberg "Opinion" gave another reason why the church should abstain from any mission to pagans: nobody could be excused before God by reason of ignorance, because God had revealed himself to all people through nature as well as through the preaching of the apostles. We once again encounter Nicolai's belief that the word of God had been proclaimed to all, even to the peoples of the Americas. Prior to the Wittenberg "Opinion", and following Nicolai, the great Jena theologian Johann Gerhard (1582-1637) also supplied proof of the fact that all nations had long before been reached with the gospel: the ancient Mexicans received Christianity from the Ethiopians, an unknown missionary had gone to Brazil, the Peruvians, Brahmins, and others must also have been evangelized centuries ago, since their religions reveal Christian elements, etc (cf Warneck 1906:28-31). If these nations were still pagan, in spite of having been evangelized at one time or another, there could be one explanation only — their heedlessness and ingratitude. Those who were still not Christians thus had no excuse and should not be given a second chance.

This theme became particularly dominant in Ursinus' refutation of the passionate plea for missionary involvement published in three tracts (in 1663 and 1664) by the nobleman Justinian von Welz (1621-1666).[4] Welz believed that the "Great Commission" continued to have unqualified validity, and severely censured the provincialism of the Lutheran church of his time. He wished to reintroduce the office of hermit, but now specifically for the sake of mission. Such hermit-missionaries should be people marked by holiness and personal piety and should be sent out under the auspices of a "Jesus-Loving Society" (Scherer

1969:38-45; 62-68; 70-76). Welz was, however, ahead of his time; much of what he stood for was to be brought to fruition only a generation later, when Pietism irrupted on the German Lutheran scene.

Ursinus' refutation of Welz's proposal contains virtually all the features of orthodoxy's interpretation of mission outlined above (cf Scherer 1969:97-108): obstacles to the conversion of pagans are insurmountable and the task is impossible; God has already made himself known to all nations, in various ways; the "Great Commission" was for the apostles only and it is presumption on our part to arrogate it to ourselves; the pagan nations are, in addition, impervious to the gospel since many of them are savages who have absolutely nothing human about them; Christian rulers should see to it that no disgrace or vice goes unpunished; etc. As for Welz's "Jesus-Loving Society", such an agency is clearly un-Christian and against God and our Savior, since Jesus "can tolerate no partners". All that is called for is for everyone to "mind his own door, and everything will be fine". Dreams about a coming golden age in which Christians multiply on earth are nothing but dangerous illusions. Meanwhile, let us thank God "for preserving a small, insignificant people who trust his name". They should "work with fear and trembling that they may be saved, struggle to be silent, and do their part".

The Lutheran church of his time had no faculty for appreciating and applying Welz's ideals. His appeal for missionary volunteers fell on deaf ears. Driven by the passion of his convictions he left for Surinam in South America in 1666 where he died, probably in that same year, "a sacrifice to orthodox intransigence" (Scherer 1969:23). No trace was left of his missionary ministry.

THE PIETIST BREAKTHROUGH

With his tract, *Behauptung der Hoffnung künftiger besserer Zeiten* ("Affirming the Hope for Better Times"), published in 1693, Philipp Jakob Spener broke radically with the melancholic view of history that had characterized late orthodoxy (Beyreuther 1961:38). In the words of H. Frick (quoted in Gensichen 1961:16): for orthodoxy the proclamation of the gospel to all nations was, at best, only a *Wunschziel* ("desired aim"); for Pietism it became a *Willensziel* ("aim of the will"). The new movement combined the joy of a personal experience of salvation with an eagerness to proclaim the gospel of redemption to all. This was frequently associated with an almost unbearable impatience to go to the ends of the earth. Already at the early age of fifteen Nikolaus von Zinzendorf (1700-1760), the later founder of Moravianism who had been nurtured in the pietistic circles of Spener and Francke in Halle, together with his childhood friend, Friedrich von Watteville, pioneered a "Compact for the Conversion of Pagans". The two boys mused that (hopefully!) not all pagans would be converted before they had grown up; the remaining pagans *they* would then bring to the Savior!

In Pietism the formally correct, cold, and cerebral faith of orthodoxy gave way to a warm and devout union with Christ. Concepts such as repentance, conversion, the new birth, and sanctification received new meaning. A disciplined life rather than sound doctrine, subjective experience of the individual rather than ecclesiastical authority, practice rather than theory—these were the hallmarks of the new movement. In virtually every respect it would set itself against orthodoxy. B. Ziegenbalg, the first missionary sent out under the banner of Pietism, attacked the teachers of orthodoxy because of their view that the church had already been planted everywhere; that the office of apostle had vanished; that God's grace no longer worked as powerfully as it did in the beginning; that those who were still pagans were under a curse; that God, if he wished to convert them, would do so without human effort, etc (cf Rosenkranz 1977:165). Such criticism of the orthodox position had been expressed before, among others by Welz. What was new, was that the Pietists of Halle succeeded in mustering support for their ideas among both ordinary church members and here and there even among the leadership. What used to be the passionate concern of a few individuals had now become a movement.

There was undoubtedly a certain narrowness about Pietism, particularly insofar as it tended to be very prescriptive about the way individuals should become true believers. I am referring in particular to Pietism's insistence on the need for a so-called *Busskampf*, a fierce, inward, penitential struggle. The movement has to be praised, however, for having broken with the practice of merely formal church membership and with the superficiality of conversion that characterized much of contemporary Roman Catholic mission work (cf Warneck 1906:53, 57). In this respect it resembled Anabaptism and the latter's idea of the believers' church. Its emphasis on the individual rather than the group was both its strength and its weakness. This emerges, *inter alia*, in Pietism's (and particularly Moravianism's) view of the church.

Zinzendorf, in particular, opposed the idea of "group conversions" and emphasized individual decisions (cf Warneck 1906:66; Beyreuther 1961:40). Likewise, he was not interested in the formation of "churches" on the mission fields; to him, "church" by definition meant formality, lifelessness, lack of commitment. It was therefore one of the greatest disappointments of his life when, during his absence in North America, the community in Herrnhut organized itself into a confessional church, thus refusing to be what he intended it to be, namely, a provisional guest house (cf Beyreuther 1960:110). Mission was, for him, not an activity of the church, but of Christ himself, through the Spirit (:74). In this, however, Christ made use of people of extraordinary faith and courage, of daring energy and persistent endurance. Pietism thus introduced the principle of "voluntarism" in mission (cf Warneck 1906:55f, 59f).[5] It was not the church (*ecclesia*) that was the bearer of mission, but the small, revived community inside the church, the *ecclesiola in ecclesiae*. From here it was only one step toward mission becoming the hobby of special-interest groups, a practice that militated against the idea of the priesthood of all believers (cf Scherer 1987:73).

The church was not the bearer of mission; neither was it the goal. Ziegenbalg and Plütschau, the first Pietist missionaries sent out from Halle, arrived in Tranquebar in India without a clear idea of what was to happen to those who might embrace their message; almost by accident "churches" were formed among the converts. Zinzendorf, on the other hand, had a clearer purpose in mind for his small bands of Moravian missionaries, sent out to the ends of the earth. Following the example of the apostles, they should bring in only "first fruits", who were not to be organized into national churches as had happened in Europe. The missionaries should, rather, gather the small flocks of new believers into pioneer "pilgrim houses", or "emergency residences". Typical of Zinzendorf's thinking was the idea of improvising, of remaining open to the guidance of the Spirit and being willing to try something novel or to move on to new challenges. Everything the Brethren did stood in the sign of being provisional, of only inaugurating what was to come (cf Beyreuther 1960:102-113; 1961:41f; Rosenkranz 1977:174f).

Orthodoxy's insistence on a structural link between church and state meant that everybody in a given territory would, at least nominally, have to be regarded as Christians. Pietists and Moravians broke with this and emphasized personal decisions. Mission work could in no circumstances be regarded as the obligation of the ruler, a view that was axiomatic in orthodoxy. This was an important breakthrough, determinative for all subsequent understanding of mission, and another point of similarity between Pietists and Anabaptists. Heralds of the gospel should go out under the direction of Christ and the Spirit, and non-Christians should be won to faith in Christ irrespective of any colonial or political interests.

Naturally, in the context of the time, compromises had to be made. This was true, for instance, in the case of the very first overseas missionary enterprise of the Pietist movement, the Danish-Halle mission in Tranquebar, India. The missionaries were sent to Tranquebar by the Danish king. In the colony itself, however, the missionaries stood in almost constant tension with the local colonial authorities (for a penetrating discussion of the issue, cf Nørgaard 1988:passim).

Early Pietists were not only interested in people's souls. In 1701 Francke defined the goal of the renewal movement as the "concrete improvement of all walks of life, in Germany, Europe, in all parts of the world" (quoted in Gensichen 1975a:156 — my translation). Ziegenbalg declared that the *Dienst der Seelen* ("service of souls") and the *Dienst des Leibes* ("service of the body") were interdependent and that no ministry to souls could remain without an "exterior" side (:163; cf Nørgaard 1988:122). Neither did this remain at the level of talking. In Germany, Francke and other pietists were involved extensively in "home missions", ministering to the destitute and deprived people of Halle and environs and founding a school for the poor, an orphanage, a hospital, a widows' home, and other institutions.

It was this dynamic and comprehensive understanding of the reign of God — in which salvation and well-being, soul and body, conversion and development were not to be divorced one from the other — which Ziegenbalg and Plütschau took with them to India. To give one example, before their arrival schools were the prerogative only of Brahmins, and even then only for boys; the missionaries founded schools for members of the other castes and for girls as well. Equally important: in these schools no pressure to become a Christian was brought to

4. Calvinist mission enterprises, whether those of representatives of the Dutch "Second Reformation" or of English Puritans, were all undertaken within the framework of colonialist expansion. In the next chapter the intimate relationship between colonialism and mission will be explored more fully. Here I wish to refer only to the colonial idea as it manifested itself in the seventeenth and early eighteenth century and its relationship to Protestant missions. In order to appreciate this relationship it is important to understand that the *corpus Christianum* or Christendom idea was still completely intact in the period under discussion and would only come under fire during the Enlightenment. During the seventeenth century it was still self-evident that Europe was Christian (even if there were different "branches" of Christianity—Roman Catholic, Lutheran, Reformed, etc), and it was therefore a matter of course that the same should apply to the overseas "possessions" of European nations.

In the case of Calvinism, another dimension was added, that of theocracy. Wherever Calvinist missions were launched, the purpose was to establish in the "wilderness" a socio-political system in which God himself would be the real ruler. The missionary efforts of John Eliot clearly give evidence of this motif, particularly his "Praying Towns", a total of fourteen settlements in Massachusetts in which Indian converts were gathered and where the entire life of the community was organized according to the guidelines of Exodus 18. In similar fashion the Puritan colonies in North America were to be a manifestation of the kingdom of God on earth. Christ's rule was to be made visible in both society and church. The state bore a divine calling to function as an auxiliary agent. A perfect harmony between church and state was envisioned. In the mother country the same ideal was pursued, at least in the 1640s and 1650s, when Oliver Cromwell and others were dreaming of transforming England into a theocracy; an integration of religion and politics was intended to reflect the will of God for church and nation (cf van den Berg 1956:21-29; Rooy 1965:280).

The Enlightenment would shatter the theocratic ideal. Religion would be banished to the private sphere, leaving the public sphere to reason. The Enlightenment would thus make it impossible still to conceive of mission as building a theocracy on earth. And yet, as we shall see in the next chapter, the idea of a unity between society and religion, between state and church, would never completely die; in various ways it would continue to manifest itself, even after having been dealt a crippling blow by the Enlightenment.

5. The theocratic ideal was intimately linked to the way in which early Calvinists understood the connection between mission and eschatology. The sharp distinction between premillennialism and postmillennialism which would characterize later times (particularly the late nineteenth as well as the twentieth century) was still absent. De Jong summarizes the period well when he says that, from 1640 until, in fact, the dawn of the nineteenth century,

> millennial hopes oscillated between a highly complex chiliasm or premillennialism with adventist tendencies and a low-keyed postmillennialism with its belief in the gradual improvement of human conditions through Christian benevolent and educational programs (1970:22).

Eschatology, more than any other area of the Christian faith, has always been a field where religious fantasies have the opportunity of running free. In light of this it would be unrealistic to expect all Puritans to have thought alike. There were indeed differences. And yet there was an astounding degree of agreement here, since all shared the same theocratic vision. Their view of the relationship between mission and eschatology embraced, in essence, four elements: the anticipation of the downfall of Rome; the subsequent large-scale influx of Jews and Gentiles into the true church; the evolution of an era of true faith and material blessing among all people; and the firm conviction that England was divinely mandated to guide history to its appointed end in these matters (De Jong 1970:77; cf also Rooy 1965:241). The first three motifs were also evident in Dutch missionary circles of this period, among others in W. Teellinck and J. Heurnius (cf van den Berg 1956:20f).

Such thoughts were therefore, as it were, in the air during the seventeenth century and beyond. At the same time they reflect a shift away from Calvin's understanding of eschatology. He had postulated a tri-epochal progression of the time of the church. The first period was that of the apostles, when the gospel was offered to the whole inhabited world. Then followed the second period, when Antichrist held sway and in which Calvin himself lived; he therefore wrote a theology for the church under the cross. The final period would be that of the great expansion of the church. The Puritans accepted Calvin's scheme of history. They believed, however, that they were living at the end of the second period and at the very dawn of the third (cf Chaney 1976:32f). This explains why they were far more optimistic and confident than Calvin had been. They were convinced that they were already living in the last days. Slowly but surely the conviction grew that God's last and eminently successful attack on the forces of Antichrist would be launched from the shores of North America and that the Puritan saints would play a key role in this final drama of history (cf Hutchison 1987:38, 41).

6. Cultural uplift as an aim of mission was still relatively undeveloped in the "Second Reformation" and Puritan period. Western Christians believed that their culture was superior to those of non-Western nations, but they did not isolate cultural uplift as a goal of mission. It was simply assumed that people would live a better life once God's rule was established over their respective societies. In John Eliot's words (quoted by Hutchison 1987:27), it was "absolutely necessary to carry on civility with religion". Some decades later Cotton Mather (1663-1728) would formulate it even less unequivocally, "The best thing we can do for our Indians is to Anglicize them" (quoted by Hutchison 1987:29). In the subsequent period, as I shall illustrate in the following chapter, this view would sometimes be so dominant that it was hard to distinguish between mission and "Westernization".

7. Given the prominence of the "Great Commission" in missionary debates since the end of the eighteenth century, it is surprising that it played virtually no role in the discussions of the seventeenth century (cf Rooy 1965:319f). Perhaps the main reason for the absence of this motif is that the validity of the commission was not disputed and that the Puritans did not have to appeal to a command to justify what they were doing.

AMBIVALENCES IN THE REFORMATION PARADIGM

During the first two centuries of Protestantism the missionary paradigm tended to fluctuate between various extremes:

1. An emphasis on the sovereignty of God sometimes exercised a paralyzing influence on even the idea of missionary involvement; at other times divine sovereignty and human accountability were held in creative tension.

2. Sometimes people were seen almost exclusively in terms of the Fall—obdurate sinners en route to perdition. At other times it was Christ's love for lost humans that was emphasized—people were judged to be redeemable and worthy of redemption.

3. Protestant orthodoxy was inclined to put all emphasis on the *objective* nature of faith and to leave little room for a personal experience of salvation. Pietism went to the other extreme and overemphasized the subjective and experiential side of religion. Others, however, managed to uphold, to a degree, the indissoluble unity between the objective and subjective dimensions of faith.

4. By and large, the Protestants of the first two centuries still operated within the framework of a close liaison between church and state, and this was true also with respect to mission. Exceptions to this rule were found among the Anabaptists, the Pietists, and some exponents of the Second Reformation and Puritanism.

5. Because of its theocratic features the Calvinist branch of the Reformation put a greater emphasis than Lutheranism on the rule of Christ in society at large; this distinction also manifested itself in Calvinist missionary practice.

Other Reformation influences on missionary thinking could be identified, but these are perhaps the most important ones. None of these elements would, however, remain unaffected during the subsequent era, as the influence of the Enlightenment slowly but inexorably spread through society and church. To this we now turn.

Chapter 9

Mission in the Wake of the Enlightenment

CONTOURS OF THE ENLIGHTENMENT WORLDVIEW

This chapter continues my review of the Protestant missionary paradigm. At first glance it may appear strange to write two separate chapters on the Protestant understanding of mission. Such a procedure is, however, justified in light of the profound influence the Enlightenment had on Protestantism. This is not to suggest that Catholicism remained unaffected by it. It can, however, hardly be denied that, on the whole, Catholic theology and the Catholic Church withstood Enlightenment influences more effectively than did Protestantism and succeeded longer than the latter to remain intact. Catholicism, in effect, "postponed" its response to the Enlightenment until the Second Vatican Council. The result has been, as Hans Küng (1984:23) has suggested, that Catholicism had to effect simultaneously two paradigm shifts in the twentieth century (shifts which for Protestantism lay centuries apart), namely, in respect to both the Enlightenment and the postmodern period. In the case of Protestantism, by contrast, virtually everything that happened since the eighteenth century was, in one way or another, profoundly influenced by the Enlightenment. It goes without saying that much of this rubbed off on Catholic theology and the Catholic Church, even if fundamental differences between the two confessions remain in this respect. Most of my references will therefore be to events in Protestantism, although Catholic developments will feature occasionally.

This is not the place to discuss the Enlightenment in any detail. I shall only highlight some aspects of the movement insofar as these may contribute to a better understanding of what was happening in missionary thinking and practice during the past three centuries or so. The "modern" or Enlightenment era only began in the seventeenth century, although indications that the medieval world and worldview were beginning to disintegrate could be observed as early as the fourteenth (cf Oberman 1986:1-17).

Medieval cosmology had been structured more or less along the following lines (cf Nida 1968:48-57):

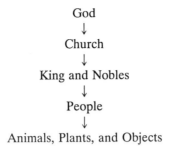

One was not to tamper with this structure. Within the divinely constituted order of things, individual human beings as well as communities had to keep their proper places in relation to God, the church, and royalty. God willed serfs to be serfs and lords to be lords. However, through a whole series of events — the Renaissance, the Protestant Reformation (which destroyed the centuries-old unity and therefore power of the Western church), and the like — the *church* was gradually eliminated as a factor for validating the structure of society. Validation now passed directly from God to the king, and from there to the people. During the Age of Revolution (primarily in the eighteenth century) the real power of *kings and nobles* was also destroyed. The ordinary people now saw themselves as being, in some measure, related to God directly, no longer by way of king or nobility and church. We find here the early stirrings of democracy. Again, in the Age of Science, *God* was largely eliminated from society's validation structure. People discovered, somewhat to their surprise at first, that they could ignore God and the church, yet be none the worse for it. With all the "supernatural" sanctions (God, church, and royalty) gone, people now began to look to the subhuman level of existence, to animals, plants, and objects, to find authentication and validation for life. Humanity derived its existence and validity from "below" and no longer from "above".

I am not suggesting that this entire process unfolded in so many clearly identifiable separate stages. Neither were people always consciously aware of what was happening. We can, however, say that, gradually, Western people began to subscribe to a new way of thinking introduced by Nicholas Copernicus (1473-1543), Francis Bacon (1561-1626), Galileo Galilei (1564-1642), René Descartes (1596-1650), and others. A generation or two later, when John Locke (1632-1704), Baruch Spinoza (1632-1677), Gottfried Wilhelm Leibnitz (1646-1716), and Isaac Newton (1642-1717) appeared on the scene, the Enlightenment worldview was firmly established. Two scientific approaches characterized the Enlightenment tradition: the Empiricism of Bacon (set out, *inter alia*, in his *Novum Organon*) and the Rationalism of Descartes (who published his *Discourse sur la méthode* in 1637 and posited the famous precept *"Cogito, ergo sum"* ["I think, therefore I am"]). Both these approaches operated on the premise that human reason had a certain degree of autonomy. However, neither Bacon nor Descartes saw their theories on scientific progress as in any sense jeopardizing the Christian faith. Bacon, in particular, operated completely within the Puritan paradigm and presumed a complete harmony between science and the

Christian faith (cf Mouton 1983:101-122; 1987:43-50). Still, in the period following their pioneering work science was increasingly regarded as being in opposition to faith.

Let me now attempt—in just a few paragraphs and therefore, once again, dangerously oversimplifying—to draw the contours of the Enlightenment paradigm before I proceed to discuss its impact on the understanding of the Christian mission. The elements I am identifying should really not be treated separately since they all impinge on each other. I am nevertheless (in true Enlightenment fashion!) going to consider them one by one.

The Enlightenment was, preeminently, the Age of *Reason*. In the course of time, Descartes' *Cogito, ergo sum* came to mean that the human mind was viewed as the indubitable point of departure for all knowing. Human reason was "natural", that is, it was derived from the order of nature, and therefore independent of the norms of tradition or presupposition. Reason represented a heritage that belonged not only to "believers", but to all human beings in equal measure.

The Enlightenment, secondly, operated with a *subject-object scheme*. This meant that it separated humans from their environment and enabled them to examine the animal and mineral world from the vantage-point of scientific objectivity. The *res cogitans* (humanity and the human mind) could research the *res extensa* (the entire non-human world). Nature ceased to be "creation" and was no longer people's teacher, but the object of their analysis. The emphasis was no longer on the whole, but on the parts, which were assigned priority over the whole. Even human beings were no longer regarded as whole entities but could be looked at and studied from a variety of perspectives: as thinking beings (philosophy), as social beings (sociology), as religious beings (religious studies), as physical beings (biology, physiology, anatomy, and related sciences), as cultural beings (cultural anthropology), and so forth. In this way even the *res cogitans* could become *res extensa* and as such the object of analysis.

In principle, then, the *res cogitans* was set no limits. The whole earth could be occupied and subdued with boldness. Oceans and continents were "discovered" and the system of colonies was introduced. It was as if previously unknown powers were unleashed. A tremendous confidence pervaded people; they felt that what was "real" was only now beginning to manifest itself, as if everything of the past was only a preparation or perhaps even an impediment. The physical world could be manipulated and exploited. And as scientific and technological knowledge advanced this became more and more possible. In his paper before the 1966 Church and Society conference in Geneva, Mesthene could therefore say:

> We are the first ... to have enough of that power actually at hand to create new possibilities almost at will. By massive physical changes deliberately induced, we can literally pry new alternatives from nature. The ancient tyranny of matter has been broken, and we know it... We can change it (the physical world) and shape it to suit our purposes... By creating new possibilities, we give ourselves more choices. With more

choices, we have more opportunities. With more opportunities, we can have more freedom, and with more freedom we can be more human. That, I think, is what is new about our age... We are recognizing that our technical prowess literally bursts with the promise of new freedom, enhanced human dignity, and unfettered aspiration (1967:484f).

Linked with the above is a third characteristic of the Enlightenment: the *elimination of purpose* from science and the introduction of direct causality as the clue to the understanding of reality. Ancient Greek and medieval scientific reflection believed in an animated causality and took purpose as a category of explanation in physics. This dimension of teleology was vital to the ancients. From the seventeenth century on, however, science has been avowedly non-teleological. It cannot answer the question by whom and for what purpose the universe came into being (cf Newbigin 1986:14); it is not even interested in the question. Instead, it operates on the assumption of a simple, mechanistic, billiard-ball-type causality. The cause determines the effect. The effect thus becomes explicable, if not predictable. Modern science tends to be completely deterministic, since unchanging and mathematically stable laws guarantee the desired outcome. All that is needed, is complete knowledge of these laws of cause and effect. The human mind becomes the master and initiator which meticulously plans ahead for every eventuality and all processes can be fully comprehended and controlled. Conception, birth, illness, and death lost their quality of mystery; they turned into mere biological-sociological processes (cf Guardini 1950:101f).

This manifests itself especially in a fourth element of the Enlightenment: its belief in *progress*. For Dante Alighieri (1265-1321), Ulysses' plans to sail beyond the Pillars of Hercules (the Straits of Gibraltar) into the open sea was blasphemy (reference in Guardini 1950:42); for the Enlightenment generation the idea was enticing and provocative. People now expressed joy and excitement at the possibility of traversing the earth and "discovering" new territories, of seeing a new day dawn over a dark world. With boldness Western nations took possession of the earth and introduced the system of colonies. An intractable confidence filled them as they prepared for their tomorrow. They were masters of their fate — a belief that was nourished from childhood by the history they studied (cf West 1971:52; Hegel 1975). They were convinced that they had both the ability and the will to remake the world in their own image.

The idea of progress expressed itself, preeminently, in the "development programs" Western nations were undertaking in the countries of the so-called Third World. The leitmotif of all these projects was that of the Western technological development model, which found its expression primarily in categories of material possession, consumerism, and economic advance. The model was based, in addition, on the ideal of *modernization*. The theorists assumed that development was an inevitable, unilinear process that would operate naturally in every culture. A further premise was that the benefits of development, thus defined, would trickle down to the poorest of the poor, in the course of time giving each one a fair share in the wealth that had been generated (cf Nürnberger 1982:240-254; Bragg 1987:23f). In this paradigm the opposite of modernism was backwardness, a condition "undeveloped" peoples should overcome and leave behind.

What was new in this model was the desire to spread wealth also among the less-privileged. It turned out to be a rather ambivalent matter, however. One study after the other, published during the last twenty-five years, has exposed the flaws in the Western development concept. The rhetoric referred to progress and affluence for all, increased security, and benefits; in the final analysis, however, the issue was neither advantages nor affluence for all, but power, since selfishness called the tune. And since religion no longer governed the right use of power it could be employed for the common good, but equally easily for the good of the already privileged. Of course, injustice had been perpetrated in the pre-Enlightenment period also, and yet, as Guardini (1950:39) argues, people then had a bad conscience about it. Now, in true Machiavellian style, expediency became more important than morality, and people could exploit others with impunity. Thomas Hobbes (1588-1679) propounded a theory of the state which declared it to be the absolute lord and judge of human life, a theory which would, in the end, lead to Auschwitz, Hiroshima, and the Gulag Archipelago.

All along, however—and this is the fifth characteristic of the Enlightenment—it was contended that scientific *knowledge was factual, value-free and neutral*. What makes a belief true, says Bertrand Russell (1970:75), "is a *fact*, and this fact does not . . . in any way involve the mind of the person who has the belief" (:75). A belief is true when there is a corresponding fact and false when there is no such corresponding fact (:78f). Facts have a life of their own, independent of the observer. They are "objectively" true. Thus Karl Popper (1979:109) defines "knowledge or thought in an objective sense" as follows (the italics are his): " (It) . . . is totally independent of anybody's claim to know; it is also independent of anybody's belief . . . Knowledge in the objective sense is *knowledge without a knower*; it is *knowledge without a knowing subject.*"

Over against *facts* there are *values*, based not on knowledge, but on *opinion*, on *belief*. Facts cannot be disputed; values, on the other hand, are a matter of preference and choice. Religion was assigned to this realm of values since it rested on subjective notions and could not be proved correct. It was relegated to the private world of opinion and divorced from the public world of facts.

Sixth, in the Enlightenment paradigm *all problems were in principle solvable.* Of course, many problems were still unsolved, but this was simply due to the fact that we had not yet mastered all the relevant facts. Everything could be explained or at least made explicable. No gaps or mysteries would permanently resist the emancipated and probing human mind. The horizon was limitless. Science was regarded as cumulative and all-encompassing. Its growth was continuous, ever onward and upward, as the fund of observational data was increased. Through the spectacles of positivism the history of intellectual life was viewed as having passed "through the dark ages of theological, metaphysical, and philosophical speculation, only to emerge in the triumph of the positive sciences" (Bernstein 1985:5). Not that there were no major advances in earlier epochs. But, says Mesthene (1967:484), "inventions in the past were few, rare, exceptional, and marvelous"; today they are "many, frequent, planned, and increasingly taken for granted". For the exuberant Mesthene the demonic, external power of nature was at last surrendering to human planning and reason, thus enabling humans to remake the world in their own image and according to their own design.

Lastly, the Enlightenment regarded people as *emancipated, autonomous individuals*. In the Middle Ages community took priority over the individual, although, as I have argued earlier, the emphasis on the individual was discernible in Western theology at least since the time of Augustine. In Augustine and Luther the individual was, however, never emancipated and autonomous but was regarded, first and foremost, as standing in a relationship to God and the church. Now individuals became important and interesting in and to themselves (cf Guardini 1950:42, 47, 64-79).

A central creed of the Enlightenment, therefore, was faith in humankind. Its progress was assured by the free competition of individuals pursuing their happiness. The free and "natural" human being was infinitely perfectible and should be allowed to evolve along the lines of his or her own choice. From the earliest beginnings of liberal thought, then, there was a tendency in the direction of indiscriminate freedom. The insatiable appetite for freedom to live as one pleases developed into a virtually inviolable right in the Western "democracies". The self-sufficiency of the individual over social responsibilities was exalted to a sacred creed. "There are no absolutes; freedom is absolute" (Bloom 1987:28).

The corollary of this view was that each individual should also allow all other individuals to think and act as they please. According to this philosophy, "the true believer is the real danger"; there is "no enemy other than the man who is not open to anything" (Bloom 1987:26, 27). So indiscriminateness was elevated to the level of a moral imperative, because its opposite was discrimination (:30).

The individual experienced himself or herself as liberated from the tutelage of God and church, who were no longer needed to legitimize specific titles, classes, and prerogatives. There were, in principle, no longer any privileged persons and classes. All were born equal and had equal rights. These were, however, not derived from religion, but from "nature". Thus human beings were, on the one hand, more important than God; on the other hand, however, they were not fundamentally different from animals and plants (cf Guardini 1950:53f). Individuals could therefore also be degraded to machines, manipulated, and exploited by those who sought to use them for their own purposes. Both capitalism and Marxism, says Newbigin (1986:118), derive from this Enlightenment vision of human beings as autonomous individuals without any supernatural reference.

ENLIGHTENMENT AND CHRISTIAN FAITH

The dominant characteristic of the modern era is its radical anthropocentrism. Prior to the Enlightenment life in all its stratifications and ramifications was pervaded with religion. Legislation, the social order, private as well as public ethos, philosophical thinking, art — all these were, in one way or another, stamped religiously. I am not suggesting that the Middle Ages were, as historical epoch, simply Christian and that what followed was, equally unequivocally, un-Christian. There was faith and unbelief both before and after the Enlightenment (cf Guardini 1950:98f, 110f). It can, however, not be denied that the Enlightenment provided people with a new "plausibility structure", that the Christian faith (or any other faith for that matter) no longer functioned in any direct way in informing scientific thinking. What distinguishes our culture from all cultures that have preceded it, then, is that it is, in its public philosophy, atheist (cf Newbigin 1986:54, 65).

So, even though the Christian faith continued to be practiced after the Enlightenment, it had lost its quiet self-evidence; it became strained and tended to overemphasize itself, for it felt itself to be operating in an alien and even hostile world (Guardini 1950:51). How can God reign sovereignly if people understand themselves to be free? Is God still active in a world in which it is believed that people take the initiative to create whatever they need? Can God still be the God of providence and of grace? Can he establish an institute — the church — which addresses the human world with divine authority? These are only some of the many questions with which modern believers are confronted. The unshaken massive and collective certitude of the Middle Ages has indeed vanished entirely. The Christian faith is severely questioned, contemptuously repudiated, or studiously ignored. Revelation, which used to be the matrix and fountainhead of human existence, now has to prove its claim to truth and validity. A new theological discipline began to emerge: Christian apologetics (:51-55).

As I shall argue below, the Enlightenment on the whole did not deny religion a place under the sun. It did, however, radically relativize the exclusivist claims of Christianity. For centuries the word "religion" was used in the sense of "devoutness" or "piety". During the Middle Ages non-Christian faiths were never referred to as "religions". In the seventeenth century, however, "religion" came to mean "a system of beliefs and practices". The word could now also be used in the plural, and the Christian faith became just one among several "religions". In essence, it was considered to be the same as any other. Its superiority over other religions was, at best, relative. This fundamental levelling of all religions also meant that the church's traditional vocabulary lost its theological content. To give one example, in its secularized form sin was perceived exclusively in moralistic terms; it referred to transgressing or failing to obey instructions. The inherent sinfulness of human nature was denied, and a remarkably optimistic view of humanity as essentially good was propagated; since evil had no inherent power over them, people would "naturally" do the right thing if left to themselves (cf Braaten 1977:18; Gründel 1983:105).

Of course, Christianity did not disappear after the Enlightenment; on the contrary, it has since spread across the entire globe. I shall return to the reasons for this and the way it happened. For the moment I just wish to argue that Christianity after the advent of the Enlightenment was different from what it

had been before. Even where it resisted the Enlightenment mentality it was profoundly influenced by it. It may perhaps be of some help to plot its influence on Christianity and Christian theology by referring to the seven characteristics of the Enlightenment paradigm listed above:

First, *reason* became supremely important also in Christian theology. This is not to suggest that in earlier times reason played no role. Frances Young (1988:307) has shown how important it was, for instance, in the patristic period, where "spirituality and rationality went hand in hand", since "faith is the reasoning of the religious mind". However, faith had priority over reason; the mind was *below* truth, not above it. Or, to put it differently, the contrast between faith and reason was really a contrast between two modes of rationality (:308).

Since the Enlightenment a different mode of rationality began to predominate. Reason supplanted faith as point of departure. Theology now differed from other academic disciplines only in its "object", not in its method or point of departure. It was basically comparable with other disciplines. In the course of time scientists were to find it increasingly difficult to allow room for God in their systems (except, perhaps, for "practical" reasons, as Kant suggested). Previously, it was believed that humans derived their existence from God. Now the opposite was proclaimed—God owed his existence to humans. Freud declared religion to be nothing but an illusion. Marx saw it as something evil, the "opiate of the people". Emile Durkheim suggested that every religious community was, really, only worshiping itself. Others were slightly more magnanimous. They conceded that there had been a time when belief in God made sense. Now, however, humans had become mature and no longer needed God. So, even if religion had at one time made sense, this prehistorical residue had no role to play in the modern world. The emergence of true humanity, which had been held in check by prejudice, superstition, and arbitrary authority, had at long last become a possibility (West 1971:73, summarizing the views of Voltaire and others).

In a thoroughly anthropocentric world there was no room left for God. It was self-evident that politics, science, the social order, economy, art, philosophy, education, etc, would have to evolve only according to their own immanent criteria. Humans still had faith . . . in themselves and in reason. No longer was a strong god needed to save them from their weakness. The inevitable consequence was that religion would gradually wither away.

Church and theology responded to this challenge in a variety of (often overlapping) ways. The first response (propagated or practiced by Schleiermacher, Pietism, and the evangelical awakenings) was to divorce religion from reason, locate it in *human feeling and experience*, and thus protect it from any possible attacks by the Enlightenment's tendency toward "objectifying consciousness" (cf Braaten 1977:22-25; Gerrish 1984:196; Newbigin 1986:44).

A second response consisted in the *privatization of religion*. It would carve out for itself a small domain in public life and for the rest remain a personal matter and leave the "public square" "naked" (cf Neuhaus 1984).

A third response was to declare *theology itself a science*, in the Enlightenment sense of the term. Thus, for some nineteenth-century Princeton theologians,

theology was "the science of God", "the greatest of the sciences", "the science of the sciences", superior, precisely as science, to any other science (for references, cf Hiebert 1985a:5).

A fourth response was for religion to attempt to establish its hegemony by *creating a "Christian society"* in which Christianity would be the official religion and public officers as well as government would have to adhere to religious principles and precepts.

A last response to the challenge of the supremacy of reason was to *embrace the secular society*. Humans have now come of age and should, in Dietrich Bonhoeffer's words, act "as if there were no God" (*etsi Deus non daretur*). A catalytic event in this regard seems to have been the World Student Christian Federation conference held in Strasbourg in 1960 where Johannes Hoekendijk urged participants to begin radically to desacralize the church and ecclesial activities. North American theologians began to espouse a theology of the "death of God". D. L. Munby in *The Idea of a Secular Society* (1963) stated that it was the peculiar glory of Western Christianity to have permitted the development of a society which explicitly refused to commit itself to any particular view. Arend van Leeuwen in *Christianity and World History* (1964) suggested that secularization, which was inspired by the gospel, was the wave of the future. Harvey Cox baptized the secular society in *The Secular City*. Many others joined in the chorus. This response was, in a sense, a modern updating of seventeenth century Deism which, using the classical illustration of God as a clock-maker, stated that God gave the world its initial impetus and then left it to run its course. This view certainly satisfied rationalists much more than did the approaches of those who tried to turn the Bible into the first book of science (third response).

Second, the Enlightenment's strict separation between *subject* and *object* in the natural sciences was also applied to theology. This was particularly the case as scholars increasingly became aware of the historical differences between their own time and those of the biblical records; in G. E. Lessing's words, a *"garstiger Graben"* (an "ugly ditch") separated us from the past. This "ditch" became evident particularly in the field of biblical scholarship, where the relationship between the biblical texts *then* and the interpretation of those texts *now* has been a central issue at least since the end of the eighteenth century. By emphasizing biblical inerrancy, Protestant orthodoxy had attempted to protect the objective truth of "pure doctrine". This was followed by Pietism with its individualization of the Word, then by idealism with its rationalization, and finally by liberalism which tended to relativize the Word as purely historical, as a document from a distant past to which modern people hardly had any relationship (cf Niebuhr 1959:37). The preoccupation with hermeneutics since Friedrich Schleiermacher (1768-1834) underlines the distance that has developed between the ancient text and the context shaped by the Enlightenment (cf Tracy 1984:95).

It is important, however, to realize that for most theologians their historical interests were subsidiary to their theological concerns. They practiced their theology for the sake of the life of the church, seeking to bridge the "ugly ditch"

caused by the many centuries which had moved in between the events concerning Jesus of Nazareth and the present. They realized that they could no longer, as their predecessors were prone to do, ignore the "ditch" and enjoy direct access to the biblical story. They believed, rather, that their task was to re-create, as far as possible, the original story and glean a message from it for today's church. In doing this, however, they increasingly ran the risk of capitulating to the Enlightenment view of history and historical research and to treat the biblical tradition as a mere object. The scholar examined the text but was not necessarily examined by it.

The *elimination of purpose* from science and the replacement of purpose by *direct causality* as the clue to the understanding of reality was another dimension of Enlightenment thinking that made deep inroads into theological thinking. The Christian faith is fundamentally interested in teleology, in the *wherefore?* question. It is the ultimate aim of our activities and the purpose of our existence that assign meaning to our lives. In the Newtonian paradigm, however, the world was increasingly governed not by purpose but by the closed cycle of cause and effect. Human planning took the place of trust in God. Little room was left for the element of surprise, for the humanly unpredictable.

Perhaps the optimism of the Enlightenment's philosophy of *progress* is the element more clearly recognizable in modern theology and the contemporary church than any of the elements listed so far. The idea of the imminent this-worldly global triumph of Christianity is a recent phenomenon and intimately related to the modern spirit. Sometimes it manifested itself as the belief that the entire world would soon be converted to the Christian faith; at other times Christianity was regarded as an irresistible power in the process of reforming the world, eradicating poverty, and restoring justice for all. This latter program was pursued particularly in circles where God was seen as a benevolent Creator, people as intrinsically capable of moral betterment, and the kingdom of God as the crown of the steady progression of Christianity. The spread of "Christian *knowledge*" would suffice in achieving these aims. Leibnitz, for instance, defined the church's task in the world as *propagatio fidei per scientiam* (the propagation of Christianity through science or knowledge). The name of the Society for the Propagation of Christian Knowledge, founded in 1699, betrays a similar sentiment. It saw its task as erecting libraries and schools and distributing Christian literature. Through knowledge and education benevolence and charity would be spread far and wide. God's kingdom became increasingly aligned with the culture and civilization of the West.

Equally far-reaching for theology was the Enlightenment's distinction between *fact* and *value*. The tolerant Enlightenment paradigm magnanimously allowed individuals to select whatever values they preferred from a wide range of options, all of which were on a par. Newbigin summarizes:

> In the physics classroom the student learns what the "facts" are and is expected in the end to believe the truth of what he has learned. In the religious education classroom he is invited to choose what he likes best (1986:39).

The logical outcome of this course was, naturally, that Christianity was reduced to one province of the wide empire of religion. Different religions merely represented different values; each was part of a great mosaic. Two different "truths" or "facts", two different views of the same "reality", cannot coexist; two different values, however, can.

Interestingly enough, there was some room left for religion in this edifice, but then only for *tolerant* religion, especially religion which had been advised by "a little philosophy" (Bertrand Russell, quoted in Polanyi 1958:271) through which one's values could, if necessary, be adjusted from time to time. Above all, the role of religion was to oppose any form of sectarianism, superstition, and fanaticism and to cultivate moral fiber in its adherents, thereby reinforcing human reason. Religion should, however, under no circumstances challenge the dominant worldview. Religion could exist alongside science, but without the first ever impinging on the latter.

The religious reaction to this dichotomy between fact and value took different forms which were sometimes but not always mutually exclusive. One reaction was to endorse the Enlightenment paradigm by turning it upside down: the tenets of the Christian faith were proclaimed to belong to the category of "facts" and not of "values". The nineteenth-century Princeton theologians provide an excellent example (cf Marsden 1980:109-118). Charles Hodge, in the introduction to his *Systematic Theology*, published in 1874, stated, "If natural science be concerned with the facts and laws of nature, theology is concerned with the facts and the principles of the Bible" (quoted in Marsden 1980:112). And Francis Turretin, the seventeenth-century theologian whose Latin text was used at Princeton, could say, "The Scriptures are so perspicuous in things pertaining to salvation that they can be understood by believers without (any) external help" (quoted in Marsden 1980:110f; cf 115). This view gave rise to the doctrine of the inerrancy of Scripture which found its classic expression in an 1881 publication by A. A. Hodge and B. B. Warfield, and which taught "the truth to fact of every statement of Scripture"; indeed, as Hodge said elsewhere, "The Bible ... is a store-house of facts" (quoted in Marsden 1980:113).

Another response to the modern dichotomy between fact and value was, in a sense, exactly the opposite of the one just mentioned, but was also predicated on Enlightenment assumptions. In this case the believer *accepted* that religious matters were concerned with values rather than facts. So facts and values were dutifully separated into non-overlapping domains; science and religion were assigned to two different realms. And in true Platonic fashion supremacy was ascribed to the transcendent, spiritual, and eternal reality over against the natural, the tangible, and the transitory. A purely scientific science was outranked by a purely religious religion. Indeed, facts and values had nothing to do with each other. One cheerfully accepted the modern scientific worldview and declared that the essence of faith belonged to a world for which neither science nor history could have anything to say (cf Newbigin 1986:49). In the process, however, faith and everything related to it became something entirely otherworldly. The kingdom of God in Jesus' ministry was "purely religious, supernational, future-oriented, predominantly spiritual and inward"; it had "no polit-

ical, national or earthly design" (Ohm 1962:247 — my translation).

The Enlightenment tenet that *all problems were in principle solvable* had an equally far-reaching effect on theology and the church. This dogma ruled out miracles and every other form of inexplicable events. Galileo regarded the physical world as a perfect machine whose future manifestations could be both predicted and controlled by somebody who had full knowledge of how it worked. All one needed was sufficient knowledge in order to understand, plan, and control events and developments. Where God was still used as a hypothesis he had become the "God of the gaps". We needed him only for exigencies such as cancer and similar incurable diseases. Step by step, however, our knowledge was expanding; the gaps were being closed. God was pushed further and further back and was becoming more and more redundant.

Similar sentiments were voiced in theological circles. I have already referred to the enthusiastic endorsement by many theologians of secularization during the 1960s (cf van Leeuwen 1964:419f). Whereas van Leeuwen, however, still warns against the "suicidal implications of future technological progress" (:408), Mesthene is much less ambivalent. He admits that technology may destroy "some values", and that this is "upsetting" since it "complicates the world", but he plays down human fear of the unknown by calling it "reminiscent of the long-time prisoner who may shrink from the responsibility of freedom in preference for the false security of his accustomed cell" (1967:487).

The last Enlightenment precept I have identified was that everyone was an *emancipated, autonomous individual*. Its most immediately recognizable effect on Christianity was the rampant individualism which soon pervaded Protestantism in particular. Its influence went further, however. The church became peripheral, since each individual not only had the right but also the ability to know God's revealed will. And because individuals were liberated and independent, they could make their own decisions about what they believed.

●

In discussing the impact of the Enlightenment paradigm on human life as a whole, not only religious life, it is of course important to realize that this view of reality did not remain unchanged and unchallenged during recent centuries. In a variety of ways the walls that so carefully divided subject from object, value from fact, ideology from science, etc, began to crack. Rationalism and empiricism increasingly proved incapable of supplying convincing answers to all the questions asked. In our next chapter the break-up of the Enlightenment paradigm will be discussed briefly. For the moment I just want to point out that all reactions to this paradigm were, until very recently, in the final analysis conditioned and even dictated by it. In each case the operative plausibility structure remained that of the Enlightenment.

Such reactions, in addition, illustrate another given: it is futile to attempt nostalgically to return to a pre-Enlightenment worldview. It is not possible to "unknow" what we have learned. To attempt to do this is, moreover, unnecessary. The "light" in the Enlightenment was real light and should not simply be discarded. What is needed, rather, is to realize that the Enlightenment paradigm has served its purpose; we should now move beyond it, taking what is valuable in it—with the necessary caution and critique—along with us into a new paradigm (cf Newbigin 1986:43). The point is that the Enlightenment has not solved all our problems. It has in fact created unprecedented new problems, most of which we have only begun to be aware of during the last two decades or so. The Enlightenment was supposed to create a world in which all people were equal, in which the soundness of human reason would show the way to happiness and abundance for all. This did not materialize. Instead, people have become the victims of fear and frustrations as never before. As far back as 1950 Romano Guardini, in his book on "the end of the modern era", again and again pointed to this legacy of the Enlightenment. The terms he used to describe it included fear, disenchantment, threat, a feeling of being abandoned, doubt, danger, alienation, and anxiety (:43, 55f, 61, 84, 94f). He summarizes,

All monsters of the wilderness, all horrors of darkness have reappeared. The human person again stands before the chaos; and all of this is so much more terrible, since the majority do not recognize it: after all, everywhere scientifically educated people are communicating with one another, machines are running smoothly, and bureaucracies are functioning well (:96—my translation).

MISSION IN THE MIRROR OF THE ENLIGHTENMENT

Church and State

It was inevitable that the Enlightenment would profoundly influence mission thinking and practice, the more so since the entire modern missionary enterprise is, to a very real extent, a child of the Enlightenment. It was, after all, the new expansionist worldview which pushed Europe's horizons beyond the Mediterranean Sea and the Atlantic Ocean and thus paved the way for a world-wide Christian missionary outreach. In the previous chapter I have shown that the very term used for this ecclesiastical and cultural expansion, namely "mission", was conceived as a concomitant of Western imperial outreach.

I shall now attempt to trace the ways in which the missionary idea has unfolded in Protestantism since the eighteenth century onward. I shall do it by means of examining the major forces and motifs that characterized Protestant mission during this period. First, however, I shall attempt to identify and delineate the major events of this period insofar as they have affected the evolution of the missionary idea.

I begin by turning to the modified relationship between *church* and *state*. Since the time of Constantine there was a symbiotic relationship between church and state, manifested during the Middle Ages in the interdependence between the pope and the ruler of the Holy Roman Empire. Even where pope and emperor were at loggerheads, they both continued to operate within the framework of interdependence and of the Christian faith—in other words, within the framework of "Christendom" or the *corpus Christianum*. The Reformation dealt a severe blow to this symbiosis, since the Western church was now no longer one. Meanwhile the Holy Roman Empire had also begun to disintegrate into several nation-states. The idea of Christendom remained intact, however; in each European country the church was "established" as state church—Anglican in England, Presbyterian in Scotland, Reformed in the Netherlands, Lutheran in Scandinavia and some of the German territories, Roman Catholic in most of Southern Europe, etc. It was difficult to differentiate between political, cultural, and religious elements and activities, since they all merged into one. This made it completely natural for the first European colonizing powers, Portugal and Spain, to assume that they, as Christian monarchs, had the divine right to subdue pagan peoples (cf chapter 7) and that therefore colonization and Christianization not only went hand in hand but were two sides of the same coin.

It was not essentially different when Protestant powers began to enter the race for the acquisition of colonies. The original inhabitants of North America, because they were "pagans", had no rights and were without further ado assumed to be subjects of the British throne. To subdue them and take their land was regarded as a divine duty similar to the Israelites' conquest of Canaan; on occasion 1 Samuel 15:3 could be applied directly to the colonists' conflict with the Indians—"Now go and smite Amalek, and utterly destroy all that they have" (reference in Blanke 1966:105). When, later, the Puritans embarked upon a mission to Native Americans (cf Beaver 1961:61), this was not because of a change of framework; it was, in a sense, just another way of affirming the hegemony of Christianity and the symbiosis of church and state.

In the Enlightenment paradigm, however, the alliance between church and state increasingly came under pressure: in the long run it could not but find such a union unacceptable. Paradoxically, Cromwell's Commonwealth (1649-1660), which sought a revival of the theocratic ideal, also set a time-bomb under the notion of the divine right of kings. It was only a matter of time before religion and politics would go their separate ways. This came sooner in England than on the European continent, yet at the same time the separation was milder than it would be in France, the Netherlands, and elsewhere, perhaps because the parties concerned were more inclined to compromise than those on the continent. The monarchy was restored in 1660 but remained under stress. Eventually, in 1689, a settlement was reached between Parliament and King William III. A Bill of Rights was adopted which, on the one hand, guaranteed the survival of the monarchy, yet at the same time curtailed royal power. The idea of an established church was not discarded, but it was brought into the sphere of practical convenience. Henceforth, theocratic dreams would belong to the past; colonial and ecclesial expansion were to be two separate things (cf van den Berg 1956:33).

On the continent events evolved differently. There the final separation between state and church came a century later than in Britain, yet when it came, it had more far-reaching consequences. The French Revolution of 1789 is the best-known example of this development but comparable, though less violent, occurrences were in evidence in the Netherlands and elsewhere.

Enlightenment ideas, bottled up for more than a century, exploded onto the scene and changed the entire face of Europe within a decade or two. In France, the tie between state and church was summarily severed. In the Netherlands the proclamation of the Batavian Republic in 1795 also terminated a centuries-old union. This also meant the end of state-mission cooperation in the overseas colonies.

In Britain's colonies, however, developments were not dissimilar to those in the colonies of Holland, Denmark, and other continental powers. In the case of the American colonies the empire continued to expand its western frontier — no longer, however, as part of a comprehensive religio-cultural-political pro-gram, but for imperialistic purposes and in order to thwart French aspirations in the area. In the East, notably in India, the empire's interests were chiefly mercantile. Thus the "secular" and the "religious" were clearly going their separate ways, even if it would still take a long time before the full implications of the new situation would manifest itself (cf van den Berg 1956:33). The *corpus Christianum*, particularly in the case of Britain, was not going to disappear in one fell swoop. The idea lingered on. From time to time in subsequent centuries colonial policies would again acquire religious overtones, especially in the first part of the nineteenth century (van den Berg 1956:33, 146, 170f, 190; I shall return to this).

The separation between the "secular" and the "religious" was particularly striking in the case of Pietism. In the previous chapter I pointed out that the first Danish-Halle missionaries, Ziegenbalg and Plütschau, succeeded in holding together "service to souls" and "service to the body" (Gensichen 1975a: *"Dienst der Seelen"* and *"Dienst des Leibes"*; cf Nørgaard 1988:34-40). This holistic approach could, however, not survive the onslaught of the Enlightenment on the European continent. A.H. Francke, one of the founders of the Pietist move-ment and spiritual father of the Danish-Halle mission, was fundamentally opposed to Rationalism and the teachings of Leibnitz, a circumstance which put Pietism (together with the pietistic missionary enterprise) and the Enlight-enment at loggerheads right from the start (van den Berg 1956:42f). The battle was an unequal one. Pietism could only survive by withdrawing into a spiritual cocoon and leaving the "world" outside the scope of its ministry. Pressure was soon exerted upon the missionaries in Tranquebar to concern themselves only with the souls of Indians. By 1727 the home board had reached the point where it distinguished categorically between the "civil" and the "religious" spheres; only the second was to be a concern of the church (Gensichen 1975a:174).

The continental churches, in contrast to those of the English-speaking world, increasingly succumbed to the Enlightenment ethos. In the course of time, Rationalism gained the upper hand in theological and ecclesiastical circles. By the end of the eighteenth century it had almost completely paralyzed the will to mission (Gensichen 1961:18). Francke and Zinzendorf, the great German missionary leaders who had towered above their contemporaries in the early part of the century (cf Warneck 1906:67), were now largely forgotten or dis-credited. The missionary enterprise had all but collapsed under the flood-tide of Rationalism (Warneck 1906:66f; van den Berg 1956:123).

In Britain, the influence of Francke and Leibnitz arrived on the scene more or less simultaneously. This led to a sort of marriage between Rationalism and Pietism (cf Gensichen 1961:31; van den Berg 1956:44; Chaney 1977:31). The dominant ecclesiastical party in the Anglican Church, Latitudinarianism,[1] was milder than the rationalism which had invaded continental churches and theology in that period; also, British evangelicalism was not as narrow as German Pietism (van den Berg 1956:124). The SPCK and the SPG (founded, respectively, in 1699 and 1701), for instance, reflected much of the "distinctly synthetic character" (van den Berg 1956:124) of British spiritual life which resists mutually exclusive extremes. Thus, what the Awakenings brought and proclaimed when they burst upon the British and American scenes from the early eighteenth century onward, was not regarded as alien to and in conflict with the ideas of the Enlightenment or with those of a warm experiential faith.

Forces of Renewal

In the event three factors converged to effect a spiritual change in the English-speaking world, a change that was to have a profound influence on missionary developments to the present day. These were the Great Awakening in the American colonies, the birth of Methodism, and the evangelical revival in Anglicanism (cf van den Berg 1956:73-78), none of which was felt to be implacably opposed to the emerging scientific age. I now turn to these *forces of renewal* and their impact on missionary thinking and practice.

Historians distinguish between the *Great Awakening*, a series of revivals in the American colonies between 1726 and 1760, and a second movement, which lasted from approximately 1787 to 1825, and which in England was called the *Evangelical Revival*. In the United States of America, however, it became known as the *Second Great Awakening*. Each of these movements exercised a profound influence on mission.

The Great Awakening began in Dutch Reformed congregations (which had been influenced by the Dutch "Second Reformation"), in the Raritan Valley of New Jersey. From there it spread to other denominations, mostly along the Atlantic seaboard, where the Presbyterian Jonathan Edwards soon became the leading figure. For America, says Niebuhr, the Great Awakening was a new beginning, "it was our national conversion" (1959:126). And it was mainly through Edwards that the Awakening succeeded in stemming the tide of shallow Rationalism, breaking the fetters of petrified Puritanism, and thus restoring dynamic to the Christian church (:172). Edwards's thought was the great intellectual and spiritual vein from which missionary theology in the period was mined (Chaney 1976:57; cf 74). This was so primarily because of the solid theological basis he had laid and because of his personal example and commitment. Orthodoxy emphasized the objective criterion of what God had done and what the Bible taught; Pietist and separatist groups stressed the subjective criterion of personal spiritual experience. Edwards and the Awakening, however, combined the two principles; they knew that Scripture without experience was empty, and experience without Scripture blind (Niebuhr 1959:109).

Edwards's eschatology—which was to be influential in North American missionary thinking into the twentieth century (cf Chaney 1976:65) — was postmillennial. It was not, however, the relaxed postmillennialism of Latitudinarianism; there was a sparkle of excitement in his eschatology, in that he believed that the Awakening really heralded the beginning of the latter days (de Jong 1970:157f). This fervent eschatological expectation was linked to the proclamation of a gospel of repentance and faith, not of inducing people to do good works. Rather than whipping up the wills of their listeners by admonitions, threats, and promises, the preachers of the Awakening guided them toward cleansing the fountains of life through an encounter with the living and present Lord. Those touched by the Awakening were characterized by a burning seriousness with regard to the ultimate issues of life. The diary of David Brainerd, Edwards's young friend, perhaps reflects better than any publication from the period the true spirit of the Awakening; it was permeated with a consuming passion for God's glory and the salvation of the lost, but also with an overpowering self-analysis (cf van den Berg 1956:78, 92; Niebuhr 1959:118f).

Robert E. Thompson's judgment (quoted in Chaney 1976:49 and 1977:20) that the Great Awakening "terminated the Puritan and inaugurated the Pietist or Methodist age of American church history", though having some validity, is only partially correct. It is probably more appropriate to describe it as a mixture of Puritanism and Pietism ground together in the crucible of the American experience (Chaney 1976:49). It was perceived as a "great effusion" (de Jong's chapter title for the period 1735 to 1776), and it launched a new era in the evolution of the American mind (Alan Heimert, reference in Chaney 1977:20). It also represented, to use Niebuhr's term, the shift from a primary emphasis on God's *sovereignty* to God's *grace* (1959:88-126).

The first Awakening did not, however, give birth directly to missionary activities, although it did lay the foundations for them.

About the time of Edwards's revival preaching in New England, in 1735, John Wesley (1703-1791) and his brother Charles (1707-1788) were sent to Georgia by the SPG. They appeared to have had no contact with the Awakening; rather, the spiritual renewal the Wesleys experienced resulted from contacts with Moravians. From 1739 onward they were, together with George Whitefield, conducting revival meetings in Britain. From these a new denomination, Methodism, evolved in the course of time. More clearly than the Great Awakening in the American colonies Methodism revealed the influence of the Enlightenment. Methodists could see no real difference between nominal Christians and pagans and could not, by implication, distinguish between "home" and "foreign" missions. The *corpus Christianum* was breaking up. The whole world was a mission field; hence John Wesley's famous adage, "The world is my parish" (van den Berg 1956:84f). The Wesleyan revival also meant that secular and spiritual interests had parted company; Methodists were concentrating on the salvation of souls (:170). Societal change was viewed as a result rather than an accompaniment of soul-saving.[2]

The *Anglican Church* was not unaffected by the Methodist revival. In particular, Methodism exercised a fertilizing influence on evangelical Anglicans who differed from Methodists mainly in that they remained loyal to the Anglican Church and wished to renew it from within. Methodism thus acted as a catalyst in helping evangelical Anglicans shake off the stranglehold of the rather anemic Latitudinarianism of the period (van den Berg 1956:70, 113, 116f, 131) and thus usher in the Evangelical Revival. Much of the renewal spilled over into non-established churches as well, particularly Presbyterian.

The Second Awakening

Meanwhile, on the other side of the Atlantic, the Great Awakening had more or less run out of steam. The churches of the religious establishment reached their nadir in the revolutionary generation. At the time of independence (1776) only about five percent of the population of the new nation were church members (Hogg 1977:201). In the words of Charles Chaney:

> In general, rationalism had invaded the ... schools and colleges, and slipped quietly into many of the churches. An unobtrusive Deism describes the religious commitment of the most influential men of the period ... The overarching interests of Americans had changed since the Great Awakening. The Enlightenment had come to the new American nation (1976:97f).

All this was soon to change, dramatically and fundamentally. Methodist, Baptist, and Presbyterian churches began to experience marked growth in the wake of the American Revolution (Chaney 1977:20-24). By the year 1800 the percentage of church membership had almost doubled; it has steadily increased ever since then, reaching a peak of about sixty percent in 1970 (Hogg 1977:361). The dramatic rise after 1776 is to be attributed almost solely to the Second Great Awakening. It was, unlike the first Awakening, not a new beginning for North America (as it was, to an extent, for Britain); rather, it could profit substantially from the first Awakening, refer back to it, learn from its failures and shortcomings, consolidate its gains, and channel the unprecedented effusion of newly released energy into a great variety of ministries, particularly domestic and foreign missions. By 1797 the awakening had reached a peak in the United States. Chaney captures the mood of the period:

> Defense turned to offense. Optimism gripped Evangelicals. Infidelity was no longer the fearsome enemy against which bulwarks must be raised but rather a vulnerable enemy against which the churches could be rallied (1976:155).

Above all, the new mood spawned a missionary spirit. By 1817 the missionary cause had become the great passion of the American churches (Chaney 1976:174). Indeed, "foreign missions had become the new orthodoxy" (J. A. Andrew, quoted by Hutchison 1987:60).

It was not very different in Britain. Carey's famous slogan, "Expect great things from God, attempt great things for God!" expressed the prevailing mood well. And it can hardly be doubted that the Enlightenment had reinforced this mood and helped to bring the entire world within reach of the gospel. Just prior to the period under discussion, James Cook had circumnavigated the earth. His story was widely read and contributed to the widening of people's horizons, in particular Carey's. Many believed that, through the explorations of Cook and others (now purely secular and mercantile enterprises and no longer intimately linked to the church and the spreading of the gospel) God in his providence was opening a way for missions also.

One of the most significant products of the Evangelical Awakening, in both Britain and North America (and, in fact, also in continental Europe and the British colonies) was the founding of societies specifically devoted to foreign mission. I shall return to the theological and missiological significance of these societies. For the moment I just wish to point out that they represent a new mood in Protestantism. The constitutive word was "voluntarism". Those touched by the awakening were no longer willing to sit back and wait for the official churches to take the initiative. Rather, individual Christians, frequently belonging to different churches, banded together for the sake of world mission.

It has become customary to hail William Carey—the Northamptonshire Baptist who in 1793 went to Serampore in India as the first missionary of the newly constituted "Particular Baptist Society for Propagating the Gospel Among the Heathen"—as the architect of modern missions. Whilst there is some validity to thus singling him out, it has to be remembered that he was only one of many similar figures from this period and as much a product as a shaper of the spirit of the time. Church renewal and mission were simply in the air. It is also noteworthy that Jonathan Edwards's *An Humble Attempt to Promote an Explicit Agreement and Visible Union of God's People, in Extraordinary Prayer for the Revival of Religion, and the Advancement of Christ's Kingdom in the Earth*, would only really be heeded more than four decades after it was first published in 1748, and become a catalyst for mission in a variety of denominations on both sides of the Atlantic (cf van den Berg 1956:93, 115, 122f, 129).

Meanwhile, on the European continent, the Enlightenment spirit succeeded in thwarting any church renewal on a scale remotely comparable to the Awakenings in Britain and North America. Political circumstances of this period also seriously inhibited renewal. It should be remembered that this was the era of the French Revolution, followed by the Napoleonic wars, which ravaged large parts of the continent. Even so, revival influences soon spilled over from England to Holland, where J.Th. van der Kemp became the catalytic figure in furthering the cause of both renewal and mission (Enklaar 1981:16-20; 1988:passim). In the German-speaking countries the situation was less promising. Pietism, which had barely survived the massive onslaught of Rationalism, was confined to small groups and was without a vision. Two men, however, Samuel Urlsperger (1685-1772) and his son Johann August (1728-1806), exerted themselves to keep alive and encourage these small and widely scattered groups. In 1780 the younger Urlsperger founded the *Deutsche Christentumsgesellschaft* (German Society for Christianity), the purpose of which was to promote "pure doctrine and true piety". In the course of time this society was to become the launching pad for German mission societies (cf Schick 1943:188-306).

It is important to note that evangelicals—whether in the United States, Britain, or the continent, and whether Anglicans, Lutherans, or members of non-established churches—were nonconformists in the true sense of the word. The "official" churches were, by and large, indifferent; they showed little interest in the predicament of the poor in their own countries or the detrimental effect of colonial policies on the inhabitants of Europe's overseas colonies. It was those touched by the Awakenings who were moved to compassion by the plight of people exposed to the degrading conditions in slums and prisons, in coal-mining districts, on the American frontier, in West Indian plantations, and elsewhere (cf van den Berg 1956:67-70; Bradley 1976:passim). William Wilberforce, who launched a frontal attack on the practice of slavery in the British Empire, was an avowed evangelical. William Carey protested against sugar imports from West Indian plantations cultivated by slaves. Christian Blumhardt, one of the founding fathers of the Basel Mission, challenged the first group of Basel missionaries never to forget "how arrogant and scandalous the poor Black people were for centuries . . . treated by people who called themselves Christians" (quoted in Rennstich 1982a:546). Many, many more similar examples could be added. Small wonder that the chartered companies administering the colonies did everything in their power to keep the missionaries out (cf van den Berg 1956:108, 146; Blanke 1966:109)! At the same time these evangelicals had no doubt that soteriological emphases had to take precedence, that they were not proclaiming mere temporal improvement of conditions, but new life in the fullest sense of the word. As such the burgeoning evangelical movement, particularly if compared with the bulk of Western Christianity and ecclesial life which by and large had succumbed to the spirit of Rationalism, represented a fairly effective opposition, in some respects even an alternative, to the Enlightenment frame of mind.

The Nineteenth Century

At the same time it could not be denied that a subtle shift had taken place between the first Awakening and the second. By and large the theocratic ideal, still basic to Edwards's thinking, lay outside of the horizon of the evangelicals of the Second Awakening. They were seeing people primarily as individuals, capable of making decisions on their own (van den Berg 1956:82). Their interest was also more narrowly soteriological than Edwards's was. The Enlightenment had steadily but relentlessly whittled away the once so broad range of the church's interests in all of life and society. Admittedly, there was something of an upsurge of theocratic interests toward the end of the Napoleonic wars, but this was fundamentally different from the older theocracy. In Britain the new theocracy was more secular, more intimately tied to patriotism. Protestant Britain's victory over Catholic France was hailed naively as the beginning of the fall of Antichrist but also as confirmation of Britain's providential destiny in world history.

Thus a religious note was again added to history, but in such a way that it tended to serve narrow nationalistic interests rather than the broad sweep of God's reign. The first generation of British evangelical missionaries, of all denominations, often fell foul of the colonial authorities. But as Victorian England sought to regain its religious dimension the second and subsequent generations of missionaries experienced less and less tension between working for God's kingdom and for the interests of the empire. Gradually, evangelicals became a respected power in the state, and missionaries, whether they intended to or not, became promoters of Western imperial expansion (cf van den Berg 1956:146, 170f). Ian Bradley, in his study on their impact on the Victorians (1976), explains how evangelicals succeeded in putting their stamp on all aspects of British life. Much of this was undoubtedly for the good of the entire community. Unfortunately, however, evangelical leaders were not free of paternalism and snobbery, which was one of the reasons why so much of Victorian England revealed two "faces"—a public face which spoke of high moral standards, and a private face where vices of many kinds abounded. Much of the vital religion of the Evangelical Awakening had been solidified into lifeless moral codes. The Victorian Age was undoubtedly an age of seriousness (cf the title of Bradley 1976), and in some of its expressions the seriousness was really all that remained.

Comparable developments took place in North America. The mood there, however, in the land of opportunities and hope, was more optimistic. In keeping with this the dominant theological position in virtually all Protestant denominations was explicitly postmillennialist. Chaney (1976:269) remarks, with reference to this period, "Not a single sermon or missionary report can be discovered that does not stress eschatological considerations". The events of the time brought the remote possibility of the millennium tantalizingly near. God's kingdom would not, however, invade history as catastrophe, but would unfold gradually and mature in an organic way. It was the old Puritan ideal in a revived form. The theology of the day, however, was no longer that of Edwards; it was the modified Calvinism of Samuel Hopkins. Evil passions would gradually fade away. Licentiousness and injustice would disappear. Strife and dissension would be wiped out. There would be no more war, famine, oppression, or slavery, neither in the United States nor on the mission fields (Niebuhr 1959:144-146). Americans saw themselves as inaugurators of a new order for the ages, an order conceived of as a return to a pristine human condition (Marsden 1980:224). At the same time the "horizontalist" interpretation of the dawning millennium was paving the way for an increasingly secularized understanding of God's reign.

By the fourth decade of the nineteenth century the impact of the Second Great Awakening was waning. Yet another revival period, this time under the able leadership of Charles G. Finney (1792-1875), simply served to underscore the fact that awakenings are apparently not destined to last; they all run out of steam and need to be revivified. The uniqueness of the renewal experience, still sensed in the first two Awakenings, was lost. Awakenings—or "revivals", as they increasingly came to be called—were becoming routine. They deteriorated into a technique for maintaining Christian America; they became "the great divine hoe, for keeping the garden clean" (Chaney 1976:295).

On the surface, however, "mainline" church life in the United States was, in spite of an ever-widening rift between the North and the South on the issue of slavery, still fairly monolithic theologically. The traumatic experience of the Civil War (1862-1865) was to change all of that. The cessation of hostilities did not usher in a golden age of the reign of righteousness, as some had predicted. The evangelical unity forged by the Awakenings—an evangelicalism in which a "commitment to social reform was a corollary of the inherited enthusiasm for revival" (Marsden 1980:12)—was about to disintegrate; "the broad river of classical evangelicalism divided into a delta, with shallower streams emphasizing ecumenism and social renewal on the left and confessional orthodoxy and evangelism on the right" (Lovelace 1981:298). By the beginning of the twentieth century the first had evolved into the social gospel, the second into Fundamentalism.

Behind the two movements lay two different eschatologies. Before the Civil War most American churches were postmillennialist—more correctly, premillennialism and postmillennialism did not fundamentally differ from each other; the proponents of the two views disagreed primarily over whether Christ would return before or after the millennium. Both groups saw history as controlled by a cosmic struggle and both expected a visible and literal parousia of Christ (cf Marsden 1980:51).

In the nineteenth-century United States, Christianity was very much an establishment religion. The virulent anticlericalism that was in evidence in many European countries at the time was absent. Little tension was felt between progress and the gospel. Rather, scientific advance was regarded in a rather simplistic way as heralding the advent of the kingdom of God. The manifestations of secularism, such as materialism and capitalism, were blessed with Christian symbolism. As evils like slavery, oppression, and war receded, science, technology, and learning would advance to undreamed of accomplishments. Gradually, mainline theologians began to abandon the dramatically supernatural aspects of the traditional postmillennial view of history. The idea of history as a cosmic struggle between God and Satan was discarded, as was belief in the physical return of Christ. The kingdom was not future or other-worldly, but "here and now"; it was, in fact, already taking shape in the dramatic technical advances of North America (Marsden 1980:48-50). The entire development was further distinguished by a lack of urgency about evangelism. On the one hand, it was no longer believed that those untouched by the gospel would go straight to hell; on the other, it was increasingly thought that the overseas mission of the American churches consisted in sharing the benefits of the American civilization and way of life with the deprived peoples of the world (cf Hutchison 1982:169).

The Twentieth Century

By the first decade of the twentieth century the transition from Reformed postmillennialism to the Social Gospel had been completed. Sin became identified with ignorance and it was believed that knowledge and compassion would produce uplift as people rose to meet their potentials.

The other branch of North American "mainline" Protestantism held on to the supernatural elements of the Christian faith. In order to uphold these it increasingly turned to premillennialism. This switch was not unrelated to the psychological mood of the day. The devastation of the Civil War and the many problems it left unsolved gave birth to a feeling of despondency in many circles. Many Christians did not share the optimism and progress-mindedness of the "liberals". Only Christ's return in glory could really change conditions fundamentally and permanently. Until that happened, the world was doomed to becoming increasingly worse; the best one could hope for was to contain a little bit of the evil which seemed to be spreading like wildfire. In these circles evangelism was given the highest priority; increasingly people shied away from virtually any form of social involvement.

A profound and far-reaching change had taken place in North American Protestantism. This wing of the Christian church succeeded for a longer time than did European Protestantism in keeping at bay the hounds of the Enlightenment. Powerful remnants of the wholeness of life, as manifested in pre-Enlightenment Puritanism, survived in mainline North American Protestantism well into the nineteenth century, long after such remnants had lost respectability in Europe and had been confined to small and marginal groups at the edges of the established churches. The Civil War, however, in principle destroyed the belief that one could be both an evangelist and an abolitionist (as Finney had been), both postmillennialist and upholder of the belief in a supernatural kingdom of God, and define sin as both public (or structural) and private (or individual). The Enlightenment had caught up with North American churches (cf Visser 't Hooft 1928:102-125). Having originated in Puritanism and having come to full bloom in postmillennial evangelicalism, North American Protestantism split. The one wing opted for premillennialism, which developed into fundamentalism; it had learnt to tolerate corruption and injustice, to expect and even welcome them as signs of Christ's imminent return (cf Lovelace 1981:297). The other wing formally remained postmillennial, but their millennium gradually became almost completely this-worldly; it consisted, to a large extent, in an uncritical affirmation of American values and blessings, and the conviction that these had to be exported to and shared with people worldwide.

From the 1930s onward the picture would begin to change. That story, however, and its significance for mission, belongs to our next chapter.

MISSIONARY MOTIFS IN THE ENLIGHTENMENT ERA

In the preceding section the contours were drawn of ecclesial and other developments from the eighteenth to the twentieth century. My approach was diachronic. In the present section I wish to follow a different approach, attempting to identify and briefly analyze some of the most important missionary motifs of the period. This is a hazardous undertaking. To begin with, such motifs did not operate in isolation from the general flow of historical events. Perhaps more important, it is really impossible to disentangle motifs and isolate them from each other. Any one motif is, in a sense, just the opposite side of another (cf van den Berg 1956:21, 38, 186-188). If I nevertheless proceed in this way, I do so simply so as to get a handle on a very complex and at the same time crucial historical period. Also, it will not be possible to discuss in detail *all* missionary motives and motifs[3] of the period; only those I regard as particularly important will be identified and made to pass in revue.

In addition, my purpose will be to show to what extent these motives and motifs have been influenced by the Enlightenment frame of mind. It was a period in which centrifugal forces were at work. It is therefore both pointless and impossible to try to identify a completely unified and coherent pattern of thinking and action in this era. The Enlightenment macro-paradigm remains elusive and manifests itself, at best, in a variety of sub-paradigms, some of which appear to be in tension, even conflict, with others. Still, in this entire epoch, virtually everybody operated within the framework generated by the Enlightenment.

I will not attempt any exhaustive treatment but merely endeavor to show how missionary motifs since the eighteenth century related to earlier ones. In my survey I shall pay more attention to motifs in the English-speaking world than to those on the European continent. The reasons are twofold. First, it is a fact of history that during the past two centuries the English-speaking world has provided more non-Roman Catholic missionaries than any other group (Neill 1966a:261). This fact alone makes a study of Anglophone missions a high priority. Why is it that, after the continent seemed to have taken the lead in the eighteenth century, the tide changed so dramatically toward the end of that century? Second, the constituent elements of missions emanating from the English-speaking world have been researched more extensively than others. One can therefore identify and discuss these with more accuracy. The most important study on the subject, even if it really only covers the period up to 1815, remains Johannes van den Berg's *Constrained by Jesus' Love* (1956). In recent years several additional studies have, however, been published, particularly on missionary developments during and in response to the colonial expansion of the West. Still, much more has to be done in this field.

The Glory of God

In classical Calvinist missionary thinking, from Voetius to Edwards, the emphasis was on God's sovereignty over everything and on the conviction that God and God alone could take the initiative in saving people. This belief in God taking the initiative found expression in the doctrine of predestination. It is God who forgives and saves, not humans; it is God who reveals the truth and the life, not human reason. Believers stood in awe of the majesty of God, the Wholly Other. In Protestant orthodoxy, however, the emphasis on God's initiative became wooden and rigid; people were taught to wait in complete passivity upon the saving work of God in their souls (cf van den Berg 1956:73).

In the period we are surveying here, by contrast, there was a growing awareness that God's initiative did not exclude human endeavor and that his majesty was really the other side of his grace and love reaching out to humankind. In the wake of the Great Awakening, then, the motif of the glory of God became wedded to other motifs, in particular that of compassion. Still, even where the glory of God was not explicitly mentioned, it continued to constitute the silent background motif during virtually all of the eighteenth century.

In the subsequent era it began to wane. Its gradual decline is, to a significant extent, to be attributed to the influence of the Enlightenment. Theocratic ideals and the notion of the glory of God can only operate within the context of a theology deeply conscious of the unity of life and the royal dominion of Christ over every sphere of life (van den Berg 1956:185). The Enlightenment put humans rather than God in the center; all of reality had to be reshaped according to human dreams and schemes. Even in Christian circles human needs and aspirations, although originally couched in purely religious terms, began to take precedence over God's glory. So, in the late eighteenth and early nineteenth century the emphasis shifted to the love of Christ; still later the accent was on salvation of the perishing heathen and in the early twentieth century on the social gospel.

Still, the manifestation of God's glory as a motive for mission never disappeared completely. Since the middle of the twentieth century, in particular, it has once again risen to prominence.

"Constrained by Jesus' Love"?

Johannes van den Berg has chosen the words from 2 Corinthians 5:14 as the title for his excellent inquiry into the motives of the missionary awakening in Great Britain in the period between 1698 and 1815. It is therefore appropriate that we reflect briefly on the role of this motif during the period under investigation in this chapter. We meet references to the theme of love again and again.

In actual missionary motivation, promotion, and practice, this theme turned out to be a rather ambivalent one. It manifested itself in both positive and negative ways. I turn, first, to its positive expression.

In the missionary awakening love became a powerful incentive — love as gratitude for God's love in Christ and as devotion to him who "so loved the world that he gave his only begotten Son". This love, together with the desire to promote the "spiritual benefit of others" gradually became the dominant motif (cf van den Berg 1956:98-102, 156-159, 172-176; Warren 1965:52f). There was, among the Christians touched by the Awakening, a tremendous sense of gratitude for what they had received and an urgent desire to share with others, both at home and abroad, the blessings so freely shed upon them.

In conflict with the dominant views of the time, the missionaries regarded as brothers and sisters the people to whom they felt God was sending them. When the American Board of Commissioners for Foreign Missions (commonly known as the American Board) commissioned its first overseas missionaries, it was done in the conviction that distant Burma was "composed of our brethren, descended from the same common parents, involved in the consequences of the same fatal apostasy from God, and inhabiting the same world" (quoted in Hutchison 1987:47). The principal theme was that of empathy and solidarity, which found expression in compassion for others whose plight should evoke the Christian's "tenderest affections" as well as a yearning for both their temporal comfort and their immortal happiness (:48f). Though the missionaries viewed both themselves and those they considered pagans as "children of wrath", this was not where they put the emphasis; the primary accent, rather, was on the fact that all people were, first of all, objects of God's love and therefore worthy of being saved. John Wesley, in particular, was very conscious of the fact that God was above all a God of mercy. And even if, partly under the influence of the Enlightenment, there was a subtle shift away from the sovereignty of God's grace toward the view that people were inherently capable of responding to the offer of salvation, not least because all were creatures of reason, the fact that all were seen as fundamentally equal and therefore precious in the eyes of God, was something to be applauded. The missionaries were never to forget this, said Christian Blumhardt to the first missionaries of the Basel Mission sent out in 1827; therefore, in their intercourse with the people of Africa, they should be "friendly, humble, patient, . . . never boastful nor conceited, nor rude, never selfish, not quick to take offense" (quoted by Rennstich 1982a:94f).

Love for Christ and people often manifested itself in a remarkable degree of commitment and dedication. Once again the Moravians stood out as an exceptionally clear example. Zinzendorf's motto was "Wherever at the moment there is most to do for the Saviour, that is our home" (quoted in Warneck 1906:59). The Moravians made it a matter of principle to go to those most deprived and marginalized. They identified with the indigenous peoples and lived and dressed the way they did, mostly to the utter disgust of the European colonizers. Often the fury of the colonial authorities was vented on them. During a short span of forty years the Moravian missions among the American Indians in North America had to vacate their mission stations no fewer than seventeen times, because of interference from the colonial authorities (Blanke 1966:109).

Such boundless dedication to their missionary task and to the people they believed were entrusted to them was, however, not limited to the Moravians. Many similar examples from other societies could be cited. One only will have to suffice. In 1823 the Church Missionary Society sent twelve missionaries to Sierra Leone; within eighteen months ten of them had died of fever. Yet the CMS did not abandon Sierra Leone; for every one who fell there was always another willing to take his or her place (Warren 1965:29). There can, I believe, be no doubt that a primary motive of most missionaries was a genuine feeling of concern for others; they knew that the love of God had been shed abroad in their hearts and they were willing to sacrifice themselves for the sake of him who had died for them (cf Warren 1965:28, 44).

Sometimes this motif of love and utter dedication blended with another— that of asceticism. In Chapter 7, I suggested that much of the asceticism of the monastic movement was not immediately related to mission; the monk was intent on saving his own soul and in order to achieve this, he would start an abbey—which, however, gradually and almost by accident, would develop into a center for mission. Sometimes the emphasis on self-denial took on overtones of the meritoriousness of good works; a sacrificial life in mission would surely make the missionary more acceptable in God's sight! Like Catholics, Protestant missionaries were not always completely free from this sentiment. John and Charles Wesley, for instance, first went to the Indians in Georgia in the conviction that the arduous and lonely work among these primitive people would help the Wesleys themselves toward attaining true holiness and righteousness. This was, however, only a passing phase in their lives (cf van den Berg 1956:95f, 180). The validity of their attitude lies therein that they sensed that mission work was impossible without an element of sacrifice, self-denial, and preparedness to suffer for Christ (:202).

There can be no doubt that, for those touched by the Awakenings, the *soteriological* interest remained paramount. Their love expressed itself as a desire to bring "everlasting felicity" to non-Christians; the saving of souls was more important than the planting of churches or the improvement of temporal conditions (cf van den Berg 1956:101, 158; Beaver 1961:60). This was so because most Christians firmly believed that without being converted to the Christian faith people would perish eternally.

Even so, little separation between the soteriological and the humanitarian motifs was in evidence during the eighteenth and early nineteenth centuries. The missionaries persisted in the pre-Enlightenment tradition of the indissoluble unity of "evangelization" *and* "humanization" (cf van der Linde 1973), of "service to the soul" *and* "service to the body" (Nørgaard 1988:34-40), of proclaiming the gospel *and* spreading a "beneficent civilization" (Rennstich 1982a; 1982b). For Blumhardt of the Basel Mission this clearly included "reparation for injustice committed by Europeans, so that to some extent the thousand bleeding wounds could be healed which were caused by the Europeans since centuries through their most dirty greediness and most cruel deceitfulness" (quoted by Rennstich 1982a:95; cf 1982b:546). And Henry Venn, famous General Secretary of the British CMS, urged missionaries to take their stand between the oppressor and the oppressed, between the tyranny of the system and the morally and physically threatened masses of the people to whom they went (cf Rennstich 1982b:545).

Thus far our survey of the influence of the motive of love in Protestant missions has to be judged positively, by and large. There was, however, also a negative side to this motive.

It manifested itself, rather incongruously, in a curious mixture of both an optimistic and a pessimistic view of humans. The first was bolstered by the emerging romanticism of the late eighteenth century, both a result of and a reaction to the Enlightenment. J.-J. Rousseau, in particular, depicted the inhabitants of distant countries who were still untouched by Western influences as "noble savages". The descriptions of the natives of the South Sea islands by Captain Cook and others as the "sum of all earthly charm and beauty" clearly betray their indebtedness to Rousseau's views (van den Berg 1956:97f, 106, 110, 153). Such language was not, however, evidence of the fact that Westerners regarded others as their equals. Rather, the "noble savage" of Rousseau was a charming child, a *tabula rasa*, unspoiled by civilization and as yet innocent and unable to perpetrate evil. Small wonder then that this ostensibly optimistic view of humans was never far removed from its corollary, namely, a condescending attitude toward those "innocents". And this attitude could, again, easily spawn a rather pessimistic view of non-Westerners. So, by the early nineteenth century, the views of the typical evangelical concerning the pagan world, particularly with respect to its spiritual condition, began to vacillate between pessimism and romanticism. Soon pessimism was the stronger sentiment.

Furthermore, those to be saved were primarily seen as *individuals*. This approach reflected conditions on the missionaries' "home front", where the old, sheltering influence of life in a community permeated by Christian ideals was shattered by the Enlightenment worldview and "revival" consequently deteriorated to appeals made to individuals in isolation from the communities and contexts in which they lived (cf van den Berg 1956:82). The revivalists felt personally responsible for the salvation of the lost and believed that those who heard the message were, likewise, individually responsible for accepting the message; the comprehensiveness of the reign of God, which characterized the early Puritan tradition, made way for the idea of the salvation of individual souls (:186). And the same individualism was imposed upon the "objects" of Western mission on the "mission fields". In the course of the nineteenth-century it became ever more powerful and all-pervasive in mission thinking. The individual responsibility of missionaries to proclaim salvation to individuals became the hallmark of nineteenth-century missions. By the end of the century missionaries were pouring in the thousands into Africa and Asia, confident that they had something to offer to the deprived peoples of those continents and convinced that Africans and Asians were eagerly waiting to embrace what they had to offer.

With some justification one could say that the missionary text of the period was Acts 16:9, Paul's vision of the Macedonian man who beseeched him and said, "Come over ... and help us". The first seal of the Puritan colony of Massachusetts depicted an Indian from whose mouth a banner with the words from Acts 16:9 unfolded (Blanke 1966:105; Hutchison 1987:10). The seal of the SPG, founded in 1701, carried the same text in Latin: *Transiens adjuva nos*. By the nineteenth century, as Enklaar has demonstrated in a fine study of the subject (1981:5-15), the man from Macedonia became *the* archetype of non-Christians imploring Christ's messengers to come to their aid. The cover of the program for a Dutch mission festival in 1870 depicted the "Macedonian man" crying out to the missionaries on the opposite shore (:6). Various issues of the monthly of the North German Missionary Society carried a similar illustration (:7). In Holland, in particular, many missionary hymns referred explicitly to the significance of Paul's vision for their own time (for examples, see Enklaar 1981:8-12). A general missions magazine, founded in Holland in 1883, even had as title *De Macedoniër* (:9). The titles of several books and pamphlets likewise alluded to this figure (:12f). The cover illustration for the *Missionary Review of the World* of May 1920 carried the picture of an Asian toddler and the words "Come over into Asia and help us" (Hutchison 1987:11). It is clear, says van den Berg (1956:193f), "that in this period the thought was current that the heathen in their helplessness and poverty were calling upon the benevolent help of the Christian nations".

Evidently, then, a not-so-subtle shift had occurred in the original love motive; compassion and solidarity had been replaced by pity and condescension. In most of the hymns, magazines, and books of the early nineteenth century, heathen life was painted in the darkest colors, as a life of permanent unrest and unhappiness, as life in the shackles of terrible sins. Africa was the "dark" continent; there, as well as in India, on the islands of the Pacific, and elsewhere, lived only savages, cultural and spiritual have-nots, the dregs of humanity, people totally depraved and deprived of the benefits of the "Christian" world, "piteously lost souls in the thrall of the Devil and his ingenious systems" (Hutchison 1987:48), plunged into bodily and spiritual misery.

Small wonder that, particularly in the nineteenth century, the adjective "poor" was increasingly used to qualify the noun "heathen". It appears times without number in the literature of the period (van den Berg 1956:193). The patent needs of the "poor heathen" became one of the strongest arguments in favor of mission. The glory of God as missionary motive had first been superseded by the emphasis on his love. Now there was yet another shift in motivation — from the depth of God's love to the depth of fallen humanity's pitiable state (van den Berg 1956:175; Chaney 1976:225-239). Love had deteriorated into patronizing charity.

This attitude was adopted not only toward non-Christians but also toward members of the younger churches, the "fruit" of the West's missionary labors. Almost imperceptibly the constraining love of Christ (2 Cor 5:14) deteriorated into feelings of spiritual superiority among Western missionaries and an attitude of condescending benevolence to Christians from other cultures. The hearts of many of these became "the scene of a warfare between gratitude, politeness and resentment" (Paton 1953:66). Third-World Christians were regarded as minors, under the tutelage of missionaries from the West. It was only to be expected that the relationship between mission agencies and the leadership of the young churches would, in Kraemer's words, gradually become that of "controlling benefactors to irritated recipients of charity" (1947:426).

In *A Treatise on the Millennium* (1793), Samuel Hopkins still tried to escape a too anthropocentric missionary motivation by introducing the concept of "disinterested benevolence" (van den Berg 1956:101; Hutchison 1987:49-51). In the course of time, however, the "disinterested" was sometimes subtly changed into "condescending". After all, the haves — the *beati possidentes* — were morally obliged to share their spiritual wealth with others; they and they alone were equipped with power from on high and had help to offer to those sitting in darkness and the shadow of death (cf Enklaar 1981:5). The pagans' pitiable state became the dominant motive for mission, not the conviction that they were objects of the love of Christ.

It is clear that, in theory as well as in practice, much of nineteenth- and twentieth-century missionary philanthropy remained below the measure of Paul's being "constrained by Jesus' love". The purity of that motive sullied. Its fountainhead, surely, is to be looked for in the spiritual experience of a personal encounter with the living and present Lord and in a deeply personal understanding of sin and grace; but its on the whole sound origins and genuinely

Christian ingredients were unable, in the long run, to hold out against the spirit of the age.

The Gospel and Culture

The major compromises of the Christian mission across the centuries, says Eugene L. Smith (1968:72f), "have occurred in four relationships: with the state, with culture, with disunity in the church, with money". It is the compromise with culture that will be the theme of this section. This compromise was less pronounced in the eighteenth century than in the nineteenth. It was only after the Second World War that large-scale uneasiness began to manifest itself in this regard.

In the previous section I argued that, during the past few centuries, Christians did not, on the whole, have any doubt concerning the superiority of their own faith over all others. It was therefore, perhaps, to be expected that their feelings of *religious* superiority would spawn beliefs about *cultural* superiority. In itself this is no new phenomenon. The ancient Greeks called other nations *barbaroi*. Romans and members of other great "civilizations" likewise looked down upon others. More often than not, such feelings of superiority were from the powerful and dominant toward the weak and dominated. In the case of Western feelings of preeminence it was no different. There was, however, at least one fundamental difference between Western cultural, military, and political dominance of the Third World and the dominance of Greeks, Romans, etc, over other nations and cultures in the more distant past. In those instances the relationship of dominance was, at least in theory, reversible; the vanquished could, at a given moment, revolt and overpower their former masters, if not militarily, then at least culturally. The point is that, in the final analysis, both groups had at their disposal similar means and weapons and were therefore, in essence, a match for one another. All the great military and cultural empires of the world — the Assyrian, the Persian, the Macedonian, the Roman, the Mongolian, and the Turkish, to mention but a few — succumbed to forces which, in the final analysis, were their equals, since the difference between their means of obtaining and maintaining dominance and the means at the disposal of those dominated by them (again, both military and cultural) were, in the long run, only minimal.

The Enlightenment, however, together with the scientific and technological advances that followed in its wake, put the West at an unparalleled advantage over the rest of the world. Suddenly a limited number of nations had at their disposal "tools" and know-how vastly superior to those of others. The West could thus establish itself as master of all others in virtually every field. It was only logical that this feeling of superiority would also rub off on the "religion of the West", Christianity. As a matter of fact, in most cases there was no attempt to distinguish between religious and cultural supremacy — what applied to the one, applied equally axiomatically to the other. In the early years of its existence, the American Board distinguished between darkness, blindness, superstition, and ignorance among pagan nations, on the one hand, and light, vision, enlightenment, and knowledge in the West on the other (cf Chaney

1976:183). And it is virtually impossible, in this statement, to determine which of these depictions referred to the West's *culture* and which to its *religion*. The one set of characterizations presupposed the other (cf van den Berg 1956:157).

Just as the West's religion was predestined to be spread around the globe, the West's culture was to be victorious over all others. A century and a half ago G.W.F. Hegel argued that world history moved from East to West, from "childhood" in China, via India, Persia, Greece, and Rome to "adulthood" in Western Europe. He concluded, "Europe is the absolute end of history, just as Asia is the beginning" (1975:197). This understanding of the "course of world history" (:124-151) or of the "geographical basis of world history" (:152-196) is argued with complete candor and with a total absence of any fear of contradiction; it should be clear to everybody who has eyes to see. Even so, Hegel attempted to maintain the semblance of fairness, and with great detail surveyed one continent after the other, assessed its culture (or lack of it: "Chile and Peru are narrow coastal territories, and they have no culture of their own" [:157]; "Africa is characterised by concentrated sensuality, immediacy of the will, absolute inflexibility, and an inability to develop" [:215]), and in the light of his "objective" findings established the indisputable and self-evident superiority of the West.

Hegel was, of course, a child of his time (as we are of ours). Scholars of a later era — Christopher Dawson, Arnold Toynbee and others — would voice their prejudices in a more guarded fashion, but would nevertheless give pride of place to Western culture in the scheme of world development. In fact, until fairly recently virtually all Westerners (and, in many cases, non-Westerners) took it for granted that the reshaping of the entire world in the image of the West was a foregone conclusion. It was only marginally different in missionary circles. The famous Laymen's Foreign Missions Enquiry, published in 1932 under the title *Re-Thinking Missions*, had little doubt not only that every nation was en route to one world culture and that this culture would be essentially Western, but also that this was a development all should applaud. Like all other Westerners in the Third World, missionaries were to be conscious propagandists of this culture.

In the early stages of modern missions all this still happened in a rather guileless manner. That the "Christian West" had the "right" to impose its views on others, displayed a "consensus so fundamental that it operated mainly at an unconscious, presuppositional level" (Hutchison 1982:174). In the spirit of John Eliot and Cotton Mather (cf previous chapter), Samuel Worcester, in 1816, described the objectives of the American Board with respect to American Indians as making "the whole tribe English in their language, civilized in their habits, and Christian in their religion" (references in Hutchison 1987:15, 29, 65). Likewise, in 1922 a brochure was published with the title *Le rôle civilisateur des missions*. In similar fashion, Julius Richter, the German historian of missions, writing in 1927, viewed "Protestant missions as an integral part of the cultural expansion of Euro-American peoples" (references in Spindler 1967:25, 26). In virtually each of these cases there was a total absence of even the suggestion that the perceptions of others must or could be consulted; they were simply not taken seriously so that there was a general "unwillingness to grant exotic cultures the kind of hearing automatically expected for Christian and Western values" (Hutchison 1987:113; cf 168f).

Naturally, this was not viewed as an imposition. "It is certainly not by accident that it is the Christian nations which have become the bearers of culture and the leaders of world history", said Gustav Warneck (quoted by Schärer 1944:24 — my translation). It was the gospel which had made the Western nations strong and great; it would do the same for other nations. The missionaries' concern therefore was the uplift of peoples deprived of the privileges they themselves were enjoying. Culturally impoverished peoples would, in this way, be elevated to a higher level (J. Schmidlin, reference in Schärer 1944:9f; cf Spindler 1967:26). The effect of the gospel on a nation was to "soften their manners, purify their social intercourse, and rapidly lead them into the habits of civilized life" (John Abeel in 1801: reference in Chaney 1976:249). In the period following the First World War, one of the most popular missionary texts was the words of Jesus in John 10:10, "I came that they may have life, and have it abundantly", and, says Newbigin (1978:103), " 'abundant life' was interpreted as the abundance of the good things that modern education, healing, and agriculture would provide for the deprived peoples of the world".

Mission writers and speakers, then, had little doubt about the depravity of life in non-Western societies. Some of them, particularly around the transition from the nineteenth century to the twentieth, excelled in portraying the depravity of pagan life from which "Christian civilization" could rescue people. Johannes Warneck, for instance, detailed the elements of unreliability, fear, selfishness, immorality, and this-worldliness in "animistic heathenism" (1908:70-127). It was, however, the American Presbyterian, James Dennis, who, in his three massive volumes on *Christian Missions and Social Progress*, outdid all his contemporaries in his portrayal of the cultural defects of the peoples of Asia and Africa (Dennis 1897, 1899, 1906). The largest part of his first volume (1897:71-401) was devoted to a detailed analysis and enumeration of the "social evils of the non-Christian world". These were neatly arranged according to their effects on seven human categories — the individual, the family, the tribe, the social group, the nation, the commercial group, and the religious group — and included minutiae concerning cultural imperfections such as gambling, immorality, idleness, polygamy, child marriage, human sacrifice, brutalities, witchcraft, cruel customs, lack of public spirit, caste, corruption and bribery, commercial deceit and fraud, idolatry, superstition, and many more. From the inexhaustible treasure house of his vocabulary he hauled ever new depictions of the degrading cultural conditions that prevailed in heathen societies. He culled most of his examples from responses to a circular sent out to missionaries, whom he identified as people who had at their disposal the best knowledge "of the social condition and spiritual history of distant peoples" and whose testimony was "true and unimpeachable" (1897:viii).

It is against this background, and of course also many milder depictions of non-Western life, that one may get an understanding of the benefits which, according to missionary spokespersons, would accrue to those who embrace the

Christian gospel. Dennis is once again the one who wrote most profusely on the subject. The largest part of his second volume (1899:103-486) and all of the third (1906) were devoted to a detailed account of "the contribution of Christian mission to social progress". He used the same seven categories he had used in his first volume; in minute detail he elaborated on the blessings the Christian mission had bestowed upon the non-Western races. And the accomplishments in this regard were indeed impressive. Smith summarizes some of them:

> The missionary movement made a prime contribution to the abolition of slavery; spread better methods of agriculture; established and maintained unnumbered schools; gave medical care to millions; elevated the status of women; created bonds between people of different countries, which war could not sever; trained a significant segment of the leadership of the nations now newly independent (1968:71).

Among American mission advocates, the importance of the improvement in the position of women was always first and foremost (cf Forman 1982:55), usually followed by accounts of advancement in the areas of education and medicine. These achievements could indeed not be denied and have to be applauded. There is, however, also a negative side to this picture. The most seriously negative aspect was perhaps not the inordinate pride many speakers took in these accomplishments (once again Dennis is a prime example), but the almost total absence of any ability to be critical about their own culture or to appreciate foreign cultures.

The problem was that the advocates of mission were blind to their own ethnocentrism. They confused their middle-class ideals and values with the tenets of Christianity. Their views about morality, respectability, order, efficiency, individualism, professionalism, work, and technological progress, having been baptized long before, were without compunction exported to the ends of the earth. They were, therefore, predisposed not to appreciate the cultures of the people to whom they went — the unity of living and learning; the interdependence between individual, community, culture and industry; the profundity of folk wisdom; the proprieties of traditional societies — all these were swept aside by a mentality shaped by the Enlightenment which tended to turn people into objects, reshaping the entire world into the image of the West, separating humans from nature and from one another, and "developing" them according to Western standards and suppositions (cf Sundermeier 1986:72-82).

In this process, "Western theology" was transmitted unchanged to the burgeoning Christian churches in other parts of the world. Certain concessions were made, of course. In Roman Catholic missions the term commonly used in this respect was "accommodation"; Protestants preferred to speak of "indigenization". By and large, however, Catholicism endorsed the principle that a "missionary church" must reflect in every detail the Roman custom of the moment. Protestants were hardly more progressive in this regard, not least because of the Calvinist doctrine of the total depravity of human nature, which Westerners tended to recognize more easily in the peoples of Asia and Africa than in themselves. Still, "indigenization" was official missionary policy in virtually every Protestant mission organization, even if it was usually taken for granted that it was the missionaries, not the members of the young churches, who would determine the limits of indigenization.

In theory, Protestant missions aimed at the establishment of "independent" younger churches. The pervasive attitude of benevolent paternalism, however, often militated against this declared goal. The enthusiastic discussions about "self-governing, self-expanding, and self-supporting churches", so prominent around the middle of the nineteenth century, were, for all practical purposes, shelved by the beginning of the twentieth. The younger churches had, almost unnoticed, been demoted from churches in their own right to mere "agents" of the missionary societies. At the Edinburgh World Missionary Conference (1910), the missionary societies were hailed as "standard-bearers of the churches as they advance with the gospel of Christ for the conquest of the world"; the church in the "mission field", however, was merely an "evangelistic *agency*" or "*instrument*" (references in van 't Hof 1972:39). They were churches, yes, but of a lesser order than those in the West, and they needed benevolent control and guidance, like children not yet come of age.

Part of the difficulty had to do with what Smith (1968:92-97) refers to as a compromise in respect to *money*. This took at least two forms. First, there was the problem that early converts often came from the fringes of society and were the poorest of the poor. So the missionaries had to develop industries in order to make converts economically independent. The Basel Mission excelled in this. Neill (1966a:278) remarks that "Basel Mission tiles and Basel Mission textiles were famous throughout South India". A similar situation obtained in Ghana and elsewhere. There is, of course, a potential dilemma here. In Neill's words, "a mission which becomes a commercial concern may end by ceasing to be a mission". More important, such a policy makes the missionary an employer and the Indian or African Christian an employee, and easily destroys awareness of the fact that they are, first and foremost, sisters and brothers to each other. In 1880 Otto Schott (a Basel Mission director), had to complain that the missionaries controlled the industries even to the smallest detail, that they distrusted the Indians, and that the local Christians had become "slaves and pliable members" of the church who could easily be dismissed from their work (cf Rennstich 1982a:97).

The second difficulty lay in the fact that the churches on the "mission field" were structured on exactly the same lines as those on the missionaries' home front, where a completely different socio-economic system obtained. The results were often disastrous. A study group which visited India in 1920 declared, "We have created conditions and methods of work which can only be maintained by European wealth" (quoted by Gilhuis 1955:60). J. Merle Davis (1947:108) remarked that the "Western Church has made the mistake of girding the Eastern David in Saul's armor and putting Saul's sword into his hands". A report submitted to the Tambaram Conference of the IMC (1938), stated unequivocally:

An enterprise, calling for expensive buildings, western-trained leadership and a duplication of much of the equipment, paraphernalia and supple-

mentary activities that characterise the Church in the West, is beyond the
supporting power of the average Asiatic community.[4]

Many more similar examples could be quoted, but these few should suffice
to make the point that the Western church, because of its benevolent paternalism, had created conditions under which the younger churches just could
not reach maturity, at least not according to Western church standards. Willy-
nilly the Western mission agencies taught their converts to feel helpless without
money.

Surveying the great variety of ways in which Western cultural norms were,
implicitly or explicitly, imposed upon converts in other parts of the world, it is
of some significance to note that both liberals and conservatives shared the
assumption that Christianity was the only basis for a healthy civilization; this
was a form of consensus so fundamental that it operated mainly on an unconscious, presuppositional level (Hutchison 1982:174). On the surface this did not
appear to be essentially different from the early Reformation or Puritan position. However, a decisive shift had occurred since those days. For the Puritans,
culture was subsumed under religion; now, under the sway of the Enlightenment, culture really had become the dominant entity and religion one of its
expressions (cf van den Berg 1956:61). The question now asked by liberal and
conservative alike, and one that was really unthinkable before the Enlightenment, was this: Must one educate and civilize before evangelism can be effective, or should one concentrate on evangelism, confident that civilization will
follow? (cf Hutchison 1987:12).

During the eighteenth and early nineteenth century the question was still
not clearly articulated. William Wilberforce, who spent three decades cam-
paigning for the abolition of slavery in the British Empire, was also keenly
interested in evangelism; both Wilberforce and Carey bracketed together "civilization" and the "spread of the gospel" (cf van den Berg 1956:192). When
the Basel Mission was founded in 1816, it formulated its aim both as proclaiming
the "gospel of peace" and as spreading a "beneficent civilization" (cf Gensichen
1982:185). In that same year, Samuel Worcester described the American
Board's objectives as "civilizing and christianizing" (cf Hutchison 1987:65). By
the latter half of the nineteenth century, however, and even more explicitly in
the twentieth, the lines were more clearly drawn and the problem of priorities
more specifically stated.

On the one side there were those, like John R. Mott, who emphasized
"personal evangelism" as a first priority, but really only as "a means to the
mighty and inspiring object of enthroning Christ in individual life, in family life,
in social life, in national life" (quoted by Hutchison 1982:172). Here, then, the
gospel was viewed primarily as a remedy for the disorders and miseries of the
world. Others pursued a different strategy. To civilize was a *sine qua non* for
spiritual results; the forces of civilization are certainly not themselves evangelizing the world, but they open the way for those that do (for examples, cf
Hutchison 1987:99, 116). A most interesting illustration of this approach is the
policy followed in Namibia by the Rhenish missionary, Hugo Hahn (1818-1895).

Evangelism, he argued, presupposed a certain degree of cultivation of mind and manners. Without this, there is practically no point of contact for the gospel. The conditions for preaching the gospel have to be created first. The missionaries therefore have to introduce a higher culture, which would, in the course of time, facilitate the acceptance of the higher religion—Christianity (for details, see Sundermeier 1962:109-115).

By the end of the nineteenth century the rift between conservative (or fundamentalist) mission advocates on the one hand and liberals (or social gospellers) on the other was becoming ever wider. Still, representatives of both groups could argue that evangelism preceded civilization, while other spokespersons—again of both persuasions—could plead equally convincingly for introducing civilization as a precondition for evangelism. They therefore did not necessarily differ about strategy in this respect, for the simple reason that all of them, whether liberal or conservative, postmillennialist or premillennialist, were committed to the culture of the West, which they propagated equally vigorously. Where they did, however, increasingly differ was about the overall *aim* of mission. Whereas some insisted that the grand object of mission was not to bring pagans into an ordered and cultured society but to bring them to Christ and eternal salvation, others were more concerned about the creation of a gospel-centered *civilization* and the benefits this could bring to all nations than about doctrine and people's eternal destiny (cf Hutchison 1987:99, 107f; Anderson 1988:100).

Looking back upon the intertwinement of the Christian gospel with Western culture, as outlined above, a few qualifications are in order.

First, the gospel always comes to people in cultural robes. There is no such thing as a "pure" gospel, isolated from culture. It was therefore inevitable that Western missionaries would not only introduce "Christ" to Africa and Asia, but also "civilization". Robert Speer put this succinctly in 1910:

We cannot go into the non-Christian world as other than we are or with anything else than that which we have. Even when we have done our best to disentangle the universal truth from the Western form ... we know that we have not done it (quoted in Hutchison 1987:121).

Second, there is no point in denying the fact that the Western missionaries' culture has also had a positive contribution to other societies.

Third, there have always been those who realized, if sometimes only vaguely, that something was wrong somewhere and who did their best not to impose Western cultural patterns on other peoples. A persistent minority of missionaries and mission advocates questioned the right to impose on others one's own cultural forms, "however God-given and glorious" (Hutchison 1987:12). Some also were deeply aware of the West's guilt because of what it had done to other societies, particularly in respect of the horrors of the slave trade, and they attempted to make reparation (cf van den Berg 1956:151f). Still others propagated the creation of self-reliant Christian communities on the "mission field". A prominent advocate of this view was Rufus Anderson, who served as Senior

Secretary of the American Board between 1832 and 1866. The missionary, he said, was first and foremost a planter only; the harvest was up to God. What missions and missionaries had often exported, was *their* idea of the gospel that they had mistakenly associated with the gospel itself. The result of Presbyterian mission work among Syrian students had been "on the whole . . . to make them foreign in their manners, foreign in their habits, foreign in their sympathies". The explicit policy of the mission should therefore not be to control the course of the gospel but to trust the gospel and "let go". The West has no edge on the type of Christianity that should be spread throughout the world (cf Hutchison 1987:80-82).

These arguments in mitigation should carry at least some weight. And yet, when all has been said and done, a dismal picture of (admittedly well-intended) imposition and manipulation remains. Missionary advocates were, on the whole, unaware of the pagan flaws in their own culture. Too often they were on the defensive against those at home who suspected their project, and they lacked self-criticism; they were unable to appreciate the element of validity in a statement such as Herman Melville's concerning the church's programs among American Indians, namely, that "the small remnant of the natives [have] been civilised into draught horses, and evangelised into beasts of burden" (quoted by Hutchison 1987:76). They were unconscious of the inroads the Enlightenment had made into their thinking and of the fact that, because of this, the old unity of "Christianity" and "civilization" had broken asunder.

In addition, as the nineteenth century advanced and the twentieth approached, the missionaries and mission advocates were not sufficiently sensitive to a subtle yet fundamental shift in the mentality of Western nations; that is, its being permeated, slowly but inexorably, by the notion of Western nations' "manifest destiny". To this I now turn.

Mission and Manifest Destiny

The Western missionary enterprise of the period under discussion proceeded not only from the assumption of the superiority of Western culture over all other cultures, but also from the conviction that God, in his providence, had chosen the Western nations, because of their unique qualities, to be the standard-bearers of his cause even to the uttermost ends of the world. This conviction, commonly referred to as the notion of "manifest destiny", was only barely identifiable during the early decades of the nineteenth century but gradually deepened and reached its most pronounced expression during the period 1880-1920. This was also the era known as the "heyday of colonialism" (Neill 1966a: 322-396; Neill actually dates the period as running from 1858 to 1914). There is undoubtedly an organic link between Western colonial expansion and the notion of manifest destiny. Still, it is valid to treat the latter as a separate motif, since it did not always express itself in colonialism (see the next section).

"Manifest destiny" is a product of nationalism which, at least in the form we know it today, is only a recent phenomenon. Although Niccolò Machiavelli may be regarded as perhaps the earliest exponent of nationalism (cf Kohn 1945:127-129), the term "nationalism" was only coined in 1798 (Kamenka

1976:8). Until about 1700, neither nation nor tribe commanded the supreme loyalty and patriotism of Europe's inhabitants (:5). People found their mutual coherence primarily in their religion and their ruler. It was only after the revolution in the Western worldview precipitated by the Renaissance and the Enlightenment that the emphasis could be moved from God or king to the consciousness of a people as an organic entity (Kohn 1945:215-220). The catalytic event in this regard, profoundly permeated with Enlightenment ideas, was the French Revolution, which for the first time asserted the principle of national self-determination as the basis for a new political order (Kohn 1945:3f; Kamenka 1976:7-11, 17f). It substituted for the king and feudal lords the notion of the *people* as the ultimate source of authority. The Revolution's *Declaration of Human Rights* formulated this in the following words, "The principle of sovereignty resides essentially in the Nation: no body of men, no individual, can exercise authority that does not emanate expressly from it". Through the philosophical school of Romanticism, which was as much a reaction to as a consequence of the Enlightenment, these ideas were popularized in Germany and beyond. J. G. Herder submitted that it was particularly through a common language that a nation identified itself and developed its moral and political character. The concept *Volk*, infinitely vaguer and at the same time much more powerful than "citizenship", was utilized by Herder and the Romanticists (Kohn 1945:331-334, 427-441). The nation-state had replaced the holy church and the holy empire.

In the course of time, these ideas were wedded to the Old Testament concept of the chosen people. The result of this was that, at one point or another in recent history, virtually every white nation regarded itself as being chosen for a particular destiny and as having a unique charisma: the Germans, the French, the Russians, the British, the Americans, the Afrikaners, the Dutch. It was only to be expected that the nationalistic spirit would, in due time, be absorbed into missionary ideology, and Christians of a specific nation would develop the conviction that they had an exceptional role to play in the advancement of the kingdom of God through the missionary enterprise.

On the whole such notions were absent among the missionaries of the eighteenth and early nineteenth centuries. Most of the early British missionaries had no high education; they belonged to the "aristocracy of labor" and hailed from lower middle class or working-class stock (cf Warren 1967:36-57). William Carey, it will be remembered, was a cobbler by trade. A similar situation obtained in Germany. That few German missionaries at the time regarded their missionary labor as a service to the German national cause may be deduced from the fact that the very first German missionaries worked in Tranquebar under Danish supervision and that, a century later, some seventy German missionaries served in the (British) CMS. Their spiritual allegiance was to the Halle Pietist tradition, not to Germany (cf Gensichen 1982:181f).

Still, there was evidence, here and there, of impulses toward a naive German national pride even before the 1870s. Karl Graul (1814-1864), founder of the Leipzig Mission Society, became the main protagonist for a policy that emphasized the planting of autochthonous churches, a task for which, so he argued,

Germans were particularly suited (cf Gensichen 1983:258-260). A generation later Gustav Warneck would formulate this view much more explicitly: "It is a special charisma of the Germans to respect foreign nationalities and thus to enter selflessly, without prejudice and with consideration, into the peculiar qualities of other peoples"; and again: "If the missionary is no longer capable of appreciating his own *Volkstum* [peculiar national character], he cannot be expected to appreciate the foreign *Volkstum* which he is supposed to cultivate in his converts" (quoted in Gensichen 1982:188; cf also Moritzen 1982:55f and Gensichen 1985:201f).

Among Anglo-Saxons the notion of "manifest destiny" arose much earlier than among continental Protestants. In this case the notion was at a profound level linked to millennial expectations; the Puritans believed that the Anglo-Saxon race was divinely mandated to guide history to its end and usher in the millennium (cf van den Berg 1956:21; de Jong 1970:77; Hutchison 1987:8; Moorhead 1988:26). In North America the Puritan ethos lasted much longer and in a much more virile form than it did in the mother country, Britain. Since the earliest period statements were echoing and re-echoing that God had sifted a whole people in order that he might choose the best grain for New England (Niebuhr 1959:8). A key word, heard again and again, was "divine providence", which ordained that, of all peoples, it was English Puritans who were sent to cultivate a garden in the wilderness.

After the American colonies had shaken off the British yoke in 1776, these ideas began to be ventilated much more generally and confidently, gradually hardening into the notion of "manifest destiny" (cf Chaney 1976:187, 204, 295). Following, as it did, in the wake of the Revivals, it was only natural that it acquired very clear religious overtones and also that it would soon be wedded to the foreign missionary enterprise. The American Board, founded in 1810, attempted to enlist into the missionary cause not only "Christians" but also those identified as "patriots" (:249). In the early years of the nineteenth century a sense of "American exceptionalism" (Hutchison 1987:39) waxed strongly and even if the "bedrock reality" remained a demand laid upon the *church* rather than upon *Americans*, it was evident to all that *American* Christians were better equipped for the task than were others (:42). In the context of the rising tide of postmillennialism more and more spokespersons became convinced that the millennium would commence in the New World, most probably somewhere in New England (:56f). In 1800 Nathaniel Emmons could muse that God was about "to transfer the empire of the world from Europe to America, where he has planted his peculiar people"; he added, "This is probably the last peculiar people which (God) means to form . . . before the kingdoms of this world are absorbed into the kingdom of Christ" (quoted in Hutchison 1987:61).

It is worth recognizing that, after the first gush of enthusiasm for overseas missions at the beginning of the nineteenth century, interest waned after about 1845 (Chaney 1976:282). For most of the next thirty-five years the focus remained on North America, rather than on the whole world. The Monroe Doctrine of 1823, focusing on hemispheric rather than global hegemony for America, had a powerful influence also in church circles. Vast territories had been annexed in the West and Southwest of the North American continent and five new states added around the middle of the nineteenth century; Christians living on the densely populated Eastern seaboard turned their eyes westward rather than to countries beyond the continent's shores (cf Chaney 1976:281). Interdenominational mission agencies such as the American Board, which were operating outside denominational structures, had a fairly pronounced interest in overseas missions, but denominations tended to concentrate heavily on the continental United States. In 1874 the Missionary Society of the (Northern) Methodist Episcopal Church supported some three thousand missionaries within the borders of the country, but had only 145 overseas missionaries (Anderson 1988:98).

It was only in the late 1870s and particularly after 1885 that missions would be taken to the bosom of ecclesial Protestantism (Chaney 1976:282 [the date 1770 which he mentions should read 1870]; see also Hutchison 1987:43). This was the period of high imperialism, when German, Belgian, British, and French colonial empires expanded dramatically and the churches and mission organizations of those countries showed a correspondingly dramatic increase. The United States was not involved in the scramble for colonies; missions, however, provided Americans with an important "moral equivalent" for imperialism. Americans were inordinately proud of themselves for having avoided colonial entanglement and for being involved, rather, in the "fine spiritual imperialism" of proclaiming Christ's dominion over the nations (cf Hutchison 1982:167-177; 1987:91-124). Was their motivation nationalist, or was it religious? Little debate was conducted on this question, since most contemporaries saw no need for a choice. "Christian obligation and American obligation were fundamentally harmonious" (Hutchison 1987:44; cf Moorhead 1988:25).

As the nineteenth century gave way to the twentieth, the confidence and optimism that marked the American ethos of the period increasingly expressed itself in foreign missionary involvement. "The spirit of the time was expansive, vigorous, and, in one of its favorite words, 'forward-looking'. This was the 'age of energy', a time for great enterprise . . . Foreign missions matched the national mood" (Forman 1982:54). "The impatient generation" (V. Rabe, quoted by Hutchison 1987:91) was hoping for the evangelization of the world in its own time. So, in its heyday (about 1880-1930), the foreign missionary enterprise involved thousands of Americans overseas and millions at home (:1). The missionary efforts prior to 1880 were dwarfed by developments during the next half century. From relatively small numbers before 1880, the American overseas missionary force increased to 2,716 in 1890, to 4,159 in 1900, to 7,219 in 1910, and to over 9,000 in 1915 (Anderson 1988:102). The interest in missions among American students was particularly spectacular. The Student Volunteer Movement (SVM) was formed in 1886; within two years it had recruited almost three thousand students for foreign missions (cf Forman 1982:54; Anderson 1988:99).

Missionary enthusiasm reached a peak with the massive New York Ecumenical Missionary Conference of 1900. It was, by any standard, "the largest missionary conference that has ever been held" (W. R. Hogg, quoted by Anderson 1988:102), with two hundred missionary societies participating and nearly two-hundred thousand people attending the various sessions! In the spirit of the period, it was the most natural thing that political figures would participate in the program. Former president of the United States, Benjamin Harrison, was honorary president of the conference and chaired several sessions. Incumbent president, William McKinley, opened the conference (and spoke of the missionary effort having wrought "such wonderful triumphs for civilization"), and was followed by Theodore Roosevelt, then governor of the state of New York and subsequently president of the United States (cf Forman 1982:54; Anderson 1988:102). In fact, all United States presidents of the early twentieth century, from McKinley to Wilson, spoke in praise of foreign missions, which were seen as a manifestation of "national altruism" (cf Forman 1982:54). These were the terms in which McKinley, in particular, also saw the United States "involvement" in the Philippines (cf Anderson 1988:100f).

There is both continuity and discontinuity between Samuel Hopkins's "disinterested benevolence" and early twentieth-century views of foreign missions as expression of American "national altruism". Both reveal the element of "manifest destiny"; the latter, however, betrays a much clearer consciousness of "sacrifice". "Disinterested benevolence" flowed, to some extent, from the privileged Christian nations' awareness of the *debt* they owed those who still dwelt "in darkness and the shadow of death". In "national altruism" the "white man's debt" had become the "white man's *burden*" – a burden which he gladly carried, but in the hope that this would be widely acknowledged and appreciated. The new mood was not free from paternalism. Forgotten were the pleas of Rufus Anderson and others for allowing younger churches and "new" nations to stand on their own and develop along lines of their own choice. More generally than was the case in the previous century, missionaries from the West viewed peoples of the Third World as inferior to themselves and not really to be trusted with the future of the church.

Looking back upon the entire phenomenon of "manifest destiny" and mission, in North America and elsewhere, one has to beware of facile deductions. Both those who insist (as some mission apologists still do) that the missionary flame's ignition was purely religious, and those who, for whichever reasons, contend that it was merely a matter of national identity or expansiveness, miss the point that, only too often, the religious and the national impulses were fundamentally not separable (cf Hutchison 1987:44f). That the phenomenon we have reviewed here owed its very existence to the spirit of the Enlightenment can, however, not be doubted.

Mission and Colonialism

The "colonial idea" is a very old one and antedates the Christian era (Neill 1966b:11-22). The modern expression of this idea is, however, intimately linked to the global expansion of Western Christian nations. In Chapter 7 of this study attention was given to the intertwinement of colonialism and mission at the dawn of the modern era, particularly as this pertained to Catholicism and the royal patronage granted by the pope to the kings of Portugal and Spain. It was pointed out that the very origin of the term "mission", as we still tend to use it today, presupposes the ambience of the West's colonization of overseas territories and its subjugation of their inhabitants. Therefore, since the sixteenth century, if one said "mission", one in a sense also said "colonialism". Modern missions originated in the context of modern Western colonialism (cf Rütti 1974:301).

During the fifteenth to the seventeenth century both Roman Catholics and Protestants were, admittedly in very different ways, still dedicated to the theocratic ideal of the unity of church and state. No Catholic or Protestant ruler of the period could imagine that, in acquiring overseas possessions, he was advancing only his *political* hegemony: it was taken for granted that the conquered nations would also have to submit to the Western ruler's *religion*. The king missionized as he colonized (Blanke 1966:91). The settlers who, during the sixteenth and seventeenth centuries, arrived in the Americas, the Cape of Good Hope, and elsewhere, were charged not only to subdue the indigenous population, but also to evangelize them (:105).

Already in the seventeenth century a shift was detectable. The theocratic ideal was gradually, and at first certainly unconsciously, pushed back. When the Danes founded their first colony in Tranquebar on the southeastern coast of India, their considerations were primarily *mercantile* (Nørgaard 1988:11). The same applied to the Dutch when they founded a "half-way station" to the Far East at the Cape of Good Hope in 1652—in spite of lip service paid to the Calvinist notion that this territory was also to be evangelized. The various British expeditions to North America, Asia, and elsewhere were prompted by similar interests. The fact that, in most of these cases, it was mercantile companies rather than the governments of the respective European nations which took the initiative in acquiring overseas possessions, already reveals the difference with the earlier Portuguese and Spanish expeditions. The dissimilarity between the two enterprises is further highlighted by the fact that, contrary to the situation that obtained in Catholic colonies, the Dutch, British, and Danish trading companies, at least in the early stages, usually refused to allow any missionaries in the territories under their jurisdiction since they saw them as a threat to their commercial interests (cf Blanke 1966:109).

By and large, then, the colonial expansion of the Western Protestant nations was thoroughly secular. Curiously enough, in the nineteenth century colonial expansion would once again acquire religious overtones and also be intimately linked with mission! There came a time when the authorities enthusiastically welcomed missionaries into their territories. From the point of view of the colonial government the missionaries were indeed ideal allies. They lived among the local people, knew their languages, and understood their customs. Who was better equipped than these missionaries to persuade unwilling "natives" to submit to the *pax Britannica* or the *pax Teutonica*? And, once the authorities had awakened to their "sacred duty" regarding the uplift of the people "entrusted" to them, who could be more reliable educators, health officers, or agricultural instructors than the dedicated missionary force, provided the government granted adequate subsidies? What better agents of its cultural, political, and economic influence could a Western government hope to have than missionaries (cf van den Berg 1956:144; Spindler 1967:23)?

As it became customary for British missionaries to labor in British colonies, French missionaries in French colonies, and German missionaries in German colonies, it was only natural for these missionaries to be regarded as both vanguard and rearguard for the colonial powers (cf Glazik 1979:150). Whether they liked it or not, the missionaries became pioneers of Western imperialistic expansion. As far as Britain (the major colonial power of the modern period) was concerned, it was particularly during the Victorian era that there was a growing consciousness among colonial officials of the value and significance mission work had for the empire.[5] Other colonial powers were equally well aware of the contribution missionaries could make in their overseas territories. German Chancellor von Caprivi stated publicly in 1890, "We should begin by establishing a few stations in the interior, from which both the merchant and the missionary can operate; gun and Bible should go hand in hand" (quoted in Bade 1982:xiii—my translation).

It should therefore come as no surprise that, during the entire "high imperial era" (1880-1920), examples abounded of government spokespersons praising the work of missions or missionaries. Even long after this period such statements can be found. One such place was South Africa which, although not a colonial power in the classical sense of the word, used the same kind of language in its propagation of the policy of "separate development" and also regarded missionaries as government allies in executing its political blueprint. As recently as 1958 a cabinet minister, M.D.C. de W. Nel, could say that "one of the reasons why so many people are still indifferent to mission" was their inability to grasp "the political significance of mission work". Only if and when "we" succeed in incorporating blacks into the Protestant churches, "will the white nation and all other population groups in South Africa have a hope for the future" (1958:7). If this does not happen, "our policy, our program of legislation, and all our plans will be doomed to failure" (:25). Therefore, "every boy and girl who loves South Africa, should commit him- and herself to active mission work, because *mission work is not only God's work, it is also work for the sake of the nation!*" (:8; emphasis in the original); it is "the most wonderful opportunity for serving God, but also the most glorious opportunity for serving the fatherland" (:25—my translation).

If it was understandable for *politicians* to recognize the value of mission work for their colonies, it is less understandable why *missionaries* often gave expression to almost identical views. When the famous French Cardinal Lavigerie (1825-1892) sent out his "White Fathers" to Africa, he reminded them, *"Nous travaillons aussi pour la France"* ("We are working for France [as well as for the kingdom of God]"; cf Neill 1966b:349). And in a volume commemorating two centuries of (British) SPG work (1701-1900), one reads the following statement in the Preface: "It seems fitting at a time when there has been so much rejoicing over the expansion of the Empire, that the spiritual side of the Imperial shield should be presented, showing what has been done towards the building of that Empire 'on the best and surest foundations' " (Pascoe 1901:ix).

In light of such sentiments it should come as no surprise that missionaries sometimes petitioned the government of their home country to extend its protectorate to areas where they, the missionaries, were working, often with the argument that unless this happened, a rival colonial power might annex the territory. This was done, to mention only two of many examples, by Scottish missionaries in Malawi (Walls 1982a:164) and by German missionaries in Namibia (Gründer 1982:68).

In virtually all instances where missionaries became advocates for colonial expansion, they genuinely believed that their own country's rule would be more beneficent than the alternative—either the maintenance of the status quo, or some other form of European power. By and large, then, missionaries tended to welcome the advent of colonial rule since it would be to the advantage of the "natives". Sometimes, however, the modern reader gets the impression that the missionary actually meant that mission served the interests of empire rather than that colonialism served the cause of mission. John Philip, superintendent of the London Missionary Society at the Cape of Good Hope from 1819 onward—in spite of the fact that he went down in history as an indefatigable champion of the oppressed colored peoples of the colony and often clashed with colonial officials about their policies—never doubted the validity and legitimacy of British colonialism and could say astounding things about the services missions might render to the stability of the Cape Colony. He wrote, *inter alia*,

> While our missionaries . . . are everywhere scattering the seeds of civilization, social order, happiness, they are, by the most unexceptionable means, extending British interests, British influence, and the British empire. Wherever the missionary places his standard among a savage tribe, their prejudices against the colonial government give way (1828a: ixf).

And again,

> Missionary stations are the most efficient agents which can be employed to promote the internal strength of our colonies, and the cheapest and best military posts that a wise government can employ to defend its frontier against the predatory incursions of savage tribes (1828b:227).

Statements such as these (and many more could be added—for examples regarding Germany, cf Moritzen 1982:60), reflect the role of what has become known as the "three C's" of colonialism: Christianity, commerce, and civilization (or, in French, the "three M's": *militaires blancs, mercenaires blancs, missionnaires blancs*; cf Spindler 1967:23).

In supporting the colonial enterprise, not everybody would go as far as the Rhenish missionary C. H. Hahn did, who said in 1857, "Even when the Whites subjugate and enslave other peoples, they still offer them so incomparably much that even the harshest fate the enslaved have to endure may often be called a fortuitous turn of events" (quoted in Sundermeier 1962:111—my translation).[6] Most, however, would probably have agreed with Carl Mirbt, who wrote in

1910, "Mission and colonialism belong together, and we have reason to hope that something positive will develop for our colonies from this alliance" (quoted in Rosenkranz 1977:226 — my translation). With reference to the statement, "To colonize is to missionize" (by the German Colonial Secretary, Dr W. H. Solf), the Catholic missiologist, J. Schmidlin, wrote in 1913:

> It is the mission that subdues our colonies spiritually and assimilates them inwardly ... The state may indeed incorporate the protectorates outwardly; it is, however, the mission which must assist in securing the deeper aim of colonial policy, the inner colonization. The state can enforce physical obedience with the aid of punishment and laws; but it is the mission which secures the inward servility and devotion of the natives. We may therefore turn Dr Solf's ... recent statement that "to colonize is to missionize" into "to missionize is to colonize" (quoted in Bade 1982:xiii — my translation).

Blanke (1966:126) quotes Ernst Langhans as referring to the involvement of the mission agencies with the colonial enterprise as their "indirect guilt". But, Langhans added, there was also a "direct guilt": they witnessed the atrocities committed by the colonial authorities but remained silent about them. They did not comprehend that, in their attempts at playing the mediator between colonial government and local population, they were — simply by accepting the presence of the colonial lords as incontrovertible reality — actually serving the interests of the colonizers. The best they could do in the circumstances was meekly to plead with the governments to be more careful in the selection of colonial officials and to choose "practical, moral men" who would know how to treat the indigenous population "mildly and with appreciation for the people's peculiar characteristics" (references in Engel 1982:151). Few mission advocates, however, fundamentally challenged the attitude prevalent among Western Christians of the period, namely, where their power went there was the place to send their missionaries, or the corollary, where they have sent their missionaries there their power should also go — if only because it would offer protection to their missionaries.

It may be helpful, at this juncture, to dwell for a moment on the similarities and differences between mission and colonialism in British colonies and the same phenomena in German colonies.

It is important to reiterate that, on the whole, the *British* colonial venture, which goes back to the early seventeenth century, started primarily for trading purposes. It is only in the course of time that imperialist motives began to enter into the picture. There is therefore some truth in J. R. Sealey's saying that the British Empire was acquired in fits of absentmindedness. The Napoleonic wars and Britain's gaining the naval ascendancy over the world seas certainly had something to do with this. And once started on this course, there was almost no way of stopping the process of acquiring ever more territories. Commerce remained the primary purpose for a long time, however, and during this period missionaries were not welcomed. The fact that Christian spokespersons such as

William Pitt, Edmund Burke, William Wilberforce, and William Carey voiced stringent criticisms of the policies of the overseas trading companies made missionaries even less acceptable in those territories (cf van den Berg 1956: 107f).

By the second decade of the nineteenth century things began to change. In 1813 Parliament opened the door for "the introduction of useful knowledge, and religious and moral improvement" in India (and subsequently also in other colonies). This was, in effect, the beginning of what later became known as "benevolent colonialism", which meant that the colonial power consciously took responsibility for the welfare of the inhabitants of its colonies. It also meant that missionaries were henceforth allowed to operate more or less freely.

At first the newly arrived missionaries, most of whom hailed from the evangelical wing, tried to keep their distance from the colonial authorities. The LMS in the Cape Colony and particularly the ministry of John Philip are a case in point (cf Philip 1828a:253-359; 1828b:23-77; Ross 1986). In the course of the nineteenth century, however, the situation changed fundamentally; evangelicalism became a respected power in a state that tried to regain its religious aspect (van den Berg 1956:146). In practice this meant that evangelicals (and evangelical missionaries), as they got to be more respected, also became increasingly compromised to the colonial system.

With the advent of the high imperial era, after 1880, there could no longer be any doubt about the complicity of mission agencies in the colonial venture. Parallels between the high imperial and the high missionary developments became more and more obvious. The period also saw a phenomenal increase in missionary recruitment. During the first ninety years of its existence, 1799-1879, the CMS had sent out 991 missionaries; in the next twenty-six years it sent out 1,478. Similar developments took place in other societies. And several new mission agencies were founded. It would be wrong, however, simply to attribute the rise in missionary recruitment to an increased commitment to the cause of the empire. Many other factors, not least the revival movements of 1859-1860, also played a role. But these tended to dovetail with and feed on the new awareness of being sent to remake the world in the image of Britain. Also, a new kind of missionary now arrived on the scene. The universities, Cambridge above all, produced vast numbers of missionary volunteers — university-educated "gentlemen" who began to replace the previous generation of missionaries from humble backgrounds. Hundreds of women also volunteered for mission work (Walls 1982a:159-162).

The new missionary force, conscious of its assets and imbued with the desire to save the world, as a matter of course took charge wherever it went. A generation earlier, when Henry Venn propagated self-supporting, self-governing, and self-propagating churches (the so-called three selfs), there had simply not been enough missionaries available. Now there were many eager young missionaries with very clear ideas about what was best for the "young" churches, and although the three-selfs policy was never formally abandoned, it was simply forgotten. It is not unlikely that this development went hand in hand with a lower esteem of "native" talents and capabilities than had been evident in the mid-nineteenth century and earlier. There were more traces of racism in the high imperial era than there had been before (cf Walls 1982a:162-164). It was, *par excellence*, the age of the "white man's burden"; colonial officials and missionaries alike gladly but consciously took it upon themselves to be the guardians of the less-developed races. The peoples of Africa and Asia were wards dependent upon the wise guidance of their white patrons who would gradually educate them to maturity (cf Warren 1965:50-52).

In *Germany* the intertwinement between mission and colonialism evolved differently. There were basic dissimilarities between British and German nationalism. The former always put a great emphasis upon the individual and upon the human community as transcending all national divisions (Kohn 1945:178). German nationalism, by contrast, had as one of its main foundations J. G. Herder's *Volk* concept (although Herder himself remained deeply steeped in the idea of a universal civilization), which was then fecundated by two other movements: the Enlightenment and Prussianism (:354-363). Within the ambience of German nationalism, particularly as it began to reveal itself after the German Empire was created in 1871, there was much less room for the independent individual than was the case in British (or American) nationalism. This factor would also influence the relationship between German colonialism and mission.

Furthermore, German colonialism is considerably younger than its British counterpart. It only became a reality in 1885 and lasted merely three decades. It was not something which started on a small scale and gradually matured. Rather, it exploded onto the scene within the short spell of a few years and disappeared as suddenly in the conflagration of the First World War.

The entire period of German Protestant missions until shortly before the 1880s may, with reference to the issue of "mission and colonialism", be called a period of innocence. Mission, steeped in the Pietist tradition, was the hobby of rather simple and unsophisticated people on the margins of the established church; the rank-and-file church membership had difficulty in grasping "what had persuaded these peculiarly enthusiastic children of God to concern themselves with the salvation of the souls of pagans" (Gensichen 1983:258 — my translation). Any link between "colonialism and mission" was outside of their purview. Even as late as 1875 T. Christlieb could still state categorically, "We are no world-conquering nation and do not wish to become one. We have no colonies and do not wish to have any" (quoted in Moritzen 1982:55 — my translation).

This pristine innocence would, however, disappear almost completely after the Berlin Conference of 1884, when Germany joined the scramble for colonies. If we have to single out one person who contributed most to the German colonial idea, that person, by common consent, would have to be Friedrich Fabri (1824-1891), since 1857 director of the Rhenish Mission Society, a person who with good reason may be called the "father of the German colonial movement" (Gründer 1985:34). In 1879 he published a brochure entitled *Bedarf Deutschland der Kolonien?* ("Does Germany Need Colonies?"). It caused quite a stir, not least since Bismarck, at that stage, opposed the idea of Germany entering the race for overseas colonies. Fabri, however, was determined and propagated his ideas widely. Colonies would solve many of Germany's financial and social ills; since Germany was experiencing unusual population pressure at the time, Fabri pleaded for the founding of colonies where the country's surplus population could settle. In addition, German colonial rule would offer protection to German missionaries. In Namibia, in particular, missionaries were exposed to many dangers, because of the unsettled political conditions. From June of 1880 Fabri campaigned forcefully for the annexation of the territory, until he succeeded in persuading the authorities to implement his plans (cf Gründer 1982:69; Bade 1982:109). At the Continental Missionary Conference held in Bremen in 1884, Fabri spoke on "The Significance of Orderly Political Circumstances for the Development of Mission". In that same year he was forced to resign as director of the Rhenish Mission; his complicity with German colonial expansion had become an embarrassment. The remaining years of his life he dedicated virtually exclusively to the colonial cause (Bade 1982:136).

The German colonial empire consisted of German Southwest Africa (Namibia), Togo, the Cameroon, German East Africa, some islands in the Pacific Ocean, and Kiao-Chao in China (Gründer 1985:111-211). In all of these areas German missions, Protestant or Catholic, played a prominent role, often with appeal to the slogan "Only German missionaries for German colonies!" (cf Moritzen 1982:56; Gensichen 1985:195). The German charisma for mission was now widely taken for granted and used as argument in favor of explicitly sending *German* missionaries to these territories. Only in this way would "proper" results be guaranteed. The thesis of the Bavarian pastor Ittamaier — "We must rear German Christians in Cameroon" — found widespread acceptance. In addition, twelve new German mission societies were formed in the colonial period, most with the explicit purpose of working in German colonies (Moritzen 1982:62; Gründer 1982:68). The most notorious of these was a society formed for East Africa, immediately after Germany acquired Tanganyika as a colony. Carl Peters, the moving force behind the new venture, wished mission to understand itself as "German work" which should serve both "church and fatherland". It must become "mission in a national-German sense" and help to educate the colony's "Negro material" into an efficient work force (references in Gensichen 1985:196).

The barely camouflaged racism in the views of Peters just referred to was, of course, not confined to German missionaries and mission advocates. Far from it. So, if I take most of my examples from German missions history I am not suggesting that Germans were more inclined to racism than missionaries from other countries. My reason is, rather, that, after the horror of the Second World War, German mission scholars have perhaps done more than others to expose racist attitudes in their past.

It may be of interest to refer, in this respect, to the attempts of the Hermannsburg Mission in Natal and Transvaal (and, to a lesser extent, of the Rhenish Mission in Namibia) at founding "mission colonies" according to the model of early medieval monastic missions in Europe. Ludwig Harms, founder of the Hermannsburg Mission, believed that a missionary community should be sent out and new converts incorporated into it (Sundermeier 1962:103-107). Harms's attitude witnesses to a profound confidence in and concern for the mission's future African converts. He had no doubt that only *one* Lutheran church would be established in each territory and that whites and blacks alike would be members. He passionately defended the blacks against the treatment meted out to them by, among others, the white (Afrikaner) settlers, whom he called "a wild and fierce people who have permitted themselves every possible injustice and violence against the poor pagans" (quoted in Hasselhorn 1988:33 — my translation). He admonished his missionaries in no uncertain terms about the attitude required of them: "I do not believe", he said, "that you will convert pagans if you go to them as lords and gentlemen, but only if you go as faithful teachers and have a deep concern for them" (:36).

Harms's "experiment" foundered, however. Instead of only *one* Lutheran church, two different congregations developed around each mission station, one white, one black. This is not the place to investigate the merit of Harms's project as such or to pursue the question whether something that worked well in Europe in the early Middle Ages could succeed in the totally different circumstances of a European mission venture in nineteenth-century Africa. All I would like to highlight is the fact that Harms and others like him in German church and missionary circles of the mid-nineteenth century had been so free of racist ideas that they could conceive a project like this. Within a very few decades, with the advent of the high imperialist era, no Western missionary serving in Africa would even have dreamt of such a scheme. "Manifest destiny" and colonial domination activated the missionaries' latent racism and made them extremely skeptical of the aptitudes of blacks. The missionaries who went to South Africa after 1884 "were brought up in the consciousness of the superiority of the white race in general and the German people in particular" (Hasselhorn 1988:139 — my translation). Since blacks were the "descendants of the accursed Ham", equality with them was out of the question.[7]

The picture drawn in the preceding pages is a bleak one. It is a portrait of the Western missionary enterprise's compromise with and complicity in imperialism and colonial expansion. It is, however, not the whole picture, and it is simply inadequate to contend that mission was nothing other than the spiritual side of imperialism and always the faithful servant of the latter. Reality was more ambivalent. In addition, it is easy, and therefore cheap, to counsel, theorize, and dogmatize from a safe distance about what went wrong and how mission agencies and missionaries should have behaved. So let us remember, to use John Higham's distinction (quoted by Hutchison 1987:14), that retrospective criticism is in order but retrospective judging probably is not.

Such an attitude is in order also in view of the fact that, throughout the history of mission, there has always been a persistent minority which, admittedly within limits, withstood the political imposition of the West on the rest of the world. Within the crucible of Latin America's colonial history the name of Bartolomé de Las Casas will always be a shining example of a missionary who was, until the bitter end, a champion of the oppressed. Protestant missionary history tells us of comparable examples. Some of these are totally forgotten;

others are known in various degrees. I have already mentioned the tensions the first two Danish-Halle missionaries, Ziegenbalg and Plütschau, experienced with the colonial authorities in Tranquebar from the moment of their arrival there in 1706 (cf Nørgaard 1988:17-52). And South African history informs us about the selfless service of the first LMS missionary, J.Th. van der Kemp (1747-1811) (cf Enklaar 1988:110-189), of the indefatigable labors of John Philip (1775-1851) on behalf of the autochthonous population (cf Ross 1986:77-228), and of many others, such as J. W. Colenso.

Individuals like these, and the agencies in which service they stood, were often the only ones to intervene on behalf of the indigenous people in a given colonial situation. To quote a French governor of Madagascar again: "What we want, is to prepare the indigenous population for manual labor; you turn them into *people*" (cf Spindler 1967:24f). The missionaries did this in many ways. They became friends of the local people, they visited them in their homes. They proclaimed to them that God loved them so much that he sent his only Son for their salvation. They convinced them that, in spite of the way they were being treated by other whites, they had infinite worth in the eyes of the Almighty. They demonstrated this by going out of their way to heal their sick and by offering education to both their boys and their girls. They studied the local languages and in this way proved that they respected the speakers of those languages. In summary, they empowered people who had been weakened and marginalized by the imposition of an alien system.

Even during the high imperial era (and particularly in its early stages), some missionaries and mission societies were very skeptical about an alliance between nation and mission. After Fabri left the Rhenish Mission and on the eve of the commencement of Germany's colonial empire, the Home Board issued an instruction to all its missionaries in Namibia; this document (as quoted by Gensichen 1982:183) stated, "Nowhere has a European colony come into being without grave injustice. Portuguese and Spaniards, Dutchmen and Britishers have been more or less alike in this respect. The Germans will hardly be any better."

A year later, at the Continental Missionary Conference in Bremen, many delegates dissociated themselves from Fabri's paper, "The Significance for Mission of Orderly Political Circumstances" (Moritzen 1982:56). A. Reichel argued that mission was incompatible with colonialism. J. Hesse, reporting on the conference, wrote, "Mission and colonialism are as far apart from one another as *heaven* and *earth*" (quoted in Rennstich 1982a:99). After the Herero Rebellion of 1904 in Namibia, when the German press accused the missionaries of collusion with the Africans and portrayed the latter as beasts, demons, and vermin, the Rhenish Mission took the side of the Africans and mentioned the causes of the rebellion by name: the colonial system, which was inherently exploitative; and the business practices by which blacks were defrauded. The mission agency insisted that, in their own country, blacks should be entitled to more that just being "labor slaves deprived of rights and unpropertied proletarians" (Engel 1982:151-152—my translation).

At one stage or another virtually every mission agency made comparable statements. Of American missionary involvement in the Philippines, Charles Forman says, "Once American rule had been established, missionaries spent more time challenging the government to adhere to the high purposes that they had assigned to it than they did in praising its accomplishments" (1982:55). It is therefore simply not true, as Ernst Langhans claimed in 1864, that "Protestant missions have launched no protest against the rapaciousness of the colonial powers and have remained silent in the face of the malevolence perpetrated by the conquerors" (quoted in Blanke 1966:136 — my translation).

The considerations above are submitted not so as to exculpate the missionaries completely. The problem was that, even where they launched stringent criticisms against the colonial administration, they never really doubted the legitimacy of colonialism; they assumed, virtually without question, that colonialism was an inexorable force and that all they were required to do was somehow to try to tame it (cf Neill 1966b:413-415; Hutchison 1987:92). In the early stages, when the missionary idea had caught the imagination only of those on the periphery of the churches and the men and women who went to the ends of the earth to proclaim the gospel were regarded as freaks, it was still different. However, when the missionary idea was adopted by the establishment and mission agencies became respected organizations in Western society, the situation changed and the road of compromise could hardly be resisted. Willy-nilly, missions became bearers and advocates of Western imperialism, the "hounds of imperialism", set on or whistled back as it pleased "Caesar" (Engel 1982:151; Bade 1982:xiii). So, even where a mission agency criticized the authorities, it would immediately proceed to reavow its own and its missionaries' patriotic loyalty (cf Engel 1982:152). The mission agencies and the missionaries were simply not able to see reality in any other way — not until the friendly "protective umbrella" of colonialism had been abruptly withdrawn from them.

We have to probe deeper still, however. The issue is more serious than just that of the demonstrable collusion of mission with the colonial powers. If we were to define it merely in these terms we might easily be persuaded to believe that the colonialist traits of Western mission belonged only to a particular historical period, that they were merely exterior and could easily be discarded again (cf Rütti 1974:301). We would then be tempted to treat the issue too narrowly as simply a matter of the relation of mission to colonialism and overlook the fact that this relationship is but an integral part of the much wider and much more serious project of the advance of Western technological civilization. Furthermore, such a narrowness of perspective may fail to do justice to the implications of neocolonialism, which is only a continuing and more subtle form of Western dominance (cf Knapp 1977:153f). We would miss the point that, with the Enlightenment, a fundamentally new element had entered into the issue of relations between people. Whereas in earlier centuries the essential factor that divided people was *religious*, people were now divided according to the levels of *civilization* (as interpreted by the West). This led to the next criterion of division — *ethnicity* or *race* — now interpreted as the matrix out of which civilization (or the lack of it) was born. The "civilized", however, not only felt superior to the "uncivilized", but also responsible for them. In the words of D. Schellong, "Since the Enlightenment, 'good' means to know what is 'good' for *others*, and to impose it on them" (quoted by Sundermeier 1986:64 – my translation). This was also true of Western missionary "expansion". The fact that missionaries were sent not to educate and guide others but to be in their midst in a spirit of true self-surrender tended to take a back seat. A "potent blend of Providence, piety, politics, and patriotism" (Anderson 1988:100) made it hard for the missionary enterprise to be what it was called to be.

Mission and the Millennium

During the past three or more centuries Protestant missions have always revealed strong millenarian elements. It remains notoriously difficult, however, to define precisely what is meant by millennialism. Some scholars appear to use the term as a synonym for "eschatology" or "apocalypticism", and of course it cannot be divorced from these concepts. Still, it is different from either. James Moorhead suggests the following minimum definition: millennialism, he says, refers to "the biblical vision of a final golden age within history" (1988:30). This is the definition I shall also use.

The Latin term *millennium* derives from the reference in Revelation 20 to a thousand years reign of Christ. This passage has intrigued Christians since the earliest centuries of the Christian era. It became particularly prominent during the Reformation period, when various "sectarian" elements seized upon it and attempted to inaugurate Christ's reign on earth. Although the mainline Reformation reacted negatively to what it regarded as extremist manifestations of eschatological hope, Reformers such as Luther and Calvin were themselves not free from millenarian tendencies. Calvin, in particular, was looking forward to the third and final stage of history, during which the church would expand greatly (cf Chaney 1976:32f).

When the Puritans left for the New World, they took Calvin's tri-epochal scheme (see previous chapter) with them. In the course of time, and especially after the Great Awakening, millennial expectations became the common property of virtually all American Protestants. It is difficult to pinpoint precisely what they entailed. The language of Revelation 20, being "simultaneously canonical and obscure" (Moorhead 1988:28), allows for a great variety of interpretations. Still, some common features began to emerge. One of these was a much greater optimism and confidence about the ultimate success of God's cause than had been in evidence in Calvin's theology. The Puritans were in no doubt that they were well into Calvin's third epoch and on the verge of extending Christ's kingdom to the ends of the earth. It therefore became quite respectable to venture some calculations about the date of the commencement of the millennium. Samuel Hopkins, in his *Treatise on the Millennium* (published 1793 – it was one of the first American works to focus sustained attention on the theme), wrote that the golden age would probably not begin until another seventy years or perhaps even two centuries had elapsed (cf Moorhead 1988:23). Hopkins wrote during the period of the Napoleonic wars and the general social and political upheaval in Europe; these events certainly spawned high-strung apocalyptic expectations.

In spite of the burgeoning spirit of certainty about the almost imminent arrival of the millennium, all agreed that there were certain preconditions to be met. These included, since the earliest days of the Puritans, such elements as the conversion of the Jews and the "fullness of the Gentiles" being brought into the church (cf Chaney 1976:271-274). There were, at most, some minor differences about the question which should come first, the conversion of the Jews, or the great ingathering of the Gentiles (:38).

From the beginning there was an intimate correlation between mission and millennial expectations. It was, after all, only through the church's global missionary effort that the knowledge of Christ could be universally established. Originally, the vision was limited to North America; the Puritans were sent to cultivate a garden in a howling wilderness, not to move beyond the wilderness. However, as soon as it seemed that this goal was being achieved, the horizon was extended. Errand to the wilderness became "errand to the world" (cf the title of Hutchison 1987). The vision comprehended the whole of the human race. The objective was to reclaim all the nations of the world for Christ; only the renovation of the whole world corresponded to the designs of divine redemption (Chaney 1976:241). By 1820 the "missionary endeavor had become the most celebrated cause of the American churches" (:256). Every prayer for revival or for the kingdom assumed, in this period, an immediate missionary dimension (cf de Jong 1970:157). Already in 1813 the American Board stated that, whereas other times "have been times of preparation, the present age is emphatically the age of action. Shall we remain idle in this harvest time of the world?" (reference in Chaney 1976:257). God was about to bring his work of redemption to its glorious consummation. The prophecy of Revelation 14 was being fulfilled before the eyes of the faithful; the angel preaching the everlasting gospel to the whole earth had begun to fly (:271). The missionary movement became impatient; its word was "now". Christ's reign was not just a wish, a dream, a plan, an ideal. It was on the verge of being inaugurated – through the church's far-flung missionary efforts (cf Niebuhr 1959:26, 46). In a remarkable way millennial convictions were not just a *summons* to conversion activity; mission work itself became a sure *sign* of the dawn of the millennium (van den Berg 1956:161; Hutchison 1987:38).

America's role (even more particularly, New England's role) in the unfolding drama was reasonably clear. It should therefore come as no surprise if the millennium is pictured in terms of the consummation of traits already in evidence in the Massachusetts commonwealth. This was the case particularly in Hopkins's *Treatise on the Millennium* which, in the minutest details, delineated the characteristics of the coming golden age. It would be a time of "the greatest temporal prosperity", when people would have "sufficient leisure to pursue and acquire learning of every kind". Universal peace and happiness would reign, not least because there would be "great improvement in the mechanical arts" through which people would be enabled to produce utensils "with much less labor" than they used now. Because of people's "benevolence and fervent charity", all worldly things would be abundantly available to all (cf Niebuhr 1959:145f).

In this vision the reign of God had been transformed into the extension of American institutions to all the world; it would come about through a democratic revolution, the culmination of tendencies already established (Niebuhr 1959:183). It goes without saying that, in this paradigm, the millennium would not irrupt through a cataclysmic event. It would wax *gradually* and would be inaugurated through the church's ordinary missionary labors — a perfection and extension of trends already underway in history (cf van den Berg 1956:121, 162, 183; de Jong 1970:225; Chaney 1976:270, 272; Moorhead 1988:30).

Until the early nineteenth century there was a spirit of cooperation among denominations and no clear dividing line between pre- and postmillennialists. The accent fell, rather, on the responsibility of all believers in the present and on united action. After 1830, however, the united evangelical front disintegrated. A fierce spirit of competition arose among the various Protestant denominations in North America. Differences rather than similarities were emphasized during the new "era of controversy". As it became necessary, more and more, to be explicit about what one believed, the latent divergences between pre- and postmillennialists (the terms were not coined until the 1840s) began to surface.

These differences manifested themselves not only in the realm of eschatology, but across the entire spectrum, particularly in the area of the relationship between "soteriology" and "humanization". Henceforth some would put the major emphasis on "service to the body" and on the gradual improvement of society toward the dawn of the millennium, whilst others would lay stress on "service to the soul" and the gradual deterioration of the world until Christ would return to usher in the millennium. These two schools of thought have impregnated Protestant missionary thinking ever since. Both of them, in more or less opposite ways, give evidence to the church's inability to respond appropriately to the challenge presented by the Enlightenment.

Premillennialism. I turn, first, to the group broadly identifiable as *premillennialist* and its significance for the development of the missionary idea in the nineteenth and early twentieth centuries. This is by no means a homogeneous category and among at least some of them the element of premillennialism was only weakly accentuated. All of them, however, in varying degrees, began to dissociate themselves from the postmillennialism which dominated the American scene until the middle of the century, and even much more from the later Social Gospel.

The premillennialist movement sprang from "complex and tangled roots in the nineteenth-century traditions of revivalism, evangelicalism, pietism, Americanism, and variant orthodoxies" (Marsden 1980:201). It spawned a variety of subspecies: adventism, the holiness movement, pentecostalism, fundamentalism, and conservative evangelicalism. All of these, without exception, have become astonishingly active in missionary projects worldwide. And although they may sometimes differ significantly from each other, they also share a variety of common characteristics. I shall identify some of these, particularly insofar as they will help us to appreciate the movement's contribution to the understanding of mission and also illuminate the indebtedness of the movement —

certainly contrary to its own intentions—to the Enlightenment. Naturally, not all of these characteristics are found to the same degree in each of the subspecies.

As far as hermeneutics was concerned, the new movement adhered to two positions which, even if its advocates did not realize it, were in essence irreconcilable. The first was the principle, classically formulated at the launching of the (British) Evangelical Alliance in 1846, of "the right and duty of *private judgment* in the interpretation of Holy Scriptures" (emphasis added). This principle was an expression of the "modern" desire not to be told by ecclesial bodies what to believe, but for each believer to come to a personal understanding of faith and a personal commitment. Such a conviction, however, could not but stand in tension with another, namely, the doctrine of biblical inerrancy—of the Bible as "a repertory of facts, a revelation of doctrines, and a standard of appeal upon all questions to which it bears any relation" (R. G. Ingersoll, quoted in Hopkins 1940:15), as containing propositional truths which can be determined by anyone who looks at it "with impartiality" (cf Marsden 1980:112-115; cf Johnston 1978:50), and as being literally true in what it affirms. In each subgroup there was a set of non-negotiable dogmas used as shibboleths to demarcate the borders between themselves and others, and for each of these a direct appeal was made to Scripture.

A common theme in premillennialist circles was the *return of Christ*. This idea was, of course, also operative among postmillennialists, but they tended to put more emphasis on what still had to be done before Christ came. Since the 1830s, however, more and more people began to talk about the *imminence* of the parousia. William Miller (1782-1849) confidently predicted Christ's return and the beginning of the millennium for 1843 or 1844. Within a short period up to 100,000 people joined the Millerite movement. When Miller's prophecies did not come true, the movement experienced a crisis but subsequently grew significantly; today it is a worldwide fellowship known as Seventh-Day Adventism.

Also outside of Adventist circles one encounters a strong emphasis on the return of Christ, particularly as a motive for mission. Both Karl Gützlaff (1803-1851), a German missionary to China, and J. Hudson Taylor (1832-1905), founder of the China Inland Mission, were motivated by eschatological expectations. Taylor, in particular, campaigned for the evangelization of China's millions in great haste, before Christ returned. During the second half of the nineteenth century several missionary leaders and the mission organizations they founded (such as Grattan Guinness, Regions Beyond Missionary Union; A. B. Simpson, Christian and Missionary Alliance; and Fredrik Franson, The Evangelical Alliance Mission) began to use Matthew 24:14 as the major "missionary text". Christ's return was now understood as being dependent upon the successful completion of the missionary task; the preaching of the gospel was "a condition to be fulfilled before the end comes" (Capp 1987:113; cf Pocock 1988:441-444). This meant, by implication, that the "coming of the day of the Lord" could also be *hastened* (cf 2 Pet 3:12) through a concerted missionary effort. A. T. Pierson estimated the number of pennies and the number of right-hearted evangelists required to bring the millennium (cf Hutchison 1987:164). And if all tried hard, this goal could be reached before the dawn of the twentieth century (Johnson 1988 has traced the influence of Pierson on the development of the idea of the evangelization of the world before the year 1900). Here, the preaching of the message about God's future reign had become a prerequisite for its coming. Views like these persist to this day in some evangelical circles. The goal of "biblical evangelism", says Johnston (1978:52), echoing a sentiment expressed by A. B. Simpson almost a century ago (cf Hutchison 1987:118), is to "bring back the King" (cf also Capp 1987 and Pocock 1988).

Premillennialists tended to have an even more *melancholy view of non-Christians* than had prevailed among their predecessors; sometimes this view was applied even to those who professed to be Christians but clearly had a different understanding of the gospel. All reality was, in essentially Manichean categories, divided into neat antitheses: good and evil, the saved and the lost, the true and the false (cf Marsden 1980:211). "In this dichotomized worldview, ambiguity was rare" (:225). Conversion was a crisis experience, a transfer from absolute darkness to absolute light. The millions on their way to perdition should therefore be snatched from the jaws of hell as soon as possible. Missionary motivation shifted gradually from emphasizing the depth of God's love to concentrating on the imminence and horror of divine judgment.

In this whole approach it was the *individual's* choices that were decisive. The church was no longer regarded primarily as a body but was made up of free individuals who had freely chosen to join this specific denomination (cf Marsden 1980:224). Dwight L. Moody (1837-1899), the principal North American evangelist of the last quarter of the nineteenth century, rose to fame in the heyday of individualism and his thought was pervaded by its assumptions. He preached a message that viewed the sinner as standing alone before God. Also, the Holy Spirit was understood as working only in the hearts of individuals and was known primarily through personal experience (:37, 88).

Moreover, the response to Moody's preaching of the "message of salvation" was essentially a decision each person was able to make. A typical exhortation of Moody was, "Whatever the sin is, make up your mind that you will gain victory over it" (quoted in Marsden 1980:37). In this he adopted John Wesley's Arminianism (which in any case, in the democratic America of his time, was beginning to replace the inherited Calvinism), as well as Wesley's concept of sin as a "voluntary act of the will"; in the process, however, Moody distorted both to something essentially different from what Wesley, in a very different era, meant by them (cf Marsden 1980:73f).

This revealed yet another feature of the period and a typical element of Moody's "theology": *pragmatism.* Moody often tested doctrines for their suitability to evangelism and judged his own sermons by whether they were "fit to convert sinners with". This self-test kept his message simple and positive. The "three R's" adequately summarized his central doctrines: "ruin by sin, redemption by Christ, and regeneration by the Holy Ghost" (for references, cf Marsden 1980:35). His pragmatism made him averse to any doctrinal controversy. As an example of this he suggested, shortly before his death, "Couldn't they [the critics] agree to a truce, and for ten years bring out no fresh views, just to let us get on with the practical work of the kingdom?" (:33).

It was, in part, his dislike of controversy that made Moody concentrate on *personal* rather than *structural* sins in his evangelistic sermons. He stressed sins involving only the victims themselves and members of their families: the theater and other "worldly amusements" such as dancing, disregard of the Sabbath, Sunday newspapers, Free Masonry, drunkenness, the use of "narcotic poisons" (mainly tobacco), divorce, the "lusts of the body", and the like. All these together made up a rather stereotyped set of notorious vices, thoroughly familiar to revivalist audiences (cf Marsden 1980:31-37, 66).

Thus, as revivalism and evangelicalism slowly adopted premillennialism the emphasis shifted away from social involvement to exclusively *verbal* evangelism. In the course of time virtually "all progressive social concern, whether political or private, became suspect among revivalist evangelicals and was relegated to a very minor role" (Marsden 1980:86; cf 120). By the 1920s "the Great Reversal" (as Timothy Smith calls it) had been completed; the evangelicals' interest in social concerns had, for all practical purposes, been obliterated. This attitude was already in evidence in Moody's ministry (:36f).

Moody and others were, nevertheless, sure that evangelism had definite social *consequences*. Unwittingly these revivalists bought into the Enlightenment model of cause and effect; once people were evangelized and converted, moral uplift inevitably followed. So individual conversions (the "root") would eventually produce social reform (the "fruit"). This kind of metaphor was used increasingly (cf Hutchison 1987:115, 141) and is still popular in evangelical circles. Most premillennialists, however, saw little hope for society before Christ returned to set up his kingdom (cf Marsden 1980:31). As a matter of fact, a firm conviction, particularly in dispensationalist circles, was that "things on earth will get progressively worse and will culminate in a unique time of terrible tribulation" (Pocock 1988:438). Moody's most quoted statement, which summarized his entire philosophy of evangelism, was, "I look upon this world as a wrecked vessel. God has given me a lifeboat and said to me, 'Moody, save all you can' " (:38). Salvation meant being saved *from* the world. This was, no doubt, an important departure from the dominant tradition of American evangelicalism, which had a much more positive view of the reformability of society (cf Marsden 1980:38).

Curiously, however, the separation from the world propagated by Moody and other premillennialists was not a radically outward separation (as it was, for instance, in the Anabaptist tradition) but rather (only) *inward*. There was no appeal to people to "abandon most of the standards of respectable American middle-class way of life. It was to these standards, in fact, that people were to be converted" (Marsden 1980:38). The values the revivalists espoused, albeit unintentionally, were those of middle-class American culture: materialism, capitalism, patriotism, respectability (:32, 49, 207). Premillennialist churches and agencies were run in the same businesslike manner as those of their arch-rivals, the proponents of the social gospel; nobody saw any incongruence in preaching withdrawal from the world while at the same time managing the church as if it were a secular corporation. Everybody worshiped at the shrine of the cult of efficiency (cf Moorhead 1984:75; see also the penetrating study of Knapp 1977 on the relationship between mission [whether ecumenical or evangelical] and modernization).

In light of this it should not come as too great a surprise to discover that these same world-denying premillennialists were *not* really *apolitical*. In order to appreciate such an apparently incongruous phenomenon, it may help to keep in mind that, from the time of Moody's ministry in the late nineteenth century through the fundamentalist controversies of the 1920s, the constituency of the "revivalist evangelical movements appears to have been the predominantly white, aspiring middle class of Protestant heritage" (Marsden 1980:91). The lingering conviction, even in these circles, that God's kingdom would indeed be inaugurated in America, also played a part in this (:211).

After the First World War political conservatism, until then latent rather than manifest, gained a much clearer profile. In the wake of the Russian Revolution anti-socialism, a trend in premillennialism at least since the late nineteenth century, was propagated much more vigorously than before. Communism was, however, not seen in isolation; it was simply the ugly contemporary expression of everything that threatened the American middle-class value system. By the end of the Second World War this attitude had consolidated itself in the fundamentalist hyper-American patriotic anticommunism of Carl McIntire and others (Marsden 1980:210). This development, in turn, spawned the so-called New Religious Right. Those adhering to its philosophy are not necessarily all premillennialists, but they are all politically conservative and, on the whole, theologically fundamentalist, often propagating legislation in order to enforce their views. An extreme example of this trend is the circle around the Texas-based *Journal of Christian Reconstruction*. Unrelated to it and more overtly premillennialist, is the so-called Prosperity Gospel of Kenneth Hagin and others; it is, however, an expression of a similar ethos. It is attractive to the upwardly mobile to listen to a gospel which blesses their aspirations and achievements and relieves them of guilt feelings, while at the same time preaching their message of virtuous wealth as a commendable example to the poor.

The advent of the Social Gospel both confirmed the worst fears of the evangelicals and proved to them that they had been correct in severing all links with the apostate church. Their—predictable—reaction was to embrace an ever more absolute antithesis between evangelism and social concern, oblivious of the fact that, in adopting this attitude, they were in reality succumbing to the very spirit of the Enlightenment they thought they were combatting. Almost every author of the twelve famous (or notorious) volumes published from 1910 to 1915 in the series *The Fundamentals*, was making use of the rationalist framework of the Enlightenment paradigm (cf Marsden 1980:118-123).

Postmillennialism and Amillennialism. Around the middle of the nineteenth century an uncompromising premillennialist position was to be found only among religiously and socially marginal groups in the United States. In 1859 a theological journal could state, with confidence, that postmillennialism was the "commonly received doctrine" among American Protestants (cf Moorhead

1984:61). The postmillennialism of the period was still, by and large, a continuation of the earlier teachings of Edwards, Hopkins, and others, embracing a
compromise between an apocalyptic and an evolutionary view of time. Nobody
doubted that history would eventually come to a cataclysmic end, but few cared
to elaborate on this aspect; attention was focused, rather, on what should be
done *now* by way of "building the kingdom". Throughout, a hard residue of
apocalypticism persisted in postmillennialist circles (:61f). In the latter half of
the century, however, this residue came under fierce attack. The reasons were
diverse.

First, the bizarre apocalypticism of some of the recent premillennial groups
such as the Shakers and the Millerites—regarded as crackpots or fools in
"respectable" circles—caused any form of apocalyptic vision to be suspect.

Second, the Civil War, contrary to earlier expectations, was followed by a
period of malaise. In the decades preceding the war the issues were clear-cut;
most "mainline" Christians (the majority of whom were evangelicals) agreed
that slavery was a scourge that had to be eradicated. Many were convinced
that, once slavery was abolished, justice and equity would be the order of the
day. The war turned out to be much more drawn out and much more brutal
than either side had anticipated. Perhaps even worse—the end of the war did
not usher in the expected utopia. People became aware of the fact that social
problems had increased rather than decreased.

Third, unprecedented technological developments—the kind predicted a
century or more ago by Edwards and Hopkins!—were taking place and were
catching people's imagination. Factories sprang up around the nation, and tens
of thousands of rural North Americans and immigrants from Europe moved to
the cities to work in the factories. In their enthusiastic optimism Edwards and
Hopkins did not, however, anticipate the social ills that would accompany the
new technological advances. All of a sudden the churches were faced with
societal problems previously unknown, and they did not know how to respond.
The entire fabric of the nation was changing and the familiar theological certainties and solutions from the past seemed unable to provide the much-needed
guidance.

Fourth, for the first time American theological schools were exposed on a
large scale to the historical critical method in biblical studies, which had been
dominant in German theological schools since at least a century before. Scholars now argued that the Bible did not propound only *one* "canonical" view on
eschatology. And it was suggested that the books of Daniel and Revelation,
long the mainstays of millennial speculations, were of a later origin than had
always been assumed and were therefore less reliable than had been thought.
This state of affairs meant, at the very least, a complete reinterpretation of
apocalyptic; at best, it was the "shell" of a great truth, and instead of concentrating on the shell, people should search for its abiding spiritual message (cf
Moorhead 1984:63-66).

The inevitable victim of the new era was millennialism in any form, whether
pre or post. It was not rejected outright; it simply ebbed away (cf Moorhead
1984:61). The earlier expectations that the millennium was "only" about two

hundred years away now elicited little excitement. Little room was left for the "great eschatological event Christians had long awaited, namely, the Second Coming" (:67). Belief in Christ's return on the clouds was superseded by the idea of God's kingdom in this world, which would be introduced step by step through successful labors in missionary endeavor abroad and through creating an egalitarian society at home. Along with the prominent nineteenth century German theologian, Albrecht Ritschl, the proponents of the American Social Gospel perceived God's kingdom as a present ethical reality rather than a dominion to be introduced in the future (:66).[8] In 1870, Samuel Harris of Andover Theological Seminary delivered a series of lectures characteristically entitled *The Kingdom of God on Earth*, by which he meant the developments then taking place in North America (cf Hopkins 1940:21). By 1917 Walter Rauschenbusch, major exponent of the Social Gospel, could confidently declare that the doctrine of the kingdom of God was "itself the social gospel" (:20). This meant, in effect, the discarding of all supernatural features. Reality was entirely inner-worldly, anthropocentric, and naturalistic. "Is anything in the whole universe of God, when rightly understood, supernatural?" asked W. B. Brown in 1900 (quoted by Moorhead 1984:66). The miraculous was eliminated and superseded by professionalism, efficiency, and scientific planning.

The key ideas of the new mood were natural *continuity* and social *progress*. Optimism was in the air. The generator was the old postmillennialism, now, however, wedded to the Darwinian theory of evolution. The belief in natural continuity meant that no crisis was really expected. Coupled with this was the worship of the same cult of efficiency and pragmatism we have already encountered in premillennialism, only now in the service of an antithetical set of values. Here, too, and with less qualms than was the case in premillennialist circles, churches and religious organizations were run like businesses. The building of God's kingdom had become as much a matter of technique and program as religious piety and devotion.

The Social Gospel's romantic, evolutionary conception of God's kingdom involved "no discontinuities, no crises, no tragedies or sacrifices, no loss of all things, no cross and resurrection" (Niebuhr 1959:191). It was all "fulfillment of promise without judgment", so that "no great crisis needed to intervene between the order of grace and the order of glory" (:193). An indulgent God admitted "souls" to his "heaven" on the recommendation of his kindly son (:135). The coming kingdom was not regarded as involving "both death and resurrection, both crisis and promise, but only as the completion of tendencies now established" (:183).

The Puritans' understanding of the kingdom was radically different: no human plan or organization could be identified with it "since every such plan was product of a relative, self-interested and therefore corrupted reason" (Niebuhr 1959:23). Their understanding of God was also different. They indeed knew God as a God of love, but only against the dark backdrop of his awe-inspiring majesty and his wrath over sin and evil. In the Social Gospel movement, however, God was a loving and benevolent being, little more than the embodiment of all ideal human attributes, "the God who exists for the sake of human life and morality", "the synthetic unity of goodness, truth, and beauty" (Niebuhr 1988:121). God and humans were reconciled by deifying the latter and humanizing the former (Niebuhr 1959:191; cf Visser 't Hooft 1928:169-180).

All these convictions found their classical expression in the new doctrine of the *fatherhood of God and the brotherhood of all people*. It was only natural that, in this climate, the traditional soteriological perception of Jesus would disappear. Christ the Redeemer became Jesus the benevolent and wise teacher, or the spiritual genius in whom the religious capacities of humankind were fully developed (Niebuhr 1959:192; cf Barton 1925). "The sympathizing Jesus . . . replaced the Christ of Calvary" (Hopkins 1940:19; cf Visser 't Hooft 1928:38-51; Niebuhr 1988:116).

For the Christian missionary enterprise these developments had critical consequences. During this entire period, spanning the years from the middle of the nineteenth century to the Second World War, overseas missions were still predominantly a project of "mainline" churches and agencies. It was therefore only to be expected that the theological views prevailing on the home front would also be disseminated in the younger overseas churches. Basing his views on two articles published in 1915, Gerald Anderson (1988:104) concludes that, in the course of the preceding decades, four major shifts had taken place in missionary thinking: (1) other religions were no longer thought to be entirely false; (2) mission work meant less preaching and a broader range of transformational activities; (3) the accent was now on salvation for life in the present world; and (4) the emphasis in mission had shifted from the individual to society.

The conviction that *other religions were not intrinsically evil* did not necessarily mean the end of missions. James Dennis's voluminous writings referred to earlier (cf Dennis 1897, 1899, 1906) demonstrated convincingly that, although these religions were not regarded as wicked, they were undoubtedly viewed as vastly inferior to (Western) Christianity. At the World's Parliament of Religions, held in Chicago in 1893, Western Christians fraternized freely with adherents of other faiths, but not without condescension. The new view was that Christ did not come to destroy other religions but to fulfill them. Jesus, said George Gordon two years after the Chicago event, "must prove himself a better ruler to Japan, a nobler Confucius to China, a diviner Gautama to India . . . He must come as the consummation of the ideals of every nation under heaven" (quoted in Hutchison 1982:170f). Meanwhile, adherents to these faiths were not eternally lost. The theology of the earlier postmillennialists had already steadily been depopulating hell. With the virtual demise of premillennialism in liberal circles, hell was in even more rapid decline; a benevolent God would in any case not be able to tolerate the idea of such hideous punishment (Moorhead 1984:70). This meant, inevitably, that liberals not only abhorred revivalism but also lacked enthusiasm for direct evangelism, whether at home or abroad. Their emphasis was on a permeative rather than a narrowly conversionist form of Christian influence.

The shift from the primacy of evangelism to the *primacy of social involvement* was a gradual one and developed a clear profile only by the 1890s (Marsden 1980:84; Hutchison 1987:107). At the beginning of his series of lectures at Princeton Seminary, James Dennis said that the evangelistic aim was "still" first, "as it ever will be, and unimpeachable in its import and dignity". This was, however, little more than a perfunctory bow of courtesy toward the "evangelistic mandate", for Dennis immediately continued, "but a new significance has been given to missions as a factor in the social regeneration of the world" (1897:23) — and it is to this that his three volumes were devoted.

An aspect of this shift is highlighted by the history of the Student Volunteer Movement, which was formed in 1886 and had as watchword "The evangelization of the world in this generation". At its launch, "evangelization" was still understood in traditional terms, as leading people to saving faith in God through Christ. In the first half-century of its existence, nearly thirteen thousand volunteers sailed from North America for overseas missionary service. By the second decade of the twentieth century the movement was, however, already in decline and the watchword losing its influence. At a conference held in 1917 the primary question was no longer "the evangelization of the world", but "Does Christ offer an adequate solution for the burning social and international questions of the day?" Subsequent conventions pushed further the radical reorientation of the SVM (cf Anderson 1988:106).

The move from evangelism to social concern had, as its natural corollary, a shift of interest *from individual to society*. The new secular social disciplines revealed that each individual was profoundly influenced and shaped by her or his environment and that it made little sense to attempt to change individuals yet leave their context untouched. Dennis applied these insights forcefully to the overseas missionary scene. "The religion of Jesus Christ", he said, "can never enter non-Christian society and be content to leave things as they are" (1897:47). In fact, "Christian missions represent . . . accelerated social revolution" (:44f). It was the old Reformed and Puritan conviction that Christ laid claim to the whole of reality, but now in a secular garb — the fruit of the insights of sociology. Dennis argued that the fabric of "pagan" societies was almost totally unsuitable and a new fabric had to be woven. The approach of conservatives and premillennialists, namely, that of concentrating on individual regeneration, was discredited totally — if not theologically, then at least sociologically. Sin and evil reigned not only, and not even primarily, in the individual heart. Rauschenbusch and others called attention to society's corporate sins and to "the superpersonal forces of evil" (Hopkins 1940:321f).

In the course of time Social Gospel advocates such as George Davis Herron and Walter Rauschenbusch became convinced that these "superpersonal forces of evil" were somehow inherent in the capitalist system since it militated, in principle, against the creation of a social, economic, and political egalitarianism. The unbridled competition of Capitalism, "the law of tooth and nail", was the absolute antithesis of the Christian gospel of love and gravely inhibited the workers' opportunities to engage in collective bargaining. Profits should not be made at the cost of human welfare, and the workers were entitled to economic justice rather than charity or paternalistic magnanimity. Laissez faire economics, in particular, was castigated severely (cf Hopkins 1940:323-325). Still, the Social Gospel hardly addressed the problems of war, imperialism, race, or the use of force (:319); these really only began to receive serious and sustained attention from the 1960s onward.

The seed-bed in which the ideological roots of the Social Gospel found themselves most at home was Unitarianism. This movement, which evolved from elements of Congregationalism and Presbyterianism, emphasized reason and the "primary facts of human experience" rather than faith, as well as the intrinsic goodness of human nature rather than the Fall, the Atonement, and the possibility of eternal punishment. Its essentially optimistic, rational, and humanitarian character accounts for its growing proclivity toward social Christianity. The Divine remained in this system "only to give lift to the imagination"; otherwise it was a thoroughgoing "religion of humanity" (cf Hopkins 1940:4, 22, 56-61, 318).

Social Christianity did not evolve only from Unitarianism, however. Many Christian leaders, particularly postmillennialists who espoused what might perhaps be called progressive orthodoxy (cf Hopkins 1940:61-63), also slowly gravitated toward a position which ascribed primacy to social change, without, however, discarding the supernatural elements of the faith and traditional doctrines. This was particularly true of those evangelicals who felt called to one or other form of foreign missionary involvement. Their position was not enviable. They were under suspicion from both the conservative premillennialists and the thoroughgoing social gospellers. In addition, they often lacked theological sophistication, a circumstance which made them appear to be vacillating between two mutually irreconcilable positions. Still, because they refused to surrender to either manifestation of the dominant paradigm, they kept the missionary idea alive in mainstream Christianity while at the same time maintaining theological dialogue with the premillennialist wing.

In the heyday of the Social Gospel on the one hand and fundamentalism on the other, these mediators included Robert P. Wilder (1863-1938), John R. Mott (1865-1955), Robert E. Speer (1867-1947), and J. H. Oldham (1874-1969). Each of them could look back upon a profound religious experience, a factor which might have caused him to be at odds with some of the more radical elements of the Social Gospel, but each also elected to stay within "mainline" American church life, which often made him suspect in fundamentalist and other extreme premillennialist circles. Frequently, however, their stature and personal integrity helped them bridge gaps where no communication appeared possible. The result was that the movements they helped to create or in which they participated, succeeded in winning the loyalty and support of groups at both ends of the spectrum—movements such as the WSCF, the SVM, and the IMC, to mention only a few. Each of these organizations embraced both social gospellers and premillennialists. They thus succeeded in keeping alive something of the holistic understanding of the Christian faith which dated back to the times before the assault of rationalism split the Christian community into two warring factions. Sometimes Mott and his co-workers succeeded in keeping the new and fragile ecumenical boat afloat with the aid of fortuitous or unintentional ambiguities. The watchword of the SVM was one of these. There were interminable debates about what precisely "the evangelization of the world in this generation" meant, but in the end each person was both able and allowed to assign to it the interpretation he or she preferred. Another example was the World Missionary Conference held in Edinburgh in 1910. It was a curious mix of post- and premillennialism, social gospellers and soul-savers, "mainline" and evangelical mission agencies.[9]

The Inadequacies of Pre-, Post-, and Amillennialism. Inexorably, so it appears, the drift in those circles traditionally supporting the overseas missionary project was away from evangelicalism toward a more secular and inner-worldly liberalism. The heritage of evangelical faith with which the social gospellers started was gradually being used up. "The liberal children of liberal fathers", says Niebuhr (1959:194), "needed to operate with ever diminishing capital". Of Horace Bushnell (1802-1876) he says, "Bushnell protested against the faith he had learned, but he had learned it nevertheless and his protest was significant in part because it arose out of an inner tension between the old and the new" (:195). Others no longer knew this tension.

Fundamental to all the American exponents of social Christianity was the conviction that the social salvation the world stood in need of would come via Western techniques and culture. Curiously enough, it was not really different among premillennialists. In Hutchison's words, "Cultural faith . . . united liberals and premillennialists more strongly than their ideologies divided them" (1987:172); all of them "shared a vision of the essential rightness of Western civilization and the near-inevitability of its triumph" (:95). James Dennis' painstaking and ponderous chronicling of all the shortcomings of non-Western civilizations, coupled with an unbridled enthusiasm for the Western church's mission of civilizing the rest of the world, did not really differ from the views expressed by premillennialists such as A. B. Simpson and A. T. Pierson (cf Hutchison 1987:107-110, 115-118).

Both strains were, in several respects, more Western than Christian. They were, in opposite ways, expressions of the triumph of the Enlightenment in Western Christianity. The Enlightenment reached its zenith in the nineteenth century, manifesting itself in rationalism, evolutionism, pragmatism, secularism, and optimism. All these "isms" impregnated the Western churches and were exported overseas by foreign missionary agencies. Even where the proponents of pre-, post-, and amillennialism disagreed fiercely about missionary programs and priorities, they did so on the shared assumptions of the Enlightenment frame of mind.

This could not last, however. The premillennialists faced an insurmountable crisis during what has become known as the fundamentalist controversy. The very presuppositions on which fundamentalism had operated simply ceased to obtain. If an intractable fundamentalism persisted in some church and missionary circles, this should not be taken as an indication that it continued to be viable as a theological movement but as evidence of the fact that an organism often survives long after the climate in which it has first flourished no longer prevails.

But the Social Gospel also faced an insuperable crisis. Born in the late nineteenth century, it ceased to make sense in the early twentieth. The First World War and the malaise that followed it shattered to pieces the confidence that was an indispensable ingredient of the Social Gospel movement. When Walter Rauschenbusch, in 1917, presented his mature thought at Yale in his lecture series entitled *A Theology for the Social Gospel*, the entire movement was already outmoded (cf Hopkins 1940:327). This did not mean the demise of the movement, however. Far from it! The resounding victory liberal theology won over fundamentalism in the 1920s gave it a new lease of life and caused it to believe that its ultimate triumph was guaranteed. It was a Pyrrhic victory, however, and when the IMC held its first plenary assembly on the Mount of Olives in 1928, many American delegates had begun to have grave misgivings about the rise of secularism and the fact that, by and large, this was what the Western missions were exporting.

The remedy, so W. E. Hocking and others believed, did not, however, lie in disavowing the ethos that had given rise to secularism, but in redefining mission as "preparation for world unity in civilization". The Laymen's Foreign Missionary Enquiry, which convened under Hocking's leadership and in 1932 published its findings in the report *Re-Thinking Missions*, believed that this could be achieved by joining hands with other religions, discovering the common foundation of religiosity shared by all, and espousing this in the teeth of secularism. What the authors were trying to do, however, was to exorcise one nineteenth-century demon with the help of another. They sought to substitute nineteenth-century romanticism for its rationalism, little realizing that the two depended and fed on each other. John A. Mackay was one of the few to grasp this with remarkable clarity. He commented (1933:177f) that the report totally ignored the fact that a revolution had broken out in the romantic theological playground of the nineteenth century whose spirit the report perpetuated, and described it as the requiem of a dying day rather than the trumpet of dawn of a day that is coming.

By a peculiar twist, the very secularism so maligned by the Laymen's Report made a forceful comeback in the remarkable "secular sixties". Admittedly, it was no longer exactly the same thing, at least not on the surface. One now distinguished carefully between "secularism", which one rejected, and "secularization", which one welcomed and propagated. After the devastation of two world wars, the optimism of the nineteenth century and of the Social Gospel had reemerged. It was heralded first by the Strasbourg Conference of the World Student Christian Federation in 1960, where J. Hoekendijk urged the students "to begin radically to desacralize the church" and to recognize that Christianity was "a secular movement" not "some sort of religion" (cf Anderson 1988:109). In 1968 the WCC held its third general assembly, in Uppsala, where it was boldly proclaimed that "the world provides the agenda for the church". The terminology of the Social Gospel had been dropped; one now talked about "development" rather than "civilization" as the task of mission, but the dynamics remained the same. In an almost convulsive fashion the church was going to remake the world, once again in the image of the West. It was hard to define exactly how mission differed from the ethos and activities of the Peace Corps. Small wonder that, in this same year (1968), R. Pierce Beaver, respected North American theologian of mission, reported that "students are now cold, even hostile, to overseas missions" (quoted in Anderson 1988:112).[10]

In 1968 the Second General Conference of Latin American Bishops met in Medellín, an event that provided the setting and stimulus for the emergence of Latin American liberation theology, which finally ended the hegemony of Western mission's cultural and ideological assumptions (cf Gutiérrez 1988:xvii, xx-xxv).

Still, recent developments in missionary thinking only really make sense if we see them as being both a reaction to and a result of the evolution of ideas discussed in this section, that is, of the various manifestations of both premillennialism and social Christianity. The Social Gospel, in particular, has been "America's most unique contribution to the great ongoing stream of Christianity" (Hopkins 1940:3), "the first expression of American religious life which is truly born in America itself" (Visser 't Hooft 1928:186). Because North American Protestantism at the time had been contributing the lion's share to the international missionary enterprise, the influence of the Social Gospel reverberated around the world and made itself felt not only in Third-World Christianity, but far beyond.

Voluntarism

One of the most remarkable phenomena of the Enlightenment era is the emergence of *missionary societies*: some denominational, some interdenominational, some nondenominational, and some even anti-denominational. They first appeared on the scene haltingly, extremely apologetic about their existence and very uncertain about their nature and future. By the end of the eighteenth century, however, the situation had changed dramatically. New missionary societies exploded on to the scene in all traditional Protestant countries: Great Britain, Germany, the Netherlands, Switzerland, the Scandinavian countries, and the United States. In the 1880s, with the advent of the high imperial era, a second wave of new societies was in evidence; once again the entire Protestant world was involved, but by now it was clear that the United States was edging its way ahead of others, not only in the numbers of missionaries sent abroad but also in the numbers of new societies formed. The end of the Second World War saw yet another wave of missionary enthusiasm and the formation of new societies. Prior to the year 1900, a total of eighty-one mission agencies were founded in North America. During the subsequent four decades, 1900-1939, another 147 were formed. The next decade, 1940-1949, recorded the creation of eighty-three societies, followed by no fewer than 113 new agencies during the decade 1950-1959, 132 in the period 1960-1969 and another 150 in the next ten years (cf Wilson and Siewert 1986:81-314, 593f).

It is not easy to explain this astonishing phenomenon in Protestantism. Most certainly a variety of factors would have to be taken into consideration here, but it can hardly be denied that the spirit of enterprise and initiative spawned by the Enlightenment played an important role first in the genesis of the idea of missionary societies and then in their amazing proliferation. The fact is that, for more than a century after the Reformation, the mere idea of forming such "voluntary societies" next to the church was anathema in Protestantism. The institutional church, tightly controlled by the clergy, remained the only divine instrument on earth. Voetius spoke for the Reformed tradition when he said that, if there were to be any talk about mission (which there usually was not), only the institutional church — local church council, presbytery, or synod — could act as sending agency (cf Jongeneel 1989:126).

By the end of the seventeenth century, however, a new mood was beginning to develop. The Reformation principle of the right of private judgment in interpreting Scripture was rekindled. An extension of this was that like-minded individuals could band together in order to promote a common cause. A plethora of new societies was the result. Many stood in the religious mainstream and were promoting a great variety of religious and societal concerns: antislavery, prison reform, temperance, sabbath observance, the "reform of manners", and other charitable causes (cf Bradley 1976). An increasing number of new societies, however, championed the cause of foreign missions. Basically, the societies were all organized on the voluntary principle and dependent on their members' contribution of time, energy, and money.

The ideology behind the societies was that of the social and political egalitarianism of the emerging democracies (Gensichen 1975b:50; cf Moorhead 1984:73). Networks of auxiliary associations were organized in outlying districts, sent their contributions to the central office, and were fed with information from there. People of the most modest position and income became donors and prayer supporters of projects many thousands of miles away. Women also came along, to play a leading role in various agencies, "far earlier than they could decently appear in most other walks of life" (Walls 1988:151). Their involvement in mission constituted "the first feminist movement in North America" (cf the subtitle of Beaver 1980), and certainly not only there. They went out, literally to the ends of the earth, no longer just as the wives of missionaries but as missionaries in their own right. At home, women's missionary organizations undergirded the missionary movement with prayer, study, financial support, and dissemination of information. By the year 1900 there were forty-one American women's agencies supporting twelve hundred single women missionaries (cf Anderson 1988:102).

This was the Reformation principle of the office of the believer, wedded to the Enlightenment's optimistic view of the world and of humanity: people were able to do something, not only about their own circumstances, but also about the circumstances of others. The increasingly dominant postmillennialism of the period further stirred people into action. The saints saw themselves, through their many goal-oriented communities, as God's co-workers in ushering in God's kingdom (cf Moorhead 1984:73).

It has in recent years become customary to devote an enormous amount of energy to theological discussions about whether missionary societies are legitimate agents of mission. Is mission not rather to be regarded as an expression of the *church*? Without denying the merit there is in such a discussion I would like to suggest that, within the framework of the paradigm spawned by the Enlightenment, there was not much to choose between the organized *church* as bearer of mission and the mission *societies*. The point is that, in Western Protestantism, the church was increasingly fractured into a great variety of denominations which, phenomenologically speaking, were not decisively different from missionary and other religious societies. Denominations, too, were organized on the voluntary principle of like-minded individuals banding together. They were, in a sense, para-church organizations.

In those countries where there were established churches the situation only *appeared* to be different. The mere emergence and existence of "free" churches (sometimes called "non-conformist" churches or "dissenters") next to or in opposition to the established church, suggested that, even if there was some pressure on people to stay members of the established church, individuals were free to follow their conscience and join churches of their liking. Where there was no established church—for instance in the United States where all churches were treated equally before the law—a bewildering variety of denominations soon emerged.

It is important to note that the very possibility of a dispensation in which there was no established or state church was a fruit of the Enlightenment; it was only when religious belief was removed from the realm of "fact" to that of "value", about which individuals were free to differ, that a societal system could evolve in which a multiplicity of denominations could exist side by side and have equal rights. Newbigin says:

> It is the common observation of sociologists of religion that denominationalism is the religious aspect of secularization. It is the form that religion takes in a culture controlled by the ideology of the Enlightenment. It is the social form in which the privatization of religion is expressed (1986:145).

The Enlightenment was not the sole reason for denominationalism. North American denominations, for instance, were "the product of a combination of European churchly traditions, ethnic loyalties, pietism, sectarianism, and American free enterprise" (Marsden 1980:70). It was only natural that in such a climate, "free" churches would thrive. I have mentioned that magisterial Protestantism was at its lowest ebb during the two decades immediately following the American Revolution; by contrast, Methodists, Presbyterians, and Baptists were expanding rapidly in these years (cf Chaney 1977:31). They were the product of a marriage between rationalism and pietism and, as "revivalist" churches, benefited greatly from the Awakenings. None of the many Protestant denominations even dreamt of upholding the medieval idea of the identification of the empirical church with the kingdom of God.

For some five decades after Independence, a remarkable ecumenical spirit prevailed in the United States. The same obtained, by and large, in Great Britain and continental Europe (although the bewildering multiplicity of denominations which characterized the United States was unknown there). This ecumenicity was certainly to be attributed, to a large degree, to the Awakenings which were, by nature, "ecumenical". These years also saw the blossoming of interdenominational mission societies. Some of the most remarkable of these were the London Missionary Society (founded in 1795), the American Board (1810), and the Basel Mission (1816). The LMS stated its "fundamental principle" in the following terms:

> Our design is not to send Presbyterianism, Independency, Episcopacy, or any other form of Church Order and Government ... but the Glorious Gospel of the blessed God to the Heathen (quoted by Walls 1988:149).

A "denominational" society was, of course, formed three years earlier than the LMS. I am referring to the "Particular Baptist Society for Propagating the Gospel among the Heathen", founded under William Carey's leadership in 1792. It is, however, important to note that Carey advanced no theological arguments in favor of a denominational society. His arguments were purely pragmatic: "In the present divided state of Christendom, it would be more likely for good to be done by each denomination engaging separately in the work" (quoted by Walls 1988:148). As a matter of fact, Carey's pragmatic reasons for initiating a denominational society were almost identical to those of the founding fathers of the *nondenominational* LMS three years later.

There was something businesslike, something distinctly modern, about the launching of the new societies, whether denominational or not. Carey took his analogy neither from Scripture nor from theological tradition, but from the contemporary commercial world — the organization of an overseas trading company, which carefully studied all the relevant information, selected its stock, ships and crews, and was willing to brave dangerous seas and unfriendly climates in order to achieve its objective. Carey proposed that, in similar fashion, a company of serious Christians might be formed with the objective of evangelizing distant peoples. It should be an "instrumental" society, that is, a society established with a clearly defined purpose along explicitly formulated lines. So, the organizing of such a society was something like floating a mercantile company (cf Walls 1988:145f).

The new societies, even those which were consciously denominational, such as Carey's Baptist Society and the (Anglican) Church Missionary Society (founded in 1799), had nothing exclusivist or confessionalist about them. The CMS, for instance, experienced no difficulty in recognizing the validity of the office of missionaries not ordained in an Episcopal church (cf van den Berg 1956:159f). In fact, most of its first missionaries were German Lutherans.

By the fourth decade of the nineteenth century the "ecumenical" climate was, however, on the decline. In an attempt to counteract the influence of rationalism and liberalism, confessionalism was revived. The SPG became more doctrinaire and rejected any form of missionary cooperation with other societies, even with fellow-Anglicans in the low-church CMS. Writing about North America, Niebuhr says that the denominations

> confused themselves with their cause and began to promote themselves, identifying the kingdom of Christ with the practices and doctrines prev-

alent in the group ... The missionary enterprise, home and foreign, was divided along denominational lines; every religious society became intent upon promoting its own peculiar type of work in religious education, in the evangelization of the youth, in the printing and distribution of religious literature ... The more attention was concentrated upon the church the greater became the tendency toward schism (1959:177f).

Likewise, in Germany, Lutheran confessionalism (revivified, *inter alia*, by the third-centenary celebrations in 1830 of the adoption the Augsburg Confession) contributed to a new consciousness among Lutherans of being different from other Protestants. This manifested itself also in the foreign missionary enterprise (a development traced carefully and in great detail by Aagaard 1967). Several societies that were consciously transconfessional had been operating from the German-speaking world during the early decades of the nineteenth century, the most important of these being the Basel, Rhenish, and North-German Mission Societies (cf Aagaard 1967:182-306, 401-473). They were, however, not permitted to continue operating unchallenged. Tensions between Reformed and Lutheran supporters of the Basel Mission precipitated the formation, in 1836, of an exclusively Lutheran missionary society, later known as the Leipzig Mission (Aagaard 1967:357-381). Similar developments were soon to follow in other parts of Germany (:526-705).

Events in North America were only marginally different from those in Great Britain and Germany. After 1850 various churches "became markedly less willing to leave foreign missions to pandenominational or nondenominational associations" (Hutchison 1987:95) and began to sponsor denominational mission projects. Eventually even the nondenominational American Board, for a half-century the largest of all American societies (Hutchison 1987:45), became "denominational"; it evolved into the missionary arm of Congregationalism. In Britain the same happened to the LMS, and under similar circumstances.

During the heyday of nondenominational mission societies, mission had been understood predominantly as *conversio gentilium* — the conversion of individual persons. It was only natural that in the subsequent defensive reaction of denominationalism to the relativizing tendencies of the Enlightenment, mission would again, as was the case in the medieval Catholic paradigm, be defined as *plantatio ecclesiae*, church planting. The nondenominational societies, heavily influenced by the Evangelical Awakenings, had been preaching "a Gospel without a Church" (S.C. Carpenter, quoted by van den Berg 1956:159; cf Scherer 1987:75); this was now regarded as inadequate and amends had to be made. The remedy was the planting of distinctly *confessional* churches on the "mission field". The new slogan was the establishment of "self-governing", "self-supporting", and "self-propagating" (or "self-extending") younger churches. The two main personalities in this regard were the general secretaries of the two largest Protestant missionary societies of the mid-nineteenth century, Rufus Anderson of the American Board and Henry Venn of the British CMS.

One should immediately add, however, that the intentions of the two men were noble. Great strides toward church independency were indeed made in this period, not least because they were putting greater trust in the integrity of their black and brown converts than most of their contemporaries did. It should also not be forgotten that both men—but Anderson, the Congregationalist, more clearly than Venn, the Anglican—were imbued with the rising mid-nineteenth-century spirit of democracy (Hutchison 1987:77).

In spite of the admirable ideals of Anderson and Venn, things did not turn out as expected, in part because their plans were often subverted by their own missionaries. Yet, quite apart from this, one has to say that there was something incongruous about the heavy emphasis on church planting as the goal of missions. The medieval missionary policy of *plantatio ecclesiae* had still operated on the assumption that, one day, all the world would be put under the sway of the church. By the middle of the nineteenth century such an ideal was no longer deemed possible, at least not in Protestant circles. It was subconsciously assumed that the secularizing and rationalizing impact of the Enlightenment could not be undone. So the Protestant variant of *plantatio ecclesiae* was the carving out of small, exclusive "territories" of Anglicanism, Presbyterianism, Lutheranism, and the like. The "advance of the gospel" was measured by counting tangible things such as the number of baptisms, confessions, and communions, and the opening of new mission stations or outposts.

The church had, in a sense, ceased to point to God or to the future; instead, it was pointing to itself. Mission was the road from the institutional church to the church that still had to be instituted. It was the activity of professional agents of organized societies operating on the "horizontal" plane. The relationship of these churches to society and to the wider ecumenical and eschatological horizons was largely ignored. What Scherer says about the Lutheran missions of the time could, by and large, also be said of the projects of other confessional groupings,

> The kingdom of God was reduced to a strategy by which Lutheran mission agencies planted Lutheran churches around the world. Questions were seldom asked at this time about the relationship of these churches to the kingdom of God. Their very existence appeared to be its own justification, and no further discussion of mission goals was required (1987:77).

By the end of the nineteenth century the pendulum once again swung toward societal mission and a more ecumenical spirit. This was, at the same time, a reaffirmation of the principle of voluntarism. A plethora of new voluntarist missionary agencies have been formed in the course of the last hundred years or so. But precisely as expression of the spirit of voluntarism, they have also been illustrations of the modern Western mood of activism, do-goodism, and manifest destiny. The eager young missionary recruits' "crusading spirit", says Anderson (1988:98), was fuelled by "duty, compassion, confidence, optimism, evangelical revivalism, and premillennialist urgency".

Many of the newer type of Protestant missionary agencies belong to the category usually referred to as "faith missions". The pioneer and prototype of all these societies, and still the most famous, was the China Inland Mission, founded in 1865 by J. Hudson Taylor. The new societies represented an adaptation of the late eighteenth-century voluntary society, rather than a totally new departure (Walls 1988:154). Here the eschatological motif dominated. An urgent appeal was made to young men and women to sacrifice themselves without reservation so as to save the millions of China and other distant countries before the last judgment.

At the same time the new societies represented a radicalization of the voluntary principle. People were challenged to go without any financial guarantees, simply trusting that the Lord of mission would provide. In the eyes of some they were heroes of the faith; in the eyes of others they were fools; in their own eyes they were but "fools for Christ's sake". No time was left for timorous or carefully prepared advances into pagan territory, nor for the laborious building up of "autonomous" churches on the "mission field". The gospel had to be proclaimed to all with the greatest speed, and for this there could never be enough missionaries. It also meant that there was neither time nor need for drawn-out preparation for missionary service. Many who went out had very little education or training, although the recruits also included well-educated persons such as C. T. Studd and the other members of the famous "Cambridge Seven".

The weaknesses of the faith mission movement are obvious: the romantic notion of the freedom of the individual to make his or her own choices, an almost convulsive preoccupation with saving people's souls before Judgment Day, a limited knowledge of the cultures and religions of the people to whom the missionaries went, virtually no interest in the societal dimension of the Christian gospel, almost exclusive dependence on the charismatic personality of the founder, a very low view of the church, etc. The movement also had its strengths, however, particularly in the pristine form it took in Hudson Taylor and the China Inland Mission. The "home base" of the mission agency would no longer be in London, Berlin, Basel, or New York, but in China, India, or Thailand. The missionaries were not to live on "mission stations", isolated from the population, but in the very midst of the people they were trying to reach, eating the food they ate and wearing the clothes they wore. The emphasis was not on doctrinal distinctives and confessional divisions but on the simple gospel of salvation through Jesus Christ.

Some of the elements listed above, both negative and positive, became the common heritage of the modern evangelical missionary movement. There is still, among many Christians, an impatience with the cumbersome machinery of the institutional church, which tends to thwart any new initiatives. Many young people are leaving the "mainline" churches and offering their services to any one of an incredible variety of evangelical mission agencies. Today's evangelical world is full of itinerant evangelists, of magazines and Bible schools and fellowships of churches. But here, too, we notice the same curious ambiguity we identified earlier with respect to the phenomenon of denominationalism. On the one hand, evangelical groups reveal an amazing tolerance toward each other and a rejection of any doctrinal rigidity or inflexibility in favor of the free, creative adventure of serving God together. On the other hand, an equally astonishing bigotry is sometimes the order of the day, coupled with an emphasis on the exclusiveness of a given group because of its doctrinal distinctives. The "voluntary principle" appears to have an inherent predisposition to either tolerance of others or the absolutization of one's own views.

Wherever the "voluntary principle" became constitutive in Protestant missions — in nondenominational or denominational societies, in well-organized and well-prepared projects or in faith missions, in ecumenical or evangelical circles — the operative presuppositions were those of Western democracy and the free-enterprise system. It proceeded from the assumption that the missionary traffic would move in one direction only, from the West to the East or the South. It spawned an enterprise in which the one party would do all the giving and the other all the receiving. This was so because the one group was, in its own eyes, evidently privileged and the other, equally evidently, disadvantaged.

Missionary Fervor, Optimism, and Pragmatism

In spite of the fact that missionary circles in the West, on the whole, reacted rather negatively to the Enlightenment, there can be no doubt that this movement unleashed an enormous amount of Christian energy which was, in part, channelled into overseas missionary efforts. More than in any preceding period Christians of this era believed that the future of the world and of God's cause depended on *them*.

In this respect the Enlightenment era represented a significant shift away from two other developments — the one cultural, the other ecclesiastical — that preceded it. I am referring to the Renaissance and to Protestant orthodoxy, both of which were oriented backward rather than forward. The Enlightenment's orientation, by contrast, was decidedly forward and optimistic. Under its influence, the churches tended to view God as benevolent Creator, humans as intrinsically capable of moral improvement, and the kingdom of God as the crown of the steady progression of Christianity.

The idea of progress became prominent in the seventeenth century. In the eighteenth it extended into all walks of life and all disciplines. It reached its zenith in the nineteenth and early twentieth century (cf Küng 1987:17f). Protestant missions could not escape its optimism and its orientation toward the future. It found its classical expression in Kenneth Scott Latourette's famous seven-volume *A History of the Expansion of Christianity*, which exercised a profound influence in missionary circles, especially in the English-speaking world. Latourette portrayed seven major periods of Christian expansion since the first century. The pattern of expansion, he suggested, had been like seven successive waves of an incoming tide. The crest of each wave was higher than the crest that had preceded it, and the trough of each wave receded less than the one before it. Changing the metaphor slightly, Latourette wrote that, throughout its history, Christianity "has gone forward by major pulsations. Each advance has carried it further than the one before it. Of the alternating recessions, each has been briefer and less marked than the one which preceded it" (Latourette [1945] 1971:494).

Latourette penned down these words in 1944, toward the end of World War

II, somewhere down the line of the seventh period whose outcome was, humanly speaking, still uncertain. According to Latourette this era, which he designated "Advance through Storm", started with World War I in 1914. In spite of the devastation of two world wars he remained essentially optimistic, however, and could say that "never had any faith been so rooted among so many people as was Christianity in AD 1944"; it was affecting "more deeply more different nations and cultures than ever before" (:494). When Latourette's seven-volume work was republished in 1971, Ralph Winter, still operating wholly within the Latourette paradigm, added a chapter in which he surveyed developments since 1944. He called it "The Twenty-Five Unbelievable Years, 1945-1969" (Winter, in Latourette 1971:507-533). It is an excellent perusal of secular and religious developments and ends with the same "optimistic realism" (:533) that characterized Latourette's own thinking and writing.

The roots of Latourette's and Winter's optimism and pragmatism lay in the late eighteenth century. It was a period of spectacular political upheaval, which had an adverse effect especially on traditional Roman Catholic countries such as France. In Protestant circles people grew enthusiastic about the prospect of the decline of the papacy and the large-scale conversion of Jews, in the wake of their being granted full citizenship in France and elsewhere. In Britain this period was characterized by an almost apocalyptic enthusiasm (van den Berg 1956:121). Much of it spilled over to the continent and, more especially, to the United States of America. By the second decade of the nineteenth century, the missionary cause had an importance and glory "unspeakably greater" than at any previous period in Protestantism (Chaney 1976:174, 256). It was "the harvest time of the world", during which the kingdom of Satan was overturning and the reign of Jesus rising in its ruins. It was not an age to be idle (:257). Any Christian who dared raise questions about the validity of conversionist foreign missions was somehow not a genuine believer (Hutchison 1987:60). In 1818 Gordon Hall and Samuel Newell published a book entitled *The Conversion of the World*, in which they espoused the idea of the "*ability* and *duty* of the churches" to "respect" the claims of "six hundred million of heathen", suggesting that the Western churches could convert the world within twenty years (Chaney 1976:180; Johnson 1988:2f).

Indeed, the nineteenth-century envoys of the gospel, while sharing the Puritans' confidence in Protestantism's ability to renovate the world, far exceeded their spiritual forebears in their certitude that they represented a society in which this was already being realized (Hutchison 1987:9). A charter and battle plan for Christianity's final conquest of the world were called for (:51). It was not to be achieved by means of miracles, but by means of "industry and zeal" (Chaney 1976:257, 269). The "principles of reason" and the "dictates of common sense" blended happily with the "directions of scripture" and the "obvious designs of providence" (:258). The building of the kingdom of God had become as much a matter of technique and program as it was of conversion and religious piety (Moorhead 1984:75). The gospel was viewed as an *instrument* for producing a vital transformation in the total human situation, a "weapon" that alleviated woes, a "divine medicament" and "antidote", a "remedy" and "appointed means of civilizing the heathen" (Chaney 1976:240-242). The gospel was a "tool", along with all the many new tools and implements Western technology was beginning to invent. It joined the three great gods of the modern era—science, technology, and industrialization (Kuschel 1984:235)—and was harnessed with them to serve the spread of the gospel and of Christian values.

After the 1880s, that is, during the high imperial era, activism and pragmatism were propounded with renewed vigor. They were now more clearly identified as an expression of *North American* missions, but were by no means restricted to them. It was the "age of energy" and a time for great enterprises. In words reminiscent of the language later to be used by Latourette, Pierson said that "the influence of Jesus Christ was never so widespread and so penetrating and so transforming" as it was in his day (quoted by Forman 1982:54).

Pierson is also the person credited with formulating the watchword, "The evangelization of the world in this generation", adopted by the Student Volunteer Movement in 1889 (cf Anderson 1988:99; Johnson 1988). The watchword both reflected and gave birth to the scintillating missionary optimism of the period. More than anything else, it epitomized the Protestant missionary mood of the period: pragmatic, purposeful, activist, impatient, self-confident, single-minded, triumphant. It found tangible expression in the mammoth Ecumenical Missionary Conference, held in New York in 1900. Nobody could still doubt that "the cause of Christ" was soon going to be victorious. Surely, says Hutchison (1987:100), statistics such as these, together with a comparison of the "mission statistics" of the year 1800 with those of the year 1900, were such that they could lead one "to understand the sense of momentum and divine inevitability that gripped the souls of this generation, and that enabled perfectly sane people to talk of speedy world evangelization". William Dodge expressed a common conviction when he said, "We are going into a century more full of hope, and promise, and opportunity than any period in the world's history" (quoted by Anderson 1988:102).

Americans were probably not more activistic than most others. What was happening, rather, "was that Americans were doing more of everything"; amid the general enthusiasm for conquering the world for Christ or Christian civilization, "Americans were proclaiming this intention with a louder voice and a loftier idealism" than others (Hutchison 1987:93f). This frequently called forth reactions and even scathing attacks from the more "sober" continental Europeans, especially the Germans. In the course of time "both the astonishment at the Americans' zeal and efficiency, and the doubts about their haste and religious superficiality, grew exponentially" (Hutchison 1987:131). Europeans were particularly suspicious of the New York conference. G. Warneck pointed out that the missionary command "bids us 'go' into all the world, not 'fly' ", and that Jesus likened God's kingdom to a farmer's field, not to a hothouse (references in Hutchison 1987:133f).

Warneck's lifelong friend, Martin Kähler, had similar reservations, this time about the 1910 Edinburgh World Missionary Conference. The conference went ahead as planned, however, structured largely on guidelines provided by North American assumptions. This remarkable "ecumenical evangelical" conference had no difficulty in praising, in one breath, both the salvation wrought in Christ and the astonishing progress of "secular" science. The latter was naively lauded as manifestation of God's providence for the sake of the church's worldwide mission (cf Knapp 1977).

The tone of the conference was already set by Mott in his 1900 book (revised in 1902), *The Evangelization of the World in this Generation*. Chapter 5 was entitled "The Possibility of Evangelizing the World in This Generation[11] in View of Some Modern Missionary Achievements" (1902:79-101). It was in the next chapter, however — entitled "The Possibilities of Evangelizing the World in This Generation in View of the Opportunities, Facilities and Resources of the Church" (:103-129) — that Mott really succeeded, in a masterful way, in combining his faith in God's revelation in Christ with his faith in the "providential" achievements of modern science. The whole world was now open to the church, thanks to the "marvelous orderings of Providence during the nineteenth century" (:106).

Equally important were the facilities the church now had at its disposal. It had acquired a vast knowledge "of the social, moral and spiritual condition and need of all races" and could avail itself of "greatly enlarged and improved means of communication" (:109). These included railways, steamships, cable and telegraph systems, news agencies, the Universal Postal Union, and the printing press (:109-113). The "influence and protection of Christian governments" was likewise "an immense help to the work of missions" (:114f). Medical knowledge and skills, and the methods and results of science and of other branches of Western learning were at the disposal of the missionary effort (:115). Then there was the vast array of resources the church possessed. Its growing membership in the Western world provided a sure base for a worldwide mission. Its "money power" was enormous and giving to foreign missions was steadily increasing. The many missionary societies were among "the greatest resources of the Church". The Bible societies were providing bibles in ever more languages. Christian colleges were being erected in many Asian and African countries. The Christian student movement was a particularly formidable force for mission. The Sunday School movement, in some respects still "the largest undeveloped missionary resource", had incalculable potentialities for mission (:116-126). The "native Church" was the human resource which afforded the "largest promise for the evangelization of the world". In the year 1900 there were already seventy-seven thousand native evangelists, pastors, teachers, catechists, medical workers, and other helpers working full-time in this area (:126f). Of course, the "divine resources of the Church" remained "immeasurably more powerful and important than all others" (:127), but they were not essentially different from the ones just listed, as becomes evident when Mott continues and summarizes (:127-129 [the two quotations in the following paragraph are from *The Student Volunteer* and Calvin W. Mateer]),

Why has God made the whole world known and accessible to our generation? Why has He provided us with such wonderful agencies? Not that the forces of evil might utilize them . . . Such vast preparations must have been made to further some mighty and beneficent purpose. Every one of these wonderful facilities has been intended primarily to serve as a hand-maid to the sublime enterprise of extending and building up the Kingdom of Jesus Christ in all the world. The hand of God in opening door after door among the nations of mankind, in unlocking the secrets of nature and in bringing to light invention after invention, is beckoning the Church of our day to larger achievements. If the Church, instead of theorizing and speculating, will improve her opportunities, resources and facilities, it seems entirely possible to fill the earth with the knowledge of Christ before the present generation passes away. With literal truth it may be said that ours is an age of unparalleled opportunity. "Providence and revelation combine to call the Church afresh to go in and take possession of the world for Christ . . . Now steam and electricity have brought the world together. The Church of God is in the ascendant. She has well within her control the power, the wealth, and the learning of the world. She is like a strong and well-appointed army in the presence of the foe . . . The victory may not be easy, but it is sure".

I have quoted extensively from Mott's famous booklet since, more than any other publication, it conveys the spirit of optimism and confidence that characterized Western, especially North American, missionary circles at the beginning of our century. It was this spirit that prevailed also at the Edinburgh Conference. Edinburgh represented the all-time highwater mark in Western missionary enthusiasm, the zenith of the optimistic and pragmatist approach to missions.

The mood at Edinburgh was futurist rather than eschatological. The future was primarily seen as an extension of the present; as such it could be inaugurated through human efforts (van 't Hof 1972:34). Mott's earlier views were reventilated and at the same time expanded. Entire tribes on the "mission field" were being converted. Reports from the "field" pleaded desperately with home churches for more laborers to "gather in the harvest". The fact that the geographical base of mission was in the West and that the movement of missionaries was in one direction only did not yet present a problem. Western mission was an undisputed power. Mission stood in the sign of world conquest. Missionaries were referred to as "soldiers", as Christian "forces". References were made to missionary strategies and tactical plans. Military metaphors such as "army", "crusade", "council of war", "conquest", "advance", "resources", and "marching orders" abounded (:27-29). All circumstances added up to the recognition of the fact that the present moment was a mandate for mission; it was "an opportune time", "a critical time", "a testing time for the church", "a decisive hour for the Christian mission" (:34).[12]

In continental Europe this optimistic mood was shattered by World War I. Max Warren once referred to the experience of the abyss, which more surely divides continental from Anglo-Saxon theological thinking (1961:161). In North America then, and to a lesser extent in Britain, the optimistic mood continued throughout the 1950s. The world was being rebuilt feverishly and the Christian church had a decisive role to play in this. The upsurge in missionary interest during this period was astounding. Both ecumenical and evangelical mission agencies got involved on an unprecedented scale, although the former's emphasis had shifted to cooperation with the younger churches rather than unilaterally undertaking missionary, educational, and other projects.

The decade of the sixties brought with it the last, even if convulsive, attempts at reasserting the philosophy of Western programs proffering a panacea for the world's ills. There was a firm conviction that the churches were able to respond positively, adequately, and efficiently to the world's needs. Ecumenicals and evangelicals, drawing respectively on the ideas of progressive Capitalism and egalitarian Socialism, were equally convinced that they could remake the world into their respective images. Ecumenicals thought that they were equipped to penetrate the power structures of politics, economics, technology, science, and the mass media and bring about an effective change in their substance and direction. Evangelicals rallied around a revival of the SVM watchword about "the total evangelization of the world . . . in this generation"; a congress of the Interdenominational Foreign Missions Association, held in Chicago in 1960, issued a call for eighteen thousand additional missionaries (cf Anderson 1988:110; on plans for world evangelization during the second half of the twentieth century, cf Barrett and Reapsome 1988).

Both these groups resolutely followed a soteriological vision, even if their definitions of "salvation" increasingly differed.

The belief in progress and success that transpired from all these missions and visions, from the seventeenth century to the twentieth, were made possible by the advent of the Enlightenment, but also involved a subtle shift of emphasis from grace to works. Christians burdened themselves with a wide-ranging and comprehensive mission of renewing the face of the earth; the possibilities for realizing this were inherent in the present order. This entire development was, in a sense, inevitable. It was unthinkable that Christians after the advent of the Enlightenment could be the same as they had been before.

The Biblical Motif

I have indicated that in every period since the early church there was a tendency to take one specific biblical verse as *the* missionary text. Such a text was not necessarily quoted frequently. Still, even where it was hardly referred to, it somehow embodied the missionary paradigm of the period.

I have suggested that John 3:16 may be looked upon as the one verse giving expression to the patristic understanding of mission. During the medieval Roman Catholic missionary period, Luke 14:23 played a somewhat similar role. Again, the missionary text of the Protestant Reformation was Romans 1:16f.

Moving on to the missionary paradigm of the Enlightenment era, the situation becomes more ambiguous. This certainly has to do with the fact that during this period mission was much more diverse and multifaceted than ever before. It would therefore be virtually impossible to identify only *one* missionary text for this epoch. We may have to distinguish among several. Three of these have already been alluded to in this chapter. First, Paul's vision of the Macedonian man, beseeching him and saying, "Come over to Macedonia and help us" (Acts 16:9), was especially prominent in the period when Western Christians viewed peoples of other races and religions as living in darkness and deep despair and as imploring Westerners to come to their aid. Second, premillennialists were, and still are, fond of appealing to Matthew 24:14, since this verse clearly embodies their understanding of mission. Third, Newbigin (1978:103) has drawn attention to the fact that, in those circles indebted to the legacy of the Social Gospel, one of the most popular missionary texts was the words of Jesus in John 10:10, "I came that they may have life, and have it abundantly" — abundant life being interpreted "as the abundance of the good things that modern education, healing, and agriculture would provide for the deprived peoples of the world".

A fourth text has to be added, however, one that certainly was the most widely used during the entire period discussed in this chapter — the "Great Commission" of Matthew 28:18-20. Although the "Great Commission" also featured during the Reformation and Protestant orthodoxy, the person really to be credited with putting it on the map, so to speak, was William Carey in his 1792 tract entitled *An Enquiry into the Obligations of Christians to Use Means for the Conversion of the Heathen*, in which he, with the aid of a simple yet powerful argumentation, demolished the conventional interpretation of Matthew 28:18-20.

Since Carey, the appeal to Matthew 28:18-20 has always been prominent in Protestant (more especially evangelical Anglo-Saxon) missions. Chaney (1976:259) suggests that, in the United States, it became the major motive for engaging in missions after 1810. Harry Boer (1961:26) lists several early American missionaries, among them such famous figures as Robert Morrison (1792-1834) and Adoniram Judson (1788-1850), who explicitly stated that it was primarily because of obedience to Christ's command that they had gone to the mission field. Still, the appeal to the "Great Commission" in missionary sermons of the period appeared to be more or less stereotypical; since nobody doubted that the words were Christ's own, and in fact his last command, it was only natural that every preacher on mission would refer to it in every sermon, even if the text played no integral role in the overall argument. Obedience to the "Great Commission" could therefore, sometimes, appear rather far down the list of reasons for getting involved in mission (cf Hutchison 1987:48).

Johannes van den Berg is therefore much more on target when he says that the "Great Commission", at least in the early part of the nineteenth century, "was never the one and only motive, dominant in isolation", that "it never functioned as a separate stimulus", but "was always connected with other motives" (1956:165; cf 177).

This was to change, however. The spirit of rationalism, secularism, humanism, and relativism increasingly invaded the church and began subtly to undermine the very idea of preaching a message of eternal salvation to people who would otherwise be doomed. This provoked conservative, and particularly premillennialist, circles to appeal, in an almost convulsive manner, to the "Great Commission". It became a kind of last line of defense, as if the protagonists of mission were saying, "How can you oppose mission to the heathen if Christ himself has commanded it?"

In the course of time the theme of obedience to the "Great Commission" indeed tended to drown all other motifs. This happened, for instance, at the famous Mt. Hermon student conference of 1886, which was to be the beginning of the Student Volunteer Movement. William Ashmore concluded his presentation to the students with the challenge, "Show, if you can, why you should not obey the last command of Jesus Christ!" (cf Boer 1961:26). In the same year, A. T. Pierson began his most significant book on mission with the statement that Christ's command "makes all other motives comparatively unnecessary" (quoted in Hutchison 1987:113). Mott added, some years later, that Jesus' "final charges", reported in all the gospels and the Book of Acts, "define the first and most important part of our missionary obligation" (1902:5).

In continental Europe and Britain, too, mission was under attack from the side of the prevalent liberal theology. Here, also, the defense of the missionary cause took the form of a direct appeal to the commission of Jesus. By the end of the nineteenth century Matthew 28:18-20 had completely superseded other verses from Scripture as principal "mission text". Now the emphasis was unequivocally on *obedience*. The great Dutch theologian of the period, Abraham Kuyper, stated, "All mission flows from God's sovereignty, not from God's love or compassion". Elsewhere he insisted, "All mission is, formally, obedience to God's command; materially, the message is not an invitation, but an order, a burden. The Lord sends his command, 'Repent and believe!', not as a recommendation or an admonition, but as a decree" (references in van 't Hof 1980:45 — my translation). Johannes Warneck, though using less absolutist language than Kuyper, believed, like Kuyper, that "the impulse to mission only arose where the missionary idea was laid upon people's consciences as a compelling *command* of the Lord" (1913:16 — my translation).

In the period after World War II, when evangelicals became more confident of having a peculiar role to play in world missions, appeals of this nature were heard ever more frequently, as many "sought to reinstate the Great Commission as a leading, or even as an entirely sufficient, justification for missions" (Hutchison 1987:191).

There can be no doubt that this kind of appeal to the "Great Commission" has succeeded in mobilizing and bolstering evangelical missionary "forces".[13] Still, grave concerns about such an appeal have to voiced. First, it is almost always polemical, an attack on what is regarded as the watered-down understanding of mission in "ecumenical" circles. Second, it is usually couched in a most simplistic form of biblical literalism and proof-texting, with hardly any attempt at understanding the commission from within the context in which it appears in Scripture.[14] Most important, it removes the church's involvement in mission from the domain of *gospel* to that of *law*.

MODERN MISSIONARY MOTIVES AND MOTIFS — A PROFILE

Looking back at the many and varied motifs discussed in this chapter, one cannot help feeling overwhelmed. No single motif appeared to have dominated in any given period or tradition. In addition, the powerfully centrifugal forces at work frequently resulted in virtually each motif operating in two opposing ways. In the previous period there had been less discord. Several motifs — the glory of God, a sense of urgency because of the imminent millennium, the love of Christ, compassion for those considered eternally lost, a sense of duty, the awareness of cultural superiority, and competition with Catholic missionary efforts — had blended together to form a mosaic (cf Rooy 1965:282-284). Now, however, there was virtually no trace of a unified pattern of thought and practice. Sometimes Christians responded in widely divergent ways to the challenge posed to the Christian mission by the Enlightenment, as a careful study of each of the nine missionary motifs listed above would show.

The fact of the matter is that each of these motifs, as they shaped missionary thinking since the middle of the eighteenth century, betrayed the features of the Enlightenment discussed earlier in this chapter: the undisputed primacy of reason, the separation between subject and object, the substitution of the cause-effect scheme for belief in purpose, the infatuation with progress, the unsolved tension between "fact" and "value", the confidence that every problem and puzzle could be solved, and the idea of the emancipated, autonomous individual.

Since all human beings were *creatures of reason*, a very optimistic anthropology replaced the somber view of humans which had predominated in medieval Catholicism and the Protestant Reformation era. Only, in spite of lip-service paid to the "rationality" of every human being, Western superiority feelings saw to it that, in practice, Westerners were credited with more rationality than others. There was, on this score, not much difference between evangelicals and social gospellers.

The *subject-object dichotomy* meant that, in admittedly very opposite ways, the Bible and, in fact, the Christian faith as such, became objectified. Liberals sovereignly placed themselves above the biblical text, extracting ethical codes from it, while fundamentalists tended to turn the Bible into a fetish and apply it mechanically to every context, particularly as regards the "Great Commission". Each group, in its own way, celebrated the precept that each person was able to understand the Bible unaided by others. But also, representatives of both groups — because of their inveterate belief in their own "manifest destiny" — often tended to treat peoples of other cultures as objects rather than brothers and sisters.

The *elimination of purpose* implied that, as long as people succeeded in creating the right conditions, the success of their missionary enterprise was guaranteed. This was the overall thrust of James Dennis's three-volume treatise on Christian missions and social progress (1897, 1899, 1906). But ardent evangelicals could subscribe to the same philosophy: improved social conditions would guarantee an open ear for the gospel of eternal redemption or, alternatively, effective evangelism would, as a matter of course, lead to social betterment. In either case the Enlightenment tenet of a direct and causal relationship between "seed" and "fruit" reigned supreme.

The foundational Enlightenment belief in the assured *victory of progress* was perhaps more explicitly recognizable in the Christian missionary enterprise than any other element of the age. There was a widespread and practically unchallengeable confidence in the ability of Western Christians to offer a cure-all for the ills of the world and guarantee progress to all—whether through the spread of "knowledge" or of "the gospel". The gradual secularization of the idea of the millennium (which was, incongruously, also evident among conservatives, particularly those within the ranks of the "Religious Right") turned out to be one of the most sustained manifestations of the doctrine of progress.

The distinction between *facts and values* meant that Christian missionaries tried, in two radically different ways, to defend the "scientific" nature of their enterprise. Some, particularly in the more extreme manifestations of the Social Gospel, put all emphasis on tangible, demonstrable and calculable *this*-worldly achievements; others declared only *other*-worldly realities to be really real and put all emphasis on the salvation of souls.

To some extent the belief that, in principle, *everything was solvable*, underlay the eruption of voluntarist missionary agencies as early as the end of the eighteenth century and also accounted for the incredible upsurge of optimism a century later. It was hardly accidental that this upsurge was, time-wise, framed by the Berlin Conference of 1885 and the outbreak of the First World War in 1914; it was the high imperial epoch, characterized by the conviction that it was the *West* and the Christians of the West who would solve the ills of the entire world, primarily by means of the program of colonialism and the planting of Western-type churches in all parts of the world.

The Enlightenment doctrine that *individuals* were to be free, *emancipated, and autonomous* meant that, implicitly or explicitly (in Protestantism at least) God and humans were felt to be rivals. If the aim of mission was viewed as giving glory to God, this was interpreted as slighting the value and contribution of humans; if the inherent capability of human beings to make the right choices and act ethically was emphasized, this was seen as a refusal to give all credit to God. In the course of time, however, it was the latter of these two equations that triumphed. It manifested itself in the gradual "Arminianization" of Protestantism, evidenced not only by the rapid growth of (Arminian) Methodist and Baptist churches in the United States, but also in significant shifts toward an Arminian position in Lutheran, Reformed, Presbyterian, and Anglican circles.

I have, in this chapter, paid more attention to the views of missionary spokespersons than to those of missionaries themselves. Perhaps there was no great discrepancy between the two sets of views. Ultimately, however, it is more important to know what it was that made individuals go to the ends of the earth than to reflect on the opinions and predilections of those who sent them. Certainly, all the motifs discussed above, and more, were embodied in those missionaries. They were children of their time, but no ordinary children. Shorter writes about them wistfully and almost nostalgically,

> If the early missionaries had not been spiritual giants they would not have got away with what they did, but they were holy men, of immense courage and personality. Their goodness was transparent, and their intolerance,

though completely baffling to non-Christians, was nevertheless forgiven (1972:24).

Only very few of those missionaries, however, managed to escape the spell cast over them by the worldview of the Enlightenment, and even then only partially. They remained indebted, even in their "best" moments, to a world shaped by a most peculiar constellation of events and creeds. Even when they, in the words of the title of van den Berg (1956), were "constrained by Jesus' love", they could never communicate that love in its pristine form since it was always mixed with extraneous elements.

The entire Western missionary movement of the past three centuries emerged from the matrix of the Enlightenment. On the one hand, it spawned an attitude of tolerance to all people and a relativistic attitude toward belief of any kind; on the other, it gave birth to Western superiority feelings and prejudice. It is not always possible to divide these sentiments neatly between "liberals" and "evangelicals". Moreover, and only seemingly incongruously, tolerance as well as intolerance, relativism as well as bigotry could often be found side by side in the same person or group.

The Western missionary enterprise of the late eighteenth to the twentieth century remained, in spite of valid criticism which may be aimed at it, a most remarkable exercise. The influence of the Enlightenment on it was, moreover, not only negative and there is no point in trying to imagine how things might have developed had there been no Enlightenment. The entire phenomenon, in all its ramifications, was a child of Christianity and — given the overall constellation of facts and events — truly inevitable. Within the ambience of the movement Western Christians — in their emerging relationship with people of other cultures — did the only thing that made sense to them — they brought them the gospel as they understood it. For this we owe them respect and gratitude.

In our own time, however, the Christian missionary enterprise is, slowly but irrevocably, moving away from the shadow of the Enlightenment. The factors that have contributed to this are legion; in the next chapter some, and only some, of them will be identified. In the new paradigm mission will have — in spite of all elements of continuity with the past — to be different from what it was during the heyday of the Enlightenment. Some would go further and argue that the entire modern missionary enterprise is to such a profound degree an integral element and manifestation of the expanding Western world and Enlightenment spirit of the past three or four centuries that it is really impossible to salvage it as that world collapses in ruins (cf Rütti 1974:301). We shall have to reflect seriously on whether this is really required.

Few sincere Christians would be prepared to jettison the missionary idea and ideal as such. They believe that the Christian faith is intrinsically missionary. But they may be prepared for a revision of missionary theology and practice, for a missiological paradigm shift. In an article first published in 1959 Kraemer (1970:73) suggested that such a revision was needed (cf the introduction of the present book). A few years later Keith Bridston also reflected on the future and its implications for the nature of mission. The latter half of the twentieth century may prove, he said, "to be as radical in its implications for the missionary outlook of the Christian church as the Copernican revolution was for the scientific cosmology of its day" (1965:12f). A total transformation was needed, he added, the implications of which were only beginning to dawn on us (:16). The traditional forms of mission embodied a response to a world that no longer existed, and even if we do not have to negate the traditional mission response as such, we are challenged to respond in a very different way today (:17). The only ultimately effective solution to the widespread missionary malaise of today, which is sometimes hidden from our eyes because of our apparent missionary "successes", is a "radical transformation of the whole life of the church" (:19).

PART 3

TOWARD A RELEVANT MISSIOLOGY

Chapter 10

The Emergence of a Postmodern Paradigm

THE END OF THE MODERN ERA

In the preceding chapters of this study I have attempted to trace the development of the theology of the Christian mission from New Testament times up to the modern era. It has become abundantly clear that in each historical epoch of the past two millennia the missionary idea has been profoundly influenced by the overall context in which Christians lived and worked.

In chapter 5 I suggested that the "modern" or "Enlightenment" era would not be the last epoch of world history to exercise an influence on the thought and practice of mission. One more paradigm would follow, which, for the moment, I am calling the *"post*modern"[1] paradigm. All the other epochs discussed here, even the "modern" one, belong to the past; we could therefore, in a sense, look back upon them. The situation with the postmodern paradigm is fundamentally different. New paradigms do not establish themselves overnight. They take decades, sometimes even centuries, to develop distinctive contours. The new paradigm is therefore still emerging and it is, as yet, not clear which shape it will eventually adopt. For the most part we are, at the moment, thinking and working in terms of *two* paradigms.

A time of paradigm shift is a time of deep uncertainty—and such uncertainty appears to be one of the few constants of the contemporary era and one of the factors that engender strong reactions in favor of hanging on to the Enlightenment paradigm, in spite of signs from all quarters that it is breaking up.

It will be impossible to trace the developments that led to the break-up of the Enlightenment paradigm in any detail. A few broad and very general strokes will have to suffice.

Descartes, widely acclaimed as the father of the Enlightenment, employed the principle of radical doubt as the crux of his method. Only doubt, he believed, would purge the human mind of all opinions held merely on trust and open it to knowledge firmly grounded in reason (for a penetrating discussion of the "doctrine of doubt", cf Polanyi 1958:269-298). With this epistemological postulate Descartes set the tone for virtually all subsequent developments in science, philosophy, theology, etc. Naturally, many scholars moved beyond Descartes's position, but without altering it fundamentally. What happened, rather, was that the principle of doubt and the tenet of the supremacy of reason were increasingly refined as they were restated. Descartes himself emphasized a rational and deductive (or "mathematical") method in science. His slightly older contemporary, Francis Bacon (1561-1626), advocated an inductive approach, whereas Isaac Newton (1642-1717) was the first to introduce a blend of both methods (cf Capra 1983:65). The two approaches never blended completely, however, and remained, at best, two complementary models of doing science (cf Bernstein 1985:5). Twentieth-century Logical Positivism, for instance, tended to reflect the inductive trend, whereas Karl Popper's falsification theory may be viewed as continuation of the deductive tradition.

In both traditions, then, the premise of the preeminence of reason remained unassailable. Rationalism made such superb sense, particularly since its achievements in science and technology were so manifest, that it appeared absurd to question it. Small wonder then that its presuppositions were soon adopted by the human sciences as well (including theology). The very word "science" came to mean accurate knowledge, absolutely reliable data, etc. Theologians and other scholars of the humanities embraced this vision and applied it meticulously to their discipline — as much of nineteenth- and early twentieth-century theology, in all subdisciplines, attests.

Today this entire edifice is being challenged. The first fundamental assault on it did not (as one might have expected) come from the side of the human sciences. It came, quite surprisingly, from the very discipline where the Cartesian and Newtonian canons appeared totally inviolable: the field of physics, where scholars such as Albert Einstein and Niels Bohr introduced a revolution in thinking, so much so that Werner Heisenberg could say that the very foundations of science have started to move and that there was almost a need to start all over again (reference in Capra 1983:77). In the course of time it was only natural that similar upheavals would follow in other disciplines, including the humanities.

Events in world history, in particular two devastating global wars (1914-1918; 1939-1945) and everything that followed in their wake, also contributed to the steady erosion of the "naive realism" of the conventional paradigm. In theology Karl Barth, with his "theology of crisis", was the first to break fundamentally with the liberal theological tradition and to inaugurate a new theological paradigm. It was not really different in other disciplines. It became clear that the West together with its inherited understanding of reality was in trouble. Between the First and the Second World War philosophers of history like Oswald Spengler and Ptirim Sorokin attempted to trace the fundamental changes that were beginning to occur in Western culture.[2]

What was still only implicit in Spengler and Sorokin was made explicit in Guardini's *Das Ende der Neuzeit*, first published in 1950: the "modern era" — and, with it, the entire worldview on which it was built — was collapsing. Emerging from the same crucible as Guardini's book, namely the horror of the Second

World War and of Nazism, was *Dialektik der Aufklärung* (1947) by two of the leading representatives of the Frankfurt School, Max Horkheimer and Theodor W. Adorno. Like Guardini, the authors still did not discern the way forward out of the present impasse. They presented their views, for the time being, only as "fragments" (cf the book's subtitle). They recognized that science itself, as practiced according to the Enlightenment paradigm, had become questionable (:5) and that the Enlightenment was destroying itself (:7). Progress was turning into regress (:10). Their concern remained, however, a salvage operation—they wished to rescue the Enlightenment from self-destruction and "irrationalism" (:10f). The problem, as Jürgen Habermas (a junior colleague of the authors of *Dialektik der Aufklärung*) has pointed out, was that they refused (or were unable) to relinquish the view that *reason* and reason alone, in its traditional form, enables us to make normative statements—although they admitted that reason, in the Enlightenment's understanding thereof, was fundamentally corrupted.

Clearly, a more fundamental critique of the Enlightenment paradigm was called for. This came when researchers began to take more seriously the role of history, the human subject, and the social group. Two pioneering publications in this respect were Michael Polanyi's *Personal Knowledge* (1958) and Thomas Kuhn's *The Structure of Scientific Revolutions* ([1962] 1970). The opening sentence of Kuhn's book documents the influence of history and context on all human knowledge: "History, if viewed as a repository for more than anecdote or chronology, could produce a decisive transformation in the image of science by which we are now possessed" (1970:1).

In spite of differences between them, it could be argued that there is a degree of convergence between the theories propounded by Kuhn and those espoused by Polanyi. Habermas, Paul Ricoeur, and more recently John Thompson and Charles Taylor, have worked out similar ideas (cf Nel 1988). In all these views scientific theory, history, sociology, and hermeneutics go hand in hand (cf Küng 1987:162). A new vision is emerging, and it affects *all* the sciences, both human and natural. Habermas contends that, in addition to the Enlightenment's "instrumental" reason, we should create room for what he calls "communicative" reason. And Kuhn argues that scientific knowledge is not the outcome of objective, "instrumental" or "mechanistic" research but the product of historical circumstances and of intersubjective communication. In this way he challenges the Enlightenment's thesis of the priority of thought to being and of reason to action (cf Lugg 1987:176).

THE CHALLENGE TO THE ENLIGHTENMENT

After this all-too-brief survey of recent developments in the theory of science, I now wish to pick up, once again, the seven major characteristics of the Enlightenment referred to in chapter 9 and reflect briefly on the way in which each of them has been challenged by the most recent paradigm shift. I will, at this stage, not attempt to spell out in any detail the implications of this shift for missionary thinking and practice (this will follow in the next chapter); the considerations offered here are, however, important for what follows.

The Expansion of Rationality

In the previous chapter I outlined five theological "responses" to the Enlightenment's elevation of reason as the only faculty by means of which humans can arrive at knowledge and insight (cf pp 269f above). All five of these responses have been tried in the missionary program of the Christian church, particularly during the twentieth century: Christianity was propagated as a unique religious experience; as something for private life alone; as more rational than science; as a rule for all of society; and as humanity's liberator from every redundant religious attachment. In various forms all these models are still being advocated in missionary thinking and practice. Furthermore, there appears to be a basic anxiety, shared by all five approaches, that, in spite of all the attempts either to fend off the attack of reason or make common cause with it, the future of religion is in jeopardy. Because of this, each of these approaches somehow comes across as being a kind of rearguard action. There is a widespread belief, anticipated with glee by some, with apprehension by others, that religion will sooner or later die out.

The very opposite now appears to be the case, however. Not religion itself but the belief that predicted its demise proved to be an illusion (cf Lübbe 1986:14; Küng 1987:23). "Non-Christian" religions did not die out, as J. Warneck (1909) suggested. The twentieth century saw a powerful resurgence of the so-called world religions: Islam, Buddhism, and Hinduism. The same is true of Christianity, and much of this has taken place precisely in communities where the Enlightenment has reigned for centuries, as a glimpse at David Barrett's *World Christian Encyclopedia* (1982) shows. At the dawn of the twentieth century a novel and virile version of Christianity, the Pentecostal movement, made its appearance and has since grown to become the largest single category in Protestantism, outstripping the Lutheran, Reformed, and Anglican communions (Barrett 1982:838). Despite the often brutal suppression of religion in the Soviet Union and China, it is now becoming increasingly clear that Christianity is expanding rather than waning in these and similar countries. In Poland, despite almost half a century of Marxist rule, the Roman Catholic Church appears to have more support from the population than at any time in recent history. In Latin America, where (it is claimed) the christianization of the population was rather superficial,[3] there appears to be an undreamt-of vigor in Catholicism, manifested, *inter alia*, in the *comunidades ecclesiales de base* (base ecclesial communities). Predictions about the numerical growth of Christianity in Africa have to be revised often, since they are soon shown to have been too modest.

It is not easy to find an adequate explanation for this phenomenon. Much of it undoubtedly has to be judged rather negatively, as evidence of an inability to cope with the pressures of society which then results in a flight into religion (or pseudo-religion), in an individualization or privatization of faith (often producing a kind of à la carte or do-it-yourself religion) or, alternatively, in utilizing religion as buttress for a society which appears to be crumbling.

There is, however, more to the resurgence of religion than this. A fundamental reason lies in the fact that the narrow Enlightenment perception of rationality has, at long last, been found to be an inadequate cornerstone on which to build one's life. The objectivist framework imposed on rationality has had a crippling effect on human inquiry; it has led to disastrous reductionism and hence to stunted human growth.

Rationality has to be expanded. One way of expanding it is to recognize that language cannot be absolutely accurate, that it is impossible finally to "define" either scientific laws or theological truths. To speak with Gregory Bateson, neither science nor theology "proves"; rather, they "probe". This recognition has led to a reevaluation of the role of metaphor, myth, analogy, and the like, and to the rediscovery of the sense of mystery and enchantment. In this respect N. Frye's *The Great Code* (1983) is of special importance for theology (and in particular for missiology, in view of the entire new field of inculturation and contextualization of the gospel). The central doctrines of traditional Christianity, Frye says, can be expressed only in the form of metaphor; every attempt to go beyond that and "explain" doctrines has about it "a strong smell of intellectual mortality" (1983:55). In fact, when idolatry is condemned in the Bible, it "is often regarded as a 'literal' projection into the external world of an image that might be quite acceptable as a poetic metaphor" (:61). Frances Young (1988:308) argues along similar lines; that is, the early Fathers of the church, and particularly Gregory of Nazianzus (AD 330-389), often declared as heretics precisely those people who had claimed "to have mastered God by the powers of human reason".

Metaphor, symbol, ritual, sign, and myth, long maligned by those interested only in "exact" expressions of rationality, are today being rehabilitated; they create forms that "synthesize and evoke the integration of mind and will"; they "not only touch the mind and its conceptions, and evoke action with a purpose, but compel the heart" (Stackhouse 1988:104). So we see an upsurge of interest, especially in Third-World churches, in "narrative theology", "theology as story", and other nonconceptual forms of theologizing.

It is important to recognize that these modes of thinking and expression are not irrational or antirational. The problem with scientism is that it fetters human thought as cruelly as any authoritarian belief system has ever done, that it "offers no scope for our most vital beliefs and . . . forces us to disguise them in farcically inadequate terms" (Polanyi 1958:265). The best theologian, according to Gregory of Nazianzus, is not the one who can give a complete logical account of his subject, but the one who "assembles more of Truth's image and shadow" and thus moves beyond the confines of "pure" rationality (cf Young 1988:308). True rationality thus also includes *experience*. This is where the significance of Schleiermacher's theological approach lies, as well as the validity of the Pentecostal movement, the Charismatic Renewal (cf Lederle 1988), and many other manifestations of "experiential" religion.

I am therefore not suggesting the abandoning of rationality. We need to take the best of modern science, philosophy, literary criticism, historical method, and social analysis, and "constantly think through and rethink our theological understanding in the light of it all" (Young 1988:311). We should, indeed, retain and defend the critical power of the Enlightenment, but we should reject its reductionism. We are called to re-conceive rationality by expanding it to include much more than the *res cogitans*. This means that the religious dimension has to be incorporated into our overall vision of reality. It is, paradoxically, the only way in which the Enlightenment itself can be saved (cf Lübbe 1986:18). Without the religious element, says Guardini (1950:113), life is like an engine running without oil—it seizes up. When religion "falls apart or dries up, not only do people suffer meaninglessness but the civilization crumbles" (Stackhouse 1988:82). The human soul abhors a vacuum. If faith in God falls away, its place is taken by other gods: "the powers of Nature, Reason, Science, History, Evolution, Democracy, Individual Freedom, and Technology . . ." (West 1971:99), or other manifestations of secular religion, such as ideology.

Postmodern developments have shown that science is not inherently inimical to the Christian faith. This observation should not, however, lead us to postulate that there is no longer any tension between faith and reason, between religion and the world of science. This is what Fritjof Capra does, from a New Age perspective, particularly in *The Turning Point* (1983) and *The Tao of Physics* ([1976] 1984). In Capra's thinking, religion and science have embraced each other and are in perfect, tensionless harmony. It is significant, however, that Capra does not turn to the Christian faith in his attempt to argue his point, but to the Eastern religions, particularly Taoism and Buddhism. He finds the Chinese concept of *yin* and *yang* and their mutual relationship particularly amenable to his thesis.

Such views are immensely attractive, particularly in light of the long animosity between science and religion. Now that we are shaking off the shackles of rationalist thinking and are moving into the post-modern period, so it appears, the two can make peace and forever live in perfect harmony! Josuttis (1988) sounds a warning note, however, at least insofar as the Christian faith is concerned. With the easy integration of religion into its system, the postmodern paradigm has swallowed a poison which it will find difficult to digest (:16). Authentic religion imperils the emerging worldview, as it did for all earlier ones (:17). Whoever truly involves himself or herself with the Christian faith, with the biblical texts, and the ecclesial tradition, will encounter phenomena that are much more awkward and resistant than expected. The Christian faith has always designated as evil whatever destroys life. It has never affirmed its trust in God without challenging the power of anti-gods. It has concerned itself with the victims of society, but not without calling to repentance the perpetrators of injustice (:19; cf Daecke 1988).

Small wonder, then, that in those societies where structural injustice prevails and various theologies of protest are developing, there appears to be little enthusiasm for Capra's integrationism and avoidance of conflict. So, even if one can today say with confidence that many of the old battles between science and religion have become pointless and that religion can indeed look forward to playing a more vital role in society than was possible when the Enlightenment paradigm still reigned supreme, one has to recognize that the tensions will remain and that religion's role in the future will be a diffuse one (cf Küng 1987:26). There is no longer any room for the massive affirmations of faith which characterized the missionary enterprise of earlier times, only for a chastened and humble witness to the ultimacy of God in Jesus Christ.

Beyond the Subject-Object Scheme

The dominance over and objectification of nature and the subjecting of the physical world to the human mind and will—as championed by the Enlightenment—had disastrous consequences. It resulted in a world that was "closed, essentially completed and unchanging . . . simple and shallow, and fundamentally unmysterious—a rigidly programed machine" (H. Schilling, quoted in Hiebert 1985b:13).

At the same time, and paradoxically, instead of liberating humans it has enslaved them. First the machine replaced the human slave, then humans were turned into slaves of the machine. Production became the highest goal of being human, resulting in humans having to worship at the altar of the autonomy of technology.

A further disastrous consequence of the Cartesian model is found in what we today refer to as the ecological crisis. We have degraded the earth by treating it as an insensitive object; now it is dying under our very hands. We have damaged the ozone layer, and may thereby have signed our own death warrant. We are the first generation which with the help of nuclear power can destroy itself. Enlightenment culture—science, philosophy, education, sociology, literature, technology—has misinterpreted both humanity and nature, not only in some respects, but fundamentally and totally.

A basic reorientation is thus called for. One should, again, see oneself as a child of Mother Earth and as sister and brother to other human beings. One should think holistically, rather than analytically, emphasize togetherness rather than distance, break through the dualism of mind and body, subject and object, and emphasize "symbiosis".[4]

For the church's missionary existence in the world all this has profound and far-reaching consequences. It implies that nature and especially people may not be viewed as mere objects, manipulable and exploitable by others. Such a new epistemology for mission means, also, that technology must be confronted with a reality outside itself which does not depend on its canons of rationality and which therefore will not be subservient to its deterministic power. This reality may be identified as the reign of God, which stands in polemical tension with the closed system of this world.

Rediscovery of the Teleological Dimension

The elimination of purpose and the sustained linear causal reasoning of the Enlightenment paradigm ultimately rendered the universe meaningless. Humans cannot, however, continue living without meaning, purpose, and hope. Perhaps nineteenth-century Europe and North America, at least as far as the privileged classes were concerned, could afford to live in this manner. They could look at the forces inherent in the universe which guaranteed progress and improvement and could embrace the Darwinian evolution theory which suggested that, following biological laws inherent in nature, societies and individuals would gradually improve themselves; in this way the privileged could look forward to more solutions to riddles, subdue nature and, in fact, the entire world, and expect ever more privileges. In theological circles this meant, *inter alia*, that one could think in exclusively postmillennial categories, according to which the world would systematically be changed for the better until, almost imperceptibly, the kingdom of God would dawn on earth.

Toward the end of the nineteenth century, however, and more distinctly in the twentieth, there occurred a radical shift from non-eschatological to eschatological theology (cf Martin 1987:373f). This means a fundamental break with the idea that everything has to be the predictable or contrived consequence of some law, some immutable given. The category of contingency and unpredictability has been reintroduced. The notion of change — the belief that things can be different, that it is not necessary to live by old and established patterns, that everything does not operate according to unchanging laws of cause and effect — has again been recognized as both a theological and sociological category, and is creating almost boundless hope in the hearts of millions, particularly among the less privileged. The notions of repentance and conversion, of vision, of responsibility, of revision of earlier realities and positions, long submerged by the suffocating logic of rigid cause and effect thinking, have surfaced again and are inspiring people who have long lost all hope (:373f, 384), at the same time giving a new relevance to the Christian mission.

The Challenge to Progress Thinking

It was, to a large extent, the progress thinking of the Enlightenment that had given rise to the project of colonial expansion. The policy of "benevolent colonialism", however, was spawned, in part, by the Christian missionary enterprise. The same was true of the project of "development". It reflected, as far as Christian missions were concerned, a distinct evolution beyond earlier approaches.

Originally, the mission societies' involvement with people's daily needs was almost exclusively on the level of charity: disaster aid, care for orphans, the provision of rudimentary health care, and the like. During the third decade of this century, and particularly at the Jerusalem Conference of the International Missionary Council (1928), the idea of a "comprehensive approach" was propagated. The church should do more than just provide an "ambulance service"; it should get involved in "rural reconstruction", in the solution of "industrial problems", etc. After the Second World War the "comprehensive approach" philosophy was revamped and replaced with the notion of "development". Roman Catholics and Protestants alike joined enthusiastically in the new project.

It should therefore come as no surprise if we are told that the 1960s — the "decade of the secular" — was also the period of feverishly executed development plans, both governmental and ecclesial. A veritable deluge of pamphlets, books, and articles on the subject flooded the market. Development was going to solve the problems of the Third World! Optimism was in the air. Gutiérrez (1988:xvii) quotes the Medellín document of the Latin American conference of bishops (1968) which, although it had in some respects broken with the modernization model, nevertheless believed that Latin America was "on the threshold of a new epoch", which would lead people "progressively to an even greater control of nature". Such statements are reminiscent of those propounded two years earlier at the WCC Church and Society Conference in Geneva, where Mesthene (1967:484) applauded the new "massive physical changes deliberately induced", by means of which people could "literally pry new alternatives out of nature" and "create new possibilities almost at will".

The consequences of the development model were, however, contrary to what had been expected. The rich countries became richer and the poor still poorer. Within the poor countries those already privileged appeared to have benefited most from the programs. Socially and ecologically the results were often little short of disastrous (cf Bragg 1987:25-27). In retrospect the reasons are becoming clear. It has become apparent that the application of technology is not merely a technical matter, but that it is deeply influenced by the social and religious dispositions which lie behind it (Nürnberger 1982:240-248).

The process was further compounded by the fact that humans have often been regarded as mere objects in a network of planning, transfer of commodities, and logistic coordination in which the development agent was the initiator, planner, and master. Even more important was the entire area of *power*. It became clear that, deep down, this was the real issue, and that authentic development could not take place without the transfer of power. The Western developers appeared, however, to be either unwilling or unable to transfer power to poor third-world peoples.

Perhaps it would be more correct to say that the West was *both* unwilling and unable. The theory was that the Third World would be empowered without the West having to give up any of its power and privilege; however, even if the West had intended to relinquish power in favor of the Third World, it would have been impossible, given the contemporary asymmetrical relationship between the North and the South (for a detailed discussion, cf Nürnberger 1987a: passim). Because of the technological developments that had taken place during the past two or three centuries and the way these developments reshaped Western people, the West (and this includes both the capitalist and the socialist West) had a head start which made it virtually impossible for other countries ever to catch up. As a matter of fact, development projects often resulted in precisely the opposite of what they had intended: the Western developers became even more powerful than they had been and the "power gap" between the North and the South, instead of narrowing, actually widened.

Small wonder, then, that more and more Third-World countries have rejected the entire development concept and its Enlightenment presuppositions. *Desarrollismo* ("developmentalism") is used in a pejorative sense in Latin America; development did not attack the roots of the prevailing evil and merely caused confusion and frustration (Gutiérrez 1988:16f). Its obsession with "rationality" and its belief in effectiveness and evolution blinded it to the integral powers of culture and humanhood in the Third World. Development was not, as Paul VI had hoped, a new word for peace, but another word for exploitation. Underdevelopment was not a preliminary stage toward development but its consequence. The outcome of this approach was not just sobering; it was catastrophic. The "technological humanists" (as West [1971] calls those Westerners who believed in the ability of development to modernize the South) were wrong. The enemy was not nature or ignorance about technological know-how, but one structure of human power which exploited and destroyed the humanity of others (:32). The law of history is not development but revolution (West 1971:113, interpreting Karl Marx).

Thus a new model was propounded. The problem was not the relationship between backwardness and modernity, as those steeped in the thinking of the Enlightenment had thought, but the relationship between dependency and liberation (cf Nürnberger 1982:292-349; Bragg 1987:28-31; Gutiérrez 1988:13-25). Equity would not be reached via a "trickle down" of wealth from the rich to the poor, but via the overthrow of the present international system. The industrial nations accumulated their wealth by exploiting the non-Western countries during the colonial period. Indeed, there is poverty because there is wealth (Gutiérrez).

This is not the place to subject the liberation model to criticism. It will be done at a later stage in this study. For the moment, however, I just wish to suggest that the liberation model is not completely free from some of the debilitating influences of the Enlightenment from which the modernization model suffers. Even if the liberation model is eminently justified, given the sad history of Western dominance, expansion, and exploitation, it is still to a large extent built on the Enlightenment presuppositions of the innate good in (some) human beings who, once power has been transferred to them, will serve only the common good. One should, however, never forget that the Reign of Terror in France was instituted by the very people who had supported the French Enlightenment philosophers' conviction that the revolution would usher in the true humanity which prejudice, superstition and arbitrary authority had held in check (cf West 1971:73) and that this history has repeated itself several times since then, not only in the Russian Revolution and the subsequent Stalinist era, but also in other cases.

A Fiduciary Framework

Fundamental to the Enlightenment paradigm was the radical distinction between facts and values. This entire construction has, however, collapsed. The walls which Positivism and Empiricism erected between subject and object and between value and fact have begun to crumble (cf Lamb 1984:124f). It has been discovered that it is not possible to observe reality without, in a sense, altering what one sees. Every act of knowing, says Polanyi (1958:17), includes an appraisal.

The entire issue has been immensely compounded by the circumstance that modern science has released into human hands previously undreamt-of powers—powers that can no longer be regarded as neutral or value-free and for which humans are totally unprepared (cf Guardini 1950:94). The last illusions of scientific innocence, says M. Wartofsky, have been blown away by the radioactive winds over Hiroshima and Nagasaki (reference in Lamb 1984:123). Indeed, the fact-value distinction of science turned out to be the suicide of science (cf Bloom 1987:38f). "Objectivism", says Polanyi (1958:286), "has totally falsified our conception of truth".

It was not only the monsters created and then let loose by science that have helped Enlightenment science to come to its senses. Spokespersons from the Third World also began to challenge the neutrality of science by asking whose interests it was serving. They pointed out that science, far from being unbiased, was built on the cultural and imperialist assumptions of the West, that it was, in particular, a tool of exploitation and should be investigated in relation to the praxis out of which it comes.

We now know, then, that there are no "brute facts" but only *interpreted* facts and that interpretation is conditioned by the scientist's plausibility structure, which is largely socially and culturally produced. A case in point is the role *ideology* has played in the West. The great ideologies of the twentieth century — Marxism, Capitalism, Fascism, and National Socialism — were only made possible by Enlightenment scientism. It belongs to the nature of ideology to parade itself in the guise of science and to appeal to objective reason. Lübbe argues that ideologies are employing all the techniques of science in an effort to convince everybody that they are objectively true (1986:54).

In spite of (or, perhaps, because of) their professed scientific base ideologies are, however, for all practical purposes, functioning as religions (cf Lübbe 1986:53-73). More precisely, they are ersatz religions — substitutes for religion (:57) — and tend to take on explicitly religious forms and even rituals (:58f, 62).[5] They are, in the words of Raymond Aron, "the opiate of the intellectuals" (reference in Lübbe 1986:63).

All these — physics since Einstein, the discovery of the ambiguity of power, the relentless critique of the Third World on traditionally sacrosanct assumptions of science, the way in which ideologies have usurped the place traditionally occupied by religion — underline the crisis in which the Enlightenment got itself. Objectivity, as usually attributed to the "exact" sciences, has proved to be a delusion and, in fact, a false ideal (Polanyi 1958:18). The objectivist framework has imposed crippling mutilations on the human mind (:381). So Polanyi (:266) advocates the view that we should once again recognize *belief* as the source of all knowledge and consciously embrace a "fiduciary framework". "All truth", he says (:286), "is but the external pole of belief, and to destroy belief would be to deny all truth". Polanyi then promotes (:266), as a point of departure for *scientific* research, Augustine's adage: *nisi credideritis, non intelligitis* (unless you believe, you shall not understand).[6]

In this way Polanyi hopes to re-equip us with the faculties which centuries of critical thought have taught us to distrust (:381). He advocates the primacy of commitment, of "tacit" or "personal" knowledge (cf the title of his book) over "objective" knowledge, knowledge without a knowing subject (Popper 1979:109). A commitment may, of course, change; one may convert from one commitment to another. But the point is that nobody (and certainly not the Enlightenment scientist) is really completely without a commitment. As long as one lives and thinks within the pattern of a given paradigm, that paradigm provides one with a plausibility structure according to which all reality is interpreted. The paradigm may be a particular scientific worldview, or a religion, or an ideology; in each case the conceptual framework has almost all-embracing interpretative powers. It is only when one loses faith in a plausibility structure that one senses that its powers were excessive and specious (Polanyi 1958:288). In this respect Polanyi quotes Arthur Koestler who, only after he had ceased to be a Marxist, was able to write: "My party education had equipped my mind with such elaborate shock-absorbing buffers and elastic defenses that everything seen and heard became automatically transformed to fit a preconceived pattern". The point Polanyi is making is that the worldview one embraces may not be "true". It may, in fact, be the Big Lie. Still, it remains "irresistibly persuasive, since it sweeps away all existing criteria of validity and resets them in its own support" (:318).

Does this not mean that we have just jumped from the frying pan into the fire, that, having (rightly) rejected the myth of objectivity, we have now fallen prey to uncontrolled *subjectivism*? On the surface this indeed appears to be the case, particularly if someone like Kuhn (1970:94), in his eagerness to repudiate the objectivist thinking of Positivism and its heirs, states, "As in political revolutions, so in paradigm choice—there is no standard higher than the assent of the relevant community", and if he further argues (:103) that a new paradigm "is not only incompatible but often actually incommensurable with that which has gone before". Are these not examples of total relativism?

The alternative to objectivism or absolutism does not, however, have to be subjectivism or relativism. Kuhn himself later qualified his original position, which had suggested extreme subjectivism (cf Kuhn 1970:205-207). And Polanyi has argued that accepting a "fiduciary framework" does not suggest the adoption of an irrational position. It should therefore come as no great surprise that, after the early near-intoxication with the historicist or relativist position in the 1960s and 1970s, the next years witnessed to a return to a (modified) realist position in which concepts like truth and rationality are again being upheld. It is a tempered realism, however, one that remains aware of the contextuality of convictions, and operates in all disciplines. It may be a case of holding on to "unproven beliefs" (Polanyi 1958:268) and of taking "chances" (:318), but it is not a case of acting irrationally. Rather, the authentic Christian position in this respect is one of humility and self-criticism. After the Enlightenment it would be irresponsible not to subject our "fiduciary framework" to severe criticism, or not to continue pondering the possibility that Truth may indeed differ from what we have thought it to be. Whether we are aware of it or not, the developments of the past three centuries have greatly enhanced our critical powers, and we cannot go back to our earlier innocence. Polanyi expresses it as follows:

[Our critical powers] have endowed our mind with a capacity for self-transcendence of which we can never again divest ourselves. We have plucked from the Tree a second apple which has for ever imperilled our knowledge of Good and Evil, and we must learn to know these qualities henceforth in the blinding light of our new analytical powers (1958:268).

And yet, even as we are "humbly acknowledging the uncertainty of our own conclusions" (:271), for a "fiduciary philosophy does not eliminate doubt" (:318), the Christian continues to hold on to unproven beliefs. It is precisely such a self-critical posture of faith which may protect us against the "blind and deceptive" nature of a "creed inverted into a science" (:268). A post-Enlightenment self-critical Christian stance may, in the modern world, be the only means of neutralizing the ideologies; it is the only vehicle that can save us from self-deception and free us from dependence on utopian dreams (cf Lübbe 1986:63).

Since we now know that no so-called facts are really neutral or value-free, and that the line that used to divide facts from values has worn thin, we stand much more exposed than we used to. We also know, better than before, that while the future remains open and invites us to freedom, we are cautioned against new tyrannies and are facing new anxieties. At the same time we are conscious of the fact that it was precisely the prolonged attacks on religion made by rationalists that forced us to renew the grounds of the Christian faith (Polanyi 1958:286). This awareness is of critical importance for the Christian mission's and missionary's attitude to people of other faiths.

Chastened Optimism

Like other elements of the Enlightenment worldview, the belief that all problems are, in principle, solvable is also coming under increasing pressure. The West's grand schemes, at home and in the Third World, have virtually all failed dismally. The dream of a unified world in which all would enjoy peace, liberty, and justice, has turned into a nightmare of conflict, bondage, and injustice. The disappointment is so fundamental and pervasive that it cannot possibly be ignored or suppressed.

The uncritical acclamation of every manifestation of renewal, change, and liberation, so called, during the sixties and early seventies (WSCF conference, 1960; Church and Society Conference, 1966; Uppsala Assembly of the WCC, 1968; Catholic Bishops Conference in Medellín, 1968; CWME Conference in Bangkok, 1973) was the last almost convulsive illustration of the West's inability to believe that an era, the era of its hegemony, had passed. Since the seventies the horizon has progressively darkened. People are again becoming conscious of the reality of evil—in human beings and in the structures of society. The horizon is no longer limitless. We again realize, as did our forebears, that we cannot know more than a fraction of reality. It was in vain that humankind had burnt itself out in its attempt to build the tower of Babel.

All this does not, however, suggest that we should capitulate to pessimism and despair. All around us people are looking for new meaning in life. This is the moment where the Christian church and the Christian mission may once again, humbly yet resolutely, present the vision of the reign of God—not as a pie in the sky, but as an eschatological reality which casts its rays, however opaque, into the dismal present, illuminates it, and confers meaning on it. It is a road beyond Enlightenment optimism and anti-Enlightenment pessimism.

Toward Interdependence

The Enlightenment creed taught that every individual was free to pursue his or her own happiness, irrespective of what others thought or said.

This entire approach had disastrous consequences. The so-called openness of modern liberalism really means that people do not take others seriously — indeed, that they do not need others (Bloom 1987:34). It follows that individuals can no longer take themselves seriously and that, in spite of the fact that they now have the liberty to believe and do as they like, many do not believe in anything any more, and all spend their lives "in frenzied work and frenzied play so as not to face the fact, not to look into the abyss" (Bloom 1987:143, drawing on Nietzsche). Too self-confident to acknowledge or draw on their religious roots, too urbane to be duped by the lure of some irrational ideologies, all that remains in the end is the embrace of nihilism. Free to use their power any way they wish, modern humans have no referent outside themselves, no guarantee that they will use their freedom responsibly and for the sake of the common good. The autonomy of the individual, so much flaunted in recent decades, has ended in heteronomy; the freedom to believe whatever one chooses to believe has ended in no belief at all; the refusal to risk interdependence has ended in alienation also from oneself.

Two things are needed in order to break the grip of the spurious doctrine of autonomy and retrieve what is essentially human. First, we must reaffirm the indispensableness of conviction and commitment. In the long term, nobody can really survive without them. What is called for is the willingness to take a stand, even if it is unpopular — or even dangerous. Tolerance is not an unambiguous virtue, especially the "I'm ok, you're ok" kind which leaves no room for challenging one another.

Secondly, we need to retrieve togetherness, interdependence, "symbiosis" (cf Sundermeier 1986: passim). The individual is not a monad, but part of an organism. We live in one world, in which the rescue of some at the expense of others is not possible. Only *together* is there salvation and survival. This includes not only a new relationship to nature, but also among humans. The "psychology of separateness" has to make way for an "epistemology of participation". The "me generation" has to be superseded by the "us generation". The "instrumental" reason of the Enlightenment has to be supplemented with "communicative" reason (Habermas), since human existence is by definition intersubjective existence. Here lies the pertinence of the rediscovery of the church as Body of Christ and of the Christian mission as building a community of those who share a common destiny.

Chapter 11

Mission in a Time of Testing

Never before in the history of humankind have scholars in all disciplines (including theology) been so preoccupied as they are today, not with the study of their disciplines themselves, but with the metaquestions concerning these disciplines (cf Lübbe 1986:22). This state of affairs in itself is indicative of the presence of a crisis of major proportions or, to put it in Kuhnian terms, of the advent of a significant "paradigm shift" in *all* branches of science. And since all the modern academic disciplines are essentially *Western* phenomena and products, it is only to be expected that it is above all the West that finds itself in the midst of a crisis of gigantic proportions. It is becoming increasingly evident that the modern gods of the West—science, technology, and industrialization—have lost their magic (Kuschel 1984:235). Events of world history have shaken Western civilization to the core: two devastating world wars; the Russian and Chinese revolutions; the horrors perpetrated by the rulers of countries committed to National Socialism, Fascism, communism, and capitalism; the collapse of the great Western colonial empires; the rapid secularization not only of the West but also of large parts of the rest of the world; the increasing gap, worldwide, between the rich and the poor; the realization that we are heading for an ecological disaster on a cosmic scale and that progress was, in effect, a false god.

It was unthinkable that the Christian church, theology, and mission would remain unscathed. On the one hand the results of a variety of other disciplines—the natural and social sciences, philosophy, history, etc—have had a profound and lasting influence on theological thinking. On the other hand developments within church, mission, and theology (often precipitated, no doubt, by the momentous events and revolutions in other disciplines) have had equally far-reaching consequences. Theological elements which had for centuries been absent from the churches or have found a home in marginal Christian movements have once again surfaced in mainline Christianity and have, in a sense, effected a return to a pre-Constantinian position (cf Boerwinkel 1974:50-81). Adventists recovered the long neglected expectation of the parousia. Pentecostal and charismatic groups protested the loss of the gifts of the Spirit in mainline Christianity. The Brethren developed a church model without institutionalized or hierarchical offices. Baptist groups rejected infant baptism because this suggested the idea of automatic church membership and the absence of personal decision. Mennonites and Quakers distanced themselves from the church's support for violence and war. Marxism (to a significant extent a Christian "heresy") challenged the church's sanctioning of class differences and its tendency to be on the side of the rich and the powerful. And today many of these elements, initiated by protest movements on the fringes of the "official" church, have been embraced by the latter, even if not to the exclusion of other elements.

The church has also lost its position of privilege. In many parts of the world, even in regions where the church had been established as a powerful factor for more than a millennium, it is today a liability rather than an asset to be a Christian. The once-so-close relationship between "throne" and "altar" (for instance in the entire project of Western colonial expansion) has, in some instances, given way to an ever-increasing tension between the church and secular authorities. And the one-time persecutor (or, at least, conniver in the persecution) of Jews, Christian "sects", and adherents of other faiths has now taken up dialogue with these groups. Likewise, the tendency of one denomination to shun contact with other denominations (and in some cases even anathematize their members or regard them as objects of mission) has been replaced by ecumenical contact and cooperation.

In the traditional "mission fields" the position of Western mission agencies and missionaries has undergone a fundamental revision. No longer do missionaries go as ambassadors or representatives of the powerful West to territories subject to white, "Christian" nations. They now go to countries frequently hostile to Christian missions. David Barrett has calculated that countries are being closed to foreign missionary personnel at an average rate of two or three a year. The great religions of the world, once considered moribund, have become even more aggressively missionary than Christianity has ever been. Islam, in particular, is now a formidable force in many parts of the world and more resistant to Christian influences than ever before. And within the framework of the current mood of dialogue with people of other faiths, more and more missionaries are wondering whether there is still any point in going to the ends of the earth for the sake of the Christian gospel. Why, indeed, should one "suffer the pangs of exile and the stings of mosquitoes" (Power 1970:8) if people will be saved anyway? It is, after all, "bad enough to have a difficult job to do, but much worse when one is left wondering if the difficult job is worth doing" (:4).

Then there are the new relations with the "younger churches". Where Western missionaries are still welcomed (or tolerated), they go as "fraternal workers" in the service of already established autonomous churches. The rugged heroes of the faith of an earlier era, who "brought" the "gospel" to the uttermost ends of the earth and almost single-handedly (at least in their own estimation) built up new communities of faith, have evolved into "partners" who are often looked upon as expendable "spare tires". It has become clear that the missionary is not central to the life and the future of the younger churches;

in country after country (and especially in China) it has been demonstrated that the missionary is not only not central but may in fact be an embarrassment and a liability. Many of the grand institutions erected by mission agencies, often at great cost and with tremendous dedication—hospitals, schools, colleges, printing houses and the like—have turned out to be impediments rather than assets to the life and growth of the younger churches.

In the course of this century the missionary enterprise and the missionary idea have undergone some profound modifications. These came about, partly, as a response to the recognition of the fact that the church is indeed not only the recipient of God's merciful grace but sometimes also of his wrath (Paton 1953:17), that good intentions are not enough, that each of us is, in Luther's famous formulation, always *simul justus et peccator* ("at the same time justified as well as sinner"). Missionaries, perhaps more than others, have tended to regard themselves as immune to the weaknesses and sins of "ordinary" Christians; it took them a long time to discover that they were no different than the churches from which they had come, that, in the words of Stephen Neill (1960:222), they "have on the whole been a feeble folk, not very wise, not very holy, not very patient. They have broken most of the commandments and fallen into every conceivable mistake". Indeed, in many parts of the world, including its traditional home base, the Christian mission appears to be the object not of God's grace and blessing, but of God's judgment (cf the title of Paton 1953).

Writing after the Communist revolution in China, Paton makes bold to say, "When a disaster has occurred, nothing is really wise, or even kind, save ruthless examination of the causes" (1953:34). From this premise some, including many Christians, have drawn the conclusion that the Christian mission and everything it stood for now belong to a bygone era. It should be eulogized and then buried; it was an episode, not more, in the history of Christianity and may now be safely banished to the archives. Such views are expressed in many Christian circles, but especially among Roman Catholics and those Protestants often referred to as "ecumenical". Gómez (1986:28) writes that, in the wake of Vatican II, priests and religious have defected, vocations died out, venerable traditions been demolished in a frenzy, and the dirty linen of Catholic mission history washed in public, with masochistic delight; mission became a non-issue for the masses and a nonsense in intellectual, even clerical circles.

Others, by contrast, have argued that the Christian church "is missionary by its very nature" (cf AG 9) and that it is therefore totally impossible to abandon the idea and practice of mission in some form or another. To repent of past mistakes is not the same as relinquishing the essence of what one has been doing; in Paton's words (:75), "A call to repentance is not a call to drop important work, but to do it otherwise. The Mission of the Church abides".

How can the church repent of past mistakes? How can it try to rediscover the essence of its missionary nature and calling? Has it only to be on the defensive? Does it have to capitulate to the pressures of a world radically different from the one into which it first ventured to reach out missionally? Or can it respond creatively to the challenges it is encountering? These are some of the questions and issues to which we are called to hazard a response.

Repentance has to begin with a bold recognition of the fact that the church-in-mission is today facing a world fundamentally different from anything it faced before. This in itself calls for a new understanding of mission. We live in a period of transition, on the borderline between a paradigm that no longer satisfies and one that is, to a large extent, still amorphous and opaque. A time of paradigm change is, by nature, a time of crisis—and crisis, we remind ourselves, is the point where danger and opportunity meet (Koyama). It is a time when several "answers" are pressing themselves upon us, when many voices clamor for our attention.

The thesis of this study is that, in the field of religion, a paradigm shift always means both continuity and change, both faithfulness to the past and boldness to engage the future, both constancy and contingency, both tradition and transformation. This has been true of each of the five paradigm changes traced so far: they were both evolutionary and revolutionary. Of course, at the occasion of virtually each paradigm change—particularly those introduced in a more dramatic fashion, such as the early Christian paradigm and the Protestant Reformation—there was always the tendency to respond in two completely opposite ways. Some tried to oppose or at least neutralize the change that seemed to be irrupting all around them; others tended to overreact, to make a clean break with the past and deny continuity with their ancestry. During the formative years of the early church the first response was manifested, *inter alia*, in the movement known as Ebionitism, in which Jesus was viewed as just another prophet; the second response may be seen in Gnosticism, a heresy which scorned the Old Testament as well as much of the story of Jesus. Similarly, during the Reformation era much of the official Catholic response to Martin Luther's efforts was expressed in terms of counter-reformation rather than reformation; conversely, some extremist sects attempted to push aside fifteen centuries of Christian history, start with a completely clean slate, and inaugurate the reign of God without any delay.

It would be strange if the present period of uncertainty did not also throw up candidates which propagate either a convulsive clinging to the past or an even more extreme "conservative" backlash (such as some current manifestations of fundamentalism), or, contrarily, a kind of "clean slate" approach, for instance by offering alternatives to the Christian faith as the only way of responding effectively to the challenges before us. One candidate for the latter approach is the New Age Movement with its cocktail of myth and magic and its proclivity toward Eastern religions and systems of thought. In his writings, Capra has become one of the major protagonists of a paradigm shift away from the Cartesian-Newtonian worldview, but also away from the Christian worldview, toward a Taoist or Buddhist understanding of reality. He propagates a view in which all opposites are cancelled out, all barriers wiped out, all dualism superseded and all individualism dissolved into a universal, undifferentiated, and pantheistic unity.

Neither extreme reactionary nor excessively revolutionary approaches, so it seems to me, will help the Christian church and mission to arrive at greater clarity or to serve God's cause in a better way. The kind of paradigm shift discussed in this study suggests a fundamentally different model. In the case of each paradigm change reviewed so far, there remained a creative tension between the new and the old. The agenda was always—consciously or unconsciously—one of reform, not of replacement. The same will be true of my reflections on the emerging ecumenical paradigm. There will be no attempt at propagating a complete substitution of the previous paradigm, at casting it aside as utterly worthless. Rather, the argument will be that—in light of a fundamentally new situation and precisely so as to remain faithful to the true nature of mission—mission must be understood and undertaken in an imaginatively new manner today. In the words of John XXIII, spoken in 1963, shortly before his death, "Today's world, the needs made plain in the last fifty years, and a deeper understanding of doctrine have brought us to a new situation . . . *It is not that the Gospel has changed; it is that we have begun to understand it better*" (quoted in Gutiérrez 1988:xlv—emphasis added).

This means that both the centrifugal and the centripetal forces in the emerging paradigm—diversity versus unity, divergence versus integration, pluralism versus holism—will have to be taken into account throughout. A crucial notion in this regard will be that of *creative tension*: it is only within the force field of apparent opposites that we shall begin to approximate a way of theologizing for our own time in a meaningful way.

In what follows, I shall attempt to highlight some of the elements of an emerging pattern of mission. Throughout, my reflections will remain tentative, suggesting rather than defining the contours of a new model. Does the emerging postmodern paradigm proclaim a vision of unity or of diversity? Does it emphasize integration or divergence? Is it holistic or pluralistic? Is it characterized by a return to a religious consensus or by a philosophy according to which a supermarket of religions will display its wares to self-service customers (cf Daecke 1988)? Clearly, in a period of transition it is dangerous to use apodictic language. We shall, at best, succeed, in outlining the *direction* in which we ought to be moving and in identifying the overall *thrust* of the emerging paradigm.

Chapter 12

Elements of an Emerging Ecumenical Missionary Paradigm

With the qualifications mentioned in the previous chapter, I now turn to the elements which the emerging missionary paradigm comprises. Yet another warning is still in order. The elements discussed below should by no means be seen as so many distinct and isolated components of a new model; they are all intimately interrelated. This means that in discussing a specific element each other element is always somewhere in the background. The emphasis throughout should therefore be on the wholeness and indivisibility of the paradigm, rather than on its separated ingredients. As we focus our torchlight on one element at a time, all the other elements will also be present and visible just outside the center of the beam of light.

I begin with some reflections on the role of the *church* in mission. This section will be longer than the others, mainly because all the issues that will emerge in subsequent sections are, in one sense or another, already present here. Once we have discussed the place of the church in mission, we can be briefer on the other elements of the emerging paradigm.

MISSION AS THE CHURCH-WITH-OTHERS

Church and Mission

In a perceptive study Avery Dulles (1976) has identified five major ecclesial types. The church, he suggests, can be viewed as *institution*, as *mystical Body of Christ*, as *sacrament*, as *herald*, or as *servant*. Each of these implies a different interpretation of the relationship between church and mission.

Catholics have always had a high view of the church. This explains why the first two of Dulles's models have tended to predominate in Catholic ecclesiology. Highlighting the first of these, Neill (1968:74; cf Hastings 1968:28-31) says that, from the Counter-Reformation until the second half of the nineteenth century, the prevailing emphasis was on the external, the legal, and the institutional. In the course of the twentieth century the tenor of statements about the church gradually began to change. The church was now seen as the Body of Christ rather than, primarily, as a divine institution. This development culminated in the promulgation of the encyclical *Mystici Corporis Christi* in 1943. It did not, however, break with the ecclesiology that preceded it; the encyclical betrayed an unconditional identification of Christ's mystical body with the empirical Roman Catholic Church. It further strengthened the tendency to absolutize and divinize the church and hold it up as a *societas perfecta* (cf Haight 1976:623; Michiels 1989:90). The encyclical served as the main expression, indeed *the* definition of the church, until Vatican II (Michiels 1989:90). Other models of the church were rejected (:91). This did not mean, however, that the church was understood to be missionary by nature (cf Neill 1968:71-74). As van Winsen (1973:3-12; cf also Gómez 1986:46) has shown, and as was spelt out in the old Code of Canon Law, "the universal care of missions to non-Catholics (was) reserved exclusively to the Apostolic See". The pope's agents in this task were the missionary orders and congregations.

The situation was not essentially different in Eastern Orthodoxy. Protestants, on the other hand (except "High Church" Anglicans and some Lutherans), tended toward a low view of the church. Often one distinguished between the "true church" — the *ecclesiola* or little church — within the *ecclesia*, the large and nominal church; this *ecclesiola*, not the official church, tended to be viewed as the true bearer of mission. Here there was even less appreciation for the idea of the church as the bearer of mission. The "voluntary principle" (discussed in chapter 9 above) was widely followed. Groups of individuals — sometimes members of one denomination, sometimes devout believers from a variety of denominations — banded together in missionary societies which they regarded as the bearers of mission.

Gradually, however, a fundamental shift emerged in the perception of the relationship between church and mission, in both Catholicism and Protestantism, so much so that Moltmann (1977:7) can say, "Today one of the strongest impulses towards the renewal of the theological concept of the church comes from the theology of mission".

Shifts in Missionary Thinking

For an understanding of the shifts in Protestant thinking regarding the relationship between church and mission, the contributions of the world missionary conferences are of primary importance (cf, for instance, Günther 1970, who surveys the "ecclesiological reflections" of the missionary conferences from Edinburgh 1910 to Mexico City 1963). In Edinburgh, a major concern was the absence of missionary enthusiasm in the churches of the West; the theological question of the relationship between church and mission was hardly touched (cf Günther 1970:24-26). At the Jerusalem Conference of the IMC (1928), however, the relationship between "older" and "younger" churches received a considerable amount of attention and became a prominent issue, even if the subdivision of the world into two large geographical areas — the one Christian, the other "non-Christian" — remained unchallenged (:35-42).

Tambaram (1938) discussed the relationships between church and mission as well as between "older" and "younger" churches in a more theological manner. The distinction between Christian and non-Christian countries was in principle abandoned. This meant that Europe and North America, too, had to be regarded as mission fields. The dividing lines no longer ran between "Christianity" and "paganism", between the church and the world, but through the church as well. We are all, at best, "Christopagans". In a Europe traumatized by the First World War and challenged by the rise of totalitarian ideologies like National Socialism, Fascism and Marxism, the anthropocentric theology of liberal Protestantism, epitomized in the views of Adolf Harnack and Ernst Troeltsch, was found wanting. Words like sin, alienation, and judgment, like conversion, forgiveness, regeneration, and righteousness, again surfaced prominently in missionary and other discussions (cf Scherer 1968:34-37; van 't Hof 1972:108f).

This could not but have a profound impact on the perception of church and mission. For the first time the recognition that church and mission belong together indissolubly began to dawn in a way that could no longer be overlooked. And even if the famous E. Stanley Jones said that Tambaram had missed the way because it had used the church instead of the kingdom of God as its starting point (reference in Anderson 1988:107; cf also Günther 1970:64-66), it cannot be denied that Tambaram registered a significant advance over earlier positions.

The Willingen meeting of 1952, convened in the aftermath of World War II and the missionary "debacle" in China (cf Paton 1953:50), took up the same theme. In the preceding years there has been an almost imperceptible shift from an emphasis on a church-centered mission (Tambaram) to a mission-centered church. In 1948 the World Council of Churches was formed, and soon the incongruence of a council of churches and a missionary council existing side by side was making itself felt. Willingen began to flesh out a new model. It recognized that the church could be neither the starting point nor the goal of mission. God's salvific work precedes both church and mission. We should not subordinate mission to the church nor the church to mission; both should, rather, be taken up into the *missio Dei*, which now became the overarching concept. The *missio Dei* institutes the *missiones ecclesiae*. The church changes from being the sender to being the one sent (cf Günther 1970:105-114). The new mood found expression in the opening words of the Statement received by the next assembly of the IMC, which met in Achimota, Ghana, in 1958: "The Christian world mission is Christ's, not ours". In a pamphlet published soon after the Ghana Assembly, Newbigin summarized the consensus that had by now been reached: (1) "the church is the mission", which means that it is illegitimate to talk about the one without at the same time talking about the other; (2) "the home base is everywhere", which means that every Christian community is in a missionary situation; and (3) "mission in partnership", which means the end of every form of guardianship of one church over another (1958:25-38).

By this time the decision to integrate the WCC and the IMC had already been taken. It took place at the New Delhi meeting of the WCC (1961). The Assembly's Commission and Division of World Mission and Evangelism used the following words to express its views on the integration of the missionary concern into the Structures of the WCC:

> This spiritual heritage must not be dissipated; it must remain, ever renewed in the hidden life of prayer and adoration, at the heart of the World Council of Churches. Without it the ecumenical movement would petrify. Integration must mean that the World Council of Churches takes the missionary task to the very heart of its life (WCC 1961:249f; cf Neill 1968:108f).

This entire evolution indeed meant a momentous shift in the understanding of church and mission. But before we review its elements in some detail, let us have a brief look at developments in Catholicism.

The missionary encyclicals of the twentieth century prior to the Second Vatican Council—especially *Maximum Illud* (1919), *Rerum Ecclesiae* (1926), *Evangelii Praecones* (1951), and *Fidei Donum* (1957)—registered the first hesitant steps toward a missionary understanding of the church (cf also Auf der Maur 1970:82-84). On the eve of the Council the situation was, however, rather confused; salvationist (School of Münster), ecclesiocentric (School of Louvain), sacramentalist (M.-J. le Guillou), and eschatological (Y. Congar) interpretations of mission remained unintegrated (cf Dapper 1979:63-66). Contributions of French theologians—such as Yves Congar, who was building on Godin and Daniel 1943—became catalytic in opening the way toward a fundamentally new understanding of church and mission. Of primary importance in this regard was a new interest in the New Testament and, more particularly, the Pauline view of the church (cf Power 1970:17-27; Dapper 1979:66-70).

The event of the Council itself was crucial. For the first time a truly *global* council, not only a Western one, had convened. The affirmation that the "Church of Christ is really present in all legitimately organized local groups of the faithful" (LG 26) and that "it is in these and formed out of them that the one and unique Catholic Church exists" (LG 23), suggested an important break with the exclusively papal-centered understanding of the church of Vatican I (1870). This was to lead to a rediscovery of a missionary ecclesiology of the local church and to the institution of episcopal conferences (LG 37f) as well as bishops' synods (cf Fries 1986:755; Gómez 1986:38). It did not come about without a struggle. The early drafts of the Decree on Mission were prepared by representatives of the *Congregatio de Propaganda Fide* and revealed a very traditional posture. To this the African and Asian bishops objected; they would rather go without a decree on mission than subscribe to one that refused to break new ground (cf Hastings 1968:204-209; Glazik 1984b:50-56). Consequently the decree was completely rewritten.

Even so, the real breakthrough in respect to mission occurred not in the missionary decree but in *Lumen Gentium* (*Dogmatic Constitution on the Church*). Right at the outset, LG dissociates itself from traditional ecclesiology. The church is no longer described as a societal entity on a par with other societal structures like the state, but as the mystery of God's presence in the world, "in the nature of" a sacrament, sign, and instrument of community with God and unity among people. The whole tenor of the argument is new. The church is not presenting itself imperiously and proudly but humbly; it does not define itself in legal categories or as an elite of exalted souls, but as a servant community. LG's ecclesiology is missionary through and through (cf Power 1970:15f; Auf der Maur 1970:88f; Glazik 1979:153-155).

Vatican II also reflects a convergence in Catholic and Protestant views on the missionary nature of the church, even if one has to add immediately that the Catholic documents show far greater consistency and lucidity than those produced by Protestant conferences. Michiels (1989:89) suggests that modern ecclesiologies (Catholic and Protestant) employ seven main metaphorical expressions for the church, each of them implying a peculiar perspective on the understanding of mission. These are: the church as "sacrament of salvation", "assembly of God", "people of God", "kingdom of God", "Body of Christ", "temple of the Holy Spirit", and "community of the faithful" (cf also Dulles 1976). I would like to examine some aspects of these in an attempt to trace the characteristics of an emerging missionary ecclesiology.

"Missionary by Its Very Nature"

In the emerging ecclesiology, *the church is seen as essentially missionary*. The biblical model behind this conviction, which finds its classical expression in AG 9 ("The pilgrim church is missionary by its very nature"), is the one we find in 1 Peter 2:9. Here the church is not the sender but the one sent. Its mission (its "being sent") is not secondary to its being; the church exists in being sent and in building up itself for the sake of its mission (Barth 1956:725 — I am here following the German original rather than the English translation). Ecclesiology therefore does not precede missiology (cf Hoedemaker 1988:169f, 178f). Mission is not "a fringe activity of a strongly established Church, a pious cause that [may] be attended to when the home fires [are] first brightly burning. . . Missionary activity is not so much the work of the church as simply the Church at work" (Power 1970:41,42; cf van Engelen 1975:298; Stransky 1982:345; Glazik 1984b:51f; Köster 1984:166-170). It is a duty "which pertains to the *whole* Church" (AG 23). Since God is a missionary God (as will be argued in the section on the *missio Dei*), God's people are a missionary people. The question, "Why still mission?" evokes a further question, "Why still church?" (Glazik 1979:158). It has become impossible to talk about the church without at the same time talking about mission. One can no longer talk about church *and* mission, only about the mission *of* the church (Glazik 1984b:52). One could even say, with Schumacher (1970:183), "The inverse of the thesis 'the church is essentially missionary' is 'Mission is essentially ecclesial'" (my translation). Because church and mission belong together from the beginning, "a church without mission or a mission without the church are both contradictions. Such things do exist, but only as pseudostructures" (Braaten 1977:55). These perspectives have implications for our understanding of the church's catholicity. Without mission, the church cannot be called catholic (cf Glazik 1979:154; Berkouwer 1979:105-109).

All this does not suggest that the church is always and everywhere overtly involved in missionary projects. Newbigin (1958:21, 43) has introduced the helpful distinction between the church's missionary *dimension* and its missionary *intention*: the church is both "missionary" and "missionizing" (cf also Gensichen 1971:80-95, 168-186; Mitterhöfer 1974:93, 97). The missionary dimension of a local church's life manifests itself, among other ways, when it is truly a worshipping community; it is able to welcome outsiders and make them feel at home; it is a church in which the pastor does not have the monopoly and the members are not merely objects of pastoral care; its members are equipped for their calling in society; it is structurally pliable and innovative; and it does not defend the privileges of a select group (cf Gensichen 1971:170-172). However, the church's missionary dimension evokes *intentional*, that is *direct* involvement in society; it actually moves beyond the walls of the church and engages in missionary "points of concentration" (Newbigin) such as evangelism and work for justice and peace.

At least one theologian has developed his entire ecclesiology in terms of the observations above: Karl Barth. Johannes Aagaard (1965:238) calls him "the decisive Protestant missiologist in this generation". In light of Barth's magnificent and consistent missionary ecclesiology there may indeed be some justification for such a claim. Under the overarching rubric of soteriology, Barth develops his ecclesiology in three phases. His reflections on soteriology as *justification* (1956:514-642) are followed by a section on "The Holy Spirit and the *Gathering* of the Christian Community" (:643-749). His exposition on soteriology as *sanctification* (1958:499-613) leads to a discourse on "The Holy Spirit and the *Upbuilding* of the Christian Community" (:614-726). And his discussion of soteriology as *vocation* (1962:481-680) is followed by a treatise on "The Holy Spirit and the *Sending* of the Christian Community" (:681-901). From three perspectives, then, the entire field of ecclesiology is surveyed; each of these perspectives evokes, presupposes, and illuminates the other two (cf Blei 1980:19f).

God's Pilgrim People

The church is viewed as the *people of God* and, by implication then, as a *pilgrim* church. In contemporary Protestantism, this idea first surfaced clearly in the theology of Dietrich Bonhoeffer (cf Lochman 1986:58f) and at the 1952 Willingen Conference of the IMC (cf van 't Hof 1972:167). In the case of Catholicism, the notion has been promoted by Yves Congar since 1937 (cf Power 1970:17) but found little favor with the hierarchy in the preconciliar period. The classical *conciliar* references are LG 48-51 and AG 9; in fact, the church as the people of God may be viewed as *the* conciliar church model (cf Michiels 1989:90-92).

The biblical archetype here is that of the wandering people of God, which is so prominent in the letter to the Hebrews. The church is a pilgrim not simply for the practical reason that in the modern age it no longer calls the tune and is everywhere finding itself in a diaspora situation; rather, to be a pilgrim in the world belongs intrinsically to the church's ex-centric position. It is *ek-klesia*, "called out" of the world, and sent back into the world. Foreignness is an element of its constitution (Braaten 1977:56).

God's pilgrim people need only two things: support for the road, and a destination at the end of it (Power 1970:28). It has no fixed abode here; it is a *paroikia*, a temporary residence. It is permanently underway, toward the ends of the world and the end of time (cf Hoekendijk 1967b:30-38). Even if there is an unbridgeable difference between the church and its destination — the reign of God — it is called to flesh out, already in the here and now, something of the conditions which are to prevail in God's reign. Proclaiming its own transience the church pilgrimages toward God's future (cf Kohler 1974:475; Collet 1984:264-266).

Sacrament, Sign, and Instrument

In contemporary ecclesiology the church is increasingly perceived as sacrament, sign, and instrument (cf Dulles 1976:58-70). In chapter 4 of this study it has been shown that Paul saw his own mission as "priestly service of the gospel" (Rom 15:16) and challenged the Christian community to offer itself as a "living sacrifice, holy and acceptable to God" (Rom 12:1). The New Testament books list many gifts conferred on individuals for the benefit of all: teaching, healing, apostleship, etc. The gift of priesthood is never mentioned, however; instead (cf 1 Pet 2:9), God entrusted this gift to the community as a whole (cf Piet 1970:64). Other New Testament images of the church which represent the same idea are salt, light, yeast, servant, and prophet. In subsequent centuries, however, these notions disappeared almost without a trace. Only in our own time did they surface again and give birth to the idea of the church as sacrament, sign, and instrument.

The new terminology is, perhaps understandably, used more extensively in Catholicism than in Protestantism. Once again Vatican II was the catalyst. In its first paragraph, LG calls the church "a kind of sacrament — a sign and instrument, that is, of communion with God and unity among all people". Elsewhere the church is called "the visible sacrament of . . . saving unity" (LG 9) and even "the universal sacrament of salvation" (LG 48). Subsequent Catholic documents continued along the same lines. The 1975 Apostolic Exhortation, *Evangelii Nuntiandi*, asserts, "While the church is proclaiming the kingdom of God and building it up, it is establishing itself in the midst of the world as the *sign and instrument* of this kingdom" (EN 59, emphasis added). At a consultation held in Rome in 1982, "the concrete Christian community (*koinonia*) in its everyday life" was identified as sign and instrument of salvation (Memorandum 1982:462).

Gassmann (1986) has shown that the same terminology is increasingly being used in Protestant circles as well, particularly in the Commission for Faith and Order (FO). This has been happening notably since the Uppsala Assembly of the WCC (1968), although rudimentary references can already be found in the 1927 FO meeting in Lausanne and the 1937 meeting in Oxford (:3). The key formulation, often quoted, is the one drafted at Uppsala: "The Church is bold in speaking of itself as the sign of the coming unity of mankind". Subsequent

FO conferences and documents attempted to clarify what was meant by this terminology (:4-7). Two of the section reports of the Melbourne CWME Conference (1980) also referred to the church in these terms: as sacrament, sign, or instrument of the kingdom (:10f). Gassmann concludes:

> The remarkably wide reception of the ecclesiological use of the terms sacrament, sign and instrument in ecumenical debate suggests that this terminology is found to be helpful in describing the place and vocation of the church and its unity in God's plan of salvation (:13).

These images gave articulation to the idea, so well formulated by Archbishop William Temple (cf Neill 1968:76), that the church is the only society in the world which exists for the sake of those who are not members of it. The classical expression of this perception of the church was the phrase "the church for others". Its architect was Dietrich Bonhoeffer, who wrote the following sentences from a Nazi prison in 1944 (1971:382f), "The church is the church only when it exists for others. . . The church must share in the secular problems of ordinary human life, not dominating, but helping and serving".

"The church for others" was a powerful and extremely attractive phrase and was embraced widely and enthusiastically (cf Sundermeier 1986:62), not least since it so clearly echoed the New Testament picture of Jesus, particularly as the one who washed the feet of his disciples (cf also Kohler 1974:473). West (1971:262) and Sundermeier (1986:62-65) have, however, alerted us to the fact that such enthusiasm for the Bonhoeffer formula may hide from us the reality that its background is the typical liberal-humanist bourgeois climate in which Bonhoeffer had grown up, particularly the idea that Western Christians know what is best for others and, hence, that they tend to proclaim themselves the guardians of others. This helper syndrome of "pro-existence", says Sundermeier, jeopardizes the possibility of true coexistence. Instead of talking about "the church *for* others", we should rather speak of "the church *with* others".

Sundermeier's observations show that the language of "the church for others", "the church as sacrament", etc, is indeed not free from hazard. At an FO conference held in Salamanca, Spain, in 1973, Ernst Käsemann (1974) criticized the terminology. In light of the absence of intercommunion among Christians, he finds it "almost frivolous" to call the church a sacrament (:125f). This "dangerous expression" does not advance dialogue and should be avoided (:126). Käsemann fears, in addition, that this kind of terminology may blur the abiding difference between Christ and the church (:127). To call the church a sign is also problematic since there can be no doubt that the only legitimate sign of the church is the cross of Christ (:130).

Käsemann's objections have to be taken seriously. Thus, if we continue to employ this terminology, some important qualifications are in order. As the FO meeting at Louvain (1971) put it: "The church . . . *is* a sign. But it is also no more than a sign. The mystery of the love of God is not exhausted through this sign, but, at best, just hinted from afar"; and it added, "This sign of oneness is broken by the tensions and divisions in which the churches are living" (quoted in Gassmann 1986:4). A study paper for the 1973 Salamanca meeting stated that the church dares make the claim to be a sign "or even sacrament" of the coming unity of humankind "only by virtue of its relationship with Christ", who is the *real* sign of unity. Words like "sacrament" are, moreover, not attributes the church arrogates to itself: "God himself has chosen (the church) to be in Christ the sign or sacrament of the unity in his kingdom" (:5). Furthermore, in some sense these terms in fact help to *avoid* total identification of the church with Christ (:13): all three expressions clearly point *beyond* themselves. Likewise, they forcefully evoke the question of what correspondence there is between Christ and those who declare themselves his followers. Christianity purports to be a religion of grace, but then it should be remembered that a religion of grace is more vulnerable than a religion of law. In the words of John Baker:

The more we emphasize, in our description of the essential nature of the church, the divine sacramental and sanctifying life within the community, the more legitimate it becomes for the world to demand discernible results... It is no use composing in-house descriptions of the church, however faithful they may be to scripture and tradition, if within the church they have the fatal effect of giving believers a warm illusion that all is well, and when read by humankind outside the church they seem to have parted company with reality (1986:155,158).

When the church, in its mission, risks referring to itself as sacrament, sign, or instrument of salvation, it is therefore not holding up itself as model to be emulated. Its members are not proclaiming, "Come to us!" but "Let us follow him!"

Church and World

The understanding of the church as sacrament, sign, and instrument led to a new perception of the relationship between the church and the world. Mission is viewed as "God's turning to the world" (cf the title of Schmitz 1971). This represents a fundamentally new approach in theology (W. Kasper — reference in Kramm 1979:226; cf Hoedemaker 1988:168).

For centuries a static conception of the church had prevailed; the world outside the church was perceived as a hostile power (Berkhof 1979:411). Reading theological treatises from earlier centuries, one gets the impression that there was only church, no world. Put differently, the church was a world on its own. Outside the church there was only the "false church". Christian ministry and life was defined exclusively in terms of preaching, public worship, the pastorate, and charity. "Practicing" Christians were (and often still are!) defined as regular church-goers (Schmitz 1971:52f). The church filled the whole horizon. Those outside were, at most, "prospects" to be won (Snyder 1983:132). Mission was a process of reproducing churches, and once these had been reproduced, all energy was spent on maintenance. Barth asks, "Has not the work of this divine messenger and ambassador (Christ) actually ceased in the blind alley of the Church as an institution of salvation for those who belong to it?" (1962:767).

Slowly, however, a change began to take effect. Karl Barth (1961:18) sees this as a restoration of the doctrine of the prophetic office of Christ and the church. He traces six phases of this shift in the history of Protestantism (:18-38). It was, however, only after the Second World War that the essential orientation of the church toward the world was being embraced more widely in Protestantism. The church as conqueror of the world (Edinburgh 1910) became the church in solidarity with the world (Whitby 1947; cf van 't Hof 1972:140f). The Dutch "theology of the apostolate", which developed in the late forties and early fifties, also began to perceive the church primarily in terms of its relationship to the world (cf Berkhof 1979:411-413). Just as one could not speak of the church without speaking of its *mission*, it was impossible to think of the church without thinking, in the same breath, of the *world* to which it is sent (cf Glazik 1984b:53). It was rediscovered that *ekklesia* was, from the very beginning, a "theo-political category" (Hoekendijk 1967a:349).

In Catholicism the real breakthrough in respect of the relationship between the church and the world came with Vatican II. The theological foundations were laid in LG. However, the full extent of the shift in Catholic thinking on this relationship only becomes apparent once one peruses *Gaudium et Spes,* the Pastoral Constitution on the Church in the Modern World. In its opening sentence it recognizes an intimate link—which goes far beyond evangelism and church planting—between the church and the world of humanity: "The joy and hope, the grief and anguish of the people of our time, especially of those who are poor or afflicted in any way, are the joy and hope, the grief and anguish of the followers of Christ as well".

Subsequent developments reveal a convergence of Catholic and conciliar Protestant views on the inescapable connection between the church and the world as well as a recognition of God's activities in the world outside the church (cf, for instance, *Evangelii Nuntiandi* [1975] and *Mission and Evangelism* [1982]).

How is the new view to be understood?

First, it suggests that, if the church cannot be viewed as the *ground* of mission, it cannot be considered the *goal* of mission either—certainly not the *only* goal. The church should continually be aware of its *provisional* character. "The church's final word is not 'church' but the glory of the Father and the Son in the Spirit of liberty" (Moltmann 1977:19).

Second, the church is not the kingdom of God. The church "is, on earth, the seed and the beginning of that kingdom" (LG 5), "the sign and instrument of the reign of God that is to come" (EN 59). The church can be a credible sacrament of salvation for the world only when it displays to humanity a glimmer of God's imminent reign—a kingdom of reconciliation, peace, and new life (cf Schmitz 1971:58). In the here and now, that reign comes wherever Christ overcomes the power of evil. This happens (or should happen!) most visibly in the church. But it also happens in society, since Christ is Lord of the world as well.

Third, the church's missionary involvement suggests more than calling individuals into the church as a waiting room for the hereafter. Those to be evangelized are, with other human beings, subject to social, economic, and political conditions in this world. There is, therefore, a "convergence" between liberating individuals and peoples in history and proclaiming the final coming of God's reign (Geffré 1982:491). In this perspective, the church is "the people of God in world-occurrence" (Barth 1962:681-762) and the "community for the world" (:762-795).

Fourth, the church is to be viewed pneumatologically, as "a dwelling place of God in the Spirit" (Eph 2:22), as movement of the Spirit toward the world en route to the future (Memorandum 1982:461f). When we view the church as "community of the Holy Spirit" we identify it preeminently as *missionary* community, since the Spirit is the "go-between God" (Taylor 1972; cf Boer 1961).

Fifth, if the church attempts to sever itself from involvement in the world and if its structures are such that they thwart any possibility of rendering a relevant service to the world, such structures have to be recognized as heretical. The church's offices, orders, and institutions should be organized in such a manner that they serve society and do not separate the believer from the historical (Hoekendijk 1967a:349; Rütti 1972:311-315). Its life and work are intimately bound up with God's cosmic-historical plan for the salvation of the world. We are called, therefore, to be "kingdom people", not "church people", says Snyder (1983:11). He continues:

> Kingdom people seek first the Kingdom of God and its justice; church people often put church work above concerns of justice, mercy and truth. Church people think about how to get people into the church; Kingdom people think about how to get the church into the world. Church people worry that the world might change the church; Kingdom people work to see the church change the world.

Last, because of its integral relatedness to the world, the church may never function as a fearful border guard, but always as one who brings good tidings (Berkouwer 1979:162). Its life-in-mission vis-à-vis the world is a privilege (cf Rom 1:5).

Rediscovering the Local Church

The church-in-mission is, primarily, the *local* church everywhere in the world. This perspective, as well as the supposition that no local church should stand in a position of authority over against another local church, both fundamental to the New Testament (cf Acts 13:1-3 and the Pauline letters), was for all practical purposes ignored during much of Christian history. In Catholicism, church as well as mission became ever more clearly pope-centered. On the surface, at least, the Protestant "Three-Selfs" formula (self-government, self-support, and self-propagation) appeared to be more sound; soon "younger" churches would in all respects be the equals of "older" churches. Reality turned out to be different, however. The younger churches continued to be looked down upon and to be regarded as immature and utterly dependent upon the wisdom, experience, and help of the older churches or mission societies. The process toward independence was a pedagogical one; in the end, the self-appointed guardian would decide whether or not the moment for "home rule" had come. Churches and mission agencies in the West understood themselves as churches *for* others.

The first person to have attacked this entire edifice head-on was Roland Allen ([1912] 1956). He alerted his readers to the glaring differences between Paul's missionary methods and those of contemporary mission agencies. Perhaps, Allen suggested (:107), the basic difference was that Paul had founded "churches" whilst we founded "missions" in the sense of *dependent* organizations. Paul wrote the first of his letters to the church in Thessalonica—where he had spent a mere five months or so—only about a year after he had left there, and he wrote it not to a mission but to a *church* (:90; cf also chapter 4 of this study). At no point did the sending church, Antioch, have any authority over the fledgling faith communities in Ephesus, Corinth, and elsewhere. From the very first moment these were *complete* churches, with the Word and the sacraments—which were all they needed in order truly to be the church of Christ. Paul's success, Allen suggested, was due to the fact that he trusted both the Lord and the people to whom he had gone. In both these respects, modern missionaries were blatantly different from Paul (:183-190).

Gradually a shift began to take place in Protestant missions. The Jerusalem and Tambaram conferences of the IMC (1928 and 1938) began to recognize the younger churches as equals. The Whitby Conference (1947) coined the phrase "Partnership in Obedience" in an attempt to give expression to the conviction that it was theologically preposterous to distinguish between "autonomous" and "dependent" churches. The Ghana Conference of the IMC (1958) appropriately concluded "that the distinction between 'older' and 'younger' churches, whatever may have been its usefulness in earlier years, is no longer valid or helpful" (in Orchard 1958:12). And even if, in all this, practice still fell far short of theory, there could be no doubt that the die had been cast and that a change of momentous importance had begun to take place. The church-*for*-others was slowly turning into the church-*with*-others; pro-existence was changing into coexistence (cf Sundermeier 1986:65). Mission could no longer be viewed as one-way traffic, from the West to the Third World; every church, everywhere, was understood to be in a state of mission.

In *Catholicism* developments have been even more marked and dramatic. For many centuries "local churches" did not exist, neither in Europe nor on the "mission fields". What one had, at best, were affiliates of the universal church. The "mission churches", in particular, had to resemble the church in Rome in almost every detail; they "were 'missions', Churches of the second class, daughter churches, immature children, apostolic vicariates, and not yet autonomous dioceses" (Bühlmann 1977:45).

In the wake of World War I, however, the local church was discovered. *Maximum Illud* (1919) and *Rerum Ecclesiae* (1926) paved the way for a new understanding, but it was only *Fidei Donum* (1957) that constituted a true turning point (van Winsen 1973:77, 81-83) on which Vatican II was able to build. Even this council was, however, still very much run on the presuppositions of the traditional Western church. It was, in fact, only at the series of Synods of

Bishops — an ecclesial structure that originated after the Council — that the bishops of local churches[1] in the Third World really began to influence Catholic thinking in a profound way.

The fundamentally innovative feature of the new development was the discovery that the universal church actually finds its true existence in the local churches; that these, and not the universal church, are the pristine expression of church (cf LG 26); that this was the primary understanding of church in the New Testament and also the way in which, during the early centuries of our era, the church was perceived; that the pope, too, was in the first place the pastor of the local church in Rome; that a universal church viewed as *preceding* local churches was a pure abstraction since the universal church exists only where there are local churches; that the church is the church because of what happens in the local church's *martyria, leitourgia, koinonia,* and *diakonia;* that the church is an event among people rather than an authority addressing them or an institution possessed of the elements of salvation, of doctrines, and offices (cf van Engelen 1975:298f; Glazik 1979:155f; Köster 1984:169, 176-184; Fries 1986:755f; Michiels 1989:100f).

At the same time it has to be said that Catholics tend to appreciate, more clearly than Protestants do, the essential interrelatedness between the universal church and local churches. The church is, really, a *family* of local churches in which each should be open to the needs of the others and to sharing its spiritual and material goods with them. It is through the mutual ministry of *mission* that the church is realized, in communion with and as local concretization of the church universal (Stransky 1982:349; Fries 1986:756).

The rediscovery of the local church as the primary agent of mission has led to a fundamentally new interpretation of the purpose and role of missionaries and mission agencies. In 1969 Pope Paul VI told Christians in Kampala, Uganda, "You are missionaries to yourselves!" And in 1985 John Paul II said to believers in places as far apart and as different as Cameroon and Sardinia, "Like the entire Church, you are in a state of mission" (cf Gómez 1986:47f). It is in light of this new reality and realization that the Catholic Church has abolished the *ius commissionis;* no longer may foreign missionary orders and societies dictate the pattern of evangelism in the Third World. The whole world is a mission field, and the distinction between sending and receiving churches is becoming pointless. Every church is either still in a diaspora situation or has returned to it (AG 37). And churches everywhere need each other (cf Bühlmann 1977:383-394).

In the midst of these new circumstances and relationships there is still room for and need of individual missionaries, but only insofar as all recognize that their task is one that pertains to the *whole* church (cf AG 26) and insofar as missionaries appreciate that they are sent as ambassadors of one local church to another local church (where such a local church already exists), as witnesses of solidarity and partnership, and as expressions of mutual encounter, exchange, and enrichment.[2]

Much of what has been outlined above is undoubtedly still ideal rather than reality. In both confessions a donor syndrome is still very much in evidence in the affluent churches of the West and a dependency syndrome in the churches of the Third World. The Congregation for the Evangelization of Peoples (the new name for the restructured *Congregatio de Propaganda Fide*) still exercises authority over churches in Africa and elsewhere (cf Rosenkranz 1977:431-434). A quarter of a century after Vatican II, the Catholic Church in Africa has not yet held an Episcopal Conference (on this, cf Shorter 1989:349-352). It is not very different in the Protestant world. In spite of all the fine and friendly ecumenical language, it seems the final decisions are still taken in the churches and cities of the West, not least since this is where many of the subsidies needed for "running" Third World churches come from. Even so, the fundamental change in favor of the local church, everywhere, as the agent of mission both in its own environment and further afield, cannot be gainsaid and constitutes a decisive advance over positions that had been in vogue for many centuries.

Creative Tension

The new paradigm has led to an abiding tension between two views of the church which appear to be fundamentally irreconcilable. At one end of the spectrum, the church perceives itself to be the sole bearer of a message of salvation on which it has a monopoly; at the other end, the church views itself, at most, as an illustration — in word and deed — of God's involvement with the world. Where one chooses the first model, the church is seen as a partial realization of God's reign on earth, and mission as that activity through which individual converts are transferred from eternal death to life. Where one opts for the alternative perception, the church is, at best, only a pointer to the way God acts in respect of the world, and mission is viewed as a contribution toward the humanization of society — a process in which the church may perhaps be involved in the role of consciousness-raiser (cf Dunn 1980:83-103; Hoedemaker 1988:170f).

The question is whether these two images of the church have to be mutually exclusive. A few reflections on this subject may be in order. The problem, so it would seem, occurs where one is unable to integrate the two visions in such a way that the tension between them becomes creative rather than destructive. Such an integration is seldom achieved. Catholic scholars have, in this respect, referred to the inability of *Ad Gentes* to keep alive the constructive tension that was so evident in *Lumen Gentium* (cf van Engelen 1975:299-309; Weber 1978:87; Kramm 1979:36f; Dunn 1980:58-64; Glazik 1984b:54-56). Having started with a dynamic and fresh view of the church, AG made a somersault in Article 6 and proceeded to espouse a pre-Vatican II perception of church and mission: mission was again one-way traffic from West to East, and the overriding aim of mission remained *plantatio ecclesiae*.

In much of contemporary Catholicism and Protestantism, then, many of the old images live on, almost unchallenged. Traditional sending agencies — whether societies or denominational structures — are being absolutized and seduced into serving as agents or legitimizers of the status quo. This is further exacerbated by the preoccupation with numerical church growth in some circles. Donald McGavran, for instance, wishes to lift up church growth as a "chief and irreplaceable goal of mission" (1980:24). He believes that "the numerical approach is essential to understanding church growth", since the church "is made up of countable people" (:93). He defines church growth as "the sum of many baptized believers" (:147) and declares that "the student of church growth . . . cares little whether a Church is credible; he asks how much it has grown" (:159).

In this model, "achievement" in the area of mission or evangelism is frequently measured exclusively in terms of "religious" or otherworldly activities or of conduct at the micro-ethical level, such as abstinence from tobacco or profane speech. Often this also signifies a departure from engagement with the dominant social issues in a given community. Where this happens, an explosion in the numbers of converts may, in fact, be a veiled form of escapism and thus make a mockery of the true claims of the Christian faith. However, the content of a gospel without demands in respect of justice, peace, and equity suggests

> a conscience-soothing Jesus, with an unscandalous cross, an otherworldly kingdom, a private, inwardly limited spirit, a pocket God, a spiritualized Bible, and an escapist church. Its goal is a happy, comfortable, and successful life, obtainable through the forgiveness of an abstract sinfulness by faith in an unhistorical Christ (Costas 1982:80).

The first pattern, then, robs the gospel of its ethical thrust; the second, however, robs it of its soteriological depth (Costas 1982:80). This second pattern manifests itself in one of two ways: an almost complete identification of the church with the world and its agenda, or, in extreme cases, a virtually complete writing off of the church. Both these patterns—which were also mutually dependent—were in vogue particularly during the 1960s and early 1970s and reflect an extremely optimistic evaluation of the world and of humankind. Let us look briefly at these two strategies.

The idea of the world providing the agenda for the church and of the church having to identify completely with this agenda first surfaced clearly at the 1960 Strasbourg Conference of the WSCF. Speakers like D. T. Niles, Newbigin, Barth, and Visser 't Hooft appeared unable to speak to and for the students; only Hoekendijk, with his emphasis on the secular calling and role of Christianity, elicited applause (cf Bassham 1979:47f). Three years later, at the Mexico City Conference of CWME, it was said that Christians must "discover a shape of Christian obedience being written for them by what God is already actively doing in the structures of the city's life outside the Church" (quoted in Bassham 1979:65; this sentence was not, however, as Bassham seems to imply, part of the conference Message).

In 1961 the New Delhi Assembly of the WCC authorized a study project on "the Missionary Structure of the Congregation". Wieser edited an interim report on the project in 1966. A year later, and in time for the Uppsala Assembly, the final two-part report, prepared respectively by the Western European Working Group and the North American Working Group, was published (WCC 1967). Both reports (which, in the end, had precious little to say about the "missionary structure of the congregation") profoundly influenced the Uppsala meeting. The goal of mission was identified as *shalom* by the European team and as *humanization* by the North Americans. Hoekendijk called shalom a secularized concept, a social happening, an event in inter-human relations (in Wieser 1966:43). "What else can the churches do than recognize and proclaim what God is doing in the world?" asked the European group (WCC 1967:15), since "it is the world that must be allowed to provide the agenda for the churches" (:20). Conversion was something that happened on the corporate level in the form of social change, rather than on the individual-personal level. All this culminates in the following statement in the North American report:

> We have lifted up humanization as the goal of mission because we believe that more than others it communicates in our period of history the meaning of the messianic goal. In another time the goal of God's redemptive work might best have been described in terms of man turning towards God . . . The fundamental question was that of the true God, and the church responded to that question by pointing to him. It was assuming that the purpose of mission was Christianization, bringing man to God through Christ and his church. Today the fundamental question is much more that of *true* man, and the dominant concern of the missionary congregation must therefore be to point to the humanity in Christ as the goal of mission (WCC 1967:78).

By and large, the Uppsala assembly endorsed this theology. The Hoekendijk approach had become the "received view" in WCC circles. Mission became an umbrella term for health and welfare services, youth projects, activities of political interest groups, projects for economic and social development, the constructive application of violence, etc. Mission was "the comprehensive term for all conceivable ways in which people may cooperate with God in respect of this world" (Rütti 1972:307—my translation). The distinction between church and world has, for all intents and purposes, been dropped completely. In the words of J.B. Metz, "The abstract differentiation between church and world is, in the final analysis, meaningless" (quoted in Rütti 1972:274).

One can appreciate this preoccupation with the world during the 1960s and the optimism about what might be achieved soon by way of completely restructuring socio-political realities and attempts at identifying the "signs of the times". Former colonies of the West were becoming independent at a truly astonishing rate (in the year 1960 alone, eighteen African countries gained their independence). Imaginative development programs were being launched, and it was believed that, soon, these would permanently change the fate of the developing countries (although some, like Richard Shaull at the 1966 Church and Society Conference in Geneva, suggested that not the technologists, but the revolutionaries would introduce the desired restructuring of the socio-political and economic reality; cf Shaull 1967 and Dunn 1980:183-193). In church and mission circles the integration of the IMC into the WCC at New Delhi (1961) seemed to promise a completely new deal for relationships between older and younger churches. And, as far as Catholics were concerned, these were the years following Vatican II (1962-1965); many hailed "the new Pentecost, the downpouring of hope, the open windows and rejuvenation of the Church" (Gómez 1986:26).

Fact of the matter was, however, that mission—in its new definition—was overtaxed, that too much was expected of the church and its influence, that much of the euphoria sprang from human optimism rather than faith. The church was a kind of spiritual gas station from which all and sundry could draw the energy for a great variety of worthwhile projects. Sometimes the church had to supply the incentive behind grandiose development projects; sometimes it had to become a source of dissatisfaction and disruption.

It was perhaps only to be expected that the almost complete identification of the church and its calling with the world and its agenda would eventually lead to such embarrassment and frustration with the inability of the church to carry out the world's agenda that many people despaired of the church and regarded it as expendable. This view—in varying degrees—has been advocated by Hoekendijk, Aring, and Rütti (although Rütti, contrary to much of the overall thrust of his argument, admits that a "Christianity completely devoid of an institutionary nature cannot offer any true alternative"[1972:343—my translation]). For Hoekendijk, in particular, the church has little more than the character of an "intermezzo" between God and the world. Others echoed him. The church is "a reality of secondary importance", says Rütti (1972:280), and to call people to become church members is "a form of proselytism" (WCC 1967:75). The *world* rather than the church is "the locus of the continuing encounter between God and humanity" (Aring 1971:83). And God is being made present in the world through people who do not know him and cannot be regarded as members of the "church" (Rütti 1971:281).

The embarrassment with the church, and particularly with the local congregation, reached crisis proportions at the Uppsala and Bangkok conferences (1968 and 1973). Hoekendijk called the parish system immobile, self-centered, and introverted, "an invention of the Middle Ages" (quoted in Hutchison 1987:185). The classical Catholic adage, *extra ecclesiam nulla salus* ("outside the church no salvation") seemed to have been turned into its opposite—*inside* the church there was no salvation. Reflecting on the theme of the Bangkok CWME meeting, "Salvation Today", a Canadian study group asked, "Is the Church not arrogant in thinking it can offer man salvation?" (quoted in Wieser 1973:176). At both meetings the church came in for unsparing criticism. Scherer (1974:139) summarizes the mood that prevailed at Bangkok: "The church must justify itself through participation in the messianic salvation scheme, or it becomes irrelevant". The church itself needed to be saved, said Bangkok, else it cannot become a saving community: "Without the salvation of the churches from their captivity in the interests of dominating classes, races and nations there can be no saving church" (WCC 1973:89). Churches were in need of "conversion from parochial self-absorption to an awareness of what God is doing for the salvation of men *in the life of the world*" (:100).

At both conferences there were delegates who supported the Hoekendijkian position, not because they subscribed to its more extreme nuances, but because they wished to give expression to their frustration with the bourgeois nature of the church as well as to their conviction that a new understanding and praxis of mission would lead to the renewal of the church itself. In light of the terrible conditions under which millions of starving, oppressed, and exploited people were living, Uppsala and Bangkok revealed a holy impatience with any complacency on the part of the church. For the first time a world Christian body squarely faced structural evil and made no attempt at spiritualizing away its responsibilities by seeking refuge in a sacrosanct institution.

There could be no doubt—it had become fashionable to disparage the churches-as-they-exist-in-history. People lost confidence in the church. After Vatican II the Catholic Church experienced defections of priests, a drying up of vocations, and a frenzy of demolishing venerable institutions. The missionary enterprise, in particular, was attacked, often with masochistic delight (Gómez 1986:28). Visser 't Hooft (1980:393) remarks, however, that such ridicule is a form of ingratitude. Paul, who knew so much about the weaknesses of the churches to which he wrote his letters, began nearly every time by thanking God for their existence, their faith, their loyalty.

Thus one has to say that the attacks on the institutional church, launched by Hoekendijk and others, are pertinent only insofar as they express a theological ideal raised to the level of prophetic judgment (Haight 1976:633). On closer inspection, however, they represent a view that leads to absurdity. It is impossible to talk about the church's involvement in the world if its very right to exist is disputed a priori (cf Gensichen 1971:168). A "purely apostolary approach to the church is untenable" (Berkhof 1979:413).

By the mid-1970s the euphoria that had characterized the 1960s had evaporated completely. There has been something of a turning of the tide. Many of the same theologians who criticize the empirical church now hold firmly to the view that it is impossible to talk about mission as responsibility toward and solidarity with the world unless such mission is understood also in ecclesial categories (cf Schumacher 1970:183; Mitterhöfer 1974:81f; van Engelen 1975: 309). The Christian mission is always christological and pneumatological, but the New Testament knows of no christology or pneumatology which is not ecclesial (cf Kramm 1979:212, 218; Memorandum 1982:461). Mission is moored to the church's worship, to its gathering around the Word and the sacraments. " 'The visible coming together of visible people in a special place to do something particular' (Otto Weber) stands at the centre of the church. Without the actual, visible procedure of meeting together there is no church" (Moltmann 1977:334).

One may, therefore, perceive the church as an ellipse with two foci (Crum 1973:288f). In and around the first it acknowledges and enjoys the source of its life; this is where worship and prayer are emphasized. From and through the second focus the church engages and challenges the world. This is a forth-going and self-spending focus, where service, mission and evangelism are stressed (cf also Gensichen 1971:210; Bria 1975; Stransky 1982:349). Neither focus should ever be at the expense of the other; rather, they stand in each other's service. The church's *identity* sustains its *relevance* and *involvement* (Moltmann 1975:1-

4). The 1952 Lund FO meeting put it well: "The church is always and at the same time called out of the world and sent into the world". Preaching and the celebration of the sacraments call people to repentance, to baptism, to membership of the church, and to participation in God's activity in and with the world (Mitterhöfer 1974:88). The church *gathers* to praise God, to enjoy fellowship and receive spiritual sustenance, and *disperses* to serve God wherever its members are. It is called to hold in "redemptive tension" (Snyder 1983:29) its dual orientation. The report of the Vancouver Assembly Issue Group on "Taking Steps Towards Unity" expressed the conviction that

> the Church is called to be a prophetic "sign", a prophetic community through which and by which the transformation of the world can take place. It is only a church which goes out from its eucharistic centre, strengthened by word and sacrament and thus strengthened in its own identity, that can take the world on to its agenda. There will never be a time when the world, with all its political, social and economic issues, ceases to be the agenda of the Church. At the same time, the Church can go out to the edges of society, not fearful of being distorted or confused by the world's agenda, but confident and capable of recognizing that God is already there (WCC 1983:50).

It follows that the church can be missionary only if its being-in-the-world is, at the same time, a being-different-from-the-world (Berkhof 1979:415 — I am following the Dutch original here, rather than the English translation). Precisely for the sake of the world the church has to be unique, *in* the world without being *of* the world (cf van 't Hof 1972:206f). Christ's body, his own "earthly-historical form of existence", is "the one holy catholic and apostolic church" and as such "the provisional representation of the whole world of humanity justified in Him" (Barth 1956:643), "the experimental garden of the new humanity" (Berkhof 1979:415). There is, thus, a legitimate concern for the inalienable identity of the church and there should not be any premature amalgamation and confusion between it and the world. A witnessing and serving church "can only exist when she is intensely driven by the Spirit. She can give only in the measure that she herself receives" (:413f). It is therefore striking that even Hoekendijk, who throughout his entire life relentlessly castigated the church and argued that there was no room for an "ecclesiology", found it impossible to turn his back on it. He chastised the church, but for its own sake. He could, for instance, say that "the church is (nothing more, *but also nothing less!*) a means in God's hands to establish shalom in this world" (1967b:22 — emphasis added; cf also Blei 1980:5-7).

This does not mean that we simply accept the concrete community of faith positivistically and resign ourselves to its actual mode of life (cf also Lochman 1986:71). We know today — what many of our spiritual forebears would have found difficult to accept — that the empirical church will always be imperfect. Every church member who loves the church will also be deeply pained by it. This does not, however, call for discarding the church, but for reforming and renewing it. The church is itself an object of the *missio Dei*, in constant need of repentance and conversion; indeed, all traditions today subscribe to the adage *ecclesia semper reformanda est* (cf Rickenbach 1970:70; Memorandum 1982:462). The cross which the church proclaims also judges the church and censures every manifestation of complacency about its "achievements". A church that pats itself on the shoulder frustrates the power of the cross in its life and ministry.

Still, the cross conveys a message not only of judgment but of forgiveness and hope as well, also for the church. It is therefore incorrect for the church to allow itself constantly to be goaded into action, as though it has to prove itself, has to earn its credibility through its own imposing schemes and in this way secure its own salvation. To flagellate itself and relentlessly prod itself to accomplish more and more simply intensifies guilt, frustration, and despair. If the injunction to repent does not go hand in hand with the free offer of forgiveness and new life, we have law without gospel, judgment without mercy, and works without grace. There is an abiding tension between the Christian community for which we long and the Christian community as it actually is. However, the dream or ideal and the factual community belong together. In the words of Bonhoeffer, "He who loves the dream of a Christian community more than the community itself, often does great damage to that community, no matter how well-intentioned he might be" (quoted in Michiels 1989:84).

There is another side to this. Sometimes, when Christians announce what they think they should accomplish by way of transforming the world, they run the risk of exceeding the competence of the church, of talking and acting pretentiously on matters about which Christians have no more expertise than the world outside the church has (cf Rickenbach 1970:78). There is therefore something both captivating and problematic in Christians endeavoring to distinguish the "signs of the times" and thereby verifying where precisely God is at work in history.[3] We should be constantly aware of the risks we are taking and refrain from glibly stating, "Thus sayeth the Lord!" Even if secular history and the history of salvation are inseparable they are not identical, and the building of the world does not directly lead to the reign of God; as M. D. Chenu says, "Grace is grace, and history is not the source of salvation" (quoted in Geffré 1982:490).

Another way of saying this is to affirm that the church, since it is an *eschatological* community, may not commit itself without reservation to any social, political, or economic project. As first fruits of the reign of God it anticipates that reign in the here and now. It is the knowledge of this that gives it confidence to work for the advance of God's reign in the world, even if it does so with modesty and without claiming to have all the answers. Even if oppressive and sinful circumstances are not wiped away as if by magic, Christians confess that these circumstances have already been brought into the force field of God's reign, relativized, and robbed of their ultimate validity (Lochman 1986:67). It is this knowledge that grants us the certainty that we are no longer prisoners of an omnipotent fate. The "church in the power of the Spirit" is not yet the reign of God; it is blundering and often unfaithful, and yet it is the anticipation of that reign in history. Christianity is not yet the new creation, but it is the working of the Spirit of the new creation; it is not yet the new humankind, but it is its vanguard (cf Moltmann 1977:196; Collet 1984:262f).

The perception of the church as an entity completely separate from the human community—which, for instance, still dominated the deliberations of the 1952 Willingen Conference of the IMC—has been shown to be false and untenable. The church exists only as an organic and integral part of the human community. As soon as it tries to view its own life as meaningful in independence from the total human community it betrays the major purpose of its existence (Baker 1986:159). Similarly, the tendency either to debunk the church as completely irrelevant, or to erase every difference between the church and its agenda on the one hand and the world and its agenda on the other, appears to be on the decline; the church has to remain identifiably different from the world, else it will cease to be able to minister to it.

For mainline Protestantism it was the Nairobi Assembly of the WCC (1975) which first clearly registered a mood about the church different from that of previous meetings. Many were now prepared to admit that reality was more complex and nuanced than delegates to previous conferences had imagined. The tone of the meeting was more subdued and the discussions more sober than those which characterized Strasbourg (1960), Geneva (1966), Uppsala (1968), and Bangkok (1973). Perhaps this is why Nairobi's message took the form of a prayer for the churches rather than a summons to the world (Vischer 1976:10,61,63). The church was again criticized, but not as haughtily as in Bangkok. The prevailing notion was rather the biblical idea that the time had come "for judgment to begin with the household of God" (1 Pet 4:17). The church had to be cleansed so as to serve the world in a more relevant way. Indeed, the cataclysmic changes taking place in the world demanded the conversion of the church (Vischer 1976:27; cf also the title of his book). So the abiding validity of the church was reaffirmed at Nairobi; the assembly's agenda was supplied by the *church* rather than by the *world* (as had happened in Uppsala).

Also at the Melbourne meeting of CWME (1980) the church was taken more seriously than had been the case previously. It appeared to have been rehabilitated in WCC circles as an instrument of mission (Scherer 1987:44). This did not, however, suggest a return to the earlier position (roughly from Tambaram 1938 to Willingen 1952), when the integration of church and mission, in effect, had bolstered the institutional nature of mission rather than impregnated the church with a missionary character. Instead, Melbourne (in spite of Orthodox protests) distinguished carefully between the church and the kingdom of God. Section III's theme for instance, was "The Church *Witnesses to* the Kingdom". The section report (III.1) states, "The whole church of God, in every place and time, is *a sacrament of the kingdom* which came in the person of Jesus Christ and will come in its fulness when he returns in glory" (WCC 1980:193—emphasis added). Again, Section II.13 refers to the church as "a *sign* of the kingdom of God" and as being called "to be an *instrument* of the kingdom by continuing Christ's mission to the world" (:193f—emphasis added). Uppsala and Bangkok had tended to regard the churches as belonging to the court of Pharaoh; at least Sections III and IV at Melbourne viewed them, despite many defects, as essentially belonging to the camp of Moses. The church, by the grace of God capable of repenting, of being renewed and equipped for missionary service, attained its rightful place not as final expression of God's reign, but as its servant and herald (Scherer 1987:144).

The same tone is echoed in the 1982 WCC document, *Mission and Evangelism*. It unequivocally affirms the centrality of the church in God's divine economy; the unity of the church is deemed indispensable (ME 20-27), not only, but certainly also for the sake of "mission in six continents" (ME 37-40). A year later the Vancouver Assembly of the WCC endorsed the new ecumenical consensus on the crucial importance of the church in mission. This emerges, among other ways, in the subtle differences between its language and that of Uppsala 1968 (cf WCC 1983:50). The deliberations at the San Antonio Meeting of CWME (1989) followed a similar pattern, particularly in Section I.

We now recognize that the church is both a theological and a sociological entity, an inseparable union of the divine and the dusty. Looking at itself through the eyes of the world, the church realizes that it is disreputable and shabby, susceptible to all human frailties; looking at itself through the eyes of the believers, it perceives itself as a mystery, as the incorruptible Body of Christ on earth. We can be utterly disgusted, at times, with the earthliness of the church, yet we can also be transformed, at times, with the awareness of the divine in the church (Smith 1968:61). It is *this* church, ambiguous in the extreme, which is "missionary by its very nature", the pilgrim people of God, "in the nature of" a sacrament, sign, and instrument (LG 1), and "a most sure seed of unity, hope and salvation for the whole human race" (LG 9).

MISSION AS *MISSIO DEI*

During the past half a century or so there has been a subtle but nevertheless decisive shift toward understanding mission as *God's* mission. During preceding centuries mission was understood in a variety of ways. Sometimes it was interpreted primarily in soteriological terms: as saving individuals from eternal damnation. Or it was understood in cultural terms: as introducing people from the East and the South to the blessings and privileges of the Christian West. Often it was perceived in ecclesiastical categories: as the expansion of the church (or of a specific denomination). Sometimes it was defined salvation-historically: as the process by which the world—evolutionary or by means of a cataclysmic event—would be transformed into the kingdom of God. In all these instances, and in various, frequently conflicting ways, the intrinsic interrelationship between christology, soteriology, and the doctrine of the Trinity, so important for the early church, was gradually displaced by one of several versions of the doctrine of grace (cf Beinert 1983:208).

After the First World War, however, missiologists began to take note of recent developments in biblical and systematic theology. In a paper read at the Brandenburg Missionary Conference in 1932, Karl Barth ([1932] 1957) became one of the first theologians to articulate mission as an activity of God himself.

ın *Die Mission als theologisches Problem* (1933), Karl Hartenstein gave expression to a similar conviction. A few years later, at the Tambaram meeting of the IMC (1938), a statement by the German delegation became another catalyst in the development of a new understanding of mission. The delegation confessed that only "through a creative act of God His Kingdom will be consummated in the final establishment of a New Heaven and a New Earth", and "We are convinced that only this eschatological attitude can prevent the Church from becoming secularised".[4]

Throughout, the Barthian influence was crucial. Indeed, Barth may be called the first clear exponent of a new theological paradigm which broke radically with an Enlightenment approach to theology (cf Küng 1987:229). His influence on missionary thinking reached a peak at the Willingen Conference of the IMC (1952). It was here that the idea (not the exact term) *missio Dei* first surfaced clearly. Mission was understood as being derived from the very nature of God. It was thus put in the context of the doctrine of the Trinity, not of ecclesiology or soteriology. The classical doctrine on the *missio Dei* as God the Father sending the Son, and God the Father and the Son sending the Spirit was expanded to include yet another "movement": Father, Son, and Holy Spirit sending the church into the world. As far as missionary thinking was concerned, this linking with the doctrine of the Trinity constituted an important innovation (Aagaard 1974:420). Willingen's image of mission was mission as participating in the sending of God. Our mission has no life of its own: only in the hands of the sending God can it truly be called mission, not least since the missionary initiative comes from God alone (cf van 't Hof 1972:158f). Mission was not seen in triumphalist categories, though. Willingen recognized a close relationship between the *missio Dei* and mission as solidarity with the incarnate and crucified Christ. Whereas the Willingen meeting was convened under the theme "The Missionary Obligation of the Church", the addresses delivered at the meeting were published under the title *Missions Under the Cross* (1953). Thus, next to the affirmation that the mission was God's, the emphasis on the cross prevented every possibility of missionary complacency (van 't Hof 1972:160f; cf Dapper 1979:27).

In attempting to flesh out the *missio Dei* concept, the following could be said: In the new image mission is not primarily an activity of the church, but an attribute of God. God is a missionary God (cf Aagaard 1973:11-15; Aagaard 1974:421). "It is not the church that has a mission of salvation to fulfil in the world; it is the mission of the Son and the Spirit through the Father that includes the church" (Moltmann 1977:64). Mission is thereby seen as a movement from God to the world; the church is viewed as an instrument for that mission (Aagaard 1973:13). There is church because there is mission, not vice versa (Aagaard 1974:423). To participate in mission is to participate in the movement of God's love toward people, since God is a fountain of sending love.

Since Willingen, the understanding of mission as *missio Dei* has been embraced by virtually all Christian persuasions—first by conciliar Protestantism (cf Bosch 1980:179f, 239-248; LWF 1988:5-10), but subsequently also by other ecclesial groupings, such as the Eastern Orthodox (cf Anastasios 1989:79-81, 89) and many evangelicals (cf Costas 1989:71-87). It was also endorsed in Catholic mission theology, notably in some of the documents of the Second Vatican Council (1962-1965) (cf Aagaard 1974). After having stated that the church is missionary by its very nature, since "it has its origin in the mission of the Son and the Holy Spirit", the Council's *Decree on Mission* defines missionary activity as "nothing else, and nothing less, than the manifestation of God's plan, its epiphany and realization in the world and in history" (AG 2, 9). Mission is here defined in trinitarian, christological, pneumatological, and ecclesiological terms (Schumacher 1970:182f; cf Snijders 1977:171f; Fries 1986:761; Gómez 1986:31).

For the *missiones ecclesiae* (the missionary activities of the church) the *missio Dei* has important consequences. "Mission", singular, remains primary; "missions", in the plural, constitutes a derivative. With reference to the post-Willingen period, Neill (1966a:572) boldly proclaims, "The age of missions is at an end; the age of mission has begun". It follows that we have to distinguish between mission and missions. We cannot without ado claim that what we do is identical to the *missio Dei*; our missionary activities are only authentic insofar as they reflect participation in the mission of God. "The church stands in the service of God's turning to the world" (Schmitz 1971:25 — my translation). The primary purpose of the *missiones ecclesiae* can therefore not simply be the planting of churches or the saving of souls; rather, it has to be service to the *missio Dei*, representing God in and over against the world, pointing to God, holding up the God-child before the eyes of the world in a ceaseless celebration of the Feast of the Epiphany. In its mission, the church witnesses to the fullness of the promise of God's reign and participates in the ongoing struggle between that reign and the powers of darkness and evil (Scherer 1987:84).

After Willingen (and, already at Willingen, in the American report) the *missio Dei* concept gradually underwent a modification—a process traced in great detail by Rosin (1972). Since God's concern is for the entire world, this should also be the scope of the *missio Dei*. It affects all people in all aspects of their existence. Mission is God's turning to the world in respect of creation, care, redemption and consummation (Kramm 1979:210). It takes place in ordinary human history, not exclusively in and through the church. "God's own mission is larger than the mission of the church" (LWF 1988:8). The *missio Dei* is God's activity, which embraces both the church and the world, and in which the church may be privileged to participate.

In *Gaudium et Spes*, Vatican II's "Pastoral Constitution on the Church in the Modern World", this wider understanding of mission is expounded *pneumatologically* rather than christologically (cf Aagaard 1973:17f; Aagaard 1974:429-433). The history of the world is not only a history of evil but also of love, a history in which the reign of God is being advanced through the work of the Spirit. Thus, in its missionary activity, the church encounters a humanity and a world in which God's salvation has already been operative secretly, through the Spirit. This may, by the grace of God, issue in a more humane world which, however, may never be seen as a purely human product—the real author of this humanized history is the Holy Spirit. So *Gaudium et Spes* 26 can say, with reference to the social order and its development toward service to the common good, "The Spirit of God, who, with wondrous providence, directs the course of time and renews the faith of the earth, assists at this development". And even if paragraph 39 sounds a warning that "we must be careful to distinguish earthly progress clearly from the increase of the kingdom of God", it adds that "such progress is of vital concern to the kingdom of God, in so far as it can contribute to the better ordering of human society".

There can be little doubt that this wider understanding of the scope of the *missio Dei* meant a development contrary to the intentions of Barth and also of Hartenstein, who first used the term. By introducing the phrase, Hartenstein had hoped to protect mission against secularization and horizontalization, and to reserve it exclusively for God. This did not happen. Others, following in the footsteps of Barth and Hartenstein, were equally upset by subsequent developments. Rosin (1972:26) calls *missio Dei* a "Trojan horse through which the (unassimilated) 'American' vision was fetched into the well-guarded walls of the ecumenical theology of mission".[5]

Those who supported the wider understanding of the concept tended to radicalize the view that the *missio Dei* was larger than the mission of the church, even to the point of suggesting that it *excluded* the church's involvement – as we have seen in the previous section. In the volume prepared by a WCC study committee on "The Missionary Structure of the Congregation" (Wieser 1966), it could, for instance, be said, "The church serves the missio Dei in the world . . . (when) it points to God at work in world history and name him there" (:52). It appeared that God was primarily "working out his purpose in the midst of the world and its historical processes" (:53). The influence of Hoekendijk is clearly discernible in formulations like these. Hoekendijkian sentiments also characterize the theological position of Aring (1971). It seems the church has become unnecessary for the *missio Dei*: "*We* have no business in 'articulating' God. In the final analysis, 'missio Dei' means that God articulates himself, without any need of assisting him through our missionary efforts in this respect" (:88 – my translation). In fact, it is unnecessary for the world "to *become* what it already *is* since Easter: the reconciled world of God" (:28). It therefore does not stand in any need of the missionary contribution of Christians. After all, God is not imaginable without the reconciled world, neither the world without God's dynamic presence (:24).

Developments like these have prompted Hoedemaker (1988:171-173) to challenge the usefulness of the *missio Dei* concept. It can, he argues, be used by people who subscribe to mutually exclusive theological positions. Hoedemaker may be right – to some extent at least. On the other hand, it cannot be denied that the *missio Dei* notion has helped to articulate the conviction that neither the church nor any other human agent can ever be considered the author or bearer of mission. Mission is, primarily and ultimately, the work of the Triune God, Creator, Redeemer, and Sanctifier, for the sake of the world, a ministry in which the church is privileged to participate (cf LWF 1988:6-10). Mission has its origin in the heart of God. God is a fountain of sending love. This is the deepest source of mission. It is impossible to penetrate deeper still; there is mission because God loves people.

The recognition that mission is God's mission represents a crucial break-through in respect of the preceding centuries (van 't Hof 1972:177). It is inconceivable that we could again revert to a narrow, ecclesiocentric view of mission.

MISSION AS MEDIATING SALVATION[6]

Traditional Interpretations of Salvation

Some years ago, the Catholic journal *Studia Missionalia* devoted two consecutive volumes (vol 29, 1980, and vol 30, 1981) to the theme "salvation in world religions". Salvation is indeed a fundamental concern of every religion. For Christians, the conviction that God has decisively wrought salvation for all in and through Jesus Christ stands at the very center of their lives. After all, the very name Jesus means "Savior" (cf Wiederkehr 1976:9f; 1982:329f; Beinert 1983:217f; Greshake 1983:15).

It follows from this conviction that the Christian missionary movement has been motivated, throughout its history, by the desire to mediate salvation to all. The "soteriological motif" may indeed be termed the "throbbing heart of missiology" since it concerns the "deepest and most fundamental question of humanity" (Gort 1988:203 – my translation). It therefore makes sense that international missionary conferences would be devoted in their entirety to this theme. One may think, for instance, of the 1973 Bangkok Conference of CWME, the theme of which was "Salvation Today." More recently, in October 1988, the Roman Catholic Congregation for the Evangelization of Peoples, meeting at the Urban University in Rome, devoted a week-long consultation to the same subject.[7] That these were *missionary* consultations makes eminent sense, since one's theology of mission is always closely dependent on one's theology of salvation; it would therefore be correct to say that the scope of salvation – however we define salvation – determines the scope of the missionary enterprise.

Just as there have been paradigm shifts in respect of the understanding of the relationship between church and mission, there have also been shifts in the understanding of the nature of the salvation the church had to mediate in its mission. Our reflections on mission in the early church has revealed that salvation was interpreted in comprehensive terms. This is not to suggest that all New Testament authors have exactly the same understanding in this respect. Luke, for instance, uses "salvation language" in respect of a very wide spectrum of human circumstances – the termination of poverty, discrimination, illness, demon possession, sin, and so forth – or as Scheffler (1988) puts it, in respect of economic, social, political, physical, psychological, and spiritual suffering. Moreover, for Luke salvation is, above all, something that realizes itself in *this* life, *today* (see, in particular, Jesus' sayings recorded in 4:21; 19:9; 23:43). For Luke, salvation is *present* salvation (cf Stanley 1980:74f).

In *Paul* the accent appears to be elsewhere; he puts a greater emphasis on the *inchoative* nature of salvation – it only *begins* in this life (cf Stanley 1980:63-69). Salvation is a *process*, initiated by one's encounter with the living Christ, but complete salvation is still outstanding. The Holy Spirit is only God's *first* gift to us (Rom 8:23). We are saved *in hope* (8:24). *Reconciliation* (a key concept in Paul) indeed occurs here and now, but Paul normally refers to salvation in the future tense: "For if while we were enemies we *were reconciled* to God . . . much more, now that we *are reconciled, shall* we be saved by his life" (Rom 5:10). These delicate nuances certainly have to do with the fact that Paul thinks in *apocalyptic* categories and wishes to emphasize that comprehensive salvation is reserved for the coming triumph of God (Beker 1984). For the moment, Paul still *awaits* Jesus Christ as Savior (Phil 3:20). This does not, however, detract from the reality of radical renewal—both personal and social—which the believer may already experience in the here and now (cf Rom 8:14f and 2 Cor 5:17). Neither does this only hold good for the believer's "religious" life. The experience of reconciliation with God and the new birth has far-reaching *social* (cf Paul's letter to Philemon) and *political* consequences (Christ is called *Kyrios* and *Soter* in the face of the public confession that *Caesar* is lord and savior). But all of this remains within the framework of a fervent eschatological expectation.

In the Greek Patristic period, however, the eschatological expectation waned. Salvation now took the form of *paideia*, of a gradual "uplift" of believers to a divine status (the *theosis*). The emphasis was on the "origin" of Christ. The incarnation stood at the center, as instrument of the divine *paideia* (cf Lowe 1982:200; Beinert 1983:204).

Whereas salvation was understood as a "pedagogical" progression in the Byzantine church, the West (Catholic and Protestant) stressed the devastating effect of sin as well as the restoration of the fallen individual by means of a crisis experience mediated by the church. Not Christ's preexistence and incarnation, but his substitutionary death on the cross (a doctrine perfected in Anselm's theory of the *satisfactio vicaria*) now stood at the center (cf Beinert 1983:203-205). Salvation was the redemption of individual souls in the hereafter, which would take effect at the occasion of the miniature apocalypse of the death of the individual believer.

In this design, the "person" and "work" of Christ were increasingly separated from each other. Eventually christology was made subservient to soteriology (Lowe 1982:219; Greshake 1983:72f; Beinert 1983:202, 205, 208). By the same process, God's "salvific" activities were distinguished more and more from his "providential" activities in respect of the well-being of individuals and society. Thus even if—throughout all the centuries of Christian missionary history—remarkable service has always been rendered in respect of the care of the sick, the poor, orphans, and other victims of society, as well as in respect of education, agricultural instruction, and the like, these ministries were almost always viewed as "auxiliary services" and not as missionary in their own right. Their purpose was to dispose people favorably toward the gospel, "soften them up", and thereby prepare the way for the work of the *real* missionary, namely, the one who proclaimed God's word about eternal salvation. In most cases, then, a strict distinction was maintained between "horizontal" and "external" emphases (charity, education, medical help) on the one hand and the "vertical" or "spiritual" elements of the missionary agenda (such as preaching, the sacraments, church attendance) on the other. Only the latter had a bearing on the appropriation of salvation.

This attenuated definition of salvation inevitably led to a preoccupation with narrowly defined ecclesiastical activities, which, for their part, severely complicated the believers' involvement in society since such involvement had nothing to do with salvation except to draw people toward the church where they might get access to salvation proper.

Salvation in the Modern Paradigm

The theological constellation just outlined could only survive unscathed as long as people continued to live in the context of *Christendom* and felt themselves to be completely dependent on the comprehensive, transcendent activity of God as the sole explanation for everything that happened in the world. With the advent of the Enlightenment this entire interpretation of salvation came under severe pressure, with the result that traditional soteriology was increasingly challenged. The idea of salvation coming from outside, from God, totally out of reach of human power and capability, became extremely problematic (cf Wiederkehr 1976:77-122; 1982:331-336; Beinert 1983:209; Greshake 1983:26,74; see also chapter 9 of this study).

The modern critique of religion took its point of departure here. Religion as expression of total dependence upon God and as eternal salvation in the hereafter was an anachronism and remnant of humankind's period of childhood. Salvation now meant liberation from religious superstition, attention to human welfare, and the moral improvement of humanity. An alternative soteriology emerged, an understanding of salvation in which humans were active and responsible agents who utilized science and technology in order to effect material improvements and induce socio-political change in the present. In this respect, the critique of religion became, in essence, the critique of soteriology (Wiederkehr 1982:331-333). Salvation remained the motivating force in the life of modern people, but it was redefined radically.

The reaction of church and mission to the challenge of modernism was—very generally put—twofold. The first reaction—in both Catholic and Protestant circles—was for people to continue to define salvation in traditional terms, ignoring, as it were, the challenges of the Enlightenment, and proceeding as if nothing had changed.

The second reaction was to attempt to take the challenges of modernism seriously, also with respect to its understanding of salvation. One way in which Christianity was "salvaged" was by rejecting the view according to which Jesus died a substitutionary death for humankind and thereby propitiated God. Jesus was, rather, the ideal human being, an example to emulate, a moral teacher. Here not the *person* of Jesus was at the center but the *cause* of Jesus; the *ideal*, not the One who embodied the ideal; the *teaching* (particularly the Sermon on the Mount), not the Teacher; the *kingdom* of God, but without the King (cf Greshake 1983:76).

In this paradigm, then, guilt and salvation no longer primarily divide and unite God and humans, but humans among themselves. Luther's cry, "Where do I find a merciful God?" is changed to "How can we be merciful neighbors to each other?" God's "vertical" coming into this world manifests itself in changed, felicitous, "horizontal" relationships: the saving relationship of the human with God is made concrete in a person's conversion to his or her brother and sister. Sin is—in categories borrowed from Marx—alienation between humans. Salvation does not come through change in individuals but through the termination of perverted and unjust structures (cf Greshake 1983:26-29; Gründel 1983:113-115, 122). The apocalyptic pessimism of fundamentalism is refuted with the aid of evolutionary optimism. It is believed that people will soon be freed from *every* form of servitude to ignorance, hunger, misery, and oppression. The "paradise of the future" is being painted in vivid utopian colors, particularly in the American "Social Gospel". Salvation, defined in the American way, had to be exported to the "mission fields" (cf Dennis 1897, 1899, 1906). In this paradigm, sin is defined preeminently as *ignorance*. People only had to be *informed* about what was in their own interest. The Western mission was the great educator, which would mediate salvation to the unenlightened.

After the "Barthian interlude" (the 1920s to the 1950s) caused an interruption in this general trend, a new era of optimism dawned in the 1960s. For Johannes Hoekendijk, *shalom* was a more comprehensive notion than salvation, and if one *had* to choose, it was by no means self-evident that one would choose salvation. After all, we impose an antiquated anthropology upon our contemporaries if we continue to act as if they have to be on the lookout for a merciful God who could forgive their sins (Hoekendijk 1967a:348).

At the Geneva Conference on Church and Society (1966), both Emmanuel Mesthene and Richard Shaull utilized Hoekendijkian categories of salvation, even though they did so in very different ways. Both agreed that *this* world was the main arena of God's activity and the (only?) place where salvation could be effected. Where Mesthene's frame of reference was the modern industrialized and secularized West, and where he saw the solutions to the world's problems in technological progress, Shaull's frame of reference was the Third World, more particularly its experience of injustice, exploitation, and poverty. Mesthene's theology attempted to respond to the challenges of the Enlightenment, Shaull's to the challenges of Karl Marx and colonial exploitation. For Mesthene, salvation meant the large-scale expansion of technological development so that all may get a share in the wealth of the West; for Shaull, salvation meant liberation, which could be achieved only by overthrowing the existing order.

The Uppsala Assembly of the WCC (1968) attempted, in a sense, to reconcile these two positions, as the two reports on the "Structures for Missionary Congregations" demonstrated (WCC 1967). It was, however, left to the next conference of CWME (Bangkok, 1973, with the theme "Salvation Today") to attempt to determine, once and for all, what salvation was. The "spirit" of the conference, it seems, emerges where salvation is defined exclusively in this-worldly terms. Section II depicts salvation in four dimensions. It manifests itself in the struggle for (1) economic justice against exploitation; (2) for human dignity against oppression; (3) for solidarity against alienation; and (4) for hope against despair in personal life (WCC 1973:98). In the "process of salvation", we must relate (only?) these four dimensions to each other (:90).

Catholic missionary thinking on salvation paralleled that of Protestantism, particularly after Pope John XXIII announced the Second Vatican Council in 1959. As in Protestantism, it was believed that salvation could not be defined only in "religious" (or "ecclesial") terms but also in terms of what happened elsewhere. *Gaudium et Spes* devoted particular attention to this (e.g. in paragraph 4). It was, furthermore, especially in Roman Catholic *liberation theology* that a wider interpretation of salvation emerged.

There can be no doubt that the interpretation of salvation that has emerged in recent missionary thinking and practice has introduced elements into the definition of salvation without which it would be dangerously narrow and anemic. In a world in which people are dependent on each other and every individual exists within a web of inter-human relationships, it is totally untenable to limit salvation to the individual and his or her personal relationship with God. Hatred, injustice, oppression, war, and other forms of violence are manifestations of *evil*; concern for humaneness, for the conquering of famine, illness, and meaninglessness is part of the *salvation* for which we hope and labor. Christians pray that the reign of God should come and God's will be done *on earth* as it is in heaven (Mt 6:10); it follows from this that the *earth* is the locus of the Christian's calling and sanctification.

Crisis in the Modern Understanding of Salvation

In the course of the 1970s, however, the "secularist" as well as the "liberationist" definitions of salvation came under pressure. I have already referred to the more sober atmosphere that has characterized WCC meetings since the Nairobi Assembly (1975). Much the same has been true of Catholicism since the 1974 Bishops' Synod and the publication of *Evangelii Nuntiandi* (1975). It has gradually become clear that the "horizontalist" model was riddled with inconsistencies, both theological and practical. It was self-deception to begin to think and act as if salvation lay in our grasp, was at our disposal, or was something *we* could bring about. We began to realize once again that, in spite of the deeply rooted heretic conviction that we can bring about salvation through our own good works, even Christians have no ready-made answers to the needs of society. Christians promised themselves too much, for instance at Uppsala and Medellín (both in 1968), when statements were made to the effect that within the foreseeable future *all* injustice, *all* poverty, and *every* form of servitude would be something of the past and that salvation was just around the corner. Thomas Wieser, the WCC staff member responsible for coordinating the "Salvation Today" project, sounds the following sobering warning:

> The task of identifying God's saving purpose in the midst of historical events requires solid theological criteria on the basis of which critical judgments can be made. Here an important task remains to be undertaken in order to ensure that the Church's credibility will not again be lost in a dash for short-lived "relevance" (1973:177).

Indeed, the euphoric sense of a breakthrough which the delegates to the Bangkok Assembly had experienced at the time was deceptive. The ringing statements about the meaning of salvation actually raised more questions than they answered. This was further underscored when, during the past two decades, we have become conscious of the "limits of growth". Unchecked technological development has become nonsensical, since earth's nonrenewable resources are being exhausted, while the rich become richer and the poor poorer. Even if humans could live by bread alone, there is simply no longer enough bread for all because of structures which appear to be unalterable. We have, in addition, become conscious of the real possibility that our technological and scientific know-how may lead to our irreversibly ruining the ecosystem. We are, reluctantly, arriving at the conclusion that not everything that is technologically possible *should* be manufactured. The modern story of success tends toward becoming a story of catastrophe, and some people even try to withdraw into an illusory pre-technological world. Meanwhile the dreams about the "paradise of the future" are disappearing in the smoke of interminable wars and, much worse, in the radioactive winds of nuclear explosions which threaten to destroy all life on earth. The optimism and euphoria of the sixties are no longer part of our experience.

Christians are, in addition, forced to ask whether the tendency to allow theology and mission to be submerged in social ethics must not unavoidably lead to a relativizing of the person of Jesus Christ. Beinert rightly remarks, "The indispensable christological element of soteriology is not (always) made sufficiently clear" (1983:215 – my translation). The inescapable result of much of the modern paradigm is that the world's needs and solutions are being portrayed in terms which, to an extent, are independent of Jesus Christ (Lowe 1982:220). The church, however, is called in its mission to give witness to what God has "once for all, absolutely new, unrepeatably and finally done in Jesus Christ for the sake of the salvation of the world" (Glazik 1979:160 – my translation). It is Jesus Christ who "accomplishes all salvation. No one can complete his work if he does not achieve it himself" (Memorandum 1982:459).

To summarize, salvation and well-being, even if they are closely interlocked, do not coincide completely. The Christian faith is a critical factor, the reign of God a critical category, and the Christian gospel not identical with the agenda of modern emancipation and liberation movements (cf Beinert 1983:214f; Gort 1988:213f).

We cannot, however, simply return to the classical interpretation of salvation, even if that position upholds and defends elements which remain indispensable for a Christian understanding of salvation. Its problem lies, first, in the fact that it dangerously narrows the meaning of salvation, as if it comprises only escape from the wrath of God and the redemption of the individual soul in the hereafter and, second, in that it tends to make an absolute distinction between creation and new creation, between well-being and salvation. This is, for instance, what Donald McGavran does when he writes

Salvation is a vertical relationship . . . which issues in horizontal relationships. . . The vertical must not be displaced by the horizontal. Desirable as social ameliorations are, working for them must not be substituted for the biblical requirements of/for "salvation" (1973:31).

Over against this kind of approach we have to affirm that redemption is never salvation *out of* this world (*salus e mundo*) but always salvation *of* this world (*salus mundi*) (Aagaard 1974:429-431). Salvation in Christ is salvation in the context of human society en route to a whole and healed world.

Toward Comprehensive Salvation

The challenges of the modern world to the mission of the church in respect of the interpretation of salvation cannot simply be ignored. New challenges call for new responses. We are forced by circumstances to reflect anew on this entire matter. Perhaps a rereading of the biblical notions of salvation, done from the perspective of the realization that both the traditional and modern interpretations of salvation have proved inadequate, will help us here.

For its understanding of salvation the first model—that of the Greek Patristic mission—was oriented to the *origin* and *beginning* of Jesus' life—his preexistence and incarnation. The orientation of Western mission was toward the *end* of Jesus' life—his death on the cross (formulated classically in the Anselmian satisfaction theory). In both instances salvation was located on the edges of the life of Jesus (Wiederkehr 1976:34; Beinert 1983:211). The third model, that is, the ethical interpretation of salvation, was oriented to Jesus' *earthly life and ministry*. It admittedly introduced a more dynamic element into our understanding of salvation, but in such a way that, in the final analysis, it made Christ himself redundant.

We stand in need of an interpretation of salvation which operates within a *comprehensive* christological framework, which makes the *totus Christus*—his incarnation, earthly life, death, resurrection, and parousia—indispensable for church and theology. All these christological elements taken together constitute the praxis of Jesus, the One who both inaugurated salvation and provided us with a model to emulate (cf Wiederkehr 1976:39-43).

It therefore makes sense that in missionary circles today, but elsewhere as well, the mediating of "comprehensive", "integral", "total", or "universal" salvation is increasingly identified as the purpose of mission, in this way overcoming the inherent dualism in the traditional and more recent models (cf, for instance, the titles of Waldenfels 1977; Müller 1978; and Weber 1978).[8] Missionary literature, but also missionary practice, emphasize that we should find a way *beyond* every schizophrenic position and minister to people in their *total* need, that we should involve individual as well as society, soul *and* body, present *and* future in our ministry of salvation.

Never before in history has people's social distress been as extensive as it is in the twentieth century. But never before have Christians been in a better position than they are today to do something about this need. Poverty, misery, sickness, criminality, and social chaos have assumed unheard-of proportions. On an unprecedented scale people have become the victims of other people; *homo homini lupus* ("The human being is a wolf to other human beings").

Marginalized groups in many countries of the world lack every form of active and even passive participation in society; inter-human relationships are disintegrating; people are in the grip of a pattern of life from which they cannot possibly wrench themselves free; marginality characterizes every aspect of their existence (cf Müller 1978:90). To introduce change, as Christians, into all of this, is to mediate salvation; after all — to quote GS 1 again — "the joy and hope, the grief and anguish of the men of our time, especially of those who are poor or afflicted in any way, are the joy and hope, the grief and anguish of the followers of Christ as well". Precisely because our concern is salvation, we may no longer regard ourselves or others as prisoners of an omnipotent fate; in its mission the church constitutes a resistance movement against every manifestation of fatalism and quietism.

On the other hand, since we may never overrate our own or others' capabilities, we have to ask critical questions in respect to all current theories of human self-redemption. Final salvation will not be wrought by human hands, not even by *Christian* hands. The Christian's eschatological vision of salvation will not be realized in history. For this reason Christians should never identify any specific project with the fullness of the reign of God. We are, at best, erecting bridgeheads for the reign of God (cf Geffré 1982:490; Beinert 1983:215, 218; Beker 1984:86f; Gort 1988:213). We therefore hold on to the transcendent character of salvation also, and to the need of calling people to faith in God through Christ. Salvation does not come but along the route of repentance and personal faith commitment (cf Wiederkehr 1982:334).

The integral character of salvation demands that the scope of the church's mission be more comprehensive than has traditionally been the case. Salvation is as coherent, broad, and deep as the needs and exigencies of human existence. Mission therefore means being involved in the ongoing dialogue between God, who offers his salvation, and the world, which — enmeshed in all kinds of evil — craves that salvation (Gort 1988:209). "Mission means being sent to proclaim in deed and word that Christ died and rose for the life of the world, that he lives to transform human lives (Rom 8:2) and to overcome death" (Memorandum 1982:459). From the tension between the "already" and the "not yet" of the reign of God, from the tension between the salvation *indicative* (salvation is already a reality!) and the salvation *subjunctive* (comprehensive salvation is yet to come!) there emerges the salvation *imperative* — Get involved in the ministry of salvation! (Gort 1988:214). Those who know that God will one day wipe away all tears will not accept with resignation the tears of those who suffer and are oppressed *now*. Anyone who knows that one day there will be no more disease can and must actively anticipate the conquest of disease in individuals and society *now*. And anyone who believes that the enemy of God and humans will be vanquished will already oppose him *now* in his machinations in family and society. For all of this has to do with *salvation*.

MISSION AS THE QUEST FOR JUSTICE

The Legacy of History

In our next section (on evangelism) it will be argued that although evangelism may never simply be equated with labor for justice, it may also never be divorced from it. The relationship between the evangelistic and the societal dimensions of the Christian mission constitutes one of the thorniest areas in the theology and practice of mission. In subsequent sections we shall return to it again and again.

There can be no doubt that social justice was at the very heart of the prophetic tradition of the Old Testament. Since most of Israel's kings at least professed to believe in Yahweh, prophets like Amos and Jeremiah could, in the name of God, challenge them insofar as they had tolerated or perpetrated injustice in their kingdoms. The socio-political context in which the early church began to engage in mission was, however, fundamentally different. Christianity was a *religio illicita* in the Roman Empire. It was, at best, tolerated; at worst, it was persecuted. No Christian could address the authorities on the basis of a shared faith. This circumstance has led many Christians of later generations to the erroneous view that the New Testament is more "spiritual" than the Old and is, because of this, superior to it. At the same time the innate justice dimension of the Christian faith has often been overlooked, mainly because it was—in the prevailing circumstances—couched in terms which differed substantially from those we encounter in the Old Testament (cf also chapters 2 to 4 of this study).

During the reign of Constantine Christianity not only became a *religio licita*, it actually soon was the *only* legitimate religion in the empire. The situation was similar to that which prevailed in certain periods of the history of Israel as an independent nation. As had happened then, so also now the new situation led to compromises. And frequently the compromise was in the area of social justice, the "court prophets" finding it either impossible or imprudent to criticize the authorities when the latter had connived and even colluded in injustice. Still, since the membership of church and state for all practical purposes overlapped during the entire period from Constantine to the dawn of the modern era, and since the rulers explicitly acknowledged that they were as much responsible for the religious and moral life of their subjects as they were for politics, the realms of religion and politics were, somehow, held together.

As early as Augustine, however, there was a trend to divide reality starkly into two irreconcilable opposites, spelled out forcefully in *The City of God,* Book 4 Chapter 28 (cf also chapter 6 of this study). In spite of counter-currents (in late medieval Catholicism the name of Thomas Aquinas may be mentioned) there has always, since Augustine, been a tendency to construe a contrast "between the ... radiance of divine holiness and the darkness of the world" (Niebuhr 1960:69). This legacy was passed on from Catholicism to Protestantism in all its forms (though it manifested itself more clearly in the Lutheran and Anabaptist traditions than in Calvinism). The world was evil and unredeemable, and changing its structures did not really fall within the sphere of the church's responsibilities.

With the advent of the Enlightenment and its thoroughgoing differentiation between the public world of facts and the private world of ideas, politics and the state were assigned to the former, religion and morals to the latter. The organic link between church and state had been severed and the church could no longer appeal to the state on the basis of a shared faith commitment. The church's ministry—outside its walls—was by and large limited to charity and development. To challenge unjust societal structures fell outside of its purview and would also have been totally unacceptable to the political rulers. When, in 1926, a group of ten bishops (one of whom was William Temple, later Archbishop of Canterbury) attempted to mediate in a dispute between coal miners, coal-owners, and the British government, an irate Stanley Baldwin, then prime minister, asked how the bishops would like it if he were to refer to the Iron and Steel Federation the revision of the Athanasian Creed! (cf Temple 1976:30).

The "interference" of the bishops with politics was one of the earliest manifestations of an "established" church breaking out of the mold of harmony and neat division of labor between church and state.[9] Much of the convolution in church-state relationships in the twentieth century flowed from attempts at redefining this relationship.

The Tension between Justice and Love

In order to appreciate the issues involved, it may help to highlight an observation made by Reinhold Niebuhr (1960). A *rational* ethic, Niebuhr suggests, aims at *justice*, whereas a *religious* ethic makes *love* the ideal (:57). The latter ideal is supported by viewing the soul of one's fellow human being "from the absolute and transcendent perspective" (:58). This leads to the presence—in every vital religion—of a millennial hope for a society in which the ideal of love and equity will be fully realized (:60f). However, this is complicated by the fact that, *within* the religious ideal, a "mystical" emphasis exists side by side with a "prophetic" emphasis (:64). The mystical dimension tends to make an individual or a group withdraw from the world, devalue history, claim that one's true home is not here but in heaven, and seek communion with God without attending to one's neighbor (cf Haight 1976:623). The prophetic dimension prompts the believer to get involved in society for the sake of the neighbor.

Attempts to deal with this unresolved tension in the Christian ethic have, by and large, taken two different forms.

In the Protestant *ecumenical* movement, and to a lesser extent in contemporary Catholicism, it seems it is the *prophetic* motif that predominates. In some manifestations of ecumenicalism, however, it seems that the rational ethic, which aims at justice, is more powerful than the religious ethic of love. The Social Gospel, for instance—particularly after the year 1900—"emphasized social concern in an exclusivistic way which seemed to undercut the relevance of the message of eternal salvation" (Marsden 1980:92), thereby, seemingly, jettisoning completely any idea of transcendence in Christianity. The same appeared to be true, by and large, of much of what was said and done in "mainline" Christianity during the "secular sixties". The Geneva Church and Society Conference (1966), the WCC Uppsala Assembly (1968), and the CWME meeting in Bangkok (1973) again come to mind as manifestations of the trend to give "a blanket endorsement of any political movement" (Wieser 1973:177) without adequately identifying criteria for judging whether it truly belonged to the mission of God (cf Bassham 1979:94). The religious ethic of love, says Niebuhr (1960:80f), will always aim at leavening the idea of justice with the ideal of love; it will prevent it from becoming purely political, with the ethical element washed out. Love demands more than justice (:75). The "ultra-rational hopes" in religion provide courage and keep love alive.

This is what EN 27 has in mind when it warns against reducing the mission of the church "to the dimensions of a simple temporal project". In similar vein Bonhoeffer ([1932] 1977) refers to the "secularist temptation" of identifying the reign of God, consciously or unconsciously, with some earthly goal, of trying to be the architects not only of our own future but also of God's. Here the "eschatological reservation" has almost completely disappeared. However, Bon-hoeffer also refers to the other extreme where—in the pious radiance of oth-erworldly realities—earth pales into insignificance and ultimately becomes meaningless. This is the danger in the *evangelical* position on the church's calling in respect to justice in society. The problem, says Niebuhr (1960:74) is that the religious ideal tends to be more interested in the perfect *motive* of the believer than in fleshing out the consequences of love. Such a preoccupation with motive—which has its own virtues—is perilous to society. As the institution of slavery has shown, sincere Christians, motivated by love, might not move vig-orously against the social injustices in the larger society, which they know to be in conflict with their religious and moral ideals (:77f). The consistent God-world, spirit-body dualism, inherited from Augustine and the Greeks and rein-forced by the Enlightenment mind-set, defeats the ideal of love.

The Two Mandates

One attempt to solve the enigma of the relationship between evangelism and social responsibility is to distinguish between two different *mandates*, the one spiritual, the other social. The first refers to the commission to announce the good news of salvation through Jesus Christ; the second calls Christians to responsible participation in human society, including working for human well-being and justice (cf Bassham 1979:343). Perhaps this distinction—as far as North American Protestantism is concerned—goes back to Jonathan Edwards (1703-1758). According to Edwards, God's work of redemption has two facets. One consists in the converting, sanctifying, and glorifying of individuals; the other pertains to God's grand design in creation, history, and providence (cf Chaney 1976:217). Still, for Edwards these two "mandates" were inseparable. The same was true of those who had been touched by the Evangelical Awak-enings. The evangelical commitment to social reform was a corollary of the enthusiasm for revival (Marsden 1980:12).

Gradually, however, a subtle shift toward the primacy of the "evangelistic mandate" was discernible. This coincided with the rise of premillennialism in what later became known as fundamentalism and the latter's growing protest against the this-worldliness of the Social Gospel. Between 1865 and 1900 inter-est in social and political action diminished, though it was not completely dis-continued, among revivalist evangelicals. Between 1900 and 1930, however, all progressive social concern became suspect among them and disappeared dra-

matically (Marsden 1980:86-90). The broad sweep of the involvement and interest of the eighteenth- and nineteenth-century Awakenings had shrivelled to
narrow and intolerant sectarianism. The "Great Reversal" (Timothy Smith —
cf Marsden 1980:85) had set in. The Awakening, says Lovelace (1981), had
never been completed.

Much of this mentality still prevails in fundamentalist circles around the
world. In the main body of evangelicalism, however, a change began to set in.
Catalytic in this respect was Carl F. H. Henry's *The Uneasy Conscience of Modern
Fundamentalism* (1947). He wrote (quoted in Bassham 1979:176):

> Whereas once the redemptive gospel was a world-changing message, now
> it was narrowed to a world-resisting message ... Fundamentalism in
> revolting against the Social Gospel seemed also to revolt against the
> Christian social imperative ... It does not challenge the injustices of the
> totalitarianisms, the secularisms of modern education, the evils of racial
> hatred, the wrongs of current labor-management relations, and inade-
> quate bases of international dealings.

Henry concludes, "There is no room ... for a gospel that is indifferent to
the needs of the total man nor of the global man". It took some time for this
perspective to begin to filter through, not least because much evangelical energy
at the time was dissipated in attempts to attack the young and energetic WCC.
The "Wheaton Declaration" (produced by an evangelical conference which
convened in Wheaton, Illinois, in 1966) conceded that evangelicals in the eighteenth and nineteenth century had led in social concern and stressed the importance of ministering to physical and social needs, but stated that this should
happen "without minimizing the priority of preaching the gospel of individual
salvation" (Lindsell 1966:234). Henceforth, whenever the "social mandate" was
emphasized in evangelicalism, it would always be accompanied by a statement
about the primacy of evangelism. The Berlin Congress, also held in 1966, a few
months after the Wheaton Congress, reaffirmed the participants' "unswerving
determination to carry out the supreme mission of the Church" (Henry and
Mooneyham 1967a:5). In his address, Billy Graham spoke for many evangelicals
when he included a social dimension within evangelism but then added that
improved social conditions were a *result* of successful evangelism (:28),

> I am convinced if the Church went back to its main task of proclaiming
> the Gospel and getting people converted to Christ, it would have a far
> greater impact on the social, moral and psychological needs of men than
> any other thing it could possibly do. Some of the greatest social move-
> ments of history have come about as the result of men being converted
> to Christ.

By this definition evangelism relates to social responsibility as seed relates
to fruit; evangelism remains primary (the church's "main task") but it generates
social involvement and improved social conditions among those who have been
evangelized (cf McGavran 1973:31).

All these and similar interpretations of the relationship between evangelism and social responsibility could not but increasingly come under tremendous pressure. Several evangelical scholars began to reflect anew on the issues, building on nineteenth-century social ethics and taking up some of the challenges articulated by Henry in his 1947 book.[10] So-called radical evangelicals—Mennonites and others—began to move out of their centuries-old self-imposed isolation from mainstream Christianity and made vital contributions to social thinking and practice among evangelicals (cf Yoder 1972). So by 1974, when the International Congress on World Evangelization met in Lausanne, many evangelicals, particularly those from the Third World, were ready for a new advance. John Stott, in a book published soon after the Lausanne conference, candidly confessed that he had changed his mind on the interpretation of the "Great Commission": at Berlin 1966 he had interpreted it exclusively in terms of evangelism (in Henry and Mooneyham 1967a:37-56). Now he would prefer to express himself differently:

I now see more clearly that not only the consequences of the commission but the actual commission itself must be understood to include social as well as evangelistic responsibility, unless we are to be guilty of distorting the words of Jesus (Stott 1975:23).

It was in line with this new understanding that the LC 5 affirmed that

(evangelism and socio-political) involvement are both part of our Christian duty. For both are necessary expressions of our doctrines of God and man, our love for our neighbor and our obedience to Jesus Christ.

However, both the Congress and the Covenant continued to operate in terms of the two-mandate approach and to uphold the priority of evangelism. It affirmed that "in the church's mission of sacrificial service evangelism is primary". It was also explicitly stated that "reconciliation with man is not reconciliation with God, nor is social action evangelism, nor is political liberation salvation".

In spite of the advantages of this approach over the one-mandate strategy ("evangelism only") that dominated evangelicalism for so long, Stott's understanding of mission as "evangelism *plus* social responsibility" was under pressure from the very beginning. The moment one regards mission as consisting of two separate components one has, in principle, conceded that each of the two has a life of its own. One is then by implication saying that it is possible to have evangelism without a social dimension and Christian social involvement without an evangelistic dimension. What is more, if one suggests that one component is primary and the other secondary, one implies that the one is essential, the other optional. This is precisely what happened. The *Thailand Statement*, released by the Pattaya conference of LCWE (1980), affirmed the movement's commitment to LC's emphasis on both evangelism and social action but went on to say that "nothing contained in the Lausanne Covenant is beyond our concern, *so long as it is clearly related to world evangelization*" (emphasis added). The significance of this sentence lies in what it does *not* say — that nothing in LC is beyond our concern, *so long as it clearly fosters Christian involvement in society.*

In 1982, two years after the Pattaya conference, some forty scholars met in Grand Rapids, Michigan, at a "Consultation on the Relationship Between Evangelism and Social Responsibility" (CRESR), sponsored by LCWE and the WEF. The consultation's report conceded that some participants "felt uncomfortable" about LC's stand on the primacy of evangelism and attempted to explain that its priority may not always be *chronologically* prior to social engagement. It continued,

> Seldom if ever should we have to choose between satisfying physical hunger and spiritual hunger, or between healing bodies and saving souls, since an authentic love for our neighbor will lead us to serve him or her as a whole person. *Nevertheless, if we must choose, then we have to say that the supreme and ultimate need of all humankind is the saving grace of Jesus Christ,* and that therefore a person's eternal, spiritual salvation is of greater importance than his or her temporal and material well-being (CRESR 1982:25, emphasis added).

The dichotomy was thus upheld at CRESR. The official evangelical position remained: evangelism is primary, and where it has been successful, it has led to "fruits" in the form of social justice. In fact, this cause-effect thinking (a legacy of the Enlightenment?) still remains powerful within evangelicalism. The greatest single step the church can take toward creating a new world order, says McGavran (1983:21), is to multiply in society, "cells of the redeemed". Once this has happened, God "inevitably . . . causes them to seek a better social order" (:28).

The question is whether this cause-effect thinking can really be maintained. Apart from the fact that it could be argued, on empirical grounds, that converted individuals do not "inevitably" (McGavran's word) get involved in restructuring society, one has to ask whether this approach is *theologically* tenable. It is of interest to note that this question is increasingly asked by evangelicals themselves. Already at the Lausanne Congress several hundred delegates sided with a statement called *A Response to Lausanne,* in which LC was criticized on this point. The response states, among other things, that

> there is no biblical dichotomy between the word spoken and the word made visible in the lives of God's people. Men will look as they listen and what they see must be at one with what they hear . . . There are times when our communication may be by attitude and action only, and times when the spoken word will stand alone: but we must repudiate as demonic the attempt to drive a wedge between evangelism and social concern.

This powerful response found an echo at the Pattaya 1980 meeting of LCWE when some two hundred participants signed a "Statement of Concern on the

Future of the LCWE", in which the conference leadership was criticized in no uncertain terms for the way in which it had emphasized the evangelistic mandate to the almost total exclusion of the church's calling in the area of justice and peace. In the same year, and shortly before the Pattaya Conference, the WEF unit on Ethics and Society held two meetings at High Leigh near London, one on development, one on lifestyle.[11] Both consultations moved beyond the themes and scope which characterized evangelical meetings in the 1960s and 1970s, not least because of the strong Third-World representation. Scherer comments on the second of the two consultations,

> The actual content of the London consultation went far beyond simple living, stewardship, or benevolence, and touched precisely on God's preferential option for the poor, divine judgment on oppressors, the pattern of Christ's own identification with the poor, the risk of suffering for Christ's sake, and Christian support for changes in the political structures — themes seldom articulated with such passion in evangelical mission circles (1987:180).

In 1983 another significant step forward was taken at a WEF consultation in Wheaton devoted to "The Church in Response to Human Need".[12] For the first time in an official statement emanating from an international evangelical conference the perennial dichotomy was overcome. Without ascribing priority to either evangelism or social involvement, the *Wheaton '83 Statement,* paragraph 26, declared,

> Evil is not only in the human heart but also in social structures. . . . The mission of the church includes both the proclamation of the Gospel and its demonstration. We must therefore evangelize, respond to immediate human needs, and press for social transformation.

By the early 1980s, then, it seemed that a new spirit was establishing itself in mainstream evangelicalism. Regional evangelical groupings followed suit. One of the most remarkable documents in this respect was the *Evangelical Witness in South Africa,* produced by a group of "Concerned Evangelicals" in 1986.[13] In the context of the apartheid system and the experience of repression and police brutality during a state of emergency, evangelicals felt forced to respond and articulate their views on evangelism, mission, structural evil, and the church's responsibility with respect to justice in society. They had no doubt that they were called to a ministry of proclaiming Christ as Savior and of inviting people to put their trust in him, but they were equally convinced that sin was both personal and structural, that life was of a piece, that dualism was contrary to the gospel, and that their ministry had to be broadened as well as deepened. This represents an important shift in evangelicalism and not simply a return to a nineteenth-century position. At that time, and due to the prevalent optimistic mood, Christians tended to believe in a "natural" and evolutionary improvement of societal conditions. Today both evangelicals and ecumenicals grasp in a more profound manner than ever before something of the depth of evil in the world, the inability of human beings to usher in God's reign, and the need for both personal renewal by God's Spirit *and* resolute commitment to challenging and transforming the structures of society.[14]

A Convergence of Convictions

In many respects, then, an important segment of evangelicalism appears poised to reverse the "Great Reversal" and embody anew a full-orbed gospel of the irrupting reign of God not only in individual lives but also in society. A similar turning of the tide, but in the opposite direction, has been in evidence in ecumenical circles since the middle of the 1970s, more particularly since the Nairobi Assembly of the WCC (1975). This is particularly in evidence in the 1982 *Mission and Evanqelism* document. It states, among other things:

> There is no evangelism without solidarity; there is no Christian solidarity that does not involve sharing the knowledge of the kingdom which is God's promise to the poor of the earth. There is here a double credibility test: A proclamation that does not hold forth the promises of the justice of the kingdom to the poor of the earth is a caricature of the Gospel; but Christian participation in the struggles for justice which does not point towards the promises of the kingdom also makes a caricature of a Christian understanding of justice (para 34).

A similar convergence of ideas is witnessed in Catholicism. *Evangelii Nuntiandi*, in particular, underscores the important advance in Catholic thinking that took place since Vatican II. Refusing to limit the church's ministry to the dimensions of economics, politics, or cultural life, the pope nevertheless does not allow a return to a preconciliar position, maintaining that salvation most certainly begins in this life to find its fulfillment in eternity (EN 27; cf also Snijders 1977:172f)

Many ambiguities remain and much still has to be done in sorting out the nature of the church's involvement in society, not least because of "the general failure of theologians to deal adequately with this problem" (Snijders 1977:173). And yet, churches—Catholic, Protestant, and Orthodox—are learning afresh "to overcome the old dichotomies between evangelism and social action. The 'spiritual Gospel' and 'material Gospel' were in Jesus one Gospel" (ME 33). The alternative "between evangelization and humanization, between interior conversion and improvement of conditions, or between the vertical dimension of faith and the horizontal dimension of love" is untenable (Moltmann 1975:4). Speaking to the Uppsala Assembly, Visser 't Hooft lamented the "rather primitive oscillating movement of going from one extreme to the other", and added,

> A Christianity which has lost its vertical dimension has lost its salt and is not only insipid in itself, but useless to the world. But a Christianity which would use the vertical preoccupation as a means to escape from its responsibility for and in the common life of man is a denial of the incarnation (WCC 1968:318).

MISSION AS EVANGELISM[15]

Evangelism: A Plethora of Definitions

Our discussion on the meaning and scope of salvation and on the church's mission in respect to social justice leads us, almost as a matter of course, to reflections on the nature of evangelism. The concept "to evangelize" and its derivatives have actually been around much longer than the word "mission" and, of course, also occur fairly frequently in the New Testament (*euangelizein* [or *euangelizesthai*] and *euangelion*). However, these terms fell into almost complete disuse during the Middle Ages (Barrett 1987:21f). Even today they are hardly ever used in English Bible translations; *euangelion* is usually translated "gospel" and *euangelizesthai/euangelizein* "preach the gospel". Since the early nineteenth century the verb "evangelize" and its derivatives "evangelism" and "evangelization" were, however, rehabilitated in church and mission circles. They became particularly prominent around the turn of the century because of the slogan "The evangelization of the world in this generation" (:30).

After a temporary lull in usage, from the 1920s to the 1960s, the terms again became very prominent and have been widely used since 1970 in Protestant (ecumenical and evangelical) as well as Catholic circles (Barrett 1987:60-66). An "epochal watershed" (:66) in this respect was the publication, in 1975, of Pope Paul VI's Apostolic Exhortation, *Evangelii Nuntiandi*; equally significant were the Nairobi Assembly of the WCC in the same month that EN was released and the publication, in 1982, of *Mission and Evangelism — An Ecumenical Affirmation* (ME). In fact, these meetings and documents mark a significant revival in Catholic and Protestant interest in evangelism (cf Gómez 1986:35).

As far as the noun is concerned, it is worth noting that the Protestant evangelical movement as well as Roman Catholics appear to prefer "evangelization", whereas Protestant ecumenicals favor "evangelism". I shall use "evangelism" to refer to (a) the activities involved in spreading the gospel (however we may wish to define these; see below), or (b) theological reflection on these activities. "Evangelization" will be used to refer to (a) the process of spreading the gospel, or (b) the extent to which it has been spread (for instance in the expression "the evangelization of the world has not yet been completed") (cf also Barrett 1982:826; 1987:25f; Watson 1983b:7).

It remains difficult, however, to determine precisely what authors mean by evangelism or evangelization. Barrett (1987:42-45) lists seventy-nine definitions, to which many more could be added. Broadly speaking, controversy prevails in two areas: the differences (if any) between "evangelism" and "mission", and the scope or range of evangelism. These issues are, moreover, intimately interrelated.

First, some suggest that "mission" has to do with ministry to people (particularly those in the Third World) who are *not yet* Christians and "evangelism" with ministry to those (particularly in the West) who are *no longer* Christians. The existence of such "no longer" Christians reflects a new situation. Prior to the Enlightenment and the Age of Discovery all people outside the West were "pagans", whereas everybody in the West was considered Christian. Now there are "non-believers" in the West also. It is argued, however, that a difference in terminology is needed when referring to the church's work among these two groups. Mission, it is suggested, is concerned with first conversion, with Christianization, with *vocare*, with a first beginning, with the stranger far away; evangelism has to do with re-conversion, re-Christianization, *revocare*, a new beginning, the estranged neighbor (cf Barth 1957). Within (Western) Christendom, then, evangelism is in order, not mission. "Home Missions" (evangelism) is judged to be *theologically* distinct from (foreign) mission. The differentiation is, at the same time, *geographical*. In the words of Margull, "The distinctive feature of foreign mission is to proclaim the gospel where no church as yet exists, where the Lordship of God has never yet — historically — been proclaimed, where *pagans* are the object of concern" (1962:275). Mission, then, takes place in a *pre*-Christian milieu. Over against this, Margull defines evangelism, which he also distinguishes sharply from the church's "regular" preaching to its members, as the proclamation of the gospel among those who have left the church or those living in a *post*-Christian milieu, such as Eastern Europe (1962:277f).

Margull reflects a wide consensus in Roman Catholic and Protestant circles (cf Barth 1962:872-874; Ohm 1962:53-58; *Ad Gentes;* Verkuyl 1978b:passim). At the same time, he argues (:275-277) that "evangelism" should never have a life of its own, since it is derived from the reality of the foreign mission and must always be seen in close relationship to it. "Mission" remains primary, "evangelism" secondary. One reason for such a "synchronizing" of mission and evangelism (Margull 1962:274) lies in the fact that the distinction between work among "not yet Christians" ("mission") and "no longer Christians" ("evangelism") is increasingly breaking down; there are now also "not yet Christians" (people who are not only alienated from the church but who have never had any link whatsoever with it) in the West, just as there are "no longer Christians" (people who were once Christians but have become alienated from the church) in the traditional "mission" territories (cf also Gensichen 1971:237-240; Verkuyl 1978b:72-74).

Second, and in addition to the distinction just identified, there has often been a tendency to define "evangelism" more narrowly than "mission". And as Roman Catholics and ecumenical Protestants increasingly tended to use the word "mission" for an ever-widening range of ecclesial activities (this happened particularly at the Uppsala Meeting of the WCC), evangelicals began to avoid the term "mission" and to use only "evangelism", also for the "foreign" enterprise. This polemic use of "evangelism" by evangelicals suggested that, in their view, the WCC had wrongfully broadened the scope of the original enterprise to what it is today. Johnston (1978:18), for instance, claims, "Historically the mission of the church is evangelism alone" (cf McGavran 1983:17 — "Theologically mission was evangelism by every means possible"). The more "inclusive" understanding of the enterprise, Johnston says (:36) actually began with the Edinburgh Conference of 1910.

Third, there has been, over the last four decades or so, a trend to understand

"mission" and "evangelism" as synonyms. The church's task—whether i.. ...
West or the Third World—is *one*, and it is immaterial whether we call it "mission" or "evangelism". As far as evangelicals are concerned this already
emerges in the definitions of Johnston and McGavran just quoted.[16] In WCC
and Roman Catholic circles there is a similar tendency. The formation of the
Commission for World Mission and Evangelism after the WCC New Delhi
Assembly (1961) attests to this; Philip Potter was therefore correct when he
said that, in ecumenical literature, "mission", "evangelism", and "witness" are,
as a rule, interchangeable concepts. And a Roman Catholic memorandum
claims, "*Mission, evangelization and witness* are nowadays often used by Catholics
as synonymous" (Memorandum 1982:460).

Further confusion was added when, fourth, the term "evangelism" or "evangelization" began to *replace* "mission" in recent years, not only in conservative
evangelical circles but also among Roman Catholics and ecumenical Protestants. In the case of the latter grouping, "evangelism" or "evangelization",
understood to be identical with "mission", was deemed more acceptable than
"mission" because of the colonialist overtones still associated with the latter
term (cf Geffré 1982:479; Gómez 1986:36). The most thoroughgoing example
of "evangelization" supplanting mission is to be found in EN. The document
shuns the word "mission" and, in its English translation, uses "evangelization"
and its cognates no less than 214 times (Barrett 1987:66). "Evangelization" is
understood as an umbrella concept embracing the whole activity of the church
sent into the world: "One single term—evangelization—defines the whole of
Christ's office and mandate" (EN 6; cf Snijders 1977:172; Geffré 1982:489;
Scherer 1987:205). In like manner, Geijbels (1978:73-82) understands evangelization to include proclamation, translation, dialogue, service, and presence.
And Walsh (1982:92) states that "human development, liberation, justice, and
peace are *integral* parts of the ministry of evangelization".

In the case of evangelicals, "evangelism" (or, more commonly, "evangelization") is often preferred to "mission" because of what evangelicals believe
ecumenicals to understand by "mission" (or because of the way "mission" had
been "reconceptualized" at Uppsala 1968 and "implemented" as "new mission"
at Bangkok 1973 [Hoekstra 1979:63-109]). Thus, if Johnston (1978) writes about
"the battle for world evangelism" and Hoekstra (1979) of "the demise of evangelism" in the WCC, they reveal a preference for the term "evangelism" as
opposed to the term "mission".

Toward a Constructive Understanding of Evangelism

Convolutions in meaning such as the ones identified above are symptomatic
of the prevailing state of flux in missionary thinking and of the period of transition in which we find ourselves. In what follows I shall attempt to outline an
understanding of evangelism which will, hopefully, contribute to the kind of
mission that will be relevant to the present hour. Basic to my considerations is
the conviction that mission and evangelism are not synonyms but, nevertheless,
indissolubly linked together and inextricably interwoven in theology and praxis.

1. *I perceive mission to be wider than evangelism.* "Evangelization is mission,

but mission is not merely evangelization" (Moltmann 1977:10; cf Geffré 1982:478f). Mission denotes the total task God has set the church for the salvation of the world, but always related to a specific context of evil, despair, and lostness (as Jesus defined his "mission" according to Luke 4:18f — cf also Chapter 3 of this study). It "embraces all activities that serve to liberate man from his slavery in the presence of the coming God, slavery which extends from economic necessity to Godforsakenness" (Moltmann 1977:10). Mission is the church sent into the world, to love, to serve, to preach, to teach, to heal, to liberate.

2. *Evangelism should therefore not be equated with mission.* Where this happens, the need arises to supplement "evangelism" with neologisms like "pre-evangelization" and "re-evangelization" (cf Rahner 1966:52f; Gómez 1986:36), in an attempt to introduce elements which may otherwise be lost. It is therefore better to uphold the distinctiveness of evangelism within the wider mission of the church. It is, however, impossible to dissociate it from the church's wider mission (Geffré 1982:480). Evangelism is integral to mission, "sufficiently distinct and yet not separate from mission" (Löffler 1977a:341). One may never isolate it and treat it as a completely separate activity of the church. "If it is not related to everything the church does, then the church is suspect" (Spong 1982:15). Authentic evangelism is imbedded in the total mission of the church, "our opening up of the mystery of God's love to all people inside that mission" (Castro 1977:10). ME's holding together both mission (ME 1-5) and evangelism (ME 6-8) rightly makes it impossible to choose between mission and evangelism.

3. *Evangelism may be viewed as an essential "dimension of the total activity of the Church"* (1954 Evanston Assembly of the WCC, quoted in Löffler 1977b:8), the heart or core of the church's mission (Löffler 1977a:341). If we accept this, we would have to rule out the idea, propounded by Stott (1975) and the *Lausanne Covenant*, that evangelism is one of two segments or components of mission (the other one being social action). Evangelism may never be given a life of its own, in isolation from the rest of the life and ministry of the church (cf Castro 1978:88). In light of this, and of the apparent absence of conspicuous programs of evangelism in WCC member churches, it is perhaps rash to talk about the "demise" of evangelism in the WCC (Hoekstra 1979).

4. *Evangelism involves witnessing to what God has done, is doing, and will do.* This is the way Jesus began his evangelistic ministry according to the synoptic gospels: "The time is fulfilled, and the kingdom of God is at hand" (Mk 1:15). Evangelism is announcing that God, Creator and Lord of the universe, has personally intervened in human history and has done so supremely through the person and ministry of Jesus of Nazareth who is the Lord of history, Savior and Liberator. In this Jesus, incarnate, crucified and risen, the reign of God has been inaugurated (cf ME 6, 8). Evangelism thus includes the "gospel events" (Stott 1975:44f). It is, essentially, not a call to put something into effect, as if God's reign would be inaugurated by our response or thwarted by the absence of such a response (cf Kramm 1979:220). It is a response to what God has already put into effect. In light of this, evangelism cannot be defined in terms of its results or effectiveness, as though evangelism has only occurred where

there are "converts". Rather, evangelism should be perceived in terms of its nature, as mediating the good news of God's love in Christ that transforms life, proclaiming, by word and action, that Christ has set us free (cf Gutiérrez 1988:xxxvii, xli).

5. *Even so, evangelism does aim at a response.* On the basis of the reality of the fullness of time and the irruption of God's reign, Jesus summons his listeners, "Repent, and believe the gospel". "The calling is to specific changes, to renounce evidences of the domination of sin in our lives and to accept responsibilities in terms of God's love for our neighbour" (ME 11); after all, *metanoia* involves the "total transformation of our attitudes and styles of life" (ME 12; cf Costas 1989:112-130). To dispense with the centrality of repentance and faith is to divest the gospel of its significance. Conversion "involves a turning *from* and a turning *to*" — "*from* a life characterized by sin, separation from God, submission to evil and the unfulfilled potential of God's image, *to* a new life characterized by the forgiveness of sins, obedience . . . renewed fellowship with God in Trinity" (ME 12). Conversion is, moreover, an ongoing, lifelong process (cf Löffler 1977b:8).

6. *Evangelism is always invitation* (Löffler 1977a:341; Sundermeier 1986:72, 92). To evangelize is to communicate joy (Gutiérrez 1988:xxxvii). It conveys a positive message; it is hope we are holding out to the world (Margull 1962:280). Evangelism should never deteriorate into coaxing, much less into threat. It is not the same as (1) offering a psychological panacea for people's frustrations and disappointments, (2) inculcating guilt feelings so that people (in despair, as it were) may turn to Christ, or (3) scaring people into repentance and conversion with stories about the horrors of hell. People should turn to God because they are drawn by God's love, not because they are pushed to God for fear of hell. It is only in the light of our experience of the grace of God in Christ "that we know the terrible abyss of darkness into which we must fall if we put our trust anywhere but in that grace" (cf Newbigin 1982:151). As was explained in Chapter 4, it is the "solution" in Christ that reveals to us the "plight" from which we have been saved.

7. *The one who evangelizes is a witness not a judge.* This has important consequences for the way we evaluate our own evangelistic ministry and often facilely divide people into the "saved" and the "lost". As Newbigin formulates it,

> I can never be so confident of the purity and authenticity of my witness that I can know that the person who rejects my witness has rejected Jesus. I am witness to him who is both utterly holy and utterly gracious. His holiness and his grace are as far above my comprehension as they are above that of my hearer (1982:151).

8. *Even though we ought to be modest about the character and effectiveness of our witness, evangelism remains an indispensable ministry.* It is not an optional extra but a sacred duty, "incumbent on (the church) . . . This message is indeed necessary. It is unique. It cannot be replaced" (EN 5). It cannot be assumed

that the evangelistic dimension of the church's mission is included in all that the church says and does; it has to be made explicit (Watson 1983a:68f). "Each person is entitled to hear the Good News" (ME 10).

9. *Evangelism is only possible when the community that evangelizes — the church — is a radiant manifestation of the Christian faith and exhibits an attractive lifestyle.* "The medium is the message" (Marshall McLuhan). In the words of the (British) *Nationwide Initiative in Evangelism*: "What we are and do is no less important in this respect than what we say" (NIE 1980:3). If the church is to impart to the world a message of hope and love, of faith, justice and peace, something of this should become visible, audible, and tangible in the church itself (cf Acts 2:42-47; 4:32-35). The witness of life of the believing community prepares the way for the gospel (cf EN 59-61; see also, once again, the criteria for a missionary church identified by Gensichen 1971:170-172). Where this is absent the credibility of our evangelism is dangerously impaired. "How many of the millions of people in the world who are not confessing Jesus Christ have rejected him because of what they saw in the lives of Christians! *Thus the call to conversion should begin with the repentance of those who do the calling, who issue the invitation*" (ME 13 — emphasis in the original). These words are particularly pertinent where a Christian community fails to demonstrate the fact that in Christ God has shattered all the barriers that divide the human family. In this respect, in particular, the very *being* of the church has an evangelistic significance, either positively or negatively (cf Barth 1956:676f, 706f).

10. *Evangelism offers people salvation as a present gift and with it assurance of eternal bliss.* People are, even without realizing it, desperately searching for a meaning to life and history; this impels them to look for a sign of hope amid the widespread fear of global catastrophe and meaninglessness. We may, through our evangelism, mediate to them "a transcendent and eschatological salvation, which indeed has its beginning in this life but which is fulfilled in eternity" (EN 27; cf Memorandum 1982:463).

However, if the offer of all this gets center-stage attention in our evangelism, the gospel is degraded to a consumer product. It has to be emphasized, therefore, that the personal enjoyment of salvation never becomes the central theme in biblical conversion stories (cf Barth 1962:561-614). Where Christians perceive themselves as those enjoying an indescribably magnificent private good fortune (:567f), Christ is easily reduced to little more than the "Disposer and Distributor" of special blessings (:595f) and evangelism to an enterprise that fosters the pursuit of pious self-centredness (:572). Not that the enjoyment of salvation is wrong, unimportant, or unbiblical; even so, it is almost incidental and secondary (:572, 593). It is not simply to *receive* life that people are called to become Christians, but rather to *give* life.

11. *Evangelism is not proselytism* (cf Löffler 1977a:340). At the founding of the *Sacra Congregatio de Propaganda Fidei* (1622) it was explicitly stated that the interest of the new organization would be focused, not on "non-Christians", but on "non-Catholics"; indeed, until around 1830 its spotlight was on Protestant Europe (Glazik 1984a:29f). Only too often, then, evangelism has been used as means of reconquering lost ecclesiastical influence, in Catholicism *and*

Protestantism. Particularly in contexts where the church (or "denomination") is viewed as made up of individuals who have made a free choice to join it, there is an implicit (and sometimes explicit) suggestion that competition is necessary. Thus people in the surrounding community, whether they belong to other churches or not, are perceived as "prospects" to be won. Much of this reflects the tendency toward empire-building—the church "cannot resist the temptation to open yet another branch office in an area that looks promising" (Spong 1982:13). Whether intended or not, this mentality suggests that it is not by grace, but by becoming adherents of our denomination, that people will be saved.

12. *Evangelism is not the same as church extension.* During the period that the adage "no salvation outside the (Catholic) Church" was in vogue, this was the quintessence of evangelism. It is the view that lies behind the encyclical *Rerum Ecclesiae* of Pope Pius XI (1926). Evangelism meant "adding to the Catholic Church the greatest number of newly-baptized"; this happened in stages, via the catechumenate, the probation period, and the introduction to the liturgical life of the church. Evangelism became the expansion of the church through increased membership. Conversion was a numerical affair. Success in evangelism was measured by counting the numbers of baptisms, of confessions, and of communions (Shorter 1972:2).

Also in Protestantism evangelism was, by and large, understood as church extension. In recent years this has been true especially of the Church Growth Movement. McGavran pleads for "gospel-proclaiming, sinner-converting, church-multiplying evangelism" (1983:71; cf 21). Moreover, the purpose of church growth is further church growth. Those who have become church members should win others for church membership; this is a main thrust, perhaps *the* main thrust of the New Testament (McGavran 1980:426). A "theology of harvest" has to take priority over a "theology of seed-sowing" (:26-30). Numerical or quantitative growth should have first priority in a world where three billion people are not Christian. "Resistant" populations constitute a problem for this approach, of course. Still, McGavran does not plead for complete withdrawal from fields of low receptivity; he adds, however, that these fields should be occupied lightly and that evangelists should concentrate on "winnable" populations (:262).

This kind of thinking distorts evangelism, however, not least since reasons why people join the church may vary greatly and may often have little to do with commitment to what the church is supposed to stand for. A talk-alike, think-alike, look-alike congregation (Armstrong 1981:26) may reflect the prevailing culture and be a club for religious folklore rather than an alternative community in a hostile or compromised environment. This emerges particularly in situations where church membership is declining and the church, reluctantly, decides that, if it is to stay in business, it had better resign itself to an evangelistic campaign. The focus in evangelism should, however, not be on the church but on the irrupting *reign of God* (cf Snyder 1983:11, 29).

13. *To distinguish between evangelism and membership recruitment is not to suggest, though, that they are disconnected* (Watson 1983a:71). After all, "it is at

the heart of the Christian mission to foster the multiplication of local congregations in every human situation" (ME 25). We cannot be indifferent to numbers, for God is "not wishing that any should perish, but that all should reach repentance" (2 Pet 3:9). AG 6 therefore rightly includes church planting and growth in its definition of the goal of mission. The monomaniac rejection of the empirical church in Hoekendijkian and similar theologies is totally inappropriate. Without the church there can be no evangelism or mission.

Still, as a measure of how effectively and how responsibly a church has evangelized, membership statistics are less helpful (Watson 1983a:73). As a matter of fact, authentic and costly evangelism may cause a church's membership to decline rather than increase. Numerical growth is, therefore, in a sense nothing more than a byproduct when the church is true to its deepest calling. Of greater importance is organic and incarnational growth.

14. *In evangelism, "only people can be addressed and only people can respond",* as WCC moderator M. M. Thomas said in Nairobi (in WCC 1976:233). Authentic evangelism thus doubtless has a personal dimension. The gospel is "the announcement of a personal encounter, mediated by the Holy Spirit, with the living Christ, receiving his forgiveness and making a personal acceptance of the call to discipleship" (ME 10). It is inaccurate to argue—as often happens—that individualism is simply an "invention" of the West. Rather, the Christian gospel of necessity emphasizes personal responsibility and personal decision; therefore individualism in Western culture is primarily a fruit of the Christian mission. Rosenkranz (1977:407, drawing on E.E. Hölscher and H. Gollwitzer) argues that this constitutes the only *real* revolution in the structure of human nature, since it introduced the doctrine of the individual worth of every human being; thus, if people today think and act as free and responsible individuals—a way of thinking that diametrically opposes ancient thought and practice—it is because of the influence of the gospel.

Since only persons—individuals—can respond to the gospel, it is confusing the issue to talk of "prophetic evangelism" as the calling of "societies and nations to repentance and conversion" (Watson 1983b:7) or to say that the "call to conversion, as a call to repentance and obedience, should also be addressed to nations, groups and families" (ME 12). Principalities and powers, governments and nations cannot come to faith—only individuals can. So, even if this ministry is necessary and is an integral part of mission, it is not, strictly speaking, evangelism.

Even so, the gospel is not individualistic. Modern individualism is, to a large extent, a perversion of the Christian faith's understanding of the centrality and responsibility of the individual. In the wake of the Enlightenment, and because of its teachings, individuals have become isolated from the community which gave them birth. In evangelism, this trend has been prominent particularly since the ministry of D. L. Moody (1837-1899). For him, sin was exclusively an individual affair, with the sinner standing alone before God—a sinner who, in the democratic United States of Moody's time, was perfectly able to make up his or her mind and gain victory over sin (cf Marsden 1980:37). Since the individual was understood to be the basic unit in the work of salvation, the emphasis, increasingly, was on the saving of individual *souls*. And biblical sayings such as Matthew 16:26, "For what is a man profited, if he shall gain the whole world, and lose his own soul?" (King James Version) were interpreted as pointing in this direction. People are, however, never isolated individuals. They are social beings, who can never be severed from the network of relationships in which they exist. And the individual's conversion touches all these relationships. Christian Keysser (1980) recognized this when, during his years in Papua New Guinea, he always emphasized the need for the social group to be involved in the conversion of every individual.

15. *Authentic evangelism is always contextual* (Costas 1989:passim). An evangelism which separates people from their context views the world not as a challenge but as a hindrance, devalues history, and has eyes only for the "spiritual" or "nonmaterial aspects of life" (H. Lindsell, quoted in Scott 1980:94), is spurious. The same is true of an evangelism which couches conversion only in micro-ethical terms, such as regular church attendance, abstinence from alcohol and tobacco, and daily bible reading and prayer (cf Wagner 1979:3; for a critique of this view, cf Scott 1980:156f; 220-222), or limits the evangelistic message to an offer of release from loneliness, peace of mind, and success in what we undertake (cf Scott 1980:208f). In fact, much so-called evangelism, it appears, aims at satisfying rather than transforming people. In the West (at least in the past) Christianity used to be identified with social respectability. Churches had public prestige going for them. In this, evangelism came to their aid: "Dominant community pressure made church membership not only a necessity but also the mark of civilization, good manners and decent living" (Spong 1982:12). Much of this mentality had been exported to Africa and other parts of the Third World. The church was for the upwardly mobile; to become a Christian meant to identify with the ethos and value system of the aspiring middle class.

All of this is a far cry from authentic evangelism. It led to a conversion to the predominant *culture*, not to the Christ of the gospels. In much of the "electronic church" materialism is baptized. The Jesus of revivalism appears to have more in common with the Chamber of Commerce and the entertainment world than with a simple cave in Bethlehem or a rugged cross on a barren hill (Armstrong 1981:22, 41, 49). Preachers steer clear of controversial social issues and concentrate on those personal sins of which most of their enthusiastic listeners are not guilty. However, what criterion decides that racism and structural injustice are social issues but pornography and abortion personal? Why is politics shunned and declared to fall outside of the competence of the evangelist, except when it favors the position of the privileged in society? How is it that preachers who appear to have an interest only in the otherworldly destiny of their listeners can be so thoroughly worldly in their ethos and methods?

Of course, to those who are experiencing personal tragedy, emptiness, loneliness, estrangement, and meaninglessness the gospel *does* come as peace, comfort, fullness, and joy. But the gospel offers this only within the context of it being a word about the lordship of Christ in all realms of life, an authoritative word of hope that the world as we know it will not always be the way it is.

16. *Because of this, evangelism cannot be divorced from the preaching and practicing of justice.* This is the flaw in the view according to which evangelism is given absolute priority over social involvement, or where evangelism is separated from justice, even if it is maintained that, together with social justice, it constitutes "mission". If we understand evangelism not just as recruiting church members, not just as offering individual souls eternal salvation, and not as seeking to hasten the return of Christ, it cannot be divorced from the larger mission of the church. And even if we include recruiting of new members and offering eternal salvation in the aim of mission, the question remains: What are people becoming church members *for*? What are individuals being saved *for*?

In our reflections on Matthew's use of the term "disciple" (chapter 2), it has been suggested that to become a disciple of Jesus includes a whole range of commitments. Primarily, it means accepting a commitment to Jesus and to God's reign. At its heart, Jesus' invitation to people to follow him and become his disciples is asking people whom they want to serve. Evangelism is, therefore, a call to *service*. This is not to be contrasted with the blessings—including eternal blessings—which the new convert will receive; as a matter of fact, it is pointless to play the one perspective out against the other. Still, since it is the perspective on eternal bliss that has usually been emphasized, it is high time that the perspective of service to the kingdom be stressed as forcefully. An evangelistic invitation oriented toward discipleship, says Scott,

> will include a call to join the living Lord in the work of his kingdom. It will direct attention to the aspirations of ordinary men and women in society, their dreams of justice, security, full stomachs, human dignity, and opportunities for their children. It will forthrightly name the "principalities and powers" opposed to the Kingdom (1980:212).

Evangelism, then, means enlisting people for the reign of God, liberating them from themselves, their sins, and their entanglements, so that they will be free for God and neighbor. It calls individuals to a life of openness, vulnerability, wholeness, and love (cf Spong 1982:15; Snyder 1983:146). To win people to Jesus is to win their allegiance to God's priorities. God wills not only that we be rescued from hell and redeemed for heaven, but also that within us— and through our ministry also in society around us—the "fullness of Christ" be re-created, the image of God be restored in our lives and relationships. LC 4 puts it well:

> In issuing the gospel invitation we have no liberty to conceal the cost of discipleship. Jesus still calls all who would follow him to deny themselves, take up their cross, and identify themselves with his new community.

Evangelism, then, is calling people to mission.

17. *Evangelism is not a mechanism to hasten the return of Christ, as some suggest* (for example Johnston 1978:52). The ushering in of the *eschaton* has been an important missionary motif since the last decades of the nineteenth century.

Agencies like the China Inland Mission (Hudson Taylor) and the Regions Beyond Missionary Union (Grattan Guinness) were formed because their founders believed — on the basis of a biblicist interpretation of Matthew 24:14 — that the return of Christ was dependent on the completion of the proclamation of the gospel to all people worldwide (cf Beaver 1961). Johnson (1988) traces the waxing enthusiasm, particularly between 1887 and 1893, for the idea of the evangelization of the entire world before the year 1900 (:24-44), but also the decline after 1893, when it had become clear that the goal was unattainable (:45-50). Most of the leading figures in the movement, such as A. T. Pierson, A. B. Simpson, and H. Grattan Guinness, defined evangelism strictly in individualistic and verbalistic categories and shunned any idea of missionaries getting involved in other projects or in the structures of society (:53-55). The mere preaching of the word, it was believed, would bring the world's millions into the fold of the redeemed and hasten Christ's second coming.

Barrett and Reapsome (1988) calculate that there have, in fact, been 788 "global plans" to evangelize the world since the beginning of the Christian era, and that most of these were intimately linked to eschatological expectations. The slogan, "the evangelization of the world in this generation", popularized by John R. Mott around the beginning of the twentieth century, did not specifically interpret evangelism as ushering in the parousia, but certainly had apocalyptic overtones. Of the almost 800 plans identified by Barrett and Reapsome, only some 250 were still alive as of 1988. But as the third millennium draws nearer, more and more new plans are being launched, and virtually all of them link evangelism with the parousia. Frequently expectations are expressed in premillennialist terms. Contemporary evangelical literature vibrates with contributions on "world evangelization before the year 2000". Modern technologies, notably computers, are utilized not only to assess the gigantic dimensions of the task, but also to devise effective strategies. One such plan, DAWN (Discipling A Whole Nation), proceeds from the premise that we need a church for every thousand people in order to evangelize the world effectively; since there will be about seven billion people by the year 2000, the DAWN strategy is to facilitate the planting of churches so as to reach a total of seven million by the end of the century (Montgomery 1989). Various conferences devote their attention to a similar goal. In 1980 a "World Consultation on Frontier Missions" was held in Edinburgh; it formulated its goal as "A Church for Every People by the Year 2000". A similar conference was held in Sao Paulo in 1987, with a focus largely, but not exclusively, on Latin America. In January 1989 a "Global Consultation on World Evangelization by AD 2000 and Beyond" convened in Singapore. And the program of Lausanne II, the conference of the Lausanne Committee for World Evangelization held in Manila in July 1989, included an "AD 2000 Track".[17]

As Glasser (1989) has argued, however, this entire project, and its fascination with the year 2000, is highly questionable. It proceeds from the doubtful assumptions that the world economy will become ever more buoyant, that parachurch income will skyrocket, and that the main bearers of mission in the coming decades will still be Western-type mission agencies (:6). More important, however, are the theological flaws in this philosophy, particularly that this kind of evangelism appears deliberately to ignore the growing poverty and injustice in the world.

18. *Evangelism is not only verbal proclamation* (as Watson 1983b:6f suggests; cf McGavran 1983:190). Even so, evangelism does have an inescapable verbal dimension. In a society marked by relativism and agnosticism it is necessary to name the Name of the One in whom we believe. Christians are challenged to give an account of the hope that is in them (cf 1 Pet 3:15); their lives are not sufficiently transparent for others to be able to recognize whence that hope comes.

There is no single way to witness to Christ, however. The word may therefore never be divorced from the deed, the example, the "Christian presence", the witness of life. It is the "Word made flesh" that is the gospel. The deed without the word is dumb; the word without the deed is empty. Words interpret deeds and deeds validate words, which does not mean that every deed must have a word attached to it, nor every word a deed (Newbigin 1982:146-149; Jongeneel 1986:8).

If we now, finally, attempt a definition of evangelism, it is important that we should not delineate the content of our evangelism too sharply, too precisely, and too self-confidently (R. Jones, in NIE 1980:28). We cannot capture the evangel and package it in four or five "principles". There is no universally applicable master plan for evangelism, no definitive list of truths people only have to embrace in order to be saved. We may never limit the gospel to our understanding of God and of salvation. We can only witness in humble boldness and bold humility to our understanding of that gospel. Still, "as we humbly but joyfully reflect God's reconciling love for all humanity, in friendship and mutual respect, the Holy Spirit uses our witness and service to make God known" (NIE 1980:3).

In awareness of the essentially preliminary nature of our evangelistic ministry, yet at the same time conscious of the inescapable necessity to be involved in this ministry, we may, then, summarize evangelism as that dimension and activity of the church's mission which, by word and deed and in the light of particular conditions and a particular context, offers every person and community, everywhere, a valid opportunity to be directly challenged to a radical reorientation of their lives, a reorientation which involves such things as deliverance from slavery to the world and its powers; embracing Christ as Savior and Lord; becoming a living member of his community, the church; being enlisted into his service of reconciliation, peace, and justice on earth; and being committed to God's purpose of placing all things under the rule of Christ.

MISSION AS CONTEXTUALIZATION

The Genesis of Contextual Theology

The word "contextualization" was first coined in the early 1970s, in the circles of the Theological Education Fund, with a view particularly to the task of the education and formation of people for the church's ministry (cf Ukpong

1987:163). It soon caught on and became a blanket term for a variety of theological models. Ukpong (1987:163-168; cf Schreiter 1985:6-16; Waldenfels 1987) identifies two major types of contextual theology, namely, the indigenization model and the socio-economic model. Each of these can again be divided into two subtypes: the indigenization motif presents itself either as a translation or as an inculturation model; the socio-economic pattern of contextualization can be evolutionary (political theology and the theology of development) or revolutionary (liberation theology, black theology, feminist theology, etc). In what follows, this broad definition of contextual theology will be used and its nature and qualities as manifestation of a new paradigm highlighted. I shall, however, qualify Ukpong's categorization somewhat. In my view, only the inculturation model in the first type and only the revolutionary model in the second qualify as contextual theologies proper. In two subsequent sections liberation theology and inculturation will be reviewed.

A basic argument of this book has been that, from the very beginning, the missionary message of the Christian church incarnated itself in the life and world of those who had embraced it. It is, however, only fairly recently that this essentially contextual nature of the faith has been recognized. For many centuries every deviation from what any group declared to be the orthodox faith was viewed in terms of heterodoxy, even heresy. This was the case particularly after the Christian church became established in the Roman Empire. Arianism, Donatism, Pelagianism, Nestorianism, Monophysitism, and numerous similar movements were all regarded as doctrinally heterodox and their adherents excommunicated, persecuted, or banned. The role of cultural, political, and social factors in the genesis of such movements was not recognized. The same happened at the occasion of the Great Schism in the year 1054; henceforth, the Eastern and Western churches would declare each other to be theologically unorthodox. History repeated itself in the sixteenth century when, after the Reformation, Protestants and Catholics denied each other the epithet "Christian". In subsequent centuries the formulations of the Council of Trent and the various Protestant confessions were employed as shibboleths to determine the difference between acceptable and unacceptable creedal formulations.

Under the influence of the Greek spirit ideas and principles were considered to be prior to and more important than their "application". Such an application was both a second and a secondary step and served to confirm and legitimize the idea or principle, which was understood to be both suprahistorical and supracultural. Churches arrogated to themselves the right to determine what the "objective" truth of the Bible was and to direct the application of this timeless truth to the everyday life of believers. With the advent of the Enlightenment this approach received a new lease of life. In the Kantian paradigm, for instance, "pure" or "theoretical" reason was superior to "practical reason".

The Baconian view gave birth to a complementary approach. Here, the earlier deductive thinking made way for an inductive or empirical method in science. Instead of starting from classically derived principles and theories one now started with observation. In ecclesial and theological circles where this method was adopted (and which, in the course of time, was termed liberal) creeds and dogmas were no longer judged on the basis of their conformity to eternal truth but in terms of their usefulness (cf Stackhouse 1988:92f). "Churches", in the sense of bodies which claim an ultimate and uncontestable correspondence between their own teachings and the divine revelation, became "denominations", bodies of like-minded individuals, each of which magnanimously conceded to others the right to exist and practice its faith in the way it chooses. Denominations coexisted peacefully with one another. Debates no longer centered around what was *true*, but around what were *practically* (more specifically, *pragmatically*) the right things to do. The Christian faith was preferred not because it was the only true religion, but because it was manifestly the best (cf Dennis 1897, 1899, 1906).

Both these approaches were, each in its own way, attempts at salvaging theology as "science". For both, theology remained rational knowledge. Both were responses to the challenge of the Enlightenment and, more particularly, to the growing awareness of the "ugly ditch" (G.E. Lessing) that had opened between the time and culture of the Bible and the fundamentally different modern world. Each experienced ongoing history as a threat, since the distance between the then and the now was increasingly becoming unbridgeable. At the same time, no effort was spared to bridge the "ugly ditch". Indefatigably biblical scholars researched the ancient texts in an attempt to uncover the mind of the author and, in this way, put the modern reader in the immediate company of the original author, as it were, so that he or she may hear the author unhampered by the events of the intervening history. In true Enlightenment fashion, science was understood to be cumulative; if scholars could only persist hard enough and amass more and more data, they would reach the point where the original text and the intention of the original author would be established beyond any reasonable doubt.

Friedrich Schleiermacher (1768-1834) was one of the first theologians to realize that something was fundamentally wrong with this entire modus operandi. He interpreted the Protestant Reformation not as an attempt at restoring the primitive or apostolic church. What has once been cannot simply be brought back in a later period. The Christian church is always in the process of *becoming*; the church of the present is both the product of the past and the seed of the future. For this reason, theology must not be pursued as an attempt at reconstructing the pristine past and its truths; rather, theology is a reflection on the church's own life and experience (for references, cf Gerrish 1984:194-196, 201).

Thus Schleiermacher pioneered the view that all theology was influenced, if not determined, by the context in which it had evolved. There never was a "pure" message, supracultural and suprahistorical. It was impossible to penetrate to a residue of Christian faith that was not already, in a sense, interpretation. Every text, it was now recognized, had a peculiar *Sitz im Leben*, which the scholar had to determine, particularly with the aid of form criticism. During the nineteenth century and, more particularly, in the twentieth, the recognition of the way in which theology was conditioned by its environment became the received view in critical theological circles. Chapters 1 to 4 of this study have shown that this was true even of the earliest New Testament writings themselves.

Neither Schleiermacher nor the form critics, such as Bultmann, were able to execute the next step, however. They did not realize that their own interpretations were as parochial and as conditioned by their context as those they were criticizing. Their explications of the biblical texts thus, unconsciously, served to legitimize predetermined views and positions. Martin (1987:379f) explains the problem in respect to professional theologians such as those who are members of the Society for New Testament Studies. In conducting its "business", the SNTS preserves a fair degree of equilibrium, with only minor fluctuations, and is happy with the academic standards it is maintaining. This is so mainly because of its composition: its membership is predominantly male and white. If, however, the SNTS would admit to its ranks a large membership of feminist interpreters, of Jewish scholars, or of liberation theology exponents, this would gradually introduce a major flux in the system.

Where this state of affairs is recognized, scholars may succeed in moving beyond the important accomplishments of the historical-critical method and of the form and redaction critics of the middle twentieth century. Paul Ricoeur and other recent literary critics have, in a great variety of ways, advanced the view that every text is an interpreted text and that, in a sense, the reader "creates" the text when she or he reads it. The text is not only "out there", waiting to be interpreted; the text "becomes" as we engage with it. And yet, even this new hermeneutic approach is not going far enough. Interpreting a text is not only a literary exercise; it is also a social, economic, and political exercise. Our entire context comes into play when we interpret a biblical text. One therefore has to concede that *all* theology (or sociology, political theory, etc) is, by its very nature, contextual.

The real breakthrough in this respect came with the birth of Third-World theologies in their various forms. This was perceived to be so pivotal an event that Segundo (1976) referred to it as "the liberation of theology". Contextual theology truly represents a paradigm shift in theological thinking (cf Frostin 1988:1-26).

The Epistemological Break

Contextual theologies claim that they constitute an epistemological break when compared with traditional theologies. Whereas, at least since the time of Constantine, theology was conducted *from above* as an elitist enterprise (except in the case of minority Christian communities, commonly referred to as sects), its main source (apart from Scripture and tradition) was *philosophy*, and its main interlocutor the *educated non-believer*, contextual theology is theology *"from below"*, "from the underside of history", its main source (apart from Scripture and tradition) is the *social sciences*, and its main interlocutor the *poor* or the *culturally marginalized* (cf also Frostin 1988:6f).

Equally important in the new epistemology is the emphasis on the priority of praxis. Theology, says Gutiérrez, is "critical reflection on Christian praxis in the light of the word of God" (1988:xxix) or "critical reflection on the word of God received in the church" (:xxxiii). Sergio Torres explains the difference between the traditional Western epistemology and the emerging epistemology in the following way:

The traditional way of knowing considers the truth as the conformity of the mind to a given object, a part of Greek influence in the western philosophical tradition. Such a concept of truth only conforms to and legitimizes the world as it now exists. But there is another way of knowing the truth — a dialectical one. In this case, the world is not a static object that the human mind confronts and attempts to understand; rather, the world is an unfinished project being built. Knowledge is not the conformity of the mind to the given, but an immersion in this process of transformation and construction of a new world (in Appiah-Kubi & Torres 1979:5).

The following features of the new epistemology emerge from the above programmatic statement:

First, there is a profound suspicion that not only Western science and Western philosophy, but also Western theology, whether conservative or liberal, in spite of (or because of?) their claim that knowledge was neutral, were actually designed to serve the interests of the West, more particularly to legitimize "the world as it now exists". Nietzsche's "hermeneutics of suspicion" is here radicalized and applied particularly to Western scholarship in all its forms since it has developed into a rationale for imperialistic domination (cf Segundo 1976). Even where this has happened unintentionally, or "innocently", it is time to say farewell to this kind of innocence (cf the title of Boesak 1977), since it is nothing but pseudo-innocence (see also Frostin 1988:151-169).

Second, the new epistemology refuses to endorse the idea of the world as a static object which only has to be *explained*. Like Marx, it says, "The philosophers have only tried to interpret the world; the point, however, is to change it". It is history and the *human and physical* world that have to be taken seriously, not metahistory or metaphysics.

Implicit in Torres's statement, and worked out in great detail by many contextual theologians is, third, an emphasis on *commitment* as "the first act of theology" (Torres and Fabella 1978:269) — more specifically, commitment to the poor and marginalized. The point of departure is therefore orthopraxis, not orthodoxy. Orthopraxis, says Lamb,

> aims at transforming human history, redeeming it through a knowledge born of subject-empowering, life-giving love, which heals the biases needlessly victimizing millions of our brothers and sisters. *Vox victimarum vox Dei*. The cries of the victims are the voice of God. To the extent that those cries are not heard above the din of our political, cultural, economic, social, and ecclesial celebrations or bickerings, we have already begun a descent into hell (1982:22f).

Fourth, in this paradigm the theologian can no longer be "a lonely bird on the rooftop" (Barth 1933:40), who surveys and evaluates this world and its agony; he or she can only theologize credibly if it is done *with* those who suffer.

Fifth, then, the emphasis is on *doing* theology. The universal claim of the hermeneutic of language has to be challenged by a hermeneutic of the deed, since doing is more important than knowing or speaking. In the Scriptures it is the doers who are blessed (cf Míguez Bonino 1975:27-41). There is, in fact, "no knowledge except in action itself, in the process of transforming the world through participation in history" (:88).

Last, these priorities are worked out in contextual theology by means of a hermeneutical circle (or, better, circulation) (cf Segundo 1976:7-38). The circulation begins with experience, with praxis, which, in the case of most people in the Third World or those on the periphery of power in the First World and the Second World, is an experience of marginalization. Allan Boesak says, "The black experience provides the framework within which blacks understand the revelation of God in Jesus Christ. No more, no less" (1977:16). The Ecumenical Association of Third World Theologians (EATWOT) concurs: "The experience of the Third World as a source of theology must be taken seriously" (Fabella and Torres 1983:200).

From praxis or experience the hermeneutic circulation proceeds to reflection as a second (not a secondary—cf Gutiérrez 1988:xxxiii) act of theology. The traditional sequence, in which *theoria* is elevated over praxis, is here turned upside down. This does not, of course, imply a rejection of *theoria*. Ideally, there should be a dialectic relationship between theory and praxis. "Faith and the concrete, historical mission of the church are mutually dependent" (Rütti 1972:240—my translation). The relationship between theory and praxis is not one of subject to object, but one of intersubjectivity (cf Nel 1988:184). Where this occurs, contextual theology is a clear example of the paradigm that is emerging in all disciplines. Traditionally, thought and reason were firmly placed on the one side and being and action on the other. But, as Kuhn (1970) has argued, in the new paradigm thought is no longer conceived to be prior to being or reason to action; rather, they stand and fall together (cf Lugg 1987:179-181). In the best of contextual theologies it is therefore no longer possible to juxtapose theory and praxis, orthodoxy and orthopraxis: "Orthopraxis and orthodoxy need one another, and each is adversely affected when sight is lost of the other" (Gutiérrez 1988:xxxiv). Or as Samuel Rayan puts it: "In our methodology, practice and theory, action and reflection, discussion and prayer, movement and silence, social analysis and religious hermeneutics, involvement and contemplation, constitute a single process" (quoted in Fabella and Torres 1983:xvii).

The Ambiguities of Contextualization

There can be no doubt that the contextualization project is essentially legitimate, given the situation in which many contextual theologians find themselves. "The theologians of liberation", says Dapper (1979:92—my translation), "live in an emergency situation; they are involved in mission, speak, preach, and act in an emergency situation. They no longer have any need of deliberating what should happen in case of an emergency". In light of this, "there is no socially and politically neutral theology; in the struggle for life and against death, theology must take sides" (Míguez Bonino 1980:1155).

Still, some ambiguities remain, particularly insofar as there is a tendency in contextual theology to overreact in one of the two manners identified in chapter 11 of this study—in this case, to make a clean break with the past and deny continuity with one's theological and ecclesial ancestry. Let me try to explain.

1. *Mission as contextualization is an affirmation that God has turned toward the world* (cf the title of Schmitz 1971). As soon as we talk about God, the world as theater of his activity is already included in the discussion (Hoekendijk 1967a:344). The historical world situation is not merely an exterior condition for the church's mission; rather, it ought to be incorporated as a constitutive element into our understanding of mission, its aim and its organization (Rütti 1972:231). Such a posture is in full accord with Jesus' understanding of his mission, as reflected in our gospels; he did not soar off into heavenly heights but immersed himself into the altogether real circumstances of the poor, the captives, the blind, the oppressed (cf Lk 4:18f). Today, too, Christ is where the hungry and the sick are, the exploited and the marginalized. The power of his resurrection propels human history toward the end, under the banner "Behold, I make all things new!" (Rev 21:5). Like its Lord, the church-in-mission must take sides, *for* life and against death, *for* justice and against oppression.

We therefore have to adopt a firm stand against every attempt at a non- or under-contextualized approach in mission. As Manfred Linz (1964) has illustrated in his investigation into German sermons on four so-called "missionary texts", many sermons ignore the world completely, even where the biblical text clearly centers on the world. The sermons only serve to strengthen the faith of the listeners and create in them some interest for a mission understood as calling people out of the world. Sin and evil in the world render the situation so hopeless that all we can do is build dikes against them and their destructive effects. But this kind of thinking spawns pious self-sufficiency, hypocrisy, a retreat from responsibility toward other people and toward society, and a condescending offer of the salvation we already possess to the "poor, benighted heathen" (cf Günther 1967:21f).

To see an antithesis between the glorification of God and the search for a truly human life on earth is, however, contrary to the gospel. Much talk about "leaving everything to God" is nothing but an escape from our responsibilities in the world. Here, a docetic Christology reigns supreme. Christ's incarnation is not taken seriously. The humanity of Christ is a cloak behind which the hidden God alone deals with us (Wiedenmann 1965:199).

This does not mean that God is to be identified with the historical process. Where this happens, God's will and power too easily become identified with the will and power of Christians and with the social processes they initiate. It is difficult, however, if not impossible, says Niebuhr (1959:9f) to fit Amos, Isaiah, Jeremiah, Jesus, and others into a system determined by social factors; there is in Christianity a revolutionary and creative strain which does not allow it to be reduced to a human, albeit Christian, project. The "new creation" Paul talks about irrupts not so much because of Christian involvement in history; it comes about through Christ's work of reconciliation (cf 2 Cor 5:17), that is, primarily through God's intervention (see also Günther 1967:20). Some duality between God and the world remains. Precisely this creates the "identity-involvement dilemma" to which Moltmann (1975:1; cf also Küng 1984:70-75) refers; it is of the essence of the Christian faith that, from its birth, it again and again had to seek, on the one hand, how to be relevant to and involved in the world and, on the other, how to maintain its identity in Christ. These two are never unrelated; neither are they the same. Christians find their *identity* in the cross of Christ, which separates them from superstition and unbelief but also from every other religion and ideology; they find their *relevance* in the hope for the reign of the Crucified One by taking their stand resolutely with those who suffer and are oppressed and by mediating hope for liberation and salvation to them (Moltmann 1975:4).

2. *Mission as contextualization involves the construction of a variety of "local theologies"* (cf Schreiter 1985). Hiebert (1987:104-106) refers to the period from 1800 to 1950 as the "era of noncontextualization" as far as Protestant missions are concerned. It was hardly any different in Catholic missions. In each case theology (singular) had been defined once and for all and now simply had to be "indigenized" in Third World cultures, without, however, surrendering any of its essence. Western theology had *universal* validity, not least since it was the *dominant* theology (cf Frostin 1985:141; 1988:23; Nolan 1988:15). The Christian faith was based on eternal, unalterable truth, which had already been stated in its final form, for instance in ecclesiastical confessions and policies. Ostensibly, of course, Protestants did not ascribe the same status to their traditions and creeds as they did to Scripture. Even so, the sixteenth-century Protestant confessions were soon treated as universals, valid in all times and settings and, through the missionary enterprise, exported in their unaltered—and unalterable—forms to the younger churches in the Third World (cf Conn 1983:17).

Contextualization, on the other hand, suggests the experimental and contingent nature of all theology. Contextual theologians therefore, rightly, refrain from writing "systematic theologies" where everything fits into an all-encompassing and eternally valid system (cf Míguez Bonino 1980:1154). We need an experimental theology in which an ongoing dialogue is taking place between text and context, a theology which, in the nature of the case, remains provisional and hypothetical (Rütti 1972:244-249).

This should not, however, lead to an uncritical celebration of an infinite number of contextual and often mutually exclusive theologies. This danger—the danger of *relativism*—is present not only in the Third World but also, for instance, in Western historical-critical biblical scholarship, where one sometimes gets the impression that each scriptural text is viewed as being so deeply shaped by its context that it actually constitutes an isolated theological world in itself. Such historicism and unbridled relativism, however, is inadmissible. There *are* faith traditions which all Christians share and which should be respected and preserved. We therefore—along with affirming the essentially contextual nature of all theology—also have to affirm the universal and context-transcending dimensions of theology. The purely contingent perspectives in theology need to be counterbalanced by an emphasis on the metatheological perspectives (for a discussion of the difference between and interrelatedness of these perspectives in theology and culture, cf Kraft 1981:291-300).

The best contextual theologies indeed hold on to this dialectic relationship. In the new introduction to *A Theology of Liberation*, Gutiérrez not only stresses his union with and allegiance to the Catholic Church worldwide, but also emphasizes that particularity does not mean isolation and that any theology is a discourse about a universal message (1988:xxxvi). Every *theologia localis* should therefore challenge and fecundate the *theologia oecumenica*, and the latter, similarly, enrich and broaden the perspective of the former. Naturally, this does not only mean that Third-World Christians should study Western theology, but also that First-World Christians should study Third-World theologies. The former has always been taken for granted; the latter, however, not. Still, this is changing (even if it is happening too slowly—cf Frostin 1988:24). A generation or so ago, no theological institution in the West would have deemed it necessary to offer courses on theological developments in the Third World; today more and more of them have integrated such courses into their curricula—not as interesting oddities but as an essential dimension of theological education.

3. *There is not only the danger of relativism, where each context forges its own theology, tailor-made for that specific context, but also the danger of absolutism of contextualism.* This is, in fact, what has happened in Western missionary outreach where theology, contextualized in the West, was in essence elevated to gospel status and exported to other continents as a package deal. Contextualism thus means universalizing one's own theological position, making it applicable to everybody and demanding that others submit to it. If Western theology has not been immune to this tendency, neither are Third-World contextual theologies. A new imperialism in theology then simply replaces the old. During the Melbourne Conference of CWME (1980), for instance, Latin American spokespersons were inclined to promulgate their peculiar brand of contextual theology as having universal validity. Delegates from other Third-World situations did not always take kindly to this. The Christian Conference of Asia, for instance, argued that it would be inappropriate if Latin American liberation theology were simply to

> take the place of western theology in Asia. Not because we do not stand in need of liberation. Simply because the liberation we must have is from our captivities, and for such liberation we need other perspectives and other sensitivities.[18]

4. *We have to look at this entire issue from yet another angle, that of "reading the signs of the times", an expression that has invaded contemporary ecclesiastical language* (cf Gómez 1989:365). There can be no doubt that such an enterprise has profound validity. Like the other Semitic religions, it is innate to Christianity to take history seriously as the arena of God's activity—as has also been argued above. Such an affirmation then begs the question *how* we are to interpret God's action in history and so learn to commit ourselves to participation in this. Which are the *signs* in human history that reveal God's will and God's presence? How do we identify God's *vestigia*, God's footprints in the world? This is an

enterprise fraught with danger on all sides, but one of which we cannot absolve ourselves (cf Berkhof 1966:197-205; Gómez 1989:passim).

The first and perhaps most vexing problem is that, with the benefit of hindsight, we can now establish that the signs of the times have often been misread in the past. There was a time when the "benevolent colonialism" of the West was widely viewed — to some extent even by the colonized — as a sign of God's providential intervention in history. For many decades the policy of separate development — apartheid — was hailed by serious Christians in South Africa as a just and God-willed solution to that country's problems. The same was true of Nationalism Socialism in Germany, where the *Deutsche Wende* ("German turning point") of 1933 was applauded unreservedly by many Christians as proof of divine intervention and favor. In the 1960s secularism was similarly embraced by Mesthene, Harvey Cox, van Leeuwen, and many others. Again, many Christians saw political events and developments in the Soviet Union, Eastern Europe, and other socialist countries as divine signs of the times (one may, for instance, refer to the fascination with Cuba among members of a Nicaraguan community of *campesinos*, as it emerges from Cardenal 1976:49, 64). Today, all of these signs of the times have been discredited, to the point of being an acute embarrassment to those who hailed them so enthusiastically. Compassion and commitment, apparently, are no guarantee that one will not produce bad sociology, practice poor politics, and pursue debatable historical analysis (cf Stackhouse 1988:95).

The problem seems to be that Christians tend to sacralize "the sociological forces of history that are dominant at any particular time, regarding them as inexorable works of providence and even of redemption" (Knapp 1977:161). Examples abound. Speaking at the CWME Conference in Melbourne (1980), Julia Esquivel saw in the victory of the people of Nicaragua a "glorious experience of the resurrection of Christ"; Israel *en route* from Egyptian slavery "may for us today mean Zimbabwe, El Salvador, Nicaragua or Guatemala". Again, at the San Antonio Meeting of CWME (1989), it was stated without qualification in Section II.6: "The rising up of the people against injustice is the creative power of God for the people and for the whole world . . . The acts of the people become God's mission for justice through creative power" (WCC 1990:40). Albert Nolan (1988:166) writes in similar vein about the struggle of the South African people against an oppressive system: "The power of the people that is manifested in the struggle is indeed the power of God . . . What the system is up against now is not 'flesh and blood' but the almighty power of God".[19]

The situation is further compounded when exponents of contextualization claim a special or privileged knowledge about God's will and declare those who do not agree with them as suffering from "false consciousness". Their own clairvoyance, on the other hand, equips them with the ability to know exactly not only what God's will is, but also what will happen in the future. With reference to South Africa, for instance, Nolan (1988:144; cf 184) avers "that we can be quite sure that our future will not be oppressive and alienating". The one thing South Africans need not fear "is the kind of take-over whereby another group of people simply replaces the present rulers and maintains the same type of system. . . That possibility is gone forever".

Contextual theology is right in stressing the need for a "hermeneutic of suspicion", particularly as concerns the religion of the ruling classes. The danger in this is, however, "that suspecting tends to become an end in itself" (Martin 1987:381). Where this happens, theological conversation becomes "less and less a dialogue about the most important questions and more and more a power struggle about who is to be allowed to speak" (Stackhouse 1988:22f). Only those who have access to "privileged knowledge" may interpret the context and are able to say what the gospel for the context is. In this paradigm, anything "non-victims" think is irremediably tainted; if they do not immediately endorse a particular orthopraxis, they are unofficially excommunicated (because of their "false consciousness") and judged to be beyond the pale of God's justice (:102f, 186).

This approach ends up having a low view of the importance of *text*, as coming from outside the context (Stackhouse 1988:38). The very idea that texts can judge contexts is, in fact, methodically doubted (:27). The message of the gospel is not viewed as something that we bring *to* contexts but as something that we derive *from* contexts (:81). "You do not incarnate good news into a situation, good news arises out of the situation", writes Nolan (1988:27); after all, "the prophets did not 'apply' their prophetic message to their times, they had it revealed to them through the signs of the times".

The problem, however, is that "facts" always remain ambiguous. It isn't the facts of history that reveal where God is at work, but the facts illuminated by the gospel. According to GS 4, the church, in reading the signs of the times, is to interpret them *in the light of the gospel* (cf Waldenfels 1987:227). In all major ecclesial traditions—Catholic, Orthodox, and Protestant—people look not only at where they are at the present moment, but also at where they come from. They look for a real, reliable, and universal guide to the truth and justice of God, to apply as criterion in evaluating the context. This means that it is the *gospel* which is the *norma normans*, the "norming norm". Our reading of the context is also a norm, but in a derived sense; it is the *norma normata*, the "normed norm" (Küng 1987:151). Of course, the gospel can only be read from and make sense in our present context, and yet to posit it as criterion means that it may, and often does, critique the context and our reading of it.

There is no doubt, then. We *have* to interpret the "signs of the times". Our interpretations of the signs only have relative validity, however, and they involve tremendous risks. Matthew's parables of the reign of God emphasize the need for watching (Mt 25). Watching flows from not knowing; at the same time, however, watching is a form of interpreting signs (Berkhof 1966:187f), at the risk of interpreting them incorrectly. Our initial assumptions may be erroneous; we could have asked completely inappropriate questions and looked for the wrong clues. And yet, we are not without a compass. We are given some crucial guidelines, some lodestars which indicate God's will and presence in the con-text. Where people are experiencing and working for justice, freedom, community, reconciliation, unity, and truth, in a spirit of love and selflessness, we may dare to see God at work. Wherever people are being enslaved, enmity between humans is fanned, and mutual accountability is denied in a spirit of individual or communal self-centrism, we may identify the counter-forces of God's reign at work (cf Rütti 1972:231, 241; Lochman 1986:71). This enables us to take courage and make decisions, even if they remain relative in nature (Berkhof 1966:204), since our judgments do not coincide with God's final judgment (:199f). Even if we are not equipped to decide between absolute right and absolute wrong, we should be able to distinguish between shades of grey and to choose *"for* the light grey and *against* the dark grey" (:200).

5. *In spite of the undeniably crucial nature and role of the context, then, it is not to be taken as the sole and basic authority for theological reflection* (cf also Stackhouse 1988:26). Praxis can mean too many things (:91). So, even if it may be very bad form in some circles today to raise any questions about the absolute priority of praxis (:96), the fact of the matter is that there is no praxis without theory, even where the theory is not spelled out.

For this reason, praxis needs the critical control of theory—in our case, a critical theology of mission, which is dependent upon the context without, however, elevating operational effectiveness to the highest norm. The dynamics of particular contexts always involve "abstract" issues of truth and justice, "abstract" metaphysical-moral visions, and "theoretical" questions of epistemology (Stackhouse 1988:11). All praxis is dependent on "a quite specific, highly schematized and synthetic, social and historical dogma" and demands "a previous, and a rather elaborate, *theoria* about what is true and just" (:96; cf 103). The issue, therefore, is less one of the primacy of praxis over theory than it is one of "which *theoria* is sufficiently true and just that *praxis* ought to be carried out in its service" (:98). There is a legitimate suspicion today of the positing of a doctrinally "orthodox" position and an immutable *depositum fidei*; still, where some such agreed-upon faith tradition is completely absent, contextualization just spawns new sects of fideist politics (:103) and renders theological discourse utterly useless (:102f).

6. *Stackhouse has argued that we are distorting the entire contextualization debate if we interpret it only as a problem of the relationship between praxis and theory.* We also need the dimension of *poiesis*, which he defines as the "imaginative creation or representation of evocative images" (1988:85; cf 104). People do not only need truth (theory) and justice (praxis); they also need beauty, the rich resources of symbol, piety, worship, love, awe, and mystery. Only too often, in the tug-of-war between the priority of truth and the priority of justice, this dimension gets lost. In a profound sense, Niebuhr (1960:75) is correct: "Love demands more than justice"; indeed, it signifies more than truth. Of faith, hope, and love, love is the greatest—but, of course, it may never be divorced from the other two.

7. *The best models of contextual theology succeed in holding together in creative tension theoria, praxis and poiesis*—or, if one wishes, faith, hope, and love. This is another way of defining the missionary nature of the Christian faith, which seeks to combine the three dimensions. Like the other great missionary religions of the world, says Stackhouse, Christianity holds

to some great "unveiling" of ultimate truth believed to be of universal import. This "unveiling" induces a passion for transcendent justice; it frees adherents from localistic practices, from the absolute claims of contextual loyalties, and from conventional social conditions. It induces a certain "homelessness", a divine alienation — a willingness to adopt practices that are more just than what may be found at home, an eagerness to bring all other individuals into contact with this new truth, a desire to carry the universal message to peoples and nations who do not yet know of it and to transform personal identity and whole societies on the basis of its justice (1988:189).

It goes without saying that not every manifestation of contextual theology is guilty of any or all of the overreactions discussed above. Still, they all remain a constant danger to every (legitimate!) attempt at allowing the context to determine the nature and content of theology for that context. With this in mind, we now turn, consecutively, to liberation theology and to inculturation.

MISSION AS LIBERATION

From Development to Liberation

In this section I will continue my reflections on mission as contextualization, sharpening the focus to explore the nature of liberation theology as one of the most dramatic illustrations of the fundamental paradigm shift that is currently taking place in mission thinking and practice.

The theology of liberation is a multifaceted phenomenon, manifesting itself as black, Hispanic and Amerindian theologies in the United States, as Latin American theology, and as feminist theology, South African black theology, and various analogous theological movements in other parts of Africa, Asia, and the South Pacific. One could certainly also categorize the various theologies of *inculturation* as liberation theologies; at the same time, the movements we are discussing here are sufficiently different from the theologies of inculturation, which will be surveyed in the following section, to warrant separate treatment.

For all intents and purposes, all theologies of liberation and of inculturation, except some feminist theologies, are Third-World theologies or theologies of the Third World within the First World. They have their primary focus in EATWOT (the Ecumenical Association of Third World Theologians), which was founded in Dar es Salaam in 1976. The label Third World was consciously chosen; it expresses the experience of those who feel that they are being treated as third-class people and exploited by the powers of the First and Second Worlds. Most EATWOT members would therefore reject the term "Two-Thirds World", increasingly common in evangelical circles, since it only reflects the geographical size and population of the Third World, not its political and socioeconomic position at the "underside of history" (cf Fabella and Torres 1983:xii).

To a significant extent, theologies of liberation, particularly the classical Latin American variety, evolved in protest against the inability in Western church and missionary circles, both Catholic and Protestant, to grapple with the problems of systemic injustice. Not that there was no concern for liberation in missionary circles prior to the 1960s! One could, for instance, refer to some individuals and mission agencies mentioned in the earlier parts of this study: Bartolomé de Las Casas; the early Pietist, Basel, and CMS missionaries; and William Wilberforce. By and large, however, churches tended to claim a sort of "extra-territoriality", a position *above* the flux and conflicts of history, merely spelling out gospel principles (cf Míguez Bonino 1981:369). It was agreed that social ills had to remedied, but without challenging societal and political macrostructures. The 1937 conference on "Church, Community, and State", held at Oxford, could still claim that the church's task was supranational, supra-class and supraracial.

Confronted by Nazism in the 1930s, the church in Germany slowly began to realize that it had deluded itself in thinking that the principalities and powers were just "in the heavens"; they were incarnate on earth, as demonic forces within societal structures. As far as the Protestant mission was concerned, it was not until the Tambaram meeting of the IMC (1938), however, that there was a clear focus on the wider structures and a conviction that improvement was not enough; what was called for, was radical renewal (cf van 't Hof 1972:119-123). Since Tambaram, the church's prophetic voice would be heard ever more clearly.

Even so, Tambaram did not usher in an era of intense confrontation with unjust societal and political structure in the Third World. For thirty years or so after the first Church and Society Conference (Stockholm 1925) the focus of the ecumenical movement remained on the social problems of the *West* and the (Marxist) *East*, particularly those caused by the tension between Socialism and free enterprise. In 1955, however, the study project on Christian responsibility toward areas of rapid social change was introduced. The axis had begun to tilt: henceforth North-South relationships would grow in importance (cf Nürnberger 1987a:passim).

In missionary circles it was recognized that neither the traditional charity model nor the model of the "comprehensive approach" (which was initiated in the 1920s and concentrated, in particular, on education, health ministries, and agricultural training) was adequate. A more fundamental strategy was needed. The concept which gave expression to the contemporary challenge was *development*. Governments of the First and the Second Worlds were going to contribute to the solution of the problem of Third-World poverty by pouring their resources into ambitious development projects. Hurriedly, Western churches and mission agencies got onto the bandwagon as well.

For the West, development meant modernization (cf Bragg 1987:22-28). The entire project was, however, based on several flawed assumptions: it supposed that what was good for the West would be good for the Third World also (in this respect, then, it was culturally insensitive); it operated on the Enlightenment presupposition of the absolute distinction between the human subject and the material object and believed that all the Third World stood in need of was technological expertise; it assumed one-way traffic without any reciprocity — development aid and skills moved from Western "donors" to Third-World "recipients" who had often not even been consulted; and it operated on the assumption that nothing in the rich North needed to change (cf also Nürnberger 1982:233-391; Sundermeier 1986:63f, 72-80; Bragg 1987:23-25). By and large, the project miscarried disastrously. A small elite benefited; the majority of the population found themselves in an even more desperate plight. The rich got richer, the poor poorer. Smith (1968:44) mentions that, before World War II, a Brazilian could buy a Ford car for five sacks of coffee; now (1968) two hundred and six sacks were needed. In spite of (because of?) billions of dollars of development aid, the socio-economic situation in many Third-World countries was getting more desperate by the day. It was not recognized that poverty was not just the result of ignorance, lack of skills, or moral and cultural factors, but rather that it had to do with global structural relationships.

In the 1960s, however — because of the infatuation with secularization and technology — it was virtually impossible to convince Western churches and their leadership that the development model was riddled with inconsistencies. At the Geneva Church and Society Conference (1966) Mesthene and other "technological humanists" could not believe that the salvation of the poor could lie anywhere but in helping them to catch up with the West through modern technology. As late as 1968, the Uppsala WCC Assembly — in spite of its radical political stance on many issues — could devote an entire section (III) to "World Economic and Social Development" and produce a report (cf WCC 1968:45-55) which appears to be almost oblivious of the fact that the entire development philosophy had been challenged fundamentally.

Even in 1973 the German Protestant churches would still produce a memorandum which spoke in glowing terms of the exciting prospects in store for humankind and of the technological possibilities which may help to make the dreams of the whole world come true (reference in Sundermeier 1986:72f). Utopian language was characteristic of the development philosophy. "Development", said Pope Paul VI in *Populorum Progressio* 76 (1967), was "the new name for peace". The underdeveloped nations were just late in the race toward welfare; if only they could be helped to run faster and learn quicker the techniques of the advanced countries, the end to their misery was just around the next corner (cf Gómez 1986:37).

Since the 1950s, however, the mood had been changing in Third-World countries themselves, particularly in Latin America. Socio-politically, development was replaced by revolution; ecclesiastically and theologically by *liberation theology*. By the time the term "liberation theology" was coined (in 1968, just before Medellín — cf Gutiérrez 1988:xviii), its main themes had already been around for almost a decade (:xxix, cf Segundo 1986:222, note 243). Soon "liberation" was cropping up everywhere in the ecclesiastical landscape. The opposites we were dealing with were not development and underdevelopment, but domination and dependence, rich and poor, Capitalism and Socialism, oppressors and oppressed (cf Waldenfels 1987:226f; Frostin 1988:7f). Poverty would not be uprooted by pouring technological know-how into the poor countries but by removing the root causes of injustice; and since the West was reluctant to endorse such a project, Third World peoples had to take their destiny into their own hands and liberate themselves through a revolution. Development implied evolutionary continuity with the past; liberation implied a clean break, a new beginning.

"God's Preferential Option for the Poor"

Modern capitalism, building on the philosophy of Adam Smith, has created a world totally different from anything known before. Two hundred years after the Enlightenment, says Newbigin (1986:110), "we live in a world in which millions of people enjoy a standard of material wealth that few kings and queens could match then". As their wealth accumulated, rich Christians increasingly tended to interpret the biblical sayings on poverty metaphorically. The poor were the "poor in spirit", the ones who recognized their utter dependence upon God. In this sense, then, the rich could also be poor — they could arrogate all biblical promises to themselves.

Gradually, however, the faces of the poor forced themselves on to the attention of the rich Christians of the West in a way that could no longer be ignored or allegorized. The Mexico City meeting of CWME began to notice these faces, but was still to preoccupied with secularization to draw theological consequences from this (cf Dapper 1979:39). After the Geneva Conference of 1966 the climate changed. In its "Message", the Uppsala Assembly stated:

> We heard the cry of those who long for peace; of the hungry and exploited who demand bread and justice; of the victims of discrimination who claim human justice; and of the increasing millions who seek for the meaning of life (WCC 1968:5).

Dapper writes, "Nobody can doubt that these are new tones in the World Council; there is no longer any attempt to evade the cry by resorting to metaphorical speech" (1979:45 — my translation). Bangkok (1973) confirmed the new emphasis: terms like "salvation" were now translated as "liberation", "fellowship" as "solidarity" (cf Dapper 1979:53). At Melbourne (1980) the poor were put in the very center of missiological reflection; indeed, the conference made "an unalloyed affirmation that solidarity with these is today a central and crucial priority of Christian mission" (Gort 1980a:11f). In a sense, the poor became the dominant hermeneutical category at Melbourne. In at least three of the four sections (I, II, and IV) the poor were prominent. Reflecting after the conference, Emilio Castro (1985:151) suggested that, at Melbourne, the affirmation of the poor was the "missiological principle par excellence" and the church's relation to the poor "the missionary yardstick".

Even more dramatic was the "discovery of the poor" in Roman Catholic circles, particularly as this was demonstrated at the Second and Third General Conferences of Latin American Bishops at Medellín, Colombia (CELAM II, 1968) and at Puebla, Mexico (CELAM III, 1979). It was at Puebla that the phrase "preferential option for the poor" was coined. And as Gutiérrez has explained (1988:xxvf), the very word "preference" denies all exclusiveness, as though God would be interested *only* in the poor, whilst the word "option" should not be understood to mean "optional". The point is rather that the poor are the first, though not the only ones, on which God's attention focuses and that, therefore, the church has no choice but to demonstrate solidarity with the poor. The poor have an "epistemological privilege" (Hugo Assmann, quoted in Frostin 1988:6); they are the new interlocutors of theology (Frostin 1988:6f), its new hermeneutical locus.

The danger in all of this, of course, is that one may again easily fall into the trap of "the church *for* others" instead of "the church *with* others", "the church *for* the poor" rather than "the church *of* the poor". Melbourne helped to move away from the traditional condescending attitude of the (rich) church toward the poor; it was not so much a case of the poor needing the church, but of the church needing the poor — if it wished to stay close to its poor Lord. The poor were beginning to discover and affirm themselves. Just as, in their reaction to the development model, the poor "refused to dream by order" (Ivan Illich, quoted in Dapper 1979:91 — my translation), they now refused to be defined by the West, the rich, or the whites. The poor were no longer merely the *objects* of mission; they had become its *agents* and bearers (cf Section IV.21 of Melbourne — WCC 1980:219). And this mission is, above all, one of liberation. Gutiérrez even defines liberation theology as "an expression of the right of the poor to think out their own faith" (1988:xxi). Once the church was the "voice of the voiceless"; now the voiceless are making their own voices heard (Castro 1985:32).

During the past two decades or so numerous studies have appeared on who the poor are and on how they have traditionally been viewed and treated by the church. There can be no doubt that both in the Old Testament and in the ministry of Jesus there was a significant focus on the poor and their plight (cf chapter 3 of this study, and De Santa Ana 1977:1-35). "The entire Bible, beginning with the story of Cain and Abel, mirrors God's predilection for the weak and abused of human history" (Gutiérrez 1988:xxvii). Much of this ethos was preserved during the first centuries of the Christian church (De Santa Ana 1977:36-64). After Constantine, and as the church got richer and more privileged, the poor were increasingly neglected or treated condescendingly. Yet even then powerful voices, particularly from the circles of the monastic movement, continued to stress the Christian's inescapable responsibility in this regard. Basil the Great, in particular, was an indefatigable champion of the poor (:67-71). In a sense, then, the rediscovery of the poor in our own time is also a reaffirmation of an ancient theological tradition.

Being poor is quite incontrovertibly a material reality. We may, however, not think of the poor in modern socio-economic categories only. In my reflections on Luke (chapter 3) I have shown that, whenever Luke recorded words of Jesus about those who suffered, he either put the poor at the head or at the very end of the list. This seems to suggest that the poor were an all-embracing category for those who were the victims of society. Liberation theology interpretations of the poor follow a similar hermeneutic. The poor are the marginalized, those who lack every active or even passive participation in society; it is a marginality that comprises all spheres of life and is often so extensive that people feel that they have no resources to do anything about it (Müller 1978:80, drawing from Hugo Kramer). It is a "subhuman condition" (Gutiérrez 1988:164), "an evil, scandalous condition" (:168), "a total system of death" (Míguez Bonino 1980:1155).

From this perspective, then, the "preferential option for the poor" does not apply to Latin America only, as is sometimes suggested. The practice of *racism* is a form of poverty inflicted on people (and, of course, those racially discriminated against are often also materially poor). In this respect, black theology — as the North American and South African rendition of liberation theology — is a situational application of the "preferential option for the poor" (cf Kritzinger 1988:172-236).

Traditionally, in Western theology, one's relationship with the poor has been understood only as a question of ethics, not of theology proper or of epistemology (Frostin 1985:136; 1988:6). "Political action in our view has its place in Christian ethics, not in soteriology", says Brakemeier (1988:219). This position is today being challenged, not only from the side of liberation theology but also in Catholic, Reformed, and other circles elsewhere. Gort (1980b:52, 58) affirms that, in the Reformed position, theology and ethics belong together. Ethics is the hands and feet and face of theology, and theology the vital organs, the soul of ethics.

Such a position, of course, has tremendous consequences for our understanding of mission. In this model, liberation and black theologies become "a challenge to mission" (cf the title of Kritzinger 1988). This was the model that predominated at Melbourne (1980); solidarity with the poor and the oppressed was a central and crucial priority in Christian mission (cf Gort 1980a:12). Once we recognize the identification of Jesus with the poor, we cannot any longer consider our own relation to the poor as a social ethics question; it is a gospel question (Castro 1985:32; cf Sider 1980:318). Or, to put it in the words of Nicholas Berdyaev: While the problem of my own bread is a material issue, the problem of my neighbor's bread is a spiritual issue.

This does not preclude God's love for the non-poor. In their case, however, a different kind of conversion is called for, which would include admitting complicity in the oppression of the poor and a turning from the idols of money, race, and self-interest (cf Kritzinger 1988:274-297). This is needed, not only because they have been acting unethically, but because they have, through their "pseudo-innocence" (Boesak) actually denied themselves access to knowledge.

It seems we have, in this respect, an increasingly unified theological perspective. The Orthodox churches, many of which have for many centuries lived in situations where the church was persecuted or at least marginalized, have always held to this intrinsic link between theology and ethics as regards the church's attitude to the poor. Catholics and ecumenical Protestants today also subscribe to this position. And evangelicals, after the "Great Reversal" during the first decades of this century, have likewise gradually begun to see the indissoluble connection between theology and social ethics. Today many evangelicals, such as Ronald J. Sider, speak in a very candid manner on the church and the poor. Sider accepts the "doctrine" that God is on the side of the oppressed

(1980:314). And if the privileged are really the people of God, they, too, would be on the side of the poor; indeed, those who neglect the needy are not really God's people at all, no matter how frequent their religious rituals are (:317f). Jesus will not be our Savior if we persistently reject him as Lord of our total life. In similar vein a consultation on simple lifestyle, co-sponsored by the Lausanne Committee for World Evangelization and the World Evangelical Fellowship (1980), went far beyond simple living and touched precisely on God's preferential option for the poor, divine judgment on oppressors, and the pattern of Jesus' own identification with the poor (cf Scherer 1987:180).

Liberal Theology and Liberation Theology

It is often contended that the theology of liberation is merely a variant of what may broadly be termed liberal theology—the classical liberal theology of the nineteenth century, the Social Gospel, the secular theologies of the 1960s, or European political theology (cf, among others, Braaten 1977:139-148, 153; Knapp 1977:160f). And there are indeed some important similarities. Like most liberal theologies, the theology of liberation has a strong social concern and rejects both the tendency to interpret the Christian faith in otherworldly categories and excessive individualism. In spite of its critique of the West and Western theology, liberation theology is also committed to the motif of earthly prosperity via the modernization model (Sundermeier 1986:76). Both theological tributaries appear to be anthropocentric rather than theocentric; like those Western theologies, liberation theology is accused of immanentism and "an evaporation of faith" (cf Frostin 1988:12, 193).

If these assessments of liberation theology were true in their entirety, it would hardly have moved out of the shadow of the Enlightenment into a new paradigm. There are, however, two general areas in which the two projects differ rather fundamentally.

1. All the Western theologies alluded to grapple primarily with the reality of modernity, of secularism, that is, with the question whether it still makes sense to talk about God in a secular age. Their response is to affirm the basic tenets of secularism whilst trying to salvage something of their religious heritage in the process. They often do this by jettisoning evangelism as a call to personal faith and by replacing mission with "humanization". They claim that the discovery of the political, societal, and economic dimensions of life have rendered the subjectivist, individualist, and existentialist reduction of theology obsolete (cf Daecke 1988:631). They assert that the entire world is moving toward one global culture, which is irreversible, which will be shaped in the image of the West, and where religious faith in its traditional form will lose its "sacralizing relevance" (cf Fierro 1977:265-267). A "restoration of the sacred" is futile (:339-348); we should embrace the secular (:348-341). In true Enlightenment fashion, these "technological humanists" assume a separation between fact and value and believe that the human being, as detached rational subject, is capable of delivering reliable information and of making the necessary adaptations (also on the socio-political level) intelligible (and therefore acceptable) to fellow rational human beings (cf West 1971:26f). Westerners, including Western the-

ologians, says West (:51), are by instinct technological humanists; the history they study and the assumptions of each science they absorb generate in them an instinctive faith in reason (:52), which is only to be enlightened by revelation (:63).

Liberation theologians, in contrast, tend to be almost naively religious, sometimes even biblicist (cf the critique of Desmond Tutu and Allan Boesak by fellow-liberationist Mosala 1989:26-42). The cross of Jesus, an embarrassment to the Social Gospel, is at the very center of liberation theology. The "practice of Jesus" (Echegaray 1984) includes the life, death, and resurrection of Christ. There is an avowal that "theology must remain theology through and through" and refuse "to dissolve its fundamental epistemological principle" (Míguez Bonino 1980:1156). In his study of Paul, Segundo refers again and again to the "transcendent data" (1986:152, 157, and elsewhere), which may in no circumstances be relinquished. Liberation theology's question is not knowing whether God exists, but knowing on which side God is (Fabella and Torres 1983:190). And this is a *post*modern question.

2. Western progressive theologies tend to be evolutionary in their philosophy and are therefore all, in the final analysis, oriented toward an upholding of the status quo, even if in an adapted form (cf Lamb 1984:138). Even where they are committed to a form of socialism this tends to be a Fabian socialism (cf Hopkins 1940:323). Their view of society is often romantic, utopian, naive, and sentimental (:323, 325). Even the radical statements of Uppsala 1968 revealed little more than, "on the whole, a chastened technological rationalism and a sober liberal optimism laced with moral urging" (West 1971:33, note 10). As such, progressive theologies reflect the language of the privileged. It is theology "from above".

Liberation theology, however, is theology "from below". It is counter-hegemonic (Frostin 1988:192). It believes that the law of history is not development, but revolution—"an inexorable law that molds but is not subject to the human will" (West 1971:113). The enemy of humanity is not nature (as is the case in technological humanism), but one structure of human power which exploits and destroys the powerless (:32).

In light of the above, and in spite of the undeniable similarities between these two genres of theology, it would therefore be facile to regard them as mirror images of one another. Liberation theology is not just the radical, political wing of European progressive theology (Gutiérrez 1988:xxix). There is a difference here so basic that each side must misinterpret the other in order to make sense (cf West 1971:32). Both may indeed be termed "signs of the times" theologies but, as I have argued above, we have no alternative but to try and interpret the signs of the times, even if this remains an extremely hazardous venture. We cannot escape this responsibility; after all, what is worth doing is also worth doing badly. Rather than being a simple logical extension of the Social Gospel and the secularist theologies of the 1960s, various forms of liberation theology stand in the tradition of the evangelical awakenings, of Reformed theology (cf the centrality of the Reformed tradition in Boesak 1977) and of the theological breakthrough associated with the name of Karl Barth (note the way in which James Cone and Míguez Bonino extrapolate their theologies from their Barthian roots; cf also Lamb 1984:129).

The Marxist Connection

Contextual and liberation theologies are often accused of having surrendered the Christian gospel to Marxist ideology. In itself, this is to be expected, given the fact that both Marxism and liberation theology reject the capitalist model (cf, for instance, Míguez Bonino 1976). It is also understandable in light of the bourgeois nature of most Western churches and their complicity with colonialism and capitalism. The status quo orientation of much of Christianity and the conventional interpretation of Christian social involvement as not going beyond charity and relief has been eloquently expressed in Dom Hélder Câmara's oft-quoted words: "When I build houses for the poor, they call me a saint. But when I try to help the poor by calling by name the injustices which have made them poor, they call me subversive, a Marxist". There are, thus, sound reasons for Third-World theologians to resort to a Marxist critique of traditional Christianity. Marx himself was consumed by the desire to bring an end to the exploitation and oppression of the poor, and this can hardly be faulted.

It is, however, not always recognized that liberation theology's use of Marxism and Marxist categories is selective and critical. Liberation theologians tend to use Marxist analysis as an instrument of critique rather than in a prescriptive way. Even somebody as outspokenly Marxist as José P. Miranda (whose book *Communism in the Bible* opens with a chapter entitled "Christianity Is Communism") criticizes many revolutionaries who call themselves Marxists and makes critical use of Marxist categories.

Moreover, it would seem that, as far as Latin American liberation theology is concerned, there has in recent years been a move away from Marxist analysis. This is particularly true in respect to the Marxist critique of religion. Segundo, for instance, criticizes Marxism's inability to take into account the reality of "Christian *transcendent data*". His problem, he says, is with Marxism's "simplistic, mistaken eschatology, which raises false hopes and hence in the long run will only intensify people's desperation and despair" (1986:179), and with the "paralyzing utopia" which has crept into liberation theology because of this alliance. Also Míguez Bonino (1976:118-132) is careful to point to crucial flaws in Marxism, such as its abuse of power, its arbitrariness, its personality cults, and its bureaucratic cliques. The alliance with Marxism thus has both "promise" and "limits".

At the same time, whereas Marxist analysis appears to be on the decline in Latin America, it has been introduced more vigorously into South African Black Theology since about 1981 — again for very obvious reasons, given the situation of repression and disenfranchisement of Blacks in South Africa. In a sense, then, a reverse development has taken place in South Africa, compared to Latin America. The "first phase" of Black Theology (1970-1980) was almost completely free of Marxist influences; theologians of the "second phase", however, after 1980, are using Marxist categories much more consciously and consistently (for the two "phases", cf Kritzinger 1988:58-84).

There can hardly be any problem with using Marxist *theory* as a tool in social analysis. As such, it certainly can be of tremendous value. The question is, however, whether some proponents of liberation theology have not adopted Marxist *ideology* as well, and whether this can be deemed compatible with the Christian faith. In attempting to respond to this question, one may point out, first, that Marxism shares, with Capitalism, the presuppositions of the Enlightenment paradigm, particularly in respect to its subject-object thinking, its utopianism, and its belief in modernization and in human beings as autonomous and innately good. Newbigin, with some justification, calls it "Capitalism's rebellious twin sister"; the two are "the twin products of the apostasy of the European intellectuals of the eighteenth century" (1986:8). The difference may perhaps only be that the one pursues freedom at the cost of equality and the other equality at the cost of freedom (:118).

Second, Christianity, as a religion, proceeds from the premise that there is another reality behind and above the visible and tangible reality around us; its reference is not only to this world. Marxism, by contrast, is an ideology, which means that it lacks any reference to a trans-empirical reality (which does not preclude it from having founders, sacred scriptures, martyrs, official creeds, an eschatology, heretics, and soon; for a superb summary of the "religious elements in Marxism," cf Nürnberger 1987b:105-109). In the classical Marxist model, religion is an illusion and the opiate of the people. It is important to note that this thoroughgoing atheistic dimension of Marxism is increasingly rejected by liberation theologians. In this respect, secularist theologians are actually closer to the classical Marxist premise than liberation theologians are. By and large, the latter refuse to jettison what Segundo calls the "transcendent data". For Gutiérrez, salvation "embraces every aspect of humanity: body and spirit, individual and society, person and cosmos, time and eternity" (1988:85) — a statement no Marxist can assent to. Leonardo Boff likewise distinguishes between "partial liberation" and "integral liberation" (1984:14-66; cf Boff 1983). Only the latter deserves to be called salvation and has to do with "the eschatological condition of the human being" (1984:56-58). Salvation and liberation may never be divorced from each other (as so often happens in conventional theology); neither, however, should they be confused (:58-60).

Third, there is the matter of violence. Support for violence is intrinsic to Marxism. Without condoning the violence of the status quo and Christians' blessing of it (which is actually the bigger problem), one has to express concern about the support for revolutionary violence (which is actually the lesser problem, since it is really a response to the violence of the system) in some branches of liberation theology. It becomes especially problematic when the Marxist idea of a continual revolution is adopted by theologians, in the sense of Albert Camus' philosophy, "I rebel, therefore we are", or Ché Guevara's slogan, "The duty of a revolutionary is to make a revolution". In this kind of approach revolutionary action is raised almost to the level of a sacred liturgy, conflict becomes an all-embracing hermeneutical key, and the mobilization of hatred and demagogy an inescapable duty. At the same time, it perpetuates the fixation on the "opponent" as the implacable enemy and imputes the blame for every misery on others (cf Sundermeier 1986:67, 76), while condoning everything the oppressed may choose to do in trying to rid themselves of the shackles of oppression.

In spite of the fact that some liberationists unequivocally support violence (such as Shaull 1967) whilst others appear to be equivocal on the issue (for instance, the *Kairos Document*), the majority are committed to nonviolence (for instance, Desmond Tutu and Allan Boesak). In this vein, the Melbourne CWME Conference asserts that "Jesus of Nazareth rejected coercive power as a way of changing the world" (Section IV.3; WCC 1980:209) whilst EN 37 declares, "Violence is not in accord with the gospel". The "spiral of violence" (Câmara) is an all too well-known specter in many parts of the world. This alone makes nonviolent strategies such as those of Ghandi and Martin Luther King worthy of serious consideration. Human power has its limits; it can coerce, but it can hardly heal (West 1971:230). Christians should always remain open to the "possible impossibility" that the "enemy" may change into a friend and that the oppressor may be persuaded to pursue another course (de Gruchy 1987:242). To the chagrin of many, the gospels tell us that Jesus ate with sinners and righteous ones, with exploiters and the exploited, and that both Levi the collaborator and Simon the Zealot were among his disciples (unless, of course, our hermeneutics of suspicion prompts us radically to doubt the entire gospel tradition on these and similar points, as Mosala 1989 seems to suggest). And since Christians believe that the decisive battle has already been won by Christ, they may believe in the possibility of forgiveness, justification, and reconciliation. In view of the harsh realities of oppression and exploitation such reconciliation will be costly. It is "utterly destructive of human continuities, of theories of progress, of the old self and the old society, because it leads also to the affirmation of the adversary" (West 1971:47; cf de Gruchy 1987:241f). In this sense, then, the element of conflictual analysis in liberation theology should not be an alternative to reconciliation but an intrinsic dimension of restoring community between those who are now the privileged and the underprivileged (Frostin 1988:180).

Integral Liberation

Liberation theology has helped the church to rediscover its ancient faith in Yahweh, whose outstanding qualification—which made him the Wholly Other—was founded on his involvement in history as the God of righteousness and justice who championed the cause of the weak and the oppressed (cf Deut 4:32, 34f; Ps 82). It has helped us to understand the Holy Spirit afresh, in particular his ability to change inert things into living things, to bring people back from death to life, to empower the weak, and to recognize the Spirit's presence not only in people's hearts but also in the workaday world of history and culture (cf Krass 1977:11). It has rekindled faith in the great renewal of history that had been inaugurated in the death, resurrection, and ascension of Christ and reawakened the confidence that nothing need to remain the way it is: Christians may assume a critical stance vis-à-vis the authorities, traditions, and institutions of this world and match the age-old adage, *ecclesia semper reformanda*, with its corollary, *societas semper reformanda* (cf Gort 1980b:54). This applies especially to the conditions of the poor and the lowly. They deserve preference not because they are morally or religiously better than others, but because God is God, in whose eyes "the last are first"; or, in the words of Las Casas, "God has the freshest and keenest memory of the least and most forgotten" (quoted in Gutiérrez 1988:xxvii).

Since faith and life are inseparable (Gutiérrez 1988:xix), this is a liberation that is to be effected at three different levels: from social situations of oppression and marginalization, from every kind of personal servitude, and from sin, which is the breaking of friendship with God and with other human beings (:xxxviii; 24f; cf Brakemeier 1988:216). Orthodoxy and orthopraxy need each other, and each is adversely affected if sight is lost of the other; we mutilate the message of Jesus if we choose where no choice is possible (:xxxiv). And we are liberated by our participation in the new life bestowed upon us through the gratuitousness of God (:xxxviiif).

The three levels are intimately interconnected but they are not the same. The tendency in some quarters to elevate the political to a position of indisputable primacy is therefore to be challenged. In his study on the humanist christology of Paul, Segundo has some important reflections on this theme. The Yahwist faith of Israel, he says, had political liberation as one, but only one, of its dimensions (1986:169f). Liberation theologians, however, have tended either to read the whole Bible—even the seemingly most apolitical parts—with the aid of the political key, or to slight those parts which could not be read in this way (:169-171). This happened because they were trying to glean ready-made answers from Scripture, looking for an immediate pragmatic connection between the problems arising on their own horizon and the message of the Bible (:172f). He then proposes a rereading of Paul, understanding him within his own context where socio-political freedom is not everything and extrapolating from there to today. Paul shows us that there are indeed aspects of being human that are not reducible to the socio-political.

Segundo then addresses the question of who the real bearers of the idea of the theology of liberation are. There is a tendency in liberation theology, he says, to blur the distinction between the church and "the people" or "the poor", and to sacrifice the church as a distinct community. This tendency is found also outside the strict confines of liberation theology. At the Melbourne CWME Conference, for instance, a messianic quality was often conferred on the poor, as though the poor and the church were completely synonymous. A suggestion to say that the poor are blessed *insofar as* they are longing for justice was defeated in Section I. The report now asserts (emphasis added), "The poor are 'blessed' *because* of their longing for justice and their hope of liberation. They *accept* the promise that God has come to their rescue" (I.2; WCC 1980:172). Segundo warns against this kind of discourse and says that there is much empty rhetoric in superficially dazzling formulas, for instance that people should put themselves "under the discipleship of the poor", for (according to Gutiérrez), it is only to the poor that the grace of receiving and understanding the kingdom has been granted, so that there can be no authentic theology of liberation until it is created by "the People" (in Segundo 1986:182, 224, note 257; cf 226, note 262).

Segundo, however, pleads that our overarching theological category should be the *church* rather than "the People". The praxis of liberation theology presupposes justification by grace through faith. "The People", however, is a sociological category and may not be turned into a theological term and treated as a synonym for church. All liberation must pass by way of the judgment of the cross of Christ (cf Brakemeier 1988:217-221). In the *Kairos Document*, too, the line between the church and the political movements gets blurred (cf de Gruchy 1987:241). Lamb's conviction, quoted earlier, that "the voice of the victims is the voice of God" (1982:23), is an immensely powerful and moving statement, but it suffers from the same blurring of categories. To say that God hears and responds to the cries of the oppressed is one thing; to say that these cries *are* the voice of God is another. Bishop Alpheus Zulu once said, "The statement, 'God is on the side of the oppressed' cannot simply be turned round: 'The oppressed are on the side of God'". Segundo's admonitions in this respect need to be heeded. And it seems Gutiérrez is indeed beginning to heed him. In the new introduction to *A Theology of Liberation* he warns against "the facile enthusiasms that have interpreted [the theology of liberation] in a simplistic and erroneous way by ignoring the integral demands of the Christian faith as lived in the communion of the church" (1988:xviii; cf xlii).

There is yet another side to this: humankind's innate optimism. In this respect liberation theology — at least in its early manifestation — shared the optimism of the secularist theologians, the "technological humanists". Both located sin in the structures of society rather than in the human heart. Both were inherently optimistic about the future and about humankind and were, for this, indebted to the Enlightenment worldview. The difference was perhaps only that, whereas the technological humanists considered *all* people to be essentially good, liberation theology tended to believe that only the poor and the oppressed were innately good — the rich and the oppressors, however, were evil.

The optimism of the 1960s and of the early stage of liberation theology was almost tangible. Gutiérrez (1988:xvii) quotes a paragraph from the CELAM II document (Medellín 1968, where Latin American liberation theology was first officially sanctioned) which epitomizes this:

Latin America is obviously under the sign of transformation . . . It appears to be a time of zeal for full emancipation, of liberation from every form of servitude, of personal maturity and collective integration . . . We cannot fail to see in this gigantic effort toward a rapid transformation and development an obvious sign of the Spirit who leads the history of humankind and of the peoples toward their vocation. We cannot but discover in this force, daily more insistent and impatient for transformation, vestiges of the image of God in human nature as a powerful incentive.

At the time, Gutiérrez himself shared this excitement and endorsed the optimism. What really makes utopian thought viable and highlights its wealth of possibilities is the revolutionary experience of our times (1988:135) — indeed, authentic utopian thought postulates, enriches, and supplies new goals for political action (:136).

This sort of language was indicative of the euphoria of the mid-1960s. Israel's liberation from slavery in Egypt was the undisputed theological paradigm for liberation theology (Segundo 1986:169). Medellín fanned the enthusiasm and inspired the church and the people of Latin America. And there were indeed many promising events. The capitalist system, so it appeared, was under severe pressure, in Chile and elsewhere. The socialist golden age was just around the corner. By the mid-1970s, however, much of this had disappeared. Hopes for a social and political transformation were dashed to pieces in Chile, in Uruguay, in Argentina, and in Bolivia. Brutal regimes inspired by "national security" ideology had imposed their police repression and economic policies on much of the continent (cf Míguez Bonino 1980:1154). Also where socialist regimes were introduced, the situation hardly changed. Repression just took on new forms. And it became even more difficult to attack the morality of it all, since the socialist rulers claimed to have the backing of the people for what they were doing. Often, then, people were liberated without becoming free. . .

In this climate, the triumphalist elements began to disappear from the liberation theology discourse. Segundo (1986:224, note 254) criticizes Gutiérrez's *The Power of the Poor in History*, and asks, "What 'power' is he talking about? Where has this 'power' been hiding for the past four centuries, since the days of European colonialism?" Elsewhere he reflects on the darkening of the horizon:

> It seems that everything has been tried, every possible approach used, yet the result is the same. By some inflexible law, more keenly felt as time passes, we find it impossible to be even partially free, to choose the kind of societal life we want, to even discuss it much less fight for it. Every day we see a road closing to us that seemed open the day before (:175).

In the new introduction to his book, Gutiérrez also takes cognizance of these changed circumstances. Often, he says, the theology of liberation has "stirred facile enthusiasms" (1988:xviii). The second phase of Latin American liberation theology thus appears to be more modest, more sober, than the first. For Segundo (1986:157-180) this means, among other things, a "deutero-reading" of Paul, particularly his sayings about slaves. Paul calculates the energy costs entailed in various social situations (:222, note 240). With respect to the institution of slavery — a form of being dominated by Sin — Paul realizes that he, and the Christian slaves, are faced with a limited option, a problem of efficacy, an energy calculus; if the preoccupation of the slave is to win civil liberation, and the slave invests all his or her energy in doing that, Paul thinks that the cost is too high. So Paul makes a choice, a choice which, of course, has its limitations; that is, Paul opts to humanize the slave from within (:164). In the circumstances that he faces, he postpones commitment to the concrete socio-political cause of liberating the slaves (:165). But this does not paralyze him, for faith sees what we ourselves cannot see; faith represents a change in our (and the slave's) epistemological premises (:159). We now have a new way of interpreting events, so that Paul can even say (Rom 8:28), "Everything works together for the good of those who love God" (:221, note 237).

We cannot simply apply Paul to our present situation. Still, we have to allow ourselves to be informed by Paul's spirituality and ask what his "energy calculus" might mean in a given context. And what is true of Paul is also true of Jesus. It is hard to imagine Jesus being silent in the face of the reality we must live through today, says Segundo (1986:173), but it is equally difficult to picture him challenging the established power over us in a totally unrealistic way and merely for the sake of principle. Paul, and Jesus, were not escaping to the "private" sector; they were simply stressing that the dehumanizing *status* of slaves need not prevent them from attaining human maturity. This they could do by adhering to faith in Christ and to the "transcendent data" brought by him (:180). In the circumstances, this was the only way in which Jesus or Paul could humanize the slave. It is the way in which the Christian can triumph qualitatively even if he or she does not escape the quantitative victory of Sin (:160).

Segundo is pioneering a new course within liberation theology. The Christian can triumph, even where circumstances do not change, even where liberation does not come. Liberation and salvation overlap with each other to a significant degree, but they do not overlap totally. We should not deceive ourselves into believing that everything lies in our grasp and that we can bring it about, now; we would then, also, diminish "the importance and decisive character of the next generation" (Segundo 1986:160). Paul's (and Segundo's) is a "spirituality for the long haul" (Robert Bilheimer, reference in Henry 1987:279f), not that of a Pelagius, who believed that "we have the power of accomplishing every good thing by action, speech, and thought" (Pelagius, quoted in Henry 1987:272). For the Pelagian, true justice and true unity can coalesce fully in this world if we just try hard enough (:274; cf Gründel 1983:122). But the hope that human beings can shoulder the burdens of the world is an illusion that leads them through anxiety to despair (cf Duff 1956:146, summarizing a report of the Advisory Committee on the theme of the WCC Evanston Assembly). It simply heightens our guilt feelings and leads to increasing self-flagellation because of our inability to achieve what we convinced ourselves we ought to accomplish. We are then trapped into the belief that justice must be our justice, that we can and must cancel our guilt by restitution, overcome our frustration by more action, and relentlessly drive ourselves from one "involvement" to the other. In addition, it is easy for those whose cause is just to blur the line between what they are working for and their own reputation and glory. Work for justice can easily slip into a kind of ideological dogmatism, with the result that we may be perpetrating injustice while fighting for justice (Henry 1987:279).

Segundo wishes to break this vicious circle of frustration, from which liberation theology is by no means exempt. We should recognize, however, that Segundo's position does not reflect a compromise or a pragmatic adjustment to and reconciliation with "realities". That would be contrary to the heart of liberation theology. And Segundo remains firmly committed to the agenda of liberation. If Christianity would lose its counter-cultural and world-transforming role, other forces would take its place. We need a vision to direct our action within history. Indifference to this vision is a denial of the God who links his presence to the elimination of all exploitation, pain, and poverty. As soon as our hope is compromised, as soon as we stop expecting the wholesale trans-formations *within* history that the Scriptures talk about, we kill that vision (cf Krass 1977:21). We have to turn our backs resolutely on our traditional dualistic thinking, of setting up alternatives between the body and the soul, society and the church, the *eschaton* and the present, and rekindle an all-embracing faith, hope, and love in the ultimate triumph of God casting its rays into the present.

The theology of liberation is often misunderstood, attacked, and vilified. I believe that one such case of misunderstanding, one that had far-reaching con-sequences, was the *Instruction on Certain Aspects of the "Theology of Liberation"*, released by the Vatican in 1984 and aimed rather particularly at Leonardo Boff. I have not intended to whitewash liberation theology in these paragraphs, nor to "put the record straight". I have simply attempted to point out that this movement, in spite of its flaws (and there are several) represents "a *new stage*, closely connected with earlier ones, in the theological reflection that began with the apostolic tradition" (John Paul II, in an April 1986 letter to Brazilian bish-ops, quoted in Gutiérrez 1988:xliv; emphasis added). The pope put it well. It is not a "new theology" but a new stage in theologizing, and as such both continuous and discontinuous with the theologizing of earlier epochs. It is not a fad but a serious attempt to let the faith make sense to the postmodern age. Precisely for this reason it will never be a finished product. At every stage, says Gutiérrez, "we must refine, improve, and possibly correct earlier formulations if we want to use language that is understandable and faithful both to the integral Christian message and to the reality we experience" (:xviii).

MISSION AS INCULTURATION

The Vicissitudes of Accommodation and Indigenization

Inculturation represents a *second* important model of contextualizing the-ology (cf Ukpong 1987) and is, like liberation theology, of recent origin — even though it is not without precedent in Christian history. Inculturation is one of the patterns in which the pluriform character of contemporary Christianity manifests itself. Even the term is new. Pierre Charles introduced the concept "*en*culturation", at home in cultural anthropology circles, into missiology, but it was J. Masson who first coined the phrase *Catholicisme inculturé* ("incultur-ated Catholicism") in 1962. It soon gained currency among Jesuits, in the form of "*in*culturation". In 1977 the Jesuit superior-general, P. Arrupe, introduced the term to the Synod of Bishops; the Apostolic Exhortation, *Catechesi Traden-dae* (CT), which flowed from this synod, took it up and gave it universal currency (cf Müller 1986:134; 1987:178). It was soon also accepted in Protestant circles and is today one of the most widely used concepts in missiological circles.

The Christian faith never exists except as "translated" into a culture. This circumstance, which was an integral feature of Christianity from the very beginning, has hopefully been made abundantly clear in the course of this study. Lamin Sanneh rightly says (cf Stackhouse 1988:58) that the early church, "in straddling the Jewish-Gentile worlds, was born in a cross-cultural milieu with translation as its birthmark".[20] It should therefore come as no surprise that in the Pauline churches Jews, Greeks, barbarians, Thracians, Egyptians, and Romans were able to feel at home (cf Köster 1984:172). The same was true of the post-apostolic church. The faith was inculturated in a great variety of liturgies and contexts—Syriac, Greek, Roman, Coptic, Armenian, Ethiopian, Maronite, and so forth. Moreover, during this early period the emphasis was on the local church rather than the church universal in its monarchical form.

After Constantine, when the erstwhile *religio illicita* became the religion of the establishment, the church became *the* bearer of culture. Its missionary outreach thus meant a movement from the civilized to "savages" and from a "superior" culture to "inferior" cultures—a process in which the latter had to be subdued, if not eradicated. Thus Christian mission, as a matter of course, presupposed the disintegration of the cultures into which it penetrated. Where such disintegration did not take place, mission had only limited success (as in the case of some Asian cultures—cf Gensichen 1985:122; Pieris 1986).

In chapter 9 of this study, and elsewhere as well, I have stressed the decisive influence Western colonialism, cultural superiority feelings, and "manifest destiny" exercised on the Western missionary enterprise and the extent to which this compromised the gospel. Without repeating what has been said there, let me just mention some ways in which these circumstances have affected the subject under discussion here.

By the time the large-scale Western colonial expansion began, Western Christians were unconscious of the fact that their theology was culturally conditioned; they simply assumed that it was supracultural and universally valid. And since Western culture was implicitly regarded as Christian, it was equally self-evident that this culture had to be exported together with the Christian faith. Still, it was soon acknowledged that, in order to expedite the conversion process, some adjustments were necessary. The strategy by which these were to be put into effect was variously called adaptation or accommodation (in Catholicism) or indigenization (in Protestantism). It was often, however, limited to accidental matters, such as liturgical vestments, non-sacramental rites, art, literature, architecture, and music (cf Thauren 1927:37-46).

The ramifications were manifold. First, accommodation never included modifying the "prefabricated" Western theology. Second, it was actually understood as a *concession* that Third-World Christians would now be allowed to use some elements of their culture in order to give expression to their new faith. Third, only those cultural elements which were manifestly "neutral" and naturally good, that is, not "contaminated" by pagan religious values, could be employed (cf Thauren 1927:25-33; Luzbetak 1988:67). Fourth, the word "elements" further implied that cultures were not regarded as indivisible wholes but, in Enlightenment fashion, as separate components that could be put together or disassembled at will; it would thus be perfectly in order if one were to isolate some components and employ them in the service of the Christian church. Fifth, it went without saying that indigenization or accommodation was a problem only for the "young" churches. In the Western church indigenization had for many centuries been a *fait accompli*; the gospel was perfectly at home in the *West* but still foreign elsewhere (cf Song 1977:2). Sixth, a term like "adaptation" could not help but convey the idea of an activity that was peripheral and therefore nonessential, even superficial, as far as the essence of the Christian mission was concerned; it was something optional and, in any case, only a matter of *method*, of *form* rather than *content* (cf Shorter 1977:150). The philosophy behind all of this was that of a division between "kernel" and "husk". The faith, as understood and canonized in the Western church — in other words, the *depositum fidei* — was the unalloyed kernel, the cultural accoutrements of the people to whom the missionaries went were the expendable husk. In the accommodation process, the kernel had to remain intact but adapted to the forms of the new culture; at the same time, these cultures had to be adapted to the "kernel" (cf Fries 1986:760). Seventh, this entire project suggested, implicitly and often also explicitly, that the younger churches needed the older churches, but that the latter were in no respect dependent on what they might receive from the former; the traffic was decidedly one-way. Last, often the initiative in respect of indigenization did not come from the newly converted but from missionaries with a sentimental interest in exotic cultures, who insisted on the "otherness" of the young churches and treated them as something that had to be preserved in their pristine form.

Still, Catholic missionaries, in particular early Jesuits like de Nobili and Ricci, tried to move beyond the kernel-husk model in their accommodation of the faith to the peoples of India and China. So, in fact, did *Propaganda Fide* (founded 1622). In an extraordinary policy statement in 1659 it advised its missionaries not to force people to change their customs, as long as these were not opposed to religion or morality. The statement went on to say:

> What could be more absurd than to carry France, Spain, or Italy, or any part of Europe into China? It is not this sort of things you are to bring but rather the Faith, which does not reject or damage any people's rites and customs, provided these are not depraved.

In spite of this instruction (which was remarkably similar to a directive of Pope Gregory the Great more than a thousand years earlier — cf Markus 1970), the Jesuits soon ran into difficulties, particularly because of what became known as the "Rites Controversy", in both China and India. In 1704 the papal envoy, T. M. de Tournon, released a decree in which he condemned the Jesuit praxis in sixteen points. The pope sided with de Tournon — two papal decrees (1707 and 1715) sanctioned de Tournon's ruling. The controversy continued until 1742, when another decree, *Ex quo singulari*, endorsed the earlier rulings. A papal bull of 1744, *Omnium sollicitudinum*, forbade all but the most trivial concessions to local custom and ordered an oath of submission, which was to be taken by all missioners; also forbidden was any further discussion of the issue (cf Thauren 1927:131-145; Shorter 1988:157-160). In 1773 the Society of Jesus was suppressed. Soon after, all Jesuit missionaries were recalled. Not until 1814 were they restored by papal decree. The oath introduced in 1744 was not repealed until 1938.

Protestant missions only *appeared* to be different; instead of subordinating the expression of the faith to magisterial authority as in Catholicism, Protestants unwittingly subordinated it to the presuppositions of Euro-American culture. Protestants were, on the whole, even more suspicious of "non-Christian" cultures than Catholics, not least because of their emphasis on humankind's total depravity (Müller 1987:177). They allowed some freedom but in the main worked for an exact reproduction of European models. This could even be seen in cases where they deliberately set out to encourage indigenization, as in the celebrated case of the "three-selfs" as the aim of mission (self-government, self-support, and self-propagation), formulated classically by Rufus Anderson and Henry Venn almost a century and a half ago. These *notae ecclesiae* were derived from the Western idea of a living community, which was one which could support, extend, and manage itself; these, then, were the criteria according to which the younger churches were judged. The Western churches, which had long ago achieved these aims, represented the "higher" form, the others, struggling to rise up to these expectation, the "lower". In both Catholicism and Protestantism, then, the prevailing image was a *pedagogical* one—over an extended period of time and along a laborious route the younger churches were to be educated and trained in order to reach selfhood or "maturity", measured in terms of the "three-selfs". In practice, however, the younger churches, like Peter Pan, never "grew up", at least not in the eyes of the older ones. Most of them could only survive, and thereby also please their founders, if they resolutely segregated themselves from the surrounding culture and existed as foreign bodies.

Twentieth-Century Developments

The "rigid system" of accommodation (Thauren 1927:130) could not last interminably. Forces that contributed to the breakdown of the model included the emergence, already in the nineteenth century, of nationalism in the Third World; the rise of anthropological thought, which gradually revealed the relativity and contextuality of all cultures (including those of the West); and—of particular importance for our purpose—the maturation of the younger churches, which frequently went hand in hand with the founding of independent churches free from any missionary control. In spite of the flaws inherent in the "three-selfs" model, it did help to inspire subjugated peoples to seek independence also in areas other than the strictly ecclesiastical. Even somebody as fiercely critical of the entire Western missionary enterprise as Hoekendijk had to admit that, in this respect, the church really was ahead of the world (1967a:321). Around 1860 the autonomy of the young churches could be seen in large print on every sensible missionary program, long before anybody in the West even dreamt about other kinds of autonomy for colonized countries. There certainly were more sensitivities in this respect in Western missionary circles than there were in the various colonial offices.

Pope Benedict XV, particularly in his encyclical *Maximum Illud* (1919), was one of the first to promote the right of the "mission churches" to cease being ecclesiastical colonies under foreign control and to have their own clergy and bishops. *Rerum Ecclesiae* (Pius XI, 1926) and *Evangelii Praecones* (Pius XII, 1951) elaborated further along similar lines (cf Shorter 1988:179-186). Since then, local hierarchies have been introduced everywhere. Bühlmann (1977) describes the new development as "the coming of the third church", a reality which he elsewhere calls "*the* epoch-making event of current church history" (quoted in Anderson 1988:114). The new reality also finds expression in the fact that there are today (according to the calculations of Barrett 1990:27) many more Christians outside than inside the traditional missionary-sending countries—914 million compared to 597 million—and that many of these younger churches have themselves begun to send out missionaries.

In the period immediately after World War II a host of adjustments had to be made in both Catholic and Protestant circles. For our purpose, two are of special importance. First, there were the events in China, culminating in the victory of the Communists in 1949—an event which symbolized, in a special way, the breakup of the entire old missionary order. Then there was the circumstance that—in spite of the war during which they had been "orphaned"— many fledgling Third World churches had not only survived, but some had actually grown spectacularly during the years of the missionaries' absence. Whitby's slogan (1947) "Partnership in Obedience" and the formation of the WCC as a council of autonomous churches from all corners of the globe, were two ways of giving recognition to the new reality and to the need for a new relationship. This found expression in the idea of "mission as reciprocal assistance" and in such ecumenical projects as "Interchurch Aid", "Ecumenical Sharing of Personnel", and "Joint Action for Mission" (cf Jansen Schoonhoven 1977; for the Catholic scene, cf van Winsen 1973).

Mission as interchurch assistance was, however, a transitional phenomenon (cf van Engelen 1975:294). By the late 1960s it became evident that a decisive shift had taken place, even in the mind of Westerners, from a Europe-centered world to a humankind-centered world. Henceforth the churches of the West would increasingly take cognizance of the views of and developments in the younger churches. Yet even at the Second Vatican Council the voices of Third World church leaders were still muffled, as they were in Protestant ecumenical gatherings of the time. Only since the Catholic Synods of Bishops and, in Protestantism, since the Bangkok CWME meeting (1973), has it become clear that global ecclesiastical leadership is inexorably passing toward Third World Christians. The "rediscovery" of the local church, during and after Vatican II, contributed tremendously to the new sense of maturing of relationships. The birth of basic Christian communities, first in Latin America and then elsewhere, meant much to the self-image of local Christian communities in the Third World, so much so that Leonardo Boff (1986) refers to it as "ecclesiogenesis", or as "reinventing" the church.

It was now also high time that a "fourth self" be added to the classical "three-selfs"—*self-theologizing*, an aspect about which the missionary theorists of the nineteenth century never thought (cf Hiebert 1985b:16). Of course a lot of self-theologizing had already been taking place, often unnoticed or clandestine, more frequently outside of the "mission churches" and thus of the purview of missionaries – to whom much of this was at any rate unacceptable since it was deemed to be syncretistic.[21] Since the 1930s, however, Asian (especially Indian) theologians from "mission churches" had begun consciously and publicly to chart new ways theologically. In Africa, such developments only rose above the surface after World War II. In 1956 a group of African priests from Francophone countries published *Des prêtres noirs s'interrogent*, a book that was to have wide influence in Catholic circles. Shortly afterward, Tharcisse Tshibangu, a student at the Catholic Theological Faculty in Kinshasa, began to challenge his Belgian mentors' ideas about a universally valid theology. In 1965 he published his *Théologie positive et théologie speculative*. These and other developments were the first steps toward remedying a situation which John Mbiti once described as follows: "[The church in Africa] is a church without a theology, without theologians, and without a theological concern" (1972:51). The stage was set for the vigorous development of autochthonous African theology.

Toward Inculturation

The developments outlined above paved the way for what was later to be known as "inculturation". It was finally recognized that a plurality of cultures presupposes a plurality of theologies and therefore, for Third-World churches, a farewell to a Eurocentric approach (cf Fries 1986:760; Waldenfels 1987:227f). The Christian faith must be rethought, reformulated and lived anew in each human culture (Memorandum 1982:465), and this must be done in a *vital* way, in depth and right to the cultures' roots (EN 20). Such a project is even more needed in light of the way in which the West has raped the cultures of the Third World, inflicting on them what has been termed "anthropological poverty" (cf Frostin 1988:15).

At first, the Western church leadership embraced the new development only reluctantly. Snijders (1977:173f) has shown how Paul VI, for instance, wavered between embracing and rejecting the inculturation idea – much the way an earlier pope, Gregory the Great, wavered with respect to missionary accommodation in the sixth century (cf Markus 1970). In the end, however, Paul VI resolutely chose in favor of inculturation, as did John Paul II, particularly in CT. The latter's commitment to the project was further underscored when he founded the Pontifical Council for Culture in 1982 (cf Shorter 1988:230f). A similar evolution can be observed in Protestantism. Here, evangelicals were often in the forefront (perhaps because ecumenical Protestants revealed a greater interest in mission as liberation rather than in mission as inculturation?). A landmark event was the Consultation on Gospel and Culture, sponsored by the Lausanne Committee on World Evangelization and held in 1978 in Willowbank, Bermuda (cf Stott and Coote 1980). The Willowbank Report (:311-339) was widely acclaimed (cf Gensichen 1985:112-129). By and large, Willowbank opted for the "dynamic equivalence" model of inculturation (Stott and Coote 1980:330f), thus following in the steps of the pioneering work done by Eugene Nida and, more recently, Charles Kraft. "Dynamic equivalence", a variation of the "translation model", is, however, only one of several current inculturation patterns. Others include the anthropological, praxis, synthetic, and semiotic models. An excellent example of the last is Schreiter's *Constructing Local Theologies* (1985). It is clear, then, that inculturation does not necessarily mean the same to everybody. Still, there are some basic traits all these models share and which set them off against the earlier accommodation, indigenization, and similar approaches.

In which respects does inculturation differ from its predecessors?

First, it differs in respect of the *agents*. In all earlier models it was the Western missionary who either induced or benevolently supervised the way in which the encounter between the Christian faith and the local cultures was to unfold. The very terms "accommodation", "adaptation", etc, suggested this. The process was one-sided, in that the local faith community was not the primary agent. In inculturation, however, the two primary agents are the Holy Spirit and the local community, particularly the laity (cf Luzbetak 1988:66). Neither the missionary, nor the hierarchy, nor the magisterium controls the process. This does not mean that the missionary and the theologian are excluded. Schreiter even regards their participation as indispensable; to ignore the resources of the professional theologian "is to prefer ignorance to knowledge" (1985:18). Missionaries no longer go with a kind of Peace Corps mentality for the purpose of "doing good", however. They no longer participate as the ones who have all the answers but are learners like everybody else. The *padre* becomes a *compadre*. Inculturation only becomes possible if all practice *convivência*, "life together" (Sundermeier 1986).

Second, the emphasis is truly on the *local* situation. "The universal word only speaks dialect" (P. Casaldáliga, quoted in Sundermeier 1986:93). Vatican II's new emphasis on the local church already pointed in this direction. The one, universal church finds its true existence in the particular churches (LG 23, 26) — something Third World churches take much more seriously than the church in the West (cf Glazik 1984b:64). At this local level, inculturation comprises much more than culture in the traditional or anthropological sense of the term. It involves the entire context: social, economic, political, religious, educational, etc.

Inculturation is, however, not only a local event. It also has a *regional* or macrocontextual and macrocultural manifestation. To a significant extent the various paradigms I have traced in the earlier part of this study evolved because each time the Christian faith entered another macrocultural context — the Greek, Slavic, Latin, or Germanic worlds. The theological disputes which arose in this process should be attributed at least as much to cultural as to genuine doctrinal differences. Looked at from this perspective, it could be argued that the Protestant Reformation was a case of the (overdue?) inculturation of the faith among Germanic and related peoples. The same is true of many regional differences today. The decisive consideration may, then, not be whether a church is Roman Catholic, Anglican, Presbyterian, or Lutheran, but whether it has its home in Africa, Asia, or Europe. Regional differences tend to become more decisive than confessional ones. It is noteworthy, for instance, that black Americans, after having been assaulted by an alien culture for several centuries, still retain a unique religio-cultural identity. In part, then, these differences on the macro-level explain why, in Latin America, inculturation takes the form of solidarity with and among the poor; in Africa it may be solidarity and communion within and across autonomous cultures; and in Asia the search for identity amid the density of religious pluralism. In various regions of the world we thus observe the burgeoning of autochthonous ecclesiologies, christologies, and the like.

Fourth, inculturation consciously follows the model of the *incarnation* (cf John Paul II, quoted in ITC 1989:143). The Willowbank Report refers specifically to John 17:18, 20:21, and Philippians 2 (cf Stott and Coote 1980:323). In fact, the kenotic and incarnational dimension of authentic inculturation is mentioned again and again in all theological traditions (cf Bühlmann 1977:287; Scott and Coote 1980:323f; Geffré 1982:480-482; Gensichen 1985:123-126; Müller 1986:134; 1987:177; cf also CT 53 and ME 26, 28). This incarnational dimension, of the gospel being "en-fleshed", "em-bodied" in a people and its culture, of a "kind of *ongoing* incarnation" (P. Divarkar, quoted in Müller 1986:134 – my translation) is very different from any model that had been in vogue for over a thousand years. In this paradigm, it is not so much a case of the church being *expanded*, but of the church being *born anew* in each new context and culture.

In the fifth place, and following directly from the previous point, the earlier models did indeed suggest an interaction between gospel and culture, but one in which the theological content of the interaction remained obscure. The coordination of gospel and culture should, however, be structured *christologically* (Gensichen 1985:124). Still, the missionaries do not just set out to "take Christ" to other people and cultures, but also to allow the faith the chance to start a history of its own in each people and its experience of Christ. Inculturation suggests a *double movement*: there is at once inculturation of Christianity and Christianization of culture. The gospel must remain Good News while becoming, up to a certain point, a cultural phenomenon (Geffré 1982:482), while it takes into account the meaning systems already present in the context (cf Schreiter 1985:12f). On the one hand, it offers the cultures "the knowledge of the divine mystery", while on the other it helps them "to bring forth from their own living tradition original expressions of Christian life, celebration and thought" (CT 53). This approach breaks radically with the idea of the faith as "kernel" and the culture as "husk" – which in any case is, to a large extent, an illustration of the Western scientific tradition's distinction between "content" and "form". In many non-Western cultures such distinctions do not operate at all (cf Hiebert 1987:108, who refers to Mary Douglas). A more appropriate metaphor may therefore be that of the flowering of a seed implanted into the soil of a particular culture. This is also the metaphor AG 22 employs (without, of course, explicitly using the term "inculturation").

Sixth, since culture is an all-embracing reality, inculturation is also all-embracing. EN 20 could still state that the reign of God makes use only of "certain elements of human culture and cultures". It is now, however, recognized that it is impossible to isolate elements and customs and "christianize" these. Where this is being done the encounter between gospel and culture does not take place at a meaningful level (cf Gensichen 1985:124f). Only where the encounter is inclusive will this experience be a force animating and renewing the culture from within (cf Müller 1987:178).

The Limits of Inculturation

Inculturation also has a *critical* dimension. The faith and its cultural expression—even if it is neither possible nor prudent to dislodge the one from the other—are never completely coterminous. Inculturation does not mean that culture is to be destroyed and something new built up on its ruins; neither, however, does it suggest that a particular culture is merely to be endorsed in its present form (cf Gensichen 1985:125f). The philosophy that "anything goes" as long as it seems to make sense to people can be catastrophic.

Of course, the churches of the West have to say this first to themselves, before they dare say it to and of others. Often in the West the inculturation process has been so "successful" that Christianity has become nothing but the religious dimension of the culture—listening to the church, society hears only the sound of its own music. The West has often domesticated the gospel in its own culture while making it unnecessarily foreign to other cultures. In a very real sense, however, the gospel is foreign to every culture. It will always be a sign of contradiction. But when it is in conflict with a particular culture, for instance of the Third World, it is important to establish whether the tension stems from the gospel itself or from the circumstance that the gospel has been too closely associated with the culture through which the missionary message was mediated at this point in time (cf Geffré 1982:482).

There are two principles at work here, says Walls (1982b), and they operate simultaneously. On the one hand there is the "indigenizing" principle, which affirms that the gospel is at home in every culture and every culture is at home with the gospel. But then there is the "pilgrim" principle, which warns us that the gospel will put us out of step with society—"for that society never existed, in East or West, ancient time or modern, which could absorb the word of Christ painlessly into its system" (:99). Authentic inculturation may indeed view the gospel as the liberator of culture; the gospel can, however, also become culture's prisoner (cf Walls 1982b).

Inculturation's concern, says Pedro Arrupe, is to become "a principle that animates, directs, and unifies the culture, transforming it and remaking it so as to bring about a 'new creation'" (quoted in Shorter 1988:11; cf ITC 1989:143, 155). The focus, then, is on the "new creation", on the transformation of the old, on the plant which, having flowered from its seed, is at the same time something fundamentally new when compared with that seed.

Interculturation

In the nature of the case inculturation can never be a *fait accompli*. One may never use the term "inculturated". Inculturation remains a tentative and continuing process (cf Memorandum 1982:466), not only because cultures are not static but also because the church may be led to discover previously unknown mysteries of the faith. The relationship between the Christian message and culture is a creative and dynamic one, and full of surprises. There is no eternal theology, no *theologia perennis* which may play the referee over "local theologies". In the past, Western theology arrogated to itself the right to be such an arbitrator in respect to Third-World theologies. It implicitly viewed itself as fully indigenized, inculturated, a finished product. We are beginning to realize that this was inappropriate, that Western theologies (plural!) — just as much as all the others — were theologies in the making, theologies in the *process* of being contextualized and indigenized.

This insight has important consequences. We are beginning to realize that all theologies, including those in the West, need one another; they influence, challenge, enrich, and invigorate each other — not least so that Western theologies may be liberated from the "Babylonian captivity" of many centuries. In a very real sense, then, what we are involved in is not just inculturation, but "*inter*culturation" (Joseph Blomjous — cf Shorter 1988:13-16). We need an "exchange of theologies" (Beinert 1983:219), in which Third-World students continue (as they have been doing for a long time) to study in the West but in which Western students also go to study in Third-World contexts, in which one-way traffic, from the West to the East and the South, is superseded, first by bilateral and then by multilateral relationships.[22] Where this happens, the old dichotomies are transcended and the churches of the West discover, to their amazement, that they are not simply benefactors and those of the South and the East not merely beneficiaries, but that all are, at the same time, giving and receiving, that a kind of osmosis is taking place (cf Jansen Schoonhoven 1977:172-194; Bühlmann 1977:383-394). This calls for a new disposition, particularly on the part of the West and Western missionaries (and perhaps increasingly also on the part of missionaries from the South to the West!), who have to rethink the necessity and blessedness of receiving, of being genuinely teachable. The missionary, Daniel Fleming said almost seventy years ago, must realize that he or she is "temporary, secondary and advisory" (quoted in Hutchison 1987:151). This does not make missionaries redundant or unimportant. They will remain, also in the future, living symbols of the universality of the church as a body that transcends all boundaries, cultures, and languages. But they will, far more than has been the case in the past, be ambassadors sent from one church to the other, a living embodiment of mutual solidarity and partnership.

Interculturation assumes, furthermore, that local incarnations of the faith should not be *too* local. On the one hand, a "homogeneous unit" church can become so ingrown that it finds it impossible to communicate with other churches and believes that its perspective on the gospel is the only legitimate one. The church must be a place to feel at home; but if only *we* feel at home in our particular church, and all others are either excluded or made unwelcome or feel themselves completely alienated, something has gone wrong (cf Walls 1982b). On the other hand, we may be tempted to over-celebrate an infinite number of differences in the emergence of pluralistic local theologies and claim that not just each local worshiping community but even each pastor and church member may develop her or his own "local theology" (cf Stackhouse 1988:23, 115f). Over against these positions it has to be said that our churches and worshiping communities also have to be de-provincialized (:116). This can only happen if vital contact with the wider church is nurtured. While acting locally we have to think globally, in terms of the *una sancta*, combining a micro- with a macro-perspective. It is true that the church exists primarily in *particular* churches (LG 23), but it is also true that it is *in virtue of the church's catholicity* (cf LG 13) that the particular churches exist — and this holds true not only for the Roman Catholic Church as an international ecclesiastical structure, but for all those communities that call themselves "Christian". If the church is the Body of Christ it can only be one. In this sense, then — and not as an idealistic supra-cultural entity — the church is a kind of "universal hermeneutical community, in which Christians and theologians from different lands check one another's cultural biases" (Hiebert 1985b:16). Particularity does not mean isolation; so, even if we may celebrate our various local theologies, let us remember that it is equally true that "any theology is a discourse about a universal message" (Gutiérrez 1988:xxxvi). This discourse certainly leads to tension, but it can be a creative tension if we pursue the model of "unity within reconciled diversity" (H. Meyer, reference in Sundermeier 1986:98). If we follow this road, our understanding of mission and church will indeed be qualitatively different from all earlier models, while we will at the same time experience vital communion with those former epochs.

MISSION AS COMMON WITNESS

The (Re)birth of the Ecumenical Idea in Mission

I have called the emerging theological paradigm "ecumenical" (see the title of this chapter). This leitmotif has been *implicit* throughout this entire chapter. It is now necessary to make it more *explicit*.

As far as Protestantism is concerned, the ecumenical idea was a direct result of the various awakenings and the subsequent involvement of churches from the West in the worldwide missionary enterprise. The first clear example of this was the emergence of the Pietist movement at the beginning of the eighteenth century. Lutherans, Calvinists, and Anglicans in Germany, Scandinavia, the Netherlands, and Britain experienced a newfound unity of Christians, which transcended denominational differences, and felt urged to involve themselves in a new, trans-denominational missionary movement (cf Rosenkranz 1977:168). The ecumenical spirit manifested itself, for example, in the bible societies and, at the end of the nineteenth century, in youth movements such as the YMCA, YWCA, and WSCF. But it was especially in the foreign missionary movement that the ecumenical idea thrived. Several of the earliest mission societies were non- or transdenominational. One may, for instance, think of the LMS, the American Board, the Basel and the Barmen Missionary Societies. Others, such as the Berlin Missionary Society, were only mildly confessional (cf Rosenkranz 1977:198).

By the third decade of the nineteenth century, however, the fervor for both mission and cooperation had declined. A new and often fierce denomination-alism took its place. The signals were, in fact, there almost from the beginning of the Awakenings. The LMS (1795) was deliberately formed as a nondenom-inational society, but only four years later the Anglicans withdrew to found the (denominational) CMS. The LMS itself also gradually evolved into a denomi-national society (of the Congregational Church), as did the American Board on the other side of the Atlantic. On the continent, Lutherans increasingly experienced difficulties with the "mixed" nature of the Basel Mission Society; in 1836 the Leipzig Mission Society was formed on a confessional Lutheran basis, as an alternative to the Basel society (cf chapter 9).

This meant, of course, that it was no longer only "the Glorious Gospel of the blessed God" (one of the "fundamental principles" of the LMS) that was exported to other lands, but Lutheranism, Presbyterianism, Anglicanism, and the like. On the "mission fields" it inevitably led to rivalry and competition, often on a large scale. This was particularly evident in China, traditionally the "darling of Protestant missions". Already in 1855 twenty Protestant societies were working in China's six port cities. By 1925 there were 130 societies oper-ating in all of China (Rosenkranz 1977:210). It was only to be expected that such a state of affairs would have very negative effects and lead to incredible confusion. As recently as 1953 Beaver could still write: "The non Roman-Catholic missionary enterprise appears as a chaotic conglomeration of unre-lated, overlapping, often competing units seemingly incapable of common plan-ning and action" (quoted in Hoekendijk 1967a:332f, note 66).

Prior to the last quarter of the nineteenth century the only new form of ecumenism evolving in Protestantism was that of global confessional alliances, for such churches as the Lutheran, Presbyterian, Methodist, and Anglican. On the mission fields, however, a degree of mutual acceptance began to develop. This led to so-called comity agreements, according to which the areas to be evangelized were subdivided among different mission agencies. A kind of denominationalism by geography resulted. Of course, this only worked in the case of those denominations willing to waive their claim to absoluteness and usually excluded any agreement with Roman Catholics and Anglicans. The aims were laudable, but purely pragmatic—to avoid competition, to realize better stewardship of resources, and to provide more effective witness to non-Chris-tians (cf Anderson 1988:102). This was also the purpose of the first conferences, on the mission fields, of representatives from various mission agencies.

In the course of time these pragmatic considerations, quite unintentionally, led to the rediscovery of a basic theological *datum*: the oneness of the church of Christ. In the last two decades of the nineteenth century, then, the scene changed dramatically, with the emergence first of the international student movement, then of the international missionary movement and, early in the twentieth century, with the first hesitant steps toward a global and inclusive ecumenical movement. The most important milestone in this regard was the 1910 World Missionary Conference in Edinburgh. Because of its pragmatic agenda (it was essentially a "how to" conference), Edinburgh succeeded to a remarkable degree in transcending denominational differences (cf Scherer 1968:20).

In spite of its pragmatic nature, Karl Barth (1961:37f) hailed the movement that began at Edinburgh as a fundamental ecclesiological breakthrough. Earlier, church unity had been understood as the result of reaching doctrinal consensus via theological debate, but *the world was ignored*; in the new style, the interest in church unity was motivated by a *concern for the world*. Still, "ecumenism new style" was present only in embryo at Edinburgh. Martin Kähler was one of the first to grasp the theological significance of unity; he regarded church unity as an expression of faith and disunity as a manifestation of unbelief. In a letter to John Mott, Kähler ([1910] 1971:259) referred to the strife between churches as a *"Zerrissenheit"* ("disruption") on a par with that caused by the absence of faith. Two years earlier ([1908] 1971:179) he had commented that the deficit of unity in mission was far more pressing than any financial deficits the societies might be experiencing. And as early as 1899 he had written — almost with melancholy — that Jesus' prayer in John 17:21 had not yet been answered: "So far the Lord has *not* led his people on *this* road toward the victory of faith" ([1899] 1971:462 — my translation).

Edinburgh 1910 suggested, without spelling it out, that authentic unity could not be had without authentic mission, without an open window toward the world. In the course of time those first halting steps toward unity in mission and mission in unity would lead to the conviction that it is impossible to choose in favor either of unity or of mission: "The only possible choice for the Church, or any part of the Church, is *for or against both*" (Saayman 1984:127 — italics in original).

The International Missionary Council, founded in 1921, which provided the non–Roman Catholic world with its first organ of international and interconfessional cooperation (cf Neill 1968:107), was the first tangible expression of the new paradigm. It was soon to be followed by two other movements, which could also trace their origins to Edinburgh 1910: *Faith and Order* and *Life and Work*. The latter two merged in 1948 to form the World Council of Churches. The dichotomy between unity and mission — epitomized in the existence, side by side, of the WCC (a council of churches) and the IMC (a council of societies) — increasingly came under pressure. A WCC Central Committee meeting at Rolle in Switzerland (1951) reflected on "the calling of the church to mission and to unity" (cf Saayman 1984:14f). It recognized that it was inconceivable to divorce the obligation of the church to take the gospel to the whole world from its obligation to draw all Christ's people together; both were viewed as essential to the being of the church and the fulfillment of its function as the Body of Christ. It was also urged that the word "ecumenical" should be used "to describe everything that relates to the whole task of the whole Church to bring the Gospel to the whole world".

The dichotomy — on the global structural level — between unity and mission was overcome only at the WCC's New Delhi assembly (1961), where the IMC integrated with the WCC. Whatever criticism one might have about the way the integration took place, there can be no doubt that a crucial *theological* point was made: unity and mission belong together. The rediscovery of the essentially missionary nature of the church could not but lead to the discovery that the Christian mission could only be truly called Christian if it was borne by the *one* church of Christ. This "discovery" confirms an age-old tenet of (Eastern) Orthodoxy. Since mission and unity belong together, we may not view them as consecutive stages; if this is not consistently kept in mind, we would only be converting people to our own "denomination" while at the same time administering to them the poison of division (Nissiotis 1968:198). It is through the universality of the gospel it proclaims that the church becomes missionary (Frazier 1987:13). To say that the church is catholic is another way of saying that it is essentially missionary (cf Berkouwer 1979:105-107). Therefore, to claim — as some do — that the ecumenical age has now taken the place of the age of mission, is to misunderstand both; and to neglect one of the two is to lose both (Linz 1974:4f).

It was this theological perspective that stood behind the decision of the WCC New Delhi Assembly (1961) to integrate the IMC with the WCC. Newbigin, speaking to the Assembly, said, "For the churches which constitute the World Council this means the acknowledgment that the missionary task is no less central to the life of the church than the pursuit of renewal and unity" (WCC 1961:4). In keeping with the new insight, New Delhi amended the WCC's "basis". Originally, it had identified itself as "a fellowship of churches which *accept* our Lord Jesus Christ as God and Savior". At New Delhi, "accept" was changed to "confess". At the same time the words "and therefore seek to fulfil together their common calling to the glory of one God, Father, Son and Holy Spirit" were added (cf WCC 1961:152-159). The "common calling" was understood to refer to "confess" and thus had a clear missionary thrust, something that was absent in the original basis (cf also WCC 1961:116, 121, 257). Neill (1968:108) calls this decision "a revolutionary moment in Church history". He adds,

> More than two hundred Church bodies in all parts of the world . . . had solemnly declared themselves in the presence of God to be responsible as Churches for the evangelization of the whole world. Such an event had never taken place in the history of the Church since Pentecost (:108f).

The Nairobi Assembly (1975) endorsed the New Delhi perspective. The Section Report, "What Unity Requires", formulated this as follows: "The purpose for which we are called to unity is 'that the world may believe'. A quest for unity which is not set in the context of Christ's promise to draw all people to himself would be false" (WCC 1976:64).

ME 1 also makes mention of the "inextricable relationship between Christian unity and missionary calling, between ecumenism and evangelization". The San Antonio CWME meeting (1989) took up the same theme and interpreted, "Christian mission is the humble involvement of the *one* body of Christ in liberating and suffering love" (Section I.10; WCC 1990:27), and "To be called to unity in mission involves becoming a community that transcends in its life the barriers and brokenness in the world, and living as a sign of at-one-ment under the cross" (I.11; WCC 1990:28).

Whether the vision of New Delhi, Nairobi, ME, and San Antonio is being realized is a question that cannot be pursued here. The goal of *structural* church unity ("in one faith and in one eucharistic fellowship" [Vancouver – cf WCC 1983:43-52]), it would appear, has in recent years been put on the back burner. Also, many would say that the ecumenical movement and many member churches of the WCC have virtually lost their missionary vision (depending, of course, on how one defines "mission"). This may be true, or partially true. Even so, there can be little doubt that the WCC and its member churches are giving expression to a notion that is fundamental to the Christian faith: the indissoluble link between unity and mission (cf Saayman 1984:112-116, 127).

Many evangelical agencies withdrew from the wider ecumenical movement after the New Delhi integration of the IMC into the WCC. And few evangelical denominations have joined the WCC. This does not mean that all evangelicals are anti-ecumenical. It simply means that the ecumenical movement is wider than the WCC. There is today an evangelical ecumenical movement which operates in its own right and which runs from Wheaton 1966 and Berlin 1966 via Lausanne 1974 to Manila 1989. The evangelical emphasis on unity differs in a significant respect from the ecumenical understanding, however. Evangelicals tend to regard unity as something almost exclusively *spiritual* and as an attribute of the *invisible* church. Where "visible" unity is mentioned it tends to be stressed only for the sake of more effective evangelism and not as non-negotiable theological premise. LC 7, for instance, states: "Evangelism also summons us to unity, because our oneness strengthens our witness, just as our disunity undermines our gospel of reconciliation". The concern is for a pragmatic unity, involving planning, mutual encouragement, and the sharing of resources and experiences. It is further circumscribed by a heavy emphasis on doctrinal purity. At the Pattaya Conference (1980) of the Lausanne Committee for World Evangelization, for instance, a suggestion that the LCWE should be open to fraternal relationship with anybody "in sympathy" with the *Lausanne Covenant* was amended to read "in full support of" the Covenant. Such a mentality easily leads to the situation where instead of witnessing to people who are not Christians, one witnesses against Christians whose priorities differ from one's own. By and large, then, the paradigm shift which is in evidence in the ecumenical movement is absent among evangelicals.

Catholics, Mission, and Ecumenism

Developments in Catholicism have – if anything – been even more dramatic than in Protestantism. This is illustrated, for example, by the change in the way official Roman Catholic documents refer to Protestants. From being called "children of Satan" and "heretics" or "schismatics", the appellations for Protestants have been modified to refer to "dissenters", "separated brethren", and eventually, "brothers and sisters in Christ" (cf Auf der Maur 1970:88f; van der Aalst 1974:197). The foundations for the earlier position had been laid firmly at the Council of Trent. The restoration of Catholicism manifested itself as

Counter-Reformation. The very word "mission" had an anti-Protestant ring to it; not least since the term "mission" in the sense of "propagation of the faith" first surfaced as designation for the Jesuit settlements in northern Germany, where their task was to reconvert Protestants (Glazik 1984b:29). After the founding of *Propaganda Fide* (1622), and, in fact, until about 1830, the main focus of the *Propaganda* was on calling Protestants back to the true faith. And the missionary encyclicals of the twentieth century, from *Maximum Illud* (1919) to *Fidei Donum* (1957), were unashamedly anti-Protestant (cf Auf der Maur 1970:83f). *Rerum Ecclesiae* (1926), for instance, referred to the importance of calling "the separated brethren back to the unity of the church" and of "tearing away non-Catholics from their errors" (cf Auf der Maur 1970:85). Even the joint praying of the Lord's Prayer, for instance, was proscribed for Catholics until 1949. Because of the paradigm shift from Catholicism to Protestantism — says Pfürtner (1984:179) — two different "linguistic communities" came into existence; their followers, even where they used the same words, no longer meant the same by them.

Against this background the events of Vatican II were little short of a miracle. A new spirit permeated virtually all the proceedings and documents of the Council. It is true that the use of the term "church" remains ambiguous (sometimes it clearly refers to the Roman Catholic Church; sometimes, however, it seems to have a wider reference), but there can be no doubt that Vatican II spoke about the church in a manner very different from what had been customary. LG 15 states categorically that those "who are sealed by baptism which unites them to Christ . . . are indeed in some real way joined to us in the Holy Spirit". In light of the guidelines of AG 15 it has, furthermore, become impossible to continue to regard non-Catholic Christians as objects of mission.

It was, however, especially the Decree on Ecumenism (*Unitatis Redintegratio*) that spoke in clear language about the need for improved relations and mutual acceptance. Crumley describes its adoption by the Council as "the most important single event in the somewhat checkered history of the ecumenical movement" (1989:146). In its first paragraph it describes "the restoration of unity among all Christians" as one of the principal concerns of the Council and states that division among Christians "contradicts the will of Christ, scandalizes the world, and damages that most holy cause, the preaching of the Gospel to every creature". AG 6 takes up the same theme and intimately links the unity of the church to its mission. All baptized people are called upon to come together in one flock, that they might bear unanimous witness to Christ their Lord before the nations. The Decree goes on to say, "And if they cannot yet fully bear witness to one faith, they should at least be imbued with mutual respect and love". Frequently (in paragraphs 3 and 19 to 23), the Decree on Ecumenism has subtly changed the (already less judgmental) "separated brethren" to "the brethren divided (or separated) from us", drawing attention to the fact that the separation had been mutual (cf Auf der Maur 1970:89). The Council's Declaration on Religious Freedom (*Dignitatis Humanae*) and Pope John XXIII's creating the Secretariat for Promoting Christian Unity set the seal on this entire development, which was also welcomed by the WCC (cf Meeking 1987:5-7).

Vatican II together with recent developments in Protestantism hailed the advent of a new era (cf Saayman 1984:33-67). After the Council the Catholic Church proceeded further on its new road (:67-70). EN 77 (published 1975) insists on "a collaboration marked by a greater commitment to the Christian brethren with whom we are not yet united in *perfect unity*" (emphasis added). Dialogue projects between the Catholic Church and various other confessional communities, including evangelicals, are today part and parcel of the ecclesial scene. In 1980 John Paul II called Martin Luther "a witness to the message of faith and justification". On December 11, 1983, he praised Luther in a Lutheran Church. The two "linguistic communities" (Pfürtner) were at long last beginning to understand and even speak each other's language. Controversy and confrontation have made room for ecumenical encounter. And the Reformation doctrine of justification by faith alone is no longer regarded as ground for separation (cf Pfürtner 1984:168; Crumley 1989:147).

The new term, which enunciates the ideas of both unity and mission and which found expression in various study documents, is "common witness" (cf Common Witness 1984; see also Meeking 1987 and Spindler 1987). The impulse to a common witness, it is claimed, does not flow from any strategy; rather, "awareness of the communion with Christ and with each other generates the dynamism that impels Christians to give a visible witness together" (Common Witness 1). The renewal the Holy Spirit spawns in Christians and in their communities "centres in Christ and calls forth a new obedience and a new way of life which is itself a witnessing communion" (Common Witness 13). The "striking and clear convergences" on evangelism which emerged from Bangkok (1973), the Lausanne Congress (1974), and *Evangelii Nuntiandi* (1975) are applauded (Common Witness 11). Spindler (1987:20; cf Meeking 1987:9-17) rightly makes mention of "the tremendous reality" and "emerging tradition" of common witness. Not that the idea is without problems. Common witness is still extremely rare in the area of evangelism, and particularly insofar as mission is defined almost exclusively as "church planting" (cf Auf der Maur 1970:97; Spindler 1987:21, 25). Also, what is written in church documents or joint statements is not necessarily practiced at the local level, where it really matters. In addition, ecumenism seems to have lost much of its momentum. In light of all this we are at the moment, at best, involved in "intermediate ecumenism" (Spindler 1987:26f).

Unity in Mission; Mission in Unity

At his enthronement as Archbishop of Canterbury in 1942, William Temple referred to the existence of a worldwide Christianity as "the great new fact of our time" (quoted in Neill 1966a:15). Intimately related to this, says Jansen Schoonhoven, is a second "great new fact of our time": the ecumenical movement, in all its forms. It was a Roman Catholic, W. H. van de Pol, who, in 1948, alluded to the formation of the WCC as "something absolutely new in history". In 1960 another Catholic, M. J. le Guillou, called the WCC "a community of a fundamentally new type, without precedent in history" (references in Jansen Schoonhoven 1974b:7f — my translation).

Since Vatican II much the same can be said about Catholicism. It has become impossible to say "church" without at the same time saying "mission"; by the same token it has become impossible to say "church" or "mission" without at the same time talking about the *one* mission of the *one* church. This represents a paradigm shift of momentous proportions. It did not come about because of the accumulation of new (and better!) insights, but because of a new self-understanding (cf Pfürtner 1984:184). It is part of the new search for wholeness and unity and for overcoming dualism and dividedness (Daecke 1988:630f). It is not the result of lazy tolerance, indifference, and relativism but of a new grasp of what being Christians in the world is all about. For this reason, all the unions of churches that have been taking place since the 1920s and all the national "councils of churches" that have been formed during the past half century or so, only make sense if they serve the *missio Dei*. Ecumenism is not a passive and semi-reluctant coming together but an active and deliberate living and working together. It is not merely the replacement of hostility by correct but noncommittal politeness.

Let me now attempt to draw some of the contours of the new paradigm.

First, the mutual coordination of mission and unity is *non-negotiable*. It is not simply derived from the new world situation or from changed circumstances, but from God's gift of unity in the one Body of Christ. God's people is one; Christ's Body is one. It is therefore, strictly speaking, an anomaly to refer to the "unity of *churches*"; one can only talk about the "unity of *the church*". As H. de Lubac puts it:

> The Church is not catholic because she is spread abroad over the whole of the earth and can reckon on a large number of members. She was already catholic on the morning of Pentecost, when all her members could be contained in a small room . . . For fundamentally catholicity has nothing to do with geography or statistics . . . Like sanctity, catholicity is primarily an intrinsic feature of the Church (quoted in Frazier 1987:47).

In light of this, we are creating a false dichotomy if we play truth out against unity. A hallmark of Paul's theology was his refusal to entertain the possibility of a disjunction between the truth of the gospel and the divinely willed unity of the church; for him the supreme value was indissolubly this unity and this truth (cf Beker 1980:130; Meyer 1986:169f, note 12).

Second, holding onto both mission and unity and to both truth and unity *presupposes tension*. It does not presume uniformity. The aim is not a levelling out of differences, a shallow reductionism, a kind of ecumenical broth. Our differences are genuine and have to be treated as such. Whenever the church takes seriously its mission in respect to the various human communities which stand in conflict with one another—whether these conflicts are doctrinal, social, or cultural in nature, or due to different life situations and experiences—there is an inner tension which cannot be disregarded. Rather, this tension calls us to repentance. Mission in unity and unity in mission are impossible without a self-critical attitude, particularly where Christians meet with others, fellow-believers or non-believers, who, by human standards, should be their enemies. But this is what the church is for—"to take up the deepest conflicts of the world into itself and to confront both sides there with the forgiving, transforming power which breaks and remakes them into a new community, with a new hope and a new calling" (West 1971:270). Ecumenism is only possible where people accept each other despite differences. Our goal is not a fellowship exempt from conflict, but one which is characterized by unity in reconciled diversity. The modern paradigm, says Daecke (1988:631) suggested that the choice is between diversity without unity or unity without diversity; the postmodern paradigm manifests itself as unity which preserves diversity and diversity which strives after unity. Divergences are not a matter of regret, but part of the struggle within the church to become what God wants it to be (cf NIE 1980:12; Crumley 1989:147).

In the midst of all diversity, however, there is a center: Jesus Christ. When John XXIII opened the Second Vatican Council on October 11, 1962, he spoke on what had remained unaltered after almost two thousand years; namely, that Jesus Christ was still the center of the community and of life. It is this common foundation, this point of orientation, which enables us to engage in joint service and united witness in the world (cf Verstraelen 1988:433). Unity in mission is no lost cause as long as the Bible, which witnesses to this Christ, is opened, read, and proclaimed in all Christian churches (cf de Groot 1988:155). Listening to God's word and listening to each other belong together, however; we can have the first only if we are also prepared to have the second (:163; cf also Küng 1987:81-84).

Third, a united church-in-mission is essential in light of the fact that the church's mission *will never come to an end*. There was an age when it was believed in all sincerity that it was only a matter of time before we would actually complete the missionary task. Much nineteenth-century missionary policy was built on this premise. Today we know that we shall never reach the stage where we can say "mission accomplished!" We know that the world can no longer be subdivided into "sending" and "receiving" countries, between "home base" and "mission field". The home base is everywhere, and so is the mission field. This was the shocking message of Godin and Daniel (1943): France, the "eldest daughter of the church", had again become a mission field. A new "Age of Discovery" had begun for the churches in Europe—not the exploration of new lands overseas, but of the worlds of atheism, secularism, and superstition, of the "new pagans" of Europe (cf Köster 1984:156f). Everywhere the church is in the diaspora, in a situation of mission.

Fourth, mission in unity means an end to *the distinction between "sending" and "receiving" churches*—something for which John Mott called as early as the Jerusalem Conference of 1928 (cf Hutchison 1987:180). Ten years later, Kraemer found it necessary to remind the delegates to the Tambaram Conference that the "younger" churches are the *fruit* of missionary labor, not the *possession* of mission societies ([1938] 1947:426). Many phrases and slogans were conceived to give expression to the need for new relationships: "three-selfs", "partnership in obedience", "living as comrades", "equality", "cooperation", "a fifty-fifty basis", "solidarity". Marvellous phrases! The younger churches, however, experienced most of them as hollow and meaningless. Alluding to the Whitby (1947) slogan, an Indonesian pastor once trenchantly remarked to a Dutch professor: "Yes, *partnership* for *you*, but *obedience* for *us!*" (Jansen Schoonhoven 1977:48). It is, however, useless to talk about the "autonomy of the younger churches" (quite apart from the question whether one may *ever* refer to *any* church's "autonomy"!) while leaving existing structural patterns intact. No superficial modernization of missionary policies or adaptation to the current practices and techniques of the West will effect any fundamental changes (cf Rütti 1974:291). This applies not only to Protestants but also to Catholics; there, too, the relationship between the churches in the West and those in the Third World is often still shot through with paternalism (cf Rosenkranz 1977:431-434). For the sake of unity and of mission, we need new relationships, mutual responsibility, accountability, and interdependence (not independence!) — not just because the Western church is now operating in the context of a world in which the West's dominance, numerically and otherwise, appears to have ended definitely, but rather because there can be no "higher" or "lower" in the Body of Christ.

Fifth, if we accept the validity of mission-in-unity we cannot but take a stand against the *proliferation of new churches*, which are often formed on the basis of extremely questionable distinctions. This Protestant virus may no longer be tolerated as though it is the most natural thing in the world for a group of people to start their own church, which mirrors their foibles, fears, and suspicions, nurtures their prejudices, and makes them feel comfortable and relaxed. If Wagner (1979) is praised (on the dust cover of his book) for having transformed "the statement that '11 A.M. on Sunday is the most segregated hour in America' from a millstone around Christian necks into a dynamic tool for assuring Christian growth", then something is drastically wrong. The apostle Paul sought to build communities in which, right from the start, Jew and Greek, slave and free, poor and rich, would worship together, learn to love one another, and learn to deal with difficulties arising out of their diverse social, cultural, religious, and economic backgrounds. This belongs to the essence of the church. By contrast, the essence of heresy, says Hoekendijk, is the "fundamental refusal to participate in a common history" (1967a:348). There is a tendency in Protestantism to stress the vertical relationship between God and the individual in such a way that it is distinct from the horizontal relationship between people; however, the "vertical line" is also a covenant line with the community (cf Samuel and Sugden 1986:195). Theologically — and practically — this means that christology is incomplete without ecclesiology (:192f) and without Pneumatology (cf Kramm 1979:218f; Memorandum 1982:461). We cannot speak about Christ, the Lord and Savior, without speaking about his Body — his liberated and saved community. By the same token, the Spirit, in the New Testament dispensation, is not given to individuals, but to the community. If our mission is to be christological and pneumatological, it also has to be ecclesial, in the sense of being the *one* mission of the *one* church.

Sixth, ultimately unity in mission and mission in unity do not merely serve the church but, through the church, stand in the service of *humankind* and seek to manifest *the cosmic rule of Christ* (cf Saayman 1984:21-55). The church (but only insofar as it is the *one* church) is "the sign of the coming unity of mankind" (Uppsala, Section I.20 – WCC 1968:17). The 1989 San Antonio Conference of CWME concurs: "The church is called again and again to be a prophetic sign and foretaste of the unity and renewal of the human family as envisioned in God's promised reign" (Section I.11; WCC 1990:28). The reign of God is not only the *church*'s final fulfillment but also the *world*'s future (Limouris 1986:169).

Lastly, we have to confess that the *loss of ecclesial unity is not just a vexation but a sin.* Unity is not an optional extra. It is, in Christ, already a fact, a given. At the same time it is a command: "Be one!" We are called to be one as the Father, the Son, and the Spirit are one, and we should never tire of striving toward that day when Christians in every place may gather to share the One Bread and the One Cup (cf Crumley 1989:146, 149). At the moment, this appears to be nothing more than an eschatological lightning on a distant horizon. Both the "world church" and the "unity of humankind" are, in a sense, fictions. But both fictions are indispensable if we wish to do justice to what it means to be church and to live creatively and missionally in the face of the eschatological tension which belongs to our very being as Christians (cf Hoedemaker 1988:174).

MISSION AS MINISTRY BY THE WHOLE PEOPLE OF GOD

The Evolution of the Ordained Ministry

The movement away from ministry as the monopoly of ordained men to ministry as the responsibility of the whole people of God, ordained as well as non-ordained, is one of the most dramatic shifts taking place in the church today. Boerwinkel (1974:54-64) has identified the "institutionalization of church offices" as one of the characteristics of the Constantinian dispensation and the contemporary "laicization" of the church as indicative of the end of Constantinianism. Moltmann (1975:11), in addressing the task of church and theology in our time, formulates six theses, one of which reads: "Christian theology . . . will no longer be simply a theology for priests and pastors, but also a theology for the laity in their callings in the world".

The crisis we are facing in respect to ministry is part and parcel of the crisis church and mission face in this time of paradigm shifts, when virtually every traditional element of faith and polity is under severe pressure. For almost nineteen centuries and in virtually all ecclesiastical traditions ministry has been understood almost exclusively in terms of the service of ordained ministers. In order to grasp something of the magnitude of the shift that is now taking place and its significance for the mission of the church today, it will be necessary to survey, very briefly, the developments that have led to the present impasse.

There can be no doubt that Jesus of Nazareth broke with the entire Jewish tradition when he chose his disciples not from among the priestly class, but from among fisherfolk, tax-collectors, and the like. This was part of his "wineskin-breaking ministry", of the "reversal" feature in Jesus' teaching, of turning the proprieties of the time upside down by going contrary to normal human expectations (cf Burrows 1981:44f). I have argued, in chapter 1 of this study, that the Jesus movement began as a renewal movement within Judaism, not as a separate religion. This may be the reason why the terminology used for the movement and its members was borrowed neither from Jewish nor (after the movement consciously began to recruit non-Jews) from Greek religious culture. The main word for the community, *ekklesia*, was a term from the secular sphere. Meeks (1983:81) draws attention to the fact that the Pauline churches are not called "synagogues". Neither, in fact, are they called *thiasoi*, the common Greek word for cultic or religious meetings. The believers simply "gather" (cf 1 Cor 11:17, 18, 20, 33, 34; 14:23, 26), mostly in private homes (cf Beker 1980:319). Indeed, the *household* may be regarded as the basic unit in the establishment of Christianity in any city (Meeks 1983:29). The church has offices—if we wish to call them that—particularly those of *episkopos*, *presbyteros*, and *diakonos* (all of them secular terms). But, first, these offices are always understood as existing within the community of faith, as never being prior to, independent of, or above the local church (cf de Gruchy 1987:27), and, second, it would be grossly inaccurate simply to plug these terms into a later sacral-juridical understanding of ecclesiastical office (Burrows 1981:77, drawing upon H. von Campenhausen and H. Conzelmann). Most of the "leaders" in the early church are charismatic figures, natural leaders, both men and women.

By the eighties of the first century AD it was, however, clear that Christianity had become a new religion and could no longer be contained within Judaism. This also meant that the terminology used by adherents of the new faith was increasingly understood in a strictly religious sense. The church now had to cope with heresy from without and a hollowing-out of faith from within. In these circumstances the most reliable antidote appeared to have been to encourage believers to follow the directives of the clergy, in particular the bishops, who soon—particularly because of the writings and influence of Ignatius and Cyprian—were regarded as the sole guarantors of the apostolic tradition and the ones endowed with full authority in matters ecclesiastical. Henceforth the ordained minister would hold a dominant and undisputed position in church life, a situation that was further bolstered by the doctrines of apostolic succession, the "indelible character" conferred on priests in the rite of ordination, and the infallibility of the pope.

The clericalizing of the church went hand in hand with the sacerdotalizing of the clergy. Apart from a questionable reference in Ignatius, the term "priest" was not applied to Christian clergy until around the year 200. After that the term, and the theology behind it, was the "received view", strengthened by an elaborate "sacrament of holy orders", which gave the ordinand the power to represent sacramentally the sacrifice of Christ and brought about a mystical and ontological change in the soul of the priest (cf Burrows 1981:61). At the same time it cut off the priest from the community, putting him over against it as a mediation figure and as a kind of *alter Christus* ("another Christ") (:60, 88). The priest had *active* power to consecrate, forgive sins, and bless; "ordinary" Christians, enabled thereto by their baptism, had only a *passive* role to play, namely, to *receive* grace (:105). The church consisted of two clearly distinct categories of people: the clergy and the laity (from *laos*, "people [of God]"), the latter understood as immature, not come of age, and utterly dependent on the clergy in matters religious.

It was inevitable that, in this arrangement, it would be believed that the church's sole business was the sacred (even if clergy, in particular bishops, often wielded secular power!). In reviewing the five models of the church identified by Dulles (1976), Burrows (1981:38) points out that all of them (the church as institution, mystical communion, sacrament, herald, and servant) actually understand the church almost exclusively as a means of communicating grace and thus reinforce the sacerdotal picture of the church. The church is a community mainly concerned with mediating eternal salvation to individuals. The ordained ministry is the primary vehicle for that work, so the shape of the church is built around it (:61f).

As the hegemony of the Catholic Church was not disputed in medieval Europe, it became customary for the church to understand itself as the actual kingdom of God on earth. The simple sociological fact at work here is that any dominant religion tends to adopt this sort of position. In this case, the Catholic Church viewed itself as stocked with a supply of heavenly graces which the clerical proprietors could disburse to customers. When, in the sixteenth century, its supremacy was challenged by the Protestant Reformation, it reacted (in the Council of Trent) by dismissing the Protestant claims out of hand. At the same time it embarked on "mission", an activity of a corps of "specialists", priests and religious, authorized by the pope to extend the church's hegemony to other parts of the world. In those countries, ecclesiastical structures identical to those on the "home front" were erected and an analogous leadership cadre installed.

The question is whether *Protestants* have really done any better. It is true that Luther is to be credited with the rediscovery of the notion of the "priesthood of all believers". In his thesis that "the Christian . . . congregation has the right and power to judge all teaching and to call, install and dismiss teachers" (quoted in Pfürtner 1984:184 — my translation), Luther most certainly broke with the dominant paradigm. However, when Luther's understanding of church and theology was under assault from Anabaptists (some of whom had jettisoned the idea of an ordained ministry altogether) and Catholics alike, he reverted to the inherited paradigm. In the end, he still had the clergyman at the center of his church, endowed with considerable authority (cf Burrows 1981:104).

The other Reformers and their heirs followed Luther in this. To be sure, they rejected Catholicism's sanctioning of the form of the priesthood as it had stood at the end of the fourth century and settled, instead, for the shape the offices had taken at the close of the formation of the New Testament. The key to this was the "threefold office of Christ" — King, Prophet, and Priest — which, in the Protestant view, had clearly crystallized in the three offices of pastor, elder, and deacon. Instead of showing appreciation for the fact that, in the early stages, these offices had evolved only to a rudimentary degree, they took them to be explicitly instated by Christ and therefore immutable. In practice, most denominations in mainline Protestantism today are muddling along with an understanding of the ordained ministry vacillating between the traditional Reformation definition and a view closer to that of Catholicism. On the other hand, many evangelical denominations, which tend to follow a congregationalist polity, are struggling to avoid one of two pitfalls: either the minister becomes a little pope whose word is law, or the congregation regards him as their employee who has to dance to their tune.

The net result was not fundamentally different from the dominant Catholic view. The church remained a strictly sacral society run by an in-house personnel. Only, the focus for the "cure of souls" was not, as in Catholicism, the sacraments but the proclamation of the word of God (cf de Gruchy 1987:18, on Bonhoeffer). For the rest, what Protestants and Catholics shared regarding the role of the ordained ministry was far more significant than their disagreements — in both traditions the clergyman-priest, enshrined in a privileged and central position, remained the linchpin of the church (cf Burrows 1981:61, 74). With the increasing specialization of theological training, the elitist character of the "clerical paradigm" was further reinforced (cf Farley 1983:85-88). Like Catholic missions, Protestant missions as a matter of course exported their dominant clergy pattern to the "mission fields", imposing it on others as the only legitimate and appropriate model, clothing David in Saul's armor, and making it impossible for the young church either to execute its particular ministry or to survive without help from outside.

It was highly unlikely that any change would appear in the dominant pattern until a transformation of profound proportions would manifest itself in both church and society. This is what has begun to happen in our time, in respect of the rediscovery of the "apostolate of the laity" or the "priesthood of all believers".

The Apostolate of the Laity

Catholic missions have always had a significant lay involvement. Their participation in the missionary enterprise was, however, clearly auxiliary and firmly under the control and jurisdiction of the clergy. In Protestant missions the prospects were more auspicious, particularly as the "voluntary principle" (see chapter 9) gained momentum.

Actually, from the very beginning Protestant missions were, to a significant extent, a lay movement. The voluntary societies were not restricted to ecclesiastics. Normally there were clergy involved in the founding of mission societies but they were often, as in the case of the CMS, clerical nobodies, who usually cooperated closely with prominent laypersons (Walls 1988:150). Walls (:142) describes the societies as free, open, responsible, embracing all classes, both sexes, all ages, the masses of the people — a truly democratic and anti-authoritarian movement, to some extent also anti-clergy and anti-establishment. North American societies, in particular, attracted large numbers of women. In some instances, women founded their own mission societies (by 1890 there were thirty-four of these in North America alone) and periodicals, and raised their own support (cf Anderson 1988:102f). On the "mission fields", even in the case of societies run by men, women were soon the majority (cf Hutchison 1987:101).

And they did all the things men used to do, including preaching (excluding the administering of the sacraments, of course).

After World War II the "home front" slowly began to catch up. It dawned upon the churches, both Catholic and Protestant, that the traditional monolithic models of church office no longer matched realities. The theological *aggiornamento* in both main Western confessions discovered again that apostolicity was an attribute of the entire church and that the ordained ministry could be understood only as existing within the community of faith.

In various ways Vatican II gave expression to the new theological and societal mood and to a new awareness about the central role of the laity in the church, particularly in respect to the church's missionary calling. The mood was, in this respect, fundamentally different from that of several earlier councils. Y. Congar has noted that words repeatedly used in Vatican II had never been used by Vatican I—words like *amor* ("love") 113 times, and *laicus* ("layperson") 200 times (quoted in Gómez 1986:57). LG 33 states: "The apostolate of the laity is a sharing in the salvific mission of the Church. Through Baptism and Confirmation all are appointed to this apostolate by the Lord himself." It adds that the laity have "the exalted duty of working for the ever greater spread of the divine plan of salvation to all people of every epoch and all over the earth". AG 28 (cf LG 12) urges every member of the church "to collaborate in the work of the Gospel, each according to his opportunity, ability, charism and ministry". It even states categorically (AG 21), "The Church is not truly established and does not fully live, nor is it a perfect sign of Christ unless there is a genuine laity existing and working alongside the hierarchy". The *Decree on the Pastoral Office of Bishops* defines bishops primarily as pastors, not as "holders of the fullness of priestly power" (cf Burrows 1981:109). Most important, however, Vatican II produced *Apostolicam Actuositatem*, the *Decree on the Apostolate of Lay People*, a document which describes the laity preeminently in terms of the church's *mission*, having the "right and duty to be apostles" (paragraph 3).

Not that all problems were suddenly solved. Far from it! Vatican II still refers to laypersons as "auxiliaries" of the "sacred ministries" (cf Gómez 1986:51). Also in other respects the old dichotomy between clergy and laity seems to be firmly upheld, so much so that Boff (1986:30) maintains that, in spite of Vatican II, the participation of the faithful in decision-making is totally mutilated. It seems, in fact, as if the tension between the "top" and the "base" has been increasing rather than decreasing in recent years, as more and more base communities, so-called "ecclesias", "critical congregations", and the like are being formed within the Catholic Church (cf Blei 1980:1). There is, on the part of the hierarchy, a certain apprehension about the consequences of according a larger role to the laity, a fear of what N. Lash (quoted in de Gruchy 1987:35) has called "the rediscovery of the 'congregationalist' element in Catholicism" (cf also Burrows 1981:39f; Michiels 1989:106f).

In respect to the laity, post-Vatican Catholicism thus reveals both old and new versions of ecclesiology. It is not essentially different in Protestantism. This is understandable if one keeps in mind the almost two millennia during which the ordained clergy model persisted unchallenged. The watertight division between the "teaching" church and the "learning" church (the *ecclesia docens* and the *ecclesia discens*), between the active mediating of grace and the passive receiving of grace, is too deep-seated to be expunged without some ado.

Even so, an unmistakable shift is taking place. Laypersons are no longer just the scouts who, returning from the "outside world" with eyewitness accounts and perhaps some bunches of grapes, report to the "operational basis"; they *are* the operational basis from which the *missio Dei* proceeds. It is, in fact, not *they* who have to "accompany" those who hold "special offices" in the *latter's* mission in the world. Rather, it is the *office bearers* who have to accompany the laity, the people of God (cf Hoekendijk 1967a:350). In the New Testament dispensation the Spirit (just as the priesthood) has been given to the whole people of God, not to select individuals. "The clergy, then, come *from the community*, guide it, and act *in Christ's name*" (Moltmann 1977:303).

For it is the *community* that is the primary bearer of mission. The project on the "missionary structure of the congregation", launched by the WCC's New Delhi Assembly in 1961 (a project which, however, to a large extent aborted), together with the rediscovery of the local church in Catholicism, are perhaps — from a missiological perspective — the most far-reaching contributions of the WCC and Vatican II. Mission does not proceed primarily from the pope, nor from a missionary order, society, or synod, but from a community gathered around the word and the sacraments and sent into the world. Therefore the ordained leadership's role cannot possibly be the all-determining factor; it is only one part of the community's total life (Burrows 1981:62). Gradually, churches are beginning to adjust to the new theological insight. The vertical, linear model, running from the pope via the bishop and the priest to the faithful (a model which has its parallels in Protestantism) is gradually being replaced by one in which all are directly involved (cf Boff 1986:30-33).

It goes without saying that a new model of church is of great significance for the entire debate about the ordination of women (cf, among other examples, Burrows 1981:134-137; Boff 1986:76-97). Their ordination is, however, only one component of the issue involved, as is the notion of authorizing laypersons to be directly involved in the celebration of the Lord's Supper (cf Boff 1986:70-75). The problem with this undoubtedly legitimate and crucial debate is that it still suggests that some form of ordained ministry and some form of authority to celebrate the sacraments is the be-all and end-all of what the church is all about.

Forms of Ministry

If it is true, as has been argued throughout this study, that the entire life of the church is missionary, it follows that we desperately need a theology of the laity — something of which only the first rudiments are now emerging. But also, such a theology is only now becoming possible again, as we are moving out of the massive shadow of the Enlightenment. For a theology of the laity presupposes a break with the notion, so fundamental to the Enlightenment, that the private sphere of life has to be separated from the public (cf also Newbigin 1986:142f). Moltmann, in his thesis that the theology of the future will no longer be simply a theology for priests and pastors but also for the laity, goes on to say:

> It will be directed not only toward divine service in the church, but also toward divine service in the everyday life of the world. Its practical implementation will include preaching and worship, pastoral duties, and Christian community, but also socialization, democratization, education toward self-reliance and political life (1975:11).

One must therefore say, emphatically, that a theology of the laity does not mean that the laity should be trained to become "mini-pastors". Their ministry (or perhaps we should say their "service", for "ministry" has come to be such a churchy word—cf Burrows 1981:55f) is offered in the form of the ongoing life of the Christian community "in shops, villages, farms, cities, classrooms, homes, law offices, in counselling, politics, statecraft, and recreation" (:66f). The contingent form this ministry will take must be recognized—as we should, in fact, recognize the contingent shape of the ordained ministry. It will not be the same for every age, context, and culture. In some parts of the Third World, in particular, the ministry of both laity and ordained will be much more extensive than it is in the West. Its wider scope may be occasioned by the circumstance that in a developing country the church's efforts may be more comprehensive than those of the government (:72) or, in a country like South Africa—which is going through a painful process of democratization—by the fact that, where the voices of political and community leaders have been silenced, the church is left as almost the only voice of the voiceless. In most such cases, it will be a combined ministry of clergy and laity, to the extent that it becomes impossible to distinguish who is doing what.

A striking example of lay ministry is to be found in the phenomenon of "base" or "small" Christian communities which, having begun in Latin America,[23] are today spreading across the entire globe, even in the West. It takes many forms: house church groups in the West, African independent churches, clandestine gatherings in countries where Christianity is proscribed, etc. The movement is, as far as Catholicism is concerned, so exceptional that scholars are easily tempted to become too starry-eyed in their evaluation (cf, for instance, Boff 1986:1, 4). Still, it is a development of momentous significance. Bühlmann (1977:157) even ventures to say that these "experiments" are more significant than the theology of liberation and can, with better reason, be taken as the contribution offered by Latin America to the universal church. And their significance lies particularly in the fact that here the laity have come of age and are missionally involved in an imaginative way.

It took a very long time before the Christian church discovered that Christ, who had turned upside down the hallowed forms of ministry of the Jewish establishment of his time, might perhaps also challenge the established "theology of ministry" of the Christian church (cf Burrows 1981:31f). But, as always, Christ is not intent on destroying, but in fulfilling. This applies also to the ordained ministry. Nothing will be gained by abolishing it. Boff (1986:32), in spite of all his criticism of the structures of the Catholic Church and all his enthusiasm for the base communities, repudiates any attempt at "despoiling the bishop and priest of their function in a sham liberation process". Indeed, clericalism is not overcome by rejecting an ordained ministry or by downplaying its significance and task. De Gruchy (1987:26) quotes E. Schillebeeckx in this respect: "If there is no specialized concentration of what is important to everyone, in the long run the community suffers as a result".

Therefore, Hoekendijk's tendency to regard church offices merely as functional and therefore, in the final analysis, as contingent (cf also Rütti 1972:311-315) leads us nowhere. Some form of ordained ministry is indeed essential and constitutive (see also Moltmann 1977:288-314), not as *guarantor* of the validity of the church's claim to be the dispenser of God's grace, but, at most, as *guardian*, to help keep the community faithful to the teaching and practice of apostolic Christianity (cf Burrows 1981:83, 112). The clergy do not do this alone and off their own bat, so to speak, but together with the whole people of God, for all have received the Holy Spirit, who guides the church in all truth. The priesthood of the ordained ministry is to enable, not to remove, the priesthood of the whole church (Newbigin 1987:30). The clergy are not prior to or independent of or over against the church; rather, with the rest of God's people, they *are* the church, sent into the world. In order to flesh out this vision, then, we need a more organic, less sacral ecclesiology of the whole people of God.

MISSION AS WITNESS TO PEOPLE OF OTHER LIVING FAITHS[24]

The Shifting Scene

The *theologia religionum*, the "theology of religions", is a discipline that has evolved only since the 1960s. The same impetus that made Christians of a given theological denomination ask, Who are these Roman Catholics, Anglicans, Methodists, Orthodox? also led to the question, Who are these people of other faiths, these Hindus, Buddhists, and Muslims? At least in this *formal* sense, then, there is a relationship between ecumenism and the theology of religions.

The issue of the attitude Christians and Christian missions should adopt to (adherents of) other faiths is, of course, an ancient one, with roots in the Old Testament. For many centuries, however, this was hardly ever debated. Emperor Theodosius' decrees of 380 (which demanded that all citizens of the Roman Empire be Christians) and 391 (which proscribed all non-Christians cults), inexorably paved the way for Pope Boniface's bull, *Unam Sanctam* (1302), which proclaimed that the Catholic Church was the only institution guaranteeing salvation; for the Council of Florence (1442), which assigned to the everlasting fire of hell everyone not attached to the Catholic Church; and for the *Cathechismus Romanus* (1566), which taught the infallibility of the Catholic Church. In the context of this model it was unthinkable that people should be allowed to believe as they chose; as late as 1832 Gregory XVI rejected the demand for freedom of religion not only as error, but as *deliramentum*, "insanity" (reference in Fries 1986:759). Protestants, it is true, did not have anything comparable to papal bulls. Still, their mentality often hardly differed from that of Rome; where the Catholic model insisted on "outside the *church* no salvation", the Protestant model adhered to "outside the *word*, no salvation" (Knitter 1985:135).

In both these models mission essentially meant *conquest* and *displacement*. Christianity was understood to be unique, exclusive, superior, definitive, normative, and absolute (cf Knitter 1985:18), the only religion which had the divine right to exist and extend itself. For most of the Middle Ages, Christianity's archenemy was Islam. Mohammed was a "second Arius"; Islam was a post-Christian *imitatio diaboli*, a menace that had to be crushed before it crushed the church. Hence the crusades which, on the whole, miscarried. This did not change the Christian attitude toward Islam, however (cf Erdmann 1977; Kedar 1984).

Given the circumstances and the general climate of the time, one can hardly blame the church for the attitude it adopted. This makes the exceptions to the rule so much more remarkable, however – people like Raymond Lull in the fourteenth century and Las Casas in the sixteenth. And half a century before Las Casas there was the German cardinal, Nicholas of Cusa, who – tired of the religious wars between Christians and Muslims – hoped for the day when all would recognize the *one* religion in the plurality of religious rites (*religio una in rituum varietate*). Even Nicholas did not for a moment, however, doubt the absolute superiority of Christianity over Islam (cf Gensichen 1989:196f), just as Las Casas assumed, as a matter of course, that the "superstitions" of the American Indians were infinitely inferior to the Christian faith.

The unshaken, massive, and collective certitude of the Middle Ages, which existed until the eighteenth century, has, however, vanished. Christianity, says Kraemer (1961:21) is severely questioned, repudiated, or condescendingly ignored. A major factor in this breakdown was, of course, the Enlightenment. As far as the world of values (to which religion was assigned) was concerned, the Enlightenment in principle adopted a relativistic attitude. In the course of time this would erode hitherto unshakable Christian certainties and slowly make the church aware of the existence of a dilemma it had never needed to recognize. With the collapse of colonialism it lost its hegemony – even in the West, its traditional home – and today has to compete for allegiance on the open market of religions and ideologies. There are no longer oceans separating Christians from other religionists. In Western countries Christians, Muslims, Hindus, Sikhs and Buddhists rub shoulders on every street. Serious Christians have also discovered that those "other" religions are, incongruously, both more different from and more similar to Christianity than they had thought.

In the Enlightenment paradigm it was expected that religion would eventually disappear as people discovered that *facts* were all they needed to survive, and that the world of values – to which religion belongs – would lose its grip on them. And much indeed seemed to point in this direction. Marxism dismissed religion as the "opiate of the people" and propagated a world in which it would have no place. Even outside the Communist world, religion – Christianity in particular – appeared to be in decline. Arnold Toynbee (1969:327) says that in his student days in Oxford, during the first decade of our century, he and his fellow-students believed that religions had no future and would disappear. At the IMC Jerusalem Conference (1928) John Macmurray put forward the thesis that religions would disappear with the rise of scientific thinking—although he did not believe that Christianity, too, would vanish (cf Newbigin 1969:31). Still, in a 1948 poll, thirty-four percent of France's population declared themselves "atheist" (cf Gómez 1986:30), thus corroborating the thesis of Godin and Daniel (1943). With the "secular sixties", so it seemed, the final hour for religion had arrived; the only way of securing the survival of Christianity was to turn it into a thoroughly secular religion.

Strangely, however, religion, did not perish. Quite the contrary! We are discovering today the indisputable reality of "religion after the Enlightenment" (cf the title of Lübbe 1986). Human nature, said the octogenarian Toynbee in 1969 (:322), abhors a vacuum; so, if one religion goes, another takes it place; contrary to his earlier view that religions were moribund (:327), he now held that they had an enduring role to play (:328). Apparently Bonhoeffer's idea of the nonreligious human being and of the "worldly world" was a misconception. Since the "secular sixties" more and more scholars have been writing on the resurgence of a transcendent longing that is both open to spiritual insight and critical of science as an adequate means of knowing the whole truth; one may think, for instance, of Peter Berger's *A Rumor of Angels* (1970), Theodore Roszak's *Where the Wasteland Ends* (1972), and Harvey Cox's *The Seduction of the Spirit* (in which, incidentally, he adopts a stance rather different from his *The Secular City*, but which differs significantly from Roszak and others).

The revival of religion is not only a Christian phenomenon, however. On the contrary, it would seem that it is especially the other religions that are experiencing revitalization. Warneck (1909) has been proved wrong—it is impossible simply to juxtapose "the living Christ" with "dying heathenism". Already in 1933 H. W. Schomerus published a study on *Das Eindringen Indiens in das Herrschaftsgebiet des Christentums* ("India's Infiltration Into the Domain of Christianity"). In some instances (particularly in the case of Islam) the revitalization of traditional religions has been intimately linked to burgeoning nationalism and projects of nation building and the like. Often these religions are involved in far more aggressive "evangelism" than the Christian churches are. Hinduism is not only self-assertive at home, but its sects are proselytizing with success in the West. Buddhism has become militant in Sri Lanka and elsewhere. Whereas the number of Christians has increased threefold since the beginning of the century, the number of Muslims has increased fourfold (cf Barrett 1990:27). In Western countries freedom of religion has a high premium, which enables all faiths to propagate their beliefs freely; in several Islamic countries, however, the propagation of the Christian faith is prohibited—with important consequences for Christian mission (cf Gensichen 1989:199-201). Indeed, Christians in the West have been jolted out of their complacency.

All these circumstances cause the Christian church of today to be faced with totally unprecedented challenges. It would probably be correct to say that we have reached the point where there can be little doubt that the two largest unsolved problems for the Christian church are its relationship (1) to *world views which offer this-worldly salvation*, and (2) to *other faiths*. On the first page of *On Being a Christian*, Hans Küng (1977:25) says that, in the face of this twofold challenge of the world religions and of modern humanism, today's Christian is confronted with the question whether Christianity is indeed something essentially different, something special. Sharpe (1974:14) believes the challenge of the religions to be even more important than that of secular ideologies — although matters such as the relationship between mission and the world, mission and politics, mission and social action, are important, it is the *theologia religionum* which is the epitome of mission theology.

The question is whether the Christian church and mission are equipped to respond to the challenge emanating from the religions. After the Tambaram Meeting of the IMC in 1938, Karl Hartenstein declared, "We have no theology with which we could even begin to take up the challenge presented to Christianity by Buddhism and Hinduism" (quoted in Gensichen 1989:195 — my translation). During the past half-century little seems to have changed in this respect. The recent Dutch introduction to missiology (Oecumenische inleiding 1988: 475f) suggests that much confusion and uncertainty still prevails in this area and that, as we approach the twenty-first century, much new ground still has to be broken, since we are totally unprepared for facing the challenge before us. If these scholars are correct, one may appreciate the frustration and distress of Cracknell and Lamb (1986:10-16) who, surveying the British scene, find that the theology of religions (indeed, the entire area of missiology) is either virtually unknown in theological institutions or relegated to the position of an unimportant subsection of pastoral theology.

Postmodern Responses?

Since the 1960s few themes have dominated missiological (and, indeed, general theological literature) the way the entire area of the theology of religions has done. A deluge of books and articles have been published and no end to this torrent appears to be in sight. There can be little doubt that the contemporary world situation and the increasing exchange of ideas between peoples and religions have created an unprecedented situation. Before an attempt is made to order the ideas in some manner, it may be of importance to point out that much of the current interest in our theme has to do with the fact that, by and large, Christianity has not been very successful among those peoples who are adherents to what often (perhaps incorrectly) is termed the great religions — Islam, Hinduism, Buddhism, etc. Many explanations for this failure have been put forward in the course of history. In light of what I have written on contextualization and inculturation earlier in this chapter it may, however, be illuminating to refer to one such explanation, that of A. Pieris (1986). He argues that these models proceed from Latin Christianity's practice of separating religion from culture. What is really called for, however, is not just in*cultur*ation but "in*religion*ization" (1986:83). Song, using the example of the spread of Buddhism in Asia, says essentially the same. No sooner did Buddhism leave the land of its birth than it became *Chinese* Buddhism, *Thai* Buddhism, *Japanese* Buddhism (1977:5; cf Pieris 1986:85), intrinsic to the soil and the people of each of these countries. This, Song claims, was truly a mission of *enfleshment*. Christian mission, by contrast, was a mission of *disembodiment* (:54). We should never have transplanted Christianity to Asia without breaking the pot in which the plant came, says Pieris. He calls the "inculturation-fever" a desperate last-moment bid to give an Asian facade to a church which has failed to strike roots in Asian soil, because no one dares to break the Greco-Roman pot in which, for centuries, it has been existing like a stunted *bonsai* (1986:84). Maybe, says Pieris (:85), Christianity has missed its chance because it arrived too late on the Asian scene, except perhaps in the Philippines. Now its only hope lies not in trying to create (for instance) just an *Indian* Christianity, but—as M. Amaladoss, R. Panikkar, and others are suggesting—a *Hindu* Christianity (:83).

I have mentioned the thesis of Pieris (and Song) simply to highlight the fact that, all around, there is today a new urgency to grapple with the entire issue of a Christian *theologia religionum* and a sometimes almost desperate attempt to make up for earlier shortsightedness. The bewildering diversity of these attempts (Nürnberger 1970:42f lists no fewer than twenty-seven varieties!) is an indication that, thus far, no clear direction seems to be emerging. Nürnberger subdivides the twenty-seven types into three broad categories which he terms relativistic, dialectical, and antithetical. Perhaps, however, Küng's subdivision into *four* "fundamental positions" (1987:278-285) is more helpful for our present purposes. The first position, that of atheism ("no religion is true" or "all religions are equally untrue") can be ignored for our purposes since it is not a view entertained by any branch of the Christian theology of religions. The other three are (my terms): exclusivism, fulfillment, and relativism. Each of these carries within itself elements of both the modern and the postmodern paradigm. It will not be possible to display the three views in any detail; only those dimensions which reveal the elements within each of them which, unconsciously, strives to move beyond the modern position will be touched upon.

1. *Exclusivism*: The traditional Western Catholic and Protestant exclusivist attitude in respect to other religions was decidedly premodern or (in some of its manifestations) modern. The same is, by and large, true of the contemporary evangelical position. Still, there is one important example of an exclusivist position which reveals clearly postmodern elements—the theology of religions of *Karl Barth* (in this respect, then, it is erroneous on the part of Knitter [1985:80-87] to introduce Barth as a representative of the conservative evangelical position).

Barth discusses this theme in volume I/2 of his *Church Dogmatics*. Radicalizing and outbidding Luther and Calvin—his two main interlocutors—and turning consciously against the Enlightenment's evolutionary optimism and endorsement of the autonomous human being, Barth declares religion to be *unbelief*—a concern, indeed, the one great concern of *godless* human beings. This statement is, however, directed primarily not at the other religions, but at *Christianity* (a view which, in fact, brings Barth close to Feuerbach—on *this* score, at least). The human being, says Barth (1978:302), quoting Calvin, is an *idolorum fabrica*, an "idol factory", and the idol thus manufactured is religion, Christian or otherwise. He goes on to contrast, in an absolute manner, religion as a human fabrication with *revelation*, which is something totally new, coming directly from God (:301f). There is no point of contact between religion and God's revelation. If God speaks to humans (which he does) and is being understood, this does not occur on the basis of something innate to humanity, but because of a divine *creatio ex nihilo*. This also explains why we, with fear and trembling and in spite of what has been said, may refer to Christianity as *becoming* "true religion". We say this, not because of something intrinsic to the Christian religion, but because God creates, elects, justifies, and sanctifies it (:325-361). Like the justified human being, true religion is a creature of grace (:326).

There can be no doubt that Barth's was a bold, innovative, and radical attempt at solving an age-old problem. This is particularly true of the way in which he refused to take refuge in the age-old stratagem of blithely contrasting the Christian religion as true with all others as untrue.

2. *Fulfillment*: One could argue that the idea of Christianity as the fulfillment of other religions was already present in the concepts adaptation, accommodation, and indigenization (see "Mission As Inculturation" above). When Xavier, de Nobili, and Ricci attempted to accommodate Indian, Chinese, and Japanese religio-cultural values, they ascribed some worth to those cultures and religions and broke, in principle, with the dualistic view of reality sanctioned by Augustine's theology. It was, however, not until the arrival on the scene of the theory of evolution in the nineteenth century, the rise of liberal theology, and the birth of the new discipline of comparative religion, that the stage was set for an approach according to which religions could be compared and graded in an ascending scale. In the Western world there was no doubt, however, about which religion stood at the pinnacle. In almost every respect every other religion — even if it might be termed a *praeparatio evangelica* — was deficient when compared with Christianity, as Dennis illustrated so ably and amply in his three-volume study (1897, 1899, 1906).

The new discipline was brought to the attention of the general public on the occasion of the "World's Parliament of Religions", which met in Chicago in 1893 as part of the Columbian Exposition commemorating Christopher Columbus's "discovery" of the Americas (cf Barrows 1893). In the heyday of theological liberalism and under the banner of the "fatherhood of God" and the "universal brotherhood of men", the Christian organizers magnanimously invited to Chicago representatives from all the great religions.

At the parliament and in the decades that followed, Christians could indeed afford to be magnanimous. The ultimate triumph of Christianity, most likely before the end of the twentieth century, was assured — as Dahle's calculations so convincingly illustrated (cf Sundkler 1968:121). On the eve of the new century an American theological journal gave expression to this belief by changing its name to *The Christian Century*. The liberal theology of the day accepted the validity of other religions but believed that Christianity was still the best and was sure to outlive them. Other religions could prepare the way for Christianity, but it remained the "crown", as J. N. Farquhar argued in his famous study on *The Crown of Hinduism* (1913).

It was this view that also dominated at the Jerusalem Conference of the IMC (1928), particularly because of the role played by W. E. Hocking. The "Council Statement", released by the Conference, affirmed, among other things:[25]

> We recognize as part of the one Truth that sense of the Majesty of God and the consequent reverence in worship, which are conspicuous in Islam, the deep sympathy for the world's sorrow and unselfish search for the way of escape, which are at the heart of Buddhism; the desire for contact with ultimate reality conceived as spiritual, which is prominent in Hinduism; the belief in a moral order of the universe and consequent insistence on moral conduct, which are inculcated by Confucianism.

On the surface, this statement sounds relativistic and belongs in the next category. However, the "one Truth" to which Jerusalem referred was the *Christian faith*. In a sense, then, the other religions were all subsumed under Christianity. This was also the thrust of the report of the (North American) Laymen's Foreign Missions Inquiry (1932). We were all en route to one world culture and needed one world religion — undoubtedly based, largely, on Western Christian suppositions. Christian love, Hocking suggested, was the element especially needed for the spiritual rejuvenation of the world (cf Hutchison 1987:161).

This entire approach was thoroughly stamped by the assumptions of the Enlightenment. To some extent the same was still true even of Vatican II's contribution to the theology of religions. Its point of departure (spelled out in LG 16) is God's universal salvific will (cf 1 Tim 2:4)[26] and the acknowledgment of the presence of "good or truth" in the lives of people. LG 16 sees the "plan of salvation" at work in those who "acknowledge the Creator", who seek the unknown God "in shadows and images", and who "not without grace, strive to lead a good life". *Nostra Aetate* (the Council's *Declaration on the Relation of the Church to Non-Christian Religions*), elaborates further from these premises. It emphasizes what people have in common and what tends to promote fellowship, and regards religions as that which provides answers to life's unsolved riddles (NA 1). It adds that the Catholic Church rejects nothing of what is true and holy in other religions, not least since these "often reflect a ray" of the church's own truth (NA 2). What is striking about most of this is that the Council's reflections are still based on a general theory of religion. The arguments are sociological and philosophical rather than theological.

A more explicitly postmodern approach began to surface with the shift from *ecclesiocentrism* to *christocentrism*. Much of this shift was in evidence in several documents of Vatican II — not, however, in NA. Protestants, on the other hand, had always claimed to be christocentric rather than ecclesiocentric. Their christology was, however, exclusive as far as other religions were concerned. At the WCC assembly in New Delhi (1961), Joseph Sittler, a Lutheran — drawing from the Greek Patristic tradition rather than Augustine — introduced the idea of the cosmic Christ. Referring to the notion of *anakephalaiosis* ("recapitulation" or "uniting under one head") in Ephesians 1:10 (cf Colossians 1:15-20), Sittler argued in favor of a cosmic christology and the uniting of humankind under the one new Head, the cosmic Christ.

Independent of developments in ecumenical Protestant circles, Karl Rahner and others also began to plead for a shift from an ecclesiocentric to a christocentric approach to the theology of religions. It is important to take cognizance of the fact that Rahner's point of departure, when discussing other religions and their possible salvific value, is *christology*. He never abandons the idea of Christianity as the absolute religion and of salvation having to come only through Christ. But he recognizes supernatural elements of grace in other religions which, he posits, have been given to human beings through Christ. There is saving grace within other religions but this grace is Christ's. This makes people of other faiths into "anonymous Christians" and accords their religions a positive place in God's salvific plan. They are "ordinary ways of salvation", independent of the special way of salvation of Israel and the church. It is in the latter that they find fulfillment.

Rahner's thesis has been modified in several respects by H. R. Schlette, R. Panikkar, A. Camps, and others (cf Camps 1983; Knitter 1985:125-135) and may perhaps, with some reservations, be termed the dominant current Catholic perspective on the theology of religions. Camps's idea of practicing a "maieutic method" in this respect (which includes an attempt on the part of Christianity to divest itself of its Western garb) is particularly intriguing (cf Camps 1983:7, 84, 91, 155).

3. *Relativism*: I have argued that both exclusivism and fulfillment manifest themselves in some models which are clearly premodern and modern and others which show traces of a postmodern paradigm. The same is true of relativism.

Philosophers like G. E. Lessing, A. Schopenhauer, G. W. Leibnitz, and Herbert of Cherbury, all deeply imbued with the Enlightenment spirit, represented a decidedly modern understanding of religion. In their view, the reality (*if* there is such a reality) to which the various religions refer is the same for all. They just use different names for it, like the six blind Indian men who fingered an elephant and called it—depending on the part of the anatomy they had touched—a snake, a sword, a fan, a wall, a pillar, and a rope. The question in each instance is the same, only the answers differ. Thus, along their different paths the various religions guide us toward an identical spiritual summit (Toynbee 1969:328). After all, despite their amazing differences, the religions turn out to be more complementary than contradictory (Knitter 1985:220).

This extreme relativism of the Enlightenment is today hardly ever found in Christian circles. Instead, modifications are the order of the day, such as the suggestion that the various religions are historically conditioned. One of the first theologians to have used this approach was Ernst Troeltsch (1865-1923). An exponent of the history of religions school he had, throughout his life, grappled with the issue of the so-called absoluteness of Christianity. He held onto a modified claim to absoluteness until, toward the end of his life, he underwent a shift in his thinking. In his *Der Historismus und seine Überwindung* (1923) he argued for an intimate bond between a given religion and its own culture. Christianity, then, still held final and unconditional validity for Westerners, but only for them. For other peoples and cultures their traditional religions hold equally unconditional validity.

Troeltsch's thesis, often modified, is still being subscribed to by several scholars. John Hick, for instance (reference in Knitter 1985:147), combines Troeltsch's idea with the notion that all religions are different human answers to the one divine Reality and says that they embody different perceptions which have been formed in different historical and cultural circumstances. Knitter (:173-175) goes one step further and expresses his doubts about the reliability of much of the Christian tradition, notably its christology, arguing that it is a later accretion and not in keeping with Jesus' own self-understanding, which was theocentric. This interpretation, then, enables him to dispense with christocentrism, even for Christians; it becomes the basis for his central thesis that they, too, should move from christocentrism to theocentrism. He finds that Rahner and those who have proceeded beyond the Rahner tradition present us with an inadequate view, precisely because, in the final analysis, they regard faith in Christ as the definitive Savior (and thereby the Christian faith itself) as non-negotiable (:133). Knitter himself would rather identify with theologians like John Hick, R. Panikkar, and Stanley Samartha, who are clearly and seriously questioning the finality and the definitive normativity of Christ and of Christianity (:146-159).

Knitter then posits his notion of "unitive pluralism", which, he claims, is a *new* understanding of religious unity and should not be confused with the old, rationalistic idea of "one world religion". The new vision, he claims, is neither syncretism nor an example of lazy tolerance (1985:9). With Hick, he refers to the new view as a "paradigm shift" (:147). All religions are equally valid and other revealers and saviors may be as important as Jesus Christ. Knitter does not advocate the idea of a world faith embracing all religions, as Hocking did. Rather, he advances the notion of a wider ecumenism (:166). He thus consciously opts for religious plurality, but without either mutually exclusive claims or indifference. Interreligious encounter should be based on personal religious experience and firm truth-claims (:207) but without suggesting that any partner in the encounter possesses the final, definitive, irreformable truth (:211).

From this position, Knitter then also ventures a few words on Christian *mission*. What he says about this (:222) turns out to be a rehash of what Swami Vivekananda said at the World's Parliament of Religions a century ago:

> Do I wish that the Christian would become Hindu? God forbid. Do I wish that the Hindu or Buddhist would become Christian? God forbid ... The Christian is not to become a Hindu or a Buddhist, nor a Hindu or a Buddhist to become a Christian. But each must assimilate the others and yet preserve its individuality and grow according to its own law of growth (in Barrows 1893:170 [vol I]).

So, Knitter's model appears to be less original than he claims. It is close to Vivekananda's position, as it is to Toynbee's (1969:328), who envisions the historic religions reappearing above our horizon in a spirit of mutual charity.

For the rest, Knitter would redefine mission in more or less pragmatic terms, as John Macquarrie does, who also advocates a "global ecumenism" (1977:446) and suggests that Christian mission is to restrict itself to the humanitarian fields of health, education, and the like (:445). In particular, it should not aim at converting adherents of the so-called higher religions in which God's saving grace is already recognizably at work (:445f). Rival truth-claims are simply part of the larger religious mosaic and should be treated as such.

Dialogue and Mission

I now turn to the interrelationship between dialogue and mission. In discussing this I shall, more implicitly than explicitly, critique the three models just outlined from the perspective of a postmodern missionary paradigm. At the outset, I would like to posit my belief that we are in need of a theology of religions characterized by creative tension, which reaches beyond the sterile alternative between a comfortable claim to absoluteness and arbitrary pluralism (cf Kuschel 1984:238; Küng 1986:xvii-xix). And perhaps it is precisely in this respect that the various models discussed above are found wanting. They are all too neat. They all work out too well. In the end everything — and everyone! — is accounted for. There are no loose ends, no room left for surprises and unsolved puzzles. Even before the dialogue begins, all the crucial issues have been settled. The various models seem to leave no room for embracing the abiding paradox of asserting both ultimate commitment to one's own religion and genuine openness to another's, of constantly vacillating between certainty and doubt. Each time — in all these approaches — the tension snaps.

Perhaps the theology of religions is preeminently an area which we should explore with the aid of *poiesis* rather than of *theoria* (cf Stackhouse 1988 for a discussion of these). This is the route Klaus Klostermaier follows in his captivating *Hindu and Christian in Vrindaban* (1969). For both dialogue and mission manifest themselves in a meeting of hearts rather than of minds. We are dealing with a mystery.

The first perspective called for — and this is already a decision of the heart rather than the intellect — is to accept the coexistence of different faiths and to do so not grudgingly but willingly. This is what the British Council of Churches did in 1977, in light of the multifaith situation in Britain (cf Cracknell and Lamb 1986:7). We cannot possibly dialogue with or witness to people if we resent their presence or the views they hold. Macquarrie (1977:4-18) has identified six "formative factors in theology": experience, revelation, Scripture, tradition, culture, and reason. R. Pape (in Cracknell and Lamb 1986:77) — rightly, I believe — adds a seventh formative factor — another religion. Today few Christians anywhere in the world find themselves in a situation where coexistence with other religionists is not part and parcel of their daily life. More than has ever been the case since Constantine's victory over Maxentius at the Milvian Bridge in AD 312, Christian theology is a theology of dialogue. It needs dialogue, also for its own sake (cf Moltmann 1975:12f). One-way, monological travel is out, as is militancy in any form.

Apparently, even in this day and age, it takes time for the essentially dialogical nature of the Christian faith to sink in and take root. The evolution of themes in a series of WCC consultations may illustrate my point. The CWME Mexico City Conference (1963) used the formulation "The *Witness* of Christians *to* Men of Other Faiths". A year later, at an East Asia Christian Conference meeting in Bangkok the theme was "The Christian *Encounter With* Men of Other Beliefs". Three years later, in Sri Lanka, the word "dialogue" surfaced; now the theme was "Christians in *Dialogue With* Men of Other Faiths". Throughout, the major participants were still identified as *Christians* who dialogue *about* or *with* others. Only in Ajaltoun (Lebanon) in 1970 was the mutuality of dialogue recognized; the theme was "Dialogue *Between* Men of Living Faiths" (the women were apparently still outside of the dialoguers' field of vision!). In 1977, then, in Chiang Mai (Thailand), the subject was "Dialogue in Community".

Second, true dialogue presupposes *commitment*. It does not imply sacrificing one's own position—it would then be superfluous. An "unprejudiced" approach is not merely impossible but would actually subvert dialogue. As the WCC *Guidelines on Dialogue with People of Living Faiths and Ideologies* puts it: Dialogue means witnessing to our deepest convictions, whilst listening to those of our neighbors (WCC 1979:16). Without my commitment to the gospel, dialogue becomes a mere chatter; without the authentic presence of the neighbor it becomes arrogant and worthless. It is a false construct to suggest that a commitment to dialogue is incompatible with a confessional position (cf A. Wingate in Cracknell and Lamb 1986:65).

Third, dialogue (and, for that matter, mission) is only possible if we proceed from the belief that—as D. T. Niles, Max Warren, and Kenneth Cragg have insisted—we are not moving into a void, that we go expecting to meet the God who has preceded us and has been preparing people within the context of their own cultures and convictions (cf Sharpe 1974:15f). God has already removed the barriers; his Spirit is constantly at work in ways that pass human understanding (cf ME 43). We do not have him in our pocket, so to speak, and do not just "take him" to the others; he accompanies us and also comes toward us. We are not the "haves", the *beati possidentes*, standing over against spiritual "have nots", the *massa damnata*. We are all recipients of the same mercy, sharing in the same mystery. We thus approach every other faith and its adherents reverently, taking off our shoes, as the place we are approaching is holy (Max Warren, in Cragg 1959:9f). The undialectical nature of Barth's position, particularly his definition of religion as unbelief and his view that mission means going into a void, is therefore unacceptable (cf Kraemer 1961:356-358, who criticizes Barth, "the initiator of *dialectical* thinking", for his undialectical and rationalistic arguments).

It follows from the above, fourth, that both dialogue and mission can be conducted only in an attitude of humility. For Christians, this should be a matter of course, for two reasons: the Christian faith is a religion of *grace* (which is freely received) and it find its center, to a significant extent, in the *cross* (which judges the Christian also). It is the abiding value of Barth's theology that it has taught us that the lines dividing truth from untruth and justice from injustice run not only between Christianity and other faiths but through Christianity as well. There is therefore something authentically Christian in an attitude of humility in the presence of other faiths (cf Cragg 1959:142f; Newbigin 1969:15; Margull 1974:passim; Baker 1986:156f). This is so not only as an expression of repentance for the poor track record of Christians (for instance, the vicious intolerance Christians have often unleashed on adherents of other faiths), but because such an attitude of humility is intrinsic to an authentic Christian faith. And, after all, it is when we are weak that we are strong. So, the word that perhaps best characterizes the Christian church in its encounter with other faiths is *vulnerability* (Margull 1974). We cannot approach people when we are confident and at ease but only when we are contradicted and at a loss. N.-P. Moritzen puts it as follows:

> Nobody denies that Jesus did much good, but that in no way saved him from being crucified. It belongs to the essence (of the Christian faith) that it needs the weak witness, the powerless representative of the message. The people who are to be won and saved should, as it were, always have the possibility of crucifying the witness of the gospel (quoted in Aring 1971:143 – my translation).

A qualification is in order, however. The point of our humility and our repentance is not to indulge masochistically in a bout of self-flagellation or to use our penitence as a new lever to manipulate others (cf Cracknell and Lamb 1986:9). That would be to adopt a sub-Christian position. True repentance and humility are cleansing experiences which lead to renewal and renewed commitment. Humility also means showing respect for our forebears in the faith, for what they have handed down to us, even if we have reason to be acutely embarrassed by their racist, sexist, and imperialist bias. The point is that we have no guarantees that we shall do any better than they did (cf Stackhouse 1988:215). We delude ourselves if we believe that we can be respectful to other faiths only if we disparage our own.

Fifth, both dialogue and mission should recognize that religions are worlds in themselves, with their own axes and structures; they face in different directions and ask fundamentally different questions (cf Kraemer 1961:76f; Newbigin 1969:28, 43f; Gensichen 1989:197). This means, among other things, that the Christian gospel relates differently to Islam than it does to Hinduism, Buddhism, etc (Ratschow 1987:496). In this respect both the fulfillment and the relativist models still reflect the modern paradigm, which tends to slight these differences. They are levelled down and harmonized as happened, classically, in the World's Parliament of Religions (cf Barrows 1893). What usually happens is that – consciously or unconsciously – Christianity is taken as point of departure. The "elements" of the Christian religion are generalized until they fit the phenomena of other religions and thus produce a kind of reduced copy of Christianity (cf Rütti 1972:106). This turns other religions into little more than echoes of Christianity's own voice (cf U. Schoen, reference in Gensichen 1989:197) and shows little appreciation for the fact that they are putting their own questions to Christianity (Ratschow 1987:498f, drawing on H. Bürkle; see also Gensichen 1989:passim).

This view is particularly dominant where Christianity is regarded as the fulfillment of other religions, for instance, in Rahner's notion of "anonymous Christians". It is also exhibited in the encyclical *Suam Ecclesiam* of Paul VI (1964), which creates the impression of other religions being arranged in concentric circles around the Catholic Church, which forms the center. What constitutes a non-Christian religion, in this model, is its "distance" in relation to Christianity—more particularly, to the Catholic Church. Christ is seen as working mystically, cosmically, and anonymously in other faiths, in varying degrees, yet always and ultimately as the fulfillment of those religions. Küng's trenchant criticism of this entire construct is worth noting. The notion of anonymous Christianity, he says, attempts to sweep the whole of good-willed humanity into the back door of the "holy Roman Church", thereby preserving the idea of "no salvation outside the church". Meanwhile, however, Jews, Muslims, and people of other faiths know only too well that they are "unanonymous". So Küng dismisses the entire notion as a pseudo-solution (1977:98).

It would seem that Knitter, Hick, and others are at least more honest in that they explicitly debunk the idea of any need for Christ and the church. Yet Knitter's "unitive pluralism" and his postulate that the world's religions are "more complementary than contradictory" (1985:220), as attractive a hypothesis as it is, is an ahistorical one and, in the final analysis, not really different from the views expressed by the Enlightenment philosophers (cf the summary in Nürnberger 1970:42). The compatibility of different religions is a thoroughly rationalistic construct, as is Knitter's idea of "theocentrism". From another perspective his striving after holism in religion may indeed be seen as postmodern. It is, however, significant that, since 1985, Knitter has felt obliged to discard even his emphasis on theocentrism. He now recognizes only "a shared locus of religious experience" (1987:186) and opts for "soteriocentrism" instead of theocentrism (:187). What will prevent him from moving even further and ending up in close proximity to the New Age movement?

An extreme postmodern paradigm may opt for an excessive holism, for a modern version of the World's Parliament of Religions (in the style of Capra, for instance). Alternatively, it may consciously choose the path of pluralism, where rival truth claims are simply part of the mosaic, where there is no longer such a thing as orthodoxy, where we are all heretics in the original sense of the word (cf Newbigin 1986:16). In either case we would opt for a completely instrumentalist view of religion—the various faiths are either culture bound, or irrationally and arbitrarily selected, or put together in a do-it-yourself manner. However, when everything is equally valid nothing really matters any longer. Where this happens, we can no longer seriously talk about a legitimate paradigm shift; the creative tension with tradition—so basic to the idea of paradigm shifts—has disappeared. The question of truth has been completely trivialized and life itself robbed of its ultimate seriousness (cf Küng 1986:xviii; see also Bloom 1987). Authentic religion is, however, too unwieldy to fit into such a constellation (cf Josuttis 1988; Daecke 1988:629f).

In the sixth place, dialogue is neither a substitute nor a subterfuge for mission (cf Scherer 1987:162). They are neither to be viewed as identical nor as irrevocably opposed to each other. It is fallacious to suggest that, for dialogue to be "in", mission has to be "out", that commitment to dialogue is incompatible with commitment to evangelism. The San Antonio CWME Meeting put it as follows: "We affirm that witness does not preclude dialogue but invites it, and that dialogue does not preclude witness but extends and deepens it" (I.27; WCC 1990:32).

The *correspondence* between dialogue and mission is indeed striking (cf also WCC 1979:11). Both have, in the course of time, registered a shift "from ignorance through arrogance to tolerance" (Küng 1986:20-24). Neither dialogue nor mission is moving along a one-way street; neither is stubbornly dogmatic, bigoted, or manipulative. In both, faith commitment goes hand-in-hand with respect for others. Neither presupposes a "completely open mind"—which, in any case, is an impossibility. In both cases we are witnessing to our deepest convictions whilst listening to those of our neighbors (cf WCC 1979:16). In both cases we are taken "out of the security of (our) own prisons" (Klostermaier 1969:103).

The *dissimilarities* between dialogue and witness are, however, equally fundamental. If Knitter (1985:222) says that the goal of mission has been achieved when announcing the gospel has made the Christian a better Christian and the Buddhist a better Buddhist, he may be describing one of the goals of *dialogue*, but certainly not of *mission*. It is true that Christianity has—belatedly—rediscovered its integrally dialogical nature; this rediscovery should, however, not be at the expense of its fundamentally missionary nature. Today all major world Christian bodies and denominations affirm this innate missionary nature of Christianity. AG 2's famous words to this effect have been quoted frequently already. But even a "so-called anti-missionary document" (Gómez 1986:32) like *Nostra Aetate* can say (paragraph 2), "(The church) proclaims and is in duty bound to proclaim without fail, Christ who is the way, the truth and the life (Jn 14:6)".

Similar voices are heard from the ranks of the WCC. Its *Guidelines on Dialogue* (WCC 1979) almost leans over backward to establish, once and for all, the legitimacy of dialogue; yet even here there is no doubt about the church's being called to witness about life in Christ. Section I.1 of the 1975 Nairobi Assembly states, for example, "We boldly confess Christ alone as Saviour and Lord" and expresses "confident trust" ... "in the power of the gospel" (WCC 1976:43). It is in ME, however, that the commitment of the WCC to mission is unequivocally asserted. In ME 6 we read, "At the very heart of the Church's vocation in the world is the proclamation of the kingdom of God inaugurated in Jesus the Lord, crucified and risen". Again, ME 42 states that "Christians owe the message of God's salvation in Jesus Christ to every person and to every people". The San Antonio Conference built on these affirmation, declaring that "the Triune God, Father, Son and Holy Spirit, is a God in mission, the source and sustainer of the church's mission" (I.1; WCC 1990:25). Elsewhere (I.26) it asserts, "We cannot point to any other way of salvation than Jesus Christ" (WCC 1990:32).

It is necessary to highlight such affirmations today, in a climate in which, on the one hand, familiarity has robbed us of the freshness and vitality of the gospel, leaving us only a dogged loyalty to it (cf C. Lamb in Cracknell and Lamb 1986:130), or where, on the other hand, Christians are being advised, even by fellow-Christians, that it is improper to invite adherents of other faiths or of no faith to put their trust in God through Christ. The Christian faith cannot surrender the conviction that God, in sending Jesus Christ into our midst, has taken a definitive and eschatological course of action and is extending to human beings forgiveness, justification, and a new life of joy and servanthood, which, in turn, calls for a human response in the form of conversion. These inalienable elements of mission became abundantly clear in our chapters on the missionary character of the early church.

In the seventh place, however, what has just been suggested should not be construed in the sense of "business as usual", as though all we have to do is continue to preach the "old, old story". Rather, the preceding remarks should be understood within the entire framework of this section. To that some more has to be added, picking up observations made earlier in this chapter, particularly in the sections on "Mission as the Church-With-Others" and "Mission as Mediating Salvation".

Much of the debate about the relationship between the Christian faith and other faiths has been confounded by the perennial question whether other religions also "save". As the question is usually put, it refers solely to something which happens to an individual after death and suggests that people join a specific religion in order to be guaranteed this salvation, that religions expand geographically and numerically in order to ensure such salvation to ever greater numbers of people. I repudiate the notion, however, that this is all religion is about, that this is the only reason why people (should) become Christians. Such an ahistorical and otherworldly perception of salvation is spurious, particularly if one adds that all people have to do to attain it, is to subscribe to a set system of dogmas, rites, and institutions.

Conversion is, however, not the joining of a community in order to procure "eternal salvation"; it is, rather, a change in allegiance in which Christ is accepted as Lord and center of one's life. A Christian is not simply somebody who stands a better chance of being "saved", but a person who accepts the responsibility to serve God in this life and promote God's reign in all its forms. Conversion involves personal cleansing, forgiveness, reconciliation, and renewal in order to become a participant in the mighty works of God (cf Cragg 1959:142f; Newbigin 1969:111f). The believer is, after all, a member of the church, which is a sign of God's reign, *sacramentum mundi*, symbol of God's new world, and anticipation of what God intends all creation to be.

I come to my last observation on dialogue and witness in a new paradigm. This observation is really a question: How do we maintain the tension between being both missionary and dialogical? How do we combine faith in God as revealed uniquely in Jesus Christ with the confession that God has not left himself without a witness? If we are honest, also with ourselves, we encounter this tension whichever way we turn. We observe it in the Vatican II documents, for instance. Two affirmations, which seem to be mutually incompatible, speak to us from these documents—God's universal salvific will and the possibility of salvation outside the church *versus* the necessity of the church and of missionary activity. The same unresolved tension emerges from ME, which states, on the one hand, that the proclamation of God's reign in Christ is at the very heart of the church's vocation in the world (ME 6) and, on the other hand, that "the Spirit of God is constantly at work in ways that pass human understanding and in places that to us are least expected" (ME 43). It emerges more clearly still from Section I at San Antonio, where two convictions are immediately juxtaposed: "We cannot point to any other way of salvation than Jesus Christ; at the same time we cannot set limits to the saving power of God" (I.26; WCC 1990:32). The report proceeds by publicly acknowledging that there is a tension here and states: "We appreciate this tension, and do not attempt to resolve it" (I.29; WCC 1990:33).

Such language boils down to an admission that we do not have all the answers and are prepared to live within the framework of penultimate knowledge, that we regard our involvement in dialogue and mission as an adventure, are prepared to take risks, and are anticipating surprises as the Spirit guides us into fuller understanding. This is not opting for agnosticism, but for humility. It is, however, a bold humility—or a humble boldness. We know only in part, but we do know. And we believe that the faith we profess is both true and just, and should be proclaimed. We do this, however, not as judges or lawyers, but as witnesses; not as soldiers, but as envoys of peace; not as high-pressure salespersons, but as ambassadors of the Servant Lord.

MISSION AS THEOLOGY[27]

Mission Marginalized

In the first chapters of this study I have attempted to demonstrate that it is impossible to read the New Testament without taking into account that most of it was consciously written within a missionary context. I have, for example, referred to Martin Kähler's suggestion ([1908]1971:189f) that, in the first century, theology was not a luxury of the world-conquering church but was generated by the emergency situation in which the missionizing church found itself. In this situation, mission became the "mother of theology". However, as Europe became christianized and Christianity became the established religion in the Roman Empire and beyond, theology lost its missionary dimension.

In the entire premodern period, theology was understood primarily in two senses (cf Farley 1983:31). First, it was the term for an actual, individual cognition of God and things related to God. In this sense it was a *habitus*, a habit of the human soul. Second, it was the term for a discipline, a self-conscious scholarly enterprise. For many centuries there was only *one* discipline of theology, without subdivisions. There were, of course, distinctions, but they all referred back to the one "habit"—theology, the knowledge of God and the things of God (:77). Under the impact of the Enlightenment, however, this one discipline first subdivided into two areas: theology as practical know-how necessary for clerical work, and theology as one technical and scholarly enterprise among others, or, if one wishes, theology as *practice* and as *theory* (:39). From here, theology gradually evolved into what Farley (:74-80; 99-149) calls the "fourfold pattern": the disciplines of Bible (text), church history (history), systematic theology (truth), and practical theology (application). Each of these had its parallels in the secular sciences. Under the influence of Schleiermacher, this pattern became firmly established, not only in Germany but elsewhere as well; in fact, it became virtually universal for Protestant theological schools and seminaries and for theological education in Europe, North America, and elsewhere (:101).

"Practical" theology became a mechanism to keep the church going, whilst the other disciplines were examples of "pure" science. The two elements were held together by what Farley (:85-88) calls the "clergy paradigm". The horizon of theology, in both cases, was the church or, at most, Christendom. And theology was, by and large, thoroughly unmissionary. This was true even after the fifteenth century, when the Catholic Church embarked on a vigorous foreign mission program. In Protestantism the situation was even more deplorable. A case in point is the statement in 1652 of the Lutheran theological faculty in Wittenberg (quoted in Schick 1943:46) that the church had no missionary duty or calling at all. In the Reformed world, Voetius was the first to develop a comprehensive "theology of mission" (cf Jongeneel 1989), but it had little lasting effect on subsequent generations. Mission was something completely on the periphery of the church and did not evoke any theological interest worth mentioning. The "theoretical" aspect of theology had to do almost exclusively with the reality of the divine revelation or with assent in the act of faith which students had to imbibe; the "practical" component concentrated on the idea of ministry as service to the institutional church. In both modes it remained thoroughly parochial and domesticated. This was true even in the case of the new seminaries established in the Third World for the training of native clergy. Since the "daughter church" had to imitate the "mother church" in the minutest details and had to have the same structure of congregations, dioceses, clergy, and the like, it went without saying that the theology taught there would be a carbon copy of European theology. The focus was, once again, on conceptualizing and systematizing the faith along the lines that had been laid down once and for all.

As the missionary enterprise expanded and the reality of mission and of the existence of young churches in the "mission territories" more and more impressed itself upon the "home" church, it became necessary to make amends. Since the "fourfold pattern" was sacrosanct, however, other ways and means of accommodating the missionary idea had to be found. The most natural solution was to append the study of mission to one of the existing four disciplines, usually practical theology. In this respect (as in so many others) Schleiermacher was the pioneering spirit (cf Myklebust 1955:84-89). He appended missiology to practical theology and thus created a model which is still followed in some circles. Typical is, for instance, the view of Karl Rahner, who defines practical theology as the "theological, normative discipline of the self-realization of the church in all its dimensions" (1966:50). In this view, then, missiology—being one of these dimensions—becomes the study of the self-realization of the church in missionary situations (that is, of the self-*expanding* church) and practical theology proper the study of the self-realization of the existing church (that is, of the church *building up* itself). The object of missiology's theological reflection is therefore essentially the same as that of practical theology (for reflections on this view, see also Rütti 1974:292-296). Like Rahner, A. Seumois differentiates mission from those areas in which the church is already "constituted normally"—practical theology has to do with the *pastorate* of the church, missiology with the church's *apostolate*—but in such a way that the apostolate is clearly tending toward the pastorate (reference in Kramm 1979:47, 49).

A second strategy was to advocate the introduction of missiology as a theological discipline in its own right (cf Myklebust 1961:335-338). This, of course, flew in the teeth of the "fourfold pattern" (a problem encountered by other "new" theological disciplines as well, notably, theological ethics, ecumenical studies, and science of religion), but nevertheless gained ground rapidly. Charles Breckenridge was the first person to be appointed specifically to teach missionary instruction (at Princeton Theological Seminary, in 1836), although he was, at the same time, professor of pastoral theology (cf Myklebust 1955:146-151). Not so, however, with Alexander Duff's chair of evangelistic theology (as it was then called), established in Edinburgh in 1867; here missiology was taught as an independent subject in its own right (cf Myklebust 1955:19-24, 158-230). It was, however, mainly due to the indefatigable efforts of Gustav Warneck—who taught at the University of Halle (1896-1910)—that missiology was eventually established as a discipline in its own right, not just as a guest but as having the right of domicile in theology, as Warneck himself put it (quoted in Myklebust 1955:280).

Warneck's monumental contribution elicited responses not only in Protestant but also in Catholic circles. The founding of the first chair of missiology at a Catholic institution—in 1910, at the University of Münster (cf Müller 1989:67-74)—was undoubtedly influenced by developments in Protestantism and, more specifically, by Warneck's contribution. The first incumbent of the chair, Josef Schmidlin, freely acknowledged his indebtedness to Warneck, while at the same time always emphasizing the differences between him and Warneck (cf Müller 1989:177-186). The examples of Warneck and Schmidlin were soon followed elsewhere, particularly because of the tremendous impact the 1910 World Missionary Conference of Edinburgh had (Myklebust 1957:passim). In the course of time, some chairs of missiology were converted into chairs for world Christianity, comparative theology, ecumenical theology, and the like; however, many new chairs—specifically for missiology—have also been established, not only in the West but also in the Third World, particularly Africa and Asia, so there are more missiology chairs and departments today than there have ever been (cf Myklebust 1989).

This entire development turned out to be, at best, a mixed blessing. It gave no guarantee that missiology now had legal domicile in theology. Chairs were established not because theology was understood to be intrinsically missionary, but because of pressure from missionary societies, or (particularly in the United States) from students, or in some instances even from a government (as happened in the case of the chair at Münster which, at least in part, came into being because the German Ministry of Culture urged the theological faculty to attend to the "colonial system", and particularly to missions in the German protectorates, in its lectures [cf Müller 1989:69; in fact, Schmidlin's first major publication, after he took up the chair in Münster, was entitled *Die katholischen Missionen in den deutschen Schutzgebieten*, 1913]). All of this had serious consequences. Missiology became the theological institution's "department of foreign affairs", dealing with the exotic but at the same time peripheral. Other theologians often regarded their missiological colleagues with aloofness, if not condescension, particularly since they frequently happened to be retired ex-missionaries who had worked in "Tahiti, Teheran, or Timbuktu" (Sundkler 1968:114). At the same time, it meant that other teachers regarded themselves as being absolved of any responsibility to reflect on the missionary nature of theology (cf Mitterhöfer 1974:65).

All of this was further compounded when missiologists began to design their own encyclopedia of theology, naturally modelled on the "fourfold pattern" (cf Linz 1964:44f; Rütti 1974:292). "Missionary foundations" paralleled the biblical subjects, "missions theory" paralleled systematic theology, missions history had its counterpart in church history, and missionary practice in practical theology. For the rest, missiology continued to exist in splendid isolation. By duplicating the entire field of theology, it confirmed its image as a dispensable addendum; it was a science *of* the missionary, *for* the missionary.

A third approach, followed mainly in Britain—and usually dubbed integration—was to abandon the teaching of missiology as a separate subject and expect other theological disciplines to incorporate the missionary dimension into the entire field of theology. It sounds like a good solution, but has several serious defects. For instance, the teachers of other subjects usually are not sufficiently aware of the innate missionary dimension of all theology; neither do they have the knowledge to pay due attention to this dimension (cf Myklebust 1961:330-335). The study by Cracknell and Lamb (1986) illustrates the deficiencies in this model well.

From a Theology of Mission to a Missionary Theology

None of the three models—incorporation into an existing discipline, independence, or integration—succeeded (although one has to add that, at least in theory, the third model was theologically the soundest; cf, however, Cracknell and Lamb 1986:26). The basic problem, of course, was not with what *missiology* was but with what *mission* was. Where mission was defined virtually exclusively in terms of saving souls or of church extension, missiology could only be the science of and for the missionary, a practical (if not pragmatic) subject which responded to the question "How are we to execute our task?" But since the church was not understood as being "missionary by its very nature", mission and, by implication, missiology, remained an expendable extra.

By the sixth decade of this century, however, it was generally accepted, in all confessional families, that mission belongs to the essence of the church. For Protestants, the crucial dates are the Tambaram and Willingen meetings of the IMC (1938 and 1952) and the New Delhi assembly of the WCC, at which the IMC integrated with the WCC. For Catholics, Vatican II marked the occasion of mission ceasing to be a prerogative of the pope (who might delegate that responsibility to missionary orders and congregations) and becoming an intrinsic dimension of the church everywhere. Naturally, this had a profound bearing on the understanding of mission and missiology. The church was no longer perceived primarily as being *over against* the world but rather as *sent into* the world and existing *for the sake of* the world. Mission was no longer merely an activity *of* the church, but an expression of the *very being* of the church. All of this was now undisputed. At the Mexico City Conference of CWME (1963) W. A. Visser 't Hooft spoke on mission as a test of faith for the church. One could no longer think of the church except as being both called out of the world and sent forth into the world. The world could no longer be divided into "missionizing" and "missionary" territories. The whole world was a mission field, which meant that Western theology, too, had to be practiced in a missionary situation.

Only laboriously did theology begin to incorporate the new insight. Karl Barth succeeded in doing this better than most other systematic theologians (cf, for instance, Barth 1956:725). The outcome of it all was a real advance over the traditional position. In poetic language Ivan Illich gives expression to this. After defining mission as "the growth of the One Church but also the growth of the humanly ever new Church" (1974:5), he proceeds to define missiology as

> the science about the Word of God as the Church in her becoming; the Word as the Church in her borderline situations; the Church as a surprise and a puzzle; the Church in her growth; the Church when her historical appearance is so new that she has to strain herself to recognize her past in the mirror of the present; the Church where she is pregnant of new revelations for a people in which she dawns. . . . Missiology studies the growth of the Church into new peoples, the birth of the Church beyond its social boundaries; beyond the linguistic barriers within which she feels at home; beyond the poetic images in which she taught her children. . . . Missiology therefore is the study of the Church as surprise (:6f).

We can no longer go back to the earlier position, when mission was peripheral to the life and being of the church. It is for the sake of its mission that the church has been elected, for the sake of its calling that it has been made "God's own people" (1 Pet 2:9; cf Linz 1964:33). So mission cannot be defined only in terms of the church—even of the church which is mission by its very nature. Mission goes beyond the church. Illich is therefore correct when he also calls mission "the social continuation of the Incarnation", "the social dawning of the mystery", "the social flowering of the Word into an ever changing present" (1974:5). To say that the church is essentially missionary does not mean that mission is church-centered. It is *missio Dei*. It is trinitarian. It is mediating the love of God the Father who is the Parent of all people, whoever and wherever they may be. It is epiphany, the making present in the world of God the Son (cf AG 9). It is mediating the presence of God the Spirit, who blows where he wishes, without us knowing whence he comes and whither he goes (Jn 3:8). Mission is "the expression of the life of the Holy Spirit who has been set no limits" (G. van der Leeuw, quoted in Rosenkranz 1977:14). So mission concerns the world also beyond the boundaries of the church. It is the *world* God loves and for the sake of which the Christian community is called to be the salt and the light (Jn 3:16; Mt 5:13 – cf Linz 1964:33f; Neill 1968:76). The symbol "mission" should therefore not be confused with or confined to the term "missionary"; the church's missionary movement is only one form of the outward-oriented nature of the love of God (cf Haight 1976:640). Mission means serving, healing, and reconciling a divided, wounded humanity.

For our theologizing this has far-reaching consequences. Just as the church ceases to be church if it is not missionary, theology ceases to be theology if it loses its missionary character (cf Andersen 1955:60). The crucial question, then, is not simply or only or largely what church is or what mission is; it is also what theology is and is about (Conn 1983:7). We are in need of a missiological agenda for theology rather than just a theological agenda for mission (:13); for theology, rightly understood, has no reason to exist other than critically to accompany the *missio Dei*. So mission should be "the theme of all theology" (Gensichen 1971:250). Missiology may be termed the "synoptic discipline" within the wider encyclopedia of theology. It is not a case of theology occupying itself with the missionary enterprise as and when it seems to it appropriate to do so; it is rather a case of mission being that subject with which theology is to deal. For theology it is a matter of life and death that it should be in direct contact with mission and the missionary enterprise (cf Andersen 1955:60f; Meyer 1958:224; Schmidt 1973:193f).

Cracknell and Lamb (1986:2) remark that, in the first edition of their study (1980) they would not have dared to suggest that every curriculum should find some place for the study of missiology; now, however, they would insist that all theological questions should be thought about from the point of view of the theology of mission. Only in this way can a "better teaching" of every subject come about (:25f). In similar vein, a curriculum revision committee of Andover Newton Theological School identified an "almost universal corporate desire to widen our perspective to one of world concern" (Stackhouse 1988:25). One of the committee's key recommendations was to relate "each discipline specifically to a theology of mission" (:25; cf 49).

Within the broad framework of theology, missiology has a dual function. The first has to do with what Newbigin and Gensichen have termed the *"dimensional aspect"* (cf Gensichen 1971:80-95; 251f). Here missiology's task, in free partnership with other disciplines, is to highlight theology's reference to the world. Theoretically, then – and from the dimensional perspective – one might dispense with a separate subject called missiology. It is to permeate all disciplines and is not primarily one "sector" of the theological encyclopedia (cf Linz 1964:34f; Mitterhöfer 1974:103). The missionary idea is a retrieval of the universality that resides in the depth of the Good News; as such it is to infuse the entire curriculum rather than provide subject matter for a special course (Frazier 1987:47). Still it is, even if only for practical reasons, advisable to have a separate subject called missiology, for without it the other disciplines are not constantly reminded of their missionary nature. Missiology, then, accompanies the other theological subjects in their work; it puts questions to them and let them put questions to it; it needs dialogue with them for their and for its own sake (cf Meyer 1958:224; Linz 1964:35; Schmidt 1973:195). It is in terms of its dimensional aspect that missiology challenges and responds to the challenges of specific disciplines (cf Andersen 1955:59-62; Meyer 1958:221-224; Sundkler 1968:113-115; Gensichen 1971:252f; Schmidt 1973:196-198).

After what has already been said in the early chapters of this study, it would be superfluous to argue for the missionary dimension of Old and New Testament studies. The same would be true of the discipline of church history. The church has a history only because God has granted it the privilege of participating in the *missio Dei*. Gerhard Ebeling has suggested that church history is the history of the exegesis of Scripture; but would it not be equally appropriate to view it as the history of the sending of God? Instead, we have turned it into a series of *denominational* histories, where each denomination simply writes its own chronicles, carving the faces of its own fathers into its "private totem-pole" (Hoekendijk 1967a:349). Looked at from the perspective of mission, however, church history asks fundamentally different questions concerning issues such as the failure of the early church to accommodate the Jewish people; the attitude to "heretics" after Constantine, both inside and outside the Roman Empire; the disappearance, almost without trace, of the church in once highly christianized North Africa, Arabia, and the Near East, and the ensuing virtual immunization of Islam against the gospel; the official attitude of the church concerning the enslavement of non-Christians; the complicity of the church in colonialism and in the subjugation and exploitation of other races; the paternalism and imperialism that appear to be almost endemic in Western Christians; the identification of the "official" church with the elite rather than with the marginalized classes in nineteenth-century Europe; and so forth. Is it not because it has not looked at these and related issues from a missiological viewpoint that the Western church still is—in the words of M. Austin (quoted in Cracknell and Lamb 1986:87)—a nineteenth-century middle-class church struggling to come to terms with the twentieth century on the eve of the twenty-first?

Similar questions may be put in respect to systematic theology. For more than a millennium and a half systematic theology's only dialogue partner was philosophy. How can it, however, in the contemporary world, afford to ignore the social sciences? Even more important, how can it afford to disregard anti-Christian ideologies and the beliefs of people of other faiths? Equally critical, how can Western systematic theology continue to act as if it is universally valid and dismiss the indispensable contribution to theological thinking coming out of Third World situations? Indeed, how can systematic theology be blind to its own innate missionary character? If it ignores the question "Why mission?" it implicitly also ignores the questions, "Why the church?" and "Why even the gospel?"

Then there is the missionary dimension of practical theology. Without this dimension, practical theology becomes myopic, occupying itself only with the study of the self-realization of the church in respect of its preaching, catechesis, liturgy, teaching ministry, pastorate, and diaconate, instead of having its eyes opened to ministry in the world outside the walls of the church, of developing a hermeneutic of missionary activity, of alerting a domesticated theology and church to the world out there which is aching and which God loves.

In addition to the dimensional aspect, missiology has to attend to the *intentional* aspect of mission. This does not just mean that missiology is to introduce the church in the West to the Third World and prepare "specialists" to go and work there. Rütti (1974:304) is correct when he says that church and mission in the West should overcome its inbred *"tiers-mondisme"*, which immediately thinks of what it can do for the "less fortunate". It should discover that inculturation, liberation, dialogue, development, poverty, absence of faith, and the like are not only problems for Third-World churches, but also challenges to itself in its own context. But it should recognize that it is impossible to reflect theologically and practically about these challenges if it does not, simultaneously, alert itself and its "clientele" to the realities of the Third World. And essentially the same applies to those practicing theology in the Third World. For the entire Christian community—First-, Second-, and Third-World churches—missiology means globalization. But in order to achieve globalization, it needs specificity, concretization. It is only by means of a *missiologia in loco* that we can render service to the *missiologia oecumenica* (cf Jansen Schoonhoven 1974a:21; cf Mitterhöfer 1974:102f).

What Missiology Can and Cannot Do

Missiology, then, has a twofold task: in respect to theology and in respect to the missionary praxis. This can be elucidated in yet another way.

As regards the *first*, within the context of theological disciplines, missiology performs a critical function by continuously challenging theology to be *theologia viatorum*; that is, in its reflecting on the faith theology is to accompany the gospel on its journey through the nations and through the times (Jansen Schoonhoven 1974a:14; Mitterhöfer 1974:101). In this role, missiology acts as a gadfly in the house of theology, creating unrest and resisting complacency, opposing every ecclesiastical impulse to self-preservation, every desire to stay what we are, every inclination toward provincialism and parochialism, every fragmentation of humanity into regional or ideological blocs, every exploitation of some sectors of humanity by the powerful, every religious, ideological, or cultural imperialism, and every exaltation of the self-sufficiency of the individual over other people or over other parts of creation (cf Linz 1964:42; Gort 1980a:60).

Missiology's task, furthermore, is critically to accompany the missionary enterprise, to scrutinize its foundations, its aims, attitude, message, and methods—not from the safe distance of an onlooker, but in a spirit of co-responsibility and of service to the church of Christ (Barth 1957:112f). Missiological reflection is therefore a vital element in Christian mission—it may help to strengthen and purify it (cf Castro 1978:87). Since mission has to do with the dynamic relation between God and humankind, missiology consciously pursues its task from a faith perspective. Within the broad field of missiology every viewpoint is debatable; the faith perspective, however, is not negotiable (cf Oecumenische inleiding 1988:19f).

The faith perspective does not mean that the missiologist can, through careful exegesis of Scripture, get access to biblical "laws" of mission which determine, in detail, how mission has to be performed. It is improper to treat the present and the future simply as extension of what the "laws" of mission, revealed in Scripture or tradition, have once and for all ordained mission should be (cf Nel 1988:182f; 187). This traditional approach treats the missionary praxis as mute, as being subject to "remote control", as being allowed only to respond to stimuli coming from far back in history; as "application" of what has been established since all eternity.

This brings us, *second*, to the responsibility missiology has in respect of interacting with the missionary praxis. Mission is an *intersubjective* reality in which missiologists, missionaries, and the people among whom they labor are all partners (Nel 1988:187). This reality of the missionary praxis stands in creative tension with mission's origins, with the biblical text, and the history of the church's missionary involvement. It is, however, inappropriate to construe the divine origins of mission and its historical realization as opponents or competitors (:188). Rather, "faith and concrete-historical mission, theory and praxis determine each other" (Rütti 1972:240—my translation) and are dependent on each other. Present-day missiology's concern will be a contextual elucidation of the relationship between God, God's world, and God's church (Verstraelen 1988:438). It is, if one wishes, a "dialogue" between God, God's world, and God's church, between what we affirm to be the divine origin of mission and the praxis we encounter today.

In this dynamic tension text and context remain separate. We may neither, in a fundamentalist manner, force the context into the straitjacket of what we perceive the text to say, nor treat the text, Rorschach-like, as a normless blob into which we project our context-derived interpretations of what mission should be (cf Stackhouse 1988:217f). Traditionally, the first danger was the greater one. Nowadays the second danger is more real. It is the danger of contextualism, already discussed in the section on "Mission as Contextualization". We may not, however, without ado convert the context into the text. Missiology's task is not a purely pragmatic one. Its task is not simply maintenance of the missionary operation. Its primary goal is not recruiting candidates for missionary service or sanctioning existing missionary projects—our cherished "missions and missionlets" (Hoekendijk 1967a:299). This is indeed the way missiology and the role of the missiologist have often been viewed; the latter was appointed to the faculty mainly to generate interest in the "missionary idea" and, where necessary, to try and reverse the waning tide of interest in mission. And since this was the missiologist's main responsibility, missiology could make do with a minimal theological basis, just enough to keep the concern going (cf Mitterhöfer 1974:99). Where this happens, however, missiologists should not be surprised to discover that the really relevant missionary issues are being addressed outside rather than inside the department of missiology (cf Hoekendijk 1967a:299; Rütti 1972:227). Theology (and this, naturally, includes missiology), however, is not in itself proclamation of the message, but reflection on that message and on its proclamation. It does not in itself mediate the missionary vision; it critically examines it (cf Barth 1957:102-104). Missiology cannot, as such, issue in missionary involvement (:111). In short, a missionary vision is *caught*, not *taught* (Scherer 1971:149).

A shift to a subjectivistic basis for mission, then, will end in complete relativism. There *are* criteria by means of which we can assess and critique the context. It may not be easy to find criteria on which all can agree, but we must try. Stackhouse (1988:9) suggests that, since we can have some prospect of knowing something reliable about God, truth, and justice in sufficient degree to recognize it in views and practices of others, we should judge every context by establishing what is and what is not *divine*, *true*, and *just* in that context. Stackhouse hesitates to take the context as the basic authority (:26). This seems to me to be correct; it is Scripture (and, if we wish, tradition) that relates us and our context to the church and mission of all ages, and we cannot do without this. But equally, we cannot do without grounding our faith and our mission in a concrete, local context. So perhaps, as a strategy (if nothing else), we might give up all talk about what has priority, text or context, and concentrate on the *intersubjective* nature of the missionary enterprise and of missiological reflection on it.

Perhaps van Engelen's formulation sums it up best. He says that the challenge to missiology is "to link the always-relevant Jesus event of twenty centuries ago to the future of the promised reign of God for the sake of meaningful initiatives in the present" (1975:310 — my translation). In this way, new discussions on soteriology, christology, ecclesiology, eschatology, creation, and ethics will be initiated, and missiology will be granted the opportunity to make its own unique contribution (cf Oecumenische inleiding 1988:474).

This remains a hazardous undertaking. Every branch of theology — including missiology — remains piecework, fragile, and preliminary. There is no such thing as missiology, period. There is only missiology in draft. *Missiologia semper reformanda est.* Only in this way can missiology become, not only *ancilla theologiae*, "the handmaiden of theology" (cf Scherer 1971:153), but also *ancilla Dei mundi*, "handmaiden of God's world".

MISSION AS ACTION IN HOPE

The "Eschatology Office" Closed

Ernst Troeltsch once said of nineteenth-century (liberal) theology: "The eschatology office is mostly closed" (quoted in Wiedenmann 1965:11 — my translation). One of the most striking characteristics of twentieth-century theology is the rediscovery of eschatology, first in Protestantism, then in Catholicism. In our century the "eschatology office" has been working overtime.

It should come as no surprise that the recovery of the eschatological dimension is manifested particularly clearly in missionary circles. From the very beginning of the Christian church there appeared to have been a peculiar affinity between the missionary enterprise and expectations of a fundamental change in the future of humankind.

Only in our own time, however, have we begun to rediscover the fundamentally *historical* nature of biblical faith and eschatology. Chapters 1 through 4 of this study have attempted to trace this notion. It certainly does not begin with Jesus of Nazareth, however. In chapter 1, we referred to G. E. Wright, who argues that it belongs to the essence of the biblical faith, Old and New Testament, to perceive God primarily as a God *acting* in history (1952:22). "Revelation" does not mean making known what used to be hidden (this is what the Greek word *apokalypsis* primarily means); nor does it refer to the disclosing of God's will which was previously kept secret. Rather, revelation is the word for God making himself known in *historical acts* (:23, 25). The question, Who is God?, was answered with a reference to history—He is the God of Abraham, Isaac, and Jacob. And the story of Jesus of Nazareth is part of that history, unintelligible without it (:32).

The recovery of eschatology as ingredient of religion is a phenomenon thoroughly at variance with the Newtonian views of time and space as these were assumed in the classical historical-critical method of the "mechanical paradigm" (cf Martin 1987:373f). Eschatology stands for the hope element in religion. Even a Marxist philosopher like Ernst Bloch can say, "Where there is hope, there is religion" (quoted in Moltmann 1975:15). The Enlightenment has, for all intents and purposes, destroyed the category of hope. It discarded teleology and operated only in terms of cause and effect, not of purpose. "The god of physics gives us what we wish. But he does not tell us what we should wish", said George Santayana (quoted in Moltmann 1975:24). Only religion can tell us that.

Religion's answer to this question is twofold, however. One answer has been classically formulated by Mircea Eliade as "the myth of the eternal return"— what we hope for is what was but has been lost. At the beginning stood a paradise, a tension-free state of bliss, which we lost; salvation means the regaining of paradise. The Jewish and Christian answers differ from this. The future we hope for is not simply a repetition of or a return to the origin. Rather, the future is open toward a new beginning that will surpass the first beginning. The exodus, says Moltmann (1975:18), was understood in the Old Testament not as a mythical event of the origin but as a historic event which pointed beyond itself to a greater future of God. In Greek and Oriental mythology, the past is made present as a perpetual origin; in the Israelite perspective, the past is a promise of the future. As we can see in the constant controversy between Yahweh and the *baalim* in Canaan, the God of the future sets himself against the gods of the origin, of the cycle of nature, of the "eternal return".

This is—admittedly extremely oversimplified—also the way Jesus of Nazareth and the early church understood what God was doing in their time. Much of the New Testament gives evidence to a vibrant expectation that what has begun in Jesus is only the beginning of a new era—in which God will no longer be dealing only with Israel. In spite of the fact that the early Christians were convinced that, in Christ, history has entered into an unprecedented rapid, that, in fact, the future has now already invaded the present, they looked forward to events even greater than those they had experienced—those who believe in this Jesus would not only do the works he had done, but even "greater works than these" (Jn 14:12).

The Blurring of the Eschatological Horizon

Our study has, however, illustrated that the Christian church found it impossible to hold on to the eschatological-historical character of the faith. Christian proclamation shifted from announcement of the reign of God to introducing to people the only true and universal religion (cf Rütti 1972:128). In this development it was only natural that the Old Testament would be underplayed, even neglected. Compared to Christianity as the true and universal religion it was, at best, provisional but now largely antiquated (:95).

To a significant extent this was the result of the hellenization of the Christian faith. In the Greek culture even historians—such as Herodotus and Thucydides—understood history as a continuing circle. Philosophers likewise interpreted events in human history mainly as adumbrations of what was to come, as prototypes of the return to the origin. History—events in human life—became above all a manual for moral philosophy, a mirror for human use, illustration material for right conduct (cf van der Aalst 1974:143). This thinking made deep inroads into Christianity. The Logos was interpreted not so much as reference to the *historical* incarnation but was painted in purely metaphysical colors derived from Platonism. Origen's doctrine of the *apokatastasis* reintroduced the cyclical element into Christian theology. And even if this doctrine was not sanctioned, it did contribute to a growing ahistorical trend in Christianity (:144). Attention was transferred from eschatology to protology, a development which became abundantly clear in the trinitarian and christological controversies of the patristic period; discussions about the "origin" of Christ, his preexistence, dominated the theological agenda (cf Beker 1984:108).

During subsequent centuries eschatological expectations were channelled, largely, into two avenues (which were not, however, mutually exclusive). First, there was the tendency toward what may, very inadequately, be called the *mystical*. It took several forms, for instance *theosis* in the Eastern church and salvation as individual bliss in the Western church. Second, there was the tendency toward ecclesiocentrism. In this model the church is the extension of the incarnation and the logical fulfillment of Jesus' preaching about the coming reign of God. Braaten (1977:50) rightly calls this "the most conservative possible model of eschatology"—the church only has to sit on its past and raise up leaders to function as guardians of the heavenly treasure entrusted to it. Of course, neither of these models surrendered the belief in the return of Christ; this would, however, only be an unveiling of what, at the moment, is hidden from unbelievers because of their hardness of heart.

The two models predominated in all three major branches of Christianity:

Orthodox, Catholic, and Protestant. The onslaught of the Enlightenment on the Western church merely reinforced the prevailing trends. Being banished from the public sphere of facts to the private sphere of values and opinion, religion found refuge in the metahistory of mysticism, the eternal, suprahistorical redemption of the soul, or the safe enclave of the empirical church. Protestant missions gradually moved from the first: Pietism with its emphasis on the redemption of souls, to the second: the planting of self-governing, self-supporting, and self-expanding churches.

Better than most other branches of Protestantism, Puritanism succeeded in keeping alive a form of eschatological hope which was not merely individual or ecclesial (cf chapters 8 and 9 of this study). Increasingly, this hope was expressed in millennial categories. Authors like Jonathan Edwards and Samuel Hopkins fanned missionary enthusiasm and stimulated the dispersion of North American missionaries across the globe; the garden they had planted in the howling wilderness of North America produced seeds in abundance, enough for the whole world. The dominant theology, at least between the American Revolution and the Civil War, was postmillennial (Marsden 1980:49). More and more, however, it was a very domesticated postmillennialism, optimistic in the extreme, and concentrating on earthly happiness and prosperity. The primary assumption was the immanence of God—a conception derived from the influence of science, in particular Darwinian evolution theory, upon Protestant theology: the indwelling God was working out his purposes in the world of people, here and now. Only in premillennial circles did the original Puritan idea of a cataclysmic overthrow of the existing order survive—but then, in the late nineteenth and early twentieth century premillennialists were completely marginalized.

Developments on the European continent were similar—only there premillennialists were even more marginal to the mainstream. For liberal theology, the eschatology of the New Testament was an expendable husk, and in any case an embarrassment. In the theology of Warneck—even if it distinguished itself from the prevailing liberal theology—eschatology played no role (cf Wiedenmann 1965:187). In this respect, then, liberal and conservative theology, both European and Anglo-Saxon, were of one mind. Eschatological thinking was, for instance, hardly in evidence at the 1910 World Missionary Conference (cf van 't Hof 1972:48). Mission consisted, to a large extent, in the christianizing and civilizing of nations via church planting, to which German missiology further added that the emerging church had to be adapted to a particular people's *Volkstum* (cf Hoekendijk 1967a). And all of this was interpreted in terms of organic growth toward maturity.

The "Eschatology Office" Reopened

At the turn of the century New Testament scholars like Johannes Weiss and Albert Schweitzer argued that—contrary to the tenets of liberal theology—eschatology was not an expendable husk for Jesus and the early church, but integral to their entire life and ministry. Still, neither Weiss nor Schweitzer knew what to do with their discovery (cf Käsemann, quoted in Beker 1980:361).

It was only the trauma of two world wars that created a climate in which eschatological thinking once again began to make sense in mainline church and theology circles. This happened sooner in continental theology than in the Anglo-Saxon world, as the conferences of the IMC at Jerusalem (1928) and Tambaram (1938) demonstrated.[28] At Tambaram, Kraemer's book ([1938] 1947) reflected the vision of only a minority of delegates, mostly those from the European continent, as the so-called "German Eschatological Declaration" (which was, however, not signed only by Germans) illustrated. Only after World War II, at the occasion of the Willingen Conference of the IMC (1952), can one in more general terms refer to the "entrance of the eschatological foundation of mission into the ecumenical discussion" (Margull, quoted in van 't Hof 1972:173).

The "new eschatology" was, however, far from uniform. Wiedenmann (1965:26-49; 55-91; 131-178) distinguishes four major eschatological "schools" in German Protestantism, each of which had a significant impact on missionary thinking. These are the dialectical eschatology of the younger Barth (which influenced missiologists like Paul Schütz, the younger Karl Hartenstein, Hans Schärer, and Hendrik Kraemer), the existential eschatology of R. Bultmann (which was applied missiologically by Walter Holsten), the actualized eschatology of Paul Althaus (which inspired Gerhard Rosenkranz), and the salvation-historical eschatology of Oscar Cullmann (traces of which may be detected in the missiological thinking of Walter Freytag and the older Hartenstein).

In the *first* model, the absolute transcendence of God and his being totally separate from the world are stressed. God is in heaven; we are on the earth. The only link between God and humans is God's intervention in judgment and grace. In Barth's terminology, this divine intervention is eschatological through and through. In the 1921 edition of his *Römerbrief* he writes, "Christianity which is not totally and altogether eschatology has nothing at all to do with Christ" (quoted in Jansen Schoonhoven 1974a:34—my translation). In this tradition, "eschatology" simply becomes a hermeneutical term for what is ultimate and transcendent, an expression with which to repel even the slightest hint at human collaboration in bringing in the end. Barth holds onto the future coming of the reign of God in its fullness, but views it as being inaugurated solely by God, at the end of history.

The *second* model, associated primarily with the name of Bultmann, has some affinities with the first and stems from the same root. Radicalizing the Lutheran statement that "the Word alone will do it", Bultmann views eschatology as the event which unfolds itself between the proclaimed word—the *kerygma*—and the individual human being. Holsten applies this missiologically in his *Das Kerygma und der Mensch* (1953). Mission is limited to the offer of the possibility of a decision and of a new self-understanding in light of the *kerygma*. Wiedenmann, who throughout his study censures Protestantism for its low view of the church and of the societal dimension of the Christian faith, finds in Holsten the climax of "modern Protestant singularism, occasionalism and actualism" (1965:168—my translation). This eschatology had no ethic for public life and left the church helpless in the face of the demons of power-politics, particularly the challenge presented by National Socialism. Neither was there room for any expectation of a different future, of the irruption of the reign of God. All that remained was the "private apocalypse" occurring in the life of the individual.

The *third* model, Althaus's "actualized" eschatology, shows some resemblance to C. H. Dodd's "realized" eschatology (although Althaus would prefer to talk about "eschatology in the process of being realized"). Since the world has in principle its end in the judgment of the kingdom in Christ, every moment in history, and likewise history as a whole, is end-time, always equally close to the end (Beker 1980:361, summarizing Althaus's position). The early Christian confession that the Lord is at hand is as applicable today as it was then. The parousia is not to be looked forward to as an historical event, but is the *suspension* of all history. Therefore it is immaterial whether the end is "chronologically" close or distant—it is "essentially" always near. Rosenkranz, taking up the Althaus theme, interprets mission as the proclamation of a kingdom already present but yet hidden.

Wiedenmann judges all three of these interpretations to be examples of ahistorical eschatologies. Only the *fourth* model, the salvation-historical school, takes history seriously. It became increasingly clear, since the 1930s, that the dialectical eschatology of the early Barth as well as the views on eschatology of the schools of Bultmann and Althaus were leaving people helpless in the face of the challenges of the modern world.

The fourth approach distinguishes itself from the other three in several respects. First, it puts a special emphasis on the reign of God as a hermeneutical key. Equally fundamental to it is the idea of the reign of God as both present and future. Israel looked to the future for salvation, but now that future was split in two. The new age has begun; the old has not yet ended. We live between the times, between Christ's first and his second coming; this is the time of the Spirit, which means that it is the time for mission. As a matter of fact, mission is the most important characteristic of and activity during this interim period. It fills the present and keeps the walls of history apart—as even Hoekendijk could still put it in 1948 (the German translation [1967a:232] conceals the powerful metaphor and only says, "History is kept open by mission"). It is a preparation for the end and—in Cullmann's earlier writings—even a precondition. In keeping with this he interprets the reference to *ho katechon* and *to katechon* ("the one who restrains", "that which restrains") in 2 Thessalonians 2:6,7 as references to mission. Until the missionary task is completed, it is "holding up" the end.

Cullmann thus interprets mission in radically salvation-historical terms. At the same time he lends academic respectability to a view widely held in rank-and-file missionary circles and which again, as we approach the end of the second millennium, fans enthusiasm for efforts aimed at the evangelization of the entire world before the year 2000.

Perhaps somewhat surprisingly, however, the salvation-historical school of mission is turning out to be much less homogeneous than one might expect. As a matter of fact, one could make a case for the view that practically all contemporary schools of eschatology and of missionary thinking, in one way or another, are offshoots of the salvation-history approach — even if some of them might prefer to deny this ancestry.[29] Beker's reading of Paul as standing in the apocalyptic tradition and the significance of this for Christian mission (1980, 1984) also reveals some parallels with Cullmann (cf Cullmann 1965:225-245). Salvation-history thinking has, furthermore, inspired both conservative evangelical missionary scholars and liberation theologians — José Míguez Bonino, for instance, contributed to a Festschrift in Cullmann's honor in 1967.

It is also important to note that Cullmann has — from the first articles on the subject, published in the 1930s, through his *Christ and Time* (first German edition 1945) to his *Salvation as History* (first German edition 1965) — refined and redefined his own understanding of the relationship between eschatology and mission. In this development he has put more and more emphasis on the world-historical dimension of mission. I would therefore suggest that — barring some of Cullmann's rather crude formulations, particularly in his earlier writings, and his preoccupation with attempts to delineate salvation history as something entirely different from world history — the salvation history approach, broadly speaking, constitutes the most significant advance over earlier positions, both Catholic and Protestant (cf also Wiedenmann 1965:194-196), and the soundest base for an understanding of the eschatological nature of mission from a postmodern perspective. Still, it remains a hazardous enterprise to trace the contours of a reasonably reliable model of the eschatological nature of mission, as the following two sections will show.

Extreme Eschatologization of Mission

Throughout its history there were periods when Christianity was running a high eschatological fever. Our own time also seems to be such a period. Once again, predictions about the future are pouring in and, as we near the end of the second Christian millennium, we may expect the fever to reach an even higher pitch. Christian eschatology, in particular, seems to lend itself to becoming a playground for fanatical curiosity, as the writings of Hal Lindsey and others witness. At the same time, it would not do simply to label all millenarians as crackpots. The validity of their views lies in the anger and protest they voice against the complacency of the main Christian body, and against an understanding of history as a crisscrossing of chance impulses, an accidental flow of bodies tumbling over the cataract of time to their destruction (cf Braaten 1977:97-99).

In the past (and certainly also in Lindsey's writings) the preoccupation with the end has led to a paralysis in respect of mission, to an absence of missionary involvement. This was true of much of seventeenth-century Protestant orthodoxy. Its philosophy appeared to have been not that all must be saved but that most must be damned. It was only with the advent of Pietism that the time before the end was viewed not as a season of waiting but as time allowed for witness and for bringing in as many of the lost as possible.

Protestant orthodoxy, Pietism and much of their spiritual offspring shared one sentiment, however: boundless pessimism about the world. In his analysis of almost a century of German preaching on missions, Linz (1964) has shown that, in most of these sermons, the world was understood as totally forsaken by God or, alternatively, as having resolutely turned its back on God (:179). The world needs the church if it wishes to be saved, but the church does not need the world in order to be church (:136). The only positive remark we can still make about the world and about history is that they make mission possible as long as God's patience lasts (:178; cf Freytag 1961:213f). All the good lies in the past and the future. In this essentially Manichean view history is a conspiracy, set in motion by demonic forces. As was true of the Qumran community of the first century AD, Christian conversion means that individuals should separate themselves from the masses, who are on their way to eternal damnation.

Sometimes, however, this pessimism about the world may go hand in hand with great optimism about the missionary enterprise. This was already true of much of Pietism but is also in evidence in some contemporary evangelical circles. At the LCWE Consultation held in Pattaya (Thailand) in 1980, the key notion was *opportunities* — the world was waiting for the gospel of eternal redemption and people were ready to respond positively to the invitation to become Christians. McGavran often exudes a similar confidence about the opportunities awaiting the church-in-evangelism (cf 1980:49). The only real history is the history of missions (Linz 1964:136, 178); it is the hand on the clock of the world, telling us what time it is and when we may expect Christ's second coming (:132). The overriding purpose of mission is the preparation of people for the hereafter, ensuring for each a safe passage to heaven. At best, history is a prologue, a preparation, a provisional stage. At worst, it is the believer's enemy, an abiding threat, and a possible source of contagion, since the continuation of history only increases the "distance" between the dreary present and the glorious future.

It is to be expected that such a pessimistic understanding of history would discourage virtually every attempt at reforming the world and human conditions. For Freytag, progress in world history consists, at most, in an increase of catastrophes (1961:216). The New Testament knows no other progress in history than that the end is drawing near (:215). Human history, meanwhile, stands under the sign of the advance of the demonic (:189). Our task is not to build up God's kingdom in this world, to christianize society, or to change structures (:200). There are limits set to what we can and should do, and we should not anticipate now what will only become visible at the arrival of the new creation (:96f).

Freytag must be understood in his context, however. He wrote against the immediate background of the catastrophe of World War II; he had seen what human "achievements" can produce and wished his readers to be modest about their abilities. Referring to Freytag's missiology, Warren (1961:161) says that it was the experience of the abyss which divided continental from Anglo-Saxon thinking about almost every subject, and not least about mission. In this respect Freytag was decidedly postmodern and very different from those today who, judged on the surface, are saying more or less the same as he did. Freytag was pleading that we should abandon our incurable success-thinking, that we should do what has to be done regardless of the results (cf Freytag 1961:222). He also criticized those missionaries and mission agencies which were blind to service *in* and *for the sake of* this world, for whom the reign of God was an exclusively otherworldly entity (:211), and who sometimes even appeared to welcome the decay of society as a sure sign of the imminence of the parousia. Freytag supported the entire comprehensive missionary program of his time as well as the activities of the ecumenical movement. By contrast, many who appear to stand in the Freytag tradition are actually victims of an insidious dualism, where the emphasis on being saved for the next life alienates and separates the individual from involvement in this world, even if they may magnanimously state, "Social service is of course important, but *our* task is evangelism". If, in addition, their refusal to challenge unjust societal structures is rooted in a view about the inviolability of the "orders of creation", they cannot appeal to Freytag or, for that matter, to Cullmann, who states that the "already" of the reign of God outweighs its "not yet" (1965:164).

The validity of the views of Freytag and Cullmann lies in their unflagging insistence that there is no authentic mission without a fundamental eschatological disposition. For Freytag, in particular, this finds expression in his ever recurring references to the *basileia*, the reign of God as the substance and goal of mission. It was therefore fitting that the Festschrift published in his honor should bear the title *Basileia*. God's reign remains, essentially, a gift; we can never identify it with an empirical structure. And yet, even if Freytag would add that God's reign is not only gift but also challenge, his emphasis on *waiting* can easily lead to quietism. We may become guilty of the sin of temerity, confusing God's reign with what we have achieved in this world; we may, however, also become guilty of the sin of timidity, hoping for less than has been promised. This world may indeed be enemy-occupied territory, but the enemy has no property rights in it (cf Warren 1948:53). He is a usurper. We are not called to act as God's fifth columnists, carrying out commando raids and snatching lost souls from the "prince of this world". Rather, we are to claim this entire world for God, as part of God's reign. God's future reign impinges upon the present; in Christ, the future has been brought drastically closer to the present. A fixation on the parousia at the end simply means that we are evading our responsibilities in the here and now. Submitting to Christ as Savior is inseparable from submitting to him as Lord not only our personal lives but also political and economic systems in the corporate life of society.

History as Salvation

As intimated above, the salvation-history school has not only given rise to an extreme eschatologization of mission, but also to an entirely this-worldly interpretation of the eschatological character of mission. One can, after all, either interpret salvation history as something completely separate from and untouched by world history, or one can take the opposite course; that is, secularize salvation history and thus, by implication, sacralize world history (cf Beyerhaus 1969:49). This happens where one abandons any idea of the uniqueness of the church and concentrates, rather, on the uniqueness of what happens in the world outside the church. Instead of talking about "salvation as history" (cf the title of Cullmann 1965), one then talks about "history as salvation". History is not only the "context" of mission, but its "text" (Rütti 1972:232).

Usually, this is not done with the help of purely secular terminology. Rather, one continues to use religious, even ecclesiastical, language. History needs a "spiritual base". So the incarnation of Christ becomes the symbol of the world-historical salvation process that emerges progressively and immanently through cultural, moral, social, political, and even revolutionary enlightenment (cf Braaten 1977:50). Having become impatient with the slowness of the coming of God's reign, we take things into our own hands, redefine the kingdom, and seek to build it with instant techniques, while continuing to use the name of Christ to endorse our party or program of self-improvement and world betterment (:101). Then the kingdom of God, in the words of W. Rauschenbusch (quoted in West 1971:77), is "the energy of God realizing itself in human life", in the form of whatever happens to be the socio-political ideals of the age or of the group in question. "Mission" and "missionary" merely become shorthand for the discharge of societal responsibilities, since there is no human activity for the sake of the world which is not in itself mission (Linz 1964:206). The question, after all—as it was put at the Uppsala meeting of the WCC (1968)— is not nearly so much what God has spoken in the Bible as what God is doing in the world today. The "divine" is to be experienced *only* in historical risk and engagement, since God is *only* God insofar as he is acting in the world. Thus Christians can recognize their mission *only* in the midst of worldly processes (Rütti 1972:232f). Where liberation to true humanity has taken place, we may conclude that the *missio Dei* has reached its goal (Hoekendijk 1967a:347). All people already belong to the new humanity, constituted in Christ, whether they are aware of it or not.

However, if one rejects the extreme eschatologization of mission, one also has to reject its twin—the extreme historicization of mission. The world, once it has been emancipated, cannot but dictate the conditions under which it would be prepared to accept a "missionary" encounter with itself (cf Gensichen 1986:116). It will decide, on its own terms, which kind of political ideology or praxis is kosher. But where this happens, the gospel gets converted into law. Our incurable tendency to spoil everything we touch and our inveterate drive to self-seeking then become the ultimate arbiters of what action is appropriate. Far from being the climax of *our* ideals, however, the reign of God passes a sovereign judgment on them; it remains a critical category and often goes against the grain of our history (cf Lochman 1986:63). It is this focus on the reign of God, both present and future, that may grant us some appropriate perspective on our mission in the world. Without this eschatological dimension our "gospel" becomes reduced to ethics (cf Braaten 1977:39, 152).

Eschatology and Mission in Creative Tension

There is some validity to Aagaard's observation (1965:256) that, generally speaking, and until the sixth decade of the twentieth century, the stricter eschatological perspective was evidenced in continental European missionary circles, with the North Americans emphasizing social involvement. Since then, the scene has become blurred, so that it is no longer possible to distinguish in this manner. In every Christian tradition and in every continent we are still in the midst of a movement to reformulate a theology of mission in the light of an authentic eschatology (cf Braaten 1977:36). Meanwhile, we can say that there is today widespread agreement that eschatology determines the horizon of all Christian understanding, even if we are still groping for its precise meaning. It has become clear, however, that neither the eschatologization nor the historicization of mission satisfies. In its fixation on the parousia, the first has neglected the problems of this world and thereby crippled Christian mission. In its preoccupation with this world to the exclusion of the transcendent dimension, the second has robbed people of ultimate meaning and of a teleological dimension without which nobody can survive (cf Moltmann 1975:20-24).

We need a way beyond both. We need an eschatology for mission which is both future-directed and oriented to the here and now. It must be an eschatology that holds in creative and redemptive tension the already and the not yet; the world of sin and rebellion, and the world God loves; the new age that has already begun and the old that has not yet ended (Manson 1953:370f); justice as well as justification; the gospel of liberation and the gospel of salvation. Christian hope does not spring from despair about the present. We hope because of what we have already experienced. Christian hope is both possession and yearning, repose and activity, arrival and being on the way. Since God's victory is certain, believers can work both patiently and enthusiastically, blending careful planning with urgent obedience (:149), motivated by the patient impatience of the Christian hope. The disciples' being sent to the uttermost ends of the earth (Acts 1:8) is the only reply they get to their question about *when* God's reign would be inaugurated in its fullness.

There is no choice, then, between becoming involved in *either* salvation history *or* profane history. Salvation history is not a separate history, a separate thread unfolding itself inside secular history. There are not two histories, but there are two ways of understanding history. The distinction therefore only has noetic significance. The Christian is not preoccupied with a different set of historical facts, but uses a different perspective. The secular historian will turn salvation history into profane history, whilst the believer will see the hand of God also in secular history. Not that history (either salvation or secular history) will always be transparent to the believer. There are paradoxes, gaps, discontinuities, riddles, and mysteries in all history (cf Braaten 1977:95f). Thus the history of salvation is, for the Christian, both revealed and hidden, both transparent and opaque (cf Blaser 1978:35-42).

Christian eschatology, then, moves in all three times: past, present, and future. The reign of God has already come, is coming, and will come in fullness. It is because God already rules and because we await the public manifestation of his rule that we may, in the here and now, be ambassadors of his kingdom. Christians can never be people of the status quo. They pray, "Your kingdom come . . . on earth as in heaven!" and interpret this both as a petition to God and as a challenge to themselves to attack evil structures around them (Käsemann 1980:67). The fullness of the reign of God is still coming, but precisely the vision of that coming kingdom translates itself into a radical concern for the "penultimate" rather than a preoccupation with the "ultimate", into a concern for "what is at hand" rather than for "what will be" (cf Beker 1984:90). In Christ's death and resurrection the new age has irreversibly begun and the future is guaranteed; living in the force-field of the assurance of salvation already received and the final victory already secured, the believer gets involved in the urgency of the task at hand. In this sense, eschatology is taking place right now.

Looked at from this perspective we have to agree with Cullmann (1965:164) that the "already" outweighs the "not yet". This, in a nutshell, is what the postmodern paradigm proclaims in respect to eschatology, particularly since the 1938 Tambaram meeting of the IMC (cf van 't Hof 1972:119; Bassham 1979:24). The new perspective is not merely a variation on an earlier position but something fundamentally different (cf Rütti 1972:73 [note 38], 76). Instead of seeking to know God's future world plan, we ask about the Christian's involvement in the world (:221). The world is no longer viewed as a hindrance, but as a challenge. Christ has risen, and nothing can remain the way it used to be. It was a stupendous victory of the evil one to have made us believe that structures and conditions in this world will not or need not really change, to have considered political and societal powers and other vested interests inviolable, to have acquiesced in conditions of injustice and oppression, to have tempered our expectation to the point of compromise, to have given up the hope for a wholesale transformation of the status quo, to have been blind to our own responsibility for and involvement in a world en route to its fulfillment. In assuming a critical stance vis-a-vis the authorities, prescriptions, traditions, institutions, and ideological predilections of the existing world order, we are to become a ferment of God's new world (cf Gort 1980b:54).

Without taking back anything just said and without again pleading for some degree of moderation or compromise, a note of warning is nevertheless in order. By nature, we are all romantics and Pelagians (which amounts to the same thing—cf Henry 1987:275), confident that we have both the will and the power to usher in a new world. We too easily identify God's will and power with ours. In essence, however, Weiss's and Schweitzer's studies should already a century ago have sounded the death knell to any immanental, progressivistic, evolutionary, and ethical concept of the reign of God as a human product (cf Braaten 1977:40). We will never realize our blueprint for a societal and political order that will match the will and rule of God. In fact, it belongs to the essence of Christian teleology that it doubts that the eschatological vision can be fully realized in history (Stackhouse 1988:206). God's transformation is different from human innovations. God takes us by surprise. God is always before us, his coming triumph bidding us to follow—as Beker (1980, 1984) has so lucidly illustrated in respect of Paul's theology (see chapter 4 above). From this perspective, then, the future holds the primacy. The ultimate triumph remains uniquely God's gift. It is *God* who makes all things new (Rev 21:5). If we turn off the lighthouse of eschatology we can only grope around in darkness and despair.

The two affirmations made in the previous two paragraphs are not to be seen as mutually exclusive, however. On the contrary. The transcendent message of God's sure triumph gives us the necessary distance and sobriety in respect to this world as well as the motivation to involve ourselves in the transformation of the status quo. Precisely the vision of God's triumph makes it impossible to look for sanctuary in quietism, neutrality, or withdrawal from the field of action. We may never overrate our own capabilities; and yet, we may have confidence about the direction into which history moves, for we are not, like Sartre, peering into the abyss of nothingness, nauseated by the emptiness of our freedom, leaping into a future which only confirms the meaninglessness of the present moment (cf Braaten 1977:98).

We do distinguish between hope for the ultimate and perfect on the one hand, and hope for the penultimate and approximate, on the other. We make this distinction under protest, with pain, and at the same time with realism. We know that our mission — like the church itself — belongs only to this age, not to the next. We perform this mission in hope. So, if Margull (1962) was correct in referring to the evangelism dimension of our missionary calling as *"hope in action"*, it may be correct to label our entire, comprehensive mission in the context of our eschatological expectation as *"action in hope"* (cf also Sundermeier 1986:60f). But then we must define our mission — with due humility — as participation in the *missio Dei*. Witnessing to the gospel of present salvation and future hope we then identify with the awesome birthpangs of God's new creation.

Chapter 13

Mission in Many Modes

IS EVERYTHING MISSION?

There can be no doubt that the last decades have seen a surprising escalation in the usage of the term "mission"—surprising, that is, in light of the fact that these decades have also witnessed unparalleled criticism of the missionary enterprise. The inflation of the concept has both positive and negative implications. One of the negative results has been the tendency to define mission too broadly—which prompted Neill (1959:81) to formulate his famous adage, "If everything is mission, nothing is mission", and Freytag (1961:94) to refer to "the spectre of panmissionism". Even if these warnings have to be taken seriously, it remains extraordinarily difficult to determine what mission is. This entire study has evolved from the assumption that the definition of mission is a continual process of sifting, testing, reformulating, and discarding. Transforming mission means both that mission is to be understood as an activity that transforms reality and that there is a constant need for mission itself to be transformed.

Attempts to define mission are of recent vintage. The early Christian church undertook no such attempts—at least not consciously. And yet, our surveys of the "mission theology" of Matthew, Luke, and Paul have shown that their writings may be interpreted as sustained endeavors at defining and redefining what the church was called to do in the world of their day. More recently, however, it has become necessary to design definitions of mission in a more conscious and explicit manner. Since the nineteenth century such attempts have been legion.

Around the time of the Jerusalem Conference of the IMC (1928) it became clear that most definitions were hopelessly inadequate. Jerusalem coined the notion "Comprehensive Approach", which marked a significant advance over all earlier definitions of mission. The Whitby Meeting of the IMC (1947) then used the terms *kerygma* and *koinonia* to summarize its understanding of mission. In a famous paper, first published in 1950, Hoekendijk (1967b:23) added a third element: *diakonia*. The Willingen Conference (1952) made the expanded formula its own, adding the notion of "witness", *martyria*, as the overarching concept: "This *witness* is given by *proclamation, fellowship* and *service*" (quoted in Margull 1962:175). For the next three decades the expression dominated missiological discussions as the most appropriate and comprehensive portrayal of what mission is or is supposed to be. One encounters it in almost every book on the theology of mission after 1952. There are, naturally, some variations in the definitions. Sometimes *martyria* and *kerygma* are treated interchangeably and as synonyms (cf Snyder 1983:267). Others add *leitourgia*, "liturgy," as a further element (cf Bosch 1980:227-229).

The formula, even in adapted form, has severe limitations, however. Rütti (1972:244) concedes that it has served to lead mission out of the straitjacket of defining it only in terms of proclamation or church planting and that, here and there, it may still serve some purpose. However, he laments the fact that, in the final analysis, it only helps to illuminate traditional ideas and activities. I tend to agree with Rütti. We do need a more radical and comprehensive hermeneutic of mission. In attempting to do this we may perhaps move close to viewing everything as mission, but this is a risk we will have to take. Mission is a multifaceted ministry, in respect of witness, service, justice, healing, reconciliation, liberation, peace, evangelism, fellowship, church planting, contextualization, and much more. And yet, even the attempt to list some dimensions of mission is fraught with danger, because it again suggests that we can define what is infinite. Whoever we are, we are tempted to incarcerate the *missio Dei* in the narrow confines of our own predilections, thereby of necessity reverting to one-sidedness and reductionism. We should beware of any attempt at delineating mission too sharply. And perhaps one cannot really do this by means of *theoria* (which involves "observation, reporting, interpretation, and critical evaluation") but only by means of *poiesis* (which involves "imaginative creation or representation of evocative images") (Stackhouse 1988:85).

FACES OF THE CHURCH-IN-MISSION

Our mission has to be multidimensional in order to be credible and faithful to its origins and character. So as to give some idea of the nature and quality of such multidimensional mission, we might appeal to images, metaphors, events, and pictures rather than to logic or analysis. I therefore suggest that one way of giving a profile to what mission is and entails might be to look at it in terms of six major "salvific events" portrayed in the New Testament: the incarnation of Christ, his death on the cross, his resurrection on the third day, his ascension, the outpouring of the Holy Spirit at Pentecost, and the parousia.

1. *The Incarnation*: Protestant churches, by and large, have an underdeveloped theology of the incarnation. The churches of the East, Roman Catholics, and Anglicans have always taken the incarnation far more seriously—albeit the Eastern church tends to concentrate on the incarnation within the context of the preexistence, the "origin", of Christ. In recent years it has, however, been liberation theology which, far more explicitly than has hitherto been the case, viewed the Christian mission in terms of the incarnate Christ, the human Jesus of Nazareth who wearily trod the dusty roads of Palestine where he took com-

passion on those who were marginalized. He is also the one who today sides with those who suffer in the *favelas* of Brazil and with the discarded people in South Africa's resettlement areas. In this model, one is not interested in a Christ who offers only eternal salvation, but in a Christ who agonizes and sweats and bleeds with the victims of oppression. One criticizes the bourgeois church of the West, which leans toward docetism and for which Jesus' humanness is only a veil hiding his divinity. This bourgeois church has an idealist understanding of itself, refuses to take sides, and believes that it offers a home for masters as well as slaves, rich and poor, oppressor and oppressed. Because it refuses to practice "solidarity with victims" (Lamb 1982), such a church has lost its relevance. Having peeled off the social and political dimensions of the gospel, it has denatured it completely.

Our survey of the early church's (and particularly Luke's) understanding of mission has proved the validity of this perspective. The Western church has been tempted to read the gospels—in Kähler's famous phrase—as "passion histories with extensive introductions". The recent emphasis on the significance of the incarnation—which has been accepted into the ecumenical movement at least since the 1980 Melbourne CWME Conference—is calling our attention precisely to these "extensive introductions" and their significance for our mission. Melbourne concentrated, to a large extent, on "the earthly Jesus, the Jew, the Nazarene, who lived as a simple Galilean man, suffered and was executed, dying on the cross" (J. Matthey in WCC 1980:ix). The "practice of Jesus" (Echegaray 1984) has indeed much to say about the nature and content of mission today.

2. *The Cross*: Kähler's phrase, just quoted, betrays the preoccupation of the Western church—Catholic and Protestant—with the passion and crucifixion of Jesus. To the question, What is the essence of the gospel?, most Western Christians would probably reply, "It is that Christ died for my sins on the cross". Without embarking on a discussion of the doctrine of the atonement, let it suffice to say that it would seem that such a view indeed has a biblical basis; according to sayings such as Mark 10:45 and several utterances of Paul, one may conclude that, for many in the early church, Christ was the new "place of expiation" which replaced the temple (cf Pesch 1982:41f). Those who accept him as Savior have their sins forgiven. This opens to them the way to become members of a new, saved community, called church, a unique body of those with whom God has a special relationship.

Jesus' death on the cross should not, however, be isolated from his life. The "extensive introductions" to the gospels are themselves already passion stories. Jesus' *kenosis*, his self-emptying, began at his birth. And it was because of his identification with those on the periphery and his refusal to act according to the conventions of the day that he was crucified. But there is more to it than this. The cross of Jesus is, uniquely, the badge of distinction of the Christian faith (cf Moltmann 1975:4). And when the risen Christ commissioned his disciples to go on the same mission that he had received from the Father, it was the scars of his passion that revealed to them who he was (Jn 20:20). Without the cross, Christianity would be a religion of cheap grace (cf Koyama 1984:256-

261). The cross goes against the grain of any human being. It is not natural. And if, in the postmodern era, it may seem as if religion is once again acceptable and natural — as Capra and others argue — it has to be pointed out that a religion of the cross cannot be natural; the cross constitutes a permanent danger to any religiosity (Josuttis 1988; cf Koyama 1984:240-261).

The scars of the risen Lord do not only prove Jesus' identity, however; they also constitute a model to be emulated by those whom he commissions: "As the Father has sent me, even so I send you" (Jn 20:21). It is a mission of self-emptying, of humble service — herein lies the abiding validity of Bonhoeffer's idea of the "church for others". In the series of international missionary conferences it was especially Jerusalem (1928) and Willingen (1952) which stood in the sign of a theology of the cross. Willingen convened under the theme "The Missionary Obligation of the Church"; its report was, however, published as *Missions Under the Cross*. All mission, said Hartenstein with respect to Willingen, is ministry to truth in humility (quoted in van 't Hof 1972:160). In the presence of the cross the church-in-mission has to repent before it engages in mission. In the words of Käsemann, in his address to the Melbourne conference, "Churches that do not repent deny their reality and reject the Lord who also had to die for them. They fail to stand under the cross where all our sins come to light and where we in our humanity are crucified with him" (WCC 1980:69). Paul discovered that it was not in spite of but because of the death he found himself dying every day that he was an apostle, a missionary (cf 1 Cor 15:31; 2 Cor 12:10). "When Christ calls a man, he bids him come and die", wrote Bonhoeffer in the midst of the German church struggle (quoted in West 1971:223). Herein lies the missionary significance of the cross. "Suffering is the divine mode of activity in history. . . The church's mission in the world, too, is suffering . . . is participation in God's existence in the world" (Schütz 1930:245 — my translation).

The cross also stands for reconciliation between estranged individuals and groups, between oppressor and oppressed. Reconciliation does not, of course, mean a mere sentimental harmonizing of conflicting groups. It demands sacrifice, in very different but also in very real ways, from both oppressor and oppressed. It demands the end to oppression and injustice and commitment to a new life of mutuality, justice, and peace. And yet, without taking away anything from this assertion, it has to be added that there may be wrongs that cannot be repaired by human means, that we should not allow ourselves to be trapped in "helpless, desperate guilt feelings" or in the idea "that justice must be our justice, that we can and must cancel our guilt by restitution, or . . . overcome our frustration by mere action" (H. Bortnowska, in WCC 1980:150).

Among the moral teachers of the world Christ alone does not make everything depend on moral success. In addition to reconciliation, then, the cross — missiologically speaking — also means a ministry of love of enemies, of forgiveness. It is an assertion "that *loving is worthwhile*, whatever it may cost in self-giving and even death" (Segundo 1986:152 — italics in original). It was for this above all, says Baker (1986:162), that Jesus gave his life. He adds a quotation from the Staretz Silouan: "Without love of enemies there is no following of

Christ". This is a hard saying, for it spells the absolute end to any form of self-righteousness. So the cross is also a critical category. It tells us that mission cannot be realized when we are powerful and confident but only when we are weak and at a loss. Nothing we do is exempt from the judgment of the cross. There is no righteous action which does not also need to be forgiven, not least since the power which works for justice today may be unjust tomorrow (cf West 1971:229; Henry 1987:279).

3. *The Resurrection*: In the Eastern churches it is the resurrection of Christ which is God's salvific event *par excellence*. The planners of the Melbourne conference (1980) had assigned to Section IV the theme "The Crucified Christ Challenges Human Power". Orthodox participants, however, criticized the formulation. So the theme was rephrased and changed to "Christ — *Crucified and Risen* — Challenges Human Power". The Orthodox intervention was appropriate. Jesus' death on the cross remains meaningless without the resurrection. Early Christians viewed the Easter event as the vindication of Jesus. Cross and resurrection are not in balance with each other; the resurrection has the ascendancy and victory over the cross (Berkhof 1966:180). The most common summary of the early church's missionary message was that it was witnessing to the resurrection of Christ. It was a message of joy, hope, and victory, the first fruit of God's ultimate triumph over the enemy. And in this joy and victory believers may already share. This is, among other things, what the Eastern church gives expression to in its doctrine of *theosis*, of divinization; it is the beginning of "life in incorruption" (Clement of Rome). In the resurrection of Christ the forces of the future already stream into the present and transform it, even if everything that meets the eye appears to be unchanged. The Christian's life continues on two planes, as it were (cf Segundo 1986:159). God's promise and our hope are already full reality in Christ, before they are fully realized in human history; in Christ eternity has entered time, life has conquered death (Memorandum 1982:463).

Missiologically this means, first, that the central theme of our missionary message is that Christ is risen, and that, secondly and consequently, the church is called to live the resurrection life in the here and now and to be a sign of contradiction against the forces of death and destruction — that it is called to unmask modern idols and false absolutes (Memorandum 1982:463).

4. *The Ascension*: The Calvinist tradition, one could say, focuses on the ascension. For John Calvin, Christians live between the ascension and the parousia; from that position they seek to comprehend what their mission is (cf Krass 1977:1). The ascension is, preeminently, the symbol of the enthronement of the crucified and risen Christ — he now reigns as King. And it is from the perspective of the present reign of Christ that we look back to the cross and the empty tomb and forward to the consummation of everything. Christian faith is marked by an inaugurated eschatology (:10). This is true not only of the church — as if the church is the present embodiment of God's reign — but also of society, of history, which is the arena of God's activity (:8). Salvation history is not opposed to profane history, nor grace to nature. Therefore, to opt out of civil society and set up little Christian islands is to subscribe to a truncated and disjunctive

understanding of God's workings (:5). In the Calvinist tradition there is, therefore, a positive attitude toward what may be achieved in human and world history.

Together with the emphasis on the incarnation, one may say that this theological tradition more than any other has exercised a profound influence on the ecumenical movement. It is committed to the view that Christ's order of life already forcefully progresses throughout the world (Berkhof 1966:170). Mission from this perspective means that it should be natural for Christians to be committed to justice and peace in the social realm. God's reign is real, though as yet incomplete. We will not inaugurate it, but we can help make it more visible, more tangible. Within this unjust world, we are called to be a community of those committed to the values of God's reign, concern ourselves with the victims of society and proclaim God's judgment on those who continue to worship the gods of power and self-love. In the words of Section IV.3 of the Melbourne conference, "The proclamation of God's reign is the announcement of a new order which challenges those powers and structures that have become demonic in a world corrupted by sin against God" (WCC 1980:210).

The glory of the ascension remains intimately linked to the agony of the cross, however. The same paragraph from Melbourne (Section IV.3) refers to "the most striking image ... of a sacrificed lamb, slaughtered but yet living, sharing the throne ... with the living God himself". Likewise, the words of Jesus in John 12:32 – "When I am *lifted up* from the earth" – have traditionally been interpreted as reference both to his being "lifted up" on the cross and to his ascension. The Lord we proclaim in mission remains the suffering Servant. "The principle of self-sacrificing love is ... enthroned at the very centre of the reality of the universe" (:210). And this principle has to be transparent in our missionary praxis. It is thus not strange that Melbourne was the conference at which both the weakness of the incarnate Jesus and the power of the ascended Christ were celebrated. Käsemann, in particular (in WCC 1980:61-71), stressed the identity of the Crucified with the *Kyrios*.

5. *Pentecost*: The Pentecostal and charismatic movements tend to view the Pentecost event as God's deed *par excellence*. Some would even say that, after an era in church history in which the emphasis was on God the Father, followed by the era of the Son, we have now – particularly since the beginning of the twentieth century – entered into the era of the Spirit. In this new dispensation we strive after the total wealth of heaven and unceasing ecstasy now. So one encounters in these circles claims about the occurrence of miraculous events and the exhilaration of an unbroken chain of mountaintop experiences.

Without denying the element of validity in this interpretation of Pentecost, I wish to suggest that, from a missiological viewpoint, there is more to say. First, when the risen Christ was asked by his disciples about the restoration of the kingdom to Israel (Acts 1:6), he replied by promising them the Spirit of witness. Our study of Luke's writings, in particular, has revealed the Holy Spirit as the Spirit of boldness (*parresia*) in the face of adversity and opposition. So "the Church continues Christ's mission in the power of his spirit" (Memorandum 1982:461).

The era of the Spirit is, furthermore, the era of the church. And the church in the power of the Spirit (Moltmann 1977) is itself part of the message it proclaims. It is a fellowship, a *koinonia*, which actualizes God's love in its everyday life and in which justice and righteousness are made present and operative. We cannot ignore this community, indeed are forbidden to do so (Lochman 1986:70). It is a *distinct* community, but not a club, not a ghetto society. The Spirit may not be held hostage by the church, as if his sole task were to maintain it and protect it from the outside world (:71). The church exists only as an organic and integral part of the entire human community, "for as soon as it tries to understand its own life as meaningful in independence from the total human community it betrays the only purpose which can justify its existence" (Baker 1986:159).

Even its worship, its celebration of the Eucharist, does not fall outside this frame of reference. The Orthodox churches teach us that the Eucharist is the most missionary of all the activities of the church (cf Bria 1975:248). On the one hand it is a celebration and anticipation of the coming triumph of God (Moltmann 1977:191f, 196, 242-275); on the other hand it is, each time we celebrate it, an invitation to share our bread with the hungry (cf Melbourne, Section III.31 [WCC 1980:206]; Memorandum 1982:462).

6. *The Parousia*: Ever since the first century there have been adventist groups whose central focus was on the second coming of Christ. They have tended to regard the reign of God as an exclusively future reality and this world as a vale of tears, in the grip of the evil one. In this model the church is merely a waiting room for eternity. The eyes of the faithful are fixed on the distant horizon and on the clouds, whence Christ will return as Lord, to change everything in the twinkling of an eye.

The validity in this view is that, in the Christian faith, the future indeed holds the primacy. Mission can be understood only when the risen Christ himself has still a future, a universal future for the nations (Moltmann 1967:83). This has emerged, particularly, from our survey of Paul's missionary theology; mission, for him, was a response to the vision of the coming triumph of God. Segundo (1986:179) recognizes the fidelity of Paul's eschatology to the thrust of Jesus and describes it as "the only kind (of eschatology) capable of giving real meaning to human history". In an authentic eschatology the vision of God's ultimate reign of justice and peace serves as a powerful magnet—not because the present is empty, but precisely because God's future has already invaded it.

The church is not the world, because God's reign is already present in it. So, the unity between church and world can only be recognized and practiced dialectically in hope—that is, in the light of God's reign (cf Lochman 1986:68). But also, the church is not God's reign. It has no monopoly on God's reign, may not claim it for itself, may not present itself as the realized kingdom of God over against the world (:69). The kingdom will never be fully present in the church. Still, it is in the church that the renewal of the human community begins (:70). But precisely as vanguard of God's reign, of the new earth and the new humankind, the church should neither try to provoke the irruption of the end nor just preserve itself for the end. The place of both these is taken by the mission of the church (Moltmann 1967:83; 1977:196). In its mission, the church affirms its own preliminariness and contingency (cf Küng 1987:122). Practicing "expectant evangelism" (Warren 1948:133-145), it always anticipates its own abrogation. Aware of its provisional character, it lives and ministers as that force within humanity through which the renewal and community of all people is served ("Report" in Limouris 1986:167).

WHITHER MISSION?

The six christological salvific events may never be viewed in isolation from one another. In our mission, we proclaim the incarnate, crucified, resurrected, ascended Christ, present among us in the Spirit and taking us into his future as "captives in his triumphal procession" (2 Cor 5:14, NEB). Each of these events impinges on all the others. Unless we hold on to this, we will communicate to the world a truncated gospel. The shadow of the man of Nazareth, crucified under Pontius Pilate, falls on the glory of his resurrection and ascension, the coming of his Spirit, and his parousia. It is the Jesus who walked with his disciples who lives as Spirit in his church (cf Eph 2:20); it is the Crucified One who rose from the dead; it is the One who had been lifted up on the cross who has been lifted up to heaven; it is the Lamb slaughtered yet living who will consummate history.

But who, which church, which human body of people, is equal to such a calling? (cf 2 Cor 2:16). This was the question Mott put to Kähler just before the Edinburgh Conference: "Do you consider that we now have on the home field a type of Christianity which should be propagated all over the world?" (in Kähler 1971:258). Today we would not phrase the question as naively as Mott. But it continues to nag us. From all sides the Christian mission is under attack, even from within its own ranks. For Rütti (1972, 1974), the entire modern missionary enterprise is so polluted by its origins in and close association with Western colonialism that it is irredeemable; we have to find an entirely new image today. Speaking at a consultation in Kuala Lumpur in February, 1971, Emerito Nacpil (1971:78) depicts mission as "a symbol of the universality of Western imperialism among the rising generations of the Third World". In the missionary, the people of Asia do not see the face of the suffering Christ but a benevolent monster. So he concludes, "The present structure of modern mission is dead. And the first thing we ought to do is to eulogize it and then bury it". Mission appears to be the greatest enemy of the gospel. Indeed, "the most *missionary* service a missionary under the present system can do today to Asia is to go home!" (:79). In the same year John Gatu of Kenya, speaking first to an audience in New York, then to a meeting of the American Reformed Church in Milwaukee, suggested a moratorium on Western missionary involvement in Africa. Much earlier, in May 1944, Bonhoeffer, writing from a Gestapo prison and reflecting on the German church as he had come to know it, wrote:

Our church, which has been fighting in these years only for its self-preservation, as though that were an end in itself, is incapable of taking the word of reconciliation and redemption to mankind and the world. Our earlier words are therefore bound to lose their force and cease, and our being Christians today will be limited to two things: prayer and righteous action among men (1971:300).

Bonhoeffer probably also viewed the church's foreign missionary enterprise as a fight for self-preservation. With less reserve than Bonhoeffer, James Heissig (1981) has termed Christian mission "the selfish war".

Contrary to what some of these authors might suggest, they are not describing a new phenomenon. Throughout most of the church's history its empirical state has been deplorable. This was already true of Jesus' first circle of disciples and has not really changed since. We may have been fairly good at orthodoxy, at "faith", but we have been poor in respect of orthopraxis, of love. Van der Aalst (1974:196) reminds us that there have been countless councils on right believing; yet no council has ever been called to work out the implications of the greatest commandment—to love one another. One may therefore, with some justification, ask whether there has ever been a time when the church had the "right" to do mission work. What Neill says about missionaries has been true of missionaries of all times, from the great apostle who boasted in his weakness to those who still call themselves "missionaries": "(They) have on the whole been a feeble folk, not very wise, not very holy, not very patient. They have broken most of the commandments and fallen into every conceivable mistake" (1960:222).

The critics of mission have usually proceeded from the supposition that mission was only what Western missionaries were doing by way of saving souls, planting churches, and imposing their ways and wills on others. We may, however, never limit mission exclusively to this empirical project; it has always been greater than the observable missionary enterprise. Neither, to be sure, should it be completely divorced from it. Rather, mission is *missio Dei*, which seeks to subsume into itself the *missiones ecclesiae*, the missionary programs of the church. It is not the church which "undertakes" mission; it is the *missio Dei* which constitutes the church. The mission of the church needs constantly to be renewed and re-conceived. Mission is not competition with other religions, not a conversion activity, not expanding the faith, not building up the kingdom of God; neither is it social, economic, or political activity. And yet, there is merit in all these projects. So, the church's concern *is* conversion, church growth, the reign of God, economy, society and politics—but in a different manner! (cf Kohler 1974:472). The *missio Dei* purifies the church. It sets it under the cross— the only place where it is ever safe. The cross is the place of humiliation and judgment, but it is also the place of refreshment and new birth (cf Neill 1960:223). As community of the cross the church then constitutes the fellowship of the kingdom, not just "church members"; as community of the exodus, not as a "religious institution", it invites people to the feast without end (Moltmann 1977:75).

Looked at from this perspective mission is, quite simply, the participation of Christians in the liberating mission of Jesus (Hering 1980:78), wagering on a future that verifiable experience seems to belie. It is the good news of God's love, incarnated in the witness of a community, for the sake of the world.

Notes

1. REFLECTIONS ON THE NEW TESTAMENT AS A MISSIONARY DOCUMENT

1. In more recent times Ernst Käsemann has advocated the thesis that *apocalyptic* was "the mother of theology" (1969a:102; 1969b:137). This is undoubtedly true, particularly in regard to Paul (see below, chapter 4). In a sense, the assertions of Kähler and Käsemann actually complement each other.

2. A "proselyte" (from the Greek: *proselytos*) was, literally, "one who has come over" or "one who has come in" (from a "pagan" religion to Judaism, rather than one who has been won for the Jewish faith through the active involvement of Jewish "missionaries".

3. The "God-fearers" (Greek: *sebomenoi* or *phoboumenoi ton Theon*) were more numerous than the actual proselytes (cf K. G. Kuhn, art *proselytos* in *Theological Dictionary to the New Testament*, vol VI) and were generally of a higher social standing than proselytes (cf Malherbe 1983:77). Whereas the dominant Jewish attitude toward the "God-fearers" was negative, it was more ambivalent toward proselytes (cf Kuhn, op cit).

4. On entering the community, a new member had to swear to love only the members of his own community and to hate all "children of darkness", that is, all non-members (cf 1QS 1:9-11).

5. Q, from "Quelle" (the German word for "source") was a collection of sayings of Jesus that Matthew and Luke drew upon, in addition to the use they made of Mark's gospel, when they wrote their gospels (though both also had access to other minor sources). As far as can be established Q consisted almost exclusively of *sayings* of Jesus (hence the name *Logia*, "words").

6. In recent years several scholars (notably Gerd Theissen) have argued that the *Logia* were used especially by wandering preachers or "prophets" who had confined their ministry to Israel. I draw particularly on Schottroff and Stegemann (1986:38-66) for my interpretation of the missionary thrust of the ministry of the Q prophets. Much of what is said about Q remains extremely hypothetical, particular the existence of a group of wandering prophets who—in the decades following Jesus' earthly ministry—roamed the Jewish land, preaching to all and sundry. If in what follows I refer to them (with Theissen, Schottroff and others) as a distinct and identifiable body of preachers, I do this as a kind of imaginative extrapolation from the tradition rather than as an attempt to make a historical point. Such an approach may assist us in appreciating the unique character of this body of the early Christian tradition.

7. The term *basileia* is, however, only prominent in the synoptic gospels. Perhaps one can say that "(eternal) life" in the fourth gospel intends essentially the same

reality as "God's reign" in the synoptic gospels, as does *dikaiosyne Theou* in Paul (cf Lohfink 1988:2).

8. Schweitzer (1952:368f) describes Jesus' futile attempt at precipitating the irruption of the reign of God in a moving way: "In the knowledge that He is the coming Son of Man, He lays hold of the wheel of the world to set it moving on that last revolution which is to bring all ordinary history to a close. It refuses to turn, and He throws Himself on it. Then it does turn; and crushes Him. Instead of bringing in the eschatological conditions, He has destroyed them. The wheel rolls onward, and the mangled body of the one immeasurably great Man, who was strong enough to think of Himself as the spiritual ruler of mankind and to bend history to His purpose, is hanging upon it still".

9. In a recent article Gerhard Lohfink (1988) has, however, argued passionately for the *present* character of God's reign in Jesus' coming. Lohfink's views are not simply to be equated with the traditional "realized eschatology" position.

10. In the 1960s several scholars (particularly S.G.F. Brandon in *Jesus and the Zealots* [New York: Charles Scribner's Sons, 1967]) described Jesus as a kind of proto-Zealot. In more recent years New Testament scholars have, on the whole, agreed that Jesus differed fundamentally from the (later) Zealots and their ethos (cf, for instance, Hengel 1971). Even so, as late as 1981 George Pixley still put forward the thesis that the Jesus movement differed from the Zealots only in strategy: Jesus first wanted to put an end to the "temple domination" before taking on the Roman oppressors; only the latter were the concern of the Zealots (Pixley 1981:64-87).

11. Lapide (1986:41-48) takes issue with Christian theologians who argue that Jesus abrogated the Law. In his attempt to explain Jesus consistently from within contemporary Judaism Lapide, however, tends to overstate his case. Still, his warnings against the tendency of many Christians completely to "dejudaize" Jesus have to be taken seriously.

12. The same is true of modern apocalyptic movements (cf Beker 1984:19-28). I shall return to this issue in more detail when I discuss Paul's understanding of mission (see below, chapter 4). Cf also Lohfink 1988.

13. The exact situation with Jamnia Pharisaism toward the end of the first century AD remains obscure, however. It went through a long period of development before it reached its more or less final form. One should therefore be careful not to read attitudes and views which were typical of Pharisaism after the Bar Kochba revolt (which was squashed around AD 135) into the period when our gospels were written. It is, among other things, impossible to reconstruct either the exact wording or precise meaning of the *Eighteen Benedictions* in the decades immediately after the end of the Jewish War.

2. MATTHEW: MISSION AS DISCIPLE-MAKING

1. For a detailed discussion of *dikaiosyne* in Matthew, see further Giessen 1982:79-112, 122-146, 166-194. Giessen also compares *dikaiosyne* in Matthew and Paul (:237-263). See further Michael H. Crosby, *House of Disciples: Church, Economics and Justice in Matthew* (Maryknoll, N.Y.: Orbis Books, 1988), pp 145-195.

2. For the meaning of the participle "go" (*poreuthentes*), I refer to what I have written elsewhere (cf Bosch 1980:68f; 1983:229f). Suffice it to say here that I do not believe that geographical distance (*going* from one locality to another) is of any particular significance here.

3. Naturally, I am not thinking of this author as a lone theological giant who on his own has set out to construct an original "theology of mission" or "local theology". I am assuming, rather, that Matthew reflects many of the views and convictions that were alive in his community. Perhaps we should see him, at best, as a kind of catalyst who regarded it as his task to bring everything together into some kind of coherent whole.

3. LUKE-ACTS: PRACTICING FORGIVENESS AND SOLIDARITY WITH THE POOR

1. In another recent essay on the understanding of mission in Luke's gospel, I have followed an approach which differed quite significantly from the procedure followed here (cf D.J. Bosch, Mission in Jesus' Way: A Perspective from Luke's Gospel, *Missionalia* vol 17, 1989, pp 3-21). I have suggested there that Jesus' mission, according to Luke, consisted of three thrusts: empowering the weak and the lowly, healing the sick, and saving the lost. The views expressed there may be seen as complementing those articulated here.

2. The "religious" nature of some of the English words in the RSV may cause us some difficulty in understanding Luke's terminology. We could, however, translate *paraklesis* in 2:25 as "restoration" (RSV: "consolation"); *soterion* in 2:30 as "deliverance" (RSV: "salvation") and *lytrosis* in 2:38 as "liberation" (RSV: "redemption").

3. I am aware that there is wide disagreement on Luke's attitude to and appreciation of the Jewish people. A recent symposium volume, to which eight scholars (including Jervell, Tiede, J. T. Sanders and Tannehill) have contributed, gives a fair reflection of the spectrum of opinions on the subject. See Joseph B. Tyson, ed., *Luke-Acts and the Jewish People* (Minneapolis: Augsburg, 1988).

4. Luke has, however, omitted the reference to the poor we always have with us (Mk 14:7; Mt 26:11; see also Jn 12:8), probably because the saying had already in his time been interpreted to mean that, since the poor will always be with us, we need not do anything about their circumstances.

5. The RSV translates *apolyo* in Luke 6:37 with "forgive", which is a secondary meaning of the verb. The context, however, calls for a translation in terms of the word's *primary* meaning, "release", "acquit", or "pardon" (cf Schottroff and Stegemann 1986:115).

6. Walaskay (1983) proposes that we should regard Luke's two volumes as an elaborate apology for the Roman Empire. He argues that Luke (almost?) always goes out of his way in his attempt to present the Empire in a favorable light. In particular, he does his best to emphasize the positive aspects of Roman involvement in the early history of the church. God is at work in the world, not only through the church but through the secular realm as well. From a Black Liberation Theology perspective, Mosala (1989:173-179) presents a more radical version of this assessment of Luke and suggests that, in the process, Luke may have destroyed the *raison d'être* of the very movement he was trying to save (:177).

7. Walaskay (1983) certainly goes too far when he suggests that Luke wrote his two-volume work as an apology for the Roman Empire. Talbert (1984:107-109) may be more on target when he says that the Lukan Jesus and the Luke of Acts were *indifferent* to the political rulers. From this point of view, the church does not make the state's cause its own, nor does it "attack the social structure of society directly,

as one power group among others, but indirectly, by embodying in its life a transcendent reality" (:109).

8. Holmberg (1978) provides an excellent study of the authority structures in the primitive church, also insofar as they pertain to missionary outreach.

4. MISSION IN PAUL: INVITATION TO JOIN THE ESCHATOLOGICAL COMMUNITY

1. We should therefore, perhaps, have put this chapter before those on Matthew and Luke (which is what Senior and Stuhlmueller 1983 do). However, the gospels cover events which took place long before Paul's ministry, so there may be some justification for examining their understanding of mission before we study Paul's.

2. Sometimes, however, and particularly in his letters to the Galatians and the Corinthians (cf Gal 1:11-16; 1 Cor 9:1), there is an element of apologetic in Paul's claim that his encounter with Jesus and his apostolic commissioning coincided completely. He has to defend his apostleship (cf also Wilckens 1959:275). For a detailed discussion of the issues involved, cf Lategan 1988.

3. A careful rereading of Galatians has led Martyn (1985:307-324) to postulate the existence of a well-organized, Law-observant Christian mission to Gentiles, perhaps even before and certainly in opposition to Paul's missionary venture.

4. The essential reason for this re-conception, to which I shall return in a slightly different context, lies in the fact that Paul increasingly understands his mission in eschatological terms. For a long time there was, in Judaism, the expectation of the Gentiles flocking to Zion at the end of the ages; in Paul's judgment that moment has now arrived.

5. I have developed these ideas in greater detail in *A Spirituality of the Road* (Scottdale, Pa.: Herald Press, 1979), a booklet in which I tried to draw the contours of a missionary spirituality based on Paul's second letter to the Corinthians. See also Horst Baum, *Mut zum Schwachsein — in Christi Kraft* (St Augustin: Steyler Verlag, 1977).

6. It should, however, be remembered that, for Paul, the word *ethne* does not as such carry a negative connotation, as do the terms "pagans" or "heathens" in our own time. Paul uses *ethne* primarily in the sense of "non-Jews" and can therefore also apply it to non-Jewish Christians. For this reason the translation "Gentiles" for *ethne* is to be preferred (cf Kertelge 1987:371).

7. Paul does not accept the Stoic view that all people have an innate capacity to know God, which must be developed through reason (cf Malherbe 1987:31-33). The higher echelons of Hellenistic society (to which most of the "God-fearers" also belonged) tended to be monotheistic, but this was not a monotheism that conflicted with syncretism; even a "monotheist" could participate in the cults of other gods. For an enlightened pagan the idea of a "jealous" God, who requires exclusive allegiance, was an absurd notion (*moria*, "folly" — 1 Cor 1:23). On this whole matter, see Dahl 1977b:178-191; Walter 1979:422-442; Grant 1986:45-53).

8. From Paul's letters we can deduce little about the actual sermons he preached to Gentile audiences, but we can assume that the elements just indicated formed a regular component of those sermons, which certainly must have been presented with much passion. Their thrust would have been to convict rather than to inform (cf Malherbe 1987:32). For the possible form and content of Paul's missionary sermons, cf Haas 1971:94-98; Senior and Stuhlmueller 1983:185-187; Mal-

herbe 1987:28-33; and particularly Bussmann 1971:passim.

9. *Kerdaino* is a "technical missionary term" (cf van Swigchem 1955:141-143; Bieder 1965:34; Sanders 1983:177). For its Jewish background and its significance as a conversion term (also in the sense of calling sinners back to faith), see David Daube, "A Missionary Term", in *The New Testament and Rabbinic Judaism* (New York: Arno Press, 1973 [reprint of 1956 edition]), pp 352-361.

10. Van Swigchem suggests that *idiotai* (the "uninstructed" or "ignorant"; the RSV translates "outsiders"), a term Paul uses a few times in 1 Corinthians, refers not to outsiders proper (as *hoi exo* does), but to inquirers, people who attend meetings regularly but have not yet taken the final step of embracing the Christian faith (1955:189-192).

11. Not so, however, in 1 Peter! It is interesting that van Swigchem (1955), who inquired into the missionary character of the church according to the letters of Paul and Peter, found most of the explicitly "missionizing" references not in Paul's letters but in the very short first letter of Peter (cf also Lippert 1968).

12. In Greek literature, *katallassein* is a completely profane concept, employed in the diplomatic sphere and normally meaning "to exchange hostility for friendship". Until Paul, it is never used theologically. Paul, however, and the New Testament authors dependent on him, use it in the sense of God reconciling Jews and Gentiles to himself through the substitutionary death of Christ. Cf Breytenbach 1986:3-6, 19-22. (In addition to this essay, Breytenbach has provided a detailed treatment of the subject in a monograph entitled *Katallage: Eine Studie zur paulinischen Soteriologie* [Neukirchen-Vluyn: Neukirchener Verlag, 1986]).

13. In this respect Beker refers to the exclusion of apocalyptic literature not only from the Old Testament but also from the New Testament canon, the repudiation of millennial apocalyptic at the Council of Ephesus (AD 432), and its condemnation by the Reformers (for instance in the Augsburg Confession) (Beker 1984:61).

14. Cf also Stendahl's altercation with Bornkamm and Käsemann on this matter, and his argument that to declare justification by faith as *the* key to Paul is to miss the point about the historical nature of Paul's arguments and to read him through the eyes of Augustine and Luther (Stendahl 1976:127-133; cf Beker 1980:17). Kraemer (1961:198f) criticizes the Lutheran missiologist, Walter Holsten, in similar fashion for declaring the doctrine of justification to be the be-all and end-all of biblical and Pauline theology. Kraemer calls this a "Procrustean theology", which "overlooks the fact that the apostolic *kerygma* is a full orchestra and not a single flute" (:199). Needless to say, justification by faith is indeed a fundamental Pauline theme (acknowledged today by Protestants and Catholics alike – cf Pfürtner 1984:168-192), which is, however, not the same as saying that it is the overriding motif in Paul. Beker (1984:56) is right when he says, "Key terms like the righteousness of God, justification, redemption, or reconciliation are not to be measured over against each other as if one term is *the* permanent key to which all others are subservient". Cf also Beker 1988.

15. De Boer (1989) prefers to use the term "apocalyptic eschatology" when interpreting Paul's theology.

16. This interpretation of *prosphora ton ethnon* is, in fact, widely accepted; cf, *inter alia*, Dahl 1977a:87; Beker 1980:332; Senior and Stuhlmueller 1983:183; Sanders 1983:171-173; Hultgren 1985:133-135. Luz (1968:391) proposes a different interpretation, but it should be kept in mind that he denies any connection between mission and the parousia in Paul's thinking (:390f).

17. The question whether Paul teaches that all *Israel* will be saved will be addressed below. For the moment my concern is with universalism as regards the *Gentiles*.

18. For a different (and more comprehensive) discussion of this entire subject, cf D. J. Bosch, "Paul on Human Hopes", *Journal of Theology in Southern Africa* 67 (June 1989), pp 3-16.

19. Cf also Räisänen: "I join the ranks of those who doubt the assertion that post-Biblical Judaism was a man-centred achievement religion which invited its adherents to earn the favour of God by doing meritorious works of the law ... An average Jew observed the law because he held it to embody God's will" (1987:411).

20. De Boer (1989:172-180) argues that it is necessary to distinguish between two major "tracks" in Jewish apocalyptic before AD 70, namely, "cosmological apocalyptic eschatology" (where "this age" will be replaced by "the age to come" after a cosmic confrontation between God and the evil angelic powers) and "forensic apocalyptic eschatology" (according to which God has given the Law as a remedy and human accountability to God is stressed). Evidence indicates that Track 2 completely overtook and displaced Track 1 after the disaster of AD 70.

21. Räisänen (1983:16-198) has contended that Paul lacks a coherent theology of the Law. In a subsequent work (*The Torah and Christ* [Helsinki: Publications of the Finnish Exegetical Society 45, 1986]), he has refined and moderated his views somewhat. Cf also Räisänen 1987. De Boer (1989) suggests that, in Paul's letter to the Romans, sometimes cosmological apocalyptic eschatology dominates, and at other times forensic apocalyptic eschatology.

22. It is significant that only in his letter to the Galatians does Paul use the expressions *Ioudaismos*, *Ioudaikos*, and *ioudaizein* (all derivatives of *Ioudaios*, "Jew").

23. Martyn (1985:316) summarizes the "major point" in the preaching of the Law-observant missionaries: "They necessarily view God's Christ in the light of God's Law, rather than the Law in the light of Christ, and this means that Christ is secondary to the Law".

24. I am not suggesting that Paul's theology was ready-made at the moment of his conversion. There certainly was development in his thinking, particularly as regards his interpretation of the Law (his earliest letter, 1 Thessalonians, contains virtually no references to this) and certainly also because of his contact with Hellenistic Jewish Christians. See also Senior and Stuhlmueller 1983:169 and Räisänen 1987:416.

25. At the same time, we should not lose sight of the need of similar humble and sensitive missionary approaches in other situations as well. In light of the way whites have treated blacks in Southern Africa and the United States—to mention only these two examples—white Christians are challenged to witness to blacks primarily by means of practicing justice and solidarity, and not only by means of verbal witness.

26. Pixley (1981:90-96) totally misinterprets Paul when he says that Paul's message was exclusively "individually-centered" and "did not extend to the real social relations in the public world", that he preached only a "spiritual religion" and conceived of the kingdom of God merely as a "spiritual reality" and as "the end of history, to be entered by purified persons".

27. See further my *Spirituality of the Road* (Scottdale, Pa: Herald Press, 1979),

particularly pp 74-90. Cf also Michael Prior, "Paul on 'Power and Weakness' ", *The Month* 1451 (Nov 1988), pp 939-944.

5. PARADIGM CHANGES IN MISSIOLOGY

1. The epistemological approach I am advocating here is sometimes referred to as critical hermeneutics (cf Nel 1988). To practice this approach means that I accept that I am open to change and to the reexamination of my existing convictions. In the case of theology, critical hermeneutics recognizes that Christians will disagree in their understandings of Scripture and the Christian faith, but that they share a commitment to the same Lord.

2. I devoted a major section of *Witness to the World* to the theology of mission through the ages (cf Bosch 1980:85-195). I have no intention of repeating here what I did there, although some degree of overlap is, in the nature of the case, unavoidable.

6. THE MISSIONARY PARADIGM OF THE EASTERN CHURCH

1. This is the way Pliny the Younger and others often referred to Christianity. To call it a *superstitio* was to classify it as "a non-Roman worship of non-Roman gods" (W. M. Ramsay, *The Church in the Roman Empire Before* AD 170 [London: Hodder & Stoughton, no date], p 206). Pliny actually called Christianity a *superstitio prava immodica*, a degrading and improper superstition.

2. The Orthodox doctrine of *theosis*, union with God or divinization, has its roots here. In the words of Athanasius, "God became human, so that we might become God". Stamoolis (1986:9) suggests that this view is similar to the Western Christian doctrine of the believer's union with Christ, but that *theosis* is far more central in Orthodoxy than its counterpart is in Western theology and church life. It expresses "in essence the Eastern understanding of the purpose of the incarnation and the ultimate end of humankind" (:10; cf also Bria 1986:9).

3. Contrary to popular opinion, Christians were persecuted only during short periods. Most emperors showed no particular eagerness to wipe out the new religion by force. Empire-wide persecutions were extremely rare; in most cases persecutions were sporadic and confined to specific regions. The most widespread, bloody, and long-lasting persecution broke out under Emperor Diocletian in AD 303 and lasted until AD 311. For a concise and reliable discussion, cf Jacques Moreau, *Die Christenverfolgung im Römischen Reich* (Berlin: Alfred Töpelmann, 1961).

7. THE MEDIEVAL ROMAN CATHOLIC MISSIONARY PARADIGM

1. As I shall argue in the next chapter, the Protestant theological paradigm was not going to be decisively different on this point. In this respect, then, Protestantism, like Catholicism, betrays continuity with Greek patristic theology.

2. The Latin word used by the Donatists, *traditor*, literally meant somebody who had committed *traditio*, or the "surrender" of the Scriptures during the recent persecutions, and thus "betrayed" (that is, had become a traitor to) the Christian cause.

3. In recent years several scholars have argued that the Donatists may truthfully be regarded as the first "African Independent Church". There can be little doubt

that the Catholic Church, by and large, represented the Latin element in North Africa, and the Donatists the indigenous African (Berber) element.

4. It should, of course, be remembered that, since the sixteenth century, many Protestants adopted exactly the same attitude to Catholics and often even to fellow-Protestants.

5. It is, in any case, important not to regard the work—as has often been done—as an attempt at presenting a "Christian philosophy of history". The problem with such an approach to the *City of God* is that it is read against the background of the intellectual and cultural development of the seventeenth and subsequent centuries. For a careful refutation of this view, cf Ernst A. Schmidt, "Augustins Geschichtsverständnis," *Freiburger Zeitschrift für Philosophie und Theologie*, vol 34 (1987), pp 361-378.

6. As I shall argue below, it was in particular the Benedictines who revealed the qualities I have enumerated. Their unswerving dedication to selfless service and to virtue equipped them for the task of recreating society and shaping a Christian civilization. Coupled with their awareness that things take time and that we have to persevere faithfully and doggedly in what we have set out to do, they provide an example which particularly in our own day is worth emulating. In his perceptive analysis of the malaise of our contemporary society, entitled *After Virtue* (London: Duckworth, 1981), Alasdair MacIntyre insists that it is of the very character of virtue that it be exercised without regard to consequences, that we should practice virtues irrespective of whether in any particular set of contingent circumstances they produce any rewards (:185). This is consonant with the Benedictine view of virtue. On the final pages of his monograph, MacIntyre refers to the impact of monasticism on Europe during the Middle Ages, when new forms of community were constructed within which the moral life could be sustained, "so that both morality and civility might survive the coming ages of barbarism and darkness" (:244). With reference to our own time, he concludes: "What matters at this stage is the construction of local forms of community within which civility and the intellectual and moral life can be sustained through the new dark ages which are already upon us. And if the tradition of the virtues was able to survive the horrors of the last dark ages, we are not entirely without grounds for hope. This time however the barbarians are not waiting beyond the frontier; they have already been governing us for some time. And it is our lack of consciousness of this that constitutes part of our predicament. We are waiting not for a Godot, but for another—doubtless very different—St Benedict" (:245).

8. THE MISSIONARY PARADIGM OF THE PROTESTANT REFORMATION

1. Protestants tend to see the late Middle Ages only in terms of decay, theologically and morally. This is doubtless a dangerous oversimplification. Cf, for instance, H. Oberman, *The Harvest of Medieval Theology* (Grand Rapids: Eerdmans, 1967 [revised edition]). Oberman writes, *inter alia*, "The later Middle Ages are marked by a lively and at times bitter debate regarding the doctrine of justification, intimately connected with the interpretation of the works of Augustine on the relation of nature and grace" (p 427). In light of this, some would prefer to see the Protestant Reformation paradigm as a subdivision of a wider "Western Christian" paradigm, as an important chapter in the medieval period, not as something essentially new. I believe, however, that there is justification for treating the Reformation

paradigm as a theological model in its own right, as a break with both Scholasticism and the *via moderna* of Occam and others (cf Gerrish 1962).

2. Holl's tendentiousness reveals itself, *inter alia*, in his statement that "the German mission may pride itself in the fact that, unlike churches from other nations, it has never been guilty of harboring any ulterior political motives and that, in this, it had remained faithful to Luther's principles" (1928:241 — my translation). Cf, however, the section on colonialism and mission in the next chapter.

3. It is therefore incorrect to argue, as still happens frequently, that William Carey's 1792 tract was the first example of a Protestant promoting mission with an explicit appeal to the "Great Commission". Saravia did this more than two centuries before Carey, as did the Dutchman J. Heurnius in 1648 and the Lutheran nobleman Justinian von Welz in 1664.

4. Some years ago J. A. Scherer republished Welz's plea, together with Ursinus's reply, and provided it with an introduction (Scherer 1969; cf also Schick 1943:44-66).

5. I shall return to this important principle in Protestant missions in the next chapter.

9. MISSION IN THE WAKE OF THE ENLIGHTENMENT

1. This term signifies a theological temper rather than a set of doctrines. The Latitudinarians or "Broad Churchmen" were people of the middle road who opposed both rationalistic Deism and Puritanism.

2. I am aware that this rather summary statement needs some qualifications. John Wesley himself was adamant that the church's service to people's souls could not be divorced from its service to their bodies. This side of Wesley's ministry has only recently become the object of serious and sustained research. A fine guide to the "social Wesley" is L. D. Hulley's *To Be and to Do* (Pretoria: University of South Africa, 1988). Of particular importance is Wesley's attack on the institution of slavery, long before William Wilberforce (1759-1833) and others began to address this issue. He published his *Thoughts upon Slavery* in 1744. On this entire subject, cf W. T. Smith, *John Wesley and Slavery* (Nashville: Abingdon Press, 1986), in which the third edition of Wesley's brochure is reproduced (pp 121-148).

3. Although I shall concentrate on *motifs* (the dominant missionary themes or ideas of the period), I shall also pay some attention to *motives* (the reasons for people's getting involved in mission). It is not always possible to separate motifs from motives.

4. The Tambaram Conference is, to my knowledge, the only large international missionary meeting to have paid extensive attention to the issue I am discussing here. The entire fifth volume (633 pages) of the Tambaram Series is devoted to "The Economic Basis of the Church". The quotation above comes from p 155. Cf also Davis 1947:73-182, and Gilhuis 1955:98-157.

5. For Britain, the Victorian era was a highly *religious* age as much as it was a *national* age without parallel. This no doubt has to do with the fact that English nationalism has always been "closer to the religious matrix from which it arose" (Kohn 1945:178), a circumstance which again points to a factor previously referred to — in Britain the Enlightenment did not, as it did on the continent, completely break asunder "religious" and "secular" life.

6. A similar attitude is recorded by Hasselhorn (1988:138). The occasion this

time was the Bambatha Rebellion in Zululand in 1906 and the effects it had on the Hermannsburg Mission in Natal. Before the rebellion broke out, Missions Director Harms remarked, "The Kaffirs are arrogant, since the government is weak. (Because of the authorities') current lax attitude, the (black) people will go to wrack and ruin. A black man is not much upset by an injustice — he easily overcomes that — but he can absolutely not stand it to be treated weakly" (my translation).

7. British missionaries, let me reiterate, were as racist as Germans, not least because of the influence of "social Darwinism" (cf Cochrane 1987:19f; Villa-Vicencio 1988:54-64). And those from other Western countries were hardly any better. Racism in South Africa presents us, in a sense, with a special case, not least because racism there became entrenched through legislation. So much has been and is still being written about this peculiar brand of racism that I find it unnecessary to cover the ground in detail. In addition, the theme of this section is racial prejudice in *missionary* circles, and although South African missionaries, including those hailing from the white Afrikaans-speaking churches, were certainly as racist as other white missionaries, the particular phenomenon of racism and its role in Afrikaner *missionary* circles has not yet been studied in much detail. See further J. W. de Gruchy, *The Church Struggle in South Africa* (Cape Town: David Philip, 1979), pp 1-85; J. W. de Gruchy and C. Villa-Vicencio, eds., *Apartheid is a Heresy* (Cape Town: David Philip, 1983), in particular the contributions by Chris Loff, "The History of a Heresy", pp 10-23, and David Bosch, "Nothing but a Heresy", pp 24-28; and Villa-Vicencio 1988:22-30, 145-150.

8. The Social Gospel was fecundated by European theological ideas, particularly those of theologians such as Albrecht Ritschl, Richard Rothe, Ernst Troeltsch, and Adolf Harnack. The differences between the American Social Gospel and the Germans, however, should not be ignored (cf Niebuhr 1988:116). The Social Gospel remained a peculiarly American phenomenon.

9. The ambiguous character of Edinburgh is revealed, *inter alia*, in the fact that two plenary addresses were devoted to the subject of "Christianity the Final and Universal Religion", the one on Christianity as religion of *redemption* (by W. Paterson), the other on Christianity as an *ethical ideal* (by Henry Sloan Coffin).

10. This was, of course, only one side of the equation; the other side was the astonishing upsurge in missionary enthusiasm and involvement — admittedly defined in terms very different from those of the Uppsala Assembly — in conservative evangelical circles during this same period.

11. One should keep in mind that Mott never understood the watchword of the SVM as suggesting that the whole world would be *converted* in a single generation. He interpreted it in the sense of "reaching the whole world with the gospel", of "offering each person a valid opportunity to accept Christ as Savior".

12. Immediately after the Edinburgh Conference Mott published another book, entitled *The Decisive Hour of Christian Missions* (London: Young People's Missionary Movement, 1910). It reflected the same spirit as the conference and Mott's earlier book. The selection of the photograph facing the title page — the caption of which read, "Railway penetrating the old wall of Peking" — may surprise the modern reader, but made perfect sense to Mott since it portrayed the "advance" of the gospel.

13. At the same time we should be reminded of the fact that the "Great Commission", in its various forms, is also the most often quoted text in the documents

of Vatican II (cf Gómez 1986:32); one should therefore not regard its use as restricted to Protestant evangelicals.

14. As such, it is a manifestation of fundamentalism and the doctrine of biblical inerrancy, both of which betray the influence of the Enlightenment (as argued in the early part of this chapter). In chapter 2 of this study an attempt has been made to interpret the "Great Commission" within the overall context of the Gospel of Matthew.

10. THE EMERGENCE OF A POSTMODERN PARADIGM

1. It should be noted that the preposition "post" in no sense suggests a value judgment. "Postmodern" does not signify "antimodern" (as Jürgen Habermas interprets it). I use it, rather, in the sense Küng also uses it (1987:16-27), namely as a *heuristic* notion, as a *search* concept. The term "post" looks backward and forward at the same time and "does not mean a simple return to precritical, premodern, preliberal discourse, but a 'pro-volution' toward an emerging new ... paradigm" (Martin 1987:370). It is, nevertheless, an awkward term, which I shall later replace with the notion "ecumenical".

2. Cf Spengler, *The Decline of the West* (London: Allen & Unwin, no date; the title of the German original, *Der Untergang des Abendlandes*, carried numinous undertones absent in the English translation) and Sorokin, *The Crisis of Our Age* (New York: E. P. Dutton, 1941 — a summary of his four-volume work, *Social and Cultural Dynamics*, 1937-1941).

3. A cardinal (quoted in Bühlmann 1977:154) once said during the pontificate of Pius XII, "When the Pope thinks of Latin America in the evening, he cannot sleep that night"!

4. A penetrating exposition, from a theological perspective, of such symbiosis, such living together, is found in Sundermeier 1986. The title of his essay, translated into English, would be "Symbiosis [literally, life together] as Fundamental Structure of Ecumenical Existence Today".

5. For a perceptive summary of Marxist eschatology and its similarities with classical Christian eschatology, cf K. Nürnberger, "The Eschatology of Marxism," *Missionalia* vol 15 (1987), pp 105-109.

6. The more commonly known version of this adage is *Credo ut intelligam*, "I believe in order to understand"; cf also Anselm's *Fides quaerens intellectum*, "Faith seeking understanding."

12. ELEMENTS OF AN EMERGING ECUMENICAL MISSIONARY PARADIGM

1. It should be noted that, in contemporary Catholicism (as in Anglicanism), a "local church" is understood as a *diocese* and not as a local parish or congregation. In a given diocese all parishes together share one pastor, the bishop.

2. One of the most exciting developments in this respect, in both Catholic and Protestant circles, is the new wave of Third-World missionaries. For Protestantism, cf Lawrence E. Keyes, *The Last Age of Missions: A Study of Third World Missionary Societies* (Pasadena: Wm Carey Library, 1983) and Larry D. Pate, *From Every People: A Study of Third World Missionary Societies* (Pasadena: Wm Carey Library, 1989); for Catholicism, see Omer Degrijse, CICM, *Going Forth: Missionary Consciousness*

in Third World Catholic Churches (Maryknoll, NY: Orbis Books 1984).

3. This notion, introduced into contemporary theological discussion by Pope John XXIII just before Vatican II, has found an echo in several theological traditions (cf Gómez 1989:365f). For a Catholic bibliography on the notion, cf Kroeger 1989:191-196. (I shall return to this notion in the section on "Mission as Contextualization".)

4. *Tambaram Series*, vol I: *The Authority of the Faith* (London: Oxford University Press, 1939), p 183, 184.

5. Aagaard (1965:251f) is therefore correct in saying that while Willingen may be considered the consummation of the Barthian impact on missionary thinking, it was at the same time the beginning of the end of the Barthian influence as the decisive and unifying force. Cf also Hoedemaker 1988:172.

6. For a more comprehensive discussion of this theme, cf my contribution entitled "Salvation: A Missiological Perspective", *Ex Auditu*, vol 6 (1989), pp. 139-157.

7. The papers presented at this consultation have been published under the title *La salvezzia oggi* (Rome: Urban University Press, 1989).

8. In a sense, of course, it is tautological to add any adjective to the noun "salvation"; salvation is, in the nature of the case, comprehensive and integral — or it is not salvation.

9. It is certainly not the earliest example. Throughout the history of missions (as has been pointed out in this study) there have been courageous individuals like Bartolomé de Las Casas and hundreds of others who have spoken out against the injustices perpetrated by colonial governments in "their" colonies. They were, however, mostly peripheral to the church and hardly spoke for the official church. What makes this example unique is that in this case a very prominent official body of church representatives was involved.

10. Cf, for instance, Timothy L. Smith, *Revivalism and Social Reform: American Protestantism on the Eve of the Civil War* (New York: Harper & Row, 1957); David O. Moberg, *Inasmuch: Christian Social Responsibility in the Twentieth Century* (Grand Rapids: Eerdmans, 1965); Sherwood E. Wirt, *The Social Conscience of the Evangelical* (London: Scripture Union, 1968); David O. Moberg, *The Great Reversal: Evangelism and Social Concern* (Philadelphia: J.B. Lippincott Co, 1972, 1977); and Neuhaus & Cromartie 1987.

11. The proceedings of both conferences were edited by Ronald Sider and published by Paternoster Press in Exeter. They are *Evangelicals and Development: Toward a Theology of Social Change* (1981), and *Lifestyle in the Eighties: An Evangelical Commitment to Simple Lifestyle* (1982).

12. This was one of three parallel "tracks" of a conference which met under the overall theme of "The Nature and Mission of the Church". Samuel and Sugden (1987) contains all the papers presented at the consultation as well as *The Wheaton '83 Statement*.

13. The document was reprinted in *Transformation* 4 (1987) pp 17-30.

14. It goes without saying that all of this is by no means true of all evangelicals. There are those identified with the political far right (cf Jerry Falwell and Jeffrey K. Hadden in Neuhaus and Cromartie 1987:109-123; 379-394; there are those who continue to put an exclusive emphasis on evangelism and church planting alone (cf Donald A. McGavran, "Missiology Faces the Lion", *Missiology* 17 [1989], pp 335-341); and there are countless other groups who call themselves evangelical, fun-

damentalist, or charismatic, who are not interested in relationships of any sort with other groups of believers.

15. In several publications I have addressed the theological issues concerning the understanding of evangelism, as well as the relationship between evangelism and mission: "Evangelism", *Mission Focus* vol. 9 (1981), pp 65-74; "Mission and Evangelism—Clarifying the Concepts", *Zeitschrift für Missionswissenschaft und Religionswissenschaft* 68 (1984), pp 161-191; "Evangelism: Theological Currents and Crosscurrents Today", *International Bulletin of Missionary Research* 11 (1987), pp 98-103; "Toward Evangelism in Context", in Samuel and Sugden 1987:180-192; "Evangelisation, Evangelisierung", in Müller and Sundermeier 1987, pp 102-105.

16. This trend is also attested by the fact that North American evangelical agencies have been sending thousands of "missionaries" (not "evangelists") to Europe. For that matter, in evangelical parlance the term "evangelist" is usually reserved for an *itinerant* preacher.

17. In passing, it may be of interest to point out that similar projects are operative in Catholicism. In response to Pope John Paul II's call for a "New Evangelization", a worldwide effort called *Evangelization 2000* was launched to promote a "Decade of Evangelization" from Christmas 1990 to Christmas 2000. A major difference between this project and the evangelical plans referred to is that *Evangelization 2000* is essentially a *prayer campaign*. Nearly four thousand contemplative houses and fourteen hundred intercessory groups and individuals were approached in this respect in 1988 only. A booklet, *Praying for a New Evangelization*, has been made available in various languages.

18. *CCA News*, 15, no. 6 (June 1980), p 6.

19. It is immensely instructive, in this respect, to read the open letter Paul Tillich wrote to Emanuel Hirsch in 1934 (the English translation, "Open Letter to Emanuel Hirsch", is published in J. L. Adams, W. Pauck, and R. L. Shinn, eds., *The Thought of Paul Tillich* [San Francisco: Harper & Row, 1985], pp 353-388), just after Hirsch had published his *Die gegenwärtige geistige Lage im Spiegel philosophischer und theologischer Besinnung*: Akademische Vorlesungen zum Verständnis des deutschen Jahres 1933 (Göttingen: Vandenhoeck & Ruprecht, 1934). Tillich quotes Hirsch as writing that the events in Germany (particularly Hitler's rise to power) were "to be perceived as the work of the Almighty Lord, whose instruments we essentially must be" (1985:364). He accuses Hirsch of having "perverted the prophetic, eschatologically conceived Kairos doctrine into a sacerdotal-sacramental consecration of a current event" (:363). Hirsch did this by drawing "a theological and therefore absolute value judgement" from specific historical events (:365), thereby absolutizing "a finite possibility" (:366). In doing this, Hirsch turned current history into "a source of revelation alongside the biblical documents" (:371). (For the reference to Tillich I am indebted to Stackhouse 1988:97, who observes that "many of the terms used in the analysis of modern society and history celebrated by *praxis*-based liberation thought today were present in Hirsch's work".)

20. In this respect, Sanneh adds, Christianity is fundamentally different from Islam. The notion that the Qur'an contains the very thoughts of Allah since they were directly dictated to the Prophet in Arabic, limits Islam's capacity to contextualize in ways that other faiths have. (Of course, the same notion is present in excessively fundamentalist quarters in Christianity).

21. In this respect, the African Independent Churches have to be mentioned specifically. Since Bengt Sundkler's pioneering *Bantu Prophets in South Africa*

(1948), a large body of literature on this exciting archetype of self-theologizing has been built up. Pride of place has in this regard to be given to M. L Daneel's multivolume series, *Old and New in Southern Shona Independent Churches*. Three volumes have been published thus far: Volume I on "Background and Rise of the Major Movements" (The Hague: Mouton, 1971); Volume II on "Church Growth — Causative Factors and Recruitment Techniques" (Mouton, 1974); and Volume III on "Leadership and Fission Dynamics" (Gweru [Zimbabwe]: Mambo Press, 1988). Two more volumes are anticipated, one of which will be devoted in particular to the emerging theology of the movement.

22. For instance in the *Communauté Evangélique d'Action Apostolique*, a fellowship of forty-six churches worldwide, which has replaced the former Paris Evangelical Missionary Society, or the Council for World Mission, which is a structure consisting of some thirty churches, which have "resulted" from the work of the London Missionary Society.

23. The best missiological study of the Latin American movement, written from a Protestant viewpoint, is Guillermo Cook, *The Expectation of the Poor: Latin American Basic Ecclesial Communities in Protestant Perspective* (Maryknoll, NY: Orbis Books, 1985). For a Catholic evaluation, cf Boff 1986.

24. Cf D. J. Bosch, "The Church-in-Dialogue: From Self-Delusion to Vulnerability", *Missiology*, 16 (1988), pp 131-147, for a complementary discussion of this theme.

25. Cf *The Christian Life and Message in Relation to Non-Christian Systems: Report of the Jerusalem Meeting of the IMC*, vol I (London: Oxford Univ. Press, 1928), p 491.

26. Spindler (1988:147) draws attention to a striking discrepancy in the way 1 Timothy 2:4 is used in LG 16 and in AG 7 (and 42). AG 7 quotes the entire verse, as well as the following one, and thereby clearly limits God's saving activity to those who embrace Christ, the Mediator, in faith. LG 16 quotes only the first half of 1 Timothy 2:4 ("The Savior wills all to be saved") and uses it to support the idea that those who do not know the gospel but live exemplary lives may also achieve eternal salvation.

27. Cf also D. J. Bosch, "Theological Education in Missionary Perspective", *Missiology* vol. 10 (1982), pp 13-34.

28. As late as 1965, Cullmann (:207) still complains about the "almost excessive fear" among Anglo-Saxon exegetes to attribute to Jesus sayings concerning "a cosmic end-event".

29. Outside the specific field of mission studies one may, for instance, think of the approaches to history and eschatology of scholars as different from each other and from Cullmann as Wolfhart Pannenberg and Jürgen Moltmann. The latter, in particular, emphasizes "that eschatology without the future of the eschaton is not eschatology at all, but only axiology or mysticism" (Braaten 1977:36). I have — in some detail — discussed both the similarities and the differences between Cullmann's and Moltmann's views on eschatology and mission (making use, particularly, of Moltmann's *Theology of Hope*, the first German issue of which appeared in 1964) in my "Heilsgeschichte und Mission" (*Oikonomia: Heilsgeschichte als Thema der Theologie* [Oscar Cullmann zum 65. Geburtstag gewidmet]. Hamburg: Herbert Reich, 1967, pp 386-394). It is equally worth noting that Cullmann has had a significant influence on contemporary Roman Catholic thinking. One may, in this respect, refer to AG 9.

Bibliography

AAGAARD, Anna Marie. 1974. Missio Dei in katholischer Sicht, *Evangelische Theologie* vol 34, pp 420-433.

AAGAARD, Johannes. 1965. Some Main Trends in Modern Protestant Missiology, *Studia Theologica* vol 19, pp 238-259.

———1967. *Mission, Konfession, Kirche: Die Problematik ihrer Integration im 19. Jahrhundert in Deutschland* (two volumes) Lund: Gleerup.

———1973. Trends in Missiological Thinking During the Sixties, *International Review of Mission* vol 62, pp 8-25.

ADAM, Alfred. 1974. Das Mönchtum der Alten Kirche, in Frohnes & Knorr, pp 86-93.

ALBERTZ, Rainer. 1983. Die "Antrittspredigt" Jesu im Lukasevangelium auf ihrem alttestamentlichen Hintergrund, *Zeitschrift für die Neutestamentliche Wissenschaft* vol 74, pp 182-206.

ALLEN, Roland. 1956. *Missionary Methods: St Paul's or Ours?* London: World Dominion Press (first published in 1912).

———1962. *The Ministry of the Spirit: Selected Writings by Roland Allen*, ed. David M. Paton. Grand Rapids: Eerdmans.

ANASTASIOS of Androussa. 1965. The Purpose and Motive of Mission, *International Review of Missions* vol 54, pp 281-297.

———1989. Orthodox Mission — Past, Present, Future, in George Lemopoulos (ed), *Your Will Be Done: Orthodoxy in Mission*. Geneva: World Council of Churches, pp 63-92.

ANDERSEN, Wilhelm. 1955. *Towards a Theology of Mission: A Study of the Encounter Between the Missionary Enterprise and the Church and Its Theology*. London: SCM Press.

ANDERSON, Gerald H. 1988. American Protestants in Pursuit of Mission: 1886-1986, *International Bulletin of Missionary Research* vol 12, pp 98-118.

ANDERSON, Hugh. 1964. Broadening Horizons. The Rejection at Nazareth Pericope of Luke 4:16-30 in Light of Recent Critical Trends, *Interpretation* vol 18, pp 259-275.

ARING, P.G. 1971. *Kirche als Ereignis: Ein Beitrag zur Neuorientierung der Missionstheologie*. Neukirchen-Vluyn: Neukirchener Verlag.

APPIAH-KUBI, Kofi & TORRES, Sergio (eds). 1979. *African Theology En Route*. Maryknoll, New York: Orbis Books.

ARMSTRONG, James. 1981. *From the Underside: Evangelism from a Third World Vantage Point*. Maryknoll, New York: Orbis Books.

AUF DER MAUR, Ivo. 1970. Die Aussagen des II. Vatikanischen Konzils über Mission und Ökumene, in Stirnimann, pp 81-102.

AUS, Roger D. 1979. Paul's Travel Plans to Spain and the "Full Number of the

Gentiles" of Rom XI 25, *Novum Testamentum* vol 21, pp 232-262.

BADE, Klaus J. (ed). 1982. *Imperialismus und Kolonialmission: Kaiserliches Deutschland und koloniales Imperium.* Wiesbaden: Franz Steiner Verlag.

BAKER, John. 1986. A Summary and Synthesis, in Limouris, pp 152-162.

BAKER, L.G.D. 1970. The Shadow of the Christian Symbol, in Cuming, pp 17-28.

BARRETT, David B. 1982. *World Christian Encyclopedia.* Nairobi: Oxford University Press.

———1990. Annual Statistical Table on Global Mission: 1990, *International Bulletin of Missionary Research* vol 14, pp 26f.

BARRETT, David B. & REAPSOME, James W. 1988. *Seven Hundred Plans to Evangelize the World: The Rise of a Global Evangelization Movement.* Birmingham: New Hope.

BARROWS, J.H. (ed). 1893. *The World's Parliament of Religions* (two volumes). Chicago: The Parliament Publishing Co.

BARTH, Gerhard. 1965. Das Gesetzverständnis des Evangelisten Matthäus, in Bornkamm, Barth & Held, pp 54-154.

BARTH, Karl. 1933. *Theologische Existenz Heute!* Munich: Chr. Kaiser.

———1956. *Church Dogmatics IV/1.* Edinburgh: T. & T. Clark.

———1957. Die Theologie und die Mission in der Gegenwart, in *Theologische Fragen und Antworten* vol 3. Zollikon-Zürich: Evangelischer Verlag, pp 100-126 (first published in 1932).

———1958. *Church Dogmatics IV/2.* Edinburgh: T. & T. Clark.

———1961. *Church Dogmatics IV/3* (first half). Edinburgh: T. & T. Clark.

———1962. *Church Dogmatics IV/3* (second half). Edinburgh: T. & T. Clark.

———1978. *Church Dogmatics I/2.* Edinburgh: T. & T. Clark.

BARTON, Bruce. 1925. *The Man Nobody Knows: A Discovery of the Real Jesus.* Indianapolis: The Bobbs-Merrill Co.

BASSHAM, Rodger C. 1979. *Mission Theology 1948-1975: Years of Worldwide Creative Tension, Ecumenical, Evangelical, and Roman Catholic.* Pasadena: William Carey Library.

BEAVER, R. Pierce. 1961. Eschatology in American Missions, in *Basileia* (Walter Freytag zum 60. Geburtstag). Stuttgart: Evang. Missionsverlag, pp 60-75.

———1977. (ed) *American Missions in Bicentennial Perspective.* Pasadena: William Carey Library.

———1980. *American Protestant Women in World Mission: The History of the First Feminist Movement in North America.* Grand Rapids: Eerdmans.

BEINERT, Wolfgang. 1983. Jesus Christus, der Erlöser von Sünde und Tod. Überblick über die abendländische Soteriologie, in Rivinius, pp 196-221.

BEKER, J. Christiaan. 1980. *Paul the Apostle: The Triumph of God in Life and Thought.* Philadelphia: Fortress Press.

———1984. *Paul's Apocalyptic Gospel: The Coming Triumph of God.* Philadelphia: Fortress Press (2d printing).

———1988. Paul's Theology: Consistent or Inconsistent? *New Testament Studies* vol 34, pp 364-377.

BERGQUIST, James A. 1986. "Good News to the Poor"—Why does this Lucan Motif appear to run dry in the Book of Acts?, *Bangalore Theological Forum* vol 28, pp 1-16.

BERKHOF, Hendrikus. 1964. *The Doctrine of the Holy Spirit.* Richmond: John Knox.

———1966. *Christ the Meaning of History.* London: SCM.

————1979. *Christian Faith*. Grand Rapids: Eerdmans.

BERKOUWER, G. C. 1979. *The Church*. Grand Rapids: Eerdmans (first published in 1976).

BERNSTEIN, Richard J. 1985. *The Restructuring of Social and Political Theory*. London: Methuen & Co (first published in 1976).

BEYERHAUS, P. 1969. *Humanisierung* — Einzige Hoffnung der Welt? Bad Salzuflen: MBK-Verlag.

BEYREUTHER, Erich. 1960. Mission und Kirche in der Theologie Zinzendorfs, *Evangelische Missionszeitschrift* vol 17, pp. 65-76, 97-113.

————1961. Evangelische Missionstheologie im 16. und 17. Jahrhundert, *Evangelische Missionszeitschrift* vol 18, pp 1-10, 33-43.

BIEDER, Werner. 1964. *Das Mysterium Christi und die Mission*. Zürich: EVZ-Verlag.

————1965. *Gottes Sendung und der missionarische Auftrag der Kirche nach Matthäus, Lukas, Paulus und Johannes* (Theologische Studien 82). Zürich: EVZ-Verlag.

BLANKE, Fritz. 1966. *Missionsprobleme des Mittelalters und der Neuzeit*. Zürich/Stuttgart: Zwingli Verlag.

BLASER, Klauspeter. 1978. *Gottes Heil in heutiger Wirklichkeit*. Frankfurt/Main: Otto Lembeck.

BLEI, K. 1980. Kerk voor de wereld, *Kerk en Theologie* vol 31, pp 1-21.

BLOOM, Allan. 1987. *The Closing of the American Mind*. New York: Simon & Schuster.

BOER, Harry. 1961. *Pentecost and Missions*. London: Lutterworth.

BOERWINKEL, Feitse. 1974. *Einde of nieuw begin? Onze maatschappij op de breuklijn*. Bilthoven: Amboboeken.

BOESAK, Allan A. 1982. *Farewell to Innocence*. Maryknoll, NY: Orbis Books.

BOFF, Leonardo. 1983. *The Lord's Prayer: The Prayer of Integral Liberation*. Maryknoll, New York: Orbis Books.

————1984. Integral Liberation and Partial Liberations, in L. & C. Boff, *Salvation and Liberation*. Maryknoll, New York: Orbis Books, pp 14-66.

————1986. *Ecclesiogenesis: The Base Communities Reinvent the Church*. Maryknoll, New York: Orbis Books.

BONHOEFFER, Dietrich. 1971. *Letters and Papers from Prison*. The Enlarged Edition. London: SCM Press.

————1977. Thy Kingdom Come on Earth, *The Expository Times* vol 88, pp 147-149 (English summary of a sermon preached in 1932).

BORING, M. Eugene. 1986. The Language of Universal Salvation in Paul, *Journal of Biblical Literature* vol 105, pp 269-292.

BORNKAMM, G., BARTH, G., HELD, H. J. 1965. *Überlieferung und Auslegung im Matthäusevangelium*. Neukirchen-Vluyn: Neukirchener Verlag (4., vermehrte Auflage).

BORNKAMM, Günther. 1965a. Enderwartung und Kirche im Matthäusevangelium, in Bornkamm, Barth & Held, pp 13-53.

————1965b. Der Auferstandene und der Irdische, Mt. 28:11-20, in: Bornkamm, Barth & Held, pp 289-310.

————1966. The Missionary Stance of Paul in 1 Corinthians 9 and Acts, in *Studies in Luke-Acts*, ed. L. E. Keck & J. L. Martyn. Nashville: Abingdon, pp 194-207.

BOSCH, David J. 1959. *Die Heidenmission in der Zukunftsschau Jesu: Eine Untersuchung zur Eschatologie der Synoptischen Evangelien*. Zürich: Zwingli Verlag.

———1980. *Witness to the World: The Christian Mission in Theological Perspective*. Atlanta: John Knox.

———1983. The Structure of Mission: An Exposition of Matthew 28:16-20, in Wilbert R. Shenk (ed), *Exploring Church Growth*. Grand Rapids: Eerdmans, pp 218-248.

BOVON, Francois. 1985. *Lukas in neuer Sicht*. Gesammelte Aufsätze. Neukirchen-Vluyn: Neukirchener Verlag (= Biblisch-Theologische Studien No 8).

BRAATEN, Carl E. 1977. *The Flaming Center*. Philadelphia: Fortress Press.

BRADLEY, Ian. 1976. *The Call to Seriousness: The Evangelical Impact on the Victorians*. London: Jonathan Cape.

BRAGG, Wayne G. 1987. From Development to Transformation, in Vinay Samuel & Chris Sugden (eds), *The Church in Response to Human Need*. Grand Rapids: Eerdmans, pp 20-51.

BRAKEMEIER, Gottfried. 1988. Justification, Grace, and Liberation Theology: A Comparison, *The Ecumenical Review* vol 40, pp 215-222.

BRAUER, J. 1984. Herausforderungen an das Christentum heute, in Küng & Tracy, pp 11-17.

BREYTENBACH, Cilliers. 1984. *Nachfolge und Zukunftserwartung nach Markus*. Eine methodenkritische Studie. Zürich: Theologischer Verlag (Abhandlungen zur Theologie des Alten und Neuen Testaments vol 71).

———1986. Reconciliation: Shifts in Christian Soteriology, in W. S. Vorster (ed), *Reconciliation and Reconstruction: Creative Options for a Rapidly Changing South Africa*. Pretoria: Univ. of South Africa, pp 1-25.

BRIA, Ion. 1975. The Church's Role in Evangelism — Icon or Platform?, *International Review of Mission* vol 64, pp 243-250.

———1976. Renewal of the Tradition through Pastoral Witness, *International Review of Mission* vol 65, pp 182-185.

———1980. *Martyria/Mission: The Witness of the Orthodox Churches Today*. Geneva: World Council of Churches.

———1986. *Go Forth in Peace: Orthodox Perspectives on Mission*. Geneva: World Council of Churches.

———1987. Unity and Mission from the Perspective of the Local Church: An Orthodox View, *The Ecumenical Review* vol 39, pp 265-270.

BRIDSTON, Keith. 1965. *Mission Myth and Reality*. New York: Friendship Press.

BRIGHT, John. 1953. *The Kingdom of God: The Biblical Concept and Its Meaning for the Church*. Nashville: Abingdon.

BROWN, Schuyler. 1977. The Two-fold Presentation of the Mission in Matthew's Gospel, *Studia Theologica* vol 31, pp 21-32.

———1978. The Mission to Israel in Matthew's Central Section (Mt. 9:35-11:1), *Zeitschrift für die Neutestamentliche Wissenschaft* vol 69, pp 73-90.

———1980. The Matthean Community and the Gentile Mission, *Novum Testamentum* vol 22, pp 193-221.

BRUEGGEMANN, Walter. 1982. The Bible and Mission: Some Interdisciplinary Implications for Teaching, *Missiology* vol 10, pp 397-411.

BÜHLMANN, W. 1977. *The Third Church*. Maryknoll, New York: Orbis Books.

———1990. *With Eyes To See: Church and World in the Third Millennium*. Maryknoll, New York: Orbis Books.

BURCHARD, Chr. 1980. Jesus für die Welt. Über das Verhältnis von Reich Gottes und Mission, in *Fides pro mundi vita*. Hans-Werner Gensichen zum 65. Geburtstag. Gütersloh: Gerd Mohn, pp 13-27.

BURROWS, William R. 1981. *New Ministries: The Global Context*. Maryknoll, New York: Orbis Books, first published 1980.

BUSSMANN, Claus. 1971. *Themen der paulinischen Missionspredigt auf dem Hintergrund der spätjüdisch-hellenistischen Missionsliteratur*. Bern: Herbert Lang; Frankfurt/Main: Peter Lang.

CAMPS, Arnulf. 1983. *Partners in Dialogue: Christianity and Other World Religions*. Maryknoll, New York: Orbis Books.

CAPP, Philip L. 1987. Eschatology: Its Relevance to Mission from an Evangelical Perspective, *Missionalia* vol 15, pp 110-118.

CAPRA, Fritjof. 1983. *The Turning Point: Science, Society and the Rising Culture*. New York: Bantam Books (first published in 1982).

————1984. *The Tao of Physics: An Exploration of the Parallels Between Modern Physics and Eastern Mysticism*. New York: Bantam Books (2d ed., rev. and updated; first published in 1976).

————1987. Für ein neues Weltbild. Gespräch mit Fritjof Capra, *Evangelische Kommentare* vol 20, pp 519-522.

CARDENAL, E. 1976. *The Gospel in Solentiname* vol 3. Maryknoll, New York: Orbis Books.

CASTRO, Emilio. 1977. Some Awkward Questions, *One World* no 29, pp 10f.

————1978. Liberation, Development, and Evangelism: Must We Choose in Mission?, *Occasional Bulletin of Missionary Research* vol 2, pp 87-90.

————1985. *Freedom in Mission*: The Perspective of the Kingdom of God. Geneva: World Council of Churches.

CHANEY, Charles L. 1976. *The Birth of Missions in America*. Pasadena: William Carey Library.

————1977. The Missionary Situation in the Revolutionary Era, in Beaver, pp 1-34.

CHRISTENSEN, Torben, & HUTCHISON, William R. (eds). 1982 *Missionary Ideologies in the Imperialist Era: 1880-1920*. Aarhus: Forlaget Aros.

CLARK, K. W. 1980. *The Gentile Bias and Other Essays*. Leiden: Brill (The first essay in the volume was originally published in 1947).

COCHRANE, James R. 1987. *Servants of Power: The Role of English-Speaking Churches in South Africa: 1903-1930*. Johannesburg: Ravan.

COLLET, Giancarlo. 1984. *Das Missionsverständnis in der gegenwärtigen Diskussion*. Mainz: Matthias-Grünewald-Verlag.

COMMON WITNESS. 1984. *Common Witness: A Study Document of the Joint Working Group of the Roman Catholic Church and the World Council of Churches*. Geneva: World Council of Churches (2d printing; first published in 1982).

CONN, Harvie M. 1983. The Missionary Task of Theology: A Love/Hate Relationship?, *Westminster Theological Journal* vol 45, pp 1-21.

CONZELMANN, Hans. 1964. *The Theology of Saint Luke*. Translated by Geoffrey Buswell. London: Faber & Faber (3d impression).

COSTAS, Orlando E. 1982. *Christ Outside the Gate: Mission Beyond Christendom*. Maryknoll, New York: Orbis Books.

————1989. *Liberating News: A Theology of Contextual Evangelism*. Grand Rapids: Eerdmans.

CRACKNELL, Kenneth, & LAMB, Christopher (eds). 1986. *Theology on Full Alert* (revised and enlarged ed.). London: British Council of Churches.

CRAGG, Kenneth. 1959. *Sandals at the Mosque: Christian Presence Amid Islam.* New York: Oxford University Press.

CRESR. 1982. *Evangelism and Social Responsibility: An Evangelical Commitment.* Exeter: Paternoster.

CROSBY, Michael H., OFMCap. 1977. *Thy Will Be Done: Praying the Our Father as Subversive Activity.* Maryknoll, New York: Orbis Books. London: Sheed & Ward.

————1981. *Spirituality of the Beatitudes: Matthew's Challenge for First World Christians.* Maryknoll, New York: Orbis Books.

CRUM, Winston. 1973. The *Missio Dei* and the Church, *St. Vladimir's Theological Quarterly* vol 17, pp 285-289.

CRUMLEY, James. 1989. Reflections on Twenty-Five Years After the Decree on Ecumenism, *Ecumenical Trends* vol 18, pp 145-149.

CULLMANN, Oscar. 1965. *Heil als Geschichte: Heilsgechichtliche Existenz im Neuen Testament.* Tübingen: Mohr.

CUMING, G.J. (ed). 1970. *The Mission of the Church and the Propagation of the Faith.* Cambridge: University Press.

DAECKE, Sigmund M. 1988. Glaube im Pluralismus: Gibt es eine postmoderne Theologie? *Evangelische Kommentare* vol 21, pp 629-632.

DAHL, N. A. 1977a. The Missionary Theology in the Epistle to the Romans, in *Studies in Paul: Theology for the Early Christian Mission.* Minneapolis: Augsburg Publishing House, pp 70-94.

————1977b. The God of Jews and Gentiles (Romans 3:29-30), in *Studies in Paul,* pp 178-191.

DAPPER, Heinz. 1979. *Mission — Glaubensinterpretation — Glaubensrealisation: Ein Beitrag zur ökumenischen Missionstheologie.* Frankfurt/Main: Peter Lang.

DAVIES, W.D. 1966. *Worship and Mission.* London: SCM Press.

DAVIS, J. Merle. 1947. *New Buildings on Old Foundations: A Handbook on Stabilizing the Younger Churches in Their Environment.* New York & London: International Missionary Council.

DAWSON, Christopher. 1950. *Religion and the Rise of Western Culture.* London: Sheed & Ward.

————1952. *The Making of Europe.* New York: The New American Library (first published in 1932).

DE BOER, Martinus C. 1988. Paul and Jewish Apocalyptic Eschatology, in Marcus & Soards, pp 169-190.

DE GROOT, A. 1988. De ene Schrift en de vele interpretatie-contexten: de hermeneutiek in de missiologie, in *Oecumenische inleiding,* pp 155-166.

DE GRUCHY, J. W. 1986. The Church and the Struggle for South Africa, *Theology Today* vol 43, pp 229-243.

————1987. *Theology and Ministry in Context and Crisis.* London: Collins.

DE JONG, J. A. 1970. *As the Waters Cover the Sea: Millennial Expectations in the Rise of Anglo-American Missions 1640-1810.* Kampen: Kok.

DENNIS, James S. 1897, 1899, 1906. *Christian Missions and Social Progress: A Sociological Study of Foreign Missions* (three volumes). Edinburgh & London: Oliphant, Anderson & Ferrier.

DE SANTA ANA, Julio. 1977. *Good News to the Poor: The Challenge of the Poor in the History of the Church.* Geneva: World Council of Churches.

DIETZFELBINGER, Christian. 1985. *Die Berufung des Paulus als Ursprung seiner Theologie*. Neukirchen-Vluyn: Neukirchener Verlag.

DILLON, R. J. 1979. Easter Revelation and Mission Program in Luke 24:46-48, in D. Durken (ed), *Sin, Salvation and the Spirit*. Collegeville: The Liturgical Press.

DIX, (Dom) Gregory. 1953. *Jew and Greek: A Study in the Primitive Church*. Westminster: Dacre Press.

D'SA, Thomas. 1988. The Salvation of the Rich in the Gospel of Luke, *Vidyajyoti* vol 5, pp 170-180.

DUFF, Edward, SJ. 1956. *The Social Thought of the World Council of Churches*. London: Longmans, Green & Co.

DUFF, Nancy J. 1989. The Significance of Pauline Apocalyptic for Theological Ethics, in Marcus & Soards, pp 179-196.

DULLES, Avery, SJ. 1976. *Models of the Church*. Dublin: Gill & Macmillan.

DUNN, Edmond J. 1980. *Missionary Theology: Foundations in Development*. Washington: University Press of America.

DUPONT, Jacques, OSB. 1979. *The Salvation of the Gentiles: Essays on the Acts of the Apostles*. New York: Paulist Press.

DÜRR, H. 1951. Die Reinigung der Missionsmotive, *Evangelisches Missions-Magazin* vol 95, pp 2-10.

DU TOIT, A. B. 1988. Gesetzesgerechtigkeit und Glaubensgerechtigkeit in Röm 4:13-25: In Gespräch mit E. P. Sanders, *Hervormde Teologiese Studies* vol 44, pp 71-80.

ECHEGARAY, Hugo. 1984. *The Practice of Jesus*. Maryknoll, New York: Orbis Books.

EHRHARDT, Arnold A.T. 1959. *Politische Metaphysik von Solon bis Augustin*, Die Christliche Revolution. Tübingen: J.C.B. Mohr.

ENGEL, Lothar. 1982. Die Rheinische Missionsgesellschaft und die deutsche Kolonialherrschaft in Südwestafrika 1884-1915, in Bade, pp 142-164.

ENKLAAR, I. H. 1981. *Kom over en help ons! Twaalf opstellen over de Nederlandse zending in de negentiende eeuw*. The Hague: Boekencentrum.

———1988. *Life and Work of Dr. J. Th. van der Kemp 1747-1811*. Missionary Pioneer and Protagonist of Racial Equality in South Africa. Cape Town/Rotterdam: A. A. Balkema.

ERDMANN, Carl. 1977. *The Origin of the Idea of Crusade*. Princeton: Princeton University Press (German original published in 1935).

FABELLA, Virginia, MM, & TORRES, Sergio (eds). 1983. *The Irruption of the Third World*. Maryknoll, New York: Orbis Books.

FARLEY, Edward. 1983. *Theologia: The Fragmentation and Unity of Theological Education*. Philadelphia: Fortress Press.

FIERRO BARDAJI, Alfredo. 1977. *The Militant Gospel: A Critical Introduction to Political Theologies*. Maryknoll, New York: Orbis Books.

FISHER, Eugene J. 1982. Historical Developments in the Theology of Christian Mission, in Martin A. Cohen & Helga Croner (eds), *Christian Mission—Jewish Mission*. Ramsey, New Jersey: Paulist Press, pp 4-45.

FLENDER, Helmut. 1967. *St Luke—Theologian of Redemptive History*. Philadelphia: Fortress Press.

FORD, J. Massyngbaerde. 1984. *My Enemy is my Guest: Jesus and Violence in Luke*. Maryknoll, New York: Orbis Books.

FORMAN, Charles W. 1982. Evangelization and Civilization: Protestant Missionary

Motivation in the Imperialist Era. II. The Americans, *International Bulletin of Missionary Research* vol 6, pp 54-56.

FRANKEMÖLLE, Hubert. 1974. *Jahwebund und Kirche Christi: Studien zur Form- und Traditionsgeschichte des "Evangeliums" nach Matthäus.* Münster: Verlag Aschendorff.

————1982. Zur Theologie der Mission im Matthäusevangelium, in Kertelge, pp 93-129.

FRAZIER, William, MM. 1987. Where Mission Begins: A Foundational Probe, *Maryknoll Formation Journal* (summer), pp 13-52.

FREND, W.H.C. 1974. Der Verlauf der Mission in der Alten Kirche bis zum 7. Jahrhundert, in Frohnes & Knorr, pp 32-50.

FREYTAG, Walter. 1961. *Reden und Aufsätze* vol II. Munich: Chr. Kaiser Verlag.

FRIEDRICH, Gerhard. 1983. Die formale Struktur von Mt. 28, 18-20, *Zeitschrift für Theologie und Kirche* vol 80, pp 137-183.

FRIES, Heinrich. 1986. Katholische Missionswissenschaft in neuer Gestalt, *Stimmen der Zeit* vol 111, pp 755-764.

FROHNES, H. & KNORR, U. W. (eds). 1974. *Kirchengeschichte als Missionsgeschichte. Bd. I: Die Alte Kirche.* Munich: Chr. Kaiser Verlag.

FROSTIN, Per. 1985. The Hermeneutics of the Poor—The Epistemological 'Break' in Third World Theologies, *Studia Theologica* vol 39, pp 127-150.

————1988. *Liberation Theology in Tanzania and South Africa.* A First World Perspective. Lund: Lund University Press (Studia Theologica Lundensia 42).

FRYE, Northrop. 1982. *The Great Code: The Bible and Literature.* London: Ark Paperbacks.

FUETER, P. 1976. Confessing Christ Through Liturgy: An Orthodox Challenge to Protestants, *International Review of Mission* vol 65, pp 123-128.

FUNG, Raymond. 1980. Good News to the Poor—A Case for a Missionary Movement, in WCC 1980, pp 83-92.

GASSMANN, Günther. 1986. The Church as Sacrament, Sign and Instrument: The Reception of this Ecclesiological Understanding in Ecumenical Debate, in Limouris, pp 1-17.

GAVENTA, Beverly Roberts. 1982. "You will be my Witnesses": Aspects of Mission in the Acts of the Apostles, *Missiology* vol 10, pp 413-425.

————1986. *From Darkness to Light: Aspects of Conversion in the New Testament.* Philadelphia: Fortress Press.

GEFFRÉ, Claude, O.P. 1982. Theological Reflections on a New Age of Mission, *International Review of Mission* vol 71, pp 478-492.

GEIJBELS, M. 1978. Evangelization, Its Meaning and Practice, *Al-Mushir* vol 20, 73-82.

GENSICHEN, Hans-Werner. 1960. Were the Reformers Indifferent to Missions?, in *History's Lessons for Tomorrow's Mission.* Geneva: WSCF, pp 119-127.

————1961. *Missionsgeschichte der neueren Zeit.* Göttingen: Vandenhoeck & Ruprecht.

————1971. *Glaube für die Welt: Theologische Aspekte der Mission.* Gütersloh: Gerd Mohn.

————1975a. "Dienst der Seelen" und "Dienst des Leibes" in der frühen pietistischen Mission, in H. Bornkamm et al, *Der Pietismus in Gestalten und Wirkungen* (Martin Schmidt zum 65. Geburtstag). Bielefeld: Luther-Verlag, pp 155-178.

————1975b. Über die Ursprünge der Missionsgesellschaft, in Nils E. Bloch-Hoell (ed), *Misjonskal og forskersglede* (Festschrift til professor O.G. Myklebust). Oslo: Universitetsforlaget, pp 48-69.

————1982. German Protestant Missions, in Christensen & Hutchison, pp 181-190.

————1983. Evangelisieren und Zivilieren. Motive deutscher protestantischer Mission in der imperialistischen Epoche, *Zeitschrift für Missions-und Religionswissenschaft* vol 67, pp 257-269.

————1985. *Mission und Kultur: Gesammelte Aufsätze.* Munich: Chr. Kaiser Verlag, pp 112-129 ("Evangelium und Kultur: Variationen über ein altes Thema" [first published in 1978]), and pp 189-202 ("Die deutsche Mission und der Kolonialismus" [first published in 1962]).

————1986. Akzente und Problemstellungen in der gegenwärtigen Missionstheologie, *Zeitschrift für Missions- und Religionswissenschaft* vol 70, pp 112-127.

————1989. Erwartungen der Religionen an das Christentum, *Zeitschrift für Missions-und Religionswissenschaft* vol 73, pp 197-209.

GERRISH, Brian A. 1962. *Grace and Reason: A Study in the Theology of Luther.* Oxford: Clarendon Press.

————1984. Das Paradigma in der modernen Theologie: Der Übergang vom Alt- zum Neuprotestantismus nach Troeltsch, in Küng & Tracy, pp 193-203.

GIESSEN, Heinrich 1982. *Christliches Handeln: Eine redaktionskritische Untersuchung zum dikaiosyne-Begriff im Matthäus-Evangelium.* Frankfurt/Main: Peter Lang.

GILHUIS, J. C. 1955. *Ecclesiocentrische aspecten van het zendingswerk.* Kok: Kampen.

GILLILAND, D. 1983. *Pauline Theology and Mission Practice.* Grand Rapids: Baker Book House.

GLASSER, Arthur F. 1989. Mission in the 1990s, *International Bulletin of Missionary Research* vol 13, pp 2-8.

GLAZIK, Josef. 1979. *Mission — der stets grössere Auftrag* (Gesammelte Vorträge und Aufsätze). Aachen: Mission Aktuell Verlag.

————1984a. Die neuzeitliche Mission under der Leitung der Propaganda-Kongregation, in *Warum Mission?* (1. Teilband). St. Ottilien: EOS-Verlag, pp 27-40.

————1984b. Das Zweite Vatikanische Konzil und seine Wirkung, in *Warum Mission?* (2. Teilband). St. Ottilien: EOS-Verlag, pp 49-72.

GODIN, H. & DANIEL, Y. 1943. *France, pays de mission?* Paris: Editions du Cerf.

GÓMEZ, Filipe, SJ 1986. The Missionary Activity Twenty Years After Vatican II, *East Asian Pastoral Review* vol 23, pp 26-57.

————1989. Signs of the Times, *East Asian Pastoral Review* vol 26, pp 365-386.

GOPPELT, L. 1981. *Theology of the New Testament.* Vol 1. Grand Rapids: Eerdmans.

GORT, Jerald. 1980a. *World Missionary Conference: Melbourne, May 1980: An Historical and Missiological Interpretation.* Amsterdam: Free University.

————1980b. The Contours of the Reformed Understanding of Christian Mission, *Calvin Theological Journal* vol 15, pp 47-60.

————1988. Heil, onheil en bemiddeling, in *Oecumenische inleiding*, pp 203-218.

GRANT, Robert M. 1986. *Gods and the One God.* Philadelphia: The Westminster Press.

GREEN, Michael. 1970. *Evangelism in the Early Church.* London: Hodder & Stoughton.

GRESHAKE, Gisbert. 1983. *Gottes Heil — Glück des Menschen.* Freiburg/B: Herder.

GRÜNDEL, Johannes. 1983. Sünde als Verneinung des Willens Gottes. Zur Frage nach dem Ursprung von Leid, Übel und Bösem, in Rivinius, pp 105-125.

GRÜNDER, Horst. 1982. Deutsche Missionsgesellschaften auf dem Weg zur Kolonialmission, in Bade, pp 68-102.

————1985. *Geschichte der deutschen Kolonien*. Paderborn: Ferdinand Schöningh.

GUARDINI, Romano. 1950. *Das Ende der Neuzeit*. Würzburg: Werkbund-Verlag.

GUNDRY, R. H. 1987. Grace, Works, and Staying Saved in Paul, *The Best in Theology* vol 1, pp 81-100.

GÜNTHER, Walter. 1967. *Von der Sendung der Gemeinde: Der Beitrag der Weltmission zu ihrer Erneuerung*. Stuttgart: Evang. Missionsverlag.

GÜNTHER, Wolfgang. 1970. *Von Edinburgh nach Mexico City: Die ekklesiologischen Bemühungen der Weltmissionskonferenzen (1910-1963)*. Stuttgart: Evang. Missionsverlag.

GUTHEINZ, Luis, SJ. 1986. A Careful Look at a Critical Book, *East Asia Pastoral Review* vol 23, pp 482-488.

GUTIÉRREZ, Gustavo. 1988. *A Theology of Liberation* (fifteenth anniversary edition with a new introduction by the author). Maryknoll, New York: Orbis Books.

HAAS, Odo. 1971. *Paulus der Missionar: Ziel, Grundsätze und Methoden der Missionstätigkeit des Apostels Paulus nach seinen eigenen Aussagen*. Münsterschwarzach: Vier-Türme-Verlag.

HAENCHEN, Ernst. 1971. *The Acts of the Apostles: A Commentary*. Translated by Bernard Noble and Gerald Shinn. Oxford: Basil Blackwell.

HAGE, Wolfgang. 1978. Der Weg nach Asien: Die ostsyrische Missionskirche, in Schäferdiek, pp 360-393.

HAHN, Ferdinand. 1965. *Mission in the New Testament*. Translated by Frank Clarke. London: SCM Press.

————1980. Der Sendungsauftrag des Auferstandenen: Matthäus 28, 16-20, in *Fides pro mundi vita* (H.-W. Gensichen zum 65). Geburtstag. Gütersloh: Gerd Mohn, pp 28-43.

————1984. Biblische Begründung der Mission, in *Warum Mission?* (2. Teilband). St. Ottilien: EOS-Verlag, pp 265-288.

HAIGHT, Roger D., SJ. 1976. Mission: The Symbol for Understanding the Church Today, *Theological Studies* vol 37, pp 620-649.

HANNICK, Christian. 1978. Die byzantinische Missionen, in Schäferdiek, pp 279-359.

HARNACK, Adolf (von). 1924. *Die Mission und Ausbreitung des Christentums in den ersten drei Jahrhunderten*. Vierte, verbesserte und vermehrte Auflage, Band 1. Leipzig: Hinrichs'sche Buchhandlung.

————1961. *History of Dogma*. Vol 1. New York: Dover Publications.

————1962. *The Mission and Expansion of Christianity in the First Three Centuries*. Translation of vol 1 of the 1908 edition. New York: Harper & Brothers.

HASSELHORN, Fritz. 1988. *Bauernmission in Südafrika: Die Hermannsburger Mission im Spannungsfeld der Kolonialpolitik 1880-1939*. Erlangen: Verlag der Ev.-Luth. Mission.

HASTINGS, Adrian. 1968. *A Concise Guide to the Documents of the Second Vatican Council*. Vol 1. London: Darton, Longman & Todd.

HEGEL, G.W.F. 1975. *Lectures on the Philosophy of World History*. Introduction: Reason in History. Translated from the German edition of Johannes Hoffmeister by H. B. Nisbet. Cambridge: University Press.

HEISIG, J. W. 1981. Christian Mission: The Selfish War, *Verbum SVD* vol 22, pp 363-386.

HENGEL, Martin. 1971. *Was Jesus a Revolutionist?* Philadelphia: Fortress Press.

————1983a. Between Jesus and Paul: The "Hellenists", the "Seven" and Stephen, in Hengel, *Between Jesus and Paul: Studies in the Earliest History of Christianity*. London: SCM Press, pp 1-29, 133-156.

————1983b. The Origins of the Christian Mission, in Hengel, *Between Jesus and Paul: Studies in the Earliest History of Christianity*. London: SCM Press, pp 48-64, 166-179.

————1986. *Earliest Christianity*. London: SCM Press.

HENRY, Carl F. H., & MOONEYHAM, W. Stanley. 1967. *One Race, One Gospel, One Task*. World Congress on Evangelism, Berlin 1966: Official Reference Volumes (2 volumes). Minneapolis: World Wide Publications.

HENRY, Patrick G. 1987. Monastic Mission: The Monastic Tradition as Source for Unity and Renewal Today, *The Ecumenical Review* vol 39, pp 271-281.

HERING, Wolfgang. 1982. Die Kirche ist ihrem Wesen nach missionarisch, in Köster & Probst, pp 73-82.

HESS, Willy. 1962. *Das Missionsdenken bei Philipp Nicolai*. Hamburg: Friedrich Wittig Verlag.

HEUFELDER, Emmanuel, OSB. 1983. *The Way to God According to the Rule of Saint Benedict*. Kalamazoo: Cistercian Publications.

HIEBERT, Paul. 1985a. Epistemological Foundations for Science and Theology, *Theological Students Fellowship Bulletin* (March), pp 5-10.

————1985b. The Missiological Implications of an Epistemological Shift, *Theological Students Fellowship Bulletin* (May-June), pp 12-18.

————1987. Critical Contextualization, *International Bulletin of Missionary Research* vol 11, pp 104-112.

HODGSON, Peter C. & KING, Robert H. (eds). 1982. *Christian Theology: An Introduction to its Traditions and Tasks*. Philadelphia: Fortress Press.

HOEDEMAKER, L. 1988. Het volk Gods en de einden der aarde, in *Oecumenische inleiding*, pp 167-180.

HOEKENDIJK, J.C. 1967a. *Kirche und Volk in der deutschen Missionswissenschaft*. Munich: Chr. Kaiser Verlag.

————1967b. *The Church Inside Out*. London: SCM Press.

HOEKSTRA, Harvey T. 1979. *The World Council of Churches and the Demise of Evangelism*. Wheaton: Tyndale House.

HOFIUS, Otfried. 1987. Das Evangelium und Israel. Erwägungen zu Römer 9-11, *Zeitschrift für Theologie und Kirche* vol 83, pp 297-324.

HOGG, W. Richie. 1977. The Role of American Protestantism in World Mission, in Beaver, pp 354-402.

HOLL, Karl. 1928. Luther und die Mission, *Gesammelte Aufsätze zur Kirchengeschichte III*. Tübingen: Mohr, pp 234-243. (This article was first published in 1924).

————1974. Die Missionsmethode der alten und die der mittelalterlichen Kirche, in Frohnes & Knorr, pp 3-17. (This article was first published in 1928).

HOLMBERG, Bengt. 1978. *Paul and Power: The Structure of Authority in the Primitive Church as Reflected in the Pauline Epistles*. Lund: Gleerup.

HOLSTEN, Walter. 1953. Reformation und Mission, *Archiv für Reformationsgeschichte* vol 44, pp 1-32.

————1961. Von den Anfängen evangelischer Missionsarbeit, in G. Brennecke (ed), *Weltmission in ökumenischer Sicht*. Stuttgart: Evang. Missionsverlag, pp 144-152.

HOPKINS, Charles Howard. 1940. *The Role of the Social Gospel in American Protestantism 1865-1915*. New Haven: Yale University Press.

HORKHEIMER, Max, & ADORNO, Theodor W. 1947. *Dialektik der Aufklärung: Philosophische Fragmente*. Amsterdam: Querido Verlag.

HUBBARD, Benjamin J. 1974. *The Matthean Redaction of a Primitive Apostolic Commission: An Exegesis of Matthew 28: 16-20*. Missoula: Society of Biblical Literature and Scholars' Press.

HULTGREN, Arland J. 1985. *Paul's Gospel and Mission*. Philadelphia: Fortress Press.

HUMMEL, R. 1963. *Die Auseinandersetzung zwischen Kirche und Judentum im Matthäusevangelium*. Munich: Chr. Kaiser Verlag.

HUPPENBAUER, H.W. 1977. Missionarische Dimension des Gottesvolkes im Alten Testament, *Zeitschrift für Mission* vol 3, pp 37-47.

HUTCHISON, William R. 1982. A Moral Equivalent for Imperialism: Americans and the Promotion of "Christian Civilization", 1880-1910, in Christensen & Hutchison, pp 167-178.

————1987. *Errand to the World: American Protestant Missionary Thought and Foreign Missions*. Chicago & London: The University of Chicago Press.

ILLICH, Ivan. 1974. *Mission and Midwifery: Essays on Missionary Formation*. Gwelo (Gweru): Mambo Press.

INTER-ANGLICAN THEOLOGICAL AND DOCTRINAL COMMISSION. 1986. *For the Sake of the Kingdom: God's Church and the New Creation*. London: Anglican Consultative Council.

IRIK, J. 1982. Lukas, evangelie voor de volken, evangelie voor Israel?, *Kerk en Theologie* vol 33, pp 278-290.

ITC. 1989. Faith and Inculturation, *The Irish Theological Quarterly* vol 55, pp 142-161 (Report of the International Theological Commission).

JANSEN SCHOONHOVEN, Evert. 1974a. *Variaties op het thema "zending"*. Kok: Kampen.

————1974a. *De ontwikkeling van het Christendom in de nieuwste tijd*. Leiden: Inter-university Institute for Missiological and Ecumenical Research.

————1977. *Wederkerige assistentie van kerken in missionair perspectief*. Leiden: Inter-university Institute for Missiological and Ecumenical Research.

JEREMIAS, Joachim. 1958. *Jesus' Promise to the Nations*. London: SCM Press.

JERVELL, Jacob. 1972. *Luke and the People of God: A New Look at Luke-Acts*. Minneapolis: Augsburg Publishing House.

JOHNSON, Todd M. 1988. *Countdown to 1900: World Evangelization at the End of the Nineteenth Century*. Birmingham: New Hope.

JOHNSTON, Arthur P. 1978. *The Battle for World Evangelism*. Wheaton: Tyndale House.

JONGENEEL, J.A.B. 1986. *Het christendom als wereldzendingsgodsdienst*. The Hague: Boekencentrum. (Inaugural Lecture).

————1989. Voetius' zendingstheologie, de eerste comprehensieve protestantse zendingstheologie. In J. van Oort (ed), *De onbekende Voetius*. Kampen: Kok, pp 117-147.

JOSUTTIS, Manfred. 1988. Religion — Gefahr der Postmoderne, *Evangelische Kommentare* vol 21, pp 16-19.

KAHL, Hans-Dietrich. 1978. Die ersten Jahrhunderte des missionsgeschichtlichen Mittelalters, in Schäferdiek, pp 11-76.

KÄHLER, Martin. 1971. *Schriften zur Christologie und Mission*. Munich: Chr. Kaiser Verlag.

KAMENKA, Eugene. 1976. *Nationalism: The Nature and Evolution of an Idea*. London: Edward Arnold.

KANNENGIESER, Charles. 1984. Origenes, Augustin und der Paradigmenwechsel in der Theologie, in Küng & Tracy, pp 151-167.

KÄSEMANN, Ernst. 1969a. The Beginnings of Christian Theology, in *New Testament Questions of Today* (English Translation by W. J. Montague). Philadelphia: Fortress Press, pp 82-107.

———1969b. On the Subject of Primitive Christian Apocalyptic, in *New Testament Questions of Today*, pp 108-137.

———1969c. The Righteousness of God in Paul, in *New Testament Questions of Today*, pp 168-182.

———1969d. Worship and Everyday Life: A Note on Romans 12, in *New Testament Questions of Today*, pp 188-195.

———1969e. Paul and Early Catholicism, in *New Testament Questions of Today*, pp 236-251.

———1974. Zur ekklesiologischen Verwendung der Stichworte "Sakrament" und "Zeichen", in R. Groscurth (ed), *Wandernde Horizonte auf dem Weg zu kirchlicher Einheit*. Frankfurt/Main: Otto Lembeck, pp 119-136.

———1980. The Eschatological Royal Reign of God, in WCC 1980, pp 61-71.

KASTING, Heinrich. 1969. *Die Anfänge der urchristlichen Mission*. Munich: Chr. Kaiser Verlag.

KEDAR, Benjamin Z. 1984. *Crusade and Mission: European Approaches Toward the Muslims*. Princeton: Princeton University Press.

KERTELGE, Karl (ed). 1982. *Mission im Neuen Testament*. Freiburg-Basel-Vienna: Herder.

———1987. Paulus, in Müller & Sundermeier, pp 369-375.

KEYSSER, C. 1980. *A People Reborn*. Pasadena: William Carey Library (German original first published in 1929).

KIRK, Andrew. 1986. The Middle East Dilemma: A Personal Reflection, *Anvil* vol 3, pp 231-258.

KLOSTERMAIER, Klaus. 1969. *Hindu and Christian in Vrindaban*. London: SCM Press.

KNAPP, Stephen C. 1977. Mission and Modernization: A Preliminary Critical Analysis of Contemporary Understandings of Mission from a "Radical Evangelical" Perspective, in Beaver, pp 146-209.

KNITTER, Paul F. 1985. *No Other Name? A Critical Survey of Christian Attitudes Toward the World Religions*. Maryknoll, New York: Orbis Books.

———1987. Toward a Liberation Theology of Religions, in John Hick & Paul F. Knitter (eds), *The Myth of Christian Uniqueness — Toward a Pluralistic Theology of Religions*. Maryknoll, New York: Orbis Books, pp 178-200.

KOENIG, John. 1979. Vision, Self-Offering, and Transformation for Ministry, in D. Durken (ed), *Sin, Salvation, and the Spirit*. Collegeville: The Liturgical Press, pp 307-323.

KOHLER, Werner. 1974. Neue Herrschaftsverhältnisse als Grund der Mission, *Evangelische Theologie* vol 34, pp 462-478.

KOHN, Hans. 1945. *The Idea of Nationalism: A Study of its Origins and Background.* New York: The Macmillan Co.

KÖSTER, Fritz. 1984. Ortskirche—Weltkirche: Mission in Sechs Kontinenten, in *Warum Mission?* (2. Teilband). St. Ottilien: EOS-Verlag, pp 157-186.

KÖSTER, Heinrich M. & PROBST, Manfried (eds). 1982. *Wie mich der Vater gesandt hat, so sende ich euch. Beiträge zur Theologie der Sendung.* Limburg: Lahn-Verlag.

KOYAMA, K. 1980. *Three Mile an Hour God.* Maryknoll, New York: Orbis Books.

———1984. *Mount Fuji and Mount Sinai: A Pilgrimage in Theology.* Maryknoll, New York: Orbis Books. London: SCM Press.

KRAEMER, Hendrik. 1947. *The Christian Message in a Non-Christian World.* London: Edinburgh House Press (first published in 1938).

———1961. *Religion and the Christian Faith.* London: Lutterworth (first published in 1956).

———1970. *Uit de nalatenschap van dr H. Kraemer.* Kampen: Kok.

KRAFT, C. H. 1981. *Christianity and Culture: A Study in Dynamic Biblical Theologizing in Cross-Cultural Perspective.* Maryknoll, New York: Orbis Books (3d printing).

KRAMM, Thomas. 1979. *Analyse und Bewährung theologischer Modelle zur Begründung der Mission.* Aachen: Missio Aktuell Verlag.

KRASS, Alfred C. 1977. On Dykes, the Dutch and the Holy Spirit, *Milligan Missiogram* vol 4, no 4, pp 1-26.

———1978. *Five Lanterns at Sundown: Evangelism in a Chastened Mood.* Grand Rapids: Eerdmans.

KREMER, Jacob. 1982. Weltweites Zeugnis für Christus in der Kraft des Geistes. Zur lukanischen Sicht der Mission, in Kertelge, pp 145-163.

KRETSCHMAR, Georg. 1974. Das christliche Leben und die Mission in der frühen Kirche, in Frohnes & Knorr, pp 94-128.

KRITZINGER, J.N.J. 1988. *Black Theology—Challenge to Mission.* Pretoria: Univ. of South Africa (unpublished DTh dissertation).

KROEGER, James H., MM. 1989. "Signs of the Times": A Thirty-Year Panorama, *East Asian Pastoral Review* vol 26, pp 191-196.

KUHN, Thomas S. 1970. *The Structure of Scientific Revolutions.* Chicago: The University of Chicago Press (2d ed., enlarged).

KÜNG, Hans. 1977. *On Being a Christian.* London: Collins.

———1984. Was meint Paradigmenwechsel?, in Küng & Tracy, pp 19-26.

———1986. *Christianity and the World Religions: Paths of Dialogue with Islam, Hinduism, and Buddhism.* New York: Doubleday & Co.

———1987. *Theologie im Aufbruch: Eine ökumenische Grundlegung.* Munich: Piper Verlag.

KÜNG, Hans, & TRACY, David (ed). 1984. *Theologie—wohin? Auf dem Weg zu einem neuen Paradigma.* Zürich-Cologne: Benziger Verlag. E. T. 1989. *Paradigm Change in Theology.* New York: Crossroad.

KUSCHEL, Karl-Josef. 1984. Ein kleiner Rückblick als Hinführung, in Küng & Tracy, pp 233-240.

LABUSCHAGNE, C. J. 1975. De godsdienst van Israel en de andere godsdiensten, *Wereld en Zending* vol 4, pp 4-16.

LAMB, Matthew L. 1982. *Solidarity with Victims: Toward a Theology of Social Transformation*. New York: Crossroad.

———1984. Die Dialektik von Theorie und Praxis in der Paradigmenanalyse, in Küng & Tracy, pp 103-147.

LAMPE, G.W.H. 1957. Early Patristic Eschatology, in *Eschatology* (Scottish Journal of Theology Occasional Papers, No 2). Edinburgh: Oliver & Boyd, Ltd. Reprint (first published in 1953).

LANGE, Joachim. 1973. *Das Erscheinen des Auferstandenen im Evangelium nach Matthäus: Eine traditions- und redaktionsgeschichtliche Untersuchung zu Mt. 28, 16-20*. Würzburg: Echter Verlag.

LAPIDE, Pinchas. 1986. *The Sermon on the Mount: Utopia or Program for Action?* Maryknoll, New York: Orbis Books.

LATEGAN, Bernard. 1988. Is Paul Defending His Apostleship in Galatians?, *New Testament Studies* vol 34, pp 411-430.

LATOURETTE, Kenneth Scott. 1971. *A History of the Expansion of Christianity* vol 7. Advance Through Storm: 1914 and After. Exeter: Paternoster (first published in 1945).

LaVERDIERE, Eugene A., & THOMPSON, William G. 1976. New Testament Communities in Transition, *Theological Studies* vol 37, pp 567-597.

LEDERLE, H. I. 1988. *Treasures Old and New: Interpretations of "Spirit-Baptism" in the Charismatic Renewal Movement*. Peabody, Massachusetts: Hendrickson.

LEGRAND, L. 1987. The Missionary Command of the Risen Lord, Mt. 28:16-20, *Indian Theological Studies* vol 24, pp 5-28.

———1988. *Le Dieu qui vient: La mission dans la Bible*. Paris: Desclée. E. T. 1990. *Unity and Plurality: Mission in the Bible*. Maryknoll, New York: Orbis Books.

LIMOURIS, Gennadios (ed). 1986. *Church-Kingdom-World: The Church as Mystery and Prophetic Sign*. Geneva: World Council of Churches (Faith and Order Paper No. 130).

LINDER, Amnon. 1978. Christlich-jüdische Konfrontation im kirchlichen Frühmittelalter, in Schäferdiek, pp 397-441.

LINDSELL, H. (ed). 1966. *The Church's Worldwide Mission*. Waco: Word Books.

LINZ, Manfred. 1964. *Anwalt der Welt: Zur Theologie der Mission*. Stuttgart: Kreuz-Verlag.

———1974. Missionswissenschaft und Ökumenik, in R. Bohren (ed), *Einführung in das Studium der evangelischen Theologie*. Munich: Chr. Kaiser Verlag, pp 33-54.

LIPPERT, Peter. 1968. *Leben als Zeugnis: Die werbende Kraft christlicher Lebensführung nach dem Kirchenverständnis neutestamentlicher Briefe*. Stuttgart: Verlag Katholisches Bibelwerk (Stuttgarter Biblische Monographien, No 4).

LITTELL, Franklin H. 1972. *The Origins of Sectarian Protestantism*. New York: The Macmillan Company (3d printing).

LOCHMAN, Jan M. 1986. Church and World in the Light of the Kingdom, in Limouris, pp 58-72.

LÖFFLER, Paul. 1977a. The Confessing Community. Evangelism in Ecumenical Perspective, *International Review of Mission* vol 66, pp 339-348.

———1977b. Evangelism, *One World* no 29, pp 8f.

LOHFINK, Gerhard. 1988. Die Not der Exegese mit der Reich-Gottes-Verkündigung Jesu, *Theologische Quartalschrift* vol 168, pp 1-15.

LOHMEYER, Ernst. 1951. "Mir ist gegeben alle Gewalt!" Eine Exegese von Mt.

28, 16-20, in *In Memoriam Ernst Lohmeyer*. Stuttgart: Evang. Verlagswerk, pp 22-49.

———1956. *Das Evangelium des Matthäus*. Göttingen: Vandenhoeck & Ruprecht.

LOISY, Alfred. 1976. *The Gospel and the Church*. Philadelphia: Fortress Press.

LOVELACE, Richard. 1981. Completing an Awakening, *The Christian Century* vol 98, pp 296-300.

LÖWE, Heinz. 1978. Pirmin, Willibrord und Bonifatius. Ihre Bedeutung für die Missionsgeschichte ihrer Zeit, in Schäferdiek, pp 192-226.

LOWE, Walter. 1982. Christ and Salvation, in Hodgson & King, pp 196-222.

LÜBBE, Hermann. 1986. *Religion nach der Aufklärung*. Graz/Vienna/Cologne: Verlag Styria.

LUGG, Andrew. 1987. "The Priority of Paradigms" Revisited, *Zeitschrift für Allgemeine Wissenschaftstheorie* vol 18, pp 175-181.

LUZ, Ulrich. 1968. *Das Geschichtsverständnis des Paulus*. Munich: Chr. Kaiser Verlag.

LUZBETAK, Louis J., SVD. 1988. *The Church and Cultures*. Maryknoll, New York: Orbis Books.

LWF. 1988. Together in God's Mission. A Lutheran World Federation Contribution to the Understanding of Mission, *LWF Documentation*, no 26.

MACKAY, John A. 1933. The Theology of the Laymen's Foreign Missions Enquiry, *International Review of Missions* vol 22, pp 174-188.

MACQUARRIE, John. 1977. *Principles of Christian Theology*. New York: Charles Scribner's Sons. (2d ed.; first published in 1966).

MALHERBE, Abraham J. 1983. *Social Aspects of Early Christianity* (2d ed., enlarged). Philadelphia: Fortress Press.

———1986. *Moral Exhortation: A Greco-Roman Sourcebook*. Philadelphia: The Westminster Press.

———1987. *Paul and the Thessalonians*. Philadelphia: Fortress Press.

MANN, Dietrich. 1981. Der Ruf zur Umkehr, *Zeitschrift für Mission* vol 7, pp 67-69.

MANSON, William. 1953. Mission and Eschatology, *International Review of Missions* vol 42, pp 390-397.

MARCUS, Joel, & SOARDS, Marion L. (eds). 1989. *Apocalyptic and the New Testament*. Essays in Honor of J. Louis Martyn. Sheffield: Sheffield Academic Press.

MARGULL, Hans J. 1962. *Hope in Action: The Church's Task in the World*. Philadelphia: Muhlenberg Press.

———1974. Verwundbarkeit: Bemerkungen zum Dialog, *Evangelische Theologie* vol 34, pp 410-420.

MARIUS, R. J. 1976. The Reformation and Nationhood, *Dialog* vol 15, pp 29-34.

MARKUS, R. A. 1970. Gregory the Great and a Papal Missionary Strategy, in Cuming, pp 29-38.

MARSDEN, George M. 1980. *Fundamentalism and American Culture. The Shaping of Twentieth-Century Evangelicalism: 1870-1925*. New York/Oxford: Oxford University Press.

———1987. *Reforming Fundamentalism: Fuller Seminary and the New Evangelicalism*. Grand Rapids: Eerdmans.

MARTIN, James P. 1987. Toward a Post-Critical Paradigm, *New Testament Studies* vol 33, pp 370-385.

MARTYN, J. Louis. 1985. A Law-Observant Mission to Gentiles: The Background of Galatians, *Scottish Journal of Theology* vol 38, pp 307-324.

MATTHEY, Jacques. 1980. The Great Commission according to Matthew, *International Review of Mission* vol 69, pp 161-173.

MAZAMISA, L. W. 1987. *Beatific Comradeship: An Exegetical-Hermeneutical Study on Lk 10:25-37*. Kampen: Kok.

MBITI, J.S. 1972. Some African Concepts of Christology, in G.F. Vicedom (ed), *Christ and the Younger Churches*. London: SPCK, pp 51-62.

McGAVRAN, Donald A. 1973. Salvation Today, in Ralph Winter (ed), *The Evangelical Response to Bangkok*. Pasadena: William Carey Library, pp 27-32.

————1980. *Understanding Church Growth* (fully rev.). Grand Rapids: Eerdmans.

————1983. What Is Mission?, in A. F. Glasser & D. A. McGavran, *Contemporary Theologies of Mission*. Grand Rapids: Baker Book House, pp 15-29.

McNALLY, Robert E. 1978. Die Keltische Kirche in Irland, in Schäferdiek, pp 91-115.

MEEKING, Basil. 1987. An Obedient Response: The Common Witness of Christians, *Verbum SVD* vol 28, pp 5-18.

MEEKS, Wayne A. 1983. *The First Urban Christians: The Social World of the Apostle Paul*. New Haven: Yale University Press.

MEIER, John P. 1977. Two Disputed Questions in Matt 28:16-20, *Journal of Biblical Literature* vol 96, pp 407-424.

MEMORANDUM. 1982. Memorandum from a Consultation on Mission (Produced by a Consultation held in Rome, May 1982, and Organized by the Secretariat for Promoting Christian Unity), *International Review of Mission* vol 71, pp 458-477.

MERKLEIN, H. 1978. *Die Gottesherrschaft als Handlungsprinzip: Untersuchung zur Ethik Jesu*. Würzburg: Echter Verlag.

MESTHENE, Emmanuel. 1967. Technology and Religion, *Theology Today* vol 23, pp 481-495.

MEYER, Ben F. 1986. *The Early Christians: Their World Mission and Self-Discovery*. Wilmington: Michael Glazier, Inc.

MEYER, Heinrich. 1958. Die Existenz junger Kirchen als Frage an die abendländische Theologie, in J. Heubach & H.-J. Ulrich (eds), *Sammlung und Sendung* (Eine Festgabe für Heinrich Rendtorff). Berlin: Christlicher Zeitschriftenverlag, pp 218-224.

MICHEL, Otto. 1941. Menschensohn und Völkerwelt, *Evangelische Missions-Zeitschrift* vol 2, pp 257-267.

————1950/51. Der Abschluss des Matthäusevangeliums, *Evangelische Theologie* vol 10, pp 16-26.

MICHIELS, Robrecht. 1989. The Self-Understanding of the Church after Vatican II, *Louvain Studies* vol 14, pp 83-107.

MIGUEZ BONINO, J. 1975. *Doing Theology in a Revolutionary Situation*. Philadelphia: Fortress Press.

————1976. *Christians and Marxists: The Mutual Challenge to Revolution*. London: Hodder & Stoughton.

————1980. For Life and Against Death. A Theology that Takes Sides, *The Christian Century* vol 97, pp 1154-1158.

————1981. Doing Theology in the Context of the Struggles of the Poor, *Mid-Stream* vol 20, pp 369-373.

MINEAR, Paul S. 1961. Gratitude and Mission in the Epistle to the Romans, in *Basileia*. Walter Freytag zum 60. Geburtstag. Stuttgart: Evang. Missionsverlag, pp 42-48.

———1977. *Images of the Church in the New Testament*. Philadelphia: Fortress Press (3d printing).

MITTERHÖFER, Jakob. 1974. *Thema Mission*. Vienna: Herder.

MOFFETT, Samuel H. 1987. Early Asian Christian Approaches to Non-Christian Cultures, *Missiology* vol 15, pp 473-486.

MOLTMANN, Jürgen. 1967. *Theology of Hope*. New York: Harper & Row.

———1975. *The Experiment Hope*. London: SCM Press.

———1977. *The Church in the Power of the Spirit: A Contribution to Messianic Ecclesiology*. London: SCM Press (first published in 1975).

MONTGOMERY, Jim. 1989. *Dawn 2000: 7 Million Churches to Go*. Pasadena: William Carey Library.

MOO, Douglas. 1987. Paul and the Law in the Last Ten Years, *Scottish Journal of Theology* vol 40, pp 287-307.

MOORHEAD, James H. 1984. The Erosion of Postmillennialism in American Religious Thought, *Church History* vol 53, pp 61-77.

———1988. Searching for the Millennium in America, *The Princeton Seminary Bulletin* vol 9, pp 17-33.

MORITZEN, Niels-Peter. 1982. Koloniale Konzepte der protestantischen Mission, in Bade, pp 51-67.

MOSALA, Itumeleng J. 1989. *Biblical Hermeneutics and Black Theology in South Africa*. Grand Rapids: Eerdmans.

MOTT, John R. 1902. *The Evangelization of the World in This Generation*. London: Student Volunteer Movement (first published in 1900).

MOUTON, Johann. 1983. Reformation and Restoration in Francis Bacon's Early Philosophy, *The Modern Schoolman* vol 60, pp 101-122.

———1987. The Masculine Birth of Time — Interpreting Francis Bacon's Discourse on Scientific Progress, *South African Journal of Philosophy* vol 6, pp 43-50.

MÜLLER, K. 1978. "Holistic Mission" oder das "umfassende Heil", in Waldenfels, pp 75-84.

———1986. Die Welt setzt die Tagesordnung. Akzentverschiebungen im Missionsverständnis, *Zeitschrift für Missions- und Religionswissenschaft* vol 70, pp 128-135.

———1987. *Mission Theology: An Introduction*. Nettetal: Steyler Verlag.

———1989. *Josef Schmidlin (1876-1944)*. Papsthistoriker und Begründer der Katholischen Missionswissenschaft. Nettetal: Steyler Verlag.

MÜLLER, K., & SUNDERMEIER, T. (eds). 1987. *Lexikon missionstheologischer Grundbegriffe*. Berlin: Dietrich Reimer.

MUSSNER, Franz. 1976. "Ganz Israel wird gerettet werden" (Römer 11, 26), *Kairos* vol 18, pp 241-255.

———1982. Die Juden im Neuen Testament, *Bibel und Liturgie* vol 55, pp 4-14.

MYKLEBUST, O. G. 1955 & 1957. *The Study of Missions in Theological Education*. Oslo: Egede Instituttet (2 volumes).

———1961. Integration or Independence? Some Reflections on the Study of Missions in the Theological Curriculum, in *Basileia* (Walter Freytag zum 60. Geburstag). Stuttgart: Evang. Missionsverlag, pp 330-340.

———1989. Missiology in Contemporary Theological Education, *Mission Studies* vol 6, pp 87-107.

NACPIL, Emerito. 1971. Whom Does the Missionary Serve and What Does He Do?, in *Missionary Service in Asia Today*. Hong Kong: Chinese Christian Literature Council, pp 76-80.

NEILL, Stephen. 1959. *Creative Tension*. London: Edinburgh House Press.

————1960. *The Unfinished Task*. London: Edinburgh House Press (first published in 1957)

————1966a. *A History of Christian Missions*. Harmondsworth: Penguin (first published in 1964).

————1966b. *Colonialism and Christian Missions*. London: Lutterworth.

————1968. *The Church and Christian Union*. London: Oxford University Press.

NEL, D. T. 1988. *Kritiese Hermeneutiek as model vir sendingwetenskaplike navorsing*. Pretoria: Univ. of South Africa (unpublished doctoral dissertation).

NEL, M.D.C. de W. 1958. Enkele vraagstukke van ons sendingtaak onder die Bantoe, *Op die Horison* vol 20 (March), pp 6-26.

NEUHAUS, R. J. 1984. *The Naked Public Square*. Grand Rapids: Eerdmans.

NEUHAUS, R. J. & CROMARTIE, M. (eds). 1987. *Piety and Politics: Evangelicals and Fundamentalists Confront the World*. Washington: Ethics and Public Policy Center.

NEWBIGIN, Lesslie. 1958. *One Body, One Gospel, One World*. London & New York: International Missionary Council.

————1969. *The Finality of Christ*. London: SCM Press.

————1978. *The Open Secret: Sketches for a Missionary Theology*. Grand Rapids: Eerdmans.

————1979. Context and Conversion, *International Review of Mission* vol 68, pp 301-312.

————1982. Cross-currents in Ecumenical and Evangelical Understandings of Mission, *International Bulletin of Missionary Research* vol 6, pp 146-151.

————1986. *Foolishness to the Greeks: The Gospel and Western Culture*. Geneva: World Council of Churches.

————1987. *Mission in Christ's Way*. Geneva: World Council of Churches.

NEWMAN, John Henry (Cardinal). 1970. *Historical Sketches*. Vol II. Westminster, Maryland: Christian Classics Inc. (first published in the 1830s).

NIDA, E. A. 1968. *Religion Across Cultures*. New York: Harper & Row.

NIE. 1980. *Evangelism: Convergence and Divergence*. London: Nationwide Initiative in Evangelism.

NIEBUHR, H. Richard. 1959. *The Kingdom of God in America*. New York: Harper & Brothers (first published in 1937).

————1988. The Social Gospel and the Mind of Jesus, *The Journal of Religious Ethics* vol 16, pp 115-127.

NIEBUHR, Reinhold. 1960. *Moral Man and Immoral Society*. New York: Charles Scribner's Sons (first published in 1932).

NISSEN, Johannes. 1984. *Poverty and Mission: New Testament Perspectives* (IIMO Research Pamphlet No 10). Leiden: Inter-university Institute for Missiological and Ecumenical Research.

NISSIOTIS, Nikos A. 1968. *Die Theologie der Ostkirche im ökumenischen Dialog*. Stuttgart: Evang. Verlagswerk.

NOCK, A. D. 1933. *Conversion: The Old and the New in Religion from Alexander the Great to Augustine of Hippo*. London: Oxford University Press.

NOLAN, Albert. 1976. *Jesus Before Christianity*. Maryknoll, New York: Orbis Books. Cape Town: David Philip.

———1988. *God in South Africa: The Challenge of the Gospel*. Cape Town/Johannesburg: David Philip.

NØRGAARD, Anders. 1988. *Mission und Obrigkeit: Die Dänisch-Hallesche Mission in Tranquebar 1706-1845*. Gütersloh: Gütersloher Verlagshaus.

NÜRNBERGER, Klaus. 1970. Systematisch-theologische Lösungsversuche zum Problem der anderen Religionen und ihre missionsmethodischen Konsequenzen, *Neue Zeitschrift für Systematische Theologie und Religionsphilosophie* vol 12, pp 13-43.

———1982. *Die Relevanz des Wortes im Entwicklungsprozess*. Frankfurt/Main: Peter Lang.

———1987a. *Ethik des Nord-Süd-Konflikts*. Das globale Machtgefälle als theologisches Problem. Gütersloh: Gütersloher Verlagshaus.

———1987b. The Eschatology of Marxism, *Missionalia* vol 15, pp 105-109.

OBERMAN, Heiko. 1983. *Luther: Mensch zwischen Gott und Teufel*. Berlin: Severin & Siedler.

———1986. *The Dawn of the Reformation: Essays in Late Medieval and Early Reformation Thought*. Edinburgh: T. & T. Clark.

OECUMENISCHE INLEIDING. 1988. *Oecumenische inleiding in de Missiologie* (eds A. Camps, L. A. Hoedemaker, M. R. Spindler, & F. J. Verstraelen). Kampen: Kok.

OHM, Thomas. 1962. *Machet zu Jüngern alle Völker: Theorie der Mission*. Freiburg/B: Erich Wevel Verlag.

OLLROG, W.-H. 1979. *Paulus und seine Mitarbeiter*. Neukirchen-Vluyn: Neukirchener Verlag.

ORCHARD, R. K. 1958. *The Ghana Assembly of the International Missionary Council*. London: Edinburgh House Press.

OSBORNE, Grant R. 1976. Redaction Criticism and the Great Commission, *Journal of the Evangelical Theological Society* vol 19, pp 73-85.

PASCOE, C. F. 1901. *Two Hundred Years of the S.P.G.* London: S.P.G.

PATON, David M. 1953. *Christian Missions and the Judgment of God*. London: SCM Press.

PESCH, Rudolf. 1969. Berufung und Sendung, Nachfolge und Mission. Eine Studie zu Mk. 1, 16-20, *Zeitschrift für Katholische Theologie* vol 91, pp 1-31.

———1982. Voraussetzungen und Anfänge der urchristlichen Mission, in Kertelge, pp 11-70.

PETERS, George W. 1980. Jesus of Nazareth—the First Evangelizer, *Studia Missionalia* vol 29, pp 105-124.

PETERSEN, Norman R. 1985. *Rediscovering Paul: Philemon and the Sociology of Paul's Narrative World*. Philadelphia: Fortress Press.

PFÜRTNER, Stephan. 1984. Die Paradigmen von Thomas und Luther. Bedeutet Luthers Rechtfertigungsbotschaft einen Paradigmenwechsel?, in Küng & Tracy, pp 168-192.

PHILIP, John. 1828a, 1828b. *Researches in South Africa*. London: James Duncan (two volumes).

PIERIS, Aloysius, S.J. Inculturation in Non-Semitic Asia, *The Month* no 1420, pp 83-87.

PIET, John H. 1970. *The Road Ahead: A Theology for the Church in Mission*. Grand Rapids: Eerdmans.

PIXLEY, George V. 1981. *God's Kingdom*. Maryknoll, New York: Orbis Books.

POBEE, John S. 1987. *Who are the Poor? The Beatitudes as a Call to Community*. Geneva: World Council of Churches.

POCOCK, Michael. 1988. The Destiny of the World and the Work of Missions, *Bibliotheca Sacra* vol 145, pp 436-451.

POLANYI, Michael. 1958. *Personal Knowledge: Towards a Post-Critical Philosophy*. London: Routledge & Kegan Paul.

POPPER, Karl R. 1979. *Objective Knowledge: An Evolutionary Approach*. Oxford: Oxford University Press (first published in 1972).

PORTEFAIX, Lilian. 1988. *Sisters Rejoice: Paul's Letter to the Philippians and Luke Acts as Received by First Century Philippian Women:* Stockholm: Almquist Wiksell.

POWER, John, SMA. 1970. *Mission Theology Today*. Dublin: Gill & Macmillan.

PRINZ, Friedrich. 1978. Peregrinatio, Mönchtum und Mission, in Schäferdiek, pp 445-465.

RAHNER, Karl. 1966. Grundprinzipien zur heutigen Mission der Kirche, in *Handbuch der Pastoraltheologie* vol II/2 (Freiburg/B: Herder), pp 46-80.

RÄISÄNEN, Heikki. 1983. *Paul and the Law*. Tübingen: Mohr.

————1987. Paul's Conversion and the Development of His View of the Law, *New Testament Studies* vol 33, pp 404-419.

RATSCHOW, C.-H. 1987. Theologie der Religionen, in Müller & Sundermeier, pp 495-505.

RENGSTORF, K. H. 1967. *Mathetes*, in *Theological Dictionary of the New Testament* vol IV. Grand Rapids: Eerdmans.

RENNSTICH, Karl. 1982a. The Understanding of Mission, Civilisation and Colonialism in the Basel Mission, in Christensen & Hutchison, pp 94-103.

————1982b. Überwindung falscher Alternativen: Missionsverständnis bei "Ökumenikern" und "Evangelikalen", *Lutherische Monatshefte* vol 21, pp 544-548.

REUTER, T. (ed). 1980. *The Greatest Englishman: Essays on St Boniface and the Church at Crediton*. Exeter: Paternoster.

RICKENBACH, H. 1970. "Erneuerung in der Mission". Zum Sektionsbericht II der Weltkirchenkonferenz von Uppsala 1968, in Stirnimann, pp 61-80.

RIVINIUS, Karl J. (ed). 1983. *Schuld, Sühne und Erlösung*. St. Augustin: Steyler Verlag.

ROBERTS, J. H. 1983. Struktuur en betekenis van Filemon, *Theologia Evangelica* vol 16, no 3, pp 59-70.

ROOY, Sidney H. 1965. *The Theology of Missions in the Puritan Tradition*. Grand Rapids: Eerdmans.

ROSE, Karl. 1960. Missionare und Missionsmethoden der Russischen Orthodoxen Kirche, *Zeichen der Zeit* vol 14, pp 453-457.

ROSENKRANZ, Gerhard. 1977. *Die christliche Mission: Geschichte und Theologie*. Munich: Chr. Kaiser Verlag.

ROSIN, H. H. 1972. *Missio Dei: An examination of the Origin, Contents and Function of the Term in Protestant Missiological Discussion*. Leiden: Inter-university Institute for Missiological and Ecumenical Research.

ROSS, Andrew. 1986. *John Philip (1775-1851): Missions, Race and Politics in South Africa*. Aberdeen: Aberdeen Univ. Press.

RUSSELL, Bertrand. 1970. *The Problems of Philosophy*. Oxford: Oxford University Press (first published in 1912)

RUSSELL, Walter B. 1988. An Alternative Suggestion for the Purpose of Romans, *Bibliotheca Sacra* vol 145, pp 174-184.

RÜTTI, Ludwig. 1972. *Zur Theologie der Mission: Kritische Analysen und neue Orientierungen*. Munich: Chr. Kaiser Verlag.

———1974. Mission—Gegenstand der Praktischen Theologie oder Frage an die Gesamttheologie?, in F. Klostermann & R. Zerfass (eds), *Praktische Theologie Heute*. Munich: Chr. Kaiser Verlag, pp 288-307.

RZEPKOWSKI, H. 1974. The Theology of Mission, *Verbum SVD* vol 15, pp 79-91.

———1983. Umgrenzung des Missionsbegriffes und das neue kirchliche Gesetzbuch, *Verbum SVD* vol 24, pp 101-139.

SAAYMAN, W. A. 1984. *Unity and Mission*. Pretoria: Univ. of South Africa.

SAMUEL, V. & SUGDEN, Chris. 1986. Evangelism and Social Responsibility: A Biblical Study on Priorities, in Bruce Nicholls (ed), *In Word and Deed*. Grand Rapids: Eerdmans, pp 189-214.

SAMUEL, Vinay, & SUGDEN, Chris (eds). 1987. *The Church in Response to Human Need*. Grand Rapids: Eerdmans.

SANDERS, E.P. 1977. *Paul and Palestinian Judaism*. Philadelphia: Fortress Press.

———1983. *Paul, the Law, and the Jewish People*. Philadelphia: Fortress Press.

SANDERS, Jack T. 1981. The Parable of the Pounds and Lucan Anti-Semitism, *Theological Studies* vol 42, pp 660-668.

SCHÄFERDIEK, Knut (ed). 1978. *Kirchengeschichte als Missionsgeschichte. Bd II/ 1: Die Kirche des früheren Mittelalters*. Munich: Chr. Kaiser Verlag.

SCHÄFERDIEK, Knut. 1978. Die Grundlegung der angelsächsischen Kirche im Spannungsfeld insular-keltischen und kontinental-römischen Christentums, in Schäferdiek, pp 149-191.

SCHÄRER, Hans. 1944. *Die Begründung der Mission in der katholischen und evangelischen Missionswissenschaft* (Theologische Studien, Heft 16). Zollikon-Zürich: Evangelischer Verlag.

SCHÄUFELE, Wolfgang. 1966. *Das missionarische Bewusstsein und Wirken der Täufer*. Neukirchen-Vluyn: Verlag des Erziehungsvereins.

SCHEFFLER, E. H. 1988. *Suffering in Luke's Gospel*. University of Pretoria: unpublished doctoral dissertation.

SCHERER, J. A. 1968. Ecumenical Mandates for Mission, in Norman A. Horner (ed), *Protestant Crosscurrents in Mission*. Nashville/New York: Abingdon.

———1969. *Justinian Welz: Essays by an Early Prophet of Mission*. Translated, annotated and with an historical introduction. Grand Rapids: Eerdmans.

———1971. Missions in Theological Education, in William J. Danker & Wi Jo Kang (eds), *The Future of the Christian World Mission*. Studies in Honor of R. Pierce Beaver. Grand Rapids: Eerdmans, pp 143-155.

———1974. Bangkok: A Lutheran Appraisal, *Dialog* vol 13, pp 137-142.

———1987 *Gospel, Church, and Kingdom: Comparative Studies in World Mission Theology*. Minneapolis: Augsburg Publishing House.

SCHICK, Erich. 1943. *Vorboten und Bahnbrecher: Grundzüge der evangelischen Missionsgeschichte bis zu den Anfängen der Basler Mission*. Basel: Basler Missionsbuchhandlung.

SCHINDLER, Alfred. 1987. Augustins Ekklesiologie in den Spannungsfeldern seiner Zeit und heutiger Ökumene, *Freiburger Zeitschrift für Philosophie und Theologie* vol 34, pp 295-309.

SCHLIER, Heinrich. 1971. Die "Liturgie" des apostolischen Evangeliums (Römer 15, 14-21), in *Das Ende der Zeit* (Exegetische Aufsätze und Vorträge III). Freiburg/Basel: Herder, pp 169-183.

SCHMEMANN, Alexander. 1961. The Missionary Imperative in the Orthodox Tradition, in G. H. Anderson (ed), *The Theology of the Christian Mission*. London: SCM Press, pp 250-257.

SCHMIDT, Johann. 1973. Die missionarische Dimension der Theologie, in Horst Balz & Siegfried Schulz (eds), *Das Wort und die Wörter* (Festschrift Gerhard Friedrich). Stuttgart: Kohlhammer, pp 193-201.

SCHMITZ, Josef. 1971. *Die Weltzuwendung Gottes: Thesen zu einer Theologie der Mission*. Freiburg/B: Imba-Verlag.

SCHNEIDER, Gerhard. 1982. Der Missionsauftrag Jesu in der Darstellung der Evangelien, in Kertelge, pp 71-92.

SCHNEIDER, Reinhard. 1978. Karl der Grosse — Politisches Sendungsbewusstsein und Mission, in Schäferdiek, pp 227-248.

SCHOTTROFF, L., & STEGEMANN, W. 1986. *Jesus and the Hope of the Poor*. Maryknoll, New York: Orbis Books. Translated by Matthew J. O'Connell.

SCHREITER, Robert J. 1982. The Bible and Mission: A Response to Walter Brueggeman and Beverly Gaventa, *Missiology* vol 10, pp 427-434.

———1985. *Constructing Local Theologies*. Maryknoll, New York: Orbis Books. London: SCM Press.

SCHUMACHER, J. 1970. Geschichte der Missionstheologie — eine Denkaufgabe, *Neue Zeitschrift für Missionswissenschaft* vol 26, pp 175-186.

SCHÜSSLER FIORENZA, E. 1976. *Aspects of Religious Propaganda in Judaism and Early Christianity*. South Bend: University of Notre Dame Press.

SCHÜTZ, P. 1930. *Zwischen Nil und Kaukasus*. Munich: Chr. Kaiser Verlag.

SCHWEITZER, Albert. 1952. *The Quest of the Historical Jesus*. London: A. & C. Black (first published in 1910).

SCHWEIZER, Eduard. 1971. *Jesus*. Richmond: John Knox.

SCOTT, Waldron. 1980. *Bring Forth Justice: A Contemporary Perspective on Mission*. Grand Rapids: Eerdmans.

SEGUNDO, Juan Luis. 1976. *The Liberation of Theology*. Maryknoll, New York: Orbis Books.

———1986. *The Humanist Christology of Paul*. Maryknoll, New York: Orbis Books.

SENIOR, Donald, CP. 1983. The Foundations for Mission in the New Testament, in Donald Senior, CP and Carroll Stuhlmueller, CP, *The Biblical Foundations for Mission*. Maryknoll, New York: Orbis Books, pp 141-312.

SEUMOIS, André. 1973. *Théologie Missionaire I*. Rome: Bureau de Presse O.M.I.

SHARPE, Eric J. 1974. New Directions in the Theology of Mission, *The Evangelical Quarterly* vol 46, pp 8-24.

SHAULL, M. Richard. 1967. The Revolutionary Challenge to Church and Theology, *Theology Today* vol 23, pp 470-480.

SHORTER, Aylward, WF. 1972. *Theology of Mission*. Cork: The Mercier Press.

———1977. *African Christian Theology — Adaptation or Incarnation?* London: Geoffrey Chapman.

———1988. *Toward a Theology of Inculturation*. Maryknoll, New York: Orbis Books.

———1989. A Council for Africa, *Euntes* vol 22, pp 349-352.

SIDER, Ronald J. 1980. An Evangelical Theology of Liberation, *The Christian Century* vol 97, pp 314-318.

SINGLETON, Michael. 1977. Obsession with Possession?, *Pro Mundi Vita: Africa Dossiers*, no 4.

SMIT, D.J. 1988. Responsible Hermeneutics: A Systematic Theologian's Response to the Readings and Readers of Luke 12:35-48, *Neotestamentica* vol 22, pp 441-484.

SMITH, Eugene L. 1968. *Mandate for Mission*. New York: Friendship Press.

SNIJDERS, Jan, SM. 1977. *Evangelii Nuntiandi: The Movement of Minds, The Clergy Review* vol 62, pp 170-175.

SNYDER, Howard. 1983. *Liberating the Church*. Downers Grove, Illinois: Inter-Varsity Press.

SOARES-PRABHU, G.M., SJ. 1986. Missiology or Missiologies?, *Mission Studies*, no 6, pp 85-87.

SONG, Choan-Seng. 1977. *Christian Mission in Reconstruction: An Asian Analysis*. Maryknoll, New York: Orbis Books.

SPINDLER, Marc. 1967. *La mission, combat pour le salut du monde*. Neuchâtel: Delachaux et Niestlé.

———1987. Meaning and Prospects of Common Witness, *Verbum SVD* vol 28, pp 18-28.

———1988. Bijbelse fundering en oriëntatie van zending, in *Oecumenische inleiding*, pp 137-154.

SPONG, John Selby. 1982. Evangelism When Certainty Is an Illusion, *The Christian Century* vol 99, pp 11-16.

STACKHOUSE, Max. 1988. *Apologia: Contextualization, Globalization, and Mission in Theological Education*. Grand Rapids: Eerdmans.

STAMOOLIS, James J. 1986. *Eastern Orthodox Mission Theology Today*. Maryknoll, New York: Orbis Books.

STANEK, Jaroslav B. 1985. Lukas — Theologe der Heilsgeschichte, *Communio Viatorum* vol 28, pp 9-31.

STANLEY, David. 1980. Jesus, Saviour of Mankind, *Studia Missionalia* vol 29, pp 57-84.

STEGEMANN, Ekkehard. 1984. "Hat Gott sein Volk verstossen? Das sei ferne!" *Pastoraltheologie* vol 73, pp 299-307.

STEIGER, Lothar. 1980. Schutzrede für Israel. Römer 9-11, in *Fides pro mundi vita* (H.-W. Gensichen zum 65. Geburtstag). Gütersloh: Gerd Mohn, pp 44-58.

STENDAHL, K. 1968. *The School of St. Matthew and Its Use of the Old Testament*. Philadelphia: Fortress Press (first published in 1954).

———1976. *Paul Among Jews and Gentiles*. Philadelphia: Fortress Press.

STIRNIMANN, H. (ed). 1970. *Ökumenische Erneuerung in der Mission*. Freiburg/ B: Paulusverlag.

STOTT, J.R.W. 1975. *Christian Mission in the Modern World*. London: Falcon.

STOTT, J.R.W., & COOTE, Robert (eds). 1980. *Down to Earth: Studies in Christianity and Culture*. Grand Rapids: Eerdmans.

STRANSKY, T. F. 1982. Evangelization, Missions, and Social Action: A Roman Catholic Perspective, *Review and Expositor* vol 79, pp 343-351.

STRECKER, Georg. 1962. *Der Weg der Gerechtigkeit: Untersuchungen zur Theologie des Matthäus*. Göttingen: Vandenhoeck & Ruprecht.

————1983. Die neue, bessere Gerechtigkeit: Zur Auslegung der Bergpredigt, *Lutherische Monatshefte* vol 22, pp 165-169.

STUHLMACHER, Peter. 1971. Zur Interpretation von Römer 11:25-32, in H. W. Wolff (ed), *Probleme biblischer Theologie* (Gerhard von Rad zum 70. Geburtstag). Munich: Chr. Kaiser Verlag, pp 555-570.

SUNDERMEIER, Theo. 1962. *Mission, Bekenntnis und Kirche: Missionstheologische Probleme des 19. Jahrhunderts bei C. H. Hahn.* Wuppertal: Verlag der Rheinischen Missionsgesellschaft.

————1986. Konvivenz als Grundstruktur ökumenischer Existenz heute, *Ökumenische Existenz Heute* 1, pp 49-100.

SUNDKLER, Bengt. 1968. Bedeutung, Ort und Aufgabe der Missiologie in der Gegenwart, *Evangelische Missions-Zeitschrift* vol 25, pp 113-124.

SWIFT, Louis J. 1983. *The Early Fathers on War and Military Service.* Wilmington: Michael Glazier.

TALBERT, C. H. 1984. *Reading Luke: A Literary and Theological Commentary on the Third Gospel.* New York: Crossroad.

TALBOT, C.H. 1970. St. Boniface and the German Mission, in Cuming, pp 45-58.

TANNEHILL, Robert C. 1985. Israel in Luke-Acts: A Tragic Story, *Journal of Biblical Literature* vol 104, pp 69-85.

TAYLOR, J.V. 1972. *The Go-Between God: The Holy Spirit and the Christian Mission.* London: SCM Press.

TEMPLE, W. 1976. *Christianity and the Social Order.* London: Shepheard-Walwyn (reprint of 1942 edition).

THAUREN, J. 1927. *Die Akkommodation im katholischen Heidenapostolat.* Münster: Aschendorffsche Verlagsbuchhandlung.

TIEDE, David L. 1980. *Prophecy and History in Luke-Acts.* Philadelphia: Fortress Press.

TORRES, S. & FABELLA, V., MM (eds). 1978. *The Emergent Gospel: Theology from the Developing World.* London: Geoffrey Chapman.

TOYNBEE, Arnold J. 1969. *Experiences.* London: Oxford University Press.

TRACY, David. 1984. Hermeneutische Überlegungen im Neuen Paradigma, in Küng & Tracy, pp 76-102.

TRILLING, Wolfgang. 1964. *Das wahre Israel: Studien zur Theologie des Matthäus-Evangeliums.* Munich: Kösel-Verlag (3d rev. ed.).

UKPONG, Justin. 1987. What is Contextualization? *Neue Zeitschrift für Missionswissenschaft* vol 43, pp 161-168.

VAN DEN BERG, Johannes. 1956. *Constrained by Jesus' Love: An Enquiry into the Motives of the Missionary Awakening in Great Britain in the Period Between 1698 and 1815.* Kampen: Kok.

VAN DER AALST, A. J. 1974. *Aantekeningen bij de hellenisering van het christendom.* Nijmegen: Dekker & van de Vegt.

VAN DER LINDE, J. M. 1973. Evangelisatie en humanisatie in de 17e en 18e eeuw, *Wereld en Zending* vol 15, pp 291-312.

VAN ENGELEN, J. M. 1975. Missiologie op een keerpunt, *Tijdschrift voor Theologie* vol 15, pp 291-312.

VAN HUYSSTEEN, Wentzel. 1986. *Teologie as kritiese geloofsverantwoording: Teorievorming in die Sistematiese Teologie.* Pretoria: Human Sciences Research Council.

VAN LEEUWEN, Arend Th. 1964. *Christianity in World History: The Meeting of the*

Faiths of East and West. London: Edinburgh House Press.

VAN SWIGCHEM, Douwe. 1955. *Het missionair karakter van de christelijke gemeente volgens de brieven van Paulus en Petrus*. Kampen: Kok.

VAN 'T HOF, I.P.C. 1972. *Op zoek naar het geheim van de zending: In dialoog met de wereldzendingsconferenties 1910-1963*. Wageningen: Veenman.

———1980. Gehoorzaamheid aan het zendingsbevel, *Kerk en Theologie* vol 37, pp 44-53.

VAN WINSEN. G.A.C., CM. 1973. *L'assistance missionaire Catholique*. Leiden: Inter-university Institute for Missiological and Ecumenical Research.

VERKUYL, J. 1978a. *Contemporary Missiology: An Introduction*. Grand Rapids: Eerdmans.

———1978b. *Inleiding in de Evangelistiek*. Kampen: Kok.

VERSTRAELEN, F. J. 1988. Van zendings- en missiewetenschap naar een gezamenlijke missiologie, in *Oecumenische inleiding*, pp 411-443.

VILLA-VICENCIO, Charles. 1988. *Trapped in Apartheid: A Socio-Theological History of the English-Speaking Churches*. Maryknoll, New York: Orbis Books & Cape Town: David Philip.

VISCHER, Lukas. 1976. *Veränderung der Welt — Bekehrung der Kirchen: Denkanstösse der Fünften Vollversammlung des Ökumenischen Rates der Kirchen in Nairobi*. Frankfurt/Main. Otto Lembeck.

VISSER 'T HOOFT, W.A. 1928. *The Background of the Social Gospel*. Haarlem: H. D. Tjeenk Willink.

———1980. Pan-Christians Yesterday and Today, *The Ecumenical Review* vol 32, pp 387-395.

VON CAMPENHAUSEN, H. 1974. Das Martyrium in der Mission, in Frohnes & Knorr, pp 71-85 (first published in 1937).

VON DOBSCHÜTZ, E. 1928. Matthäus als Rabbi und Katechet, *Zeitschr. f. die Neutest. Wissenschaft* vol 27, pp 338-348.

VON SODEN, Hans. 1974. Die christliche Mission in Altertum und Gegenwart, in Frohnes & Knorr, pp 18-31 (first published in 1956).

VOULGARAKIS, Elias. 1965. Mission and Unity from the Theological Point of View, *International Review of Missions* vol 54, pp 298-307.

———1987. Orthodoxe Mission, in Müller & Sundermeier, pp 355-360.

WAGNER, C. Peter. 1979. *Our Kind of People: The Ethical Dimensions of Church Growth in America*. Atlanta: John Knox.

WALASKAY, Paul W. 1983. *"And so we came to Rome": The Political Perspective of St Luke*. Cambridge: University Press.

WALDENFELS, Hans. 1977. Mission als Vermittlung von umfassendem Heil, *Zeitschrift für Missionswissenschaft und Religionswissenschaft* vol 61, pp 241-255.

WALDENFELS, Hans (ed). 1978. *"... denn ich bin bei Euch" (Mt 28,20): Perspektiven im christlichen Missionsbewusstsein heute* (Festgabe für Josef Glazik und Bernward Willeke). Einsiedeln: Benziger.

———1987. Kontextuelle Theologie, in Müller & Sundermeier, pp 224-230.

WALKER, G.S.M. 1970. St Columban: Monk or Missionary?, in Cuming, pp 39-44.

WALKER, R. 1967. *Die Heilsgeschichte im Ersten Evangelium*. Göttingen: Vandenhoeck & Ruprecht.

WALLS, Andrew F. 1982a. British Missions, in Christensen & Hutchison, pp 159-166.

———1982b. The Gospel as the Prisoner and Liberator of Culture, *Missionalia* vol 10, pp 93-105.

———1988. Missionary Societies and the Fortunate Subversion of the Church, *The Evangelical Quarterly* vol 88, pp 141-155.

WALSH, John, MM. 1982. *Evangelization and Justice*. Maryknoll, New York: Orbis Books.

———1990. *Integral Justice: Changing People Changing Structures*. Maryknoll, New York: Orbis Books.

WALTER, Nikolaus. 1979. Christusglaube und heidnische Religiosität in paulinischen Gemeinden, *New Testament Studies* vol 25, pp 422-442.

WARNECK, Gustav. 1906. *Outline of a History of Protestant Missions*. Edinburgh & London: Oliphant, Anderson & Ferrier (3d English ed., translated from the eighth German ed.).

WARNECK, Johannes. [1909]. *The Living Christ and Dying Heathenism*. New York: Fleming H. Revell Co. (no date).

———1913. *Paulus im Lichte der heutigen Heidenmission*. Berlin: Martin Warneck.

WARREN, M.A.C. 1948. *The Truth of Vision*. London: The Canterbury Press.

———1961. The Thought and Practice of Missions, in *Basileia* (Walter Freytag zum 60. Geburtstag). Stuttgart: Evang. Missionsverlag, pp 158-165.

———1965. *The Missionary Movement from Britain in Modern History*. London: SCM Press.

———1967. *Social History and Christian Mission*. London: SCM Press.

WATSON, David Lowes. 1983a. The Church as Journalist: Evangelism in the Context of the Local Church in the United States, *International Review of Mission* vol 72, pp 57-74.

———1983b. Evangelism: A Disciplinary Approach, *International Bulletin of Missionary Research* vol 7, pp 6-9.

WEBER, Winfried. 1978. Mission als Befreiung zum universalen Heil, in Waldenfels, pp 85-99.

WEDDERBURN, A.J.M. 1988. Paul and Jesus: Similarity and Continuity, *New Testament Studies* vol 34, pp 161-182.

WERNLE, Paul. 1899. *Paulus als Heidenmissionar*. Freiburg/B: Mohr.

WEST, Charles C. 1971. *The Power to be Human: Toward a Secular Theology*. New York: The Macmillan Company.

WIEDENMANN, Ludwig. 1965. *Mission und Eschatologie: Eine Analyse der neueren deutschen evangelischen Missionstheologie*. Paderborn: Verlag Bonifacius-Druckerei.

WIEDERKEHR, Dietrich. 1976. *Glaube an Erlösung: Konzepte der Soteriologie vom Neuen Testament bis heute*. Freiburg/B: Herder.

———1982. Die ganze Erlösung: Dimensionen des Heils, *Theologische Quartalschrift* vol 162, pp 329-341.

WIESER, Thomas (ed). 1966. *Planning for Mission: Working Papers on the New Quest for Missionary Communities*. New York: U.S. Conference for the World Council of Churches.

———1973. Report on the Salvation Study, *International Review of Mission*, vol 62, pp 170-179.

WILCKENS, Ulrich. 1959. Die Bekehrung des Paulus als religionsgeschichtliches Problem, *Zeitschrift für Theologie und Kirche* vol 56, pp 273-293.

———1963. *Die Missionsreden der Apostelgeschichte: Form- und traditionsgeschicht-*

liche Untersuchungen (2., durchgesehene Auflage). Neukirchen-Vluyn: Neukirchener Verlag.

WILKEN, Robert L. 1980. The Christians as the Romans (and Greeks) Saw them, in E. P. Sanders (ed), *Jewish and Christian Self-Understanding*, vol 1, The Shaping of Christianity in the Second and Third Centuries. London: SCM Press, pp 100-125, 234-236.

WILKENS, Wilhelm. 1985. Die Komposition des Matthäus-Evangeliums, *New Testament Studies* vol 31, pp 24-38.

WILSON, Samuel, & SIEWERT, John (eds). 1986. *Mission Handbook: North American Protestant Ministries Overseas* (13th edition). Monrovia, California: MARC.

WILSON, Stephen G. 1973. *The Gentiles and the Gentile Mission in Luke-Acts*. Cambridge: University Press.

World Council of Churches 1961. *The New Delhi Report: The Third Assembly of the World Council of Churches*. London: SCM Press.

———1967. *The Church for Others and The Church for the World*. Geneva: World Council of Churches.

———1968. *The Uppsala Report 1968: Official Report of the Fourth Assembly of the World Council of Churches*. Geneva: World Council of Churches.

———1973. *Bangkok Assembly 1973: Minutes and Report of the Assembly of the Commission on World Mission and Evangelism of the World Council of Churches*. Geneva: World Council of Churches.

———1976. *Breaking Barriers: The Official Report of the Fifth Assembly of the World Council of Churches, Nairobi 1975* (ed David M. Paton). London: SPCK.

———1979. *Guidelines on Dialogue with People of Living Faiths and Ideologies*. Geneva: World Council of Churches.

———1980. *Your Kingdom Come: Report on the World Conference on Mission and Evangelism, Melbourne, Australia*. Geneva: World Council of Churches.

———1983. *Gathered for Life: Official Report, VI Assembly of the World Council of Churches, Vancouver 1983* (ed David Gill). Geneva: World Council of Churches.

———1990. *The San Antonio Report* (ed F. R. Wilson). Geneva: World Council of Churches.

WRIGHT, G. Ernest. 1952. *God Who Acts: Biblical Theology as Recital*. London: SCM Press.

YANNOULATOS, Anastasios: see ANASTASIOS of Androussa.

YODER, J. H. 1972. *The Politics of Jesus*. Grand Rapids: Eerdmans.

YOUNG, Frances. 1988. The Critic and the Visionary, *Scottish Journal of Theology* vol 41, pp 297-312.

ZELLER, Dieter. 1982. Theologie der Mission bei Paulus, in Kertelge, pp 164-189.

ZINGG, Paul. 1973. Die Stellung des Lukas zur Heidenmission, *Neue Zeitschrift für Missionswissenschaft* vol 29, pp 200-209.

ZUMSTEIN, Jean. 1972. Matthieu 28:16-20, *Révue de Théologie et de Philosophie* vol 22, pp 14-33.

Index of Scriptural References

HEBREW BIBLE

NEW TESTAMENT

Index of Subjects

Index of Authors and Personal Names